Cold Case Hom

Practical Investigative Techniques

CRC SERIES IN
PRACTICAL ASPECTS OF CRIMINAL AND FORENSIC INVESTIGATIONS

VERNON J. GEBERTH, BBA, MPS, FBINA *Series Editor*

Practical Homicide Investigation: Tactics, Procedures, and Forensic Techniques, Fifth Edition
Vernon J. Geberth

Practical Homicide Investigation Checklist and Field Guide, Second Edition
Vernon J. Geberth

Cold Case Homicides: Practical Investigative Techniques, Second Edition
R. H. Walton

Practical Bomb Scene Investigation, Third Edition
James T. Thurman

Analyzing 911 Homicide Calls: Practical Aspects and Applications
Tracy Harpster and Susan H. Adams

Practical Aspects of Rape Investigation: A Multidisciplinary Approach, Fifth Edition
Robert R. Hazelwood and Ann Wolbert Burgess

Munchausen by Proxy and Other Factitious Abuse: Practical and Forensic Investigative Techniques
Kathryn Artingstall

Forensic Footwear Evidence
William J. Bodziak

Practical Analysis and Reconstruction of Shooting Incidents, Second Edition
Edward E. Hueske

Gunshot Wounds: Practical Aspects of Firearms, Ballistics, and Forensic Techniques, Third Edition
Vincent J. M. DiMaio

Informants, Cooperating Witnesses, and Undercover Investigations: A Practical Guide to Law, Policy, and Procedure, Second Edition
Dennis G. Fitzgerald

Practical Military Ordnance Identification
Tom Gersbeck

Practical Cold Case Homicide Investigations Procedural Manual
R. H. Walton

Autoerotic Deaths: Practical Forensic and Investigative Perspectives
Anny Sauvageau and Vernon J. Geberth

Practical Crime Scene Processing and Investigation, Second Edition
Ross M. Gardner

The Counterterrorism Handbook: Tactics, Procedures, and Techniques, Fourth Edition
Frank Bolz, Jr., Kenneth J. Dudonis, and David P. Schulz

Practical Forensic Digital Imaging: Applications and Techniques
Patrick Jones

Practical Crime Scene Investigations for Hot Zones
Jacqueline T. Fish, Robert N. Stout, and Edward Wallace

Sex-Related Homicide and Death Investigation: Practical and Clinical Perspectives, Second Edition
Vernon J. Geberth

Handbook of Forensic Toxicology for Medical Examiners
D. K. Molina

Practical Crime Scene Analysis and Reconstruction
Ross M. Gardner and Tom Bevel

Serial Violence: Analysis of Modus Operandi and Signature Characteristics of Killers
Robert D. Keppel and William J. Birnes

Bloodstain Pattern Analysis: With an Introduction to Crime Scene Reconstruction, Third Edition
Tom Bevel and Ross M. Gardner

Tire Tread and Tire Track Evidence: Recovery and Forensic Examination
William J. Bodziak

Officer-Involved Shootings and Use of Force: Practical Investigative Techniques, Second Edition
David E. Hatch and Randy Dickson

Practical Drug Enforcement, Third Edition
Michael D. Lyman

Cold Case Homicides: Practical Investigative Techniques
R. H. Walton

Principles of Bloodstain Pattern Analysis: Theory and Practice
Stuart James, Paul Kish, and T. Paulette Sutton

Global Drug Enforcement: Practical Investigative Techniques
Gregory D. Lee

Practical Investigation of Sex Crimes: A Strategic and Operational Approach
Thomas P. Carney

Principles of Kinesic Interview and Interrogation, Second Edition
Stan Walters

Practical Criminal Investigations in Correctional Facilities
William R. Bell

Practical Aspects of Interview and Interrogation, Second Edition
David E. Zulawski and Douglas E. Wicklander

Forensic Pathology, Second Edition
Dominick J. DiMaio and Vincent J. M. DiMaio

The Practical Methodology of Forensic Photography, Second Edition
David R. Redsicker

Quantitative-Qualitative Friction Ridge Analysis: An Introduction to Basic and Advanced Ridgeology
David R. Ashbaugh

Footwear Impression Evidence: Detection, Recovery, and Examination, Second Edition
William J. Bodziak

The Sexual Exploitation of Children: A Practical Guide to Assessment, Investigation, and Intervention, Second Edition
Seth L. Goldstein

Practical Aspects of Munchausen by Proxy and Munchausen Syndrome Investigation
Kathryn Artingstall

Practical Fire and Arson Investigation, Second Edition
David R. Redsicker and John J. O'Connor

Interpretation of Bloodstain Evidence at Crime Scenes, Second Edition
William G. Eckert and Stuart H. James

Investigating Computer Crime
Franklin Clark and Ken Diliberto

Practical Investigation Techniques
Kevin B. Kinnee

Friction Ridge Skin: Comparison and Identification of Fingerprints
James F. Cowger

Tire Imprint Evidence
Peter McDonald

Practical Gambling Investigation Techniques
Kevin B. Kinnee

Cold Case Homicides

Practical Investigative Techniques

R. H. Walton

CRC Press
Taylor & Francis Group
Boca Raton London New York

CRC Press is an imprint of the
Taylor & Francis Group, an **informa** business

CRC Press
Taylor & Francis Group
6000 Broken Sound Parkway NW, Suite 300
Boca Raton, FL 33487-2742

First issued in paperback 2021

Version Date: 20161031

ISBN 13: 978-0-367-77837-8 (pbk)
ISBN 13: 978-1-4822-3790-0 (hbk)

Visit the Taylor & Francis Web site at
http://www.taylorandfrancis.com

and the CRC Press Web site at
http://www.crcpress.com

Dedicated to

In memoriam

Newsome James "Jim" Gibson

S/Sgt. USMC Pacific Theater

My chief…my mentor…my friend.

Contents

Series Editor's Note

The *Practical Aspects of Criminal and Forensic Investigations* series was created by Vernon J. Geberth, a retired New York City Police Department Lieutenant Commander, who is an author, educator, and consultant on homicide and forensic investigations.

This series has been designated to provide contemporary, comprehensive, and pragmatic information to the practitioner involved in criminal and forensic investigations by authors who are nationally recognized experts in their respective fields.

Preface

The criminal justice system, indeed, the world, has changed dramatically since the first edition of *Cold Case Homicides* became the "seminal text" (Brief *Amicus Curiae* for Former and Current Law Enforcement Officials in Support of Respondent Greg McQuiggin v. Floyd Perkins USSC 12-126) on cold case homicide investigation, precipitating an upsurge in the research and writing on cold case homicide investigations. Then, as well as now, the book provides practical and convenient information to investigators, detectives, prosecutors, and others responsible for the investigation and resolution of previously investigated but unsolved cold case homicides. The content is based on my more than three decades of experience in California law enforcement as a deputy sheriff, district attorney investigator, and instructor in cold case homicide investigation techniques, years that overlapped extensive networking and research with some of the finest homicide investigators in the United States.

In presenting this material, I also draw upon a 13-year quest in which I reactivated one of America's oldest active homicide investigations, revealing a series of murders and alleged rapes set amidst official corruption during the heart of the Prohibition era. In this endeavor, in which I obtained perhaps the nation's first innocence pardon of its kind, I came to experience the same factors that the later Innocence Project identified as critical failures leading to convicting the innocent. I just did not know it at the time.

Homicide Investigation: Hot or Cold

Homicide investigation has long been considered to be the zenith for an investigator dedicated to solving violent crime. Not all who enter police work strive to be a detective or an investigator, and not all possess the drive, the energy, or the zeal to succeed in this duty slot. Nor do all possess the ability. Chief among them is the ability to look, to see, and to think independently of others. To think outside the box.

Investigation of the death of another human being is unlike any other responsibility. Whereas a homicide investigator must be able to look at a live crime scene and read it, a cold case investigator may do so only through photographs or informational documents and perhaps revisiting the locale many years later. Each must have that ability to see beyond the obvious, i.e., to "feel" it. Likewise, homicide investigation calls for strategies in approaching the investigation and approaching and interacting with people. Yet these strategies and approaches must be elastic and allow the investigator necessary freedom of thought and movement in the quest to seek the truth. This is true whether the homicide is hot or cold. Throughout, the investigator must balance education, training and experience, flexibility, understanding of human nature, and common sense with a knowledge of applicable law and techniques.

Investigators faced with a hot homicide confront situations that the unaccustomed cannot comprehend. These investigators see human tragedy set in violence, in an environment that often encompasses bloody bodies and intense human emotions. In this arena, they must sort out the basic elements of investigation—the who, what, why, how, when, and where. They ponder questions such as *MOM*, which translates to motive, opportunity, and means. In fulfilling their obligations, investigators dedicate themselves and sometimes even their relationships with their own families.

An investigator's duty, however, is to conduct a professional and intelligent investigation that seeks to bring a sense of justice to the deceased and to that person's surviving family through identification of the perpetrator and accountability through the criminal justice system. If the investigator is unable to do so, someone else may pick up the case years later. In such cases, our predecessors tried hard and did their best, but they just didn't have that one piece of evidence, that one cooperative witness, or that one bit of information. As a result, the case went cold.

The mission of today's cold case investigators is the same. Although the blood has been cleaned up and the body buried, new investigators relive the crime through photographs, reports, and follow-up interviews. What was the past is now once again the present. Like hot homicide investigators, they must detach themselves clinically and then objectively concentrate on a variety of topics, which may or may not be answered in available reports. They begin by reading a case built upon the rules and framework of another time, perhaps one far different than today. Then they must review and investigate the case with today's increased understanding of the fallibility of eyewitnesses and awareness and understanding of false confessions, as well as close scrutiny in the legal arena. Modern cold case investigators spend a lot of hours reviewing and thinking, both on and off duty. In this realm, they must struggle against personalizing the case and, instead, strive to remain objective and focus solely on the dynamics of the event. The modern cold case detective must blend experience and street knowledge with knowledge of computer systems, databases, and rapidly changing advances in forensic sciences. He/she must think forensically and still be able to exhibit skilled interview and interrogation skills with all segments of society, from hardened cons to senior citizens.

Additional frustrations for modern investigators include lost files and reports; unaccounted-for evidence; and previously unfollowed, but viable and obvious, leads. In some instances, the attitudes and unofficial policies of law enforcement agencies may appear to downplay the need to reinvestigate these most heinous of crimes. Cold case investigations demand time and fiscal, personnel, or other resources that may far surpass a hot homicide investigation. This can confound and annoy those in management. At other times, sheer incompetence or bureaucracy can stonewall the investigations. Some administrators have even suggested they see no need to go back and revisit older murder cases.

With most cold cases, the media (that fourth estate of government) is not standing in the chief's office demanding to know why these crimes are not being solved. The reality is that public pressure is sometimes a solvability factor when law enforcement agencies dedicate resources to solving a particular, high-profile crime. When I defended the proposal for my doctoral dissertation on identifying solvability factors in cold case homicide investigations, one of my professors asked why law enforcement agencies don't allocate more resources to solving cold case homicides. Another professor, a retired chief of police for a major American city, interjected, advising that he once had a group of women come into his office, asking him to allocate more resources to combat domestic violence. Because the women were proactive, the chief agreed. Soon he was running a successful domestic violence program. When asked if a similar group of people had ever demanded that he allocate more resources to solving his backlog of older unsolved murders, "No," he replied. They had not.

Teamwork and Organization

The days of the singular, jack-of-all-trades homicide investigator is over. All homicide investigations reflect modern, professional investigation methods and techniques. Both entail positive interpersonal relationships between working professionals in the law enforcement, legal, and forensic spectrums. Investigators must exhibit teamwork that fosters a positive exchange of information and knowledge and disregards personal ambition or personality differences. After all, cops are human too.

A professional homicide investigator strives to adhere to modern standards, remain objective, and seek the truth. In cold cases, however, he/she may be confronted with vestiges from the past, along with practices and attitudes that were more commonplace decades ago. Today's professional must refrain from being opinionated, tainted by racial prejudice, or prone to prejudgment. He/she must let the facts guide the actions and course of the investigation. Patience and flexibility are requisites for professional and personal success. The cold case homicide investigator must be open to new suggestions, ideas, and concepts that might be out of sync with his/her counterparts in previous investigations. As the world has changed, so have we.

Almost daily, current news reports tell us of another solved cold case. What once was uncommon is now almost common, reflecting a successful integration of these team members and their skills. Each solved case is a win and a resolution of which those involved may be justifiably proud. But another revelation has been an increased awareness of the fallibility of the criminal justice system, that in our drive to convict the guilty, we have convicted the innocent. As a result, various disciplines within the accepted forensic sciences as well as investigative procedures have been closely scrutinized. When this occurs, not only do innocent persons and their families suffer; the real perpetrators go undetected and are free to continue.

Criminal homicide generally has no statute of limitations. In the past, however, law enforcement agencies routinely investigated homicides to the degree thought possible, and when no further action was available, they filed and shelved the cases. Then, as new homicides drained department resources, many of the older homicide cases were left behind, but not forgotten by the victim's family and the perpetrators. Evidence was deliberately destroyed, and investigators moved on or passed away. During the past 30 years, we have seen the reactivation of some of the cases, however, and their solutions are presented in this book as examples of the issues and the means and methods of investigation by which such cases are resolved. Experience is a great teacher, and in these pages, we seek to learn from that of others.

Focus also is directed toward two major elements, which, when combined, offer the opportunity to solve cold case homicides. These are changes in technology and changes in relationships as enveloped in the passage of time. While the advent of DNA and other advanced forensic techniques has breathed new life into many of these old cases, modern forensics will never replace the homicide detective. A test tube cannot testify. Shoe leather, knowledge of the human character, and basic criminal investigation will continue to solve cases. These traditional methods (combined with advances in forensics) serve to ultimately bring justice to those who thought they got away with murder.

It is the purpose of this book to aid and assist the good guys in their pursuit of the bad guys.

Contents and Updates

In this updated edition of *Cold Case Homicides*, Part I addresses the background of the cold case homicide problem in America, along with an overview of previous forensics and an explanation of some of the older technology that cold case investigators may encounter when reviewing decades-old files. In addition, this segment defines and identifies cold case homicides and explores the experiences of cold case detectives in reopening and understanding their case files. Included, too, are forensic and legal considerations.

This edition features updated systems that may further assist in the identification of other cases through discussions of the Violent Criminal Apprehension Program (ViCAP), Homicide Investigation and Tracking System (HITS), and Taskforce Aimed at Catching Killers, Rapists and Sexual Offenders (TracKRS). Presented, as well, are the advances of NCIC and the National Criminal Justice Information Service, along with specialized techniques and resources involving areas not regularly encountered in homicide investigations. Since the first edition, the FBI has significantly redefined and upgraded investigative resources, and Next Generation Identification (NGI) is likewise offered here. Also revisited are techniques for interviewing senior citizens and/or others (often decades later), a review of death certificates and coroners' inquests, and the use of specialized cold case squads. The increased role of social media as well as the more traditional forms of media in the investigation of cold case homicides is similarly explored.

This updated edition also includes material on the unresolved disappearances of long-term missing persons, what the National Institute of Justice calls "the nation's silent mass disaster." Many of these cases are, without a doubt, homicides but were never investigated as such. In addition, expanded coverage is given to the investigation and prosecution of no-body murders. As the criminal landscape changes, so must we.

Part II presents technological changes that have contributed greatly to law enforcement's abilities to solve cold case homicides. What were once lumped under a general label of "fingerprints" are now "friction ridge impressions," a greatly expanded field and encompassing the role of automated fingerprint identifications systems. Building on this, the segment presents the evolution from the groupings of serology to the specificity of DNA and the future this science holds in the identification of criminal suspects. This portion also explores databases including the Combined DNA Index System (CODIS), National Integrated Ballistic Information Network (NIBIN), NGI, and the newest, the National Missing and Unidentified Persons System (NamUs), relating how they help to link people, cases, and crimes. Also provided is an expanded discussion on trace evidence in cold cases.

Part III presents additional tools and techniques that may be utilized in the investigation of cold case homicides. The contributing authors for this, and the other sections, are *outstanding* practitioners in their respective fields, allowing this text to be a grateful acknowledgment and recognition of their expertise, dedication, and professional excellence. There is no one-size-fits-all method of homicide investigation, nor is there a similar process for cold case investigations. Each brings with it a different set of circumstances and, in cold case investigations, a surviving level of documentation, original people, and evidence. The tools these authors present can contribute enormously to making an unsolved, cold case homicide a *solved* cold case homicide or resolved long-term missing-persons case.

Experienced investigators know that, not uncommonly, it is not what you know but *whom* you know. Part IV presents expanded resources that may be available to law enforcement in the course of cold case investigations. While many of these may be known to those who investigate homicides, their role in cold case investigations may be more significant. These resources and organizations are representative of the willingness of others who contribute to help their fellow citizens and to solve unsolved crimes.

This preface cannot conclude, however, without a tribute to *Vernon Geberth*, and my acknowledgment and profound gratitude to this one individual who has contributed *so much* to the betterment of law enforcement, and especially to professional homicide investigation. Vernon had the wisdom, foresight, and the vision for this original textbook. Throughout more than three decades in law enforcement, and after his retirement from the New York City Police Department as a lieutenant commander, Vernon Geberth has continued to raise the bar for those who seek to conduct criminal investigations, especially in sexual assaults and homicides. In addition to numerous professional recognitions, accolades, and achievements, Vernon Geberth has published extensively on topics relating to practical criminal investigation and forensic techniques and applied psychology. He is a nationally, and internationally, renowned author, lecturer, educator, consultant, and expert witness on the subject of death investigation. I am proud to call him a friend.

Acknowledgments

I wish to express my deepest appreciation to the many persons and agencies that have contributed to this second edition of *Cold Case Homicides: Practical Investigative Techniques.* I wish to acknowledge each individual for his/her professional expertise, suggestions, comments, photos, and case histories, which have encouraged and aided me in the completion of this first-of-its-kind book. The pages that follow are a testament to the quality of law enforcement, forensics, and their supporting disciplines in the United States, so exemplified by the following individuals. I have listed them alphabetically and apologize earnestly to any whom I have unintentionally omitted.

James Adcock, U.S. Army CID (retired), coroner and professor, Memphis, Tennessee. Detective Steve Ainsworth, Boulder County Sheriff's Office, Boulder, Colorado. Officer Robert Anderson (retired), El Cajon Police Department, El Cajon, California. Michael Arena, Criminal Intelligence Bureau, California Attorney General's Office, Division of Law Enforcement, Sacramento, California.

District Attorney Investigator Steve Baker, San Diego County District Attorney's Office, San Diego, California. Justin Bechaver, Utah Department of Public Safety. Frank Bender (deceased), forensic sculptor, Philadelphia, Pennsylvania. Capt. Tom Bevel (retired), Oklahoma City Police Department, Norman, Oklahoma. Detective Gerry Biehn, Los Angeles County Sheriff's Department Unsolved Unit, Commerce, California. Deborah Bloch, PhD, University of San Francisco, San Francisco, California. Bennett Blum, MD, Tucson, Arizona. Fred Bornhofen, chairman, Vidocq Society, Philadelphia, Pennsylvania. Sgt. Ana Peñaloza-Brackpool, Los Angeles County Sheriff's Department Homicide Bureau, Commerce, California. Tim Bradshaw, Deputy District Attorney, King County District Attorney's Office, Seattle, Washington. Detective Dave Brewer, Carbon County Sheriff's Office, Price, Utah. Chief Investigator Barry Brown (retired), Humboldt County District Attorney's Office, California. Brian Burritt, San Diego Police Department Crime Lab, San Diego, California.

Maj. George C. Cadavid (retired), Miami Police Department, Miami, Florida. Tom Callaghan, chief, CODIS Unit, Federal Bureau of Investigation, Quantico, Virginia. Detective Victor Caloca, San Diego County Sheriff's Department, San Diego, California. Anthony R. Cardoza, DDS, forensic dentist, San Diego, California. William Casper, laboratory director, California Department of Justice, Division of Law Enforcement, Bureau of Forensic Services, Eureka, California. (Late) Sgt. Alfredo Castro, Unsolved Unit, Los Angeles County Sheriff's Department, Commerce, California. Sara Chaikin, Victim-Assistance Unit, Cold Case Program, Denver Police Department, Denver, Colorado.

(Late) Judge George Clark, San Diego County Superior Court, San Diego, California. Lt. Craig Cleary (retired), El Segundo Police Department, El Segundo, California. Bonnie Collins, analyst, California Department of Justice, Sacramento, California. Detective Bob Conrad (retired), Chula Vista Police Department, Chula Vista, California. District Attorney Steve Cooley, Los Angeles County District Attorney's Office, Los Angeles, California. Gary Cordner, PhD, Eastern Kentucky University, Richmond, Kentucky. Special Agent Brad Cordts, Kansas Bureau of Investigation, Topeka, Kansas. Investigator Carl Craig, Richland County Sheriff's Department, Columbia, South Carolina. Al Crnich, Eureka, California.

Heather Davies, PhD (formerly of Police Executive Research Forum, Washington, District of Columbia), Alexandria, Virginia. John Dehaan, chief (retired), Bureau of Forensic Services, California Department of Justice, Vallejo, California. Duayne J. Dillon, DCrim, chief criminalist (retired), Alameda County Crime

Laboratory, Martinez, California. Joseph Di Zinno, DDS, deputy assistant director (retired), FBI Laboratory, Quantico, Virginia. Detective Bob Donaldson, San Diego Police Department, San Diego, California. Paul Dougherty, chief criminalist (retired), San Mateo County Sheriff's Department laboratory, Ojai, California. Capt. Jorge Duran, San Diego Police Department, San Diego, California. Marie Durina, senior forensic document examiner, San Diego County Sheriff's Department Regional Crime Laboratory, San Diego, California. Jeff Dusek, division chief (retired), deputy district attorney, Cold Case Homicide Unit, San Diego County District Attorney's Office, San Diego, California. Katharine Dyer, NIBIN Specialist, San Diego County Sheriff's Department Regional Crime Laboratory.

(Late) Detective Paul Edholm, Beverly Hills Police Department, La Palma, California. Louis N, Eliopulos, Naval Criminal Investigative Service, Virginia. Rod Englert, Chief Deputy and Commander Operations Division (retired), Multnomah County Sheriff's Department, Portland, Oregon. Julio Estrada, senior medical examiner investigator, San Diego County Medical Examiner's Office, San Diego, California.

Deputy Sheriff Dale Falicon, Los Angeles County Sheriff's Department, Los Angeles, California. Detective Sgt. James Ferguson, Cold Case Homicide Unit, El Cajon Police Department, El Cajon, California. Special Agent Carlos Field, Orange County District Attorney's Office, Santa Ana, California. John Firman, International Association of Chiefs of Police, Washington, District of Columbia. Stephen Fischer, Unit Chief, Multimedia Group, Criminal Justice Information Services, Federal Bureau of Investigation, Clarksburg, West Virginia. William Fleisher, commissioner, Vidocq Society, Philadelphia, Pennsylvania. Detective Vivian Flores, Los Angeles Police Department, Los Angeles, California. Gary Fong, *San Francisco Chronicle*, San Francisco, California. Kenneth Foote, PhD, chair, Department of Geography, University of Colorado, Boulder, Colorado. Melitta Franceschini, South Tyrol Museum of Archaeology.

Norman Gahn, assistant district attorney, Milwaukee District Attorney's Office, Milwaukee, Wisconsin. James Gannon, deputy chief of investigations, Morris County Prosecutor's Office, Morristown, New Jersey. Professor Elizabeth Gardner, Department of Justice Sciences, University of Alabama, Birmingham. Detective Ron Garvick, Sacramento County Sheriff's Department, Sacramento, California. Zach Gaskin, CEO, United Forensics, Inc., Rockwood, Pennsylvania. Capt. Duino Giordano (retired), Los Gatos Police Department, Los Gatos, California. David Godfordson, news producer, KFMB television, San Diego, California. Scott J. Goetz, Department of Geography, University of Maryland. Officer Anna Gonzales, Miami Police Department, Miami, Florida. Detective Frank Gonzales (retired), Unsolved Unit, Los Angeles County Sheriff's Department, Commerce, California. David Griffith, commander (retired), Texas Department of Public Safety, Austin, Texas. Richard Grzybowski, ATF laboratory, Walnut Creek, California. Michael Grubb, crime laboratory director, San Diego County Sheriff's Office Regional Crime Laboratory, San Diego, California.

Sharon Pagaling Hagan, supervising special agent (retired), California Department of Justice, Bureau of Investigations, Rancho Cordova, California. Thomas Hargrove, *Scripps Howard Newspaper*. Rockne "Rock" Harmon, senior deputy district attorney (retired), Alameda County District Attorney's Office, Oakland, California. Capt. Murl Harpham (retired), Eureka Police Department, Eureka, California. Detective Steve Harshberger, Michigan State Police, Alpena, Michigan. Lt. Joseph Hartshorne, Homicide Bureau, Los Angeles County Sheriff's Department, Commerce, California. Michelle Hassler, Biology Section, San Diego County Sheriff's Regional Crime Laboratory, San Diego, California. Tori Heflin, Museum of Man, San Diego, California. Detective Wally Hendricks, Carbon County Sheriff's Office, Price, Utah. Jay Henry, laboratory director, Utah Department of Public Safety.

Capt. John Hennessey, San Francisco Police Department, San Francisco, California. Robert Hickey, deputy district attorney, Gang Prosecutions Unit, San Diego County District Attorney's Office, San Diego, California. Madeleine Hinkes, PhD, D-ABFA, forensic anthropologist, San Diego, California. Detective Steve Hodel (retired), Los Angeles Police Department, Los Angeles, California. Bryan Holden, Utah Department of Public Safety. Sgt. William Holmes, Robbery Division, San Diego Police Department, San Diego,

California. Professor Frank Horvath, PhD, School of Criminal Justice (retired), Michigan State University, East Lansing, Michigan. Detective Neil Hubbard, Eureka Police Department, Eureka, California. Detective Technician Lisa Hudson, Wauwatosa Police Department, Wauwatosa, Wisconsin. Sgt. Mike Huff, homicide unit supervisor, Tulsa Police Department, Tulsa, Oklahoma. Harold Hunt, Burnt Ranch, California. Mary Ann Hunt, homicide analyst, Robbery–Homicide Division, Los Angeles Police Department, Los Angeles, California. Robert Hutton, chief of police (retired), Coronado Police Department, Coronado, California.

Jack Irvine, MD, Eureka, California. Sgt. John Jackson, Cold Case Homicide Unit, Kansas City Police Department, Kansas City, Missouri. Detective Rick Jackson, Cold Case Homicide Unit, Robbery–Homicide Division, Los Angeles Police Department, Los Angeles, California. (Late) Earl James, JD, PhD, Michigan State Police, Lansing, Michigan. Timothy Keel (detective lieutenant, Baltimore Homicide, retired), major case specialist, FBI Behavioral Analysis Unit, Quantico, Virginia. Capt. David Kelly, commander, Investigative Services Bureau, New Hampshire State Police, Concord, New Hampshire. Robert Keppell, PhD, chief investigator (retired), Washington State Attorney General's Office, Seattle, Washington. Principal criminal attorney Eric Kindall, Sacramento County District Attorney's Office, Sacramento, California. Venetia King, Criminal Information and Transition Unit, Federal Bureau of Investigation, Clarksburg, West Virginia. Supervising Special Agent Lisa Kincaid, ATF. Peter Komarinski, manager (retired), Automated Fingerprint Identification Systems, New York State Division of Criminal Justice Services, Rotterdam, New York.

Eugene J. LaChimia, criminalist, Forensic Science Section, San Diego Police Department Crime Lab, San Diego, California. Detective Dave Lambkin (retired), Cold Case Homicide Unit, Robbery–Homicide Division, Los Angeles Police Department, Los Angeles, California. Daniel G. Lamborn, deputy district attorney (retired), Cold Case Homicide Unit, San Diego County District Attorney's Office, San Diego, California. Gerry Laporte, U.S. Secret Service Laboratory, Washington, District of Columbia. Lt. Tony Leal (retired), Texas Rangers, San Antonio, Texas. Dr. Henry Lee, chief emeritus, Connecticut State Crime Lab, Meridian, Connecticut. Paul Levikow, public affairs officer, San Diego County District Attorney's Office, San Diego, California. Darren Levine, senior deputy district attorney, Los Angeles County District Attorney's Office, Los Angeles, California. John Lewin, deputy district attorney, Los Angeles District Attorney's Office, Los Angeles, California. Detective Dave Lewis (retired), Homicide Bureau, Los Angeles County Sheriff's Department, Commerce, California. Steve Loftin, forensic imaging specialist, National Center for Missing and Exploited Children, Alexandria, Virginia. Sgt. Richard Longshore, Unsolved Unit, Los Angeles County Sheriff's Department, Commerce, California. Sheriff Leon Lott, Richland County Sheriff's Department, Columbia, South Carolina. Detective Kevin Lowe (retired), Homicide Bureau, Los Angeles County Sheriff's Department, Commerce, California. Special Agent Ray Lundin, Kansas Bureau of Investigation, Topeka, Kansas.

Detective Tim Marcia, Cold Case Homicide Unit, Robbery–Homicide Division, Los Angeles Police Department, Los Angeles, California. Dan Martell, PhD, clinical assistant professor of psychiatry and behavioral sciences, Neuropsychiatric Institute, UCLA School of Medicine, Newport Beach, California. Ranger John Martin (retired), Texas Rangers, San Antonio, Texas. Special Agent Mike Matassa, ATF, Los Angeles, California. Todd Matthews, director, case management and communications, UNT Center for Human Identification, Fort Worth, Texas. Jamie Sigler McDevitt, Federal Bureau of Investigation, Clarksburg, West Virginia. Detective Dan McElderry, Homicide Bureau, Los Angeles County Sheriff's Department, Commerce, California. Sgt. Mitch McKay, Coronado Police Department, Coronado, California. Terry Melton, PhD, president and CEO (retired), Mitotyping Technologies LLC, State College, Pennsylvania. Jennifer McNair, Utah Department of Public Safety. Glen Miller, supervisor, Forensic Imaging Unit, National Center for Missing and Exploited Children, Alexandria, Virginia. Connie Milton, supervising criminalist, San Diego County Sheriff's Department Regional Crime Laboratory, San Diego, California. Matthew Mitchell, PhD, University of San Francisco, San Francisco, California. Patricia Mitchell, PhD, University of San Francisco, San Francisco, California.

Sgt. Paul Mondry, Unsolved Unit, Los Angeles County Sheriff's Department, Commerce, California. Sgt. Tim Morgan, Los Gatos Police Department, Los Gatos, California. Mitch Morrissey, district attorney, Denver, Colorado. Jeff Muckenthaler, crime analyst, Kansas Bureau of Investigation, Topeka, Kansas. Ander Murane, *Rocky Mountain News*, Denver, Colorado. Capt. Tim Murray (retired), Boston Police Department, Boston, Massachusetts.

Gerald Nance, case manager (retired), Special Case Unit, National Center for Missing and Exploited Children, Alexandria, Virginia. Linda Nance, Criminal Justice Statistics Center, California Department of Justice, Sacramento, California. Sgt. John Neff, Cold Case Homicide Unit, Austin Police Department, Austin, Texas. David O. Norris, PhD, Forensic Botany LLC, Boulder, Colorado. Patrick O'Donnell, supervisor, DNA Unit, Crime Lab, San Diego Police Department, San Diego, California. Marcutris Otani, analyst, California Department of Justice, Sacramento, California.

Edwardo Palma, certified latent print examiner (retired), Latent Print Unit, San Diego Police Department, San Diego, California. Paul Pane, information services manager, California Department of Justice, Sacramento, California. Detective Sgt. Todd Park, Salt Lake Unified Police Department, Salt Lake City, Utah. Detective David Parris (retired), Eureka Police Department, Eureka, California. William Paul, assistant civil engineer, City of San Diego, California. Capt. Raymond Peavy (retired), Homicide Bureau, Los Angeles County Sheriff's Department, Commerce, California. Sgt. Brian Pendleton, Cold Case Homicide Unit, San Diego Police Department, San Diego, California. Silvia Pettem, cold case researcher and author, Ward, Colorado. Sheriff Gary Philp (retired), Humboldt County Sheriff's Department, Eureka, California. Sgt. Darrell Price, Charlotte-Mecklenburg Police Department Cold Case Unit, Charlotte, North Carolina.

Lt. Ray Rawlins, San Diego County Sheriff's Department, San Diego, California. Tommy Ray, special agent (retired), Florida Department of Law Enforcement. Paul Redden, polygraph examiner (retired), San Diego Police Department, San Diego, California. Tony Ribera, PhD, chief of police (retired), San Francisco Police Department, San Francisco, California; Institute for International Justice, University of San Francisco, San Francisco, California. Detective Edward Reynolds (retired), Phoenix Police Department, Phoenix, Arizona. Jeff Rose, assistant chief deputy district attorney, Sacramento County District Attorney's Office, Sacramento, California. Detective Richard Rouleau (retired), Cold Case Unit, El Cajon Police Department, El Cajon, California. D. Kim Rossmo, PhD, university professor and director, Center for Geospatial Intelligence and Investigation, School of Criminal Justice, Texas State University, San Marcos, Texas.

Detective Arnold Sauro (retired), Los Angeles Police Department, Los Angeles, California. William M. Schneck, Microvision Northwest-Forensic Consulting, Inc. Anne Marie Schubert, district attorney, Sacramento County District Attorney's Office, Sacramento, California. Special agent Katie Schuetz, Kansas Bureau of Investigation, Topeka, Kansas. Sgt. Christopher Serritella, San Diego County Sheriff's Department, San Diego, California. Bonnie Shaffer, CJIS, Federal Bureau of Investigation, Clarksburg, West Virginia. Investigator Ron Shave (retired), Orange County District Attorney's Office, Santa Ana, California. Pilar Shortsleeve, Utah Department of Public Safety. Scott Snow, program director, Victim-Assistance Unit, Cold Case Program, Denver Police Department, Denver, Colorado. Susan Snyder, Bancroft Library, Berkeley, California. Norman "Skip" Sperber, DDS, forensic odontologist, forensic dental consultant, La Jolla, California. James Stam, supervising criminalist (retired), Crime Laboratory, San Diego Police Department, San Diego, California. Chief Deputy Cletis Steele, Carbon County Sheriff's Office, Price, Utah. David Steitz, public information officer, National Aeronautics and Space Administration.

Ann Stewart, FBI Laboratory, Press Section, Washington, District of Columbia. John Stewart, PhD, DNA Laboratory, Unit II, Federal Bureau of Investigation, Washington, District of Columbia. Clay Strange, attorney at law, Austin, Texas. Karen T. Taylor, forensic artist, Austin, Texas. District Attorney Investigator Ron Thill (retired), San Diego Police Department H.E.A.T. Cold Case Homicide Unit/San Diego County District Attorney's Office, San Diego, California. Assistant Director Larry Thomas, Kansas Bureau of Investigation, Topeka, Kansas. Investigator Paul Tippin (retired), Orange County District Attorney's Office,

Santa Ana, California. Katie Tobin, student intern, San Diego County Medical Examiner's Office, San Diego, California. Sgt. Frank Tona, Charles County Sheriff's Department, La Plata, Maryland. Detective James Trainum (retired), Metropolitan Police Department, Washington, District of Columbia. Maj. Larry C. Turner, commander, Criminal Investigative Division, Indiana State Police, Indianapolis, Indiana. Calvin Vine, supervising medical examiner investigator, San Diego County Medical Examiner's Office, San Diego, California.

Detective Tom Wagner, San Diego Police Department, San Diego, California. Special Agent Stanley Walker (retired), FBI, Eureka, California. William Walser, evidence technician (retired), Eureka Police Department, Eureka, California. Richard Walter, prison psychologist (retired), Montrose, Pennsylvania. Shelly Webster, Biology Section, San Diego County Sheriff's Regional Crime Laboratory, San Diego, California. Director Larry Welch (retired), Kansas Bureau of Investigation, Topeka, Kansas. Capt. Phil West (retired), Boulder County Sheriff's Department, Boulder, Colorado. Jane Whitmore (retired), ViCAP/FBI Academy, Quantico, Virginia. Eric Whitzig, major case specialist (ViCAP), FBI Academy, Quantico, Virginia. Glen W. Wildey Jr., major case specialist (ViCAP), FBI, Quantico, Virginia. Dan Williams, mortuary manager, Greenwood Memorial Park and Mortuary, San Diego, California. Sheriff Jeff Wood, Carbon County Sheriff's Office, Price, Utah. Detective Jon Woodell, El Cajon Police Department, El Cajon, California. Capt. Paul Ybarrondo (retired), San Diego Police Department, San Diego, California.

In addition, I wish to extend my deepest appreciation to the editors and staff at CRC Press for their untiring efforts in the design and production of this textbook. I wish to especially thank Misha Kydd, editorial assistant; Jay Margolis, project manager; my former senior editor, Becky McEldowney-Masterson; and my editor, Mark Listewnik, for their guidance, kindness, and support throughout the writing, editing, and publishing process; as well as Adel Rosario of MTC.

I especially wish to extend my deepest gratitude to Vernon Geberth, author of *Practical Homicide Investigation: Tactics, Procedures, and Forensic Techniques*, for his unfailing confidence, wisdom, and support. I hope he is as proud of this book as I am.

Introduction

My introduction to cold case homicide investigation began one afternoon in the early 1980s in a rural village on the north coast of California, the result of a chance conversation on a street corner while on patrol. A woman had recently died and, before passing, recanted her accusations of rape against a young Native American six decades before. If true, it meant a man had gone to prison for crimes he did not commit and justice had not been served. Everyone *knew* Jack Ryan was railroaded, I was told. If this was true, I wondered, *did he deserve to have his name cleared?*

There were no records remaining, and the current homicide rate and administrative philosophy precluded any official interest in revisiting such an old crime. Certain questions immediately needed answers. *Where to go? How to start?*

I knew nothing of this local legend, but only blocks from that street corner lived an elderly, retired newspaperman. With just a few months to live, Andy Genzoli listened to my information, retired to his study, and came back with a handful of papers. They were a start. "The law was crooked, and so was the district attorney," he told me as he handed me the bundle. The carbon paper documents were the district attorney's written account of his solution to a series murders and rapes that had occurred in the heart of Prohibition, crimes reported nationwide in the sensational journalism of the day.

As I was to learn, these events ultimately led to the imprisonment of a young Native American whose only crime was being in the wrong place at the wrong time. For this, Jack Ryan spent more than 40 years in prison and on parole for crimes later proven he did not commit. For him, justice was slow. He was commuted to time served in 1969 by Governor Ronald Reagan and granted perhaps America's first innocence pardon of its kind by Governor Pete Wilson in 1996. Posthumously. In between lay a period in which the real killers lived out their lives in freedom. Yet always looking over their shoulders.

My interest was piqued. The next 13 years would be spent reading old newspaper accounts, tracking down surviving participants or their descendants, and reconstructing a case that was never meant to be reopened. Removed and destroyed by the chief prosecutor when he himself later went to federal prison. In all, more than 400 interviews, well over half with people 65 years young or more.

For the following two years, I found myself in the newspaper morgue on my off-duty time, reading each issue of the area's two daily newspapers. These were the only surviving records that detailed what happened, the trial proceedings, and subsequent events. I copied the yellowed, dusty pages and noted names of individuals. Who they were and what they did. In this manner, I unknowingly began to build what would ultimately become, perhaps, America's oldest active homicide case. As the months became years, I filled file folders and ultimately learned to operate a revolutionary new machine—the personal computer.

The series of events that transcended the decades began with the murders of a beautiful 17-year-old girl, Carmen Wagner, and her 21-year-old male companion, Henry Sweet. The couple was shot to death while deer hunting in the remote mountains in October 1925. Jack Ryan and his half-brother, Walter David, "half-breed" Indians as they were reported in the press of the day, were arrested on "suspicion." David was later released, but Ryan was held to answer for shooting the girl. The preliminary hearing took place one month after his arrest, and trial began three months later. Events moved quickly in the 1920s.

I learned from the newspaper accounts that Ryan was acquitted in less than 24 hours after a lengthy trial by a jury of white men, a trial marked by perjury and planted evidence. This case was my introduction to Edward Oscar Heinrich, perhaps America's first academically trained forensic scientist. He collected and examined the evidence. Decades after his death, Heinrich's records allowed an in-depth review of this aspect of these events. In these pages, I saw the infancy of forensics as we know it today. The idea of blood spatter analysis and of the ability to allegedly match a fired shell casing or bullet to a specific firearm.

After the trial, Ryan returned to being a cowboy. But the politics of Prohibition had doomed him. A new DA was elected and immediately set out to solve the crimes, all the while running the biggest bootlegging ring in the county from inside the district attorney's office. Walter David was murdered shortly thereafter in a torture killing, most likely committed by bad cops. Ultimately, Ryan was arrested and charged with several rapes of young girls. To stay alive, he pled guilty to the rapes. Held overnight in the county jail, Ryan was interrogated under conditions and circumstances not uncommon for the period. Shortly after daybreak on September 14, 1928, Jack Ryan confessed to the murders. Within hours, he was given a preliminary hearing and, later that same afternoon—without an attorney—pled guilty to the murder of Sweet and was immediately sentenced to life in prison. By 7 p.m., he was en route to San Quentin State Prison, where he would spend the next 26 years before parole in 1953.

Ultimately, my efforts would officially reactivate this homicide case. The rape victim's role in a series of Prohibition-era murders, rapes, and political corruption became apparent, as indeed, the guilty suspects escaped, while an innocent Indian served time. As events unfolded, I found myself going to lengths not encountered when conducting a current homicide investigation, yet, which complement modern homicide investigation techniques.

Homicide cases can rise or fall on tiny bits of information or evidence. Without realizing it, I found myself combining current homicide investigation techniques with the fields of history, anthropology, and perhaps archaeology. I was digging up the past, events that more than a few wished left undisturbed. My landscape was not only the remote mountain crime scenes but also state and federal archives. City directories and assessors' maps, civil and probate files, and other arenas not normally encountered in a homicide investigation were exhumed to reveal the hidden skeletons left behind by parties identified in my investigation.

And, of course, years of daily newspaper review as each article was photocopied, its contents computerized for informational purposes, time line content, and value. I found myself searching for photos in old family photo albums, diaries and notes, crime scene maps, and evidence files. Coloring outside the box to find remnants of aged official records filed far from the scene of the crime. Original investigator notebooks were uncovered in the attics of time. In the course of this, I began to meet people who wanted to tell me what they had known but never told anyone else. I found myself interviewing people with direct, firsthand knowledge. Original witnesses from a series of events 60 years in the past. Slowly, the truth, and the cover-up, began to emerge.

From the White House to Wall Street, and from the governor's office in Sacramento to university archives and an old mining town in Idaho, I found myself compiling information from a myriad of sources that seem distant from those events that occur when a homicide has just been reported. Like a current homicide, however, I was looking for evidence. I was looking for witnesses, physical evidence, and persons with direct, firsthand knowledge. But there were no patrol cars with flashing lights, no crime scene tape, and no crime scene specialists responding to recover trace evidence.

I did not have the benefit of face-to-face interviews with major original participants in which I could gauge reactions to my questions or watch the body language. I did not have the benefit of experienced investigators leading me through the steps involved in my undertaking. There was no mentoring that told me I was on the right track or off on a wild goose chase. This was my first homicide investigation. Indeed, some whispered about my sanity, and certainly, the department had no interest in supporting my investigation. The more questions I asked, however, the more wrong everything seemed to be. People were evasive, and some were downright untruthful. Even my own captain of operations. *Why?* I wondered. *It was so long ago. Who cares?*

It would be years, however, before I learned that my supervising captain was related to the woman who had recanted her statements before death. "You're on your own in this one," he admonished me sternly. Interestingly enough, while never revealing what he did know, he never attempted to discourage me either. In one of the many quirks that can happen over the years in these cases, I would come to learn that a sole surviving grand juror who participated in the investigation of this case in the late 1920s had recently been murdered. He and his wife were bludgeoned to death in their farmhouse. By a nephew of the recently deceased "rape" victim.

As I tried to combine a current homicide investigation with historical research, I had one luxury. I had no TV cameras or media looking for sound bites and film clips for the evening news. Years later, I would realize how much this helped me recreate a series of infamous events that polarized the community and that saw numerous reinvestigations, state and federal, in the succeeding decades. The case was written up in the true crime magazines over the decades. Few believed, it seemed, that Ryan was guilty.

As I conducted scores of interviews with people in their 70s through their 90s, I learned a lot about life and the human experience as we age. I learned what worked and what did not when trying to elicit information under these circumstances. Theirs was a different perspective on life than it was six decades before. I came to understand that I had to overcome perspectives of the police formed in an era of the Keystone Cops and Jimmy Cagney movies, a period of well-known corruption.

Naively at first, I thought they would open up for me. After all, the 1920s were a long time ago, and the past was the past. *Wasn't it?* Surely, they did not harbor hard feelings, or fears, from so long ago. *Did they?* I came to realize that, *yes,* they did. Some were still terrified of a man who had died decades before. For some, including a killer who sat in the backseat of my car, it was yesterday. Over the years, I felt like I had one foot on a banana peel and the other on their graves as my interviews accelerated. I came to see, and to try to identify with, the emotions of those who are caught up in the fabric of murder so long ago. I didn't need clinical research and "data" to tell me that the pain and the hurt are just below the surface. It always has been and always will be, and it was increasingly visible for me. Slowly, some opened up and revealed what they knew. It was a lot.

For those with something to hide, the fear of buried events coming to the surface brought forth a terror, and a danger, which I did not immediately recognize. The fear was multifaceted. It was a fear not only for themselves but, perhaps more importantly, that their children and grandchildren would find out about their terrible secret. Grandfather executed a terrified, 17-year-old girl with two shots to her head in a remote canyon. A life spent running and hiding was in danger of exposure. I learned that although blood can be thicker than water, there are those who know something and, given the right circumstances, may come forward. Others, related to one of the victims, told me to "let it be." They did not want the case reopened. Ultimately, I would learn why.

Something else happened during this inquiry. I also began to uncover information on other murders, or secondary homicides, as former bootleggers and others who did not have long to live cautiously opened up. I had reviewed these cases as tangential issues to my case and came to believe that they were telling some truths as they fed me bits and pieces of information about crimes they participated in, or seemingly had firsthand knowledge of. I began to wonder, *How many other unsolved murders were out there? How many killers were undetected, and still alive?* Perhaps still plying their horrible crimes.

I realized that investigation of the crimes entailed understanding the era—the time, place, and circumstance in which the crimes occurred. I learned about Prohibition and the effects upon local, state, and national politics. One consequence was the trickle-down effect into the courtroom. I came to appreciate how far law enforcement practices have come in the last 25 years, a sequence of fitting the suspect to the evidence instead of fitting the evidence to the suspect, a practice once not uncommon.

DNA has brought forth a whole new chapter in our ability to identify perpetrators of violent crimes. Fingerprint and DNA databases are tremendous resources. It was not that long ago, however, when science could only tell us whether the blood on the suspect or victim came from a human or an animal, and not much else. Only in the mid–twentieth century did the science of blood pattern analysis gain a positive foothold in forensic circles.

Forensics. A mainstay of current police investigative practice, it was not many decades in the past that anyone with a camera and a test tube could call himself/herself an expert and consult on criminal cases for significant fees. Notorious criminal trials in the first half of the twentieth century, and some into the second half, have focused on the reliability and competency of the forensic evidence and the forensic practitioners. Junk science truly was junk science, and we do not know how many wrongful convictions resulted. Or how many guilty were never exposed.

Since 1930, the FBI has maintained extensive records on crime in America, including homicide. The annual FBI uniform crime report (UCR) details murder in all its categories, including victim–offender relationship, time of day, weapon, and more. Similarly, state criminal justice agencies have kept a myriad of records and publish their own annual reports about murder and other crimes. Academics, policy makers, the news media, and more can review these data in furtherance of their specific task. In doing so, we see that murder is reported both in the numbers of murders that occur each year and in the percentage of those reported that are cleared.

Missing from these reports, however, is any finding or reporting of the numbers of murders that remain open and unsolved. Some murders are solved quickly, even within hours. Others may take weeks, months, or even years to compile enough evidence to identify the suspect, link him/her to the crime, and make an arrest.

Despite our best efforts, however, some murders are not solved. When all viable leads have been followed up, and fresher cases compete for scarce resources, cases are suspended from active action. When this occurs, they are filed, pending new information. They become cold cases. There are no national statistics of unsolved cases. These reside within the domain of the responsible investigating agency and are not reported.

As the years pass, these cases grow colder. Investigators move on in their careers. They retire, but they do not forget. Time, once an enemy in homicide investigation, slowly becomes a friend. Technology and relationships change. In the past decades, we have seen a resurgence of interest in cold case investigations as more and more agencies dust off old files and utilize our newfound knowledge in pursuit of justice for those who cannot speak. These cases become a passion for those homicide cops who investigate them, an obsession to see justice done for the victim and their family. Sometimes, we find the wrong person went to jail. We need to work just as hard to exonerate the innocent as we do to convict the guilty.

There is no magic checklist, no one-size-fits-all method of cold case homicide investigation. No text can cover all the bases or consider every potential scenario involved. Some cases involve more effort than others. But in the end, they boil down to dedicated cops and prosecutors who seek justice. And their partners in the crime lab.

This text attempts to discuss some of the means and techniques used in practical cold case homicide investigation, and to present the experiences of detectives who have solved cold cases. I hope that their experiences inspire and assist those who come after.

Investigation

I

The Cold Case Problem

1

R. H. WALTON

Contents

Introduction

The purpose of this chapter is to present the background of homicide in the United States, how it has been identified and recorded, and the emergent basis for practical unsolved homicide investigation. In addition, this chapter will also review trends and patterns of twentieth-century homicides in the United States, and how these affect the investigations and operations of homicide investigators assigned to investigate unsolved, *cold case* homicides in the twenty-first century. This chapter will review homicide and homicide data to identify the scope of unsolved murders in the United States at this time, and will review trends and advances in the forensic sciences and their application to cold case homicide investigation. The chapter will conclude by reviewing circumstances that contribute to cases growing cold and to recent trends to reinvestigate such cold cases.

Hot versus Cold Case Homicide

The very use of the term *cold case* is controversial among homicide investigators and others associated with the investigation of unsolved murders. Such terminology may suggest to some that unsolved cases are unworkable and impossible, and offer no hope for future solution. This term may convey a false impression to family and friends of unsolved murder victims that their cases do not count anymore, that their case will never be resolved, and that as a result, their case is old and "cold" and has been forgotten. Counter to this philosophy is the use of the term *unsolved* when it comes to referencing to such murder cases. As will be discussed in future chapters, the wounds of murder are subsurface in the hearts and minds of those who have suffered the violent loss of a loved one or a close friend, and "closure" is a misnomer. Like the proverbial pebble cast upon still waters, the ripple effect continues. There is *no* closure.

A common perception of cold case homicides is that they are unsolved murders previously reported to law enforcement and investigated but that failed to result in the identification and arrest of a suspect and filing of criminal charges. Due to the passage of time and lack of investigative leads, they are no longer actively pursued by investigators. To the best of my knowledge, the popular application of the phrase and the concept of "cold case" homicide has been attributed to the news media in the Metro Dade region of Florida.

A high-profile rape–murder of an 11-year-old girl during a surge in homicides in the 1980s prompted the homicide section to assign a four-man team of highly experienced detectives to solve the case. They did so, and the concept of a special team of investigators to work unsolved cases that others do not have time to work grew. The effort was the first of a number of successes for the "Pending Case Squad." The media, however, coined a new term and called them the "Cold Case Squad." The name stuck. Similarly, "cold" has been used in countless western and police movies when describing a trail or a search for someone. The Los Angeles County Sheriff's Department (California) however, has maintained its unsolved unit in the Homicide Bureau since the 1970s. In the past two decades, numerous law enforcement agencies have formed their own cold case squads, with detectives and investigators tasked to reinvestigate previously investigated yet unsolved murders.

Some of these will be presented in the following chapters.

Media focus and attention on this topic in the past decade have brought about public awareness of this aspect of homicide investigation. In a positive manner, this attention has

- Stimulated public interest in rejuvenating older unsolved cases
- Provided public understanding and support when law enforcement designates resources to investigate cold cases
- Encouraged those with knowledge of unsolved homicides to come forward
- Stimulated law enforcement organizations to become more proactive in reviewing cold cases
- Reminded those who have so far gotten away with murder that law enforcement does not forget and their case has not been forgotten

Conversely, *hot* homicides are those murders that have been reported to law enforcement and are in the initial, active investigation phase. Most commonly in this scenario,

- A murder or finding of a body is reported to law enforcement.
- Officers and investigators respond to the scene.
- Witnesses are located and interviewed.
- Forensic services are enlisted.
- The victim is identified.

- The cause and manner of death are established.
- Investigators seek to identify what happened and who did it.
- In doing so, they write reports and document their actions, building the case day by day.
- These actions result in the identification and arrest of a suspect and filing of criminal charges. If not, the case may become an unsolved homicide.

Once the media coins a term, we are often stuck with it whether we like it and agree with it or not. In the past two decades, "cold case homicide" has come to be collectively understood by the public and the media as an older, unsolved murder. What is cold to one investigator or to one law enforcement agency, however, may not be shared by other investigators or agencies.

For the purposes of this book, murder is the intentional killing of one human being by another without legal justification or excuse. While it is the least frequent violent crime, it is also the ultimate crime against the person. In our culture, we value life and do not want anyone to get away with murdering another person. For the protection of society and the rule of law, it is incumbent upon the police to identify those who kill and for the criminal justice system to adjudicate their actions in accordance with the law.

In both hot and cold homicide scenarios, investigators routinely seek to answer the questions

- *What* happened?
- *Why* was the victim killed?
- *Who* had the opportunity to do it?
- *How* did it happen?
- *Why* did it happen?
- *Where* did it happen?

As in a hot homicide investigation, cold case investigators seek to learn why the victim was killed and who had the means, opportunity, and motive to do so (MOM). Over the centuries, these motives have not changed. People still commit murder for love, for money or power, in anger or rage, or for retribution of a real or imagined wrong. Cold case investigators may also consider

- Murder–suicide
- Thrill killing
- Self-defense
- Random killing
- Sex and sadism
- Love triangles
- Jealousy
- Drug connection
- Gang involvement

What + How + Why + When = Who?

Whichever the case, there is no *one-best-way* or *one-size fits-all* method of investigation. Each cold case is investigated on its own merits and the circumstances surrounding the crime, building upon those records available to modern investigators. Modern cold case investigation teams use professional law enforcement practices with forensic knowledge and technology. This combination has been successfully applied to revisiting unsolved murders dating back 10, 20, even 40 years, or more.

"Iceman"

The circumstances and cause of death surrounding Iceman illustrate a number of lessons for those who would examine cold cases. Iceman, or Iceman Ötzi, was a well-preserved human being whose mummified remains were discovered frozen face down in a glacier approximately 11,000 feet above sea level in the Ötztal Alps bordering Italy and Austria in September 1991. The reporting parties were two German hikers. It was initially believed that he was a hiker who had died from a fall, or perhaps perished from hypothermia or drowning (Figure 1.1).

Examination of the remains, clothing, and possessions—he was armed with an unfinished bow, arrows, and dagger—indicated that he was approximately 46-year-old and had died approximately 5300 years before. The find ultimately became a media sensation and attracted the interest of the public and researchers worldwide, perhaps not unlike media attention in high-profile cases today. Initial theories and findings regarding the cause and manner of death—including suggestions that he was a human sacrifice—have been revised based upon still ongoing investigation and research, and now suggest the circumstances surrounding his final meal, movements, and events preceding his death, information desirable in cold case investigations.

Forensic examination revealed an arrow point in his left shoulder. Years later, however, one of the two people who discovered the body subsequently stated that when first observed, Iceman was clutching a knife

Figure 1.1 Iceman Otzi. (© South Tyrol Museum of Archaeology, http://www.iceman.it.)

in his right hand. Such information, as in more recent cold case homicide investigations, brought a fresh examination and interpretation of the deceased and of the events surrounding his death.

A knife *had* been found at the scene but was apparently dislodged when the mummified remains were removed. A cold case investigator seeking to examine this case would inquire if there were any photographs taken *in situ*, before the body was moved. When later placed in Iceman's clenched hand, the knife did fit. Examinations revealed what appeared to be a defensive wound on his right hand, a gash on his left hand, a slash on his right forearm, and bruising on his torso. DNA examination of his effects revealed different sequences of ancient human DNA. DNA from his cloak, a broken arrow point, the arrow shaft, and his knife blade did not match Iceman's DNA.

Modern forensic disciplines and medicodisciplines involved included DNA, plant morphology, metallurgy, archeology, odontology, anthropology, and more. Ultimately, examiners concluded that he had been involved in a fight. He had been shot with an arrow from behind while fighting with at least one other assailant and most likely bled to death from the arrow wound, although scientists now believe the fatal wound was a blow to the head (Owen 2013). In many ways, this was the coldest of cold cases!

Murder in the Twentieth Century

The number of unsolved murders in the United States is unknown. No comprehensive databases for reporting or recording murder existed in the United States throughout the twentieth century, and none exist today that track unsolved cases on a national basis. The Vital Statistics Division of the National Center for Health Statistics (NCHS) records mortality information resulting from death certificate information as received from coroners and/or medical examiners.

In the early years of the twentieth century, some states reported death certificate information, while others did not. It was not until the 1930s that vital statistics reporting became fully national. Prior to this time, the reliability and presence of this information depended on which cities and states participated. While some eastern cities such as Boston and Washington, DC, furnished such information in the late nineteenth century, Georgia reportedly did not begin to provide this information until 1922, and Texas followed suit in 1933. Beginning in the mid-1930s, data based on law enforcement and mortality have been increasingly more reliable than the sporadic data of the first third of the century (NCHS 2004).

Interestingly enough, in the early part of the century, coroners in some locales in the United States practiced a fee-for-service program for enumeration. By this method, they were paid in part depending upon the manner of death they decreed for each death. A fee schedule was linked to the cause of death reported, irrelevant of the difficulty or length of time of the case. In the case of murder, the fee was often to be collected from the convicted perpetrator. One can only imagine that when a body was found with multiple gunshot wounds in the back, and with no known suspect in sight, the cause and manner of death may have been recorded as other than murder. I have reviewed some murder cases going back to the 1930s in which I wonder about the true circumstances of death.

Modern Crime Reporting

According to the U.S. Department of Justice, Bureau of Justice Statistics (BJS), homicide is of interest not only due to its severity but also because it is a fairly reliable barometer of all violent crime and is a crime most likely to be reported and investigated (BJS 1.5.04). No other crime is measured as precisely and accurately as homicide. In addition, homicide is one means by which the public gauges police operation and efficiency. In 1929, the International Association of Chiefs of Police established a system to begin to uniformly collect law enforcement statistics and record national crime information. This was done in such a way as to standardize variations in which crimes were defined in various regions of the county.

The following year, the Bureau of Investigation (later renamed the Federal Bureau of Investigation or FBI) initiated the Uniform Crime Reporting (UCR) program. Subsequently, law enforcement data at the national level began to be compiled in 1933 (FBI UCR 8.22.04). The UCR program collects and publishes criminal offense, arrest, and law enforcement personnel statistics. The program's principal objective is to generate a reliable set of criminal justice statistics for use in the administration and management of law enforcement. Information on the number of persons arrested includes numerous other additional crime types including drug abuse violations and driving under the influence (FBI).

Sources of early murder data are sometimes questionable or incomplete. Not every jurisdiction and police agency participated in this program in the early 1930s. The program's initial objective was to provide an accounting of the nature and extent of criminal activity, and was intended to serve as an administrative tool for better criminal justice management within law enforcement agencies. In the succeeding decades, the UCR has become a source to gauge the country's social order and is referenced by urban planners and scholars.

Under the UCR system, the FBI Criminal Justice Information Services Division publishes an annual report, *Crime in the United States*. The data for this report are gathered from monthly reports submitted by law enforcement as known to law enforcement. This information is reported directly to the FBI or through respective centralized state agencies. This report summarizes the amount of crime reported the previous year, categorizing these as Violent Crime (previously Part 1 offenses) or Property Crime offenses (previously Part 2 offenses). The Violent Crimes category includes

- Homicide and nonnegligent manslaughter (set as bulleted list)
- Rape
- Robbery
- Aggravated assault

Property Crimes include

- Burglary (set as bulleted list)
- Larceny–theft
- Motor vehicle theft
- Arson (added in 1979)

Together, these eight crimes reflect and gauge fluctuations in the overall volume and rate of crime. Additional categories reported include clearances, persons arrested, and others. In the UCR (2014), we find statistics reflecting victim–offender relationships in known homicides. These reflect both direct family members as well as acquaintances and friends. The UCR is a continually evolving document. Awareness of a victim–offender relationship is an important component of many homicide investigations, and this relationship may become more viable in cold case investigations.

Rates and Trends, 1900–2000

Homicide

Population and demographic changes and post-turn-of-the-century immigration changed the nation. During this period, the nation underwent transformation from agrarian and rural to more urban in nature, and the big cities saw concentrated pockets of those with similar ethnic and cultural origins. The crime patterns and

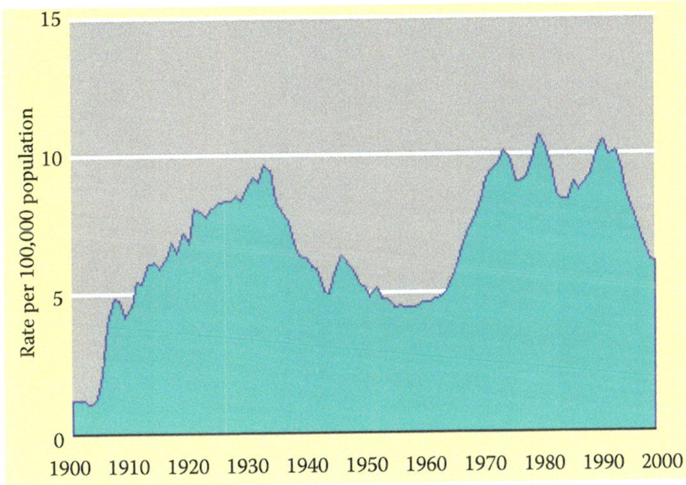

Figure 1.2 Homicide rate, 1900–2000. (Courtesy of National Center for Health Statistics, Vital Statistics.)

trends that originated during this period have in part become the basis for police, legal, and forensic practices today. During this period, the murder rate has varied significantly. This is reflected in Figure 1.2.

The compilation of homicide data from death certificates for the whole of the twentieth century makes it possible to view rises and falls in the homicide rate, the number of homicide victims per 100,000 population. This can be viewed against a backdrop of national events, and certain major occurrences appear to have contributed to changes in the crime rate during the century. According to the National Vital Statistics System, the murder rate rose from 1 homicide per 100,000 population to a peak of 9.8 in 1933; it fell to a low of 4.5 per 100,000 population between 1934 and 1958 and rose to peak at 10.2 per 100,000 population in 1980 (Report to the Nation).

Post–World War I (WWI) events saw increased reporting on crime by the national press and reaction from state and federal governments. National Prohibition, that period between 1920 and 1933 when America went dry, brought organized crime to the forefront of national attention and the efforts of federal law enforcement to assume a stronger role in criminal investigation. In part due to the use of machine guns by gangsters and others during this period, America witnessed the origins of national gun control through the beginning of the National Firearms Act in 1934, which regulated private possession of fully automatic firearms. High-profile crimes such as the 1932 Lindberg abduction brought forth federal legislation addressing kidnapping as well as the federal Bank Robbery Act of 1934. These and others paved the way for future federal legislation encompassing a wide variety of topics in the later part of the century.

The subsequent period witnessed the recovery from the Great Depression and the onset of WWII. These events affected the homicide rate, as evidenced by a sharp decline during the war years and a short time rise thereafter. The rates fell during the 1950s, but the maturity of the postwar baby boom began to emerge in the early 1960s. At this time, the homicide rate began to rise sharply. Subsequently, this increase occurred against a backdrop of the Vietnam War and the sharp increase in drugs and gangs.

Clearance Rates

Clearance rates are the number of homicides that are cleared or solved. Law enforcement agencies like to reflect high clearance rates for homicide and other violent crimes. In some instances, however, reviews have found that cases were "closed by arrest" but charges were subsequently not filed, or were dismissed at preliminary hearing. During these last decades, however, another trend became evident. This trend is a foundation for cold case investigators: the number of homicides cleared by arrest has been declining (Figure 1.3).

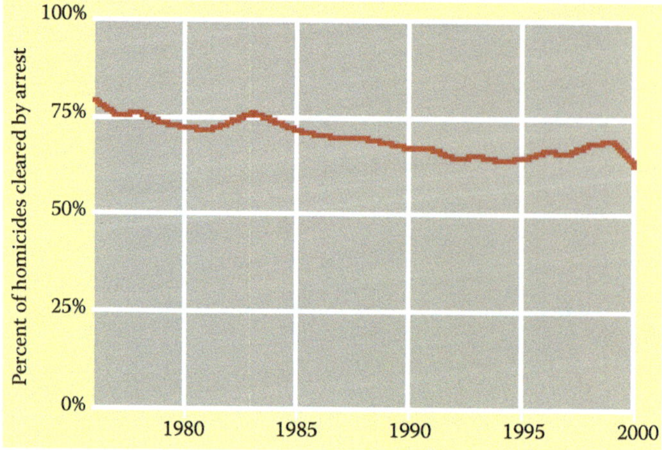

Figure 1.3 Homicides cleared by arrest, 1976–2000. (From Bureau of Justice Statistics.)

Acting as a national clearinghouse for such homicide data, the FBI uniform crime report also describes the conditions by which a homicide case is considered solved or cleared (closed) for crime report purposes. Each of these is a potential option in closing a cold case investigation.

These are as follows:

- When at least one person is arrested, charged with the commission of an offense, and turned over to a court for prosecution.
- By exceptional means. This occurs when circumstances beyond the law enforcement agency's control preclude the agency from placing formal charges against an identified offender. To clear a crime in this manner, an agency must have (1) identified the offender; (2) enough evidence to support an arrest; (3) identified the offender's location; and (4) a reason outside the agency's control that does not allow the agency to arrest, charge, and prosecute an offender. These circumstances may occur when the offender dies by suicide or is justifiably killed by police or citizenry. Official closure of the case may also result when the victim refuses to cooperate with the prosecution after the identification of the offender or denial of extradition because the offender committed a crime in another jurisdiction and is being prosecuted.

Background of Current Cold Case Problem

The last quarter of the twentieth century saw significant factors that affected homicide clearances. According to the BJS, contributing agencies provided supplemental information for 466,195 of the estimated 512,550 murders estimated to have been committed between 1976 and 2000. Additionally, supplemental information was also provided for 516,005 of the estimated 564,547 offenders. While the FBI report is based upon information reported by law enforcement agencies, not all agencies report data to it. As a result, the data reflected in the crime report are not absolute figures but are *estimates*. The most significant problem, however, in using this supplemental data to analyze offender characteristics "is the sizeable and growing number of unsolved homicides contained in the data file" (BJS).

In 2010, Scripps Howard News Service newsman Thomas Hargrove, using raw data and homicide data provided by the FBI, reported that of 565,637 known homicides between January 1, 1980, and December 31, 2008, 184,992 were unsolved. During this period, the national clearance rates ranged from a high of 76% in

1983 to a low of 61% in 2006 and 2007. He concluded, "Nearly 185,000 cases of homicide and non-negligent manslaughter went unsolved from 1980 to 2008…and that the rate at which homicides are solved has been declining during the past three decades" (Hargrove 2016).

This is significant for understanding the cold case problem in the United States as estimates suggest that perhaps 40% of the murders nationwide have remained unsolved. It is important to note that arrests made subsequent to the initial reporting would impact the total number of unsolved cases, but as this information is not tracked outside of the investigating agency, this information is not known. However, these numbers indicate the potential scope of the problem.

Analysis of long-term trends reported by the BJS (2011) suggested that the homicide rate doubled from the early 1960s to the late 1970s, peaking at 10.2 per 100,000 population in 1980, and falling off only to rise again in the late 1980s and early 1990s to peak at 9.8 per 100,000 in 1991. By 1997, the nation's murder rate fell to the lowest level in three decades. Most of this occurred in cities with more than 1 million inhabitants, where the rate fell from 35.5 per 100,000 population in 1991 to 20.3 per 100,000. Nationally, murder rates declined to 5.5 per 100,000 by 2000, levels last seen in the mid-1960s (BJS 2004). This decline allowed many law enforcement agencies the opportunity to dedicate resources to the reexamination of previously unsolved, cold case homicides.

It may be that many of the cold cases with potential for reinvestigation will fall within these periods, or later, and in this time frame, we see significant changes in investigative and forensic practices that may assist in this regard.

Figuratively speaking, however, as each decade advances, it may be fair to say that one decade's worth of unsolved cases falls off at the back end, due to this passage of time.

Advances in Forensic Science

Trace evidence, the idea that there occurred a transfer of telltale evidence from an offender to a victim or a crime scene, was formally advanced in the early twentieth century by Edmond Locard (1877–1966). A Frenchman, Locard was the founder of the anthropometric service within the Lyon Police Service shortly before WWI. Locard later served as an educator in forensics and strongly advocated analysis and examination of microscopic "trace" evidence. He noted that inculpatory evidence of a perpetrator was to be found in the examination of soil and dust, and that examination of clothing, shoes, underclothing, body parts (including skin, hair, and nails), as well as weapons and vehicles would reveal a telltale linkage between the offender and the scene or the victim. If the offender did not bring something to the scene, he certainly took something away, and proper forensic, microscopic examination would reveal it. Thus, the foundations of trace, or microscopic, evidence are to be found in the contact between people, places, and objects. With the advent of DNA technology late in the century, Locard's theories are consistent with our use of this advanced technology. See Chapter 16.

Blood and Serology

Scientific investigation in the nineteenth century, as it was, recognized the forensic potential for detecting blood at crime scenes and upon the clothing of suspected perpetrators. At the beginning of the twentieth century, science lacked a reliable method of distinguishing between bloodstains of an animal and of a human. Bloodstains did not mean much in most investigations, as a claim could be made that they came from a nosebleed or an animal, depending upon the need of the suspect. Science could not reliably differentiate.

This changed in 1901, however, when Paul Uhlenhuth discovered a method to distinguish human blood from that of animals. This was the beginning of the branch of science of serology. The precipitin test, as it came to be known, soon became a benchmark in scientific criminology. About this same time, Karl Landsteiner reasoned the existence of different blood types and the compatibility or incompatibility among certain groups of people. He identified three blood groups, A, B, and C. Shortly thereafter, C became AB, and O was recognized. Thus, the four groups we know today were identified in the first years of the twentieth century. The use of this knowledge was primarily applied to paternity issues, however. For criminal cases in America, the science did not go far beyond separating animal from human during the first half of the century. Blood spatter, or blood pattern analysis, likewise was generally not recognized for its forensic value at this time.

Firearms Identification and Other Evidence

The concept of matching a fired projectile to a specific firearm dates at least to the eighteenth century. More formal, albeit less scientific, application of this concept began to surface in the later part of the 1900s and early twentieth century. A series of high-profile crimes during the first quarter of the century focused America's attention on the application of science to the criminal justice process and the courtroom. On April 15, 1920, an armored-car robbery in Braintree, Massachusetts, resulted in the shooting deaths of a guard and a paymaster. Police arrested shoe factory worker Nicola Sacco and itinerant fish peddler Bartolomeo Vanzetti, and they were charged with the murders. This was the era of the Red Scare, and both men were active anarchists. Racial and political overtones transcended the legal aspects of the case, and it attracted international attention.

Forensic examination presented by the prosecution affirmed that their weapon fired the fatal shots, and both were sentenced to death. Others disagreed. In the courtroom process, those who testified for the prosecution that fired projectiles and shell casings came from a specific weapon were countered by experts for the defense that the suspect weapon did not fire the items. After lengthy legal appeals and controversy surrounding witness identification and forensic presentations in the courtroom, both men were executed in 1927. In this and other cases, juries were left to believe or disregard the testimony of "experts." During this period, anyone with a microscope and a camera could hold themselves out to be a "criminologist," and the field was marked by charlatans and frauds. The expert witness had come to stay.

In June 1925, the *Saturday Evening Post* reported upon the advances in forensics as pertaining to firearms examinations and "fingerprinting" of bullets. The public was informed of the advances in matching fired projectiles to specific firearms and of a new device, the comparison microscope. This piece of equipment was developed by Charles Waite, a former New York attorney general's investigator; John Fisher, a student of physics; chemist Howard Gravelle; and reserve army officer Calvin Goddard, MD. It utilized two lens systems, which, when combined with prisms, allowed an examiner to bring two images side by side for comparison. Thus, an examiner could compare a suspect projectile and a known exemplar together under conditions more conducive to accurate comparison and analysis than previous methods. Goddard and others advanced the use of forensic sciences and the establishment of formal schools for training others in the application of science to the courtroom and in the criminal investigation process. Goddard and others were the harbingers of professional standards in the area of identifying characteristics of spent bullets and shell casings, and upon examination of firearms for forensic purposes.

On the West Coast in this same time period, Edward O. Heinrich (Figure 1.4) offered law enforcement and the courtroom process the results of years of formal academic training and experience in the physical sciences. He was, perhaps, America's first academically trained forensic scientist. Upon graduation from the University of California at Berkeley with a degree in chemistry in 1908, Heinrich began to apply the field to areas in criminal investigation. As a generalist, his practice included a variety of forensic skills, including questioned document and firearms examination. During the ensuing decades, he was employed to examine evidence in a multitude of high-profile murders and other cases. Upon his death in 1953, his life works including case files, notebooks, photo archives, and other records were bequeathed to his alma mater. *Evidence is where you find it.*

Figure 1.4 Criminalist E. O. Heinrich. For the first half of the twentieth century, Edward Oscar Heinrich advanced the forensic sciences by his application of science and technology in many high-profile criminal and civil cases. (Courtesy of Duayne J. Dillon, DCrim.)

Cold case investigators can benefit from Heinrich's example. When reviewing cold cases in which any or all of the law enforcement or forensic participants have passed away, it is suggested that investigators identify those who may possess their files and records and establish what records may still exist and review them. In the 1954 "Boulder Jane Doe" case described in Chapter 22, investigators located the original pathologist, who still retained a copy of his autopsy report. My investigation into the 1925 murders and subsequent alleged rapes discovered the existence and location of Heinrich's case files, which included extensive notes, reports, and photographs. Among these records was the forensic case file for the Wagner–Sweet homicide case. Figure 1.5 illustrates Heinrich's file photograph of Ryan's jacket. An examination of the bloodstains by a research physician identified human and nonhuman stains, a fact supporting Ryan's account and discounting the prosecution. Accompanying notes and newspaper accounts reported that the

Figure 1.5 Jack Ryan's jacket. In 1925, technology only allowed differentiation between human and animal blood. In this report concerning analysis of blood found on a suspect's jacket, Dr. Ernest Victors determined that both human and animal blood were present on the jacket. This ran counter to the prosecution's theory that only human blood was present and helped exonerate the defendant, who had a logical explanation for the presence of both types. (Courtesy of University Archives, Bancroft Library, University of California, Berkeley.)

pins were used to denote the direction of blood spatter. This file and its contents provided detailed information about case events and case forensics.

As do many such investigations, methods and techniques used involve thinking *outside the box*. Successful cold case investigations are often concluded as a result of investigators who are resourceful and use imagination not normally associated with hot homicide investigations.

In the 1920s, local and state government agencies slowly began to build crime labs that could analyze physical evidence. In 1932, using a borrowed microscope, the origins of the FBI laboratory were born. By the middle of the century, the facility was conducting examinations for federal agencies and local and state law enforcement agencies. At this laboratory and others, forensic examinations included those related to firearms, serology, toolmark, paint, questioned documents, tire treads, shoe prints, and forensic geology. The field had come a long way in a short time. See Figure 1.6.

Forensic Sciences and Advanced Technology

In the 1950s, scientific breakthroughs laid the groundwork for significant advances in forensic and criminal investigation processes at the end of the century. In 1953, American scientist James Watson and Britain Francis Crick demonstrated the double helix of the deoxyribonucleic acid (DNA) molecule. This was the beginning of the ability to identify individuals not by grouping, as in ABO serology, but now down to the individual. This is further discussed in Chapter 15. In 1986, British scientist Alec Jeffries first applied DNA identification to the criminal investigative process. His efforts resulted in the identification and capture of a perpetrator for the rape–murders of two young girls in England by linking biological evidence left at the crime scene to a local baker. The forensic value of DNA quickly became apparent, but not just for conviction of criminal defendants. In 1989, the first U.S. DNA database was created, and in that year, David Vazquez reportedly became the first person in the United States exonerated through postconviction DNA testing. The forensic value of DNA became a highlight of forensic advances in the later half of the century.

Figure 1.6 1949 FBI *Law Enforcement Bulletin*. By the late 1940s, the FBI laboratory was conducting forensic examinations in a variety of fields, ranging from firearms examination to fingerprints to paint analysis. Since the 1930s, the FBI Laboratory has set high standards for forensic examination of evidence. (Author's collection.)

In 1992, the FBI introduced the Combined DNA Index System (CODIS). This system was designed to be a national database for linking crimes to criminals through DNA. In 1995, O. J. Simpson was acquitted of murder in a high-profile case despite strong DNA evidence against him. Evidence collection and custody issues were scrupulously analyzed in court and in the media, and as a result, methods of handling and testing of evidence underwent significant analysis and change. By 1994, 42% of the U.S. prosecutor's offices reported using DNA evidence in a felony case at least once, and by 2001, 68% reported such use (Prottas and Noble, 2007, 310).

Other disciplines came into their own during the latter half of this century. In 1954, Marilyn Sheppard was murdered in Cleveland, Ohio. The investigation and subsequent trial became a media circus. Her husband, Dr. Sam Sheppard, was tried for her murder and convicted. Sheppard insisted throughout his life that a "bushy-haired" intruder committed the crime, knocking him unconscious and murdering his wife. He was convicted at trial, but the verdict was overturned on appeal due to undue publicity and violation of due process. At a second trial 10 years later, University of California forensic scientist Paul Kirk analyzed bloodstains and patterns at the crime scene. In a detailed report, he concluded that Sheppard's version was credible and that the killer was left handed. Kirk's role in this notorious crime enhanced forensic and public awareness of blood spatter analysis. After serving 10 years in prison, Dr. Sheppard was acquitted at a second trial and died in 1970. This case further illustrates the value of determining the disposition of the case files, notes, and records of case personnel. In the late 1990s, legal action was brought to clear Dr. Sheppard's name. Two vials of blood from the crime scene were discovered in the property acquired by one of Kirk's students who had acquired

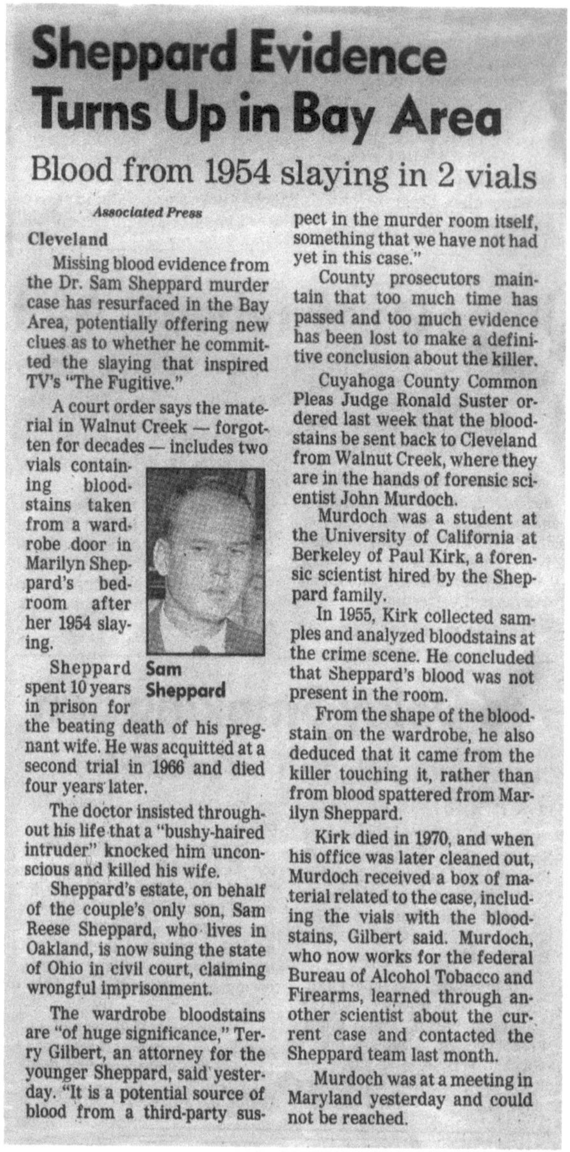

Sheppard Evidence Turns Up in Bay Area

Blood from 1954 slaying in 2 vials

Associated Press

Cleveland

Missing blood evidence from the Dr. Sam Sheppard murder case has resurfaced in the Bay Area, potentially offering new clues as to whether he committed the slaying that inspired TV's "The Fugitive."

A court order says the material in Walnut Creek — forgotten for decades — includes two vials containing bloodstains taken from a wardrobe door in Marilyn Sheppard's bedroom after her 1954 slaying.

Sam Sheppard

Sheppard spent 10 years in prison for the beating death of his pregnant wife. He was acquitted at a second trial in 1966 and died four years later.

The doctor insisted throughout his life that a "bushy-haired intruder" knocked him unconscious and killed his wife.

Sheppard's estate, on behalf of the couple's only son, Sam Reese Sheppard, who lives in Oakland, is now suing the state of Ohio in civil court, claiming wrongful imprisonment.

The wardrobe bloodstains are "of huge significance," Terry Gilbert, an attorney for the younger Sheppard, said yesterday. "It is a potential source of blood from a third-party suspect in the murder room itself, something that we have not had yet in this case."

County prosecutors maintain that too much time has passed and too much evidence has been lost to make a definitive conclusion about the killer.

Cuyahoga County Common Pleas Judge Ronald Suster ordered last week that the bloodstains be sent back to Cleveland from Walnut Creek, where they are in the hands of forensic scientist John Murdoch.

Murdoch was a student at the University of California at Berkeley of Paul Kirk, a forensic scientist hired by the Sheppard family.

In 1955, Kirk collected samples and analyzed bloodstains at the crime scene. He concluded that Sheppard's blood was not present in the room.

From the shape of the bloodstain on the wardrobe, he also deduced that it came from the killer touching it, rather than from blood spattered from Marilyn Sheppard.

Kirk died in 1970, and when his office was later cleaned out, Murdoch received a box of material related to the case, including the vials with the bloodstains, Gilbert said. Murdoch, who now works for the federal Bureau of Alcohol Tobacco and Firearms, learned through another scientist about the current case and contacted the Sheppard team last month.

Murdoch was at a meeting in Maryland yesterday and could not be reached.

Figure 1.7 *San Francisco Chronicle* news story about Sam Sheppard. It is suggested that cold case investigators seek to identify the disposition of the forensic collections of deceased forensic scientists involved in now-cold-case investigations. (*San Francisco Chronicle.*)

some of the famed scientist's property after his demise. It became a focal point in the resultant civil action. See Figure 1.7.

Role and Influence of the Media

Coupled with advances in the legal and criminal investigation processes and forensic technology, the role of the media entered into the ability of law enforcement to investigate crime. This affected investigative efforts in the field and events in the nation's courtrooms. The results have directly impacted the public perception of law enforcement and forensic science.

Cops and the Media

In the early 1950s, television began to supplement and replace newsprint as the source of America's news. Television shows about the police, including *M Squad* and *Dragnet*, popularized and glamorized the police role, especially homicide detectives. This popularization, however, sometimes misinformed the public and tainted their view of the homicide investigation process, and of police work in general. Television shows such as *The Andy Griffith Show* and *Car 54, Where Are You?* portrayed law enforcement in a comical and unrealistic setting. While vast differences did, and do, exist between large metropolitan agencies and their rural counterparts, these images have carried to this day in the minds of the baby boomer and subsequent generations through reruns of these episodes. More recently, social media and traditional media microanalysis of law enforcement actions has further contributed to public (mis)understanding of the police investigative role. Perception is reality, and these events may impact cold case investigators. In older cases, perception of the police as *Andy of Mayberry* or *Joe Friday* may affect the willingness of some to speak to the police about events long ago and to cooperate with cold case investigators. These perceptions may also carry over into the jury pool in a courtroom.

Television shows about police work saturated the airwaves during the last quarter of the century. Programs from the 1960s and 1970s such as *Adam-12* and *Police Story* gave insight into police practices and professionalized the law enforcement image. In the last decade of the century, television programs such as *NYPD Blue* and *Law and Order* impacted the way America viewed law enforcement and the court process. True-life television coverage of events such as the Los Angeles–based Symbionese Liberation Army (SLA) shootout and the Rodney King and O. J. Simpson episodes also contributed to America's perception of police and police practices.

The 1990s and beginnings of the twenty-first century marked a turning point in television's script-based portrayal of law enforcement. Programs such as *Cops* and *America's Most Wanted* portrayed the reality of law enforcement and reminded viewers that the world of police work is sometimes brutal and violent, and the police investigation process cannot be accomplished between commercials. In this evolution, however, a new trend emerged that has impacted homicide investigations and the courtroom process, and cold case investigations. This was the marriage of television with the courtroom and forensics.

Television shows based on advances in forensic sciences such as *CSI, Cold Case,* and *Cold Case Files* emerged as among the most popular and watched in television. (However, I have never seen a crime scene investigator or technician come to a scene or the laboratory in leather pants and high heels.) Together with television coverage of ongoing investigations and live courtroom proceedings, these elements have combined to impact the public's perception about forensics and police work in general (and particularly homicide investigation). As a result, advances in forensics as well as law enforcement investigative methods are perhaps more closely scrutinized now than in decades past. This is significant for cold case investigators as they must build upon the work performed during a different period and perhaps with a different level of expectation, and subsequently develop it to meet today's standards. Previous evidence identification and collection practices may directly affect their ability in these cold case investigations.

Further, media coverage of "wrongful convictions" and research and publicity about those factors that contributed to the conviction of innocent persons for crimes that they did not commit has further placed the criminal justice process under the microscope of public scrutiny. While past investigation and forensic practices have been identified as contributing factors in these miscarriages of justice, some media have contributed to the dissemination of misinformation and enhanced misconception by the public in this regard.

Law Enforcement Culture, Organization, and Practices

The changing landscape of American law enforcement has challenged and affected the ability of cold case investigators to solve cold case homicides. In the late 1960s, most of the nation's 40,000 police forces had

10 or fewer personnel. In many instances, organizational structure and practices had not changed perceptively for decades. Approximately 40 county, municipal, and state agencies had more than 1000 personnel. Coordination among agencies was sometimes sporadic and informal, and rivalries and jealousies between some police departments and sheriff's departments have carried over to this day. The result is a lack of communication and coordination. This fragmentation plays into the ability of perpetrators to commit their crimes, cross jurisdictional boundaries, and get away.

Following WWII, many states increased selection and training standards for police-empowered personnel. In the mid-1970s, some agencies were implementing variations of community policing and redesigning their organizational structure. Some agencies, such as in Lakewood, Colorado, experimented with the abandonment of the police uniform in favor of less militaristic-style attire. Many, however, remained entrenched in the traditional hierarchy of patrol, traffic, detectives, and administration (Figure 1.8). Standards for selection of detectives varied, and it was not uncommon that such personnel, especially in smaller agencies, were promoted for reasons other than demonstrated investigative ability. Knowledge of organizational structure, culture, and records and evidence practices is of importance to cold case investigators, and this will be discussed in future chapters.

America has long resisted any attempts to create a national, uniform police agency as is found in Europe and other countries. This is a condition crime writer Joseph Wambaugh has termed the "Balkanization" of the United States and is a contributing factor in the amount and nature of the cold case homicide problem

Figure 1.8 1950s police officer/dispatcher. (Courtesy of El Segundo Police Department.)

in the United States. The landscape of American law enforcement is comprised of city police departments operating within an incorporated jurisdiction while county sheriffs are responsible for investigating crimes that occur within the unincorporated regions of the state in which the county is located. In addition, states operate their own agencies with statewide jurisdiction to investigate crimes, including murder, and these may be known as state police, state troopers, or other names. Further, murders committed on federal reservations may not be reflected in local statistics, and instead, these case files are in the custody and control of agencies such as the FBI or Naval Criminal Investigative Service.

As a result, multiple jurisdictions each with their own hierarchy, policies, ranks, rules, and procedures practice their own brand of communication—or in some cases, lack of communication. Similarly, each agency maintains its own system of information retention and retrieval, as well as property and evidence rules, procedures, and methods of evidence storage. Failure in intra-agency and interagency communications has been a contributory factor to the cold case problem.

Evolving business technology also impacted law enforcement. The advent of microfiche and microfilm impacted department record keeping and retrieval. In the early 1980s, the personal computer began to revolutionize the way the world worked. Law enforcement recognized the advantages to computerizing records and communications, and a new means of recording and retrieving information evolved. These changes occurred in police agencies of all sizes, creating new sources of potential data retrieval for those investigating homicides and other serious crimes. Unfortunately, in some cases, as these records were converted to other formats, it was not uncommon for agencies to destroy the original records. These events merged to lay the foundation for a new type of homicide investigation and murder investigator, the cold case detective.

The Unsolved Problem Today

The highest homicide rates of the twentieth century occurred during its last two decades. FBI Agent Charles L. Regini summarized the background and nature of the cold case problem in his August 1997 report in the FBI *Law Enforcement Bulletin.* During this period, traditional patterns and trends were impacted by the rise in gangs and drugs, stranger killings, or drive-by shootings. The growth in drug-related homicides, crimes much more time consuming and difficult to solve, provided new challenges to law enforcement. During this era, murder became more vicious, senseless, and random. The link between victim and killer became more blurred, and motives were uncommonly thin. In addition, killers were not infrequently killed before they could be identified or located. Further, insufficient investigation allowed uncharged killers to be released back on the street to continue to kill. See Figure 1.9.

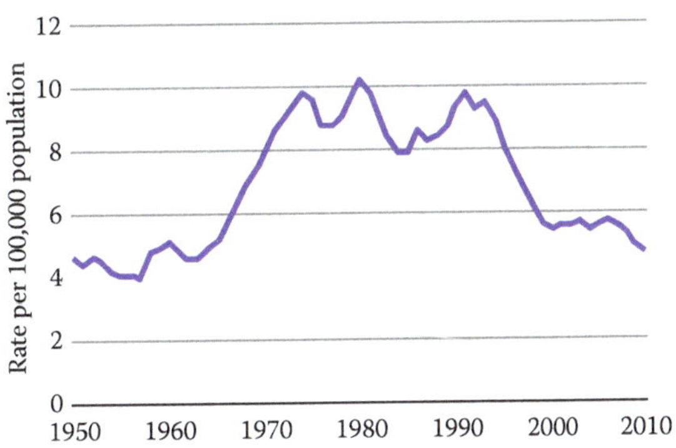

Figure 1.9 Homicide victimization, 1950–2010 graph. Note: Data are based on annual estimates of homicide from previously published versions of *Crime in the United States.* Data for 1989 to 2008 reflect updated homicide estimates from *Crime in the United States, 2008.* Data for 2009 and 2010 reflect updated homicide estimates from *Crime in the United States, 2010.* (Courtesy of FBI uniform crime reports and Bureau of Justice Statistics.)

During this period, traditional investigative approaches, such as focusing on motive, were less effective in solving these cases. Practical difficulties of identifying and locating witnesses, overcoming their hostility, and obtaining their confidence posed additional problems beyond the normal realm. Fear of retribution impacted efforts to secure witness cooperation and obtain needed testimony in court. Additionally, the lifestyles of many of these witnesses impacted credibility and compounded the difficulties in investigation and prosecution.

The ability of law enforcement to adequately investigate the sharp rise in homicides decreased under the onslaught as a steady stream of fresh murders taxed overworked investigative, forensic, and medical examiner resources. This was especially true in some of the nation's largest cities, but also in smaller jurisdictions and more rural areas. Available resources were not sufficient to keep up with the surge and spike in homicides. As a result, many agencies found themselves unable to supply the necessary fiscal, technological, educational, or manpower resources necessary to efficiently and adequately address each new homicide. In some cases, less experienced personnel lacking the skill and practice were assigned to investigate homicides (Eliopulos). The growth in stranger-to-stranger homicides further exacerbated the problem, as traditional homicide investigation focused on identifying a known victim–offender relationship.

What Are Cold Cases?

Cold case is a concept, and as such, there is no one standard definition of a cold case homicide. These are those homicides that others, perhaps more experienced, tried to solve and could not. These are homicides previously reported to law enforcement and investigated, yet lacking resolution. These are cases in which a suspect may have been known to the investigators, yet there was insufficient evidence for arrest and charging. These also include those cases in which no perpetrator has been identified, and the case is a *whodunit.*

Cold case homicides are among the most difficult and frustrating cases facing investigators. In addition to being previously reported and investigated, such cases may include homicides

- In which the primary investigator has transferred or otherwise been detached from the case and the case is not currently assigned to an investigator
- In which no current investigative activity is taking place, due to lack of investigative leads or information
- At least a year old that have had no activity on them for at least one year, or a case in which the primary investigator has been transferred from the unit and it needs to be reassigned to a new investigator

In my experience, this definition varies, and the specific designation of what constitutes a cold case rests with guidelines used by the individual law enforcement agency responsible for the investigation of the crime. Theirs is the definition they design to designate the parameters for those cases to be classified and investigated as cold case homicides within the agency. Some specify that a lengthy period of time must have elapsed since the commission of the crime. Others require that one year must have passed and/or a change of personnel involved in the investigation process must have occurred. Among the various definitions of a cold case homicide or cases to be investigated as cold case murders are those with parameters that include

- Unsolved cases prior to specific time period (i.e., 1990).
- Unsolved cases during specific intervals (i.e., 1960–1995).
- Long-term missing-persons cases that have a high probability of being a homicide.
- Cases wherein enough time has passed that the perpetrator begins to feel confident enough to speak freely about his/her involvement, suggestively four to five years or more.

- Homicide cases older than three years from the date of the offense in which no arrests have been made.
- Homicide cases older than three years from the date of the offense that are "closed–active" or cases that were closed by arrest of a suspect but the charges were dismissed without the suspect going to trial.
- Homicide cases less than three years old from the date of offense (including closed but active) in which all leads have been reasonably exhausted and investigation or assignment as a cold case homicide has been authorized by a responsible authority.
- Homicide cases in which the date that the death was ruled a homicide by the medical examiner's office is greater than one year after the original event that led to the decedent's death. This would include those cases wherein the victim dies more than one year after the fatal injuries were sustained.
- Undetermined deaths of a suspicious nature older than one year following the death.
- Any case linked to a case under active investigation by a cold case investigation unit.
- A case at least a year old that has had no activity on it for at least one year.

Why Cases Go Cold

Conventional wisdom in a homicide investigation holds that time is of the essence. For decades, this perception has guided investigators in their approach to homicide investigation. It holds that if a murder is not solved within the first 24–72 hours, the chances of solving the case rapidly diminish. Why? At the outset,

- Witnesses were still centrally located and easier to locate.
- Their recollection of events was fresh and most accurate.
- Those who may have been involved or had knowledge had not had a chance to get their stories and alibis straight among themselves.
- The chances of identifying and retrieving evidence are strongest at the outset. With the passage of time, the potential to identify evidence may diminish, or it may be damaged, lost, or destroyed (Figure 1.10).

Two primary factors may affect a homicide case becoming a cold case. Awareness of these by cold case investigators may contribute to their understanding of the strengths and weaknesses of the initial investigation in their cold case investigation. These are (1) case factors over which police have no control and (2) organizational factors within the law enforcement agency over which the police have control (Wellford, C. and Cronin, J).

1. Case factors over which the police have no control include
    - Lack of physical evidence
    - Lack of witnesses or cooperating witnesses
    - Inability to identify victim
    - Weapon used
    - Gang or drug related
    - Crime scene location (public versus private)
    - Previous technology inadequate to fully analyze evidence
2. Organizational factors within the law enforcement agency may include
    - Initial response and documentation
    - Initial investigation and gathering of evidence
    - Number of detectives originally assigned to case

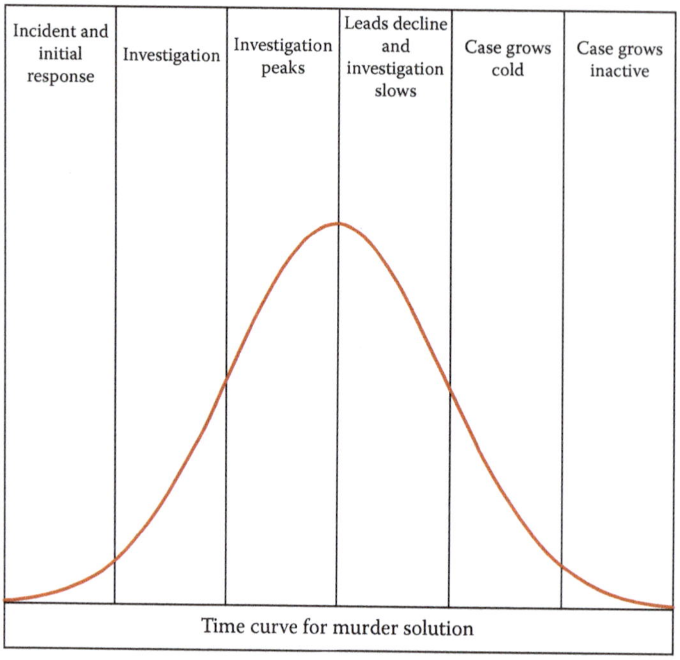

Figure 1.10 Cold case bell curve. Cold case homicides resemble the traditional bell curve. When the case is reported and investigation begins, it follows through until leads taper off, and the investigation slows. As other cases consume agency resources, the case grows cold and inactive. At any time, the bell curve may again incline when new information comes in. It is not unusual that some cold case homicides, solved and unsolved, have shown a series of bell curves. (Credit: author.)

- Detective's case load
- Leads not followed up
- Retirement
- Promotion and transfer
- Leadership and organization commitment
- Budgetary and financial considerations
- Personnel management
- Politics and personal agendas

Cases Most Likely to Go Cold

Those cases most likely to go cold include cases involving

- Missing persons
- Gang/drug related
- Immigrants, transients, and the homeless
- Unidentified
- Suicides
- Accidental
- Unclassified
- Unsolved murders of police officers (Figure 1.11)

Figure 1.11 Billboard—Who Killed Mike? Unsolved murders of police are among some of the hardest to solve. Officer Mike Edwards was murdered in 1974, and the case remains unsolved. Use of media is one means to elicit information from the public in some of the more difficult cases. (Courtesy of Detective Rick Jackson, Los Angeles Police Department, Los Angeles, California.)

How Old Is Cold?

Some departments have arbitrarily decreed that absent compelling information and circumstances, they will not proactively review cases prior to a specific date or year. This is in part due to the rationalization that the chances of the perpetrator remaining alive, witness availability, and similar case factors are minimal or nonexistent. It is also in part due to optimizing use of available resources. Also factored into this set of guidelines is the easily recognizable availability of biological evidence suitable for DNA analysis or latent fingerprint evidence. Those that have expressed this parameter to me most often cite varying time periods in the 1960s to 1970 as the arbitrary cutoff date. This issue will be addressed in future chapters.

Case Study

On the night of November 1, 1946, Miami police officer John Milledge, 48-year-old, was on duty and patrolling near a city park in which a football game was being played. Milledge was among the first black officers appointed to the department, during a time when racial segregation was a predominant factor in life in the South. The presence of black police officers was a new concept in the city, and these officers were primarily assigned to predominantly the same racial areas. While on patrol, Milledge caught some local juveniles trying to sneak into the game. He reportedly struck some with his nightstick, and they ran away. A short time later, an unknown assailant fired one shot from a .22-caliber weapon and struck Milledge in the neck. He died shortly thereafter at a local hospital. Witnesses reported seeing "some young negroes" nearby who might have been responsible, and another witness reported that one was carrying a rifle (Figure 1.12).

During the initial investigation, officers contacted two witnesses, who advised them that on the night of the shooting, an individual known locally as "FATS" came to their residence and asked for a ride out of town. He was given a ride and never seen again. FATS became a prime suspect in the shooting, and officers

Figure 1.12 Miami police officer John Milledge, one of the first African American police officers in Miami, Florida, was shot in an ambush in 1946. His murder was not solved until 1990, following revelations by a witness who had lived in fear of revealing what she knew. With the death of another, the witness now came forward. Change in relationships and no longer being in fear of another are significant solvability factors in solving cold case homicides. (Courtesy of Miami Police Department.)

learned that his true name was Leroy Strachan. Officers learned he may have gone to New York City, but he was never located or contacted during the initial investigation. Other potential suspects were investigated, and the case went cold until 1989.

On July 27, 1989, 43 years after the murder, an anonymous caller to the local Crime Stoppers program indicated knowledge about the murder of a black police officer. The call was forwarded to the homicide unit of the City of Miami Police Department. The caller identified herself and gave a sworn statement. The caller was an elderly witness, a female, who lived near the park. She reportedly was plagued by her conscience and wanted to tell what she knew but had withheld all these years.

On the night of the shooting, the witness was sitting on her porch with a male friend. A black teenager ran to her porch, almost out of breath. He was carrying a rifle. The witness described the teenager as having a bad eye. Upon seeing the rifle, her male friend went inside the house, and shortly afterwards, they learned a policeman had been shot. The witness initially misidentified the name of the teenager with the gun but noted that the teenager had a brother who was a close friend of her companion. She stated that her companion subsequently told her the teen had left town. The witness further stated that she learned the teen had gone to New York, but she was afraid of her male companion and remained silent all these years. He had recently died.

The case was reopened and assigned to Detective George Cadavid of the Cold Case Squad of the City of Miami Homicide Unit. Cadavid had been assigned to homicide for the past 10 years and assigned to this unit for approximately two years. Cadavid located the original case file within the police department and reviewed the names of those contacted during the initial investigation. In the course of his investigation, he reinterviewed some of these witnesses from 1946. Among those reinterviewed was the same male witness who gave FATS a ride out of town shortly after the shooting. With the passage of time, the witness now provided further detail of the events of that night, information not furnished to the police four decades before.

He stated that on the night of the shooting, which he remembered well, his brother and sister came home upset over the shooting of the officer. Later that night, FATS came to their house, nervous and scared, and wanted a ride out of town. During this conversation, FATS told the witness he had shot the officer. The witness stated that he now knew FATS as Leroy Strachan and that Leroy had a problem with one of his eyes. Except for the name, this information was consistent with information from the new witness.

Cadavid located Strachan, now age 62, in New York City. He learned that Strachan did have a problem with his left eye. A meeting was arranged, and Strachan gave a taped statement. Strachan stated that on the night of the shooting, he and others tried to sneak into the game. Milledge caught them and hit a number of them with his nightstick. Strachan ran to a friend's house and retrieved a .22-caliber rifle. He and the friend returned to an alley across from the park, and his friend handed him the weapon. He yelled for other boys in the alley to move, and he fired one shot at the officer. He then ran home and left Miami the next day for New York. Strachan was indicted by a grand jury for the murder of Officer Milledge and arrested in New York City on February 15, 1990.

The police and assistant state attorney recommended waiver of the death penalty. Mitigating factors considered that Strachan had no significant criminal history prior to the murder, he was 18-year-old at the time of the murder, and he had not had any criminal activity for the subsequent 43 years, in which he had been a law-abiding citizen with a wife and family. It is reported that some family members of the victim further believed that Strachan deserved a break. Strachan subsequently pled guilty to manslaughter and was given credit for 19 months in custody time served and 400 hours' community service each year for five years and placed on seven years' probation. This case illustrates cold case issues:

- Unsolved murder of police officer
- Media crime reporting program
- Tip from citizen due to conscience
- Department maintained case file
- Procedural assignment to experienced cold case detective
- Change in relationships due to passage of time
- Original investigation identified perpetrator yet never followed up
- Youthful age of offender
- Reinterview of original case witnesses
- New information by other witnesses
- Perpetrator now a religious person and admitted guilt
- Time, place, and social setting
- Legal, charging, and "justice" considerations

Suggested Readings and Bibliography

Abrahamson, S. (2002). Using DNA to solve cold cases. N. I. o. Justice. Washington, DC, U.S. Department of Justice: 22.

Anonymous. (2002). Cold Case Homicide. C.P.T. Network. Sacramento, California Commission on Peace Officer Standards and Training.

AP. (1997). Sheppard evidence turns up in Bay Area. *San Francisco Chronicle.* San Francisco: A2.

Block, E. B. (1958). *The Wizard of Berkeley.* New York, Coward-McCann, Inc.

Block, E. B. (1979). *Science vs Crime: The Evolution of the Police Lab.* San Francisco, Cragmont Publications.

Bureau of Justice Statistics. "Homicides Cleared by Arrest, 1976–2000." http://www.ojp/usdoj/bjs/homicide/cleared. Retrieved August 22, 2004.

Bureau of Justice Statistics. "Homicide Rate 1900–2000." http://www.ojp/usdoj/bjs/glance/hmrt.htm. Retrieved January 5, 2004.

Bureau of Justice Statistics. "Homicides Victimization 1950–2000." http://www.ojp/usdoj/bjs/homicide/hmrt.htm. Retrieved August 22, 2004.

Cadavid, G. (1991). Homicide Investigation F90-6184. Miami, Miami Police Department.

Carroll, R. (2002). Wounds suggest iceman was stabbed in the back, fought attacker. *The Guardian Unlimited.*

Cooper, A. and Smith, E. Homicide Trends in the United States, 1980–2010. Bureau of Justice Statistics. http://www.bjs.gov/content/pub/pdf/htus8008.pdf. Retrieved June 22, 2016.

Cooper, A. and Smith, E. L. "Homicide Trends in the United States, 1980–2008. Annual Rates for 2009 and 2010." Report NCJ236018, November, 2011.
Eliopulos, L. (2003). *Death Investigators Handbook: Expanded and Updated Edition*. Boulder, CO, Paladin Press.
Ellis, K. (2004). "Kansas City cold case squad solves string of murders." *Police Executive Research Forum* **18**: 1, 7.
FBI. (1970). Crime in the United States 1970: Uniform crime reports. U. S. D. o. Justice. Washington, DC.
FBI. (2001). Crime in the United States 2000: Uniform crime reports. Washington, DC, U.S. Government: 424.
FBI. (2002). Crime in the United States 2001: Uniform crime reports. Washington, DC.
FBI. (2014). "2014 Crime in the United States: Expanded Homicide Data Table 10. Murder Circumstances." http://www.fbi.gov. Retrieved June 21, 2016.
Fowler, B. (2000). The Iceman's last meal, *NOVA Online*.
Fox, J. A. and Zawitz, M. (1999). Homicide trends in the United States, Bureau of Justice Statistics. 2002. http://www.ojp.usdoj/bjs/homicide/homtrnd.htm. Retrieved June 23, 2003.
Geberth, V. (1996). *Practical Homicide Investigation: Tactics, Procedures, and Forensic Techniques*. New York, CRC Press.
Goddard, C. (1936). "A history of firearms identification." *Chicago Police Journal*.
Houck, M. M., Ed. (2001). *Mute Witness: Trace Evidence Analysis*. New York, Academic Press.
Hargrove, T. Project Cold Case: Cold Case Homicide Statistics, retrieved from http://www.projectcoldcase.org/cold case-homicide-stats/, December 18, 2016 and personal interview.
Hargrove, T. (2011). Scripps News. Personal Interview. June 11, 2010.
Hargrove, T. (2010). Murder Mysteries: Investigating America's Unsolved Homicides. Scripps news.com. http://scripps news.com/projects/murder-mysteries/. Retrieved June 11, 2010.
Lane, R. (1997). *Murder in America: A History*. Columbus, Ohio State University.
Lorenzi, R. (2003). Details emerge of Iceman Otzi's death, Discovery news.
McCall, P. L. and Zahn, M. A., Eds. (1999). *Trends and Patterns of Homicide in the 20th-Century United States. Homicide: A Sourcebook of Social Research*. Thousand Oaks, SAGE Publications.
National Center for Health Statistics Vital Statistics. "Homicide Rate 1900–2000: Rate per 100,000 Population." http://www.ojp.usdoj.gov/bjs/glance/hmrt.htm. Retrieved January 5, 2004.
Norrgard, D. L. (1969). *Regional Law Enforcement: A Study of Intergovernmental Cooperation and Coordination*. Danville, IL, Interstate Printers and Publishers, Inc.
Nyberg, R. (1999). "Investigations: Cold case squads re-activate old investigations." *Law and Order* **47**(10): 127–130.
Owen, J. "5 Surprising Facts about Otzi the Iceman." *National Geographic*. December 18, 2013.
Prottas, J. and Noble, A. (2007). "Use of forensic DNA evidence in prosecution offices." *Journal of Law, Medicine, and Ethics*. Summer, **35**(2): 310–315.
Regini, C. L. (1997). "The cold case concept." *Law Enforcement Bulletin* **66**(8): 1–6.
Statistics, B. of. J. (1983). Report to the nation on crime and justice. Washington, DC, U.S. Department of Justice.
Stout, W. W. (1925). Fingerprinting bullets: The expert witness. *Saturday Evening Post*: 6–7, 193, 194, 197.
Stout, W. W. (1925). Fingerprinting bullets: The expert witness. *Saturday Evening Post*: 18–19, 163, 165, 166, 169–170.
Thompson, G. and Williams E. (2003). The thin blue line's: New front line. *San Diego Union*. San Diego: G1, 5, 6.
Thorwald, J. (Unk). *Crime and Science: The New Frontier of Criminology*. New York, Harcourt, Brace & World, Inc.
Turner, R. and Kosa, R. (2003). Cold case squads: Leaving no stone unturned. *Bureau of Justice Assistance Bulletin*. U. S. D. o. Justice. Washington, DC: 2–7.
Van Natta, D. (1991). NY Man to plead guilty in 1946 Miami cop killing. *Miami Herald*. Miami: 1, 14A.
Wambaugh, J. (2002). *Fire Lover*. New York, Avon Books.
Wellford, C. and Cronin, J. (2000). "Clearing up homicide clearance rates." *National Institute of Justice Journal* (April): 3–7.

Case File Review

2

R. H. WALTON

Contents

Introduction

Cold case investigations begin with a review of the case file. The investigation of a cold case homicide is different from the investigation of a hot homicide in many ways. Cold case investigation is *proactive*, versus the *reactive* nature of a hot case. The cold case investigation initially builds upon the documented work of others, utilizing case files that may vary in the degree of completeness and record retention over the ensuing years. In addition, cold case investigations exploit the elements of time and technology in conjunction with advanced investigative techniques. While every case and each victim's family deserves the ultimate opportunity to see that justice in some form or another is rendered on their behalf, available resources require that investigation of cold cases must be selective, focused, and targeted in its method.

This chapter will begin with a review of the qualities of investigators most suitable for cold case homicide investigation and a discussion of the influence and impact of time and technology as it pertains to cold case homicide investigation. It will address the influence of past law enforcement methods in cold case investigation and how to approach a file and assess file contents. In addition, this chapter highlights administrative considerations for cold case investigations and will further discuss how to organize and prioritize multiple cases for subsequent investigation.

Causes for Review and Reactivation of Cold Cases

A single cold case is to be selected for reexamination based upon any of the following factors:

- Inquiry, single or repeated, by a family member or friend of the victim. As time passes, the parents, siblings, or others may periodically contact the police to inquire if anything new has arisen on their case. Family inquiries may cause a fresh review of the case.
- New information brought forth by family or friends of the victim. With the passage of time, friends and family of the victim may hear or otherwise obtain information that furnishes a new lead to investigators.
- New information furnished by a member of the public.
- Institutional knowledge of detectives. With the passage of time, detectives go on to other cases but, for the most part, do not forget those cases they could not solve. As the years become decades, other investigators may transfer in and out of homicide, and the case may have been rendered inactive due to leads. But those who initiated the investigation, or later followed it up, remember the unsolved. Through intentional or casual communication with homicide supervisors, homicide detectives, or others within the department, something is said that causes the case to be pulled and subject to a fresh review.
- Individual investigator curiosity.
- Secondary information from other investigations, often related to drugs or organized crime.
- Those in trouble with the law providing information to mitigate their legal burden.
- Media report.
- Political pressure.
- Sometimes by accident.

Preliminary Considerations in Cold Case Investigations

Cold Case Investigator Attributes

It is estimated that almost every law enforcement agency in the United States has unsolved homicide cases in their files. These are cases that other investigators worked but that went unsolved for various reasons. If they had been easy, they would have been solved. With the passage of time, however, and a fresh review by a new set of eyes coupled with advances in technology, these cases may offer fresh leads. Case review is more than just opening a file folder or carton. The review begins with the *mental attitude* or *mindset* of the investigator. In addition, it includes awareness of the changes wrought by *time* in technology and personal relationships. This review involves

- The ability to think and act objectively
- The ability to ask the right questions
- A positive can-do spirit
- Knowledge of modern investigative methods
- Knowledge of advances in science and technology

Case file review also entails *teamwork*. The days of the one-man homicide ace detective following gut instinct are over. Cold case homicide investigation is a team effort among law enforcement, the prosecutor's office, the medical examiner/coroner's office, and the laboratory. Each of these is an important component in the reopening and investigation of a cold case file. In addition, it requires cooperation and communication within the law enforcement community and not the territorialism or proprietary of "It's my case."

Investigators assigned a cold, unsolved homicide may be faced with a variety of start-up decisions and options to make in order to proceed expediently. Depending upon the age of the case, many factors may immediately present themselves. Some of these may appear daunting, or even insurmountable. The older the case, the higher the potential for missing reports and missing or degraded evidence, deceased investigators and witnesses, and other obstacles. The law enforcement agency may have changed physical locations one or more times. Each time files, evidence, or property is moved increases the possibility that these items will be lost, misplaced, or even destroyed. Administrative and budgetary issues may also impact the presence or absence of these items. Cases that have been inactive for a few years for lack of leads present a different arena than those revived after 20 or 30 years, or more. Those more recent are likely to be written on forms currently in use, formats to which current investigators are accustomed and that will tell them quickly where to look for desired information.

Remember—a cold case investigation builds upon the previous work of others.

Who will investigate cold case homicides is an immediate concern to law enforcement supervisors and administrators, as well as the investigators themselves. Whenever possible, those assigned to cold case homicide investigations should be experienced homicide detectives. These investigations are often prolonged, and it is important to note that all of the problems and frustrations experienced in a hot homicide may be multiplied many times over in cold case investigations and resultant court proceedings. Experience has shown, however, that these cases have been solved by properly identifying and using those with little or no homicide experience.

Desirable cold case investigator attributes would include

- Knowledgeable of the mechanics of homicide investigation
- Knowledgeable in the variations in homicide law

- Knowledgeable in the use of forensic sciences and up-to-date advances
- Skilled in interview techniques
- Excellent oral and written communication skills
- Knowledgeable and experienced in use of informants
- Open minded
- Strong deductive and reasoning skills
- A good listener
- Creative and innovative
- Knowledgeable in crime scene reconstruction
- Experienced in use of computers and report writing
- Knowledgeable of courtroom procedures and testimony
- Able and willing to work in a team atmosphere
- Knowledgeable of department resources, procedures and protocols
- Good health and stamina
- Motivated and enthusiastic
- Patience, an analytical mind, and bulldog *tenacious* (Figure 2.1)

In my experience, it appears to be a consensus among those involved in the investigation of cold case homicides that not all homicide investigators are suited to cold case investigation. Why? Cold case investigations are tedious and require an investigator who can sit for hours; review old papers; and analyze people, events, relationships, and time sequences. This is cerebral analysis. In some older cases, it may be helpful to task a more senior investigator who may have knowledge and experience in the time frame of the crime, as well as trends in department systems over the years. Younger, less experienced investigators may seek faster-paced activity.

The use of senior, experienced homicide investigators for cold case homicide investigations draws upon aspects of investigative ability that can only come from practice. These more experienced investigators

- Know what the case needs to move forward
- Know what the prosecutor needs to prosecute the case

Figure 2.1 Los Angeles Sheriff's Homicide Bulldog patch. Cold case investigation requires "Bulldog" tenacity. (Courtesy of late Sgt. Richard Longshore, Los Angeles County Sheriff's Department.)

- Have established contacts and rapport with the prosecutor's office
- Have established contacts and rapport with coroner/medical examiner office
- Through experience, have statewide and nationwide contacts
- Through membership and participation in homicide investigator associations and training programs, have expanded fields of contact
- May recognize information overlooked or blatantly obvious in the case file

Each of these is important in all stages of file review and case investigation. *What* you know is sometimes not as important as *who* you know! See Chapter 31.

Homicide investigation is part scientific but also part subjective. With experience comes the ability to *feel* or *read* a case beyond the words on paper. It is an ability to feel the *pulse* of the case. Selection of the wrong individual can further compound the difficulty in case solution. In the end, it will be the investigator who combines time, technology, and old-fashioned shoe leather to solve a cold case homicide.

Age + Experience = Wisdom

Investigators assigned to investigate cold cases must know that they may have no control over the cases they work, depending upon the political climate of their agency or community. Similarly, they may have little say in how their agency prioritizes what cases are more important and which are not as important. Conversely, however, investigators may have a say in which cases they reinvestigate, due to their experience and ability to separate those cases with a higher potential for solution from those with a lesser possibility of being solved with given resources.

Time

Modern cold case investigation turns the previous liability of time into an asset. While law enforcement labored under a conventional wisdom that murders unsolved after 48–72 hours were increasingly more difficult to close, the pendulum of time in cold cases has now reversed this adage. Time, once so unforgiving in homicide investigation, may now be an ally to law enforcement efforts to solve cold cases. This change is due primarily to two factors:

- Change in relationships
- Advances in technology

In a hot homicide scenario, witnesses or those with knowledge about the crime often remain silent due to a relationship with or fear of the perpetrator; their own lifestyle and standards; or fear, hostility, or noninvolvement with police.

With the passage of time, relationships change. Not uncommonly in these cases, people *want* to tell what they know yet cannot bring themselves to pick up the telephone and call the police. In some cases, all it takes is for an investigator to take the *initiative* and knock on their door. In a cold case scenario,

- The friendship that once existed between perpetrator and those with knowledge of the crime may have ended. It may now be adversarial.
- Marriages and former lover-partnership relations may have ended, perhaps on a sour note.
- Business relationships dissolve.
- Formerly hostile witnesses are no longer hostile.
- Religion may have entered the life of one with information or knowledge of the crime.
- Conscience may have become a factor in the lives of those with information or knowledge of the crime.

- People mature. Witnesses may have moved away from the influence of the perpetrator and lifestyle at the time of the murder. They may have married, raised a family, and become better persons.
- The witness no longer fears the perpetrator. This may be due to time having made the witness a stronger person, or the perpetrator a weaker person. Or, the perpetrator may be dead.
- The perpetrator may become complacent and talk to others about crimes committed in the past.

Technology

Advances in technology have enabled more precise examinations of evidence than were available in the past and include the following:

- DNA profiles to now be extracted from amounts of biological material previously insufficient in quantity for DNA analysis.
- DNA profiling to offer a strong potential as an investigative aid.
- Familial DNA.
- DNA data banks such as the Combined DNA Index System (CODIS) to allow for comparison of known and unknown genetic profiles between crime scenes and identified or unidentified perpetrators.
- Expanded fingerprint identification capabilities. Advanced fingerprint methods can now lift prints from surfaces once considered unprintable. Among these are cyanoacrylate fuming (superglue) and laser systems for lifting and reading fingerprints. Fingerprint databases such as Next Generation Identification (NGI) and an automated fingerprint identification system (AFIS) allow for inputting and comparing fingerprints on a state and national level.
- Other databases such as the National Integrated Ballistic Network (NIBIN) for comparing spent shell casings and projectiles or projectile fragments.
- Expanded, computer-based communications and information exchange.
- Geographical profiling.

Time + Technology

Time and technology have combined in a manner no one anticipated just a few decades ago. This includes the perpetrator *and* the police, however. Suspects who considered themselves knowledgeable, or lucky, in seemingly leaving no trace did not anticipate DNA or computer databases such as we have today. Similarly, *neither* did the police. In too many instances, evidence in homicide cases was discarded after a decade or two, and records were destroyed. The mindset of many who have committed murder is such that they have become confident after the passage of the years, and many have moved to other regions of the country away from where they committed their crimes. Some have gone on to raise families and become accepted or respectable members of their community. In a lot of cases, the original investigators moved on in their careers, retired, or have passed away. There is no free pass for those who kill, however. While those who committed murder may try to forget and put their past behind them, others have not. The family and friends of the murder victim never forget, and in most cases, neither does law enforcement. Awareness of these factors is important before an investigator opens the file.

Time may not be an ally in some cases, however. If a case is 40–50 years old, is it plausible to expect that witnesses or a suspect may still be alive? Even with a thoroughly documented case and evidence in file, does the case warrant an initial effort? In a situation such as this, a review may be justified. The investigation will involve locating friends, relatives, and other associates of the decedent. The spark needed to solve the case may be there and just needs a breath of fresh air. In addition, any subsequent investigation would seek to locate medical or law enforcement personnel involved in the initial investigation. These are concerns to be considered in the initial review. Regrettably, however, I have had senior administrative and command officers advise me that they would not review cases of this vintage.

What *if* the perpetrator in a 40-year-old homicide was 17–19 years old at the time of the crime? That person would now be 57–59 years old. Given longevity and other factors in modern life, this person may still be a suitable prospect for investigation and prosecution. Several notable investigations and convictions in these circumstances have occurred in the past few years. These include the case of Miami police officer John Milledge illustrated in Chapter 1 and those of defendants Freiburger and Wilkerson discussed elsewhere in this text.

A cold case should be evaluated upon the reasonable merits of the case and not necessarily rejected solely due to age.

Administrative and Supervisory Concerns

Hot case homicides generate media publicity. The media is often in contact with family and friends of the victim, and this is relayed in sound bites or newspaper stories. This, in return, generates a response from the law enforcement agency. In higher-profile cases, such as the Beltway sniper case in Virginia and Maryland in 2002, the sheriff or chief of police often faces the media to assure the public and answer questions.

In cold case investigations, however, the family and friends usually do not know when a case is reactivated until contacted by law enforcement. In turn, the media usually does not become aware of cold case investigations until an arrest is made. The public likes to hear that somebody did *not* get away with murder. The resultant publicity reflects positively on the agency, and not uncommonly, law enforcement uses this time to reassure the public that they are doing all they can to track down killers in unsolved cases and protect the public. Such news may also stimulate others to come forward with information on the case, or on another case. These come with a cost, however.

Cold case investigations may incur expenses and resources *exceeding* those normally found in hot homicide investigation. Further, results may be longer in coming. In addition to the normal frustrations encountered when working homicide cases, additional frustration for investigators results when an agency tasks investigators to work these cases but does not supply the necessary resources. The leadership and organizational commitment by an agency to investigate cold cases requires awareness and acceptance that such investigations often include the following:

- Added travel expenses. By this time, suspects, witnesses and others with important information may have scattered about the country. This may apply to former and retired officers and investigators as well. All witnesses and investigators will have to be located and reinterviewed, often face to face. These interviews and other investigation costs will require added travel, lodging, transportation, and related expenses.
- Overtime and associated expenses for investigators due to travel, telephone, and investigation.
- Use of other personnel and resources.
- Potential for increased laboratory costs and/or other evidentiary-related expenses. All physical evidence will need to be reprocessed.
- Conflicts within the agency. There may be those who would contest revisiting cold cases when resources are drained from investigations of current cases or other individual agendas or priorities occur within the department.
- Impact on the workload or caseload of others.

In addition, one cold case investigation may be the precursor to other cold case investigations. These investigations are often cross-jurisdictional. Investigations in these cases may lead investigators to spend time and travel to nearby or more distant law enforcement agencies. In other instances, the information spawned in one cold case may lead to reopening other cases within the department or in other agencies. It has not been unusual that information developed in the investigation of one cold case has also identified a serial killer.

Cold case homicide investigations are especially time consuming and labor intensive. The very nature and intensity of these investigations necessitates focus upon the written case and subsequent investigation. A cold case investigation begins with a review of the written record, often complex in size. In this regard, a cold case investigation builds upon the degree of thoroughness and completeness of previous investigators. It is also built upon the missed opportunities. This focus is necessary for an investigator to begin to digest and understand a multitude of names, dates, relationships, who-said-what, as well as evidence and property considerations, and to begin to formulate an investigative plan. It is a disservice to the investigator, the victims, and the agency to distract the investigator's focus from the cold case investigation.

Because these investigations originate with review of a written record and not through on-the-spot investigation as occurs with a hot homicide, investigators must have conducive working conditions and agency support in order to accomplish their task. While some agencies may assign multiple cold cases to an investigator or teams of investigators, other agencies may assign one cold case to one investigator or one team. Realistically speaking, one case at a time is an excellent ratio. In either situation, cases are worked to solution or until they can be worked no further. It is highly desirable that investigators assigned to cold case investigations not be distracted or assigned other duties during the course of these investigations.

When investigators are tasked by the administration to investigate cold cases, they must be free to do so with a minimum of resistance from other administrative personnel (who sometimes have no investigative experience and understanding of what homicide investigation entails). On some occasions, investigators will be directed to investigate a cold case by the head of the agency or other supervisory personnel, only to be stonewalled and rebuffed by those in charge of the budget and other agency resources. This creates added tension and is detrimental to the goal of the investigation, not to mention the negative impact it has on morale and interpersonal relations.

Opening the File

Where Is the Case File?

In cold case investigations, locating the original case file and original evidence is sometimes not as easy as it could be. Personnel changes, individual filing habits (quirks) or procedures, facility changes, and passage of time may complicate the simple effort of retrieving a case file or evidence. Investigator experience and knowledge of past practices and patterns of the agency may be beneficial to a cold case investigator in this sequence. Beginning in-house, investigators may look in numerous places, including

- Agency records storage area where records are normally filed
- Homicide Bureau or a specially designated storage facility for homicide files, solved and unsolved
- Agency property room (as well as for evidence logs and physical evidence)
- Off-site warehouses or storage facilities

Don't hesitate to ask those who have been around for a long time if they know of any records or other places where records may have been stored over the years. Longtime secretaries and clerks are, many times, the *best* sources of information on many different subjects. If you don't ask the question, you will not get the answer.

File Condition

Subjectively, the initial appearance of the case organization may offer an insight into the ease and potential time and resources necessary for case review and subsequent investigation. Is it together in three-ring binders or labeled envelopes and folders? See Figure 2.2. Or is it a collection thrown haphazardly into a box as shown in Figure 2.3? Or...*is* there a file?

Cases may be encountered in any one of three categories, or a combination, of completeness:

- *Organized.* An organized file suggests that the case will be complete and laid out in an orderly manner. Review of an organized file may begin with little or no reorganization by the assigned investigator. This facilitates investigator review and absorption of the case. This case may have summaries of events, evidence, and those involved in the case. These will assist in the investigator coming up to speed in a shorter period of time than otherwise. No matter which category the file appears to fall into, a cold case investigator will strive to ensure that all relevant records are identified and recovered. See Figure 2.2.

Caution is warranted, however, that if/when reports or similar material seemingly not connected to the case under review are found, you should not necessarily discard its connection to the case at hand. Someone along the line may have felt this was related to the case. Whether these reasons are documented or not, do not disregard this earlier thought at this time.

As an example, detectives Jon Wooddell and Robert Anderson of the El Cajon Police Department, California, were reinvestigating a cold case homicide that occurred in their city in 1965. Comingled with the homicide investigation case were reports and records from other seemingly unconnected sexual assaults during this same time period. Upon review, however, these reports suggested that their predecessors decades before had believed there might be a connection between these crimes. These detectives ultimately succeeded in identifying and convicting serial killer–rapist Clyde Wilkerson in 2003 for the homicide. This case is discussed further in Chapter 4.

Figure 2.2 Organized case file. An organized case file makes cold case investigation more efficient and effective. (Courtesy of Detective Richard Rouleau, El Cajon Police Department.)

(a)

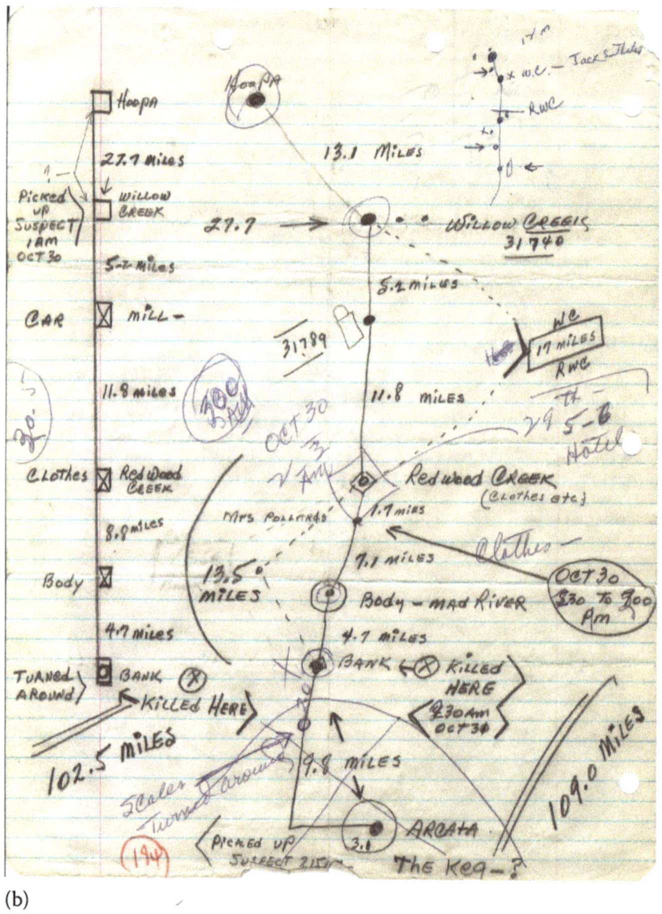

(b)

Figure 2.3 (a) Disorganized file. Disorganized files are not uncommon. Over the years, contents are scattered and dumped loosely into a box or folder. Inside these files may be found original biological or physical evidence, photos, or even bullets. (b) Old crime scene map with numerous notation and lacking authorship. (Author's collection.)

- *Disorganized.* These are not infrequently encountered in older unsolved cases and may be encountered in departments of all sizes. These are characterized as reports and other material dumped loosely into a box or file folders as shown in Figure 2.3a and b. These, in turn, may be stored haphazardly in storerooms and closets. These cases may have gone through a sequence of investigators over the decades, and documents may be such as to suggest an uncertainty as to completeness. There may be notations or other writings on reports and documents that do not appear to be those of the original author of the document. This compounds the efforts of later investigators to determine who wrote these remarks and the significance on that particular document.
- *Missing.* These are circumstances in which no case file may be retained in the department records. It has happened! In one study, data were collected on all unsolved and solved murders in the state of Washington between January 1981 and December 1986. Of the 1309 murder victims, 38 homicide case files were missing and could not be located by records personnel of the responsible agencies. This obviously poses a potential problem for investigators, and this situation has been related to me by investigators for other agencies.

Cold case investigators will often invoke methods not normally associated with homicide investigations and may successfully reconstruct events and a case file. Reconstruction of these case files may begin with review of the death certificate, media reports, and interviews with family and friends of the victim. Other methods to reconstruct these cases will unfold throughout this text.

Additional reasons for files to be missing include the following:

- Lost due to changes in physical storage location. This may occur when an old police station or courthouse is torn down and files are lost when records are moved. In these cases, it might be prudent to attempt to identify who may have had access to the homicide files and inquire if the files were taken for someone's reading pleasure.
- Destroyed due to fire, flood, or other natural disaster at the storage location.
- Inadvertently misfiled, or comingled elsewhere.
- Theft or intentional removal or destruction.
- There *never was* a case file. Yes, it has happened. Those assigned to investigate a death never wrote reports. As a result, there is no file to be found.

Organizing the Disorganized File

The first step in this instance is to organize the remaining record. It is not uncommon to find that these cases, as well as some organized cases, have items of evidentiary value comingled with the reports. This would include film negatives, x-rays, physical items, and other case material. In one case, a detective found a spent bullet and a shell casing. There was no documentation, however, and it was unknown if this was related to the case or not. Other cold case files have contained women's panties, hairs and fibers, and other items of potential physical or biological evidentiary value. If items of evidentiary value are present, contact the appropriate evidence specialist and follow evidence-handling procedures.

The initial physical opening of the file or box in any cold case may be done in a laboratory or similarly secure setting, using appropriate coverings in case items with potential trace evidence are present in the file/box. Teamwork begins with the file review, so work with your laboratory associates to ensure that you do not handle any items and potentially destroy or contaminate any evidence. These items should be secured and handled in conjunction with evidence-handling practices and department procedures.

Investigators should consider lab and legal partners in a cold case investigation to be part of the team. They must be given ownership and kept informed.

Next, organize the paperwork into chronological order. Consider the sequence of how you would begin a current homicide investigation. Begin with those records reflecting the initial report of the crime and work forward. This gives you the basis of when and how the crime came to be reported and insight into how it progressed. This is the beginning of the *who, what, when, where, why*, and *how* of the case. This may present a problem in some instances as investigative actions may have occurred on one date while the report was not written until days later and other interviews and actions occurred in between. Note the date of the interview or action in relation to when the report was written. In addition, it is not uncommon to find multiple witness interviews on one document or sequence of a single report. The object of this process is to reconstruct the sequence of reported events and steps in the investigation. This will facilitate investigator review and provide a logical basis for understanding what happened and moving forward with the review or investigation. You may also note that which is missing and/or mentally begin to construct your investigative plan as you reconstruct the file.

Keep in mind that this sequence reflects events as your predecessors came to know them, and do not be judgmental or critical with the advantages of hindsight. In addition, the investigator will have to spend additional time sorting documents, often having to review, assemble, and reconnect disconnected reports. Special attention, requiring additional time, must be paid to making sure that papers are reassembled correctly, and often, there may be multiple copies of each report. Or there may appear what seem to be multiple copies but are in fact slightly different.

Case Study

Figure 2.3a and b illustrates a disorganized file. This case consisted of a cardboard box upon which was written the victim's name and its 1958 case number. The victim was a white female in her 40s, a part-time prostitute and waitress in a blue-collar town in the Pacific Northwest. Most of the reports were separate from the file folders also found in the box, and many of these were unstapled and loose. There was no order to the documents, and contents were scattered loosely in the box. In addition, someone at a later time had renumbered in red letters all the report pages. The significance of this is unknown due to lack of documentation. The file folders themselves contained many notes and notations written by numerous, unidentified persons. *Who were they? When were they written? What did these mean?*

Photographs of the victim and other unidentified persons were scattered in the box, as well as original x-rays and personal property items of the victim. Numerous envelopes of negatives of the crime scene, victim's vehicle, and other subjects were also scattered, although it appeared none had been printed. There was an absence of documentation of the significance of what the photos may have intended to show. In addition, letters from unidentified individuals concerning a variety of topics were found in the file, including letters suggesting firsthand knowledge of events in the crime. There was no documentation to denote the status of any investigation regarding these claims.

The documents, when reassembled, revealed a pattern of investigation that began with a missing person's report in an incorporated city and the finding of her body six months later in another remote, rural jurisdiction. This is not an uncommon sequence of events, even today. After the initial investigation span of approximately one year, the case went cold. Review by local investigators was sporadic after the first year with no sign of proactive review in the succeeding decades.

Of noteworthy importance, no evidence, property, or photo logs were contained in the box. A handwritten note dated in 1979 from the property clerk to the district attorney, however, explained why: "…because the case is now 20 years old and will never be solved, request permission to destroy all the evidence in this case." Permission was granted by the prosecutor.

In 2002, all the original case investigators were still alive. Time and again, this scenario has been relayed to me by cold case investigators seeking to locate old case files and evidence.

Remember the investigator *mindset*—consider that each case offers a potential for solution. However, the ease with which investigators may quickly come up to speed in understanding the sequence of known events and in subsequent investigation is initially dependent upon how the file was organized and maintained. This degree of organization may indicate a carryover into the care and preservation of evidence, also.

Other Considerations

Past Patterns and Practices

When initially reviewing older cases, do not be alarmed if the case file appears physically rather thin. Do not necessarily assume that it is incomplete. Once subjected to follow-up investigation incorporating modern techniques and protocols, they quickly become much more massive in physical size and content. Other cases from the same time period may occupy many carton boxes or file cabinet drawers. It is not the size but the *quality* that counts!

This is one area, however, that in many instances exemplifies the difference between past and present law enforcement investigative practices. Understanding these may be of importance to cold case investigators. Each law enforcement agency has traditionally set its own practices and standards for investigating homicides and documenting these investigations. In the 1950s and forward, many states began mandating changes and implementing standardization in the selection and training of law enforcement officers. This ultimately carried over into the adoption of uniform means and methods of documentation and recording in police reports. This has been, and still is in some areas, an evolving process.

In many instances, especially prior to the early 1980s, some law enforcement agencies did *not* have policies regarding required documentation in homicide investigations. As a result, what was, or was not, recorded depended upon the individual investigator and the degree of supervision. Some investigators wrote detailed investigative reports, while others wrote a minimum if anything at all.

Who the victim was may, in some instances, have factored into the scope and quality of the initial investigation. Prostitutes, minorities, and known offenders or troublemakers may not have had the diligence applied to their investigations as found in other homicide investigations.

In addition, it may not be uncommon to find that investigation reports were more synopsis oriented than detail specific in their construction. Some agencies required no documentation in a homicide investigation unless a suspect was developed. As a result, written reports for homicide investigations may be nonexistent. The entire case record might have been kept in the notes and notebooks of the individual detective, and when that person retired, the notebooks went with him/her (if the department did not require such to be turned in). See Figure 2.4. I have spoken to old-time detectives who would tap their shirt pocket or their head and stress that they carried their investigation "right here."

Another area in which these practices have occurred was documentation of a neighborhood canvas. In decades past, if a witness reported nothing of importance, there was no requirement for any documentation. Thus, the witness who reported nothing was not identified. It was not unusual for investigators to detail uniformed officers to conduct the canvas, and in short, any documentation of a neighborhood canvas may be a hit-or-miss affair. Further discussion of this topic is covered in Chapter 4.

When opening a cold case file, never discard any papers, worn-out file folders, or other items in the file or box that may appear unrelated or of no use in the case investigation. It is advisable to note this in your report of the initial review. A defense attorney may ask if this occurred at some point and try to stress that the real killer's name was discarded.

Figure 2.4 Old investigator's notebook. During review of old homicide cases, it is prudent to identify case investigators or their descendants, and inquire if they retain any notebooks or other case memorabilia. (Author's file.)

Older Technology

When reviewing older files, investigators may encounter several types of formats not normally encountered today. Reports may be handwritten or typed on typewriters. Older homicide files may include both types. Forms may be primitive by today's standards, or lacking altogether. Word processors began to attain widespread use within law enforcement in the early to mid-1980s.

- *Onionskin paper.* This is a very thin, almost transparent type of paper that was used for making multiple copies of the same document. See Figure 2.5. It is characterized by being very fragile and tearing easily. Most often encountered in a typewritten format, reports on this paper were made using carbon paper. Carbon paper is a black paper that, when struck on the top side, leaves the impression in dark ink on a piece of paper adjacent to the bottom side. Manual (nonelectric) typewriters could often make three to five legible copies using these formats. The copy most immediate to the original face sheet is usually most legible, and the quality of print declines with the additional copies. This format is not uncommon in reports written prior to the mid-1980s.
- *Thermal paper.* This style of copy paper uses a heat source to impregnate the words and images onto the paper. See Figure 2.6. It was invented approximately 60 years ago, and variations of it are still used today in facsimile machines. A characteristic of this paper is that it begins to fade after a few

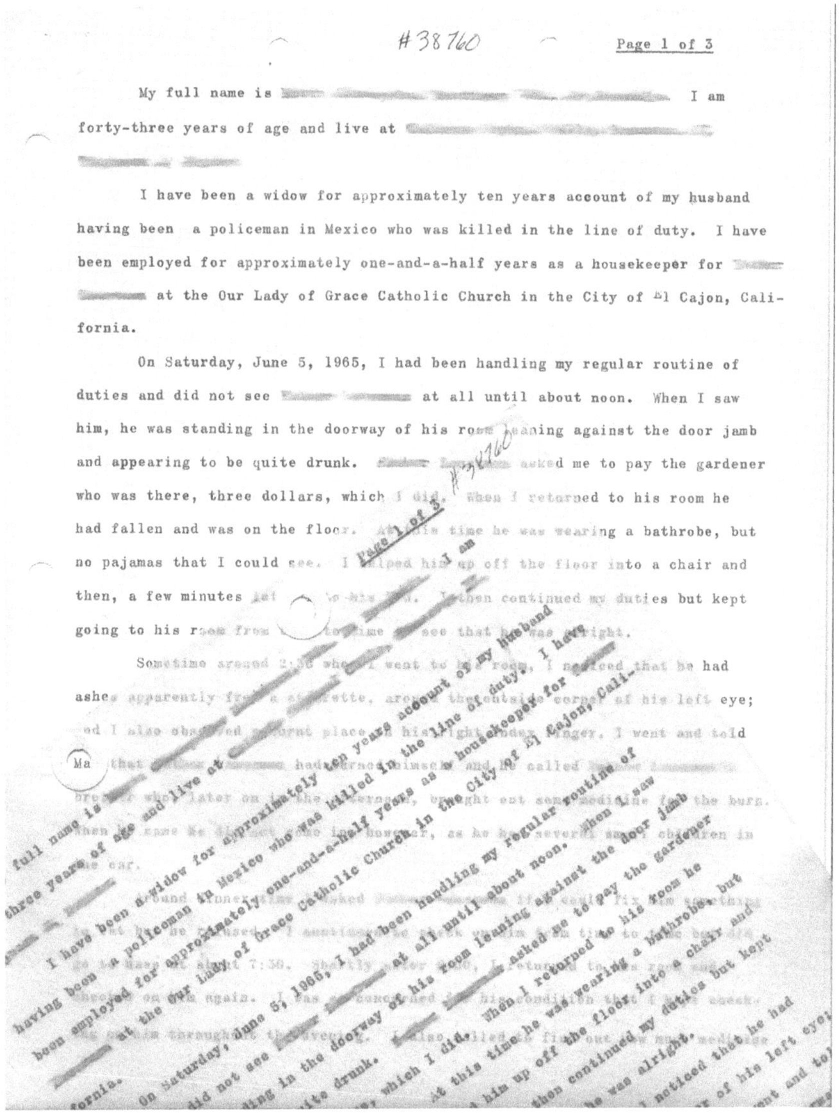

#38760 Page 1 of 3

My full name is [redacted] I am forty-three years of age and live at [redacted]

I have been a widow for approximately ten years account of my husband having been a policeman in Mexico who was killed in the line of duty. I have been employed for approximately one-and-a-half years as a housekeeper for [redacted] at the Our Lady of Grace Catholic Church in the City of El Cajon, California.

On Saturday, June 5, 1965, I had been handling my regular routine of duties and did not see [redacted] at all until about noon. When I saw him, he was standing in the doorway of his room leaning against the door jamb and appearing to be quite drunk. [redacted] asked me to pay the gardener who was there, three dollars, which I did. When I returned to his room he had fallen and was on the floor. At this time he was wearing a bathrobe, but no pajamas that I could see. I helped him up off the floor into a chair and then, a few minutes later ... I then continued my duties but kept going to his room from time to time to see that he was alright.

Figure 2.5 Carbon copies on onionskin paper. Older case files will contain copies made with carbon paper, and these are often encountered on onionskin paper, a semitransparent, fragile paper. (Courtesy of El Cajon Police Department.)

years or so, depending upon its composition and conditions to which it has been exposed, such as light and heat. Documents reproduced on thermal paper may be identified by an overall brownish tinge to the paper and a reddish-brown tinge to the letters. In addition, the paper may have a semiglossy sheen. I have encountered these in reviewing reports from the 1950s and 1970s, and this was one of the earlier forms used in office-style duplicating machines to reproduce reports or other documents now found in some older cold case files.

When thermal paper copies are found in a file, it is suggested that these be photographed or their images otherwise preserved due to the continuing degradation that may occur. In addition, a cold case investigator

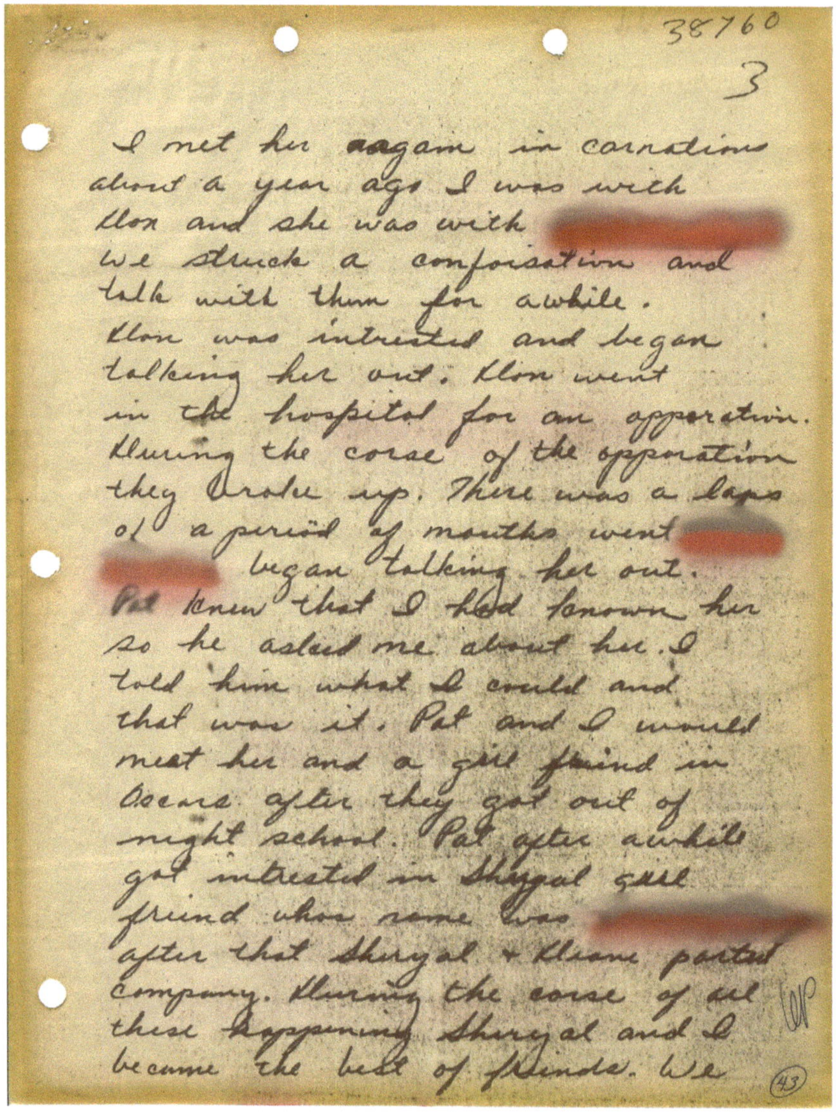
38760
3
I met her again in carnations
about a year ago I was with
Don and she was with [redacted]
we struck a comforsation and
talk with them for awhile.
Don was intrested and began
talking her out. Don went
in the hospital for an apporation.
During the corse of the opporation
they broke up. There was a laps
of a period of months went [redacted]
[redacted] began talking her out.
Pat knew that I had known her
so he asked me about her. I
told him what I could and
that was it. Pat and I would
meat her and a girl friend in
Oceana after they got out of
night school. Pat after awhile
got intrested in Sheryal girl
friend whos name was [redacted]
after that Sheryal + Diane parted
company. During the corse of all
these happening Sheryal and I
became the best of friends. We
(43)

Figure 2.6 Thermal paper. Note the reddish-brown tinge to this paper. With time, the writing will fade almost completely. (Courtesy of El Cajon Police Department.)

may ask, "Where is the original?" This may suggest possible sources for follow-up and/or retrieval of further case documents and material, or identify other contacts. *Why were copies made, and who were the recipients?*

- *Photostat.* The term is a trademark name for a style of photocopier, and copies of documents made by this process may still be found in cold case files. The device is a large camera that takes a photograph of the object. A paper negative is processed in developer, washed, and dried in a drier. The result is white letters on a black background, whereas the original of the document was black letters, such as from a typewriter, on a white background. See Figure 2.7.
- *Shorthand.* Shorthand is a method of taking notes and reporting of dialogue using a handwritten series of figures and spaces. It is a process that is formally learned through specialized training

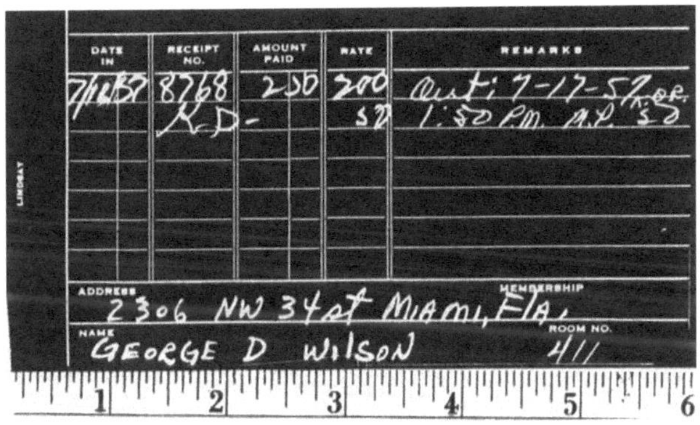

Figure 2.7 Photostat copy. This was essentially a paper negative produced by a particular camera. (Courtesy of *the late* Paul Edholm.)

and experience and was a commonplace form for taking dictation in business and in the legal profession for many decades, and mechanized forms are still in use today. The use of shorthand in the legal system dates to at least the late 1800s. In the days before courtroom reporting became mechanical, trained clerks recorded question-and answer-sessions and court proceedings using paper and pencil/pen. I have reviewed a number of cold cases in which the stenographers' notes were retained in the file. These are often the result of interrogation and interviews between investigators and witnesses or suspects.

These notes may be encountered in loose-sheet form or in spiral or similar bound tablets. In addition, there have been different styles of shorthand. Should these be encountered in reviewing cold case files, the local court reporter's office may be able to assist in deciphering and/or transcribing these notes. In addition, they may know the whereabouts or disposition of the original stenographer as well. A cold case investigator may seek to identify the stenographer who took the notes to inquire as to what they are and ask the following:

- Is this a complete statement or a partial statement?
- Was a transcribed report made? (Is it in the file, or does the stenographer have a copy?)
- Does the stenographer retain any other records pertaining to this case?

Such an instance occurred during the preparation of this text. Publicity about new developments in an early 1970s cold case brought a call to the detective. The suspect had previously been charged with the offense but was not held to answer at the preliminary hearing. Upon reading about the case, the stenographer contacted police and furnished the original notes taken during the course of the preliminary hearing. It was a treasure trove of information—under oath—in a case review that began with the only remaining documents: five newspaper clippings, the original medical examiner's report, and some faded Polaroid photos. In the fall of 2016, the suspect was charged with the murder, arrested, and pled guilty. Forty-six years later.

During the course of opening and reviewing a cold case file, investigators may discover different colored copies of report forms. When these are found, investigators may seek to determine the number of copies in the original form and their dissemination routes. This may lead investigators to other sources of case information. An example is shown in Figure 2.8. Investigators should ask, *Who was the recipient? Why did he/she need, or get, a copy? Does he/she have additional documentation relevant to this case?*

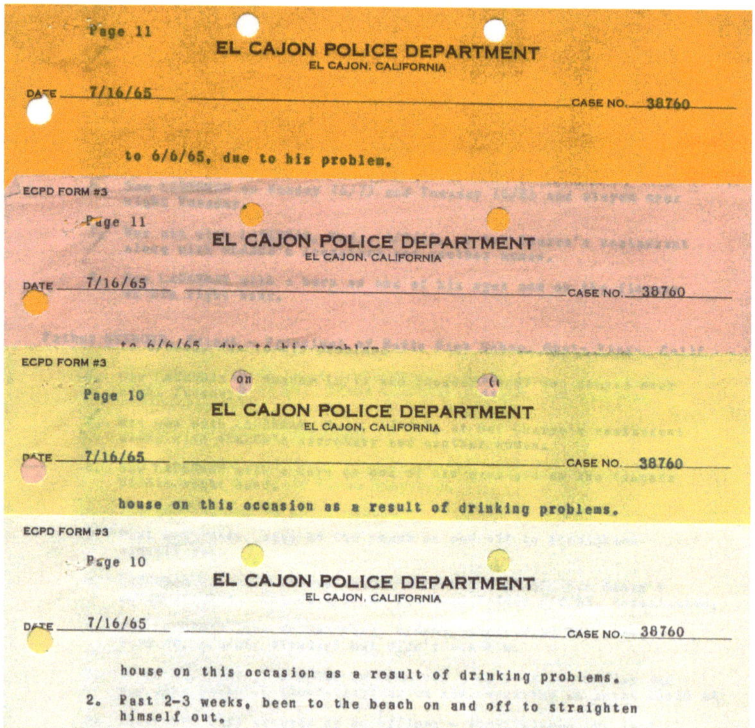

Page 11
EL CAJON POLICE DEPARTMENT
EL CAJON, CALIFORNIA
DATE 7/16/65 CASE NO. 38760
to 6/6/65, due to his problem.
ECPD FORM #3

Page 11
EL CAJON POLICE DEPARTMENT
EL CAJON, CALIFORNIA
DATE 7/16/65 CASE NO. 38760
ECPD FORM #3

Page 10
EL CAJON POLICE DEPARTMENT
EL CAJON, CALIFORNIA
DATE 7/16/65 CASE NO. 38760
house on this occasion as a result of drinking problems.
ECPD FORM #3

Page 10
EL CAJON POLICE DEPARTMENT
EL CAJON, CALIFORNIA
DATE 7/16/65 CASE NO. 38760
house on this occasion as a result of drinking problems.
2. Past 2-3 weeks, been to the beach on and off to straighten himself out.

Figure 2.8 Multicolored police report forms. When colored forms are found in a file, cold case investigators should determine who may have received the copies. These recipients may retain case documents or other material. (Courtesy of El Cajon Police Department.)

Preliminary File Review

The goal of a preliminary file review is to

- Put each file into such a condition that an investigator can (1) take that file any time following the review, (2) see a concise summary of the facts and physical evidence, and (3) begin working that case without having to track down missing information/reports.
- Create a concise summary of the facts and physical evidence as well as results of forensic examinations previously performed upon the evidence. This summary may be downloaded into appropriate computer systems, thus allowing for an immediate review of the case without having to physically locate the file.
- Update all identifying information pertaining to witnesses, suspects, and other persons of interest, allowing for the possibility of linking these persons to other cases and/or alerting other investigators who have contact with these persons of their involvement in this case.
- Download case information into the Violent Criminal Apprehension Program (ViCAP) or other local, regional, or state information sharing and/or system.
- Allow for rapid identification of cases for future forensic potential when new technology becomes available.
- Identify investigative leads.
- Prioritize cases based upon leads and evidence.

Review of cold case homicide files and selection of those cases for investigation may further occur through organizational circumstances. Agency leadership and the size and number of unsolved homicide cases may factor into this analysis. Not infrequently, the decision to undertake a preliminary file review may address legal considerations as well as personal relationships and evolving technological changes.

This review may also be the result of (1) selection of one or a few cases or (2) systematic review of all unsolved homicide cases.

Preliminary guidelines in a case file review may include these evidentiary considerations:

- There is a known suspect, and physical evidence appears to have been preserved.
- There is no known suspect, but physical evidence has been preserved.
- There is no known suspect, and physical evidence is lacking or not preserved in a manner that facilitates reexamination through advanced technology.

Initial Legal Considerations

When conducting an initial case file review, whether it is a single case or during the course of a systematic review of all unsolved cases, cold case investigators should consider potential legal issues. While there is generally no statute of limitations on first-degree murder, there may be limitations to prosecution on lesser degrees of murder. Review and potential reactivation of cold case homicides may involve other legal issues as well. In conjunction with representatives of the prosecutor's office (see Chapter 6) considerations during the review process may include the following:

- Degree of homicide.
- Jurisdiction/venue.
- Changes in the law since time of offense.
- Previous invocation of Miranda rights.
- Statute of limitations of premeditated versus manslaughter.
- Speedy trial.
- Evidence code then and now.
- Chain of custody of evidence.
- Suspect status (deceased or incarcerated).
- Sexual assault statute of limitations (if this component is present).
- Allegation of prior offenses?
- Ex post facto considerations.
- Enhancements?
- Has punishment changed?

Arrest and successful prosecution of those responsible for the murder is the ultimate goal of police and prosecutors. These are circumstantial cases. Cold case investigators should bear in mind that investigation and prosecution will fully illustrate the difference between *probable cause* and *beyond a reasonable doubt*. Good communication between law enforcement and local prosecutors is critical when examining legal questions, and serves to build rapport for the future. Keep in mind that prosecutors and judges may need to be *educated* in cold case investigation.

Cold case investigators may, in some instances, need to overcome prosecutorial belief that every possible hypothesis of innocence must be overcome. This is not normally done in the course of current homicide cases and is not necessarily so in cold case investigation and prosecution. Identifying prosecutors to assist in these cases early in the process facilitates the exchange of information and may speed up search and arrest warrants in the future. Good communication at this time will not put the investigator in a position of calling a prosecutor at 3 a.m. and hearing, "...you're calling me now on how old a case?"

Remember, the case is not done until you get a conviction.

Systematic Review of All Cases

In this method of file review, all unsolved homicide cases are identified, reviewed for potential solvability, and prioritized for further investigation. The methods and procedures utilized in this process are applicable to a single-case file review as well. During this process, reviewers may include the following:

- Current homicide detectives.
- Retired homicide detectives hired back by the organization to review these cases. This is an option that an agency may utilize in lieu of assigning detectives with current, full caseloads. When this method is used, however, it should be noted that one of the advantages in a file review is to have someone *unfamiliar* with the case do the review. A fresh pair of eyes means a fresh perspective, something that may not be possible should the original detective be hired back and assigned his/her own unsolved case.
- Civilian volunteers with homicide investigation experience. In 2002, the Charlotte Mecklenburg Police Department, (North Carolina), inaugurated a program to review unsolved homicide cases dating to the early 1960s. After concerns addressing confidentiality and potential judicial obstacles were resolved, these volunteers were assigned a case based on solvability factors such as DNA and fingerprints as well as examination for potential relationship changes. The volunteers reviewed their assigned cases and developed an organized case file. They prepared lead sheets addressing forensic evidence and suggested persons to interview. As a result of their work, a case summary was prepared for homicide detectives, and the case was given back to a detective for continued follow-up. The agency has reported favorably upon this method. See Chapter 31.

Qualifications to Review Unsolved Cases

Those persons selected to review unsolved homicide cases should be knowledgeable in homicide investigation, law, and technology. In addition, they should be

- Knowledgeable of current computer software relating to case review, including ViCAP and agency case management systems
- Knowledgeable of current sources for research of witnesses, suspects, and principals involved in unsolved cases
- Knowledgeable in locating current sources for all evidence and coroner/medical examiner documentation
- Knowledgeable in operating applicable agency computer software to document their activity

Solvability Factors

Cold case reviews focus on people (as victims, witnesses, or suspects) and evidence (physical or biological). These are the elements that constitute the crime yet may also solve it. Solvability factors are those facts and circumstances of a case that influence its potential to be solved. These reviews commonly seek to maximize the potential to be gained from (1) changes in relationships that may now result in persons providing necessary information to law enforcement or (2) utilization of advanced technology in the examination and analysis of physical or biological material. Ultimately, these solvability factors may be incorporated into the parameters that are defined when a systematic case review program is instituted.

Technology as a solvability factor includes systems such as the following:

- DNA/CODIS.
  - Potential suspect DNA recovered
  - Potential probative victim DNA recovered
  - No DNA evidence recovered
- NGI/AFIS.
  - Identified fingerprints recovered
  - Unidentified fingerprints recovered
  - No fingerprints recovered
- NIBIN/DRUGFIRE.
  - Shell casings recovered
  - Bullets recovered
  - Linked to another crime
  - No firearm evidence recovered
- ViCAP. Potential link to another crime (see Chapter 7).

People as potential solvability factors may be

- Suspect
  - Arrested but released
  - Named, no arrest
  - Incarcerated/other charge
  - Under investigation/other charge
  - Seen but unidentified
  - Deceased
  - No suspects
- Witness
  - Witness under investigation/trial
  - Witness incarcerated
  - Multiple eyewitnesses
  - Previously uncooperative
  - Previously did not tell all
  - Other

These solvability factors have been summarized by the Washington Metro Police Department, District of Columbia, and are shown in Figure 2.9.

Those homicides that have a sexual assault/biological evidence or fingerprint component often present the highest potential for solvability.

Homicide case review solvability chart

		Comments
Suspect		
Arrested but released	☐	________________
Named, no arrest	☐	________________
Incarcerated/other charge	☐	________________
Under investigation/other charge	☐	________________
Deceased	☐	________________
Seen but unidentified	☐	________________
No suspects	☐	________________
Witness		
Witness under investigation/trial	☐	________________
Witness incarcerated	☐	________________
Multiple eye-witnesses	☐	________________
Other	☐	________________
Firearm evidence		
Shell casings recovered	☐	________________
Slugs recovered	☐	________________
Linked to another crime	☐	________________
No firearm evidence recovered	☐	________________
Fingerprint evidence		
Unidentified prints recovered	☐	________________
No fingerprint evidence recovered	☐	________________
DNA evidence		
Potential suspect DNA recovered	☐	________________
Potential probative victim DNA	☐	________________
No DNA evidence recovered	☐	________________
Other crimes		
Potential link to another crime	☐	________________
Misc. solvability factors		
________________	☐	________________
________________	☐	________________

Figure 2.9 Washington Metropolitan Police Department (District of Columbia) solvability chart. (Courtesy of Detective Jim Trainum.)

Defining Parameters for a Systematic Review

Parameters may be based on elements of time, technology, and encompassing time periods. Some agencies conduct a systematic review by

- Reexamining all unsolved cases beginning with those most recently unsolved (cases prior to a date one to three years in the immediate past or similar criteria). The Kansas City Police Department (KCPD), Missouri, has utilized this method.

- Selecting a specific encompassing time period, for example, those cases unsolved from 1960 to 1995. The Los Angeles Police Department, California, has utilized this method.

In addition, these selection criteria may be combined with

- Selection of those cases in which there exists a potential to exploit changes in personal relationships due to passage of time.
- Selection of those cases in which evidence exists that may be exploited by advanced technology.

A systematic review is often conducted by an agency that has a large backlog of unsolved homicides. In conducting this style of review, an agency may seek to learn the following:

- How many qualifying cases are there in the agency?
- Where are these cases located?
- Do case summaries currently exist?

Interestingly enough, this method of review has also resulted in the following:

- Identification of cases reflected in the records as "unsolved" that are actually solved, but records were not current. Thus, the agency had less cold cases than initially thought, and records are updated.
- Identification of cases considered unsolved that had progressed through the identification of a suspect and issuance of an arrest warrant, but the warrant had not been entered into state/national computer systems.
- Identification of cases wherein an arrest warrant had been issued but erroneously recalled and needed to be reissued.
- Recognition of previously unrecognized patterns in homicides and/or sexual assaults.
- An updated database that identifies the offense and other designated criteria. This may include
  - Victim
  - Date of offense and/or report
  - Suspect name, description, and vehicle
  - Presence of physical or biological evidence
  - Physical location and availability of case and/or evidence

This method is appropriate for any jurisdictional size, and agencies of many different sizes have utilized such a method to review their unsolved homicide cases. No agency, however, has unlimited resources, and these efforts will be affected by time, number of personnel, and other available resources. While a larger department may assign more personnel to review cold cases, it most likely will have a proportionally larger number of cold cases to investigate. Similarly, smaller departments may assign one, two, or more detectives to review a smaller number of cases. They may be assigned on a full- or part-time basis to review unsolved cases. In either method, a systematic review represents a commitment by the agency to address all unsolved homicides.

Case Prioritization by Homicide Category

During a systemic review, homicides may be prioritized by type or category of homicide. These could include the following:

- Sex related. Due to DNA/CODIS potential, sexual assault–related murders may present the highest rate of solvability, depending upon the existence and preservation of biological evidence.
- *Stabbings.* Possibility of biological evidence/DNA transfer left by suspect.
- *Beating and strangulation.* Possibility of DNA transfer from suspect.
- *Shootings.* Largest category but small potential for DNA or physical evidence.
- *Closed cases.* Cases closed by arrest, but should be considered, whether or not charges were later dropped. Also, whether more than one suspect may have been involved.

Objectives Clearly Stated

In conducting a systematic review, the goal of the review should be clearly stated and understood by those who are tasked to conduct the review: (1) Is the goal of the review to obtain convictions, or (2) is the goal of the review to solve and close unsolved cases regardless of whether a conviction can be obtained?

If the purpose of the review program is to obtain convictions and the statute of limitations has expired, an agency may desire to save the resources for those cases more likely to result in a conviction. *If* the goal of the review is to solve and close unsolved cases regardless of whether a conviction can be obtained, an agency may opt to review all cases that qualify under its guidelines. This may be an important consideration during investigations of serial killers, whose criminal depredations may span years or decades.

Identifying Unsolved Cases

Using a systematic approach, each unsolved homicide is given a preliminary review and may be subsequently prioritized or ranked for possibility of successful investigation potential. When conducting a systematic review of all unsolved homicide cases, it is important to thoroughly and methodically identify all unsolved homicides within the agency. Sources of information to identify potential unsolved cases, or to assist in corroboration of unsolved cases, would include

- Local agency logbooks
- Computer databases
- Rejected cases
- Dismissed cases
- Autopsy logbooks and coroner/medical examiner records
- Crime laboratory logbooks
- Retired homicide investigators
- Prosecutor records
- State bureau of vital statistics
- Local recorder's office

Suggested Preliminary Case Review Procedure

The following is a synopsis of several cold case review protocols utilized by various law enforcement agencies. The cold case reviewer would consider (1) reports and documents, (2) evidence, and (3) review and updated condition of the case file. In-depth discussions of these topics will occur in future chapters.

1. Reports and Documents

- Locate all case files and reports.
- Read all reports and documents to determine if workable information exists.

- Listen to all audiotapes and determine if transcripts should be made or existing ones are accurate. Consider making backup copies for case work and minimizing usage of original tapes.
- Review all video recordings. Similarly, consider preserving originals, and make duplicates.
- Where possible, contact original detectives to obtain their perspective and an overview to determine whether information exists that is not reflected in the case file. During this contact, the reviewer should seek to determine whether the former detective has any notebooks, case files, photos, or other memorabilia from this case and to recover these. During this contact, the previous detective's work must not be criticized or belittled. Other events or activities that may have been concurrent with his/her investigation at the time are not known. In some rare circumstances, detectives have declined to cooperate based upon personal and professional circumstances at the time of their departure.
- The reviewer should determine whether contact needs to be made, or should be made, with the victim's family. This may be necessary to establish whether new information exists that was not known to original investigators. This may be especially true in gang-related homicides.
- The reviewer would prepare recommendations for a follow-up assigned investigator to obtain possible information from any specialized law enforcement units, such as gang units, narcotic investigative units, or other groups.

During the case file review, reviewers and investigators may begin to formulate their investigative plan by considering factors that may include the following:

- Totality of information known about the crime. Included would be
  - Date, time, location
  - Name of victim
  - Brief profile of victim
  - Finding of body
- Identified or developed suspects
  - Known relationship to victim
  - Known prior contacts with victim
  - Current location
- Agency jurisdiction for investigation of the offense.
- Previous investigation(s).
- Autopsy and medical examiner records.
- Motive.
- Witness information.
- Known physical evidence that may link a potential suspect to the crime.
- New forensic technologies that may assist in developing known physical evidence.
- What impact does the passage of time have on the case?
- Does this case have a *pulse?*

2. Evidence Review

- The reviewer would determine if evidence exists. Locations to find physical or biological evidence may include the following:
  - Agency evidence/property room.

- Coroner or medical examiner office for original slides, swabs, victim clothing, or other evidence. Even when agency biological evidence has been discarded or lost, or otherwise cannot be located, check with the coroner/medical examiner for duplicate slides/swabs that may have been retained in his/her files.
- Public or private crime laboratories (previously submitted or tested evidence and lab reports).
- Hospital/medical facilities (rape kits, medical reports, slides).
- Courthouse property rooms.
- Prosecutor's offices (previous trial or investigations).
- Retired investigators' files, including case notes and details not found in files.
- Other investigating agencies.

It is incumbent during a preliminary cold case file review, or during a subsequent in-depth case examination, to identify the location of the evidence and to *personally* inspect and examine it. During this inspection and review, the cold case investigator seeks to

- Identify the physical existence of the evidence
- Identify the physical location of the evidence
- Confirm the identity and description of the evidence
- Confirm that all evidence is properly packaged and stored
- Physically examine it to check for degradation, damage, or other conditions
- Confirm quantity (drug evidence)
- Compare physical evidence and property to be concurrent with written case records
- Examine chain-of-custody issues to ensure integrity of the evidence
- Assure that all evidence is present and accounted for
- Document this activity
- Determine and recommend what analysis may be available for existing evidence, such as DNA, NGI/AFIS, etc.

John Doe Warrants

During the initial file review, DNA-related legal issues may be identified. Due to advances in this technology, *John Doe warrants* may be a viable option. This is the method of issuing an arrest warrant for a DNA profile obtained from analysis of unsolved crime scene evidence. See Chapter 6. The warrant is issued for the DNA identifier, absent the name of the profile holder. This innovative approach was pioneered by Deputy District Attorney Norm Gahn in Milwaukee, Wisconsin. The method has allowed charges to be filed and permits old cases, primarily sexual assaults, to be prosecuted when the person matching the John Doe DNA profile is subsequently identified by name. John Doe DNA warrants are one way to permit cases to remain active and allow them the chance to be solved through future DNA technology and databases.

3. Review and Update of Case File

- Ensure that the "murder book" is complete and updated with all necessary reports (see Figure 2.10).
- Locate and inspect all photos and negatives, and ensure that they are in satisfactory condition for court purposes.
- Identify and ensure that all coroner's or medical examiner's reports and photographs and other documents are in the file and in satisfactory condition for court purposes.

Figure 2.10 Los Angeles Police Department murder investigation summaries. The larger the agency, the greater the possibility of higher numbers of unsolved homicides. (Courtesy of Detective Rick Jackson, LAPD.)

- Ensure that all available investigator's notebooks and case notes are in the file and not with the original investigator (see Figure 2.11).
- Ensure that all evidence is documented and accounted for, and that requests for needed examination or reexamination are completed and filed. In addition, the reviewer would ensure that a complete copy of the evidence list, including location, is present in the case file.
- Locate and inspect all maps and diagrams to ensure that they are present and suitable for court purposes.

Figure 2.11 Detective's notebook. (Courtesy of late Sgt. Richard Longshore, Los Angeles County Sheriff's Department.)

4. Case Synopsis and Assessment Report

Upon completion of the file review, the reviewer would prepare a complete and accurate summary of the case for entry in specified agency computer systems. This synopsis provides a review of events, a review of the persons involved, and a summary of the evidence and the case.

- *Solved cases.* If the case has been solved or resolved, the reviewer would prepare a closing supplemental report and dispose of evidence (with the approval and supervision of the homicide unit supervisor or commander).
- *Unsolved cases.* If the case is unsolved, the reviewer would ensure that the case is ready to be handed off to an assigned investigator for active follow-up investigation. This might include
  - Written recommendations and offering a comprehensive investigative plan that would suggest a high probability for the arrest and prosecution of responsible suspect(s) for criminal homicide
  - Indication of the reviewer's preparation to give an oral overview of the case and presentation of proposed investigative plan
- *Solved cases with arrest warrants outstanding.* The reviewer would evaluate the case and locate and confirm evidence. Also, he/she would
  - Ascertain and determine what information exists in the file to positively identify the defendant named in the outstanding arrest warrant.
  - Ensure that certified copies of identification that positively identifies the named defendant in the outstanding warrant exist in the case file. This documentation may include
    - Certified copy of driver's license photo with fingerprint verification
    - Latent fingerprint card
    - Other (passport, etc.)
  - Recommend or ensure ViCAP update when new information is received.
  - Prepare a written, comprehensive recommendation that the case can be assigned to a specialized unit for active investigation. In these cases, it is important to realize the necessity for *due diligence* and to document these efforts for future legal activity.
  - Be prepared to present an oral briefing or overview of the case as necessary.
  - Update the case management system.
  - Ensure that the warrant is valid and entered into state/national computer systems.

Figures 2.12 and 2.13 are examples of forms used in the review process by the Unsolved Unit of the Los Angeles County Sheriff's Department, California. Additional report forms are used for case assessment, evidence evaluation, and examination of evidence. This process is described further in this chapter.

CASE STATUS AND REVIEW

File #:			Date Received:	
			Date Received:	

Victim Name(s):	
Location of case file:	

(Library # or who has it)

Investigator responsible for	1.	
the case or investigation:	2.	
(Not the Reviewer)	3.	

INFORMATION FOR CASE NARRATIVE UPDATE:
Don't rewrite case summary or narrative unless necessary. Just write additions or update narrative already in case management system.

□	FURTHER INVESTIGATION			**(Check these only if done by Reviewer)**
□	ACTIVE WITH NO WORKABLE INFORMATION		□	CASE ASSESSMENT REPORT (6 Pages)
□	SOLVED		□	POOR-BOY INVENTORY SHEET
□	**(Mark Only If Requesting Lab Work)**		□	MURDER BOOK
□	EVIDENCE-FIREARMS		□	SUPPLEMENTARY REPORT SUBMIT
□	EVIDENCE-DNA		□	CLOSE/OUT SUPP. REPORT
□	EVIDENCE-PHYSICAL			

REVIEWED BY:		DATE:	

*****CASE MANAGEMENT SUMMARY REPORT AND CASE TRACKING FORM MUST BE ATTACHED*****

Revised 02-27-02 md

Figure 2.12 Case status and review summary. (Courtesy of Capt. Joseph Hartshorne, Los Angeles County Sheriff's Department.)

CASE ASSESSMENT REPORT

FILE #			CRIME:		
Murder Book:	□ Yes □ No	Library #		Crime Status:	
Date of Occurrence:		Time of Occurrence:		Day of Occurrence:	

LOCATION:		TYPE OF LOC:	
VICTIM:		CC#	
DESCRIPTION:			

ADD'L VICTIMS:	

SUSPECT( ):		IN CUSTODY: □YES □NO
DESCRIPTION:		

ADD'L SUSPECTS:	

****

CASE SUMMARY:

FILE #		REVIEWER:	

Figure 2.13 Case assessment report. (Courtesy of Capt. Joseph Hartshorne Los Angeles County Sheriff's Department.)

(Continued)

RECOMMENDATIONS:	

DATE:		REVIEWER:		COMPLETED:	

ORIGINAL ASSIGNED INVESTIGATORS:	

EVIDENCE EVALUATION	FILE #	

NO:	EVIDENCE ITEMS	PG #	PC #	LAB #

EVIDENCE EVALUATION	FILE #	

NO:	LAB EXAMINATION RECOMMENDED/COMPLETED	PG#	DATE

Figure 2.13 (Continued) Case assessment report. (Courtesy of Capt. Joseph Hartshorne Los Angeles County Sheriff's Department.) *(Continued)*

FILE #		SUSPECT ( ) OF ( )

NAME:		PHOTO: ☐ YES ☐ NO

AKA'S:		DOB:	

Marks/Scars/Tattoos:	

PHYSICAL:

Sex		Race		Height		Weight		Eyes		Hair	

IDENTIFIERS

ID/DL#		CII#		FBI#	

SS #		OTHER	

RESIDENCE:	

Date Arrested		Booking #		Charges:	
Case #		Charges Filed			
Arrest Warrant Issued ☐ YES ☐ NO			Warrant Status ☐ Cleared ☐ Outstanding		
Court Action:					
Sentence:					
ADDITIONAL INFORMATION:					

Figure 2.13 (Continued) Case assessment report. (Courtesy of Capt. Joseph Hartshorne Los Angeles County Sheriff's Department.)

(Continued)

WITNESS LIST	FILE #	

NAME/DESCRIPTION	ADDRESS/PHONE	RELATION TO CASE	REF PAGE

REVIEWER		FILE #	

DATE	TIME	FOLLOW-UP

Figure 2.13 (Continued) Case assessment report. (Courtesy of Capt. Joseph Hartshorne Los Angeles County Sheriff's Department.)

Prioritization Schedules

Once the preliminary case and evidence reviews have been completed, a priority of likelihood for solution building upon the following criteria may be considered. This prioritization schedule will assist in filtering those cases that offer the highest potential for solvability with given resources from those with a lesser chance of solution. The following examples reflect three different types of prioritization schedules.

By the very nature of these cases, the reality of cold case review and prioritization may be affected by who the victim is, degree of heinousness, media influence, and election politics.

1. Five-Part Schedule

- *Priority 1.* These are those cases in which an offender has been identified and an arrest warrant has been issued. These are those cases that have fallen through the cracks. Further, this review will assure that the arrest warrant is still valid and properly entered into the National Crime Information Center (NCIC), or an Unlawful Flight to Avoid Prosecution (UFAP) warrant has been obtained. Follow-up investigation to locate the suspect will be necessary, and this investigation may ultimately draw upon forensic artistry, media alerts, or national television broadcast in attempts to locate the suspect. Investigation may necessitate the review of all evidence to ascertain its existence, location, and condition as well as witness location and potential reinterviews.
- *Priority 2.* There is a known suspect, and physical evidence has been preserved. Modern technology, including DNA, NGI/AFIS, and other fingerprint-related technology, may be enlisted to develop significant information that perhaps was previously not technically feasible. In some cases, evidence was not processed. Review and follow-through may result in successful prosecution.
- *Priority 3.* There is no known suspect, but physical evidence has been preserved. Modern technology may potentially identify the suspect(s). An example would be identifying a DNA profile in conjunction with CODIS.
- *Priority 4.* There is no known suspect and insufficient physical evidence, but there are witnesses who were not previously available who may now provide material information that can assist in suspect identification. These cases may involve situations in which witnesses could not be initially located and interviewed and/or need to be reinterviewed. Investigation may be extensive.
- *Priority 5.* There are no known witnesses and no known physical evidence that can assist in identifying the suspect(s). These are those that cold case investigator Louis N. Eliopulos terms a "snowball's chance in hell."

2. Four-Part Schedule

This style is exemplified by the protocol of the San Diego Police Department Cold Case Team.

- *Priority 1.* Suspect(s) have been previously identified. A warrant of arrest has previously been issued. A suspect has been identified by forensic methods. These cases are given the highest priority for reinvestigation.
- *Priority 2.* There are witnesses who can assist in identifying the suspect(s). Information has developed that identifies possible suspect(s). Evidence has been developed that can assist in identifying

suspect(s). Initial investigation identifies witnesses who could not be located and/or need to be reinterviewed. These cases will be reinvestigated.

- *Priority 3.* Evidence has been preserved, and modern technology, NGI/AFIS, DNA, and other methods can be utilized to process and analyze evidence. These cases will be reclassified depending on the results of the additional laboratory analysis.
- *Priority 4.* There are no known witnesses who can assist in identifying suspect(s). There is no physical evidence that can assist in identifying suspect(s). These cases will not be reinvestigated.

3. Three-Part Schedule

This is a three-tiered level of investigative prioritization that is evidence based and case specific. It may also be known as a *high–medium–low* system. The following is an example as used by the Texas Rangers:

- *High.* There exist viable investigative option(s) that can be expected to generate leads and/or suspects.
- *Moderate.* There exist reasonable investigative option(s) that might generate leads and/or suspects.
- *Low.* Remote investigative option(s) exist, and these are not expected to generate viable leads and/or suspects.

In this method, a case may also be d*eclined* due to (1) the absence of any viable investigative option(s) or (2) case facts strongly suggesting that something other than a violent crime (i.e., suicide) has occurred.

Those agencies adopting a system utilizing a high–medium–low method of prioritization may also adopt a policy of investigating all high-range cases before investigating cases offering a moderate potential for solution. This may be rationalized based upon the number of cases and available resources. In turn, all moderate-range cases may be investigated before dedicating resources to those cases exhibiting a low potential for solvability.

In reality, investigative efforts, due to case numbers and resources, may never arrive at the moderate level of priority or the low level of priority. Similarly, those agencies utilizing a number-tiered system may also choose to investigate those that offer the most potential before moving to those offering a lesser potential, based upon investigative resources.

The end result, however, may be that some cases are not reinvestigated.

Agency Samples

Morris County Prosecutor's Office (New Jersey) Method

Figure 2.14 identifies 10 factors used by the Morris County Prosecutor's Office (New Jersey) to determine the priority of investigation of cold case homicides. This method utilizes a point system to rank and subsequently prioritize a cold case homicide in comparison with other unsolved homicides. The final determination of investigative priority, however, rests with the county prosecutor, chief of investigations, or their designee. This method is in keeping with identifying all unsolved homicides, management of agency resources, and optimization of investigative resources.

Factor #	Factor	If Yes, Add	If No, Add
1	Has the death been ruled a homicide?	+1	−9
2	Can the crime scene be located today and is it in Morris County?	+1	−9
3	Has the victim been identified?	+5	−3
4	Is there significant physical evidence that can identify a suspect?	+5	0
5	Is the evidence still preserved and available?	+1	−5
6	Can any evidence be reprocessed to yield further clues?	+5	0
7	Are the critical witnesses still available?	+7	0
8	Are their leads documented in the last 6 months?	+2	0
9	Are there named suspects in the file?	+5	0
10	Is there behavior in this crime that is unusual or significant enough to warrant a behavioral assessment that may identify the offender(s)?	+1–5	0

Figure 2.14 Morris County, New Jersey, solvability factors table. This agency has identified 10 factors to be considered in the reopening of an unsolved case and the resulting prioritization. (Courtesy of Deputy Chief of Investigations James Gannon.)

Kansas City Police Department (Missouri) Method

During 2002, the KCPD was scrutinized as a result of evidence disappearing in a pending homicide trial. The chief of police formed a cold case squad and tasked the detectives with two purposes: (1) examine unsolved homicides to look for new leads, and (2) audit each item of evidence and property from their assigned cold cases. In this regard, they were to determine its physical location and proper maintenance. Cases were reviewed from 2001 and working backward. The philosophy driving this directional sequence considered maximization of resources. Older cases present more difficulty due to lack of witness availability, evidence considerations, and other factors.

The department wanted the unit to be operational within a short period of time and established a method to determine which cases would be reinvestigated. Their procedure included the following:

1. Each unsolved homicide would be reviewed by a detective not originally assigned to the investigation. They felt that fresh eyes offered a fresh perspective to the case.
2. A case overview document would be prepared upon completion of the review. This overview document would cover:
   - Crime scene information overview
   - Physical evidence description, condition, and location
   - Victim/victimology information
   - Overview of witness statements
   - Citizen/informant information
   - Suspect information
   - Availability of new forensic technology
   - Impact of passage of time (is it a plus or a negative?)

Upon this review, a conclusion highlighting new information or details about the evidence would be prepared. It was the responsibility of the assigned detectives to physically locate property and evidence and to document their findings, including date and time. In addition, the conclusion specified the disposition of the case, including whether it was (1) submitted for prosecution, (2) maintained by the cold case squad for investigation, (3) exceptionally cleared, or (4) archived due to lack of follow-up leads or evidence.

If the preliminary interview suggested the likelihood of a successful investigation and solution to the crime, a more formal review and investigation would be conducted by an assigned investigator. The KCPD adopted a point system to identify cases to be worked. This system assigns a weighted value to 23 individual categories (Figure 2.15). While 50 points is the maximum possible, cases examined with as little as 2 points and as many as 24 points were successfully cleared. This format has proved to be a valuable tool for their detectives, although the overall value as a solvability indicator is unknown. The unit reported solving 22 cold case homicides within their first year.

Los Angeles County Sheriff's Department (California) Method

Beginning in July 2000, the Los Angeles County Sheriff's Department undertook a systematic review of all identified unsolved homicides that occurred from January 1, 1980, through December 31, 1999. Approximately 3000 unsolved homicide cases were initially believed to exist within these parameters. The concept of this program was to determine whether the passage of time since the murder had occurred may lead to the identification of a suspect in selected cases. The parameters for this concept involved (1) utilization of advances in forensic technology, including DNA, fingerprint visualization techniques, NIBIN, or DRUGFIRE firearm databases; (2) previously unknown witnesses that may now come forward; (3) previously reluctant witnesses that may now be more likely to cooperate; and (4) a multiyear review that may reveal previously unknown homicide patterns.

The sheriff's department employed six retired sheriff's homicide detectives, "hirebacks," and devised a protocol by which they were to identify and score those cases that held potential for solution. In addition to their previous experience within the Homicide Bureau, requirements for selection included knowledge of current scientific capabilities and proficiency with law enforcement databases and other computer technology. These rehired detectives underwent a 24-hour training program and began to review these unsolved homicides.

This training instruction entailed (1) locating and cataloging homicide file contents from within sheriff's department sources; (2) instruction in computer software for the Federal Bureau of Investigation's (FBI's) National Center for Analysis of Violent Crime (ViCAP) and department case management systems; (3) instruction in research sources for locating witnesses, suspects, and principals in unsolved cases; (4) locating all evidence and coroner's office documentation; and (5) writing and filing a case assessment report as shown in Figures 2.12 and 2.13, summarizing their case review activity.

A case review was then completed for each unsolved homicide case. The procedures utilized in this review included (1) location and receipt of the case file; (2) listening to all audiotapes and determining whether transcripts should be made or existing ones are accurate; (3) contacting original investigators, if possible, for case overview and to determine whether additional information exists that is not in the case file, and in addition, to recover any notes or notebooks still retained by the original investigator; (4) determining whether or not contact needs to be made with family of the victim to establish whether new information exists that was not known to original investigators; and (5) preparing a recommendation to the sheriff's homicide investigator as to whether to obtain information from other specialized law enforcement units.

In addition, these examiners would systematically review and update the condition of the case file. This would include ensuring the following:

- The case file folder had the appropriate information required by the Homicide Bureau and that it was up to date and complete.
- All photos and negatives were located and in satisfactory condition for investigative and court purposes.
- All coroner's reports, photos, and other documents were present in the file, complete, and in satisfactory condition for court presentation.

OFFENSE NUMBER

VICTIM

DATE OF CRIME

	EVIDENCE	YES	PT.	NO.	UNK	N/A
1	FINGERPRINTS RECOVERED?		2			
2	PRINTS CHECKED THROUGH AFIS?		–			
3	ANY PRINTS AFIS QUALITY?		3			
4	PRINTS AVAILABLE ON POSSIBLE SUSPECT?		2			
5	TRACE EVIDENCE RECOVERED FOR DNA ANALYSIS?		4			
6	DNA ANALYSIS REQUESTED?		–			
7	DNA PROFILE OBTAINED FROM ANALYSIS?		3			
8	DNA SAMPLE OBTAINED FROM SUSPECTS?		2			
9	MURDER WEAPON RECOVERED?		4			
10	PROJECTILES/CASINGS RECOVERED?		2			
11	CHECKED THROUGH NIBIN SYSTEM?		–			
12	NIBIN IDENTIFICATION MADE?		2			
13	VICTIM'S PROPERTY TAKEN IN CRIME?		2			
14	STOLEN PROPERTY ENTERED IN NCIC?		4			

	WITNESS (S)	YES	PT.	NO.	UNK	N/A
15	EYEWITNESS (S) TO THE CRIME?		3			
16	COOPERATIVE WITNESS (S)?		2			
17	HOSTILE WITNESS (S)?		1			
18	GOOD WITNESS (S) DEVELOPED IN CANVASS?		2			

	SUSPECT (S)	YES	PT.	NO.	UNK	N/A
19	SUSPECT (S) NAMED BY WITNESS(S)?		4			
20	DOES EYEWITNESS(S) KNOW SUSPECT(S)?		2			
21	SUSPECT(S) DEVELOPED IN INVESTIGATION?		2			
22	CAN WITNESS(S) IDENTIFY SUSPECT(S)?		2			
23	IS SUSPECT(S) STILL IN KANSAS CITY?		2			

TOTAL SOLVABILITY POINTS (50 possible)	
Det.	Date

Figure 2.15 Kansas City, Missouri, solvability points table. The KCPD utilizes a 23-factor table that utilizes a point system for categories of evidence, witness, and suspect in the determination of a priority ranking system for reinvestigation. (Courtesy of Sgt. Rick Jackson, Kansas City Police Department, Missouri.)

COLD CASE PROTOCOL

Victim's Name ____

Race _____ Sex _____ DOB __________

Date of Incident _______________ Incident Case # _______________

Day of Week __________ Time of Day __________

Case Materials Available?

	No	Yes
Initial Offense Report	_____	_____
Detectives Notes	_____	_____
Original Detective Available for interview	_____	_____
Crime Scene Photos	_____	_____
Crime Scene Diagrams	_____	_____
Autopsy Report	_____	_____
Body Diagram	_____	_____
Lab		
Was any evidence recovered	_____	_____
Was evidence analyzed	_____	_____
If Yes, results identify anyone besides Victim	_____	_____
Was evidence analyzed within last 5 years	_____	_____
Any remaining evidence NOT analyzed	_____	_____
Is there any DNA evidence, not the Victims	_____	_____
If Yes, is DNA profile in CODIS	_____	_____
Is there fingerprint evidence, not the Victim's	_____	_____
If Yes, is it in AFIS & IAFIS	_____	_____
Any other trace evidence recovered	_____	_____
Weapon recovered	_____	_____
If firearm, projectile	_____	_____
Casing(s)	_____	_____
If Yes to either, entered into IBIN/NIBIN	_____	_____
Was weapon analyzed for evidence	_____	_____
If Yes, any forensic/investigative value	_____	_____
Witnesses		
Any known witnesses	_____	_____
If Yes, were they formally interviewed	_____	_____
Written notes _____ Audio _____ Video _____		
Were criminal record checks conducted	_____	_____
Any criminal activity since this offense	_____	_____
Any witnesses NOT interviewed	_____	_____
Are witnesses still in area?	_____	_____

Figure 2.16 Cold case file review protocol. This protocol identifies some of those points to be considered when conducting both a case file review as well as during the investigation itself. (Courtesy of Detective Timothy Keel, Baltimore Police Department [ret'd].) *(Continued)*

Potential Person(s) of Interest	**No**	**Yes**
Any potential persons of interest identified	_____	_____
Persons Name ________________________		DOB __________
Prior criminal record ___________________________________		
Type of offenses(s) ____		
Any arrest since this offense	_____	_____
Financial Records checked	_____	_____
Relationship to Victim	_____	_____
Former paramours at time of incident	_____	_____
If Yes, bio info ____		
Arrest info ____		
Current contact info __________________________________		
Anyone offered a polygraph/CVSA that refused	_____	_____
Cell Phones		
Did victim have a cell phone	_____	_____
Were records obtained	_____	_____
Were cell site tower dumps obtained	_____	_____
Were records analyzed	_____	_____
Was a time line created	_____	_____
Any type of crime analysis from neighborhood created	_____	_____
Media		
Any newspaper or television coverage	_____	_____
Website created	_____	_____
Crime Stopper flyer out	_____	_____
Reward offered	_____	_____

Potential Motive for Offense

Drugs _____ Robbery _____ Retaliation _____

Sexual _____ Personal _____ Unknown _____

Synopsis of case :

____

____

____

____

____

Good Potential for Leads Fair Lead Potential Poor Lead Potential

Figure 2.16 (Continued) Cold case file review protocol. This protocol identifies some of those points to be considered when conducting both a case file review as well as during the investigation itself. (Courtesy of Detective Timothy Keel, Baltimore Police Department [ret'd].)

- All original investigators' notes and notebooks were in the file and not still retained by the investigator.
- All evidence is accounted for, and its location determined, as is the need for reevaluation and reexamination.
- All progress reports were up to date and in the file.
- All maps and diagrams were inspected and in satisfactory condition for court presentation.

The reviewing detective would then prepare a case assessment report. This would provide updated information and recommend any necessary fieldwork and investigation. As a result, the file would be as complete as possible and in a condition to turn over to a homicide investigator with an oral briefing.

The agency identified in excess of 2000 homicide cases that were unsolved and, as a result of the filtering process based upon parameters of time, changes in relationships, and technology, identified approximately 600 cases for further investigation. A number of the cases have been subsequently solved.

Figure 2.16 illustrates additional considerations both when conducting a preliminary file review as well as during the investigation phase itself.

Conclusion

Cold case homicides are solved by old-fashioned "shoe leather" in combination with the passage of time, advanced technology, and changes in relationships. Cold case investigators begin by finding and reviewing the original case file, a feat sometimes more difficult than it may first appear to be. These files are found in a variety of conditions. For those agencies with large numbers of unsolved cases, a systematic review may be a viable method of filtering those cases with a potential for solvability with available resources from those with a lesser possibility. After the cases are reviewed, they may be prioritized, thus providing a means for the agency to proactively move forward with cold case investigations. The following chapters discuss in-depth file reviews and investigative methods that may assist in the solution of cold case homicides.

Acknowledgments

Many persons and agencies contributed to the preparation of this edition, but the basic principles remain today although names and forms may change. In the past decade, cold case units, policies, procedures, and protocols have seemingly exemplified the old phrase "here today gone tomorrow." I would like to especially thank Detective Jim Trainum (ret'd) of the Washington Metro Police Department, District of Columbia; Lt. Tony Leal and Ranger John Martin of the Texas Rangers; Sgt. John Jackson of the Kansas City Police Department, Missouri; Sgt. John Neff of the Austin Police Department, Texas; Deputy Chief of Investigations James Gannon of the Morris County Prosecutor's Office, New Jersey; Capt. Joe Hartshorne and the late Sgt. Richard Longshore of the Los Angeles County Sheriff's Department, California; Detective Timothy Keel of the Baltimore Police Department, Maryland (ret'd); and Sgt. Brian Pendleton of the San Diego Police Department, California, for their invaluable assistance. In addition, the KCPD method was drawn from a discussion of the Kansas City cold case squad by Sgt. Kate Ellis of that agency in the July 2004 issue of *Subject to Debate*, published by the Police Executive Research Forum, and interview with department personnel. Discussion of the methods used by the Charlotte Mecklenburg Police Department, North Carolina, were drawn from an article by Mike Adams in the Jul, 2003 issue of *Subject to Debate* and personal interview with Sgt. Darrell Price. Such represent the framework that is used in varying formats today.

Suggested Readings and Bibliography

Adams, M. (2003). Cold case squad: Partnering with volunteers to solve old homicide cases. (July 2002) Subject to Debate. Police Executive Research Forum. Washington, DC. pp. 1, 7.

Anonymous. (2002). "Cold Case Homicide." C.P.T. network. Sacramento, CA, California Commission on Peace Officer Standards and Training.

Barmazel, S. (1996). "Murder on coyote flat." *California Lawyer* **16**(5): 42–45, 86–87.

Bowker, M. (1994). The case of the fateful fingerprints. *Readers Digest*: 91–96.

Eliopulos, L. N. (2003). *Death Investigators Handbook: Expanded and Updated Edition*. Boulder, CO, Paladin Press.

Ellis, K. (2004). Kansas City cold case squad solves string of murders. Washington, DC, *Police Executive Research Forum* **18**: 1, 7.

Geberth, V. (1996). *Practical Homicide Investigation: Tactics, Procedures, and Forensic Techniques*. New York, CRC Press.

Heurich, C. (2008). Cold cases: Resources for agencies, resolution for families. *NIJ Journal* (260), NCJ 222903.

Keppell, R. D. and J. G. Weis. (1994). Time and distance as solvability factors in murder cases. *Journal of Forensic Sciences* **39**(2): 386–401.

NIJ. (2002). *Using DNA to Solve Cold Cases* (Commission Report No. NIJ 194197). Washington, DC, National Institute of Justice.

Nyberg, R. (1999). Investigations: Cold case squads re-activate old investigations. *Law and Order* **47**(10): 127.

O'Brien, C. (1993). 30 years later, prints meet match. Unknown.

Roletti, A. (1992). Team's task is to look at long-unsolved murders. *San Diego Union-Tribune*. San Diego: B-1, B-4.

Spraggs, D. (2003). How to…open a cold case. *Policemag.com*: 29–31.

Reading the Book
Learning the Case

3

R. H. WALTON

Contents

Introduction

"Read the book. Before you do anything, read the *whole* book!" With these words, the late Sgt. Rudy Ortega of the Unsolved Unit, Los Angeles County Sheriff's Department, summed it up. Before you begin to investigate a cold case, read the case file to see what you have and what's already been done. As you do so, you will begin to *reconstruct the case* and formulate an *investigative plan* in your mind. You will read what is known about the victim, and about the circumstances of the crime. You will read how it was initially handled, who responded, and what was learned in the initial investigation. You may readily identify a weakness in the investigation—perhaps witnesses who appear to be less than truthful or may have been holding back, or identification of evidence that may now offer more potential due to advanced technology. As you do so, your experience will begin to identify any potential gaps, areas that you may seek to fill.

Through understanding the case file, you are *informally* reconstructing the crime, the crime scene, and postcrime behavior. This is in contrast to a formal reconstruction as might be undertaken at a later stage of investigation. This is the beginning of the new investigation as you seek answers to questions you would normally ask in a homicide investigation but are now asking years or even decades since. These questions include the following:

- What happened?
- How did it happen?
- When and where?
- Who found the body?
- Who had a motive?
- Did anyone gain financially from the victim's death?
- Do the witness statements, or those of others, make sense?
- Where are the witnesses now?
- Has the passage of time affected the willingness of others to cooperate?
- What evidence did they have?
- Does the evidence fit the crime?
- What would a timeline of events reveal?
- Have there been any relationship changes that may now be exploited?
- If a suspect was developed, where is that suspect now?
- Is the suspect in custody?
- What other crimes did the suspect commit before, or after, this crime?
- Who might he/she have talked to about this crime?
- What relationship changes may have occurred in the suspect's life?

In doing this, you will see what was done by the investigators. You may also see what they did not do. You may initially sense no weakness in the case, that the original investigators did everything humanly possible at the time but were not able to make the case. It is now your turn, and you will try to exploit the advantages of time and technology to solve the case. Maybe now a reexamination of the physical or biological evidence will reveal critical information not known before, or an informant can be generated or a witness enticed to tell *all* he/she knows.

As you do this, keep an *open mind* and do not necessarily be drawn into the theories and avenues of focus of the original investigators. I have experienced those cases, personally and through discussion with other cold case investigators, in which the focus of our predecessors was wrong. They may have had wrong information, or circumstances at the time may have suggested they were on the right track. There have been those cases, unfortunately, in which the initial investigators focused on individuals with less regard for truth or fact, and were perhaps guided by the need for a "political solution," personal feelings, or other motives.

This chapter considers these and other issues that may be addressed by the cold case investigator as he/she proceeds with the investigation. If the case has been assigned to the investigator as a result of a systematic review, it may be in order, and a synopsis or summary has been compiled from which the investigator may readily obtain an overview of the case elements. A suggested investigative plan may already be outlined, but this is a suggestion only. Cold case investigation is cerebral, and what may have sounded good at the time to a reviewer may now not seem as necessary or beneficial as it once did. All investigators have their own approaches. If a cold case investigator assumes the investigation without the benefit of a prior review, this chapter offers further assistance in understanding the file and moving forward with the investigation. If the reinvestigation is the result of specific information that has come to the attention of law enforcement, this chapter and the next address potential avenues to approach the case and its investigation.

Initial Considerations

No one person is an expert in every field, and those in law enforcement are no different. When studying the case file, keep in mind the various disciplines and experts that are used in homicide investigation today, and their possible role in a cold case investigation. Among these are

- Behavioral analysis
- Legal and prosecution considerations
- Crime scene reconstruction personnel
- Forensic laboratory
- DNA (human/plant/animal)
- Technology databases such as Combined DNA Index System (CODIS)/Next Generation Identification (NGI)/automated fingerprint identification system (AFIS)/National Integrated Ballistic Information Network (NIBIN)/National Missing and Unidentified Persons System (NamUs)
- Blood pattern experts
- Polygraph
- Specialty crime investigators or experts such as forensic document examiners
- Medical examiners and forensic pathologists
- Firearms examiners
- Advanced fingerprint technology
- Forensic odontology
- Forensic anthropology
- Forensic botanists
- Forensic artists
- Child abuse experts and resource organizations
- Nongovernment resources, including private forensic laboratories
- Media
- Technical and specialty support resources within the agency or at the state level

The Case File

The case file contains the entire written record of the investigation, including all interview reports, photographs, evidence collection and analysis reports, and other documentation. The previous chapter discussed methods and sources to determine that all known records have been assembled. It is imperative that all records be identified and collected for the reinvestigation. Some of the sources of these are

- In-house agency file systems where records are normally kept
- Archives in on-site or off-site storage areas
- District attorney/prosecutor's office
- Property/evidence storage
- Coroner/medical examiner office
  - Reports
  - Biological or physical evidence
  - Coroner's inquest
- Local laboratory
- State or Federal Bureau of Investigation (FBI) laboratory
- Retired investigators

- Other agencies involved in joint investigation of the homicide
  - Local
  - State
  - Federal

When you read the file, does it appear complete, and is it in order? As you study the file, you are beginning your investigation.

- What do you know about your victim?
- Victim's life style?
  - Friends and associates?
  - Relationships?
- By what circumstances did the victim come to be a victim?
- What more do you need to learn about your victim?
- What do you know about any developed suspect?

Where to Start

My experiences and those of most cold case investigators with whom I have spoken suggest that a cold case file review should begin at the start of the case. In other words, at the beginning. Whether it begins with the initial missing person's report, finding of a body, or report of shots fired, start at the earliest time and date of related events. The reasoning behind this is that the cold case investigator can see the investigation as it unfolded, as the events occurred, and how the pieces began to fall into place. In doing so, you may see open windows that need to be closed.

Very few investigator that I have spoken to prefer to start investigating a cold case by working *backward*. That is, once the file is in chronological order, they prefer to work backward from the most recent investigative activity to the initial report of the crime and related events. This chapter addresses the investigation in a *forward* manner from the beginning of the crime to the latest activity and to the rejuvenated investigation.

As you begin, do you have questions? Write notes down *now*. When you read it a second time, the same thought may not be repeated exactly as it was and may become a different thought pattern altogether. Quite often, our first thoughts are the best. Although many of your questions will be answered as you read further, these initial questions and thoughts are the beginning of your investigation. If they are not answered when you finish reading the book, they become the basis of your investigative plan. This plan is one that identifies and organizes your investigative action. It is based upon what has been done and what you determine *needs* to be done.

Start to think about your own organization, also.

At the outset, place a fresh page with a photograph of your victim at the start of the file. This is the person you now represent, the victim for whom you may be last chance for what passes for justice in our society.

Biography Sheet

With many cold cases, there are a lot of people—and their roles and relationships in the crime and the investigation—to come to know. Many, if not all, will need to be located, contacted, and reinterviewed. Consider a biography sheet for each individual. See Figure 3.1. This document contains summary information about an individual and provides a quick resource for the cold case investigator in lieu of reading through numerous documents. In addition, it may be used to document those who are now deceased, and other pertinent information.

INDIVIDUAL BIOGRAPHY SHEET

Case No.____________ Case Name______________

[ ] New Witness
[ ] Original Participant
[ ] Relative of Participant
[ ] Other
[ ] Role

NAME:

DOB: __________________ POB: __________________

DOD: __________________ POD: __________________

Current Address:

Current Telephone:

Previous Addresses/Time of Offense:

PHOTO/DRIVERS LICENSE

Father: Address/Phone:

Mother: Address/Phone:

Notes:

Figure No. _________

Figure 3.1 Biography sheet. A biography sheet provides quick access to individual information and is one way to summarize the role of people, and past and present investigation. (Courtesy of Detective Richard Rouleau, El Cajon Police Department [ECPD].)

As the cold case investigation progresses, investigators may learn of relationships between persons that were previously unknown, or have developed in the interim, and this may be significant. The biography sheet is a good place to note such for future investigative knowledge. As an example, I was investigating a case and contacted a man believed to have knowledge about the past events at his rural residence. After some time had passed, I identified a woman whom I believed also had critical information about the same event and drove to contact her. As I approached her rural residence, I realized that I was not very far from the man's location I had been to in the past. Upon interviewing my new witness, I casually mentioned that I had been to the nearby location in the past and inquired if she knew the man. Whereupon, my current witness said, "Oh yes, that was my uncle." This one comment tied together a number of people and opened a whole new understanding of previously unknown familial relationships that were critical to the case. Knowledge of relationships may be important in cold case investigations, especially in gang-related homicides, and this procedure is one means of quickly documenting who is related to whom.

This document may be used for

- Victim
- Victim family members, friends, and associates
- Witnesses and other parties
- Suspect
- Suspect family member, friends, and associates
- Law enforcement officers
- Forensic/laboratory personnel
- Others for a quick reference as necessary

Information to be included:

- Case number (old and new as necessary)
- Case name
- Individual role
    - New witness
    - Original participant
    - Relative of participant
    - Other
    - Role
- Name
- Also known as (AKAs)
- Date of birth (DOB)
- Place of birth (POB)
- Date of death (DOD)
- Place of death (POD)
- Current address
- Current telephone
- Previous addresses/time of offense
- Subject's picture or copy of driver's license
- Father
- Father's address/telephone
- Mother
- Mother's address/telephone
- Ex-wives or ex-husbands or other former partners
- Relationship to others in case if known

If you establish and use a computer database for your investigation, this information may be included within your case file on the computer system.

Calendars

Consider preparing a calendar of the month and year of the crime, as well as one of the month preceding and the month(s) following. Such calendars are readily available on many desktop computer programs. See Figure 3.2. Confirming accuracy may be accomplished by comparison to a period newspaper from the time of the crime or original investigation. These serve a number of purposes, including the following:

- Allow investigator to picture sequences of events as they unfolded by day of the week.
- Allow investigators to correlate witness statements to dates, days, and times.
- Illustrate potential incongruences.
- Graphically enhance investigator comprehension of the crime events and subsequent investigation.
- Aid witness recall. During witness reinterviews in the cold case investigation, it may serve as an aid to assist the witness in recalling events and time sequences. This may be especially true when interviewing senior citizens. For instance, they may not recall the *date* of an activity but remember that the activity occurred on "*Wednesday* before her body was found." The calendar assists the witness in establishing a correct orientation of events.
- At the conclusion of the investigation, such a calendar may contribute to preparing timelines, computerized slide shows, or presentations to present the case to superior officers or the prosecutor.

July

Sun	*Mon*	*Tue*	*Wed*	*Thu*	*Fri*	*Sat*
	1	**2**	**3**	**4**	**5**	**6**
7	**8**	**9**	**10**	**11**	**12**	**13**
14	**15**	**16**	**17**	**18**	**19**	**20**
21	**22**	**23**	**24**	**25**	**26**	**27**
28	**29**	**30**	**31**			

1957

Figure 3.2 Cold case calendar. A helpful technique, for investigators and witnesses, is to prepare a calendar of the period of the cold case. This helps relate days to dates and put events in context. They may be created on many desktop word processing programs.

In-House Changes

A complete case file is essential to moving forward. Knowledge of past filing systems and practices within the agency is important in locating and gathering all relevant written and evidentiary material. This includes record filing, maintenance, and storage, as well as evidence filing and storage practices. This knowledge may be learned from more senior members of the agency as well as past employees. When reviewing property lists and property records, know the evidence section filed and catalogued evidence and paperwork during the case and subsequent time period. When possible, investigators should seek to learn

- Information intake systems and dispatch procedures in place at time of reporting of crime.
- 911 or similar recordings that might still be available.
- Information-recording systems (handwritten logs or computer generated).
- Agency daily activity logs. Availability, and accessibility, of these day-to-day records of reported crimes and other activities may be of importance in reconstructing the crime or similar relevant time-frame events.
- Any "purges" or destruction of agency records since the offense?

The Case Number

Depending upon the age of the case, note whether this number style corresponds to the format still in use by the agency. If not, identify when the department or agency changed numbering systems since the homicide, and consider its relevance to the case under investigation. Identify all case file numbers associated with this case, past and present, and assure that files and evidence are searched for and located under all identified numbers. During the review and inspection of each report and document, ensure that the file or case number is accounted for. If there were additional victims, check whether separate case numbers were issued and ensure that all relevant case files pertaining to the cold case have been identified and collected.

Similarly, if the laboratory or evidence facilities have changed numbering systems, check under all numbers also. When gathering and reviewing coroner or medical examiner files, similarly ascertain whether there have been any changes in numbering systems. In these locations, changes in numbering systems may preclude a complete search and recovery of all pertinent records and evidence.

In the case of physical evidence such as rape kits or bullets and expended cartridge casings, inquire if at any time, personnel filed large groups of property under a *single* case number. This has happened, usually when suspects are unknown.

File Contents

While the layout of a "murder book" and file conditions vary between agencies, the contents detail what was done during the initial and follow-up investigations. These records serve to reconstruct the crime scene as well as the investigation. Consider that the older case files may contain all or portions of the following, and these are areas to be studied and addressed in your investigation:

- *Case chronological record.* Often over the period of years or decades, case chronological records and summaries will be compiled by a sequence of investigators. These are informative, but view these with caution: as in any instance when someone interprets and reports the work of others, misinterpretation and misreporting may result, albeit unintentionally. Always try to know and use *original* source documentation wherever possible. Upon completion of the cold case investigation, compilation of a detailed timeline and chronological record will assist those who review the completed case, as well as the prosecutor, in understanding what may often be a decades-long series of events, relationships, and technology advancements.

- *Crime scene.* Nature and extent of crime scene documentation. This would include photos and reports. Initial responding officer actions and observations:
  - Was blood dry or wet upon arrival?
  - Did the responding officer see or smell anything unusual upon arrival?
  - Weather conditions at the time.
  - Who were the technicians that responded?
  - How was evidence identified—or not?
  - What evidence collection and preservation methods were used?
  - Who turned any lights on or off?
  - Were windows and doors checked?
  - Was there evidence of what we today call *staging*?
- *Crime scene log.* Nice in theory, not always done, especially in older cases. When, and if, this document is in the case file, identify and interview
  - Who preserved the scene and their subsequent documentation
  - Subsequent officers and other agency personnel present
  - Others recorded in the log
  - Other recorded events or unusual circumstances

As with all other law enforcement or other persons involved in the response or investigation, reinterview and inquire whether they retain any notes, photographs, or other records, and also any *undocumented* observations or thoughts on the crime. When reinterviewing original-scene officers and investigators,

- Ask what they first saw.
- Discuss what they did and what evidence they recovered or did not recover.
- Review original reports with each.
  - Were there discrepancies?
  - Was the original report complete?
  - Can they add any further thoughts?
  - Were there observations or perceptions that they did not report?
- *Crime report(s).* Including initial responding officer and investigator reports. Although previously described, keep in mind that older case file reports may be much different from today's standards. Changes may include the following:
  - Personal identification information lacking specific detail. This compounds a cold case investigator's efforts to identify "John Smith" and to re-locate for follow-up interview.
  - Synopsis versus detail style of reporting.
  - Lack of reports.
  - Look for information on how the crime came to be reported, including
    - Who discovered the body?
    - Who made the call or notified police?
- *Property and evidence reports.* Review all property reports and compare these with what was seized and has since been maintained. How complete, and how detailed, are these reports? Consider the source of seizure and its relationship to the crime. In addition, consider what advances in technology may be utilized in an attempt to obtain further information from the property/evidence. During your physical inspection of each item, note whether its weight (narcotics) or other description is sufficiently detailed.
- *Forensic logs and reports.* Review the evidence gathered at the time and cross-check to other evidence and property logs. Does the case file reflect all copies of logs and reports? Compare any

original requests for forensic examination to what was done, or not done, and to copies maintained by the forensic facility. Inquire whether they retain

- Examination notebooks
- Work journals
- Photographs and diagrams
- Reports
- Biological material slides

Consider what may be accomplished by reexamination using more advanced technology. When reviewing this with laboratory personnel, explore advances such as DNA testing procedures now as opposed to the serology grouping in previous decades or earlier DNA methods. Consider the present ability to identify palm prints or fingerprints or trace evidence that was technically not possible at the time (for bloody prints on fiber background, see Chapter 26). If a knife recovered from a suspect was tested for the victim's DNA yet none was found, would advanced technology now be able to recover victim DNA from *within* the hilt of the knife due to advances in Short Tandem Repeat (STR) DNA (Figure 3.3)?

- *Vehicle reports.* Identify all vehicles involved in the case and their disposition. Were they released to family members or sold at auction? Consider running the vehicle identification number or license plate through motor vehicle registrations to re-locate the vehicle if the title has changed hands. This may be useful in reconstructing the crime scene, or other events. If the case is old and the vehicle is unable to be located, consider online web searches for similar vehicles through car collector clubs, local car clubs, auto enthusiasts, etc.
- *Related crime reports.* When reviewing names and reports, note whether other crime reports may be associated with this offense. Were there covictims whose cases may have been assigned a separate case number? Were there other victims at the same period as the homicide, or other cases suspected by original investigators to be related?
- *Follow-up and progress reports.* During the review of these reports, original investigator focus and theories may become evident. Are there numerous reports of interviews with one or a few subjects? Does the same name reappear? Are there investigator synopses detailing case progress, including their thoughts and theories?

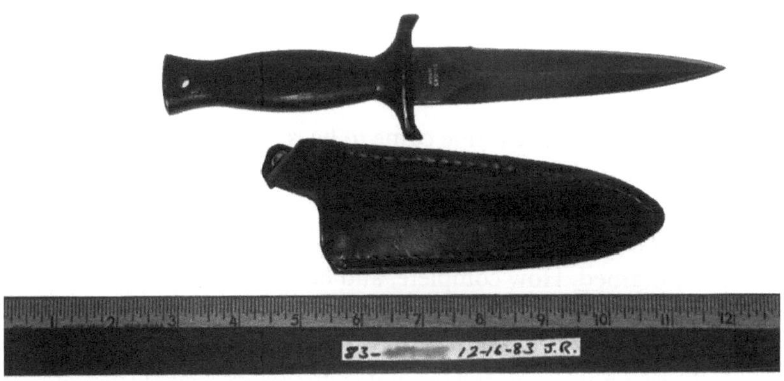

Figure 3.3 Murder weapon. With advances in DNA technology, it may now be possible to retrieve a usable DNA profile from within recesses, such as this knife hilt and blade, which previously could not be accomplished. (Courtesy of Detective Tim Marcia, Los Angeles Police Department.)

- *Crime scene canvass.* Was a canvass completed? Are the records present? How complete and thorough was it?
- *Victim information.* Victim information found in the file may or may not provide insight into motive or the victim's possible contributing role to the homicide. Keep in mind that there is often a strong possibility that the victim and his/her attacker knew one another or were acquainted. An original profile of the victim may be portrayed in the reports through interviews with family, friends, coworkers, classmates, teachers, and others. Consider the width and depth of what is known about the victim in the case file and consider follow-up investigation addressing the victim. Considerations include the following:
  - Was a psychological autopsy addressed?
  - More complete victim profile.
  - Current personal relationship at time of offense.
  - Previous or other relationships.
  - Perhaps more so than men, females have a best or close friend in whom they may confide and share private thoughts, including secrets, fears, or other intimate information. This person is not necessarily a family member and may include their hairdresser or a similar person. While reviewing witness statements, consider identifying and interviewing (or reinterviewing) the victim's best or closest friends. What *more* might they say now?
  - When viewing photos that include the victim, note other persons in the photo. Identify these people, and ascertain if they are known to the investigation.
  - Background and biographical information.
  - Criminal history including probation and parole reports.
  - Other civil or criminal reports previously reported by victim or family.
  - Any reported stalking of victim, or other reports of suspicious activity?
  - Rap sheet.
  - What *don't* you know about your victim and the circumstances?
  - Victim activity within 24–48 hours before death.
- *Suspect information.*
  - Statements
  - Alibis and witness statements
  - Photos or forensic artist/composite drawings
  - Criminal history including probation and parole reports
  - Rap sheet
  - Current custody status
  - Custody history to identify past incarcerations and identify possible cellmates, institution intelligence reports, etc.
  - Other identified relationships that may now be changed due to passage of time, including friends, intimate partners, spouses, business associates
- *Photo lineups.* Were photo lineups conducted in a previous investigation? Are they in the file? Who were they shown to? What identifications were made? What reports were generated as a result of these lineups? What processes were utilized during the procedure? Were any admonitions similar to current practice given to witnesses?
- *Witness statements and lists.* Are the reports of these statements sufficiently detailed? During the review of witness statements, including listening to recorded interviews, cold case investigators should note closely what questions were asked and what answers were given (and how these were subsequently documented).
  - What was *not* asked may be more important than what was asked.

- Note the number of interviews with repeat witnesses or suspects. Consider statement analysis of repeat interviews as discussed later in this chapter.
- Is there sufficient information to identify and re-locate the witness?

- *Crime scene notes and surveys.* Are these preserved in the file? Review and cross-check to the crime scene log, if possible. Identify officers or crime scene personnel who may have made or maintained any notes, surveys, or other documents not in the file.
- *Crime scene sketches.* Are these present in the file? If so, are they detailed and to scale? In older cases, these may be general overview and not measurement specific. Consider that in some agencies, other city or county resources may have been called upon for assistance in this regard. See Figures 3.4 and 3.5. These might include
  - City/county engineers
  - Public works
  - Private architects/draftsmen
  - State architects, engineers, or draftsmen
- *Crime scene photos.* Does the case file reflect a number of photographs that sufficiently detail the crime scene in macro and micro detail? Are they adequately documented to reflect the following?
  - What do they represent? (See Figure 3.6.)
  - What is the significance of these photos? (See Figure 3.7.)
  - When were they taken?
  - By whom were they taken?
  - Is what you now see as evidence shown in photos yet was never collected?

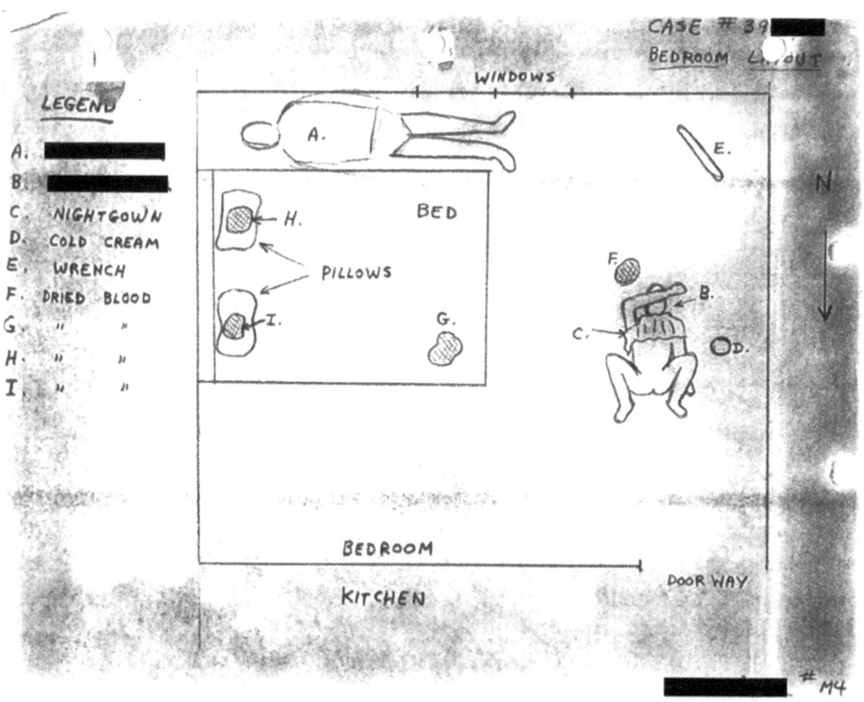

Figure 3.4 Crime scene sketch. Older crime scene sketches lack the measurement and detail present in later investigations. However, even rough sketches, coupled with photographs, can provide an informational picture of the crime scene. (Courtesy of Anderson/ECPD.)

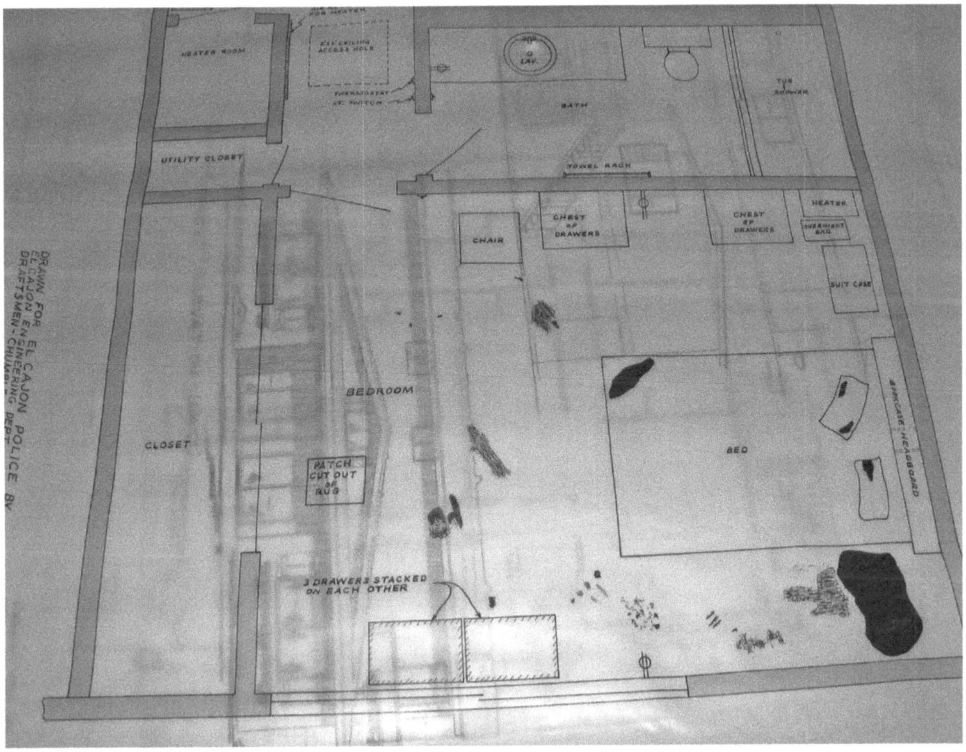

Figure 3.5 Crime scene diagram. When reviewing cold cases, consider that outside resources may have been utilized for crime scene mapping. These detailed crime scene maps were prepared by the city engineer's office in the Wilkerson case shown in Chapter 4. (Courtesy of Anderson/ECPD.)

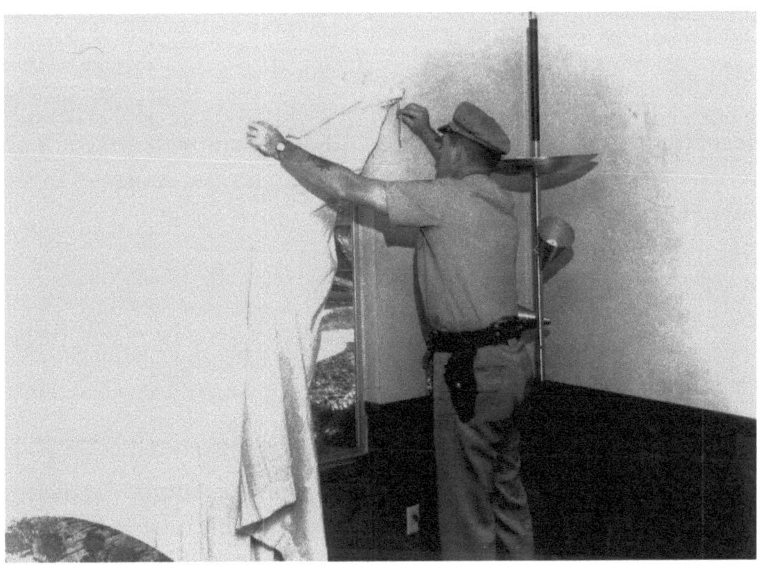

Figure 3.6 It is not uncommon in older crime scene photos to observe police practices no longer utilized. Here an officer handles a drapery cord from which a ligature was cut by a suspect, and stands within the crime scene. (Courtesy of Anderson/ECPD.)

Figure 3.7 Although there appear to be footprints in the picture, a lack of documentation makes this photo almost worthless. We do not know where it was, when it was taken, by whom, or the significance. No measurement instrument is included in the photo. (Courtesy of Anderson/ECPD.)

- *Ambulance and fire department run records.* Were emergency personnel identified and interviewed? Were their run records obtained?
- *Medical records*
  - Emergency room records
  - Doctor reports
- *Coroner's records*
  - Autopsy reports
  - Toxicology reports
  - Photos
  - Retained clothing
  - Retained biological samples
- *Death certificate, obituary, and coroner's inquest.* These documents may not always be found in the cold case file. They may provide valuable information for the course of investigation. They are further described in Chapter 10.
- *Communications*
  - Initial crime report intake information
  - Teletypes
  - Press releases
  - Newspaper clippings
  - Police bulletins
  - Other computer runs
- *Affidavit for search warrants and search warrants.* Affidavits contain detailed information about known case events and investigator knowledge at a specific time during the investigation when the affidavit is drafted and submitted. Is there evidence in the case file that affidavits for search warrants were ever prepared?
  - Are these documents still retained in the file?
  - Were they served?

    - Do court clerk or court copies remain?
    - Are there search warrant returns listing any property recovered?
- *Investigation notes.* Are any, part, or all in the file? During the follow-up interviews, cold case investigators should seek to gather all remaining notes from initial responding officers, investigators, and other persons connected with the case or its investigation.

Additional Considerations

Case Organization

While investigators have their own method of case organization, many prefer to initially organize cold cases chronologically, as noted. After doing this, it may be helpful to segregate persons, or topics, into groups and to proceed in this manner. In this context, a cold case investigator can identify all persons whose names are reflected in the reports and subsequently identify a plan of action that needs to take place with each. This will illuminate the process of the original investigation as well as identify those who need to be reinterviewed.

These persons may be categorized as

- Law enforcement
- Medical and ambulance
- Crime scene and evidence
- Coroner/medical examiner
- Laboratory and forensic
- Witnesses
- Victim's family, friends, and associates
- Suspects
- Legal
- Other persons or topics developed during the course of previous and current investigation

Some investigators find that it is helpful to organize the file utilizing a simple system of file folders that address each individual or topics (e.g., evidence) by category. All reports and news clippings and any document mentioning the individual name can be included in this file. As the records are reviewed and filed, this simple system may bring together relationships or identify inconsistent or contradictory statements, as well as illuminate the full role of the individual in the investigation. This is a simple system, although it may ultimately consume boxes of files. Each investigator has a system that works, however. What works is what is best.

All homicide investigators are guided by experience, training, and decades of insight into human nature. From this experience comes intuition and gut feeling. When reviewing the case reports, ask yourself,

- Were the right questions asked of the right people?
- Which interviews are less than incomplete now in context with the investigation to date?
- Who might have more to say now than what the original report said?

Listen to original taped interviews (it is suggested that copies be made first to preserve the original tapes). Do you perhaps hear something on the tape the original investigators did not? If there is a transcript, is it complete? Is it accurate? A simple phrase may be something that slipped out but was not caught by the investigator. Look for anonymous letters and phone calls or messages that were not returned.

Reexamination of Evidence

The importance of reexamining all physical and biological evidence is discussed throughout this book. This is necessary to update and confirm examination results due to technological or other changes. The results of these examinations may influence the investigative plan and direction of the investigation. Because of the age of many unsolved homicides, successful prosecution may depend greatly upon the use of scientific evidence. Despite old lab reports attesting that no trace evidence (such as semen) was found, or that the results are inconclusive or negative, you should *retest.* (See further discussion in Chapter 16.) Reexamination using the latest technology and forensic know-how not only provides updated results; it also provides the prosecution with an expert to subpoena when it comes time for trial.

The investigator should keep in mind that the presence of the potential evidence in the case under review and findings of the original examination are subject to (1) mistaken filing, tagging, or other association of the evidence with the case under review; (2) original error on the part of the examiner, including misidentification or inaccurate conclusions based upon, among other factors, the state-of-the-art of techniques and procedures in effect at the time of the examination; and (3) other factors that have arisen due to the passage of time. In cases such as Freiburger, discussed later in this chapter, reexamination of firearms evidence provided a positive match between the weapon linked to the suspect and bullet fragments recovered from the victim, as opposed to previously inconclusive examination results.

As a result of a fresh analysis, potentially new exculpatory or inculpatory evidence may be discovered. A previous negative finding for the presence of semen that, upon reexamination, provides a DNA profile resulting in a CODIS hit can significantly alter the direction of the investigation. Reexamination of evidence can save investigators valuable time and other resources when review of the evidence discounts that which was previously thought possible. This includes circumstances in which suspect items were believed to be associated with a homicide when in fact they were not. Conversely, reanalysis may yield new information through the discovery of new evidence that may assist police in identifying the suspect(s) and solution of the case.

Case History

While searching the evidence room for evidence in another case, officers in a small California police department discovered an old Colt revolver in a box with evidence from another case. See Figure 3.8. The case number on the evidence tag indicated that the weapon was associated with a case number that was not known to the agency. Documentation was sparse, but also found in the box were the original investigator's notebooks for an unsolved homicide that had occurred in the early 1980s.

A transcript of an interview marked with the case number of the other agency was also located in the box. These items suggested that this case encompassed investigation by more than one jurisdiction. While the case file remained, the original recording from which the transcript was made was no longer to be found. Their reports, plus the original investigator's notebook, initiated a cold case homicide investigation. When contacted, the original investigator, now retired, recalled little of the case. Officers began by reviewing all the names in the investigator's notebook and reports from the other agency, and reviewing the physical evidence remaining in the evidence room.

Also recovered from the box was the victim's clothing. The victim had been recovered from a large body of salt water when released to the medical examiner. The clothing was subsequently bagged in plastic and returned to the agency. It was stored in this condition for almost 20 years. It had not been properly dried for storage and was now in a moldy condition.

Cold case homicide investigation builds on the life and career experience of cold case investigators. An x-ray showing a number of bullets in the torso was also found in the box. See Figure 3.9. When I reviewed

Figure 3.8 Unrelated evidence. Discovery of an old revolver in the evidence room prompted reinvestigation of a cold case homicide. Officers initially thought the gun belonged with the case and fired the fatal rounds. Subsequent firearms examination dispelled this, however, and the gun proved to have no role in the homicide. (Author's collection.)

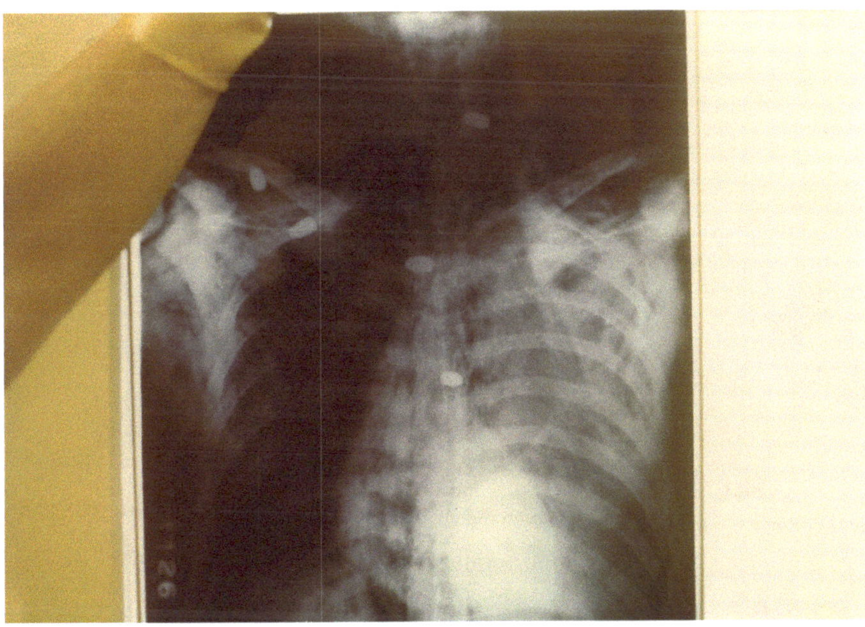

Figure 3.9 Unrelated evidence. While scant documentation existed, an x-ray of the victim was also present. (Author's collection.)

the x-ray and was given a description of the revolver, it immediately became doubtful the bullets were fired from this weapon. Observation of the bullets in the x-ray indicated that they were round-nose projectiles. The Colt was now an antique and was chambered for the .32 WCF round. This frontier-era cartridge saw double duty as a rifle cartridge in tubular feed, lever action–style rifles that necessitated the use of flat-nose bullets. When it was suggested that the weapon be reexamined to determine whether it could have fired the bullets, modern forensic examination corroborated my review, and the weapon was discovered to have no relationship to the crime. The case remains open.

Photos and Photo Analysis

While the value of crime scene photos in homicide investigation has long been recognized, nowhere is this more important than in reconstruction of a cold case homicide. The presence of sharp, quality photos that thoroughly document the crime scene in micro and macro detail provides investigators with the best representation of what the scene looked like years or decades before. While investigator or witness memory can serve to augment words on paper, nothing takes the place of original crime scene photos.

As with other trends in law enforcement, this aspect may be observed in some cold cases by a general lack of crime scene photographs, or lack of *detailed* crime scene photos. In addition, the written record to support and authenticate these photographs may be lacking in detail, if present at all. When this occurs, investigators have photographs that may not necessarily be fully relied upon for future courtroom value, due to lack of authenticating documentation. They are, however, valuable for investigative purposes as quite often, the subject or topic that the photograph seeks to represent may be apparent. In other cases, however, it may not be. See Figure 3.10.

Figure 3.10 Unidentified person pointing at ground. This person is unidentified, and there is no documentation suggesting the relevance of this photo. It may be surmised that the man is pointing to the shoeprints in the ground shown in Figure 3.8, but without documentation, the investigative and evidentiary value is significantly lessened. (Courtesy of Anderson/ECPD.)

When reviewing the photo file, it is prudent to identify agency photographic protocol at the time of the original homicide investigation. Who took the crime scene photos? Was it

- Full-time photographic and crime scene/evidence personnel?
- Responding officers responsible for own crime scene processing?
- Contract or on-call photographers from a local camera shop?
- Local news media photographers?
- Others?

Depending upon agency size, organization, and other factors, there may or may not have been a formal protocol. What was done may have varied from scene to scene, depending on the circumstances and availability of a photographer. In reviewing the photographic record, consider whether it reflects the following:

- Identity of photographer.
- Date and time of photograph.
- Exact location.
- Written record of detail being photographed.
- Compass orientation.
- Camera and film description.
- Specialized equipment used.
- Weather and light conditions.
- Processing sequences including chain of custody.
- Development record including number of prints.
- Print distribution.
- What were the processing standards? Was the film automatically developed, or was it developed and printed only at the discretion of the investigators, or the photographer?
- Where were the negatives stored?
- Where are the copies now?

If the photographer is known and available,

- Meet with the person to review each photo.
- Attempt to learn what additional information the photographer may have to offer that is not already known.
- Does the photographer have any additional photos not found in the case file, and does the photographer maintain any notes or other records of the crime or photography session?

Review of available case file photographs will reveal whether they are ground-based photos or aerial photos (see Figures 3.11 and 3.12) and whether they are black and white or color.

Aerial Photos

While the concept and earliest experiments of aerial date to the mid–nineteenth century, aerial photos have been practically utilized in some regions of the United States since the 1920s for government and private purposes. They became more commonplace in the 1940s and 1950s with reflights often updating the photo files taking place every so many years. Aerial photos may be very useful in reconstructing a crime scene decades later, especially in those areas where urban growth has redefined the landscape. Local tax assessor's

Figure 3.11 Aerial photographs. Aerial photos may be a valuable resource in reconstructing a period crime scene. This practice dates back many decades, and these may be readily available. Consider rephotographing these and using a computer to magnify areas of interest, or consult with other resources. (Author's collection.)

offices are sometimes the best sources of aerial photos. While they were most likely obtained from private contractors, these offices may have photos going back many decades. If they do not have what you are looking for, they may be able to advise on sources of older local-region aerial photos. Other sources of these photos include

- Local governments, including city and county planning departments
- Local universities and colleges
- State highway departments
- Utility companies
- Local large industries and developers
- Railroads
- Bureau of Mines
- Bureau of Reclamation
- U.S. Army Corp of Engineers
- National Park Service

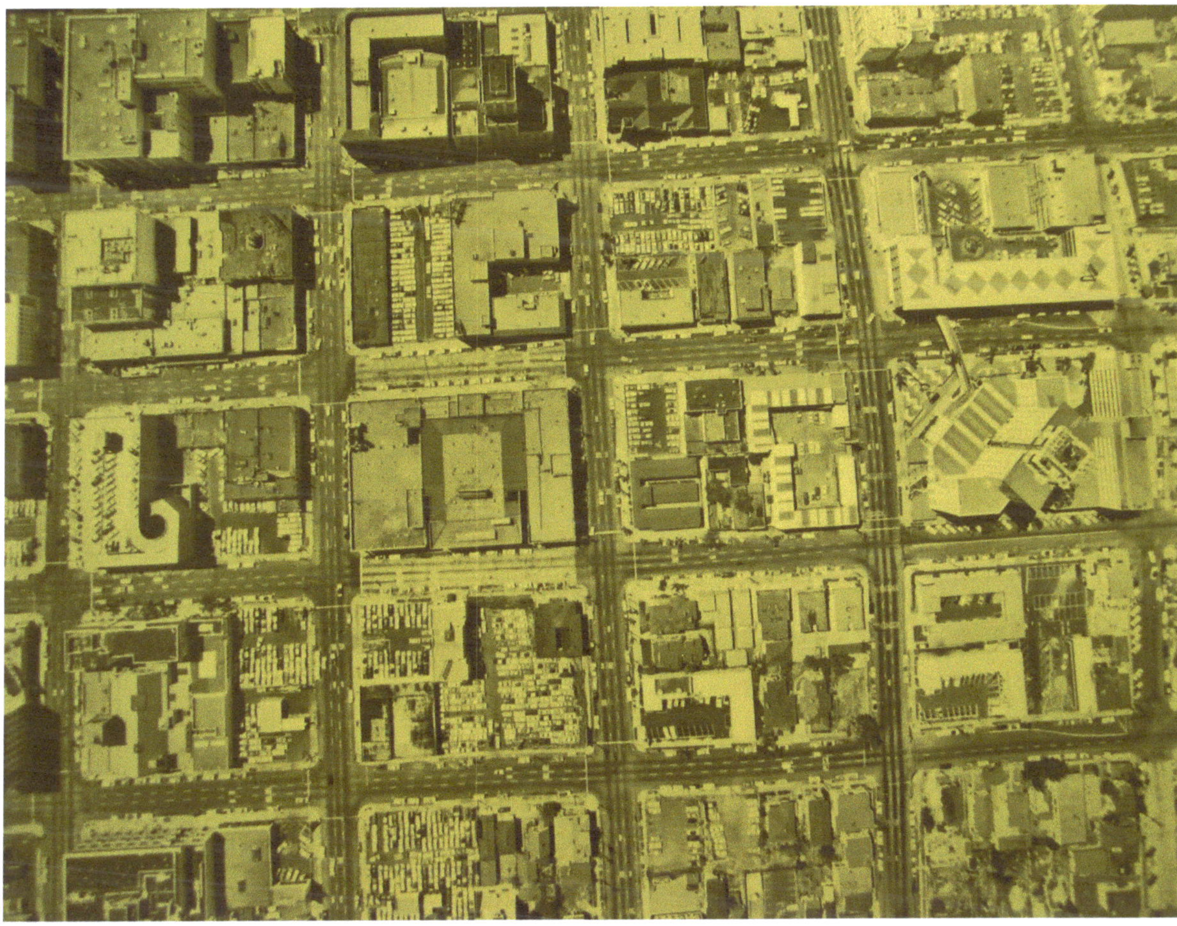

Figure 3.12 Aerial photographs. Aerial photos may be a valuable resource in reconstructing a period crime scene. This practice dates back many decades, and these may be readily available. Consider rephotographing these and using a computer to magnify areas of interest, or consult with other resources such as the National Law Enforcement and Corrections Technology Center. (Author's collection.)

- U.S. Geological Survey
- U.S. Forest Service
- Bureau of Land Management
- U.S. Department of Agriculture including National Agriculture Imagery Program
- National Environmental Satellite, Data, and Information Service
- National Aeronautics and Space Administration (NASA)
- Space imaging corporations

Photo Degradation

When reviewing the crime scene photographs in older cases, consider doing so with one knowledgeable in applicable forensic or image enhancement techniques. Due to age, crime scene photographs may be faded. This is especially true in older instant development photographs, such as those commonly referred to as Polaroids©. This problem is also encountered in 35 mm color photos. When faded or less legible photos are found in the file, consider consulting with in-agency photographic or forensic resources, state or FBI crime laboratories, or other resources.

Other Considerations in Photo Analysis

- Carefully study the photo to see what it *really* shows you in relation to what you know from reading the case reports.
- Study the photo from the center out.
- Enlarge/blow up photos. This often reveals significant detail not otherwise noticed.
- Consider reprinting from negatives without cropping the picture. Cropping may have removed vital detail from the photo.
- Is there evidence of *posing* the scene?
- Is there evidence that the victim was killed and dragged or carried to location?
- Number of perpetrators.
- Weapon used.
- Opportunity or planned.
- Ingress and egress for victim and suspect.
- Drag marks, including direction.
- What evidence do you see in the photo that you do not have today?
- Suggestion of motive.
- Possibility of witnesses.
- Remember—the primary scene is the body.
  - State of decomposition
  - Bug activity
  - Wounds or mutilation
  - Secondary scene around the body
  - Tertiary or third level including blood spatter in surrounding area

Take all photos and put them in sequence of the events during the crime. What do they tell you? Do you see anything not reflected in reports?

If persons are present in the photo, identity and reinterview to ascertain scene value and meaning of the photograph. In past decades, it was not unusual or uncommon for officers and investigators to stand in the crime scene or related locations as pictures were being taken. Other persons who might be found in crime scene photographs might be family members, coroner/medical examiner personnel, fire and ambulance personnel, or news photographers. Or they might be suspects. See Figure 3.13.

Review the photos with a crime scene reconstruction expert. What do they see that perhaps you do not?

For example, I had occasion to review a series of photographs from a late 1970s homicide. These were 35 mm color photographs, and many were now fading. The female victim had been left in a remote area that had previously been used for body dumps. A suspect had been identified in the case, but evidence to place him at the scene was lacking. Photographs of the suspect, a biker type, taken prior to the homicide had been recovered during the initial investigation. When the victim's body was recovered, a man's belt was wrapped around her legs and had been left behind, as if the suspect may have been interrupted or scared off while disposing of the body. The buckle was multisided and irregular in shape, and had the name and logo of a popular motorcycle brand embossed on it in a wavy manner. In addition, the leather belt also was stamped with an ornate pattern. Although other circumstantial evidence was present, the prosecutor wanted more evidence to link the suspect to the victim, and to the scene.

Review of the photographs recovered from the suspect identified some photos of him wearing a belt and belt buckle seemingly identical to the belt and buckle recovered with the victim's body. This was forwarded to the laboratory for further analysis, which suggested that the buckle and belt recovered with the victim were consistent with that worn by the biker suspect in the photograph.

Figure 3.13 Who is in the picture? When reviewing old crime scene pictures, consider identifying persons present. In this photo, a man holding a camera may be a newsperson. Who is he? What other crime scene pictures might he still have? (Courtesy of Los Angeles County Sheriff's Department.)

Photos Can Turn Up in the Strangest of Places

During review and investigation of cold case homicides, originals or copies of photographs not in the case file have turned up in places normally beyond the practical range of sources explored by cold case investigators. Sometimes this is the result of publicity or word-of-mouth information resulting from investigator actions. They have been found in

- Old newspapers no longer in publication.
- Off-campus university publications as shown in Figure 3.14.
- Pawnshops and secondhand stores.
- *True Detective* and similar crime magazines as illustrated in Figure 12.7.
- Private collections of local photographers.
- Historical societies.
- Family photograph albums of those who participated in the crime or its investigation. When interviewing family members, witnesses, and others, inquire if they have any photographs regarding the case and its investigation (Figure 3.15).

Practical Statement Analysis

When a case file contains multiple (more than one) statements by the same individual, or a follow-up investigation results in additional statements, it may be useful to combine these in an individual file and

Figure 3.14 Pictures are where you find them. This 1954 off-campus university magazine contained the only then-known picture of "Boulder Jane Doe" (name withheld by request) when the cold case was reactivated. This case is further discussed in Chapter 22. (Name withheld by request.)

to subject them to line-by-line scrutiny that may reveal discrepancies and inconsistencies, for example, use of the phrase "I did…" during the course of the initial interview that subsequently changes to "I did not…" when reinterviewed in proximity to the original statement, or in the course of a cold case investigation, years or decades later. While this avenue of approach is not uncommon in normal day-to-day interviews, in cold case investigations, identification of such inconsistencies may be even more valuable. While this sounds simple, consider that some cold cases consume cartons of files concerning the crime, evidence, and witness statements. Also consider that while cold case investigators are the best in the field, they are not machines. When the statements are spread out over a sequence of files, the full impact and value of what they say may not necessarily be realized. If individuals have been interviewed, and then reinterviewed, over a period of time, their statements may reveal these variations, variations that may be a segue to breaking down the discrepancies and learning the truth.

Figure 3.15 Family photograph albums with crime pictures. When recontacting persons involved or living near old crime scenes, inquire if they have any relevant photos in family albums. These are original pictures recovered in a family album and were published in the newspapers in the 1925 Wagner–Sweet case. (Author's collection.)

Sources of statements are not necessarily confined to just interview statements given to police during the course of the specific investigation. There are other sources of potential statement information that may offer opportunities to identify these discrepancies and variations. Among these are

- Initial police interview
- Follow-up police interview
- News media interviews or statements
- Statements made to other parties, including their own family or the family of the victim
- Written memorabilia including diaries, notes, or book and short story drafts
- Interviews with investigators from other agencies
- Probation and parole statements
- Wiretap conversations
- Civil actions including deposition statements
- Criminal trial actions including testimony
- Coroner's inquest testimony
- Postarrest interviews

Case Study

On the afternoon of February 28, 1961, U.S. Army Private Edward Freiburger purchased a new .32-caliber H&R model 732 revolver and a box of S&W Lubaloy ammunition at a Columbia, South Carolina, pawnshop. That same night, John Orner, a Fort Jackson (South Carolina)—area taxicab driver, did not arrive home at midnight as was his custom. See Figure 3.16. His family reported him missing to the Columbia Police Department, South Carolina, the next morning.

Figure 3.16 Victim John Orner. A military veteran, the taxi driver was murdered for about $45, $7 dollars less than what his killer paid for the gun. (Courtesy of Investigator Carl Craig, Richland County Sheriff's Department, South Carolina.)

In the meantime, Orner's taxicab had been found abandoned on a Columbia street, and a large-scale search was underway for its driver. There was evidence of blood on the back of the driver's seat, and an empty wallet was found on the backseat. The wallet's contents were scattered about, but all the money was missing. The Columbia Police Department processed the vehicle and, in doing so, observed a muddy substance on the undercarriage. A sample of this was sent to the South Carolina State Law Enforcement Division (SLED) laboratory. Chief chemist James Wilson concluded the substance was a geologic material, mica, which was found in the lower part of Richland County near the Wateree River area. Thus, the case now became multijurisdictional in scope. Sheriff Strother S. Slight and numerous members of local law enforcement, along with every available cab driver in the area, formed a search group and directed their efforts in the area described by Wilson. On March 3, 1961, Orner's body was found partially secluded at the bottom of a steep embankment about 30 miles south of Columbia in southern Richland County. See Figure 3.17.

His body was facedown, and his pants pockets were turned inside out, indicating that he had apparently been robbed. See Figure 3.18.

The autopsy revealed that the victim had been shot once in the back of the head. The single bullet fragmented into three pieces and lodged in the brain. These fragments were removed by the attending pathologist and turned over to investigators. No one at the time considered the additional value of these fragments, a value that would further contribute to solving this murder with the advent of DNA.

The bullet fragments were submitted for examination to the laboratory of the South Carolina Division of Law Enforcement. Officers were subsequently advised that the fatal weapon was an H&R 732 revolver and the type of ammunition was S&W Lubaloy.

Sheriff Slight and two deputies began a canvas of local gun dealers and pawnshops. Within 10 days of the homicide, they found that Freibuger had purchased such a weapon and given an Indiana address. The clerk who sold the gun remembered that Freiburger was wearing a U.S. Army uniform and his name tag matched the name he signed on the purchase record. The sheriff requested assistance from the U.S. Army Criminal Investigation Division (CID), and with this began a series of events that would take almost 40 years to bring Freiburger to justice. A U.S. Army CID agent at Fort Jackson, Carl Craig, became familiar with a case that he and others would finally conclude in 2002. See Figure 3.19. Freiburger was already under suspicion by military authorities for housebreaking and grand larceny

Figure 3.17 1961 crime scene. Original crime scene shown in black-and-white photo showing victim's body as well as the slope and drainage. (Courtesy of Investigator Carl Craig, Richland County Sheriff's Department, South Carolina.)

Figure 3.18 Pants pocket turned inside out. The surviving crime scene photo offered pictorial evidence that robbery was a motive in this crime, and preserved a record for cold case investigators decades later. (Courtesy of Investigator Carl Craig, Richland County Sheriff's Department, South Carolina.)

Figure 3.19 Investigator Carl Craig returns to the scene. This photo, taken from the same general direction as the 1961 crime scene photo, illustrates the relative lack of change between the scene 40 years before and when Freiburger was convicted. (Courtesy of Investigator Carl Craig, Richland County Sheriff's Department, South Carolina.)

and was AWOL. On March 29, 1961, Freiburger was apprehended in Newport, Tennessee, by Trooper Don Meredith for hitchhiking. Freiburger was dressed in civilian clothing, and as the trooper patted Freiburger down, he discovered the H&R revolver concealed in Freiburger's pocket. See Figure 3.20. During the course of this arrest, Trooper Meredith seized the weapon and wrote Freiburger a receipt for it. Almost four decades later, long after Meredith's retirement, follow-up investigators would locate the trooper, and he would provide a critical, original document linking Freiburger to this specific weapon: he still possessed his copy of the receipt.

Freiburger was arrested, pled guilty to carrying the concealed weapon, and was sentenced to 30 days. He confided to a cellmate that he was AWOL, and this was relayed to authorities, who notified the military police in Knoxville, Tennessee. The military police apprehension team picked Freiburger up but, instead of returning him to his post at Fort Jackson, transferred him to Atlanta. This complicated the sheriff's efforts to question him about the murder. After a month and a half, the sheriff was finally allowed to interview Freiburger, but this was unsuccessful. In the meantime, Freiburger was convicted of being AWOL and sentenced to one year in the Fort Leavenworth, Kansas, stockade.

Freiburger's H&R revolver was examined by a SLED examiner, who ultimately concluded that the weapon revealed an "...extremely close match as being the murder weapon." However, he did not render a conclusive written report that Freiburger's gun was the murder weapon. Sheriff Slight reinterviewed Freiburger at Fort Leavenworth in August 1961, which resulted in an 82-page typed transcript of the interview, but the officer did not have the firearms examiner's report when he conducted this interview. During this session, Freiburger made only one admission, that he bought the gun on March 22, 1961, three weeks *after* the murder of victim Orner.

Figure 3.20 H&R .32 revolver used in the crime, seized by Trooper Meredith, and the center of investigation almost four decades later. The ability of the authorities to place Freiburger with the murder weapon, to show his purchase of the gun, and to prove it fired the fatal projectile was a critical piece of evidence to evolve over the decades. (Courtesy of Investigator Carl Craig, Richland County Sheriff's Department, South Carolina.)

The records obtained by the investigators, however, revealed otherwise. See Figure 3.21. Freiburger had signed a purchase card, and the transaction was recorded in the Alcohol, Tobacco, Firearms (ATF) Register for the gun and ammunition on the afternoon of February 28, 1961, using his U.S. Army ID card and Army serial number for identification. The weapon was described by make, model, and serial number, and was the same as recovered by Trooper Meredith. In the absence of a more conclusive laboratory finding or admission of guilt, however, and lack of further information, the case was not resolved.

A New Investigation

By 1997, Carl Craig had retired from a career in the U.S. Army. He had also retired again as a criminal investigator for the South Carolina State Police. During Leon Lott's campaign for sheriff of Richland County, he and candidate Lott had discussed the possibility of forming a cold case homicide unit if Lott were elected sheriff. Lott won the election and on March 1, 1997, Craig began working pro bono to review unsolved homicides. In September 1999, Sheriff's Captain Bill Brown asked Craig if he recalled the 1960s murder of a taxi driver. Craig advised the captain of the victim's and suspect's names immediately. A relative of Orner attended church with the captain and had inquired if they could take another look at the case.

Brown retrieved the original case file and gave it to Craig. The file contained several individual folders in an accordion file folder, but ravages of time, older technology, and storage conditions had taken their toll. Approximately two-thirds of the reports were on Thermofax paper and had deteriorated significantly. Not uncommonly, the file had been stored for decades in an unshaded trailer storage facility with no heat or no air-conditioning. The photographs and newspaper clippings were still good, but reports and pages were about to fall apart. Office personnel were able to carefully reconstruct a working copy of the now-fragile documents. Included within the original file were black-and-white photos of the crime scene, Thermofax copies of numerous pawnshop documents and registers, photos of the suspect murder weapon, and a photo of Freiburger.

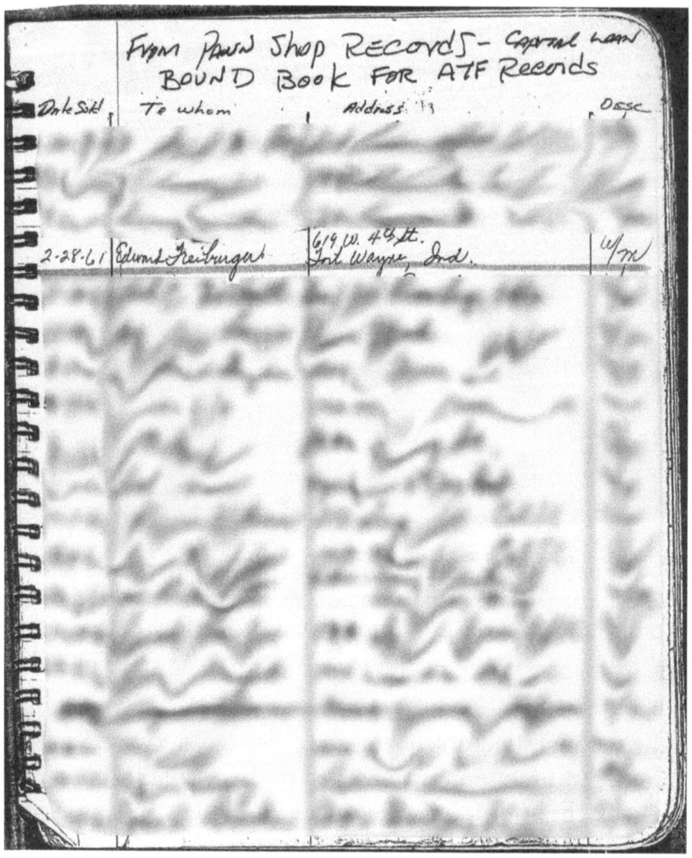

Figure 3.21 Copy of original gun store ATF record book. Cold case investigation builds on the work of earlier investigators, and this is a prime example of the good investigation shown by now-deceased law enforcement officers. Their recovery, and the preservation, of these documents helped link Freiburger conclusively to this crime. (Courtesy of Investigator Carl Craig, Richland County Sheriff's Department, South Carolina.)

Craig studied the file in depth for two weeks to familiarize himself with it and to formulate an investigative plan. He discovered that all of the original law enforcement investigators, medical staff, and forensic persons involved in the original investigation were now deceased. The original file had noted Freiburger's ties to Indiana, and a check of the state police there confirmed that Freiburger now resided near Fort Wayne, Indiana. A relative of Freiburger still lived in the same address Freiburger had used in 1961. Craig also learned that a close friend who had joined the army with Freiburger also lived in the same vicinity. Craig further discovered the whereabouts of one other witness, as well as that of Trooper Meredith. Craig located three living relatives of the victim and began to conduct a victim profile.

Craig could not find the gun and bullet fragments and contacted the state crime laboratory. A search of microfiche records revealed that, after 38 years, the lab still retained the weapon, the bullet fragments, and the test bullets. All were in pristine condition. Craig and his partner, Investigator Brian Metz, reviewed the evidence and subsequently requested that a reexamination of the gun and fragments be conducted using advanced technology now available.

It is not unusual in cold cases to find that suspects have moved to another state, and this was no exception. Craig and Metz contacted investigator Rocky Stotts of the Indiana State Police in Fort Wayne and asked for assistance. Stotts conducted a background check on Freiburger, and the investigators confirmed that the

Freiburger from the 1961 homicide case was the *same* Freiburger now living in Fort Wayne, Indiana. The two South Carolina detectives traveled to Indiana to meet with Investigator Stotts and interview Freiburger.

On October 20, 2000, Investigator Stotts contacted Freiburger at home and requested he come to the Whitley County Sheriff's Office to meet with investigators from Columbia, South Carolina. Freiburger drove there in his personal vehicle and met with Craig and Metz. The officers told him that they wanted to speak to him about a murder that occurred near Columbia, South Carolina, on February 28, 1961, while he was there as an army trainee. He was further advised that there were no warrants or restraints for him and he was free to leave at any time. Investigators noted, and documented, Freiburger's *immediate* reaction. He first turned pale and then red, and beads of sweat appeared on his forehead. He was visibly shaking and momentarily had trouble talking. When asked about his service in the army, he responded, "I was in the army?" When asked about ever being in Columbia, South Carolina, he replied, "I was in Columbia, South Carolina?"

It appeared he was faking memory loss, and Investigator Craig showed him a black-and-white picture of himself in uniform. See Figure 3.22. He then bowed his head and admitted he had been in the army. When asked about his sentence in Fort Leavenworth, he again asked if he had been there. The investigators had been prepared and showed him a copy of his FBI rap sheet. He then acknowledged he had been in the stockade.

Investigator Craig then showed him a photo of the revolver and purchase record bearing his name and Indiana address. He denied buying the gun, but his facial expressions indicated otherwise to the experienced detectives. He was shown the purchase signature and asked if it appeared to be his own, and after first declining to answer, he indicated it may or may not be his signature.

Investigators switched tracks and began talking about other events in his life since childhood, and he answered without hesitation. He discussed his life after discharge from the army in 1962 and family and work history. He was specifically asked if he was seeing a medical doctor or psychiatrist, and he replied he

Figure 3.22 Private Freiburger in U.S. Army uniform. When interviewed, the gun store clerk recalled that Freiburger purchased the weapon while in uniform and used his military identification for the transaction. The original investigators documented this fact. During an interview with investigators in 2000, however, he did not at first recall having served in the army, nor having been sentenced to Fort Leavenworth prison. Preservation of this photograph in the file proved an important piece of evidence. (Courtesy of Investigator Carl Craig, Richland County Sheriff's Department, South Carolina.)

was not. Freiburger appeared to become edgy, and then the investigators showed him a picture of the victim. Freiburger actually gasped and said, "I think I need to talk to a lawyer."

This cold case occurred before the Escobedo and Miranda decisions, but the theory and issues surrounding these U.S. Supreme Court decisions have, in my opinion, improved the quality of law enforcement in this country as well as contributing to improved safeguards for all citizens. These rules, however, do apply in pre–Miranda era investigations, and the investigators were aware of this as they terminated further interviews. Freiburger drove home but not for long. Investigators had observed apparent "selective" memory loss and that his body language, expressions, and reactions to certain questions and answers suggested perpetration, involvement, or knowledge of the murder of John Orner.

The day after their return to Columbia, however, a private attorney representing Freiburger called the investigators, intimating that they were open to a plea bargain on a lesser charge than murder one. This did not materialize but further reinforced the investigators' belief that they were on the right track.

Upon their return, Investigators Craig and Metz learned the results of the reexamination of Freiburger's H&R revolver. The laboratory had excluded the second suspect revolver but again concluded that Freiburger's gun was "a very close match, and may or may not be the murder weapon."

As the laboratory had not *excluded* the weapon, Freiburger's gun and the other weapon were submitted to a qualified private-sector firearms examiner in an attempt to obtain a definitive answer. This is a different situation, however, than might be concluded when dealing with "experts." Experienced investigators have encountered situations in which some involved in the criminal justice process, both prosecution and defense orientation, have shopped around until they found an expert who would tell them what they wanted to hear. This has led to hard feelings on both sides of the aisle but has also contributed to miscarriages of justice. No conclusion had been formally rendered by a firearms expert, and the issue was still open. Experts rely upon experience to form their opinions, but they also rely on technology.

The third examiner examined both guns as well as the fragments removed from the victim. On April 2, 2001, the examiner notified investigators that he had excluded the second revolver but had made a positive match on the Freiburger revolver. A consideration in cold cases, as in others, is chain-of-custody issues. In these cases, there may be additional opportunity for misfiling, mislabeling, loss, or contamination of evidence depending upon circumstances over the years and decades. A potential defense that the fragments belonged to someone else, however, was eliminated when DNA recovered from the bullet fragments was matched to that of the victim, Orner. An arrest warrant was obtained for Freiburger.

Freiburger had, in the meantime, secured the services of an attorney, who in turn secured the services of a local attorney. Arrangements were made for his surrender to Richland County authorities on April 10, 2001. He was subsequently arraigned and released on a $50,000 bond.

The case was assigned to Richland County Deputy Solicitors Knox McMahon and Luck Campbell. The investigators made contact with the now-retired Tennessee trooper and obtained the documents he still retained from his encounter with Freiburger. Trial began on July 29, 2002, in the Richland County General Sessions Court and lasted three days. McMahon and Campbell were able to lay foundations and enter evidence almost 40 years old, and to reconstruct for the jury a decades-long series of events. After only two hours' deliberation, the jury reached a unanimous verdict of guilty, and Freiburger was shortly sentenced to spend the rest of his natural life in the South Carolina Department of Corrections.

Irony is not a stranger in many cold cases. In this instance, Investigator Craig was in at the beginning, and the end, of this investigation. Craig, now an experienced cold case investigator, *just happened* to be in his office the day a superior officer commented casually and asked if he knew anything about a murder of a taxi driver in the 1960s. The nexus for this resulted from an encounter in church between a member of the victim's family and the captain. By chance, Investigator Craig was familiar with it already. Such knowledge is important at the start, simply identifying who and when, and building upon this knowledge. Such a chain of events was the sole factor in the reactivation of this murder, investigating one that, in most likelihood, would not have been otherwise reopened, due to age and other factors.

In additional irony, victim Orner was robbed of about $45, $7 less than he paid for the revolver. In the end, only three remaining survivors of the victim were able to see what passes for "justice" in these cases. The Richland County Sheriff's Office ultimately created a specialized cold crimes unit. From the start, Investigator Carl Craig has donated his services pro bono to this law enforcement agency and their quest to solve unsolved homicides.

Significant Cold Case Issues

This case history offers a significant number of issues for cold case investigators.

- Organizational leadership and commitment to proactive cold case homicide investigation.
- Case reactivation as a result of effort initiated by victim's family through casual conversation with a law enforcement official.
- Quality and thoroughness of initial investigation and retention of case file, including physical evidence, photographs, and firearm purchase records.
- Ability to save Thermofax documents and make a working case copy.
- Initial role of forensic geology.
- Thorough search for and location of physical evidence.
- Re-view and retesting of all evidence utilizing advanced technology. This resulted in a match of the weapon to the fragments, and the fragments, through DNA, to the victim.
- Witness recontact and interview resulting in discovery of Trooper Meredith's retention of documents 40 years after the fact that further linked Freiburger to the weapon.
- Although the nine principal investigators and other personnel were deceased, cold case investigators were able to reinvestigate this case and, through the efforts of prosecutor, to establish foundation for admission into evidence of almost 40-year-old documents and events.
- A check of the defendant's 1961 address revealed relatives still residing at same location.
- Suspect returned to his home state.
- Interstate law enforcement cooperation was so necessary in these cases.
- Reinterview with suspect and recording of immediate reaction and responses to questions, including statements and body language.
- Interview preparation by investigators including photographs and records to show suspect.
- Denials and apparent selective memory loss feigned by suspect.
- Investigator knowledge of suspect background and interview methodology.
- Dedication and perseverance of cold case investigators.
- Fate and luck.

Acknowledgments

I wish to extend my deepest gratitude to Investigator Carl Craig and his partner, Brian Metz, for providing the material used in compiling this case history as well as their work in this case. This investigation is a credit to cold case homicide investigation and to law enforcement. I further wish to acknowledge the leadership role demonstrated by Sheriff Leon Lott, Richland County Sheriff's Office, Columbia, South Carolina, in cold case homicide investigation and express my gratitude for his assistance in providing this case material.

I wish to express my gratitude and appreciation to the late Sgt. Rudy Ortega of the Unsolved Cases Unit, Los Angeles County Sheriff's Department, as well as his partner, Deputy Frank Gonzales, and Sgts. Paul Mondry and Alfredo Castro of the same unit. In addition, I wish to acknowledge and continue this appreciation to Detective Rick Jackson (ret'd) of the Los Angeles Police Department Cold Case Squad; District Attorney Investigator Ron Thill (ret'd) of the San Diego County District Attorney's Office, California; Capt. Jorge Duran of the San Diego Police Department, California; Detective Richard Rouleau (ret'd) of the El Cajon Police Department (California); Investigator Carl Craig (ret'd) of the Richland County Sheriff's Department, South Carolina; and District Attorney Anne Marie Schubert of the Sacramento County District Attorney's Office, California, for sharing their thoughts, experiences, and perspectives on the investigation of cold case homicides.

Suggested Readings and Bibliography

Anonymous. (2003). Los Angeles sheriffs cold case unit uses old fingerprints in new ways. *Crime Control Digest*, 37(6), 1.

Anonymous. (2002). Cold case homicide. C.P.T. Network, Sacramento, California. Commission on Peace Officer Standards and Training.

Adcock, J. and Stein, S. (2014). *Cold Cases: Evaluation Models with Follow-Up Strategies for Investigators*. Boca Raton, FL: CRC Press.

DiBiase, T.A. (2014). *No-Body Homicide Cases: A Practical Guide to Investigating, Prosecuting, and Winning Cases When the Victim Is Missing*. Boca Raton, FL: CRC Press.

Dieckmann, E.A. (1961). *Practical Homicide Investigation*. Springfield: Charles C Thomas.

Eliopulos, L.N. (2003). *Death Investigators Handbook: Expanded and Updated edition*.-w Boulder, CO: Paladin Press.

Geberth, V.J. (1996). *Practical Homicide Investigation: Tactics, Procedures, and Forensic Techniques* (3rd ed.). Boca Raton, FL: CRC Press.

Keel, T. (2008). *Homicide Investigations: Identifying Best Practices*. FBI Law Enforcement Bulletin. Superintendent of Documents, Washington, DC.

Keppell, R.D. and Weis, J.G. (1994). Time and distance as solvability factors in murder cases. *Journal of Forensic Sciences*, 39(2), 386–401.

Lee, H., Palmbach, T.M., and Miller, M. (2003). *Henry Lee's Crime Scene Handbook*. New York: Academic Press.

Leonard, V.A. (1970). *The Police Detective Function*. Springfield: Charles C Thomas.

Lochyer, B. (1999). *Cold Case Investigations*. Sacramento, California: California Attorney General.

NIJ. (2002). *Using DNA to Solve Cold Cases* (Commission Report No. NCJ 194197). Washington, DC: National Institute of Justice.

Nyberg, R. (1999). Investigations: Cold case squads re-activate old investigations. *Law and Order*, 47(10), 127–130.

Spraggs, D. (2003). How to open a cold case. *Policemag.com*: 29–31.

Tona, F. (2012). Cold Cases with no DNA, no Problem. *Law and Order Magazine*, September.

Walton, R.H. (2005). Identification of solvability factors in twenty-first century cold case homicide investigation. Unpublished Ed.D. dissertation. University of San Francisco. San Francisco.

Investigation

4

R. H. WALTON

Contents

Introduction

The investigation sequence and methods in a cold case homicide investigation will vary, depending upon a number of factors. These factors include those forces that caused this specific case to be reexamined (i.e., specific information has come forward regarding this specific case) and individual methods of investigation based on each investigator's training and experience, as well as the perceived investigative plan based upon file review. As no two hot homicides are investigated exactly in the same manner, neither are cold case homicides. Each takes place within an overall similar framework, however. This framework includes people, places, and evidence.

This chapter explores various considerations that may be involved in the reinvestigation of a cold case homicide. Not all cases will use all of the methods or sources of potential information presented here. Perhaps they will use others. In addition, investigators may color outside the box as they utilize combinations of other means and methods.

Reconstructing the Crime and Investigation

After reading and studying the case file, the cold case investigator is familiar with the *documented* record that has been preserved. This includes what officers and investigators did; what witnesses and others said; what evidence was collected, analyzed, and preserved; and what was photographed. In this way, the investigator has *informally* and *informationally* reconstructed the crime scene. During the course of this investigation, it may be appropriate to further consult with qualified reconstruction experts to *formally* reconstruct the crime. Reconstruction will depend upon the nature of the crime, the types of events that occurred, and the questions that need to be answered. This may involve physical reconstruction and/or psychological reconstruction (victim and suspect). Such reconstruction may involve

- Gunshot trajectory
- Muzzle-to-target distance
- Ejection pattern and other firearm-related analyses
- Blood spatter patterns
- Sharp object, including depths, angles, clothing damage, defense wounds, and antemortem or postmortem injuries
- Arson and fire burn
- Furniture and objects
- Vehicle impact
- Vehicle tire and skid-mark patterns
- Clothing and/or article patterns
- Bite mark (be careful here!)

Visit the Crime Scene

Reports and photographs provide the cold case investigator with a two-dimensional, informational view of the crime scene and the crime. In my experience, nothing serves to orient the investigator, and the investigation, more forcefully than a visit to the crime scene. Decades later, the scene may be little changed from when only a rural cabin stood (Figures 4.1 and 4.2), or condos may now stand in place of an old office building. Regardless, returning to *the scene of the crime* provides an insight that words and photographs cannot quite equal. While reading the case may allow the cold case investigator to feel the *pulse* of the crime, visiting the scene allows one to *feel* the scene of the crime (see Figure 4.3).

Reconstructing the Scene

If the location has changed, consider reconstructing the scene through interviews with those who knew the scene and the use of photographs. Such photos may be found

- From family or family members of victims (if crime occurred in or near residence)
- With neighbors of scene
- In city planning or building departments, including aerial photos
- In newspaper or local magazines
- In other media
- In historical societies
- In libraries
- In private collections

Figure 4.1 Scene of the crime, 1925. In some cold cases, the area that contained the crime scene is preserved only in photographs found outside the case file. These can provide investigators an insight into what the scene looked like at the time and aid in informational reconstruction of the crime. Pictured here is the scene of a 1925 homicide case reactivated in the 1980s. (Courtesy of the Irvine collection.)

Figure 4.2 Scene of the crime, 1988. Although the ravages of time may alter the original scene of the crime, photographs and returning to the scene with original participants or witnesses may further investigator understanding and provide information not found in the case file. In this photo, a member of the 1925 posse returns to the scene of a murder with the author to walk through the events from more than 60 years before. (Author's collection.)

When Visiting the Scene of the Crime

Revisit all scenes that are known to be associated with the crime. These may include the following:

- Homicide location.
- Body recovery location(s).
- Victim's residence or last known location.
- Suspect residence or last known location.
- All locations where evidence was located.
- Consider geographic profiling.
- Consider behavioral assessment of both victim and suspect.

Time and Distance

- Note the ingress and egress for victim and suspect.
- Visit at the time of day or night the crime occurred.
  - Lighting?
  - Who may have been present?
  - Where?
  - Businesses hours or routine activities by others that might have allowed for unknown witnesses to be present?
- For a different perspective, visit in the daytime if the crime was at night, and vice versa.
- Take the crime scene pictures with you and orient yourself and the pictures to the scene.
- Observe surrounding terrain or buildings.
- Look up, down, and around.

Figure 4.3 Crime scene, 1965 and 2001. Vegetation changes and remodeling are not uncommon in decades following a homicide. In many cases, current homeowners have allowed law enforcement to reenter the residence in order to familiarize themselves with the ins and outs of the scene. Contact of scene owners or those who control access may be a delicate situation as they may have had no knowledge of the prior homicide. (Courtesy of Anderson/ECPD.)

- Slope and lay of the land.
- Compare witness statements to the scene. Do they appear realistic as to what they said, did, and saw?
- Is evidence still present? For instance, with a rural location, tall grass, and brief scene investigation, evidence was perhaps missed and never recovered.
- Have witnesses or reporting party walk through the scene with you (see Figure 4.2).

The Neighborhood Canvass

According to homicide expert Vernon Geberth, a neighborhood canvass is the door-to-door questioning of those in the general area after a crime has been committed in an attempt to gain information about the specific incident. During this brief contact and interview with residents and others, officers or investigators attempt to locate witnesses or individuals who might provide information about the specific incident. Although this knowledge may not appear important to them, when coupled with other information known to investigators, it may play a significant role in an investigation. The canvass or a recanvass, according to Geberth, may provide

- An actual eyewitness to the crime
- Information about the circumstances of the crime
- An approximate time of occurrence and/or estimate of time of death
- Information about the deceased, including identity, habits, friends
- Information about unusual observations or individual behavior at the time
- Information about a suspect, or even identity of a suspect
- A motive for the crime

Normally, but not always, a canvass is conducted shortly after the crime or incident. A canvass may have been done by the investigators but also may have been done by other officers, who would have then forwarded the names and addresses of potential witnesses to the investigators along with a brief summary of what the witness may have to offer. The investigators would then conduct a more thorough, detailed interview. It is well to remember that due to the passage of time, a recanvass may identify those who were never interviewed and/or those who may now be more cooperative and divulge what they know.

A neighborhood canvass could be a hit-or-miss affair, depending upon the diligence of those assigned this duty, or other priorities. If a neighborhood resident had nothing to offer, the canvassing officer may have not written anything down. If a resident was not home, no one may have gone back. Some agencies may have used a form, a canvass questionnaire, in the course of this activity, and case file review should attempt to identify this practice. Not uncommonly, however, the canvassing officer used his/her notebook or perhaps an index card to make note of any information. Communication to the investigators of the identity of persons to be contacted could be verbal and the information subsequently forgotten and never followed up.

In one instance, a man hit his wife, and she died. A neighbor, who knew the couple well, approached uniformed officers at the scene and stated that she had information the investigators should be aware of. She was told that investigators would contact her. Some weeks later, she telephoned the police agency to state that she had never been contacted and possessed information regarding the couple that police should be aware of. She was never contacted.

Approximately a year later, the case was going to trial. The suspect stated he had never hit his wife before. District attorney investigators were conducting pretrial investigation in the neighborhood of the crime when they were approached by the same neighbor. The neighbor then told of past domestic violence toward the victim and how, just days before the homicide, she observed the suspect hit the victim so hard he knocked her across the room. At this time, he voiced words to the effect that next time he would kill her. The suspect pled guilty.

Reconstructing the Canvass

Going back to a neighborhood years or decades after the crime may yield valuable information. If the results of a neighborhood canvas have been found in the file, use this as a starting point to begin. What addresses were checked? Which were not? Go to the neighborhood and look around. Look for neatly maintained, older homes. Attempt to identify the older residents of the neighborhood, and elicit their help. Choose a time of day that most optimizes the chance to find people at home. When reconstructing a canvass, ascertain if the address or numbering sequences may have changed since the time of the crime.

Start going door to door as you would do for a primary canvass today. Attempt to identify those who may have been living in the neighborhood at the time of the crime. In some instances, the original resident may have moved but the current resident may be his/her tenant, or know how to contact him/her. In some circumstances, a relative may now live there, if not the same resident from the time period. Experience has shown witnesses still residing in the same location as at the time of the offense 45 years or more after the incident. It is not unheard of that witnesses resided in the same location 40–60 years later.

Call the telephone number in the report. Check the address.

Remember, while some may possess knowledge of the crime or persons involved, they can't bring themselves to pick up the telephone to call but may just be waiting for the investigator to knock on their door to tell all they know. It has happened.

When conducting the canvass, start at the point where the crime occurred. Look around; from what locations might someone see something? Don't forget to look up, also. Consider the time of day, or night, of the crime.

To reconstruct the neighborhood for a canvass, consider

- City/county directories for the time period
- Public works for street maps
- Planning department
- Public utilities for turn-ons
- Local historical societies
- Fire department
- Post office
- Local resident input

Suggested Questions

- Did you reside here at the time of the crime?
- Knowledge of crime?
- Know anyone involved?
- Firsthand knowledge of events or the crime?
- Heard of anything about the crime or individuals over the years?
- Did anybody move away suddenly after the crime?
- Any suspicious persons at that time, or other suspicious events?
- Any similar crimes before or after?
- Do you suspect anyone of this crime?

After the canvass, check criminal histories on any names that may have developed.

City/County/Business Directories

City, county, or business directories are publications produced by commercial companies that provide information about people living within the boundaries as designed by the directory and/or businesses. These directories and their variations have been around since the late 1800s and offered in many locales nationwide, both urban and rural. These publications are especially useful in reconstructing information about physical locations, including neighboring addresses and intersections as well as personal data about individuals. The cold case investigator should keep in mind that, like other print sources, the information to be found in these sources is only as good as the original source of information.

These directories were compiled and published on an annual basis, often by larger commercial publishers. They were sold commercially, often by subscription, and may have been produced in association with local chambers of commerce. These directories offered commercial and demographic information about a community, as well as personal information about its occupants. Among these directories, one may find

- Alphabetical directory of business names
- Alphabetical directory of private citizens
- Directory of householders
- Occupants of office buildings and other business places
- Street name and number guide
- Numerical telephone directory
- Classified advertising
- Other miscellaneous information

Business directories are most often compiled by the local chamber of commerce.

For example, if an investigator knows that the subject of interest operated a barber shop in San Diego, California, in a particular year, a review of the city directory for that year would include a list of barber shops in alphabetical order, as compiled by this data source. Although city or state licensing and business operation records may normally be destroyed or discarded after a prescribed length of time, city directories offer a means to locate reported information about people and places in a specific time period (see Figure 4.4).

Figure 4.4 City directories. These published directories offer cold case investigators a variety of information about people and the local community during previous decades. Such directories date to the nineteenth century in many areas and are useful in researching people and places and for may be useful in construction of timelines. (Author's collection.)

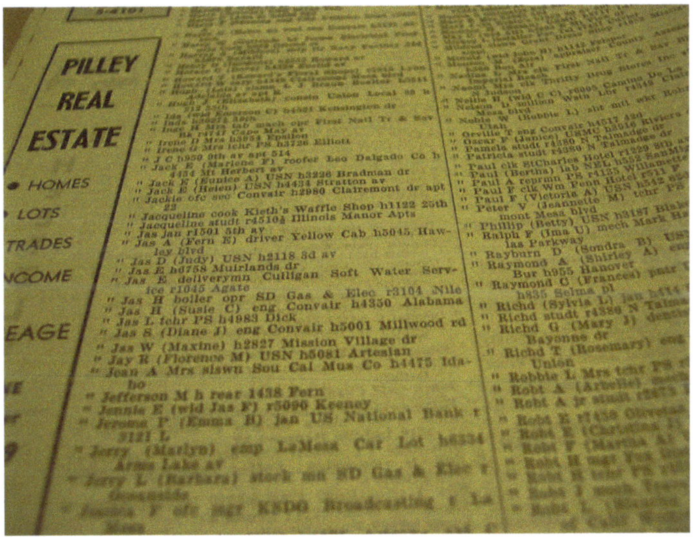

Figure 4.5 City directories may be useful in several facets of cold case investigation. In addition to listing people by name and phone number, they also provide sequential street address information. This may aid in identifying neighbors to a particular address or in reconstructing an area cold case canvass. (Author's collection.)

As a source of personal information, city directories offer a cold case investigator a thumbnail picture of people. Persons are listed in alphabetical order by last name, first name, middle initial, name of spouse (common-law, significant-other, or other nonmarried cohabitants may not be included in these older listings), address, place of employment, and/or occupation. The listing of a spouse or employment information may offer cold case investigators additional names or sources of information heretofore unknown, especially in older cases.

These directories detailed the numerical sequencing of streets and intersections. In addition, they listed individual house numbers, name of occupant, and telephone number (see Figure 4.5). City or county directory listings may also include not only the address of apartment structures but also the names of individual occupants and their telephone numbers. The passage of time between the period when the information was obtained and when it was published, however, may impact the accuracy of this information. This may be especially true in more transient populations. These listings may be useful when attempting to reconstruct addresses and occupants surrounding a subject location or crime scene. Development of this information may provide cold case investigators with names and addresses of persons not reflected in original police reports or statements. This information might be useful in preparing diagrams showing scene locations or when used in conjunction with aerial photographs. The directories might also offer confirmation or nonconfirmation of information and aid in constructing timelines and occupational profiles.

Sources of old city directories may include

- In-agency archives and library
- Local libraries
- Local chamber of commerce
- Local historical societies
- Local law enforcement agency archives
- Local offices of the Federal Bureau of Investigation (FBI) and other federal agencies

Telephone Directories

The style and format of published, softcover telephone directories has changed in the decades since the 1940s. Older telephone directories may list persons by last name, full first name, middle initial, physical location address for the specified telephone number, and telephone number. In more recent decades, there has been a transition from such inclusive personal information to a listing that includes last name, first initial, and telephone number only. As a consequence, telephone directories may offer more assistance to cold case investigators in some older cases than more recent editions.

Telephone directories may provide cold case investigators with information useful when

- Establishing residency confirmation or disconfirmation, or locations of suspects, witnesses, or other persons
- Cross-checking or indexing telephone numbers
- Searching for yellow pages business information

Victim and Family Considerations

Contacting the Victim's Family

Cold case investigators hold differences of opinion as to investigator-initiated contact with a victim's family. To contact or *not* to contact depends upon the circumstances of the case, and the investigative plan of action as it is conceived and carried out. While perhaps no such contact is planned at the start of the cold case investigation, circumstances may change, and contact then becomes necessary.

When contacting the family of a victim in these investigations, keep in mind that the pain and anxiety, the feelings from that first day of the crime, are just below their emotional surface. The family never forgets. To the family of homicide victims, the hurt is still present, even after 60 years or more. In the initial period after the crime, they sought answers from the police, from friends, and from each other. How they *perceived* their treatment by law enforcement can affect how they react to a renewed investigation. Their feelings may run the scale from desiring no contact with authority to full cooperation. On some occasions, they may not wish the case to be reopened and may want to just let it be. There may be reasons for this, and these might include family secrets or matters they do not want exposed, or culpability by a family member.

If and when contact is made with family, consider utilizing the services of the victim/witness unit (see Chapters 11 and 31). When a cold case is solved, involve this unit with the family in the postarrest and media-interest phase.

Reasons to Contact the Victim's Family

- Over the years, the victim's family may have learned direct information or have secondhand information that may be of interest to the investigation. They may also have previously contacted law enforcement investigators, who may have given them the perception that their information was not considered valuable at the time. This information may or may not have been documented in the file. In later years, with other information subsequently known, that information may now be more valuable.
- To obtain diaries, notes, photographs, or other material that now may be of importance to the investigation. These may identify previous relationships, relationship status, other friends, and acquaintances, or identify specific concerns or fears held by the victim (see Figure 4.6).
- To learn more about the victim and circumstances at the time of the homicide.
- To identify or learn further of other persons of interest who may have surfaced during the initial or subsequent investigation.
- To verify or eliminate from consideration other information.
- To inform the family that their case has not been forgotten.

Figure 4.6 Knowledge of the victim may come from many sources. During a cold case investigation, investigators seek to learn as much as they can about the victim's movements prior to the crime, as well as previous relationships. Contact with the family may provide notes, letters, and diaries with information previously unknown to investigators. In this 1925 case, a letter from the victim to her brother provided personal information and detailed a relationship that was important in the case reconstruction eight decades later. (Author's collection.)

- To obtain a photo of the victim for use when later confronting a suspect (Figure 3.16).
- To stimulate communications in the family or immediate circle of friends.
- In some instances, contact may be necessary to obtain a DNA reference sample.

Arguments against Contacting a Victim's Family

- Raises false hopes and expectations.
- Family or members begin to call every day to learn if anything is new.
- Family begins to discuss it; word may get to the suspect(s), and he/she further covers his/her tracks.
- If the cold case goes nowhere and remains unsolved, they ride another emotional roller coaster.
- A family member may be involved in the case, or may be the suspect.

Learning More about the Victim (and the Suspect)

When studying the unsolved case, investigators try to learn as much about their victim as they can. This in turn *may* begin to identify the suspect. Consider the *victimology* in the course of investigation, and try to come to know who the victim was before the murder and identify and assess what role he/she may have played in this chain of events. Apply your experience as you would in a fresh case. See Chapter 23.

- *Physical.* This includes evidence transferred from the crime and recovered at the scene, at autopsy, or in other circumstances. Interview the autopsy pathologist for case review and discussion. In older cases in which the deceased was received by a county coroner, contact that person/office as well. Always be sure and ask if they have any remaining documentation. Physical evidence may include
  - Seminal or other body fluids
  - Bruises
  - Bite marks (use caution here)
  - Bullet wounds and tracks
  - Contact distance
  - Defense wounds

- Blood spatter or patterns
- Foreign objects
- Hair and fibers
- *Lifestyle.* This is learned through observations, interviews, and document analysis and may assist in learning more about the victim as well as contributing to the identification of a suspect. As a suspect is identified, these considerations may also apply to building the case.
  - Physical residential or work environment
  - Environment where the crime occurred
  - Notes, diaries, letters
  - Church associates
  - Employment
  - Circle of friends, acquaintances, and coworkers
    - Any outliers
    - Anybody who moves away suddenly
    - Anybody who undergoes noticeable lifestyle change
  - Anyone who had access to victim
  - Then-current relationships and prior relationships (including former spouses)
  - Fears and phobias
  - Mental and physical history
  - Behavior changes
  - Hobbies and sports
  - Habits and routines
  - Neighbors
  - Social clubs and organizations
  - Physical abilities and capabilities
  - Hairdressers.
  - Financial profile and credit check
  - Review of credit card records including spending and last uses or usage profile
  - School or work problems
  - Telephone records or cell phone records reviewed
  - Sexual fetishes or interests
  - Sexual orientation
  - Drug and alcohol abuse
  - Cellmates and codefendants
  - Probation and parole reports
  - Institution intelligence reports
  - Violence or illegal activity in background
  - Enemies and adversaries
  - Former business partners and associates
  - Social services
  - Civil files
  - Known trial testimony

Other Family Dynamics

- Did any family ever hire private investigators (PIs)?
  - Were witnesses contacted by PIs?
  - Were PIs used in any aspect of the case (civil or criminal)?

- Who benefited financially from the victim's death?
  - Life insurance.
  - Mortgage insurance.
  - Review last will and testament and probate file or trusts.
  - Business insurance policies (family or partners as beneficiaries).
  - Property transfers or money movements.
- Identify family tree.
  - Use of obituary.
  - Siblings—they may now provide information they did not at the time.
  - Step-parents and relations.
  - Other relations including *black sheep*, who may tell what others will not.

Interviews and Reinterviews

Reinterviewing witnesses is an important component of the reinvestigation of cold case homicides. By this process, investigators seek to

- Affirm previous witness statements and update contact and identifier information
- Obtain information *held back* by previously identified witnesses who may now tell more due to changes in their own lifestyle, maturity, distancing from the previous crowd they ran around with, or no longer fearing the suspect
- Identify previously unidentified witnesses or associates of the suspect
- Obtain cooperation of previously uncooperative witnesses

Interview Sequence

Cold case investigators may consider the order of the witness interview process.

- Begin with law enforcement and other officials as necessary.
- Consider those witnesses on the outside periphery of those initially contacted and work toward the center, those most immediate to the victim. These on the outside may know more than they told or have heard information over the years. Of course, remember that the more people you contact, the increased likelihood that the word may get back to the suspect.
- Material witnesses. Prior to contacting material witnesses, compile as much background information on them as possible. Ascertain any pending legal difficulties, including custody, probation, or parole status.
- Run background checks on *all* subjects, including witnesses, family members, or others involved in the case, as you would if the case were a fresh homicide. Use the advantage of time to obtain further insight into various individuals.

During the background and interview process, look for

- Lifestyle changes. These include downhill slides as well as improved lifestyle and relationships, or religious embracement.
- Movements out of city, county, or state. It has been my interesting observation that many of those who commit their crimes in the vicinity of where they were raised may often move out of state, and those who commit their crimes far from where they were raised may return to their comfort zone of family and friends.

- Arrests.
- Violence.
- Changes in personal relationship or inability to maintain relationships. Keep in mind that former friends, lovers, and secretaries can be the most valuable sources of information. Identify these when possible and as necessary.
- Other evidence of self-destructive behavior.
- Be careful not to give out more than you receive!

Additional Background Resources for Victim and Suspect Information and Development

- Marriage and divorce records
- Real estate records including grantee/grantor
- Birth certificate
- Civil liens and judgments
- Reports to local police, fire, ambulance by victim, witnesses, or suspect
- Assessor
- Treasurer/tax collector
- City/county clerk
- Professional licensing and certification
- Trade unions
- Post office
- Schools
- Local voter registration

Social Media

Among the dramatic changes in law enforcement has been the continual rise of the use of social media (SM) by the public as well as in criminal investigations. A survey in 2012 by LexisNexis sought to assess the understanding by law enforcement of SM and agency tendency to use it, as well as to identify the types of investigative practices and procedures then being used. Citing the increasing use of technology by law enforcement in its follow-up survey, *2014 Social Media Use in Law Enforcement*, LexisNexis reported the results of a study that indicated significant usage of SM by law enforcement, especially investigators, and projected its usage to rise even more in coming years. Neither survey specifically identified homicide or cold case homicide investigations. According to their report,

- Eight out of every 10 law enforcement professionals (81%) actively used SM as an investigative tool, with 25% using it daily.
- More than half of responding agencies still did not have a formal process for investigative usage of SM, the largest barrier being a lack of access during work hours.
- SM can serve as a source of probable cause for search warrants; collection of evidence; and identifying criminals, their networks, and the locations of wanted persons.
- Facebook and YouTube were cited as the most commonly used SM channels.
- Seventy-three percent of respondents suggested that SM usage by investigators could help solve cases more quickly. Facebook postings and tracking cell phones can contribute in this regard, as can examining Facebook posts and photos and "friends of friends."

- Usage of SM to reach out to the public for help in solving crimes.
- Most law enforcement professionals are self-taught in its use for investigations but go to colleagues (younger?) for additional instruction.

In addition, the International Association of Chiefs of Police (IACP) Center for Social Media offers the value of SM as an investigative tool for cases involving missing and wanted persons, gang participation and recruitment, and cybercrimes. Reporting that 86.1% of agencies use SM for criminal investigations, it notes what many investigators have found—that criminals post videos, photos, and text messages bragging about or discussing their crimes. Witnesses also make SM posts.

In addition, the IACP provides suggested guidelines for getting started with SM, including strategy development, policy development, and tutorials and guides for setting up SM pages. See Chapter 5.

Victim Family Involvement through Social Media

In recent years, we have seen the families of cold case homicide victims creating Facebook and other SM or World Wide Web pages seeking information on the killers of their loved ones. Investigators may seek to ensure that any such postings to these pages are referred to the investigation.

Additional Investigative Means and Methods for Suspect Development

Time and changes in relationships as well as technology are the primary solvability factors identified in the successful resolution of cold case homicides. Many of these topics discussed in victim and witness development in this chapter are applicable to further suspect development. As the suspect is developed, many of these investigative avenues may prove useful to the investigation.

In addition to reexamination of evidence and use of resources such as the Combined DNA Index System (CODIS) and Next Generation Identification/automated fingerprint identification system (NGI/AFIS), other means and methods may assist the cold case investigator. These include

- Wiretaps
- Off-line National Crime Information Center (NCIC) checks
- Law enforcement criminal intelligence services at local, state, and federal level
- Law enforcement computer databases
- Corrections institution/incarceration records
- Corrections institution staff interviews
- Psychological profiling and behavioral assessment
- Cellmate informants and street informants
- Accomplices and codefendants in prior criminal activity
- Internet searches
- Physical surveillance
- Use of grand jury
- Federal organized crime statutes
- Undercover operations
- Search warrants
    - Home and work computers
    - Telephone records
    - Cell phone records

When investigating crime, remember crime is like water. Crooks, for the most part, are inherently lazy. Like water, they will take the path of least resistance. Don't make more out of a particular crime than it is. The easiest answer, that makes sense, is usually the answer.

Tony Leal, former Texas Ranger

Interview Considerations

Once the suspect has been identified, and located, a number of considerations occur as investigators attempt to conduct an interview, or to effect arrest.

Chief among these is a consideration of whether to arrest and *then* interview, or interview and *then* follow with arrest. At this stage of the investigation, the interview process should involve both law enforcement and prosecutorial perspectives. Department policy may subscribe parameters, and each has their own perspective and concerns although ultimately the same end result.

Law Enforcement Perspective

- Is the interview *within* the investigating agency's jurisdiction or outside, including out of state?
  - If out of state or jurisdiction, arrangements must be made with appropriate authorities.
  - Contact strategy.
    - Direct approach
    - Indirect approach (i.e., the Freiburger case study)
  - Availability of surreptitious video or recording devices.
- Type of setting for interview (formal or informal).
- Recording or video options (including agency/legal requirements) or availability.
- Custodial interview. Arrest and then interview with possibility of suspect invoking Miranda rights.
- Noncustodial interview.
  - Further inculpatory statements that may conflict with previous statements
  - Observations and appraisal of demeanor and the person
  - Negative statements
  - Admissions or confession
- Use of *forensic* psychologist or behavioral analysis to frame interview questions, techniques, and tactics.
- Strategize how to approach suspect.
- Strategize *who* will interview suspect.
  - Selection of investigator most likely to elicit suspect's cooperation and not alienate suspect from the start. As an example, perhaps it would not be wise to utilize an African American investigator to interview a white supremacist. Or would it?
  - Interviewer must be thoroughly familiar with all aspects of the case.

Strategize Interview and Interrogation

- Determine suspect's interview style. Identify and interview previous authorities who have interviewed suspect to see how he/she reacts. Learn what *pushes his buttons* and what does not.
  - Police officers and investigators.
  - Probation and parole officers.
  - Former prosecutor insight.
  - Pull all prior reports and read interviews.
  - Former psych reports.

    - Listen to previous interview tapes.
    - Determine what works and what does not.
        - Confrontation.
        - Accusation.
        - Bluff—be careful!
        - Use of props such as photos of
            - Victim
            - Crime scene
            - Grave
- Suspect's interview and interrogation history
    - How many arrests?
    - Circumstances.
    - Locations.
    - Custodial or noncustodial.
    - When/how long ago was suspect's last interview or law enforcement contact?
- Time span since crime
    - Suspect's lifestyle then/now
    - Stability as expressed through family, relationships, religion, children, career
    - Known or identified medical/mental conditions
    - Known criminal history since the cold case homicide
- Methods that have appeared to be successful

The element of surprise is a prime consideration for a successful interview.

Case Solved: Preparing the Case for Review, Arrest, and Prosecution

Not everyone necessarily understands what may be involved in cold case investigation. This sometimes includes fellow officers and superior officers within one's own agency as well as prosecutors, judges, and juries. Investigators must first convince those within their own agency of the quality of the case for submission to the prosecutor, who then must feel confident he/she can convince a jury beyond a reasonable doubt. It must be remembered that the prosecutor, who already has a full schedule, must contend with a myriad of issues now compounded by the age of the case, evidence retention, and witness matters. In addition, the prosecutor may also have to deal with potential jury pool perceptions influenced by television and media representations that, in some situations, are less than practically realistic. Sometimes they and the investigators have strong opposing viewpoints on matters. See Chapter 6.

These cases usually involve a series of events stretched out over a period of years and styles of investigation and documentation not applicable today. In addition, they usually involve many names and, sometimes, relationships that need to be explained and understood, as well as evidence and property, forensic examinations, and more.

A cold case investigation is the victim's last chance for attention from the criminal justice system, and investigators need to convince their own team as well as the prosecution that *now* is the best time to file and prosecute this case. To do this, investigators should consider other means to best explain and convey the investigation rather than just handing off the "murder book" and waiting for a response. Prepare a *road map*.

Investigators of these cases today may consider preparing a computer-generated presentation, such as PowerPoint©. In doing so, the idea is to be expressive and thorough, concise yet complete. Maps, diagrams, photos, and other means that demonstrate people, places, evidence, and relationships all contribute to making such a presentation a success. Use pictures of the victim wherever appropriate. Give the victim a place in the presentation. The prosecutor will want to make the victim come alive for a jury, so make the case come alive for the prosecutor. Everything the investigator can do to help the prosecutor in this regard may come back to pay big dividends for both. In preparing these presentations, consider using the following, mixing photos, *then and now*, as appropriate. Highlight information through the use of graphics such as lines, arrows, etc.

The Original Investigation

- Make the victim come alive through family pictures. Retrace his/her last days.
  - Victim's background
  - Victim's family, including marriage, children, responsibilities
- Known suspect information.
- Identify witnesses or others in the case.
- The crime and investigation as portrayed by
  - Original crime scene photos
  - Aerial photos
  - Maps
  - Calendars
  - Timelines
  - Newspaper clippings
- Original missing-persons report and search efforts.
- Original news video clips.
- Original agency investigation video clips.
- The killer and the relationship to events and to the victim.
- Suspect's knowledge of the victim.
- Suspect familiarity with crime scene or secondary scenes.
- Introduce the detectives and investigators, the first team.
- Victim's death.
  - Victim's clothing
  - Victim's remains
  - Weapon
  - Crime scene
  - Victim's living ingress to scene and ultimate egress
- Forensic review.
  - What was examined and what was done
  - State-of-the-art of forensics at the time of original analysis
  - Weapon analysis
  - Review of reports and criminalistics work
- Summary of defendants' original statements, if any.
- Summary of original investigation and why case went cold.

Reinvestigation

- Cause and reason for start-up.
- Discussion of remaining reports, evidence, and any other problems.
- Review of role of advanced technology.

- Review of the role of changes in relationships.
- Summary of the evidence and current investigation.
- Summary to link the suspect to the victim and the evidence.
- Time sequences.
- Rerun routes with a video camera and show times and places.
- Why now?

Arrest and Search Warrants

Search warrants may be a valuable tool during the investigation and arrest of a suspect in a cold case homicide. We seek these warrants when we conduct a hot homicide investigation, so why not in a cold case investigation? Although the element of time may be a consideration to the prosecution and to the court and the reasonable expectation to find items sought after the passage of years, this issue may be sufficiently addressed depending upon the circumstances of the case and the investigation. Research and literature soundly establish that suspects have been known to keep souvenirs of the crime and memorabilia of the case (such as newspaper reports) for decades.

In my opinion and experience, there is not necessarily a reason to believe that a suspect will not, or does not, keep something as a record or souvenir of the incident. In white-collar and fraud cases, we routinely seek search warrants to find documents often many years old. A search warrant may establish other linkages to the crime, as evidenced by the items sought by the investigators. Such may include

- Documents and memorabilia pertaining to the crime
- Documents to establish identity as the same person in the original investigation
- Documents that show dominion and control of residence or location
- Diaries, records, letters, notes, and correspondence that may indicate suspect knowledge of the victim or relationship, or commission of the crime
- Travel and movement documents
- Documents that exhibit the suspect's original handwriting
- Documents or photos that show interest in any particular aspects of the crime, i.e., bondage, torture, etc.
- Photos of the subject then and now
- Firearms and ammunition or other weapons
- DNA
- Other items particularly related to the offense

Circumstances warranting such, investigators may consider ensuring that the warrant of arrest *not* be entered into warrant systems or NCIC until shortly before service. Cold case investigators may consider the wisdom of this tactic, as it may be troublesome to have the plan in place and ready to proceed only to have the suspect stopped on a routine traffic matter and arrested. In addition, you never know who may know someone after all these years, and for security purposes, this tactic may be advisable.

As an example, I had once obtained a $6 million bail arrest warrant for a white-collar crime suspect. The suspect had relocated to a distant jurisdiction and I similarly had withheld the arrest warrant from being entered into NCIC until FBI agents and I were preparing to execute the search and arrest warrants. However, it happened that a copy of the arrest warrant was sent to a sheriff's office clerk responsible for the warrant entry. On a quiet Saturday morning, the clerk noticed the warrant and, in an attempt to be helpful, personally notified the uniform division of the police agency to which we were en route to serve the warrant. Hours before our action, two uniformed officers went to the residence and arrested the suspect on the warrant. He immediately asserted his legal rights, and no interview ensued, nor was documentation of his immediate reaction or statements made.

Officer Safety

The service of any search warrant or arrest warrant poses risk and danger for law enforcement personnel. The service of these warrants in cold cases, in my opinion, poses additional risk and uncertainty. Although the suspect may now be older, that does not necessarily mean that he/she is wiser. Suspects have had many years to think about what they have done, how they may react if confronted, and how they will react when confronted, and to estimate the results of their decisions. Flight or fight, prison, or a death penalty. Even *they* do not really know how they will react until it happens. Check available databases for any firearms purchases, updated arrests, or other resources to identify any possible intelligence.

The reality of this situation is most apparent to those who will confront a cold case suspect after the passage of time. The elevated emotions and adrenaline of the moments during and after the crime may be long past, but the consequences of their actions are suddenly a reality. Those who have committed long-past crimes may have continued to commit criminal acts and murders, or they may have gone on to become locally respectable members of the community. At this stage of the investigation, cold case investigators have been removed from the violence of the crime and have been immersed in the legal aspects of investigation and liaison with the prosecutor's office. As Los Angeles County Sheriff's detectives Dan McElderry and Kevin Lowe once told me, "…think like a policeman, not an attorney."

"Think and Practice Officer Safety"

Arrest Considerations

Most law enforcement agencies have guidelines, policies, and procedures for arrest and apprehension of suspects in violent crimes. If the arrest is to occur within your jurisdiction, you would most likely invoke normal arrest procedures. This is an area where history of the case and investigation and postcrime behavior coupled with investigator experience and perceptions influence how, when, and where the arrest is to be made. These options may range from negotiated surrender to high-risk entry tactics. In this arrest situation, you would consider potential

- Hazard assessment
  - Time of day or night
  - Type of location
  - Firearms
  - Possibility of pursuit
  - Neighbors
  - Pedestrian or other vehicular traffic
  - Hostage potential
- Tactical plan
  - Totality of knowledge of the suspect; previous arrest history, propensity for fight or flight
  - Assistance from specialized units, allied investigation agency, or neighboring agency
  - Surveillance and reconnaissance of suspect and location
  - Approach—best method to minimize hazards and execute surprise
  - Communications systems
  - Availability of ambulance and medical personnel

- Briefing and personnel assignment
- Coordination
- Execution of plan
- Consideration of advanced age and potential medical condition of suspect and wife/others

Search and Arrest Warrant Service

Serving out-of-state search warrants involves enlisting the assistance of law enforcement in the jurisdiction where the activity is to occur, and submitting the affidavit for a search warrant through local forms and format. Usually, a local law enforcement agent will act as the affiant on the warrant and prepare the search warrant for the target location. Shortly before service, the arrest warrant may/should be entered into NCIC. It is recommended that an operations plan for service of the warrants be prepared, and this may include the nearby presence of an ambulance and paramedics.

Arrest and Interview

In cold case investigations, as in other investigations, surprise is a valuable asset, not only for safety purposes, but to observe and audio/video record the immediate reaction and utterances of the suspect. Upon contact with the suspect and securing him/her, regular protocols such as a safety sweep should be made. It is recommended that the location be photographed before and after the search.

Interview of Family and Friends

When making cold case arrests, it is recommended that investigators interview family members and friends as soon as possible. Information to be sought includes length and depth of their relationship; circumstances and dates or time periods regarding their knowledge of the suspect at or about the time of the crime; as well as financial, occupational, marital, or other relationship history. This information may be useful in identifying additional crimes, victims, or witnesses, and may also be beneficial to the prosecutor in countering subsequent efforts by the defendant to portray his/her exemplary character.

News Media Considerations

The news media usually shows a high interest in these cases, and this may be especially elevated in the more sensational cases. As search warrants are served and arrests are made, investigators operate at a steady pace. They usually do not have time to respond to media interest, including questions and interviews. A competent, ranking officer experienced with media relations possesses the authority to make necessary decisions as well as to responsibility respond to media interest and departmental or prosecutorial concerns, sometimes hundreds or thousands of miles away.

Subsequent Court Proceedings

After the arrest of a suspect, it may be advisable for investigators to attend what otherwise may be considered routine hearings that they may not normally attend. What they see and hear may reveal additional investigation opportunities or provide additional information.

Case Study—Wilkerson

El Cajon is a bedroom community along the interstate highway that runs east out of San Diego, California. The city has long maintained its own police department, as have many similar communities in the region, including neighboring La Mesa. The larger San Diego Police Department and county sheriff's office border these small Southern California departments in a patchwork of jurisdictional boundaries. On June 6, 1965, a 19-year-old mother was murdered in her bottom-floor apartment in El Cajon. She had been out with friends until approximately midnight, and one of these friends stayed with her until approximately 3 a.m. Before dawn, an intruder entered through a sliding glass door and beat her with a cocktail-mix bottle. He then used a drapery cord (Figure 3.6) cut from a living room window to strangle the victim and then raped her. The victim was left in a "staged" position, with candles left to burn in a "last rite" orientation, and a candle was inserted into her vagina. The apartment was ransacked, although there was no sign of a struggle. The contents of the victim's purse were dumped on the living room floor, although cash and jewelry were not taken. The only items taken were a camera and a crucifix.

The homicide was discovered when neighbors saw the victim's young son wandering outside her apartment the next morning. She was found partially sprawled across the corner of her bed, and her legs kept her propped up off the floor. Evidence recovered at the scene indicated that she had been sexually assaulted, and that evidence decades later provided a DNA profile. While processing the crime scene, investigators recovered the ligature, and it was booked into evidence. There it remained for over three decades.

Two weeks later, on June 23, a husband, age 63, and his 57-year-old wife were preparing for bed in their apartment when an intruder entered the residence. Armed with a long-handled socket wrench (Figure 4.7) he had stolen in a vehicle burglary a short time before, he beat the husband to death, raped the wife, and beat her viciously with the wrench before leaving her for dead. An open jar of hand cream was next to her, and cream was smeared about her vagina. Her legs were doubled underneath her with the heels of her feet resting on her buttocks and her legs spread apart. She was found about 20 hours later when neighbors heard her moans and cries. Numerous individuals were investigated and cleared, but despite the best efforts of numerous detectives and other personnel, no suspects were identified. Serology and fingerprints (Figure 4.8) were the two primary means of identification utilized at this time, and no leads were developed. The socket wrench was released to its owner, and the other evidence was boxed up and put into storage.

The next month, a man in the nearby community of La Mesa reported to police that his son had seen a suspicious man emerging from some bushes. When asked what he was doing, the man replied that he was looking for his lighter. The boy did not believe him and told his father. They copied the license number

Figure 4.7 Murder weapon and lubricant. The murder weapon was brought to the scene of the crime and, afterward, released back to its owner. This was a not uncommon practice, perhaps depriving cold case investigators in some instances the chance to apply advanced technology. (Courtesy of Anderson/ECPD.)

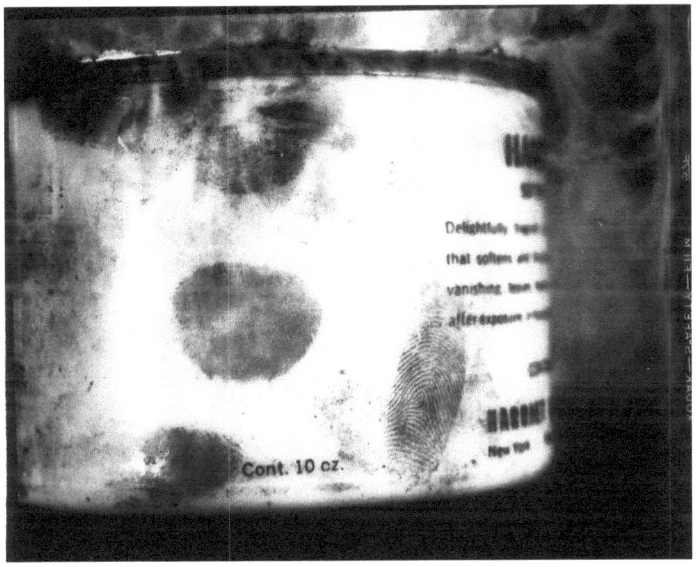

Figure 4.8 Cold cream container. Although latent prints were observed on the jar, it was broken when crushed in a vise being used to hold it. (Courtesy of Anderson/ECPD.)

from the man's red Triumph and called the police. Not long after, a similar-looking man was seen near a red Triumph in La Mesa outside the apartment of a 23-year-old nurse. Before dawn, the nurse heard noises within her apartment and dialed the operator. The suspect broke into her apartment and attempted to rape and murder her. As she fought him off, the operator heard the fight and called the police, but the suspect was gone on arrival. Based on the boy's observation and witness information regarding the red Triumph, Clyde Wilkerson, a recently released parolee, was brought in for questioning.

Wilkerson was arrested and charged for this crime after the victim positively identified him as her assailant. Although questioned in the two homicides and rapes, there was no evidence to link him to these crimes. He was convicted on the La Mesa offense in November 1965, and sentenced to five years to life in prison (Figure 4.9). He subsequently was paroled to Oklahoma in 1973.

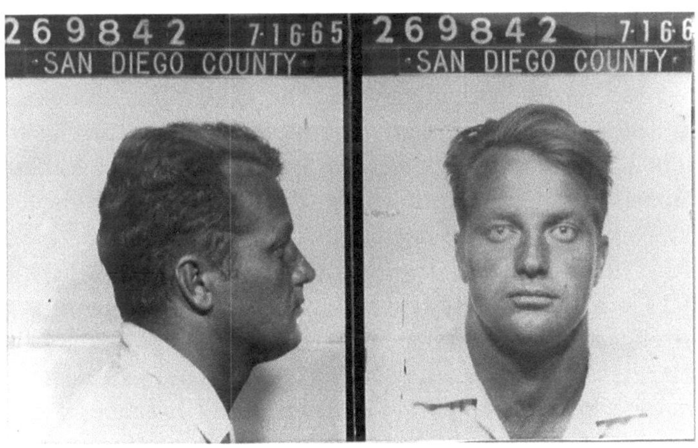

Figure 4.9 Serial killer Clyde Wilkerson after his 1965 arrest for rape. Authorities could not link him to the homicides and rapes at that time. Only the advent of DNA and the tenacity of determined investigators allowed this case to be solved. (Courtesy of Anderson/ECPD.)

In the meantime, the homicide cases remained unsolved.

In 1997, El Cajon Police Department (ECPD) Lieutenant Pat Sprecco began to assign some of the older, unsolved crimes to investigators. He believed that advanced forensic technology might assist in resolving some of these crimes. In January 1999, Detective Jon Wooddell received the homicide case of the young mother. Sometime after, Detective Robert Anderson observed a box of news clippings about the case of the older couple and began reading them. Neither case file contained a *death certificate* for the victims (see Chapter 10). Their reviews of the cases, however, had to be accomplished while carrying their normal caseload and other assigned duties. While each began working his respective case separately, they soon had reason to believe their cases might be connected. During their review of the evidence, they found that items were comingled between the two cases, suggesting that earlier detectives had considered them linked. Wilkerson was the apparent linchpin.

During this review, they encountered a situation not uncommon in cold case investigation. Although items were individually tagged and bagged, some from one case were mixed with the other case. Loose reports, photographs, correspondence, and other material were dumped into boxes, and there was no apparent chain of custody. Some pages of some reports were lost and never found. During this process, Anderson contacted other agencies mentioned in the reports to ascertain if they possessed related documents (Figure 2.8). The district attorney's office still retained reports, as did the Probation Department. In addition, the California Department of Justice retained important documents and reports.

The detectives began by putting everything on a table and sorting the two cases. In this process, they began to reassemble the record *chronologically*. As they reviewed the reports, they observed a lack of uniformity in reporting. Reports were handwritten or typed (misspellings not infrequent), and there was a noticeable lack of identifying information to be used in their efforts to relocate persons. Thermofax paper documents were fading badly, and onionskin carbon paper documents were fragile to handle. In addition, certain report entries were not politically correct by today's standards, with detectives' opinions freely inserted into the reports. In those days, suspects were not "alleged." Like the photos, the case was black and white to some earlier investigators, but the focus ultimately shifted with the later investigation.

The *photo review* similarly showed investigative actions far different from today. Officers handled crime scene evidence without gloves (Figure 3.6), or stood in the middle of the crime scene smoking a cigarette while the picture was taken. The photos were generally more overall than specific in nature. Similarly, crime scene sketches and diagrams were lacking by today's standards (Figure 4.10). The sketches showed no measurements or other detail but, for the present, did provide an overview of the scene as encountered by responding investigators.

During the course of their review and investigation to locate persons and documents, Anderson discovered that *city engineers* had subsequently diagramed the scene. These drawings had been entered into evidence (Figure 3.5). Thus, the investigators recovered more detailed drawings to supplement the photo record, and which could be used to more accurately reconstruct the scene. Although they were unable to locate the engineer who actually drew the diagrams, they did locate his supervisor, who was able to *authenticate* the period work as a course-of-business document.

An additional record of the crime and investigation was discovered when Wooddell contacted the media and discovered that a local television station still retained film footage from broadcasts of the period. As this was previously aired material, the station converted the footage to a videotape and furnished it to the investigators. A similar review of the newspapers was conducted by Anderson. Microfilm copies were located, and many hours were spent in the library reviewing old newspaper reports, in an effort to identify overlooked witnesses and information, as well as to learn what was in the public domain. Some of the newspaper reports provided better witness identification than did the police reports, as reporters interviewed neighbors and reported in the detail of the period, not unlike today. These were copied and placed in the file.

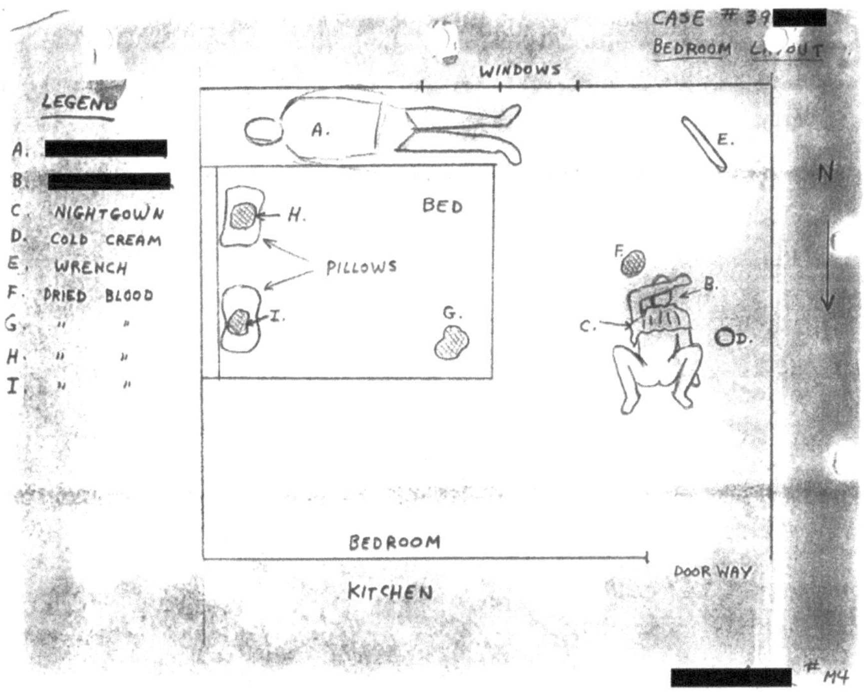

Figure 4.10 Crime scene sketch. Like other sketches of the period, no measurements were included on the sketch. This sketch, when combined with the minimal amount of photographs, does depict the crime scene. (Courtesy of Anderson/ECPD.)

The investigators continued to search for original persons who figured in the initial investigations. They located and brought on board *original detectives*, who were elated at the reinvestigation of their original, unsolved cases. Among those contacted was one detective who had interviewed Clyde Wilkerson in 1965. In addition, they located the boy who had observed Wilkerson emerge from the bushes, a grown man now living in his father's same house as in 1965.

Like other smaller agencies, the El Cajon department utilized the San Diego County Sheriff's Department crime laboratory to conduct forensic examinations. Very early in the investigation, the detectives consulted with a DNA specialist in the sheriff's crime lab, criminalist Connie Milton. Anderson was interested in DNA recovered from his crime scene. He had read the reports that earlier detectives suspected Clyde Wilkerson, and wanted to locate him to obtain a sample of his DNA. At this stage of the investigation, the two detectives were in constant contact yet handled aspects of their own investigations independently as time allowed.

Review of the remaining case file indicated that period investigators had suspected family members of the couple, and reports indicated that polygraph examinations had been utilized to clear them (the actual polygraph reports were not found in the file). The polygraph examinations had been administered by police officers and not by State Department of Justice personnel, as was often the case during this time period for smaller agencies. Similarly, the polygraph was mentioned as being used in the young mother's case, but further documentation was again lacking.

In Wooddell's investigation, events were a bit more complicated. During the course of file review and investigation, cold case investigators seek to develop as much information on the victim as they can and to learn more through the *victimology*. They attempt to identify anything the victim may have done that contributed to his/her victimization, and subsequently, to the identification of the perpetrator. While the more elderly couple's case was an apparent whodunit, the family was fully cooperative in the investigation. In Wooddell's case, the cooperation was less. The little boy found wandering outside the crime scene was now an ex-con and, when located, did not want anything to do with police nor the investigation. "Let it be," he told investigators.

In addition, Wooddell's investigation revealed that some earlier detectives had a different prime suspect, a Catholic priest. Apparently, the young mother was being tutored in catechism. The priest, an alcoholic, had made comments to various persons in the bars he frequented that he was responsible for her death. When word of this reached period detectives, they began to focus on him as a suspect. "Responsible" equated in some minds to "I killed her." The earlier detectives tried relentlessly to pursue the church representative, without success. He repeatedly denied that he killed her, and ultimately, the church transferred the priest to another locale outside the easy reach of local law enforcement. The man died in 1972, and the question remained for cold case investigators decades later—was he the guilty person? There was one way to find out: DNA.

A *forensic exhumation* is a legal process to disinter a body, and this process is presented in future chapters (see Chapter 22). Early in the investigation, the investigators had involved Deputy District Attorney Dan Lamborn in their investigation effort. Detective Wooddell sought a court order to exhume the body, and this was accomplished. DNA *excluded*, once and for all, the priest as a source of the DNA in the victim. In addition, it was also necessary to disinter the other victims as well, and permission was granted by family members in lieu of court action. As in similar cases, there were other suspects, and these were tracked down and tested, with negative results. Slowly, everyone was eliminated except for Clyde Wilkerson.

Wilkerson was a career criminal, one we now recognize as a serial killer. He had a lengthy rap sheet, and the only time he was not committing crimes was when he was in custody for previous offenses. A long-distance truck driver, Wilkerson's livelihood took him all around the nation, and to this day, there is no way of knowing how many other murders he is responsible for (see Chapter 7, "Highway Serial Killings Initiative"). He was arrested in Oklahoma in 1973 on suspicion of robbery, although charges were later dropped, and, in April 1976, convicted and sentenced for rape in Arkansas. After serving seven years in prison, he was paroled in 1983. In June 1985, he was arrested in Texas on suspicion of aggravated assault and, in March 1987, convicted of selling a controlled substance in Florida and sentenced to three years in prison, including time for violating parole.

As he began to focus on Wilkerson, Anderson formulated a *timeline* to assist in the investigation (Figure 4.11).

Timelines, Linkages, and Visual Investigative Analysis Charts

A useful and valuable tool in many situations, a timeline is an asset in homicide cases, perhaps even more so in cold case homicide investigations. These cases often involve developing, and understanding, an abundance of dates, times, events, places, and more. In a hot homicide scenario, investigators develop the information firsthand and absorb it as it happens. In a cold case investigation, the information is contained not only in the often volumes of reports and other files but also in the development of the investigation. Timelines and visual investigative analysis (VIA) charts can show the linkages, time flows, and relationships between people, places, and events, and aid in the visual informational reconstruction. They can take an apparent unconnected series of events and graphically illustrate a clear visual picture of the entire case, relating apparently unrelated events and activities. Such aids can illuminate an individual's presence, or motive. This method can highlight missing details and information and show investigators where to focus their efforts to fill these gaps. They can help reduce duplication of effort and increase investigative efficiency. In addition, they are highly effective for prosecutor and court presentations.

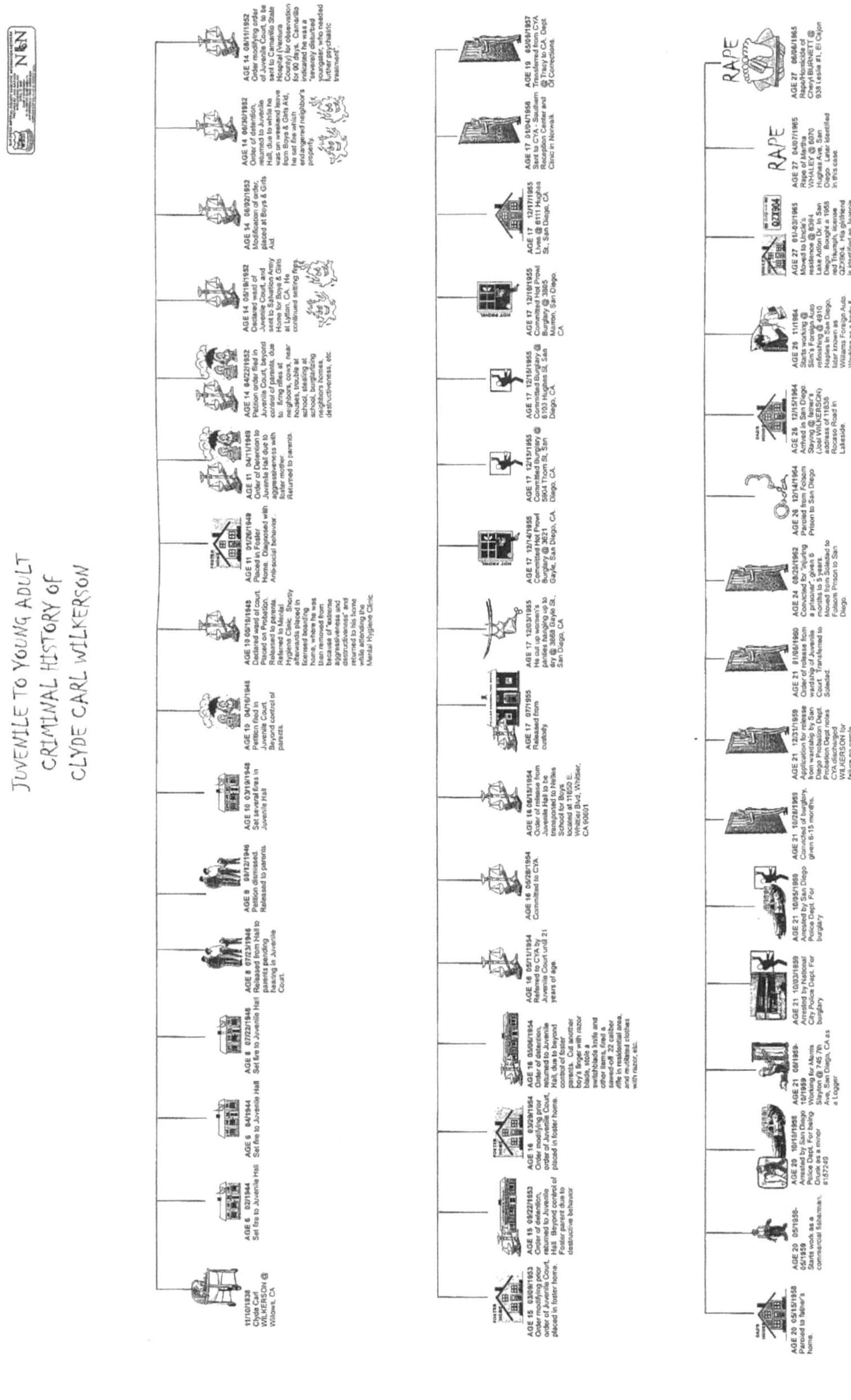

Figure 4.11 Clyde Wilkerson timeline. Timelines are an invaluable tool for investigators, prosecutors, *and* juries. They illustrate, and illuminate, more than words can say. (Courtesy of FBI.)

The concept of VIA reportedly was originated in the mid-1960s by the Los Angeles Police Department, the source of many advanced law enforcement concepts and techniques. This notion evolved from previous approaches, the critical path method (CPM) and the program evaluation and review techniques (PERTs). The VIA idea was picked up by the California Department of Justice and the Federal Law Enforcement Training Center at Glynco, Georgia, and has now become a standard investigative tool. VIA methods involving the concept of networking were first incorporated in a major criminal investigation as a result of the Robert Kennedy assassination in 1968, and in the early 1970s in the still-unsolved Zodiac killings of the late 1960s and early 1970s.

Timelines may be especially useful in understanding victim and suspect movements and how they converge.

The ability to construct useful timelines has been enhanced greatly by computers. What was once done on legal pads or rolls of butcher paper—and found in older cold case files—is now accomplished on desktop computer software (Figure 4.12). The sources of information for detailed time and date entries can include

- Law enforcement reports
- Booking sheets
- Witness statements
- Probation and parole documents
- Rap sheets
- Telephone and cell phone records
- Residence locations
- Employment records
- Trip logs

Figure 4.12 Clue management program. The Los Angeles County Sheriff's Department provides free software to law enforcement agencies to assist in clue management. This program is well suited to cold case homicide investigations as well as task force investigations or single-crime/investigator investigations and may be configured for multiple-input computers or a stand-alone desktop. (Courtesy of Detective Gerry Biehn, Los Angeles County Sheriff Unsolved Unit.)

- In-custody records
- Public utility records
- Traffic/parking tickets
- Driver's license
- Department of Motor Vehicles registrations and related documents
- Receipts (motel, gas, grocery etc.)
- Suspect statements
- Diaries, notes, and journals
- Accomplice and informant information

As the detectives discovered, Wilkerson began his life of crime at an early age, displaying behavior that later criminal profilers would come to identify as not uncommon among violent predators. This included setting fires and mutilating animals. Much of his teen years were spent in juvenile reformatories and foster homes. Every event and every known movement were now being compiled into a timeline that chronicled the life and movements of Clyde Wilkerson. Overviews provided investigators with a profile of his life, and specific timelines such as monthly trucking route, broken down by date, time, and location, were compiled (Figure 4.13).

As his profile developed, Anderson sought interstate assistance from the San Diego office of the FBI. The FBI and U.S. Marshals Service are excellent cold case homicide investigative resources, and team members often sit on agency or regional cold case task forces.

TEXAS

Date	Time	Location-City	State	Date	Time	Location-City	State
09/03/99	21:36:00	Waxzahachie	TX	12/05/99	5:38:00	Horizon Cy	TX
09/03/99	22:32:00	Waxahachie	TX	12/05/99	10:11:00	Saragosa	TX
09/03/99	22:40:00	Red Oak	TX	12/05/99	15:02:00	Ingram	TX
09/14/99	5:10:00	Horizon Cy	TX	12/06/99	5:21:00	Kirby	TX
09/14/99	10:36:00	Van Horn	TX	12/06/99	7:33:00	San Antonio	TX
09/14/99	15:44:00	Sweetwater	TX	12/06/99	10:48:00	Kirby	TX
09/15/99	0:11:00	Weatherford	TX	12/06/99	15:35:00	San Antonio	TX
09/15/99	1:19:00	Blue Mound	TX	12/06/99	15:56:00	Kirby	TX
09/15/99	7:53:00	Ft Worth	TX	12/06/99	19:18:00	San Antonio	TX
09/15/99	9:03:00	Ft Worth	TX	12/06/99	19:46:00	Kirby	TX
09/15/99	11:35:00	Rockwall	TX	12/07/99	5:58:00	Sealy	TX
09/20/99	15:30:00	Cumby	TX	12/07/99	9:44:00	Hilshire V	TX
09/20/99	19:33:00	Rockwall	TX	12/07/99	10:46:00	Houston	TX
09/21/99	7:14:00	Irving	TX	12/08/99	5:21:00	Marshall	TX
09/21/99	13:18:00	Irving	TX	12/10/99	5:16:00	Amarillo	TX
09/21/99	13:33:00	Mesquite	TX	12/17/99	5:50:00	Carthage	TX
09/21/99	15:06:00	Rockwall	TX	12/17/99	7:34:00	Burke	TX
09/21/99	15:27:00	CadoMills	TX	12/17/99	9:47:00	Hillshire V	TX
10/08/99	10:28:00	Alanreed	TX	12/17/99	16:45:00	Houston	TX
10/16/99	7:23:00	Post	TX	12/17/99	16:47:00	Hilshire V	TX
10/16/99	9:11:00	Hermleigh	TX	12/17/99	17:49:00	Jacinto Cy	TX
10/16/99	15:13:00	Elgin	TX	01/16/00	5:41:00	Amarillo	TX
10/17/99	10:16:00	Houston	TX	03/09/00	10:01:00	Tyler	TX
10/18/99	10:00:00	Heights	TX	03/09/00	11:27:00	Tyler	TX
10/18/99	11:24:00	Houston	TX	03/09/00	15:56:00	Strawn	TX
10/18/99	13:49:00	Cheek	TX	03/10/00	5:52:00	Pecos	TX
11/07/99	0:00:00	Amarillo	TX	03/10/00	8:47:00	Van Horn	TX
				03/10/00	10:56:00	Horizon Cy	TX

Figure 4.13 Timeline. Timelines are constructed from multiple sources of information and may portray a period of one day to weeks to months or years and decades. (Courtesy of El Cajon Police Department.)

Locating suspects can sometimes be difficult, at other times relatively easy. Based upon case file information for suspected places he might reside, Anderson conducted a driver's license search of various states where Wilkerson might be licensed—if he was still alive. When they located him, he was 62 years old and living in Arkansas.

Investigation revealed that Wilkerson had long been employed as an Arkansas-based truck driver. Anderson obtained a court order for employment records and, with FBI assistance, obtained Wilkerson's employment application and route invoices. The Arkansas agent inquired whether the company still retained any envelopes in which Wilkerson had mailed their invoices. They did.

Anderson conducted a further background check on Wilkerson, one that sought to determine any *relationships* that may now yield information about the crimes. Anderson located and interviewed the officers who had interviewed Wilkerson's Oklahoma rape victim, but when he attempted to interview a relative of Wilkerson, the door was slammed in his face.

Chain-of-custody documentation and collection protocols have evolved significantly over the past decades, and while reviewing the evidence, Detective Anderson had discovered a thermos bottle that they suspected contained original cotton swabs. Unopened, for fear of contaminating any potential evidence, the thermos was sent to the FBI lab. Like many investigations nationwide, the events of 9/11 impacted many facets of police work and changed the priorities for FBI operations. This investigation was no different, and ultimately, the thermos was returned unopened. Wooddell recontacted criminalist Milton.

When reviewing the original forensic reports, Milton had not suspected any usable evidence to remain. The method used in rape examinations during the time period of the crimes was no longer even a part of a modern sexual assault examination. She considered that, for lack of another container, an examining physician had emptied his thermos and stored evidence in it. It was not the usual evidence container, even then.

Inside the thermos were glass vials containing cotton swabs and a dried residue (Figure 4.14). Examination revealed the presence of sperm, but the source of the sperm was unknown. After more than 30 years, Connie Milton extracted and typed the DNA. Although Wilkerson had been questioned after both rapes and murders, there had not been enough evidence to link him to the crime scenes at the time.

Criminalist Milton had previously processed the semen evidence found on the bedsheet collected at the scene from where the young mother was raped and murdered. On a Saturday afternoon, she made the match. She now had the DNA from the trucking company envelopes as well as from the murder of the couple and the young mother. Clyde Wilkerson was the common denominator among the samples from the victims as well as the trucking company envelopes.

The case had taken over 37 years to reach this point. Technology had now enabled law enforcement to make an identification from sources almost a nation, and decades, apart. It had taken three years to complete the reinvestigation, one complicated by a process of eliminating numerous other potential suspects as the focus narrowed on Wilkerson.

Not unheard of in cold cases, Anderson and Wooddell were only a couple of years old at the time of the crime, and those who collected the evidence decades before were now quite elderly or deceased. This case was no different in that regard. Milton had not even been born when the murders occurred. Her skills, however, now identified Wilkerson's DNA print as having been at both crime scenes. The frequency of occurrence of this DNA profile for Caucasian males was now estimated at 1 in 57 quadrillion.

An arrest warrant was obtained, and the detectives, Deputy District Attorney Lamborn, District Attorney Investigator Steve Baker, and the San Diego–based FBI agent traveled to Benton, Arkansas. With the cooperation of local authorities, Wilkerson was arrested without incident on his rural property on October 29, 2002. Time had not improved his social behavior, however, and arresting officers discovered a small methamphetamine lab when he was taken into custody (Figures 4.15 and 4.16).

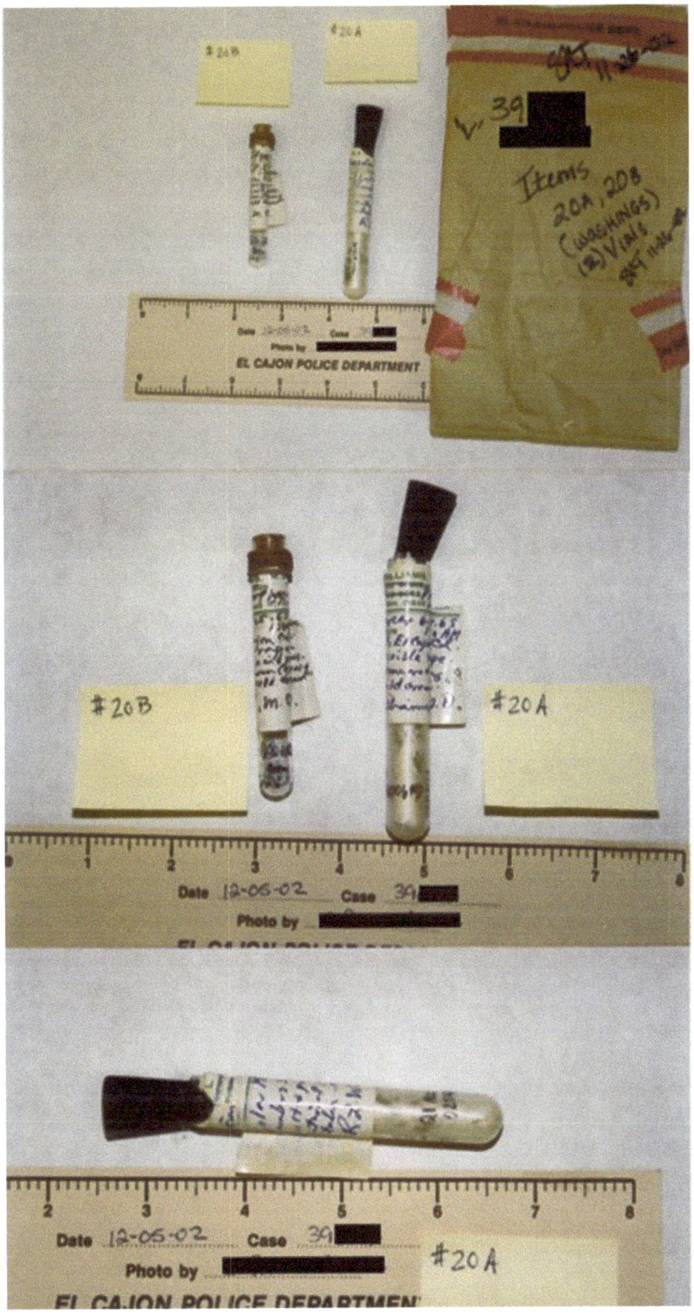

Figure 4.14 These 1965 vials containing cotton swabs were recovered in a coffee thermos that had been used to contain them for over 30 years. Criminalist Connie Milton was able to extract and type DNA, closing the forensic net on serial killer Clyde Wilkerson. (Courtesy of Anderson/ECPD.)

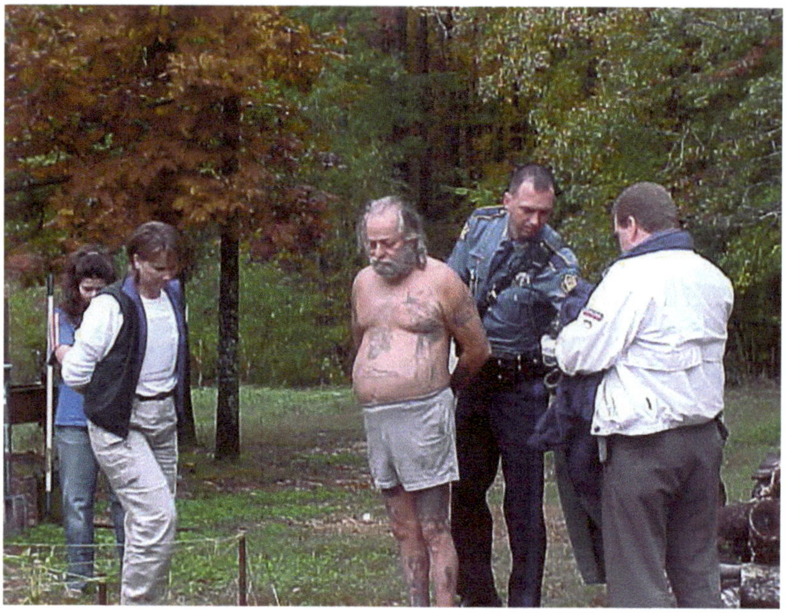

Figure 4.15 Clyde Wilkerson at his arrest. Thanks to the efforts of detectives, prosecutors, and criminalists, a serial killer's decades-long rampage came to an end. Wilkerson was arrested and subsequently pled guilty to one 1965 California murder as well as a 1975 Oklahoma murder. The investigation into his activities has continued. (Courtesy of El Cajon Police Department.)

Figure 4.16 Low-budget meth lab. Officers recovered this setup at the time of Wilkerson's arrest. (Courtesy of Anderson ECPD.)

Postarrest Interview

In cold cases, investigators have the advantage of being able to compile background history on an identified suspect and to study all aspects of the crime. As have other cold case killers, Wilkerson claimed no memory of the events, admitting that *if* he had committed these vicious crimes, he would surely have remembered. "If you get arrested, you remember it. If you don't get arrested, you don't," he said. As far as any other crimes, he told them that they would have to prove that on their own, and he stopped talking.

During the arrest period, identification and interview of those who know the suspect is a suggested tactic. At the time of Wilkerson's arrest, District Attorney Investigator Steve Baker interviewed a tenant who resided on Wilkerson's property. On his own, the tenant then contacted Wilkerson in jail. He asked Wilkerson if he had committed the crimes. "Yeah, but it took 'em 37 years to catch me," the tenant later reported his landlord had said.

Wilkerson was returned to San Diego. On March 17, 2003, almost 40 years after his crime spree, Clyde Carl Wilkerson pled guilty in a plea agreement to the murder of the husband and rape against his wife. Under the law *at the time of the murder* in 1965, Wilkerson could only be sentenced to seven years to life in prison. The other charges were not pursued, as he would receive no additional prison time and would most likely die in prison for this offense.

Continuing the Investigation—The Internet

The investigation into Wilkerson's decades-long crime spree did not end with his arrest and return to San Diego. Detective Robert Anderson believed that Wilkerson was responsible for more murders, and set out to identify other unsolved cases that fit Wilkerson's MO when he was not in custody. Such is the mark of a true detective. Wilkerson was already suspect in another unsolved San Diego homicide from July 1965 as well as a 1954 Los Angeles–area murder and attempted murder.

On his own time, from his home computer, Detective Anderson began to search the Internet and the web pages of law enforcement agencies and unsolved homicides. He discovered that the Tulsa, Oklahoma, Police Department had an unsolved rape–homicide of a junior college student from February 1975. The victim had been abducted from the parking lot of her downtown campus, and her body was found three weeks later in a vacant apartment. She had been raped and strangled. The victim suffered numerous facial injuries due to blunt force trauma, and both nipples and areolas had been amputated postmortem, with one of each inserted into her vagina. The official cause of death was ligature strangulation. The victim's clothes, jewelry, purse, checkbook, and other identification were missing. A day after the victim was reported missing, a white male cashed one of her checks and attempted to use one of her credit cards in the Tulsa area. Evidence seized from the crime scene provided a DNA profile of the offender.

Anderson contacted the Oklahoma agency, and as a result of his diligence and tenacity, the authorities there reopened their unsolved case. DNA linked Wilkerson to this crime, and on April 28, 2004, Clyde Carl Wilkerson pled guilty to the Oklahoma crime and was sentenced to life in prison. His prison time was to run concurrently with his California sentence. Under the California law at the time of the offense, Wilkerson was eligible for parole after 6 years, and after 20 years in Oklahoma. He died in custody on July 12, 2016.

Due to the serious crimes and his interstate movements, Wilkerson was the subject of a Violent Criminal Apprehension Program (ViCAP) Alert in the *FBI Law Enforcement Bulletin* in August 2003. This notice to the nation's law enforcement community detailed events of his numerous crimes, including method of operation, personal identifying information, known vehicles, and evidence. It was disseminated to alert law enforcement to Wilkerson's existence so that local agencies could review any unsolved homicides or other crimes in light of what was now known about him (Figure 4.17).

The ViCAP Alert provided additional detail regarding Wilkerson's MO, and further information may be obtained from the FBI's ViCAP. Wilkerson's DNA profile has been entered into CODIS.

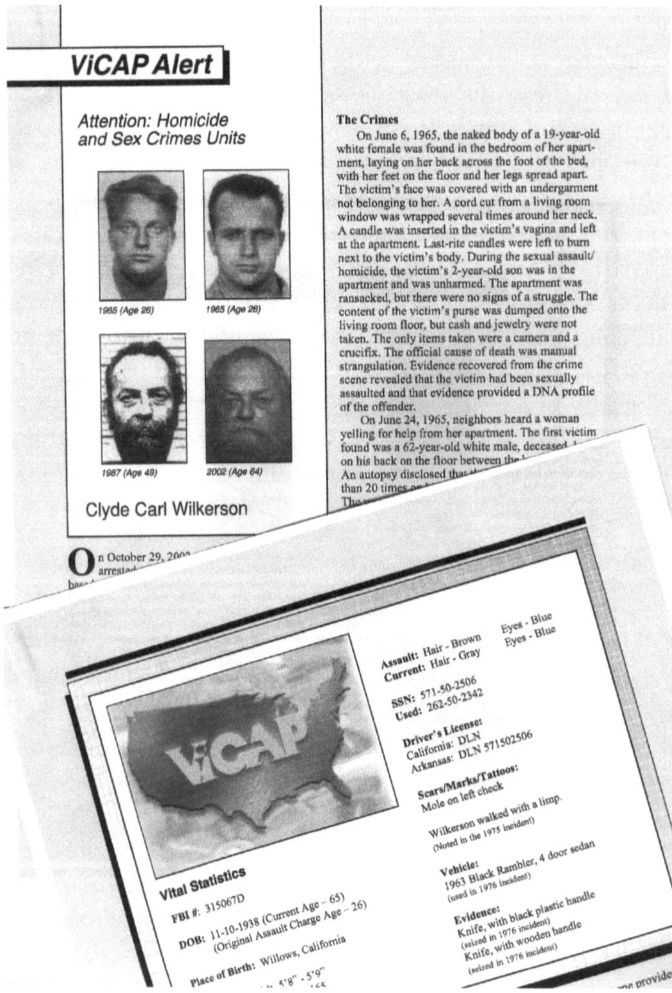
ViCAP Alert

Attention: Homicide and Sex Crimes Units

1965 (Age 26) 1965 (Age 26)

1987 (Age 49) 2002 (Age 64)

Clyde Carl Wilkerson

On October 29, 200…

The Crimes

On June 6, 1965, the naked body of a 19-year-old white female was found in the bedroom of her apartment, laying on her back across the foot of the bed, with her feet on the floor and her legs spread apart. The victim's face was covered with an undergarment not belonging to her. A cord cut from a living room window was wrapped several times around her neck. A candle was inserted in the victim's vagina and left at the apartment. Last-rite candles were left to burn next to the victim's body. During the sexual assault/homicide, the victim's 2-year-old son was in the apartment and was unharmed. The apartment was ransacked, but there were no signs of a struggle. The content of the victim's purse was dumped onto the living room floor, but cash and jewelry were not taken. The only items taken were a camera and a crucifix. The official cause of death was manual strangulation. Evidence recovered from the crime scene revealed that the victim had been sexually assaulted and that evidence provided a DNA profile of the offender.

On June 24, 1965, neighbors heard a woman yelling for help from her apartment. The first victim found was a 62-year-old white male, deceased … on his back on the floor between the … An autopsy disclosed that … than 20 times …

ViCAP

Assault: Hair - Brown Eyes - Blue
Current: Hair - Gray Eyes - Blue

SSN: 571-50-2506
Used: 262-50-2342

Driver's License:
California: DLN
Arkansas: DLN 571502506

Scars/Marks/Tattoos:
Mole on left cheek

Wilkerson walked with a limp.
(Noted in the 1975 incident)

Vehicle:
1963 Black Rambler, 4 door sedan
(used in 1976 incident)

Evidence:
Knife, with black plastic handle
(seized in 1976 incident)
Knife, with wooden handle
(seized in 1976 incident)

Vital Statistics

FBI #: 315067D

DOB: 11-10-1938 (Current Age - 65)
(Original Assault Charge Age - 26)

Place of Birth: Willows, California

Figure 4.17 ViCAP Alert for Clyde Carl Wilkerson. Wilkerson is a poster child for the need of this agency and similar state programs. The more law enforcement learns about people like this, and communicates this knowledge, the better the chances that killers such as Wilkerson will be identified and removed from society. (Picture from author's file from ViCAP Alert in *FBI Law Enforcement Bulletin*.)

Conclusion

The means and methods of cold case homicide investigation are based upon the crime, evidence, original investigation, and subsequent events. Each cold case must be weighed and evaluated on its own merits. *How to* proceed is based upon the experience, training, and best investigative plan as conceived by the investigator or investigative team. Different cases call for different tactics, and there can be no one best way. The investigation of these cases exploits the advantage of time as revealed through changes in relationships and changes in technology. Various tools are at the disposal of the cold case investigator, and the combination of these factors has allowed some cold cases to be solved. Not all will be solved, however, and many will be reshelved as unsolved, cold case homicides.

Figure 4.18 illustrates a checklist provided by the FBI ViCAP.

A Field Investigative Checklist
For Cold Case Homicides

KEY ELEMENTS

- ✓ **Get to know the case intimately**
- ✓ **Avoid tunnel vision on motive, theory of the case, or suspects**
- ✓ **Do not rule out a suspect based strictly on polygraph results**
- ✓ **Cold cases may be solvable, even without DNA/forensic evidence**

PROCESS

- ✓ **Locate, organize and read all case materials**
  - Case file, audio, video
  - Investigative notes
  - Witness and suspect statements
  - Crime scene photographs/diagrams
  - Autopsy report/autopsy photographs
  - Toxicology report
  - Laboratory reports
  - Neighborhood/roadblock canvass
- ✓ **Convert case file to electronic format (if possible)**
- ✓ **Identify all forensic evidence and lab reports**
  - Scrutinize reports, verify samples were compared against databases
  - Identify available/viable samples for testing or re-testing
  - DNA (does it qualify under current standards)
  - IAFIS
  - DHS US-VISIT
  - NIBIN
  - Electronic (cell phones, computers, GPS, social media)
- ✓ **Compile investigative timeline and case synopsis**
  - Identify any distinctive/unique *modus operandi*
  - Assess if the scene can be re-visited
  - Identify vehicles involved in the case
  - Consider possible motives
  - Identify area demographics at time of the offense
  - Consider crime rates at the time of the offense
  - Identify any similar crimes in the area
- ✓ **Complete a thorough victimology**
  - Physical characteristics
  - Lifestyle/Occupation/Hobbies
  - Victim timeline prior to incident
  - Friends, family, co-workers
  - Prior victimization
  - Risk level
- ✓ **Complete a biography sheet on all subjects associated with case**
  - Suspect(s) originally identified/developed
  - Relationship to victim
  - Run criminal history checks, financial/credit reports
  - Current location
  - Vehicle descriptions/tag information
  - Lifestyle changes
- ✓ **Identify persons to interview and questions to ask**
  - Reconstruct and re-canvass neighborhood at the time of the offense
  - Identify and locate witnesses
  - Determine if any witnesses can identify suspect
  - Identify which questions were asked in interviews conducted by original investigators
  - Identify follow-up questions that were not asked and individuals not interviewed in original investigation
- ✓ **Obtain preliminary prosecutorial opinion**
- ✓ **Conduct re-interviews**
  - Interview original case investigators
  - Interview victim's family and friends
  - Relationships change over time; this is an advantage for cold cases: Re-interview former wives, girlfriends, associates, alibis of suspects
  - Re-interview key witnesses
- ✓ **Assess media coverage**
  - Determine extent of media attention on case
  - Identify sensitive information already released
  - Consider public/media assistance value
  - Establish and monitor a cold case tip line and/or website

INVESTIGATIVE RESOURCES

FBI's National Center for the Analysis of Violent Crime (NCAVC) Behavioral Analysis Units (BAUs):

BAU-2: Crimes Against Adults/BAU-3: Crimes Against Children

- Criminal Investigative Analysis, Crime Scene Assessment, Interview/Investigative/Media/ Prosecutorial Strategies, Unknown Offender Profile, Search Warrant Assistance, etc.

BAU-4: ViCAP

- Crime Analysis, Similar Case Searches (ViCAP Web, NLETS, etc.), NCIC Off-lines, Victim/Subject Timelines, Crime Mapping, ViCAP Alerts, etc.

For further information or to discuss your case please contact: NCAVC BAU
FBI Academy
Quantico, VA 22135
703-632-4400

For Law Enforcement Use Only Revised 03/01/12

Figure 4.18 FBI cold case homicide investigation checklist. (Courtesy of FBI/ViCAP.)

Acknowledgments

I wish to express my deepest gratitude and appreciation to Captain Joseph Hartshorne and the late Sgt. Richard Longshore of the Los Angeles County Sheriff's Department as well as Officer in Charge Tim Marcia and Detective Rick Jackson (ret'd) of the Cold Case Unit of the Robbery–Homicide Division of the Los Angeles Police Department for sharing their thoughts, experiences, and suggestions for this chapter. In addition, I wish to also recognize and extend my deepest gratitude to former Texas Ranger Lt. Tony Leal for sharing his thoughts and perspectives on cold case homicide investigation.

The investigation of Clyde Wilkerson by Detectives Anderson and Wooddell exemplifies the highest abilities of cold case investigators. Their teamwork with Criminalist Connie Milton, Deputy District Attorney Dan Lamborn, the FBI, and others exemplify the results of team effort applied to cold case investigation. In addition, I wish to acknowledge the leadership of the El Cajon Police Department for their proactive efforts in identifying and reinvestigating unsolved, cold case homicides.

The case history was compiled by extensive interviews with Detectives Anderson and Wooddell and Criminalist Milton, and review of case records. In addition, I wish to acknowledge Paul Levikov of the San Diego County District Attorney's Office and his report "How a Thermos Helped Catch a Killer" in the Winter–Spring 2003–2004 edition of *Law Enforcement Quarterly.*

Suggested Readings and Bibliography

Adcock, J. and Stein, S. (2014). *Cold Cases: Evaluation Models with Follow-Up Strategies for Investigators.* Boca Raton, FL. CRC Press.

Anonymous. (2002). Cold Case Homicide. C.P.T. Network. Sacramento, California Commission on Peace Officer Standards and Training.

Anonymous. (2003). ViCAP Alert. *FBI Law Enforcement Bulletin* (August), V72, N8, p. 17.

DiBiase, T.A. (2014). *No-Body Homicide Cases: A Practical Guide to Investigating, Prosecuting, and Winning Cases When the Victim Is Missing.* Boca Raton, FL. CRC Press.

Eliopulos, L.N. (2003). *Death Investigator's Handbook: Expanded and Updated Edition.* Boulder, CO. Paladin Press.

Geberth, V. (1996). *Practical Homicide Investigation: Tactics, Procedures, and Forensic Techniques.* (Third Edition). New York. CRC Press.

IACP Center for Social Media. International Association of Chiefs of Police. http://www.iacpsocialmedia.org/Topics/Parent.aspx?termid=95&depth=2. Retrieved May 24, 2016.

Jackson, I.M. (2002). 1965 Crime spree may be solved. (October 30). *San Diego Union.* A1,9.

Jackson, I.M. (2003). Plea is guilty in '65 rape, murder. (March 18). *San Diego Union.* B3.

Johnson, R.S. (1995). *How to Locate Anyone Who Is or Has Been in the Military.* San Antonio, Texas. MIE Publishing.

Keel, T. (2008) *Homicide Investigations: Identifying Best Practices.* FBI Law Enforcement Bulletin. Superintendent of Documents, Washington, DC.

Lee, H.C., Palmbach, T., and Miller, M. (2001). *Henry Lee's Crime Scene Handbook.* New York. Academic Press.

Levikow, P. Special Report: How a Thermos Helped Catch a Killer. *Law Enforcement Quarterly.* (Winter 2003–2004). San Diego District Attorney. San Diego, CA.

LexisNexis® Risk Solutions. (2014). [Survey of Law Enforcement Personnel and Their Use of Social Media]. http://www.lexisnexis.com/investigations. Retrieved May 23, 2016.

Newcombe, B. (1990). *Paper Trails: A Guide to Public Records in California.* Oakland, CA. Center for Investigative Reporting, California Newspaper Publisher's Association.

Nyberg, R. (2004). Justice Served Cold. Police. *The Law Enforcement Magazine* (October). V28, N10, p. 44.

Pettry, M.T. (December 2014). *Social Media: Legal Challenges and Pitfalls for Law Enforcement Agencies.* FBI Law Enforcement Bulletin. http://Leb.fbi.gov/2014/December-legal-digest-social-media-legal-challenges-and-pitfalls. Retrieved May 23, 2016.

Poole, H. and Jurovics, S. (1993). "MUST: A Team for Unsolved Homicides." *FBI Law Enforcement Bulletin.* (March 1993). V62, N3. Federal Bureau of Investigation. Washington, DC.

Ray, D. (1995). *California Investigator's Handbook: A Public Records Primer.* (6th Edition). Burbank, CA. ENG Press.

Spraggs, D. (2003). How to open a cold case. *Policemag.com* (May).

Turner, R. and Kosa, R. (2003). *Cold Case Squads: Leaving No Stone Unturned* (July). Bulletin NCJ 199781. Washington, DC. Bureau of Justice Assistance.

Westvear, A. (unknown). *Death Investigation.* Federal Bureau of Investigation. Washington, DC.

Long-Term Missing-Persons and No-Body Cold Case Investigations 5

TAD DIBIASE
R. H. WALTON

Contents

Criminal homicide investigations generally begin with the response of officers to the finding of a body and a crime scene. From this, investigators develop leads, evidence, and cases, identifying and interviewing witnesses and others. Notes, reports, sketches, and photographs become the case file. Due to the severity of criminal homicide/murder, most agencies traditionally spared little expense to solve the case. Similarly, reports of missing persons begin in much the same way, but given exigent circumstances such as large-scale publicity or public status of the missing person, large-scale devotion of agency resources and investigative follow-through has often been minimal, or lacking.

When investigators identified a perpetrator in a homicide and compiled the evidence that allowed prosecutors to file appropriate criminal charges, the police agency moved the case status from *open* to *closed* in their records. If they were unable to do so, the case remained open and *unsolved*. As new cases and department priorities shifted, these unsolved cases became cold case homicides with little, if any, proactive effort. Similarly, missing-persons cases were handled in much the same way but often in a much-abbreviated form. This has been the traditional paradigm.

Sometimes, however, there is no body. Indeed, there is no evidence that a criminal homicide has occurred. The person has just disappeared. In decades past, such circumstances did not necessarily attract much departmental interest or effort, especially with missing adults. This was evidenced by only minimal documentation and little if any follow-up investigative effort. As a young new officer in the late 1960s, one of the authors observed that, not uncommonly, agencies often mandated a 24-hour waiting period before they would take a missing-persons report. With young persons, departments sometimes surmised that they were willful disappearances/runaways and would return in a day or so. Today, research and statistics suggest that three-quarters of abducted children that are killed are murdered within the first three hours (Brown et al. 2006).

In the past, the investigation of missing persons was minimal, and documentation the same. As a result, two things happened. The persons never were seen again, and the paperwork was eventually archived or destroyed, or disappeared. These and other issues plague, and confront, investigators who reinvestigate both types of unsolved cases today, often many decades later. The application of cold case homicide investigative methodologies and techniques, as they can be applied to long-time missing persons (LTMP), may assist in the reinvestigation of these cases. Like their homicide counterparts, shoe-leather detective work and forensic advances may help resolve these cases. Too often, sadly, the long-time missing persons are murder victims. They just were not investigated as homicides. A study in England showed that 1 in 7400 missing-persons cases ends in homicide but 1 of 34 homicides starts as a missing-persons case.[1] Obviously, not every missing-persons case turns into a homicide case; indeed, the vast majority do not.[2] But many homicide cases start off as missing-persons cases, and in any case where there is a suspicion that a person may be dead and not just missing, err on the side of treating it as a homicide case. It is better to have your missing person turn up alive during a homicide investigation than to learn your victim is dead during a missing-persons investigation.

See case history regarding Russell Jordan in Chapter 12.

Long-Term Missing Person Defined

As in cold case homicides, the definition is that which the individual agency designates such to be, and there is no universally accepted designation. Some consider them "long-*time* missing persons," while others denote them as "long-*term* missing persons." As utilized by the New Jersey State Police, a long-*term* missing person is "any person that has remained the subject of a missing person investigation for over thirty (30) days" (New Jersey State Police 2007).

The California Peace Officer Standards and Training (POST) guidelines for investigating such cases suggests nine categories and definitions. These are (1) *catastrophic missing*, a child or adult reported missing and assumed to be victim of natural or man-made disaster; (2) *dependent adult*, an adult reported missing and who has physical or mental limitations, such as Alzheimer's disease; (3) *lost*, a child or adult reported to have strayed away and whose whereabouts is unknown; (4) *parent/family abduction*; (5) *runaway*, a child under 18 years of age who is reported missing but has left of his/her own free will or was rejected by his/her family; (6) *stranger abduction*; (7) *suspicious circumstances*, a child or adult reported missing and circumstances give rise to belief that foul play may be involved, or the person is a danger to his/herself, due to physical/mental/emotional conditions, or the disappearance is out of character for the individual and no known reasons can be determined; (8) *unknown*, a child or adult reported missing but insufficient facts to determine circumstances; and (9) *voluntary missing adult*, an adult reported missing but has left of his/her own free will. Each of these categories will entail individualized investigative methodologies,

[1] Centrex, Developing Policing Excellence, NCOF, Operational Support Section, Missing Persons, Suggested Lines of Enquiry in Suspicious Missing Person Investigations, Version 3, September 2003.

[2] Also note that 40% of missing person cases are of missing minorities, a percentage higher than the minority population of the United States (currently 36.7%). Bui, L., 'How Many Other Relishas Are There?,' *Washington Post*, March 1, 2015; http://usnews.nbcnews.com/_news/2013/06/13/18934111-census-white-majority-in-us-gone-by-2043, accessed March 1, 2015.

but identifying the LTMP within a category may suggest or guide the investigative response (California Commission on Peace Officer Standards and Training 2011).

Case Reactivation, Locating Original Documentation, and File Reconstruction

While these issues are covered in depth in Chapters 2 through 4, these same procedures may assist in facilitating resolution of LTMP cases. Whatever the reason for reactivating a long-time missing-persons case, as in cold case homicides, basic steps must be considered. These include locating and reviewing the original case file and evidence, preliminary file review and development of an investigative plan, and investigation (including forensic review). An LTMP case can often take many years to solve. It can take so long that the original detectives on the case retire or move into other assignments and the case, now maybe years old, is assigned to a brand new-set of eyes. The benefit of new eyes is that they look at the file with no preconceived notions about the case. Every piece of paper in the file must be carefully reviewed to see if any lead was missed or not completely investigated. Remember that very often, the murderer's name is in the file, and the key is finding out which name it is.

Agency size, history, protocols, and plain human behavior may make this relatively easy or an investigative task on its own. Past patterns and practices affect file retention. While some agencies may have retained files in an orderly and retrievable manner over the decades, others routinely destroyed paperwork after a designated period of time. Current and archived record storage facilities, both on and off premises, should be checked as well.

When searching for files that are not readily available, investigators may seek to identify and contact prior personnel, active or retired, who may have knowledge of the case, and have even retained copies. Secretaries and clerks are often a treasure trove of knowledge. With the advent of computers and their usage by law enforcement beginning in the late 1970s and early 1980s, some agencies were slow to incorporate this new technology. Depending upon the age of the missing-persons case, file documentation may have incorporated computerized records, paper documentation, or a combination of both. As technology has continued to expand, agencies discarded generations of hardware and software. As a result, if technology such as 5.25-inch floppy disks or older operating systems is encountered, it is recommended that investigators seek appropriate technology support.

Absent finding the original file, such information may be reconstructed beginning with the name of the missing person and date of disappearance, if known. Identification information may or may not be learned by running the victim through available databases, including the National Center for Missing and Exploited Children and National Crime Information Center (NCIC). Investigators may review news media (including both print and film/video of the period regarding the disappearance and investigation) to begin reconstructing what was reported. Investigators are encouraged to identity each person interviewed by media, as well as their statements (to be compared with statements when reinterviewed). These sources may be maintained in libraries and universities, newspaper "morgues" or broadcast facilities, websites such as Newspapers.com, and media archives found on the Internet. As the investigation progresses, and these persons are located and reinterviewed, it may be important to note, and account for, discrepancies or variations between past and current statements.

In addition to the evidence review, examine any photographs that may be in the file and understand their purpose. These photos may be of assistance in reconstructing a neighborhood canvas. Are there pictures of

- The missing person? What is the similarity of their likeness in the photo to when they disappeared?
- Identified and unidentified persons?
- Places and locations relative to the disappearance?

Investigative Plan

During this review, the investigator attempts to understand what was known, and what needs to be learned as the investigation moves forward. As in a cold case homicide, the investigator seeks to learn the *who/what/how/why/when/where* aspects of the case, as well as *MOM*—who had *motive-opportunity-means*?

- *Who*—Who is my LTMP? My suspect? Witnesses? Are unidentified others not previously contacted? Learning as much about the LTMP as possible may open avenues of investigation heretofore unknown
- *What*—What happened to my LTMP? What evidence do I have?
- *Why*—Why did it happen? Is my LTMP's disappearance voluntary or involuntary?
- *When*—When did it happen?
- *How*—How did it happen? Did my LTMP disappear voluntarily, or is this a case of foul play?
- *Where*—Where did my LTMP disappear from? Where was my victim last seen? By who and under what circumstances?

Police must think outside the box. In one case, the family had not heard from the missing victim for some time but was receiving letters allegedly written by the victim. The family, suspicious that the victim was actually dead, wrote back and reminded the victim to send the money he owed to another family member and to not forget that same family member's birthday. A few days later, a birthday card arrived along with a check for $25. Of course, the victim did not owe that family member any money, and it was not his birthday, so the family knew that it was not the victim writing the letters. This is just one example of police and a family thinking creatively to ensnare a killer.

In addition, the investigator needs to learn, and confirm, the following:

- Who reported my LTMP missing? During the investigation, it is prudent to recontact this person(s) as well as others involved in the original investigation. Current statements should be analyzed and compared to the original statements and any discrepancies noted and investigated.
- Date and time reported? Date and time last seen? By whom? Where? Relationship?
- Where was the LTMP reported missing from?
- Exactly what were original officers told?

The most frequently asked question at the outset in a cold case homicide investigation is, "Do we notify the victim's family?" As have families of cold case homicide victims, families of these LTMPs have ridden an emotional roller coaster since the event. However, and depending upon circumstances, contact with the family is suggested to ensure that the missing person did not return home or was otherwise accounted for, without the reporting party ever notifying law enforcement. It has happened!

While such contact may also open the floodgates of emotion, it is important to ascertain if family members heard or became aware of anything in the subsequent years that investigators may not be aware of, and to confirm that which is already known or to learn new information about the LTMP or others. It is important to stay close to the family because they hear things about the case. People who would never go to the police with information often go to the family instead. Even if the family is frustrated with the pace or results of the investigation to date, and they often are, it is imperative to try to maintain cordial relationships with them so that you can both get information from them and have them assist you in sifting any new information or leads. If the LTMP had younger siblings or friends, were they interviewed? When and where, and in the presence of whom? It is worth noting that with the passage of time, and potential maturity and growth, these siblings or other young persons may now reveal information that they were previously afraid to disclose. Family name or fear of disclosure may have inhibited revealing to original investigators information that might have been important to the investigation. Such might include family dynamics that involved sexual abuse.

Go back to reinterview witnesses and suspects. As years pass, people's memory changes, and it is always good to keep memories fresh by having witnesses repeat what they have previously said (which you duly recorded in some fashion the first time they told you), see if they have any new memories, and keep the word out there that the case has not languished. Interviewing suspects also tells them you're not going away either. Guilt is a powerful emotion, and you would be surprised at how it eats away at some people and can lead to a confession years later. Also, you never know what new witnesses you might find to whom the suspect confessed because he/she felt safe so many years after the murder. Always be alert for new friends/girlfriends/boyfriends of the suspect whom you can interview. The number one rule of both cold cases and LTMP cases is simple:

NEVER, NEVER, NEVER GIVE UP.

Investigation

If known (or ascertained from the family), the investigator may revisit the location where the missing person was last seen. Over time, the scene may have altered (but do not necessarily assume that it has), and people come and go. By visiting the location, the investigator may identify possible locations of witnesses and potential locations for disposal of human remains. Investigators should keep in mind and not overlook that many persons often live in their same locations for many decades.

If the neighborhood has changed significantly during the interlude between the LTMP's disappearance and the reactivation of the investigation, investigators may reconstruct the neighborhood or location by consulting records of building and planning departments, water and other civic services, and police/fire departments, and other reconstructive methods as shown in Chapter 4. In addition, investigators may consider a neighborhood canvas.

By reconstructing who lived where at the time the LTMP went missing, investigators may locate and interview persons who might offer investigative leads. Not uncommonly, if a canvas was done at the time of the LTMP and no one was home at the time the officer knocked on the door, no follow-up occurred, and the potential witness went without contact.

In LTMP cases, the following is suggested:

- Identify, locate, and reinterview all investigators and personnel involved in the original investigation. During this, investigators should attempt to learn if these personnel have any documents or other evidence pertaining to the case and any information that they may not have reduced to written documentation.
- Identify and review similar homicide or missing-persons cases within the area and the region to try to establish links between cases.
- Consider geographic profiling, as noted in Chapter 30.
- Identify and explore individuals arrested or convicted for offenses both before and after the critical time period that may suggest potential involvement.
- Consult the National Missing and Unidentified Persons System (NamUs). Do not assume that unidentified remains have been entered into NamUs. Check local coroner and medical examiners (MEs) in this jurisdiction as well as surrounding jurisdictions for unidentified human remains discovered since/about time the LTMP went missing. Do they retain DNA samples as well as dental or skeletal x-rays, and fingerprints?

- Does the jurisdiction have access to, or is there in existence of, a state or national registry for missing persons?
  - Is there familial DNA on file? Has a family reference sample kit been obtained?
  - Was the missing person's effects examined for DNA? Sources of such might include clothing, toothbrush, and hairbrush. If not, the LTMP's family may have retained such items, and investigators are urged to explore this avenue of investigation.

Other avenues for investigation include a search for indications of the following:

- Bank account activity.
- Arrest or police contacts.
- Social Security activity.
- Requests for high school or college transcripts.
- Driver's license or identification card activity.
- Who gained financially from the LTMP's disappearance?
- Did anyone obtain a legal finding of death?
- Did anyone move away shortly after the victim disappeared?
- Did anyone exhibit unusual or strange behavior after the victim disappeared?
- Social media.
  - Obtain the passwords to all social media used by the victim through either a search warrant or the family's cooperation. You will be able to view stored messages and the victim's postings on Facebook, Twitter, Tumblr, or other media. Given the ubiquity of social media, it is essential that any interviews of friends and families include questions about what social media the victim used. It is also essential that, if you are not conversant with these technologies, you find someone who is. The face of social media changes rapidly as shown by the rise and fall of sites such as Myspace. As of this writing, Facebook, Twitter, Tumblr, and Instagram reign supreme. However, a year from now, the popular sites could be completely different. Do not let any tech phobia you may have hinder your investigation. Get help if needed.
  - It is critical that you have a skilled forensic examiner review the victim's or suspect's computer history. This is important not only so you do not miss any important clues but also so that your search is preserved and can be provided to the defense in the event of a trial.
  - You should also consider whether using social media in an undercover capacity could further your investigation. Can you reach out to the suspect through Facebook, establish a friendship, and insert an undercover that could get him/her to talk? Meeting online is so common today that it might be the best way to draw out a suspect, and people tend to let down their guard more readily online. Do not overlook blogs, social media, and other new media as a way to keep the case in people's minds. The more people who are aware of the case, the greater the chances of getting a breakthrough via a previously unknown witness and of keeping the pressure on the defendant.
  - Using social media is also a way for the family to stay involved. Setting up a Facebook page or Twitter feed about the case serves to keep the case alive, keeps family and friends productively involved, and may even lead to your killer. Once the media has been online for some time, obtain a list of the IP addresses that have viewed the site. If you have a suspect's IP address, you can see how often he/she is accessing the site and often track down who the suspect is through sites such as whois.net. See Chapter 4.

Burying is the most common method of hiding a body. Determine if there are ways to get into the air to survey the area and look for recent disturbances in the earth. Can you get a local pilot to fly you over the area if you are looking in a rural or suburban area? Is it winter, and any disturbance to the earth is going to be very noticeable? Talk to those who go out into the woods, such as hikers, hunters, and trail runners. Ask them if they've seen anything out of the ordinary or recently disturbed areas.

As a person of interest or suspect is developed, investigate what hobbies they have to help determine where he/she might go to bury a body. Is he/she hunter? Where does he/she hunt? A bird-watcher? Camper? Cross-country skier? As always, put yourself in his/her shoes and ask yourself, *If I need to get rid of a body and needed some time to do it, where would I go?* It is unlikely you would go somewhere you did not know well and risk detection since you would not know the potential traffic at the location.

When bodies are found in LTMP cases, they are often found in locations either near or familiar to the murderer. Search warrants or consent searches should be executed on any suspect's car, home, or workplace. When disposing of a body, a murderer will try not to be too obvious. Thus, while he/she may have murdered the victim in his/her own home, he/she will not necessarily hide the body there. It is still critical to search his/her home for clues to the murder, but you must also search areas outside his/her home: his/her property and nearby properties, particularly if they are wooded or belong to entities other than private citizens, such as government-owned property or property owned by commercial interests such as factories, farms, etc. Concealing a body on private property can be dangerous because a suspect will stand out while on the property and will be afraid that someone else may discover the body by accident. Burying a body on his/her own land, land owned by an absentee owner, or land that is unoccupied at night is a much safer bet.

In connection with burying, it is common to see bodies dismembered as well. A thorough search of the suspect's house must be conducted for signs of this grisly process. Because of the time and effort involved in cutting up a body, it is often conducted indoors, and needless to say, it is messy. Drains in sinks, bathtubs, and washing machines must be removed and checked for signs of blood. Basements and crawl spaces are common places to both cut up the body as well as hide the tools used to do so. It is also extremely common to see signs of a cleanup throughout a house, and often, this is the best evidence not only that a murder did occur but also of where it took place. Evidence of a cleanup can include finding cleaning products such as bleach and carpet cleaners; the removal of carpets, rugs, or furniture; and even the running of fans to get rid of a smell. Consider blood enhancement, as noted in Chapter 26.

Instruments that could have been used to cut up a body must be searched for, and with LTMP cases, what is missing is often as important as what is present. Are knives missing from the house? Saws or other cutting implements? Family members and friends are often familiar with what was in a house, apartment, or toolbox. In a case in Massachusetts, the evidence against the defendant included flesh and bone recovered from a power saw.[3] One of the first cases that brought forensic criminologist Henry Lee to fame was a Connecticut case where the defendant fed his wife through a wood chipper during a snowstorm. Pieces of her bone and hair were recovered, which helped lead to Richard Crafts' conviction.[4]

As the nation becomes more urbanized, disposing of bodies in dumpsters, which then go to landfills, or landfills themselves has become increasingly common. Obviously, in any urban location, nearby dumpsters must be carefully checked, not just for a body or body part but also for evidence of a cleanup or evidence of the victim's clothes or other possessions being disposed of. Once the dumpster has been removed to the landfill, however, it becomes much more difficult to search for a body, but it can be done. Searching a landfill is not only difficult; it can be extremely dangerous due to hazardous materials and the buildup up of dangerous gases from the decay of waste such as methane and carbon dioxide. There are actually experts on conducting landfill searches, and consulting with such an expert and working closely with the landfill

[3] http://mercuryservices.hubpages.com/video/No-Body-Trials-Locking-Up-Murderers-When-the-Victims-Corpse-Is-Missing. Last accessed March 9, 2013.

[4] http://www.trutv.com/library/crime/notorious_murders/family/woodchipper_murder/10.html. Last accessed March 9, 2013.

owners or operators are essential.[5] Landfills often track where trash came from and where it is placed in the landfill, so having close cooperation from the landfill owners, whether private or public, is critical.[6] In any event, searching a landfill can be extremely expensive and even cost too much given the difficulties of finding anything. In a recent case in the District of Columbia, the police and prosecutors opposed a defendant's request to search a landfill even though the defendant had confessed to putting the body into a dumpster that was delivered to the landfill, because of the prohibitive cost and low probability of recovering a body. Apparently, the defense hoped that recovery of the body would lead to evidence that would show that the defendant had not committed the murder or that the lack of a body would show that the confession was false.[7]

Recent advances in geophysical tools may lead to a greater ability to search landfills and other places where bodies might be buried. According to a recent article in *Science Live*, British researchers are conducting experiments with buried pigs to test ground-penetrating radars and other geophysical methods. (Pig skin is very similar to human skin.) Although their research is in the early stages, these techniques could prove to be a real boon to investigators searching for a missing body.[8]

Searches for the body are often conducted by private citizens. These private searches are often a good way for the family and friends of the victim to get involved in a positive and productive way. While it is preferable that a member of the investigative team go along on these searches, in all cases, the searches performed should be maintained in a logbook keeping track of when the search occurred, the location and areas searched, the resources used, and man-hours spent searching. All of this can be very useful at trial to demonstrate the immense effort that went into finding the victim.

It is also essential that any unidentified bodies in the area are carefully checked to make sure that an ME's office does not have your victim's body but just does not know who it is. Statistics from the Department of Justice show that every year, MEs' offices nationwide will receive 4400 unidentified bodies (Driscoll 2013). Of those 4400 bodies, an average of 1000 remain unidentified after one year (Driscoll 2013). One of the best ways to identify a body is by using NamUs. NamUs "assists law enforcement in their investigations of missing and unidentified person cases."[9] NamUs has three databases: the Missing Persons Database, the Unidentified Persons System, and the Unclaimed Persons Database. The Missing Persons Database contains information on missing persons entered by law enforcement. The information is verified before being entered into the system. The Unidentified Persons System contains information entered by MEs and coroners on unidentified bodies. The Unclaimed Persons Database contains information entered by MEs and coroners about persons who have been identified but not claimed by family. See Chapter 17.

NamUs also provides a number of free forensic services including DNA testing and anthropology and odontology services. NamUs provides analytical services that assist law enforcement with solving missing and unidentified cases. Analysts have access to multiple law enforcement databases including Accurint for Law Enforcement and Consolidated Lead Evaluation and Reporting (CLEAR). The NamUs analysts can also research the NCIC database. Additionally, NamUs analysts are experts in using social media to search for missing people, something critical in a no-body murder. They can review sites such as Facebook, Spokeo, Google, and Ancestry.com to determine whether the missing person is posting information. This evidence (or lack thereof) can prove critical to proving a person is not missing but is actually dead. It is

[5] See http://www.policechiefmagazine.org/magazine/index.cfm?fuseaction=display&article_id=2270&issue_id=122010, which profiles Ron Olive of the Naval Criminal Investigative Services (NCIS) and his expertise in searching landfills. Last accessed March 17, 2013.

[6] http://www.letsk9professionals.org/landfills.html. Last accessed March 17, 2013.

[7] http://homicidewatch.org/2011/04/27/judge-wont-compel-search-for-latisha-fraziers-body/. Last accessed on March 17, 2013.

[8] Hidden Graves Revealed with Geophysical Tools, http://www.livescience.com/31982-hidden-bodies-found-using-geophysics.html. Last accessed May 17, 2013.

[9] See Driscoll (2013). All of the information in this paragraph and the next are from this article. See also http://www.namus.gov.

important to exhaustively search both government and private databases to ensure both yourself and a jury that the victim is not somehow secretly living somewhere else.

If you have the victim's DNA, it should be entered into the Federal Bureau of Investigation's (FBI's) Combined DNA Index System (CODIS). CODIS contains DNA from persons convicted of crimes, DNA profiles taken from crime scenes, profiles from unidentified human remains, and DNA samples from the families of missing persons.[10]

Behavioral Analysis

During the investigation, investigators may seek experienced assistance in understanding behavioral aspects of both the LTMP as well as any persons of interest who may be developed. In the United States, many state criminal justice agencies as well as federal law enforcement agencies include personnel specifically trained and experienced in behavioral analysis as exhibited at the crime scene, or in individual behavior. Do not hesitate to ask for help. Many police departments in the United States have fewer than 10 officers.[11] Few if any departments of under 100 officers could reasonably handle a major case without help. Besides, the help is free, so why not use it, even of it is only to run down the bogus leads that come in any no-body murder investigation? The FBI's Behavioral Analysis Unit (BAU) does a great job at both profiling who the possible killer might be as well as suggesting approaches to a suspect during an interview or interrogation. As noted previously, the Naval Criminal Investigative Services (NCIS) does the same, although they are typically looking for a naval or armed forces connection.

Learning as much about the LTMP as possible is important in these investigations, and investigators may consider a *victimology assessment*. This may initially be undertaken by an experienced investigator to help identify whether this was a voluntary disappearance or any of the nine categories previously noted by the California POST report types. As in cold case homicides, investigators seek to identify who might have had motive, opportunity, and means, and assessment of the LTMP might also include inquiry into their

- Financial situation
- Marital/sexual relationship
- Family issues (including custody)
- Business concerns and pressures
- Emotional issues and mental state
- High-risk lifestyle, including prostitution, alcohol, and drugs
- Health issues

The National Center for Analysis of Violent Crime (NCVAC) unit at the FBI Academy assists local agencies in reviewing circumstances of these cases, analysis of behavioral characteristics, as well as consideration of investigative plans.

In any LTMP investigation, the victimology, that is, what type of person this victim is, is essential in solving the case. An investigation of a known street prostitute or drug addict is much different than the investigation of a hardworking mother of three. (Note that we did not say that one investigation is more important than the other. All LTMP cases deserve the same level of investigation, resources and, dedication

10 Behavioral Analysis Unit, National Center for the Analysis of Violent Crime, "Serial Murder, Multi-Disciplinary Perspectives for Investigators" at 37.

11 http://www.fop.net/labor/icpra/3TheFutureofLawEnforcementintheUnitedStatesofAmerica.pdf. Last accessed January 20, 2014.

no matter who they were or what their stature was in life.) Knowledge of victimology is critical to keeping your investigation on the right track. In an LTMP case, victimology is even more important because, again, your investigation focuses on not only who committed the murder but also proving that a murder occurred.

Your victim's victimology assessment can make proving the fact of his/her murder more difficult. A missing drug addict is much more likely to be thought of as dying from an overdose or simply disappearing than a young mother with no history of drug abuse. By studying and knowing your victim's victimology, you will know what types of evidence will persuade a jury that your victim is indeed dead. Remember that every victim has a victimology that can help prove he/she is dead. While it is easy to prove the death of most individuals who have a well-worn path of obligations such as families, jobs, friends, etc., even the most downtrodden victim has habits and patterns, family and friends. The absence of these patterns can demonstrate just as conclusively that a person is dead as someone missing work or an important family milestone. In one no-body murder case in the District of Columbia, the victim was an alcoholic and possible drug user who was not employed. The initial detective assigned to the case even dismissed her sister as a "crackhead" in a written report. In fact, she had five children for whom she cared deeply, and at trial, it was demonstrated that she had missed their birthdays and holidays when she had never done so before. This was proof to a jury that she was dead. One of the most poignant moments of the trial was the testimony of the victim's 12-year-old daughter, who testified that her mother had never missed her birthday or Christmas until after she went missing.

The fact that the person is presumed dead and not merely missing can also lead to your pool of suspects. As a matter of logic, an LTMP case does not lead itself to a certain type of defendant. A burglar who breaks into a home and is surprised by the owner, who he then shoots and kills, is not going to hang around to dispose of the body. Disposing of a body takes time, and that is not something an accidental killer, such as a burglar, robber, or carjacker, is typically willing to risk. There are certainly stranger-on-stranger no-body murders, but those cases typically involve the murderer deliberately seeking a victim for the thrill of the killing such child predators. He/she wants to cover up his/her crimes in order to get away with them. In cases of accidental murders where the body is hidden, there is almost always a preexisting relationship between the killer and his/her victim. A classic example is a coworker killing another coworker over a work dispute or two business associates having a falling out when one kills the other. These types of murders occur on familiar grounds for the killer, often the workplace, and the murderer can take the time to dispose of the body, safe in the knowledge that no one is likely to surprise him/her at the workplace. Since a no-body murder requires time and effort, by far, the most common suspect is a person known to the victim.

If the missing person had a computer, tablet, or other such device, and it was never analyzed, and is perhaps still in the possession of family members or others, a forensic examination is suggested. Cold case homicide and LTMP investigations involve teamwork and cooperation among many disciplines and knowledge of available resources to compliment the investigation. Among these are government resources for long-time missing persons and cold case homicides as well as nongovernment sponsored organizations.

Interagency Cooperation

With the growth and expansion of police agencies, organizational practices often lead to specialized units, sometimes physically distant. These specialized units can include missing persons, in addition to homicide, robbery, sexual assault, and more. As a result, case resolution can suffer due to lack of communication. In larger agencies, those tasked with missing-persons investigations do not always receive the same allocation of resources, or perhaps prestige, as those charged with homicide investigations.

As previously noted, LTMPs are not uncommonly homicide cases. Recognizing that their physical and organizational practices inhibited efficiency in this regard, homicide and missing-persons administrators in the Los Angeles Police Department, California, facilitated a solution to help minimize these deficiencies. At their regular meetings and reviews of missing-persons cases, experienced homicide investigators became part of the review team and were given authority to assume responsibility for the investigation of long-time missing-persons cases when, in their opinions, the case circumstances warranted homicide levels of expertise and investigation. This practice has proven successful.

Federal Agencies and Databases

Federal Bureau of Investigation (FBI)

This agency maintains numerous programs and databases, which may assist in these investigations. Included in these are NCIC, NCVAC, NGI, and the Integrated Automated Fingerprint Identification System (IAFIS), CODIS, and the Violent Criminal Apprehension Program (ViCAP). Each of these is discussed in detail in following, separate chapters.

The National Crime Information Center (NCIC)

The National Crime Information Center (NCIC) is a computerized nationwide information system supporting criminal justice agencies and is available to law enforcement 24 hours a day, 365 days a year. It consists of a series of specialized files, including those on property and persons. An archive of entries is also kept in an offline system. See Chapter 8 regarding off-line searches. While all file indices may be of assistance during the course of these investigations, the Missing Person File was originated in 1975, using defined criteria. These include whether the missing person is a juvenile, endangered, or disabled, or the disappearance is involuntary or due to catastrophic circumstances or other factors. In addition, NCIC has also maintained the Unidentified Person File since 1983 and the national Sex Offender Registry File since 1999. The IAFIS was introduced in July 1999. These systems incorporate data held at state levels as well as federal levels. See Chapter 8.

The Combined DNA Index System (CODIS)

CODIS became operational in October 1998. This tiered system is the national DNA database into which are entered DNA profiles from (1) forensic unknowns at crime scenes; (2) convicted offenders who are required to provide such samples; (3) missing persons; (4) unidentified human remains; and (5) relatives of missing persons. See Chapter 18.

National Center for the Analysis of Violent Crime (NCAVC)

This unit provides behavioral-based investigative support for local, state, national, and international law enforcement. It consists of different units, including those units tasked with providing behavioral analysis for crimes against children and crimes against adults. Within this center is ViCAP. It consists of a database and tools available to law enforcement for investigation and linkage of missing-persons and unidentified-human-remains cases as well as homicides and other offenses. These sources enable law enforcement to associate cases that are dispersed geographically and might not otherwise appear to be connected. See Chapter 7.

Next Generation Identification (NGI)/Automated Fingerprint Identification System (AFIS)

Implemented in 1999 and upgraded, this electronic database is the national fingerprint and criminal history record system of criminal arrests and civil fingerprint filings. It provides automated fingerprint searches, latent search capabilities, electronic image storage, and electronic exchanges of fingerprints. It is available and responds to inquiries and requests 24 hours a day, 365 days of the year. See Chapter 14.

National Center for Missing and Exploited Children (NCMEC)

This organization is a partnership between public and private entities. It works with law enforcement on issues related to long-time missing, missing, and sexually exploited children. Founded in 1984, it provides investigators with a number of resources. In addition to a national toll-free hotline and assistance in current case investigations, this partnership offers numerous resources to law enforcement. See Chapter 31.

Acknowledgments

I wish to express my deepest appreciation to former Assistant U.S. Attorney Thomas A. (Tad) DiBiase for his lead-authorship in this chapter. Tad has both tried a no-body homicide case during his career as a homicide prosecutor and consulted across the country on more than 30 additional no-body murder cases. He lectures on the topic to police and prosecutors and blogs on these cases at http://www.nobodymurdercases.com. He is considered the nation's leading expert on no-body murders.

Suggested Readings and Bibliography

Brown, K.M., Keppel, R.D., Weis, J.G., and Skeen, M.E. (2006). Investigative Case Management for Missing Children Homicides: Report II. https://www.ncjrs.gov/pdffiles1/Archive/218936NCJRS.pdf, accessed December 29, 2014.

California Commission on Peace Officer Standards and Training (2011). Missing Persons Investigations: Guidelines & Curriculum. http://lib.post.ca.gov, accessed May 20, 2016.

DiBiase, T.A. (2014). *No-Body Homicide Cases: A Practical Guide to Investigating, Prosecuting and Winning a Case When the Victim's Body is Missing.* CRC Press, Boca Raton, FL.

Driscoll, D. (2013). Resolving Missing and Unidentified Person Cases Using Today's Technology, *The Police Chief*, May.

New Jersey State Police. (2007). Missing Persons Investigative Best Practices Protocol. http://www.njsp.org, accessed May 20, 2016.

Pettem, S. (2009). *Someone's Daughter: In Search of Justice for Jane Doe.* Taylor Trade, Lanham, MD.

Pettem, S. (2013). *Cold Case Research: Resources for Unidentified, Missing and Cold Case Homicides.* CRC Press, Boca Raton, FL.

Regensburger, D. (2011). Law Enforcement Volunteers: An Essential Tool in the Investigation of Cold Case Homicides. *Sheriff Magazine.* May–June. Vol 63, Issue 3, pp. 22–23.

The Prosecution of Cold Case Murders

6

ANNE MARIE SCHUBERT

Contents

Introduction

On May 7, 1977, 15-year-old Penny Parker went out to collect money for her paper route with the *Sacramento Bee* newspaper. She never returned home. Two days later, Penny's body was found in a rural field in Sacramento County. She had been sexually assaulted and stabbed to death. For 25 years, her murder remained unsolved despite diligent and persistent efforts of law enforcement to find her killer. While Penny's family waited for justice. Finally, in 2002, as a result of Sacramento County's Cold Case Prosecution Program, Penny's murderer was identified and charged with her murder (Figure 6.1).

Cold case murders present unique and interesting challenges for both investigators and prosecutors. Unlike active homicide cases, there are many legal and evidentiary issues that would never arise in a fresh homicide that must be addressed in both the investigation and the prosecution in order to effectively present an old murder case to a jury.

The most significant factor in the investigation and prosecution of cold cases is—not surprisingly—the passage of time. The passage of time can both help and hinder a cold case. While time clearly has an adverse impact on the memories of witnesses, it also may become an ally if once-reluctant witnesses become forthright and cooperative. While some investigative leads can be lost with time—perhaps because physical evidence was lost or destroyed or because witnesses have died or become disabled—other avenues may open up. In the last 25 years, DNA has revolutionized the ability of investigators to evaluate physical evidence. DNA has, in essence, become the silent witness to the truth.

While the investigation of a cold case presents distinctive challenges, so too does the prosecution. In addition to learning and briefing legal issues that must be mastered in many ordinary murder trials, the prosecutor in a cold murder trial may also have to deal with legal issues arising from sometimes extensive

Figure 6.1 Penny Parker.

pretrial delay, which will be governed by the statute of limitations and constitutional standards of due process.

Additionally, the prosecutor must master the facts and, in doing so, take into account the expectations of the jury. With the introduction of cold cases in television media, jurors expect scientific evidence on par with what television writers and producers have presented to them. Satisfying these expectations in any murder case, let alone an old one, can be very difficult.

Early Involvement of a Prosecutor

Due to the legal, evidentiary, and modern-day challenges presented by cold cases, it is critical for law enforcement and the prosecution to work together at the earliest phase of the investigation. This should be done as soon as the cold case is reopened. Through this team approach, the investigator and prosecutor can effectively anticipate and prepare for any legal or evidentiary challenges that may arise in court once an individual is charged. Coordination and cooperation may involve discussing the necessity and sufficiency of search warrants, photographic or live lineups, and the chain of custody for forensic evidence. It may also involve discussing what scientific tests should be used, as well as what defenses may be raised. Through this coordination and cooperation during the investigative stage, the likelihood of a successful prosecution will increase dramatically.

Additionally, many of these cold cases will involve hundreds, if not thousands, of pages of police reports. This may be due to several reasons: the case was initially investigated by law enforcement at the time of the murder; the investigation may have continued over several years by many different investigators; and the case was ultimately solved. Further, once the perpetrator is identified, police reports will be generated not only connecting the suspect to the crime but also detailing his/her criminal background. If the defendant is charged with capital murder, a thorough review of his/her background will be required for the penalty phase. Obtaining and organizing these materials in a manner sufficient to justify arrest, conviction, and perhaps even the imposition of the death penalty requires prosecutorial involvement—and the sooner, the better.

Due to the complexity of cold cases, the involvement of a local prosecutor during the investigation will assist in the organization of the case and the presentation of evidence to a jury.

Prosecuting the Cold Case Murder

Charging Cold Case Murders

There are several considerations that must be taken into account when charging a cold case murder.

1. *Statute of limitations:* In many murder cases, additional crimes have been committed along with the homicide. In both the homicide charge as well as the other offenses, the prosecutor must determine the appropriate statute of limitations for all charges.

   In general, there is no statute of limitations for murder. There can be exceptions to the general rule, however, depending on the jurisdiction and the date of the offense. For instance, in October of 2000, Michael Skakel was charged by the state of Connecticut with the 1975 murder of 15-year-old Martha Moxley. At the time of his arrest, Skakel was 39 years old—he was barely 15 years old at the time of the crime. Numerous legal motions were filed by the defense seeking a dismissal based upon the statute of limitations. In particular, the defense claimed that the prosecution of the murder was time barred by a five-year statute of limitations in effect in Connecticut in 1975. While the trial court denied the motion to dismiss, the claim was the defendant's primary contention on appeal.

   In addition to the statute of limitations for murder, the prosecution must also become familiar with the statute of limitations for any lesser and included offenses to murder (such as manslaughter), and for any other crimes that were connected to the murder. These statutes will vary according to the jurisdiction. As a result, in many jurisdictions, the charging document may be limited to the murder charge alone.

   However, even if the statute of limitations precludes the charging of related offenses, in many jurisdictions, the prosecution can still allege special circumstances that may qualify the defendant for capital punishment. For instance, a murder case from 1981 may involve the kidnap, rape, and murder of a young female. While the statute of limitations may bar the filing of kidnap and rape as separate counts, it may not bar the filing of kidnap and rape as *special circumstances* attached to the count of murder.
2. *Law of murder:* One of the most important issues that must be confronted when charging a cold case murder is determining what the law of murder was at the time of the crime. This includes the degree of murder and any lesser included offense to the crime of murder, such as manslaughter. The simplest means of determining this is to consult the penal code for the year of the crime. Additionally, the prosecutor must determine what jury instructions will be provided to the jury at trial. This may requiring finding jury instructions that were in use at the time of the crime and determining whether those jury instructions or some more modern variant must be used.
3. *Law of special circumstances:* In jurisdictions that have capital punishment, it is imperative to know what special circumstances existed at the time of the crime. In many jurisdictions, the list of special circumstances has been expanded over the years. For instance, if a murder occurred in 1982 and involved a kidnapping and carjacking, it is necessary to know if the kidnapping and carjacking were on the list of special circumstances law in 1982. If they were not, but some related charge was (such as robbery), the prosecutor might be able to allege robbery as an alternative special circumstance in the charging document.

   Additionally, even if the death penalty was authorized under the penal code at the time of the murder, there are jurisdictions where court rulings nullified those statutes, finding that the law was unconstitutional. In such jurisdictions, the death penalty cannot be sought for offenses committed before the court ruling. For instance, the California Supreme Court found the death penalty statute of that state unconstitutional in August 1977. As a result, no defendant in California who committed murder before August 1977 can be put to death, and in fact, they face a maximum term of seven years to life in prison. Thus, in Penny Parker's murder, the prosecution was precluded from seeking the death penalty because the crime occurred in May 1977.

Clearly, the potential charges and sentence will have a significant impact on both the investigation and prosecution of a cold case. Understanding the laws that existed at the time of the murder is critical.

4. *Proper court for filing charges:* In some murder cases, the defendant may have been a juvenile at the time of the murder. In those instances, the prosecutor must determine whether his/her jurisdiction requires that charges first be filed in juvenile court or adult court. The determination of whether a juvenile defendant may be tried in adult court presents many complex issues that must be fully explored by the prosecutor.

Necessary Elements of the Investigation

The successful prosecution of a cold murder case is dependent upon the investigation conducted by law enforcement. From a prosecutor's perspective, there are several key elements to a successful cold case investigation. These include the following:

Thorough Review of Case File

A thorough review of the case file is necessary to effectively investigate and prosecute a cold case. From an investigator's point view, this is necessary to complete the investigation. From a prosecutor's perspective, this review is necessary not only for an effective prosecution but also to ensure compliance with the rules of discovery, which in most jurisdictions impose upon the prosecutor an ethical obligation to provide all reports associated with the case file to the defense.

In this case review, the following steps should be taken:

- Obtain all reports, including the following:
  - Police reports: This includes reports in the original case file as well as those maintained in the police records division. It is not uncommon for reports in the original case file not to have been submitted to the records division. It is highly recommended that the prosecutor personally review the original police file to verify that all records have been obtained.
  - Autopsy reports.
  - Laboratory reports: This includes all final reports as well as laboratory notes generated or relied upon by the laboratory analyst.
  - Medical records.
  - Psychological records.
  - Records in possession of prosecution: In some instances, the prosecutor's office may have a copy of the case file. This may be due to several reasons. The case may have been filed and later dismissed, or the case may have been submitted for filing but rejected by a prosecutor. In many instances, the prior prosecutor may have obtained records that were never seen by the original investigator.
- Locate all photographs, videotapes, audiotapes, and composites: These include those from the following agencies:

- Law enforcement: These items should be in the records division. As noted previously, however, items sometimes do not make it from the original case file to the records division. This can include original reports, photographs, tapes, composites, or Polaroid photographs of suspects and/or vehicles.
- Medical examiner's/coroner's office: The original autopsy photographs should also be obtained. While the law enforcement agency may also have taken photographs at the autopsy, the photographs taken by the medical examiner may be more comprehensive. In particular, the medical examiner may have taken photographs depicting the collection of evidence and the internal examination of the victim. Many times, these photographs will become critical for the prosecution in demonstrating the proper chain of custody in the collection of evidence or for identifying particular wound patterns for the victim.
- Hospital photographs: In some instances, a hospital may have taken photographs of injuries of the victim prior to or after death.
- Other sources of photographs: The investigator and prosecutor should also determine if other individuals have photographs relevant to the investigation. These include media sources (TV or newspapers) or those in the possession of civilian witnesses. For instance, it may be necessary to obtain photographs from the victim or suspect's family demonstrating events around the time of the homicide.

Thorough Review and Analysis of Physical Evidence

One of the most critical steps in the investigation and prosecution of a cold case involves review of the physical evidence. In many cases, the identity of the suspect is determined through forensic evidence. In particular, the introduction of forensic DNA testing and the use of convicted-offender DNA data banks have allowed investigators to identify suspects in cases that may otherwise remain unsolved. As such, it is important that both the investigator and the prosecutor understand how to handle and evaluate physical evidence. In many cases, the reliability of the evidence testing and the chain of custody will be aggressively attacked by the defense. As such, it is imperative that this review be thorough and that all necessary and relevant items of evidence be analyzed.

In reviewing the state of the physical evidence, the following steps should be taken:

- Consider all possible locations where the evidence may be located. This may include the following locations:
  - Law enforcement property room.
  - Coroner's office: In many jurisdictions, the coroner's office provides the autopsy kit to either the crime laboratory or police agency at the time of the autopsy. However, in some jurisdictions, the coroner's office keeps additional biological samples (such as smears of biological fluids placed on slides) in its own possession. Additionally, the coroner's office may have tissue samples from the victim. These autopsy and tissue samples may become vital to the investigation of the case. This is particularly true where the law enforcement autopsy kit has been either lost or destroyed.

    For instance, in Penny Parker's murder, the law enforcement agency was unable to locate the autopsy kit taken in 1977. However, the Sacramento County Coroner's Office retained autopsy samples in its possession. These samples became the vital piece of evidence for identifying Penny's killer.
  - Crime laboratory or specific laboratory analyst's possession: This should include all laboratories that have conducted analyses in the case. In many cases, several laboratories may have

conducted analyses over many years. It is vital to determine if any of these laboratories have retained any evidence in the case.
- Prosecutor's office.
- Previous investigator's possession.
- Court file.

Additionally, in reviewing the physical evidence, both the investigator and the prosecutor should consider the following:

- Do not assume evidence is lost or destroyed.

  It is not uncommon for investigators to be told that the evidence is lost or destroyed when, in fact, it isn't. The evidence may have been misplaced, or the property clerk may not know where to find it. The investigator should personally seek to find the evidence by going to all the possible locations it may be stored. A diligent and meticulous search for the evidence can oftentimes result in locating the critical items of evidence.
- Seek the assistance of an expert when conducting an inventory and review of the evidence.

  To fully understand the significance of physical evidence in a cold case, an expert will need to be consulted. The analysts employed in law enforcement crime labs will likely be able to either provide this expertise personally or know someone who can. The expert can also evaluate whether potential defenses are scientifically viable. For instance, in many cold case murders, the defendant may claim that he had consensual sex with the victim prior to her death but did not kill her. This defense, however, may be undermined by an understanding of the significance of the physical evidence that only an expert can provide. If a large amount of semen belonging to the defendant is found in the victim's body, the expert may understand that this indicates recent sexual relations, thereby possibly defeating a consent defense.
- Reevaluate old lab reports.

  Forensic science has changed dramatically over the last 20–30 years. Tests, particularly of biological substances, are much more definitive and reliable than they once were. For instance, some of the following factors should be considered in reviewing forensic testing performed in a cold case:
  - If a lab report indicates "no semen or sperm" was *found*, do not automatically assume that no semen or sperm was present. It may be that the laboratory only performed a *presumptive* test (such as acid phosphatase) at the time. In many cases, the lack of a positive response on this presumptive test does not mean there is no semen or sperm present. The investigator and/or prosecutor should confirm this through a microscopic analysis by the laboratory.

    In the Penny Parker case, for example, the victim's underwear was analyzed in 1977, and at that time, the laboratory reported that no seminal fluid was detected on the underwear (Figure 6.2).

    A review of the analysis revealed that this conclusion was based solely on a presumptive test. In 2002, the laboratory performed a microscopic analysis of the underwear, which had a large amount of sperm. DNA testing of the sperm conclusively identified the individual later charged with Penny's murder.
  - Do not rely exclusively on the autopsy and/or medical sexual assault examination to determine whether sperm is present. In many old cases, the method of evidence collection by the medical examiner may have precluded the observation of sperm. While the autopsy report may indicate "no sperm" *found*, this does not necessarily mean that there is no sperm *present* or there was no sexual assault. Thus, the autopsy kit may well have to be retested using current forensic technology.

CRIME LABORATORY TELEPHONE (916) 440-5433

Office Of The

DISTRICT ATTORNEY

SACRAMENTO COUNTY

4400 V Street Sacramento, California 95817

JOHN M. PRICE
District Attorney

GEOFFREY BURROUGHS
Chief Deputy District Attorney

May 19, 1977

John P. Kearns, Chief
Sacramento Police Department
813 6th Street
Sacramento, California 95814

LAB NO: A77-442 Supp.
CORONER: 77-711
VICTIM: PENNY PARKER
OFFENSE: 187 P.C.

ATTENTION: HOMICIDE

PHYSICAL EVIDENCE EXAMINATION REPORT

On May 11, 1977 at 3:00 P. M., the following exhibits were removed from evidence locker #13:

J. Pair of panties.
K. Pair of sandals.
L. Pair of green pants.
M. Bra.
N. Tank top.
O. Green sweater with hood.

RESULTS AND CONCLUSIONS:

No seminal fluid was detected in the pair of panties, Item J. There was a dirt stain on the back portion in the buttocks area.

Figure 6.2 1977 laboratory report.

- View and photograph the condition of the existing evidence.

  By viewing the evidence in person, both the investigator and prosecutor can better understand the significance of items that either were not photographed before or cannot be adequately portrayed in photographs. This may provide a better understanding of the circumstances surrounding the crime.

  Additionally, viewing and photographing the evidence can assist in determining the chain of custody. In many cold cases, the chain of custody is difficult to establish. In some instances, property sheets may have been lost or destroyed—if they were ever prepared at all. By viewing the evidence in person, the investigator and prosecutor can see what documentation relating to the chain of custody was maintained with the evidence itself. Photographing these items as well as documentation relating to the chain of custody will often help the prosecution in court proceedings.
- Determine whether additional forensic testing is available and advisable.

  Both law enforcement and the prosecution should consult about whether additional testing is possible and is needed in a particular cold case. For instance, further analysis may reveal that additional sexual acts were committed against the victim. As a result, it may be possible to allege additional special circumstances against the defendant.

  Furthermore, additional testing may provide greater insight into the circumstances surrounding the crime and the defendant's connection to it. This could provide useful information when the case is presented to a jury.

Reconstruct the Crime and the Defendant's Connection to the Crime

One of the most challenging aspects in both the investigation and prosecution of a cold case murder is reconstructing the crime and the defendant's connection to it. Presenting a cold case homicide to a jury presents unique challenges because many jurors expect that even an investigation conducted years ago will meet the latest scientific standards. Defense attorneys are sure to contrast modern standards with those that were actually used at the time. One way to address this issue is for the investigator and prosecutor to reconstruct the crime as fully as possible.

There are several ways that a cold case homicide can be reconstructed for a successful prosecution. These include the following:

- Reconstruct the crime scene. This can be accomplished several ways:
  - Original crime scene photographs.
  - Aerial photographs taken at or near the time (often by a government planning department or private aerial photography company).
  - Maps drawn at or near the time of the crime. This can be from the original investigation or by obtaining plot maps from private or public agencies.
  - Revisit the crime scene. In some instances, the scene has changed very little, if at all. As such, current photographs may provide useful information that may not have been photographed in the original investigation. In some instances, the original photographs taken may have been lost or destroyed. As a result, current photographs will be all the investigator or prosecutor can get.
  - Video footage: In many instances, video footage was taken at the time by either law enforcement or the news media. If possible, this footage should be obtained. If the footage is unavailable, new video photography may be useful.
- Reconstruct the circumstances surrounding the crime.

  Understanding *why* the homicide occurred is a question that every jury wants answered. While a prosecutor technically does not have to establish that a motive exists, because motive is not an element of the crime of murder, the *absence* of motive may present a viable defense to the crime. In reconstructing the circumstances of the homicide, a prosecutor may therefore want the following investigations conducted:
  - A thorough analysis of the victim's background (*victimology*)
  - Interviews of the original investigators and medical examiners
  - Current background investigation and interviews with witnesses interviewed at the time of the crime (if possible)
  - Reanalysis of all forensic evidence
  - A complete background investigation of the defendant
- Background investigation of the defendant.

  In cold cases, as in all murder cases, the defendant must be connected to both the victim and the crime scene. This is particularly true in "cold hit" cases, where the primary evidence will typically be a DNA match between biological samples obtained from the victim's body and a reference sample taken from the suspect. While it might be tempting for resource-strapped investigators and prosecutors to conclude that that is all the jury *needs*, that may not be all the evidence they *want*. In presenting a cold case to a jury, a complete background investigation of the defendant will provide the jury with a thorough understanding of the defendant's connection to the murder. Sources of information that should be considered in obtaining a complete background of the defendant include the following:
  - Interviews with the defendant's family, friends, coworkers, and previous sexual partners.
  - Police reports of all crimes committed by or involving the defendant.
  - Field identification (FI) cards on the defendant. This may assist in determining the whereabouts of the defendant around the time of the murder.
  - Registration cards, such as sexual offender, drug, or arson registration cards.

- Records relating to the defendant, including medical, mental health, and employment records.
- A complete copy of the defendant's prison file. This should include
  - Visitation logs
  - Information regarding addresses used for parole or family members
  - Family history
  - Old prison photos (particularly those near the time of the murder)
  - Psychological reports

Special Considerations in DNA Cold Hit Cases

In cold cases that are solved through a DNA cold hit, the defendant is identified through the use of an offender database, where the DNA from crime scene evidence is linked to the defendant's DNA. In these cases, there are several factors that should be considered. This includes the following:

- Once the hit is made, the most critical concern is a determination of whether the suspect is in or out of custody. Clearly, if out of custody, the law enforcement agency will need to expedite the investigation. If, however, the suspect is in custody, law enforcement will have more time and can more effectively and thoroughly prepare the case for prosecution.
- Once a hit is made, law enforcement should obtain and test an additional DNA sample from the defendant. This will confirm the analysis conducted in the case. In addition, it will allow the local DNA laboratory that conducted testing on the crime scene evidence to provide the all the necessary testimony in court.
- Prior to filing criminal charges, law enforcement and the prosecution should also determine whether additional DNA testing should be conducted. If additional items of evidence will be consumed through DNA testing, the prosecutor must also determine whether this testing should be done before or after criminal charges are filed. If the testing is done after, the prosecutor should be aware that the defense may have a right to be present during the testing analysis.

Preparation for Penalty Phase

In many cold cases, the defendant may be facing capital punishment. Because many of the solved cold case murders involve sexual assault, the prosecution may seek the death penalty against the defendant. Like many other death cases, preparation for the penalty phase is critical. One benefit for the prosecution in cold cases is that, where the defendant is already in custody for other offenses, much of this preparation can be done before the murder charges are even filed. This may be very beneficial since some witnesses—particularly the defendant's family and friends—may be more cooperative before the charges are filed.

In preparation for the penalty phase, the following avenues of investigation should be considered:

- *Interview family and friends of the defendant:* While the family and friends of the defendant will often resist providing law enforcement any helpful information, this is not always the case. Some may cooperate because they dislike the defendant or dislike what he/she has done. Others may try to limit disclosures to innocuous information but, because they don't know all the facts (particularly before charges are filed), may in fact provide information of great value. These individuals may be able to provide relevant information for the guilt phase of the trial—information that may connect the defendant to the murder. They may also provide useful information regarding the defendant's background, childhood, and any mental health issues. Once the defendant is charged, the defense will conduct an extensive background of the defendant's life in an effort to avoid the

death penalty. In cold cases, having these individuals interviewed *prior* to the filing of charges may provide useful information that can be later used at trial.
- *Interview other victims:* In all death penalty cases, it is imperative to locate and interview every person victimized by the defendant who survived encounters with him. These other crimes may be relevant in the guilt phase as evidence of such facts as common modus operandi or intent, and will certainly be relevant during the penalty phase as the jury weighs the appropriate verdict. In cold cases, it is suggested that these witnesses be identified and contacted in person at the earliest possible time. It should be anticipated that this contact may be emotionally traumatic for them.
- *Obtain all necessary records:* In preparation for the penalty phase, the prosecution should obtain all records pertaining to the defendant. In cold cases, this can be very challenging given the age of the case and the fact that many businesses or agencies have destroyed records over the years. The following types of records should be obtained, if possible:
  - Prison and jail records
  - School records
  - Employment records
  - Military records
  - Medical records
  - Mental health records
  - Police records

Legal Issues in Cold Cases

There are a several legal issues that may be present in cold cases that are rarely seen in other homicide cases, including the following:

1. *John Doe warrants*

   John Doe warrants—which identify the defendants by their physical characteristics, rather than by name—are rare but have been used for over a century. In the California case *People v. Montoya* (1967) 255 Cal.App.2d 137, for example, the court of appeals said that it was legal to issue a warrant describing the defendant as "John Doe, white male, dark hair, medium build, 30–35."

   With the introduction of DNA tests in criminal cases, John Doe warrants have been revived, with a twist. Instead of providing a physical description of the defendant in a traditional sense, these warrants have spelled out the defendant's "type" at specific genetic locations. This has proved to be a useful tool in tolling the statute of limitations. The first John Doe DNA warrant was filed in 1999 by Norm Gahn, a prosecutor in the Milwaukee County District Attorney's Office. Since that time, numerous jurisdictions have filed these warrants. Several courts have upheld the use of John Doe DNA warrants reasoning that while an individual can readily change his/her identity, name, address, or even physical appearance, a person cannot change his/her DNA. As such, there is no better way to describe a defendant than by his/her genetic code.
2. *DNA admissibility hearings*

   In cold cases that are based primarily on the use of DNA evidence, the defense may challenge the admissibility on the ground that the technology is new or novel. In some jurisdictions, the court must find that such scientific technique is "generally accepted" in the relevant scientific community.[1] In other jurisdictions, the court must first find that the DNA testing was reliable.[2]

[1] See *Frye v. United States* (D.C. Cir. 1923) 293 Fed. 1013.
[2] See *Daubert v. Merrell* (1993) 509 U.S. 579.

Even if these hurdles are overcome, the defense may argue that there are problems with the testing so grave that no jury should hear the results.

When a cold case is filed, the prosecutor must be aware of the possibility of a pretrial challenge to the DNA evidence. In particular, the defense may challenge the strength of the evidence where a cold hit is made. The prosecution must be prepared for the testimony of expert witnesses retained by the defense.

3. *Evidentiary issues in cold cases*

Cold cases present several potential evidentiary issues for the prosecution. Because these issues may have significant impact on the outcome of the case, the prosecution and investigation team should work closely throughout the investigation and prosecution of the case. The following are potential evidentiary issues that may arise in a cold case:

- *Chain of custody:* One of the most common concerns in cold case homicides is the chain of custody. In many instances, items of evidence were packaged or stored inappropriately. Additionally, there is often an incomplete log detailing the chain of custody. In some cases, items of evidence were removed from law enforcement's possession without any record of it. In other cases, witnesses integral to the chain of custody are unavailable or deceased. While an improper chain of custody should not result in the exclusion of evidence, it may present defense claims that the integrity of the evidence has been compromised. As such, the prosecution must be prepared to address this with a jury.
- *Loss or destruction of evidence:* In many cold cases, evidence may be lost or destroyed. While this presents obvious challenges for the investigator, it also presents challenges for the prosecution. If items of evidence have been destroyed, the defense may seek sanctions against the prosecution, alleging a due process violation. In some instances, the defense may seek dismissal of the charges. In order for the defendant to win this motion, however, it must demonstrate that the evidence both possessed an exculpatory value that was apparent before the evidence was destroyed and was of such a nature that the defendant would be unable to obtain comparable evidence by other reasonably available means.[3] While it is rare that a defendant can succeed in a dismissal of charges on these grounds, both the investigator and the prosecutor should be prepared to litigate the motion when it is made.
- *Use of hypnosis:* In many cold cases, the investigators relied upon hypnosis to develop information from witnesses. While this practice may have aided the investigation, it will create problems for the prosecution in many states. If a prosecutor has hypnosis evidence in his/her case, it is imperative to consult the rules of evidence regarding that evidence. For instance, in California, the testimony of a witness who has been previously hypnotized is limited to events that the witness "recalled and related prior to the hypnotic session."[4] Clearly, such limitations on admissibility of such evidence can have a significant and adverse impact on the prosecution's case.
- *Insufficient memories of witnesses:* One of the most common concerns in cold cases is the inability of witnesses to recall the events surrounding the homicide. In most cases, witnesses can refresh their memories by reviewing the statements they gave to law enforcement. However, in cold cases, there may be little or no memory left to refresh, and reviewing the police report will do little or no good.

  In cases where a witness gave a prior statement to law enforcement but no longer recalls that statement, the contents of the written statement itself may nevertheless be admissible through an exception to the hearsay rule called *past recollection recorded*.[5] Through this exception, the

[3] See *California* v. *Trombetta* (1984) 467 U.S. 479.
[4] See *People v. Hayes* (1989) 49 Cal.3d 1260, 1263, 1270–73.
[5] See *Federal Rules of Evidence* section 803.

investigator may be allowed to read the witness's statement into evidence if certain factors have been proved. Most notably, if the prosecution can show that the statement of the witness was made at or near the time of the events and the events were still fresh in the witness's mind at the time of the statement, then the statement should be admissible.

The older the case, the more likely that witness memories will fail, and the more likely that the prosecutor will have to rely on the past recollection recorded hearsay exception at trial. The investigator must therefore anticipate this issue and determine whether the facts necessary to prove this exception can be met as he/she meets and reinterviews witnesses so that the prosecutor can later prove to the court that all the requirements of this exception have been met.

- *Admissibility of prior/post crime evidence:* In many cold cases, the defendant has a criminal history that includes similar crimes that occurred either before or even after the homicide. This type of evidence, particularly in sexually motivated homicide cases, can play a decisive role in the prosecution's case if it demonstrates the defendant's modus operandi. In some jurisdictions, the prosecution may use evidence of other sexual assaults to demonstrate that the defendant has a propensity to commit such crimes.[6]

  In a cold case prosecution, a complete background investigation of the defendant's criminal behavior, whether reported to law enforcement or not, is vital. This background investigation should include not only reports made to law enforcement but also interviews with family and friends of the defendant. In many instances, the defendant may have committed crimes against family or friends, but it was never reported to law enforcement.

  The use of prior/post criminal behavior not only may be used during the guilt phase of the prosecution's case but may also play a significant role in the penalty phase of a capitol murder case.

4. *Defense motion to dismiss for precomplaint delay*

   In many cold cases, years pass before the defendant is ever arrested and/or charged with the murder. In that time, evidence may have been lost or destroyed, memories have faded, and some witnesses may have died.

   A prearrest or prefiling delay in prosecution may constitute a denial of the defendant's right to a fair trial and to due process under the state and federal constitutions.[7] If the defense moves to dismiss charges for such delay, the court will likely undertake a three-step analysis to determine whether the delay violated the defendant's due process rights to a fair trial: (1) The defendant must show that he/she has been prejudiced by the delay. (2) If prejudice is established, then the burden shifts to the prosecution to justify the delay. (3) Finally, the court balances the prejudice to the defendant caused by the delay against the justification for that delay.[8] In addition, in order for the defendant to make a claim of a due process violation under the federal Constitution, he/she must show that the delay was undertaken to gain a tactical advantage over the defendant.[9]

   In cold cases, the prosecution must be prepared for a motion to dismiss for delay in prosecution. The prosecutor should be prepared to present evidence at a pretrial hearing to justify any delay in prosecution. In many cold cases, the prosecutor will need to establish that the charges could not have been filed without the use of new scientific tests. Further, the prosecution may also need to determine whether potential defense witnesses are really unavailable or *material* to the defense. In doing so, the prosecution can demonstrate to the court that the defendant has not been prejudiced by the delay.

[6] See *California Evidence Code* section 1108.
[7] See *People v. Caitlin* (2001) 26 Cal.4th 81, 108; see also *United States v. Marion* (1971) 401 U.S. 307.
[8] See *United States v. Lovasco* (1977) 431 U.S. 783, 789–790.
[9] See *United States v. Lovasco,* (1977) 431 U.S. 795.

Discovery Issues in Cold Cases

The prosecution has a legal and ethical duty to disclose evidence favorable to a defendant.[10] With this ethical obligation, it is imperative that all discovery be provided or made available to the defense once a defendant is charged in a cold case murder. In many cold cases, because of the passage of time, it may be very difficult to find all the documents related to the investigation. In some instances, reports, photographs, or tapes have been lost or destroyed. In some cases, reports were never written at all; rather, notes from the original investigator may be found in the original investigation file.

In order to comply with the prosecution's obligation under *Brady*, the following suggestions are made:

- *Obtain and copy original "murder book"*: In most cold cases, the police agency maintains an original murder book, which was the working copy of the homicide detective. While the records maintained in this file should have been given to the police agency's records division, in some instances, they were not. It is highly recommended that the prosecutor obtain, review, and copy the original file. This file will oftentimes contain such items as investigator notes, phone logs, suspect lead information, Polaroid photographs, and composites.
- *Record keeping for the prosecutor:* Cold cases can often involve hundreds, if not thousands, of pages of documents. As a result, it is important for the prosecutor to organize these documents for trial in a logical format. In addition to an organized file, it may be helpful for the prosecutor to keep a "master discovery" file that documents exactly what items have been discovered or made available to the defense. This practice will ensure that all discovery obligations have been satisfied.

Sentencing in Cold Cases

In cold cases, the defendant will be sentenced according to the law at the time of the crime. Therefore, while a first-degree murder conviction may currently result in a 25-to-life sentence, it may be significantly different for a first-degree murder that occurred 25 years ago. Thus, in Penny Parker's murder, if the defendant were convicted of first-degree murder, his resulting sentence would have been seven years to life.

Conclusion

Cold cases are exciting and challenging cases to investigate and prosecute. Law enforcement and prosecutors have an obligation to the families of murder victims to thoroughly investigate and prosecute those responsible for these crimes. With an effective investigation and prosecution, justice—while delayed—will be served.

The advent of DNA testing in particular has revolutionized murder investigations. Not only are more fresh murder cases being solved, but also, cases that have long languished for lack of leads are being resurrected. The window of opportunity to reopen these cold cases, however, is closing; time continues to exact its toll on surviving evidence, witnesses, and memories. At some point, courts will find that further delay in investigating and prosecuting these cases is inexcusable.

Penny Parker's family had to wait a quarter of a century for answers, but in the end, they got them. With the suicide of Penny's murderer, a painful chapter in their lives could be closed. Penny mattered to

[10] See *Brady v. Maryland* (1963) 373 U.S. 83.

the officers charged with solving her murder, and they did not allow her to be forgotten. Today, there are literally thousands of families just like Penny's all over the country. They, too, deserve answers.

Acknowledgments

I wish to acknowledge and express my deepest gratitude to Sacramento County District Attorney Anne Marie Schubert for authoring this chapter. Schubert was elected as Sacramento County District Attorney in June 2014. Prior to her election, she was a veteran cold case homicide prosecutor with the Sacramento County District Attorney's Office and was a founding member of the cold case homicide training program at the California Department of Justice Advanced Training Center. That program teamed experienced homicide investigative, prosecution, laboratory, and behavioral personnel to review unsolved homicide cases presented by the case investigator in a classroom atmosphere. Schubert has presented on the topic of cold case investigation and prosecution to numerous venues, including national prosecutors' conferences. In addition, Schubert wishes to acknowledge and extend her gratitude and recognition to Assistant Chief Deputy Jeff Rose (ret'd) and principal criminal attorney Eric Kindall for their contributions to and review of this chapter.

Databases: ViCAP, HITS, and TracKRS

7

R. H. WALTON

Contents

Due in large part to the political and local diversification of American law enforcement agencies, communication and information sharing have historically been cumbersome and inefficient. Nowhere is this more illustrated on occasion than in the field of homicide investigation, as agencies sometimes labored to solve homicides, unaware that perhaps their information held the key to solving a murder in another jurisdiction, or vice versa.

This chapter presents means and methods utilized to assist in the identification of related homicides through different levels of databases and increased information technology dedicated to identifying and comparing homicides, sexual assaults, and methods of operation. This chapter presents three examples of databases that have proven useful in the investigation of homicide and cold case homicides. These are the national Federal Bureau of Investigation (FBI) Violent Criminal Apprehension Program (ViCAP), the

Washington State Homicide Investigation and Tracking System (HITS) program, and the Orange County, California, Taskforce Aimed at Catching Killers, Rapists and Sexual Offenders (TracKRS) programs.

Violent Criminal Apprehension Program (ViCAP)

The FBI-based ViCAP database, known as ViCAP Web, is a free, state-of-the-art behavior-based crime analysis tool structured to address violent crime problems impacting law enforcement agencies today. It enables these agencies to collect, collate, enter, and analyze their own violent crime information on a local level and facilitates the identification of similar cases on a regional, state, and national basis. ViCAP Web is available to law enforcement agencies nationwide through secure Internet connectivity of the Law Enforcement Enterprise Portal (LEEP) of the FBI's Criminal Justice Information Services (CJIS) Division. It is only available to persons duly employed by law enforcement, criminal justice, or public safety agencies/departments.

ViCAP Web seeks to facilitate investigative coordination among geographically dispersed agencies to better enable them to identify and link crimes committed by violent serial offenders related to the following solved and unsolved violent crimes:

- Homicides (and attempts) that are known or suspected to be part of a series and/or are apparently random, motiveless, or sexually oriented
- Sexual assaults that are known or suspected to be part of a series and/or are committed by a stranger
- Missing persons where circumstances indicate a strong possibility of foul play and the victim is still missing
- Unidentified human remains where the manner of death is known or suspected to be homicide (FBI 2016)

The Beginnings

ViCAP originated from an idea by local law enforcement and the late Pierce R. Brooks. As a detective for the Los Angeles Police Department, California, in 1956, Detective Brooks investigated the murders of two Los Angeles women who had replied to an advertisement for photographic models. Their bodies, tied with rope in such a way as to suggest that their killer practiced bondage, were later found in the desert. Detective Brooks believed that these victims were not the killer's first murders. For 18 months, he used his off-duty time to visit the Los Angeles central library and read out-of-town newspapers to look for information on murders that exhibited characteristics similar to those he was investigating. He found such an article in a newspaper and, using pieces from that case coupled with his own cases, arrested an individual who was subsequently tried, convicted, and executed for the murders.

Detective Brooks refined this idea and concluded that a computer could capture relevant information about murders. If open and closed cases were stored in a computer, investigators could query the database for similar cases when confronted with new homicide investigations. In this manner, they could use clues from other cases that exhibited similar characteristics and, in turn, solve more cases. In addition, when investigators identified offenders, a search of the computer using their modus operandi (MO) would reveal other open cases for which they might be responsible.

In 1983, the Office of Juvenile Justice and Delinquency Prevention and the National Institute of Justice (NIJ) awarded a planning grant, the National Missing/Abducted Children and Serial Murder Tracking and Prevention Program, to Sam Houston State University in Texas. From a series of workshops, the last in November 1983, emerged the National Center for the Analysis of Violent Crime (NCAVC). Initial funding was provided by the U.S. Department of Justice, and the program was established under the direction and control of the FBI training center at Quantico, Virginia.

The NCAVC was specifically authorized to maintain a computer-assisted national clearinghouse for the analysis of violent crimes with specific interest in murder, rape, child sexual abuse, arson, and bombings. ViCAP is authorized by 28 U.S.C. §534 et seq. to collect, classify, analyze, and preserve records on violent crimes and their offenders. The NCAVC reviews crimes from both a behavioral and investigative perspective. ViCAP is a *confidential* system and is *exempt* under the provisions of the Privacy Act.

ViCAP was implemented at the FBI Academy on June 1, 1985, with the goal of identifying cases exhibiting similar characteristics and providing that information to law enforcement to facilitate cooperation and communication, enhance investigative coordination, and close cases (Figure 7.1). Pierce Brooks became the unit's first program manager, and this goal has remained unchanged. In its early stages, ViCAP became a part of the NCAVC with its goal to collect and analyze information, whether or not the offender was identified or arrested, regarding solved or unsolved homicides or attempts, especially those that

- Involved an abduction
- Were apparently random, motiveless, or sexually oriented
- Were known or suspected to be part of a series
- Involved a missing person, where the circumstances indicated a strong possibility of foul play and the victim was still missing
- Involved unidentified dead bodies, where the manner of death was known or suspected to be homicide

Figure 7.1 *FBI Law Enforcement Bulletin* cover, December 1986. (Courtesy of FBI/ViCAP.)

In cases where the offender had been arrested or identified, ViCAP requested that these cases be submitted so that unsolved cases in the ViCAP system could be linked to known offenders. Unfortunately, this was not always done, in part due to the length of the submission report (189 questions) and the time it took to complete it. Cold case investigators, during the course of file or case review, should attempt to identify whether the case had previously been submitted to ViCAP (Figure 7.2). This report may assist the investigator in understanding what was known at the time and provides an overview of the case. If the case was never submitted to ViCAP, it is recommended that the case *be submitted now.*

Cases where the offender has been arrested or identified should be submitted so unsolved cases in the ViCAP system can be compared to known offenders.

The early ViCAP submission requests and crime analysis reports addressed case components including

- Case administration
- Victim and offender information
- Identified offender Information
- Vehicle description
- Offense MO
- Condition of victim when found and cause of death or trauma
- Forensic evidence
- Request for profile
- Other related cases
- Narrative summary

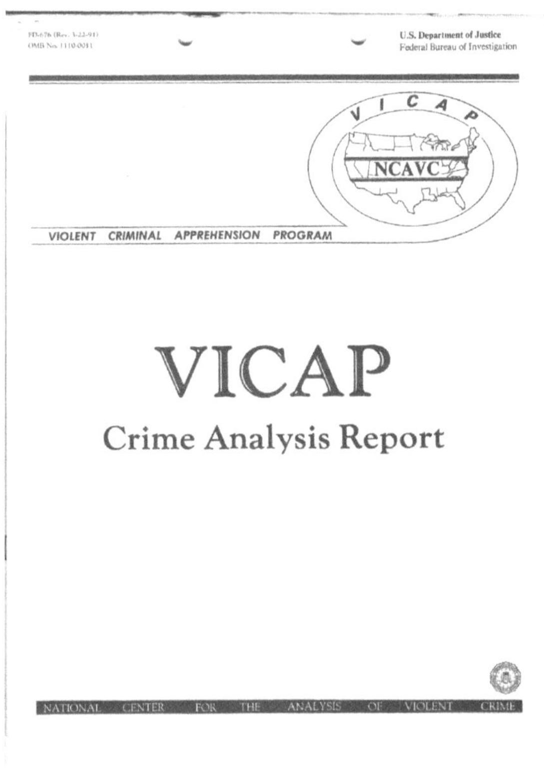

Figure 7.2 Early *ViCAP Crime Analysis Report* cover. (Courtesy of FBI/ViCAP.)

In 1994, the FBI established the Critical Incident Response Group (CIRG) to integrate tactical, negotiations, behavioral analysis, and crisis management resources into one cohesive structure to facilitate the FBI's rapid response to critical incidents. CIRG's services and capabilities include Counter–IED Operations, Strategic Information and Operations Center, Surveillance and Aviation, Tactical Operations, and Investigative and Operations Support (which includes the NCAVC) (FBI 2016).

The New ViCAP

In the mid-1990s, a business review revealed that (1) on an average, only 3% to 7% of the total numbers of annual homicides were being reported to ViCAP; (2) urban law enforcement agencies were not contributing their homicide data to the ViCAP database; (3) users were reporting that the 189-question ViCAP form was too cumbersome and difficult and they perceived that ViCAP case submissions entered a bureaucratic "black hole" never to emerge or be seen again; and (4) chronic understaffing caused a failure to address incoming case work on a timely basis. From this business review and legislative direction from Congress, changes were made. Included in these changes was a significant reduction in the number of questions.

The 189-question format was reduced to 95 questions (FBI 2016).

To increase response time to incoming work and requests, the number of analyst personnel was increased. A number of these had previous law enforcement experience. As a result of the system rework, ViCAP gave its new software and program a new name: the New ViCAP (Figure 7.3).

In 2004, the ViCAP form and software were redesigned to capture cases involving sexual assault. This was the first time ever on a nationwide basis. The questions were based upon the "Behaviorally Oriented

Figure 7.3 Later *ViCAP Crime Analysis cover.* (Courtesy of FBI/ViCAP.)

Interview of the Rape Victim" proposed by Robert Roy Hazelwood, and approved by a ViCAP working group and the ViCAP National Advisory Board. In addition to specific investigative questions, several questions related to the assault activity and suspect/offender behavior were added (FBI 2016).

In 2008, ViCAP significantly improved its platform from the client–server operation in which agencies loaded the ViCAP software on their own computer, entered their data, and then exported them to the FBI repository to a centralized web-based application, accessible in real-time by authorized users nationwide. This enhancement allowed law enforcement to quickly and efficiently share "relevant information about murders" as envisioned by Pierce Brooks more than 50 years earlier.

The events of 9/11 transformed many priorities of FBI resources. The primary mission of the NCAVC today is to provide behavioral-based investigative support to the FBI; national security agencies; and other local, state, tribal, and federal law enforcement involved in the investigation of unusual, repetitive violent crimes, threats, terrorism, cybercrimes, public corruption, and other matters. Today, it comprises five behavioral analysis units (BAUs):

- BAU 1: Counterterrorism, Arson, and Bombing
- BAU 2: Threats, Cybercrime, and Corruption
- BAU 3: Crimes Against Children
- BAU 4: Crimes Against Adults and ViCAP
- BAU 5: Strategic Initiatives Research and Training

Case Submission and Report Today

How It Works

The ViCAP case submission form and the ViCAP Web database collect detailed behavioral and investigative information through a series of 90 questions. The information is grouped into five main categories (Table 7.1), which are used to generate a report utilizing known information.

Authorized users sign on to ViCAP Web and enter case information by simply answering a series of questions utilizing radio buttons, check boxes, drop-down lists, and text boxes. On average, a single case takes less than 30 minutes to complete (Figures 7.4 and 7.5).

Once case entry is complete, users can conduct customized searches using a basic search template or an advanced search tree, to compare their case against all other cases in ViCAP (Figures 7.6 and 7.7).

In addition, each case is automatically and continuously compared against all other case submissions in the database to identify similar characteristics and to generate potential leads. ViCAP analysts review these results daily and also, as appropriate, perform additional case-specific analysis.

Thus, through ViCAP, cold case squads or investigators can store significant information about their cases without resorting to large volumes of file cabinets. With minimal information, a nickname, an address, or the name of a bar or other business, investigators can retrieve decades-old cases for further investigation. Conversely, cold case investigators looking for cases exhibiting an MO used by a suspect, or a series of cases matching a particular MO, can make those searches as well.

Despite their age, cold cases should be submitted to ViCAP today.

ViCAP Crime Analysis and the Report

The purpose of ViCAP is to collect data for analyses that will lead to the identification of patterns of violent crime throughout the county. Like any other database, however, it can only be as efficient as the data that are input into the system. A single submission received and analyzed by the ViCAP staff could initiate a coordinated effort among numerous law enforcement agencies, perhaps hundreds or thousands of miles apart, to expedite identification and solution of one or more violent crimes.

Table 7.1 ViCAP Case Submission Categories of Behavioral and Investigative Information

Basic case information
Case administration
Victim/offender names
Narrative
Dates and locations
Victim information
Demographics
Background
Suspect/offender information
Demographics
Background
Timeline
Case characteristics
Approach to victim
Trauma
Weapon
Sexual activity
Incident details
Victim release/recovery
Vehicle
Supplemental information
Forensic/physical evidence
Similar cases
Addendum
Attachments

Figure 7.4 Law Enforcement Entrance Portal. (Courtesy of FBI/ViCAP.)

Cases meeting ViCAP submission criteria with an arrested or *identified* offender can be entered into the ViCAP system by law enforcement investigators for comparison within the database to unsolved cases. Cases with an *unidentified* offender may also be submitted for database comparison.

The purpose of this continual comparison process is to detect signature aspects/traits of homicide and similar patterns of MO, which in turn may allow ViCAP personnel to pinpoint those crimes that have been

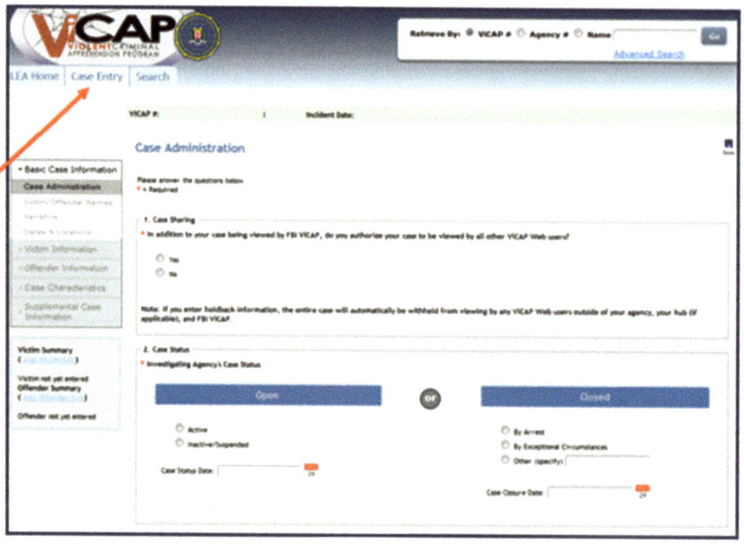

Figure 7.5 ViCAP Case Entry Screen. (Courtesy of FBI/ViCAP.)

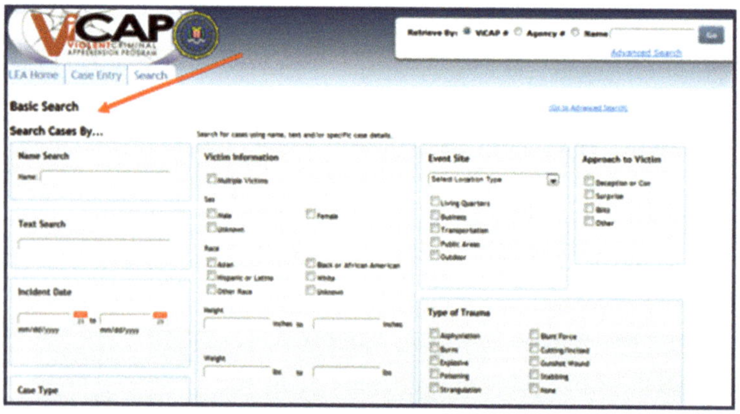

Figure 7.6 ViCAP Basic Search Screen. (Courtesy of FBI/ViCAP.)

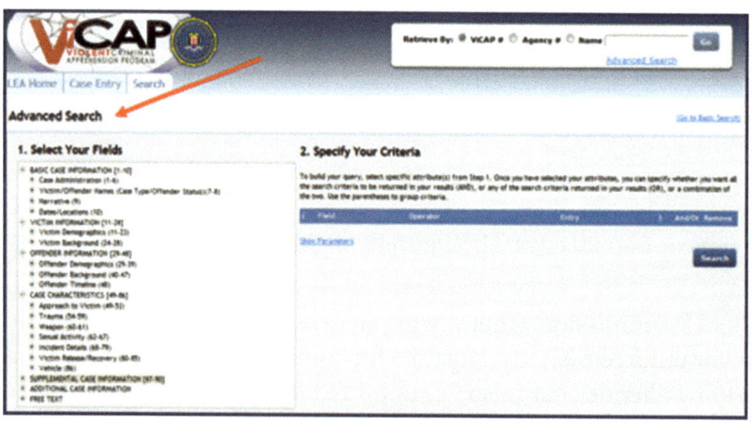

Figure 7.7 ViCAP Advanced Search Screen. (Courtesy of FBI/ViCAP.)

committed by the same offender. When such patterns are identified, involved law enforcement agencies will be notified.

When a pattern of criminal activity is discovered, ViCAP can assist law enforcement agencies by coordinating a multiagency investigative conference for case review. This may become especially important when suspects travel throughout the country, and enhances

- Information sharing
- Coordination of activities such as interview topics that may link cases
- Successful interview and interrogation techniques
- Specific evidence to be identified in search warrants
- Unique or specialty laboratory tests to be conducted

In addition, ViCAP also offers other investigative support services, including

- Timelines
- National Crime Information Center (NCIC) off-line searches
- NLETS searches
- Investigative matrix
- Case consultation, coordination, and facilitation, and training in crime analysis
- Access to
  - Military records
  - Private and non–law enforcement databases
  - Internal FBI resources
  - LexisNexis
  - Vehicle records and more

Highway Serial Killings Initiative

The case study illustrated in Chapter 4 is that of a serial killer employed as a long-distance truck driver. This is but one of hundreds of such persons suspected in cases throughout the nation.

ViCAP has undertaken an extensive effort to provide additional support to law enforcement agencies investigating violent crimes that have a nexus to the nation's highways. In April 2009, with the support of the trucking industry, it launched the Highway Serial Killings (HSK) Initiative. ViCAP analysts have developed extensive timelines on suspects through the utilization of a variety of reliable sources of information. They also enter information from cases meeting HSK criteria (see below) in a victim matrix (Figure 7.8). By comparing information in the victim matrix to suspect timelines, the analysts are able to assist in investigations by advising agencies who have contributed case information to the victim matrix about the identity of potential suspects. Additionally, when a suspect is identified or a group of cases are determined to be linked to a common offender, other behavioral analytical services can be provided in furtherance of the investigation.

HSK case criteria:

- Homicide victims whose remains were recovered along a highway or at a location associated with a highway (rest stop, truck stop, gas station, and/or restaurant located along a major highway), to include truck drivers found murdered in their trucks
- Missing persons whose last known location was along a highway or location associated with a highway

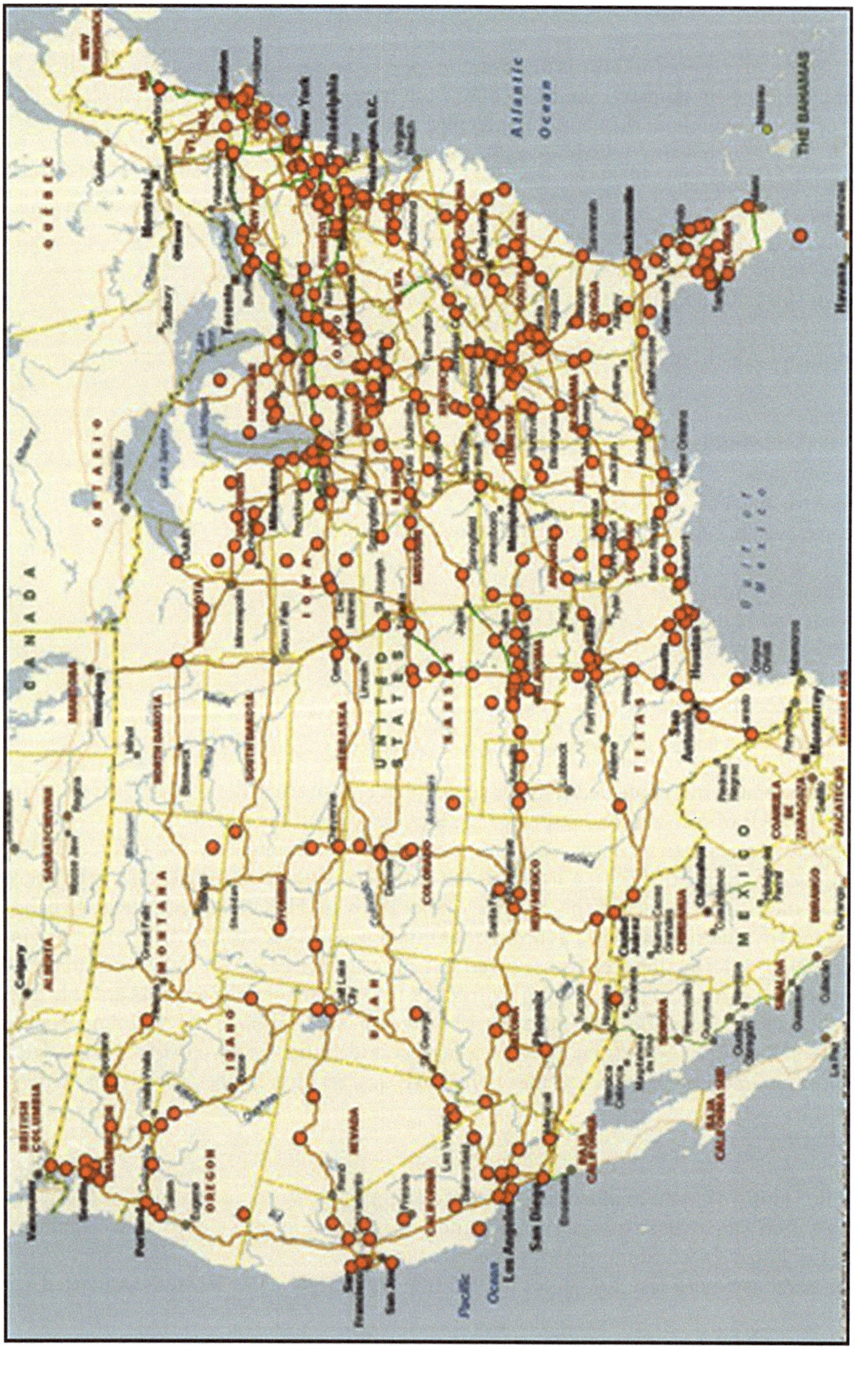

Figure 7.8 National map of murder victims found along or near U.S. highways. (Courtesy of FBI/ViCAP.)

Highway Serial Killings Initiative
An Investigative Checklist

FOR UNSOLVED CASES:

REMEMBER

- ✓ Don't be too quick to assume either the victim or the offender is local
- ✓ In these cases, the offender is highly mobile – may have no connection to the general area or the dump site specifically

Crime Characteristics

- ✓ The offender's truck is often the crime scene, meaning *the crime scene is mobile*
- ✓ Bodies dumped near areas of egress to interstates
- ✓ Victims often found nude/partially clothed

Victim Characteristics

- ✓ Victims are "picked up" at:
  - o Truck stops
  - o Service stations
  - o Along the roadway
  - o Sometimes contacted by CB
- ✓ Most are "high risk" – prostitutes, transients, hitchhikers, stranded motorists
- ✓ Consider HSK when unidentified female victims are found along the roadway

Investigative Resources

- ✓ GPS records from date of incident
  - o Request *immediately* because typically purged within 7-14 days
  - o Subpoena required
- ✓ HSK LEO SIG – for cold cases
  - o www.leo.gov (HSK-SIG)
  - o Search timelines of known offenders who were truck drivers

FOR IDENTIFIED OFFENDERS:

REMEMBER

- ✓ Be sure to request the below records not only from the subject's current employer but also previous employers.

Records to Request

- ✓ Employment application/history
  - o Especially looking for employment history and contact information such as address(es)
- ✓ Routing assignments
  - o NOTE: Driver may divert from his assigned route
- ✓ GPS records if employer tracks its vehicles
- ✓ Driver logs
  - o Driver himself may keep multiple copies
- ✓ Any time-stamped records
  - o Fuel receipts
  - o Bills of lading
  - o Scale/inspection records
  - o Maintenance receipts
  - o Toll records (ex: EZ Pass)
  - o Records of cash advances
  - o Truck stop frequent user card
    - ▪ Tracks date/location of purchases, like a receipt
- ✓ Driver history
  - o Tickets/citations, failed inspections, etc.
- ✓ Surveillance video from nearby businesses
  - o Including truck stops

Please submit your case to ViCAP Web – you can request searches for similar cases, compilation of timelines, and additional analysis on your case.

Additional resources available through the FBI's National Center for the Analysis of Violent Crime (NCAVC) Behavioral Analysis Units (BAUs):

BAU-2: Crimes Against Adults/
BAU-3: Crimes Against Children
Crime scene assessments, interview/investigative/ media/prosecutorial strategies, unknown offender profile, search warrant assistance, etc.

BAU-4: ViCAP
Crime analysis, similar case searches (ViCAP Web, NLETS, etc.), NCIC off-lines, victim/subject timelines, crime mapping, ViCAP alerts, etc.

For further information or to discuss your case please contact the NCAVC at (703) 632-4400.

For Law Enforcement Use Only

Revised 8/6/2012

Figure 7.9 HSK Checklist. (Courtesy of FBI/ViCAP.)

- Victims of sexual assault where there is a connection to a highway or a location associated with a highway
- Truck drivers or other individuals who have been investigated or arrested for the murder, kidnapping, or sexual assault of one or more victims along a highway or at a location associated with a highway (Figure 7.9) (FBI 2016)

Future Developments and Technology

Since the first edition of this text, that which was considered to be in the future has, in many cases, become reality. ViCAP is currently working on various upgrades to the existing infrastructure. Simultaneously, research and testing are being performed to incorporate geospatial mapping technology that will enable authorized users to manipulate, convert, analyze, and geographically plot violent crime data. Future development will include a powerful timeline component that can seamlessly integrate data from various sources and formats into a template with robust search functionality.

Case History: Bag of Bones

The following is reproduced from the June 2003, issue of the *FBI Law Enforcement Bulletin*.

In 2001, a ViCAP crime analyst reviewed a state police publication that mentioned a bag of human bones found by hunters in a seaboard forest of an eastern state. The victim was a white male, about 40–60 years old, and between 5'7" and 5'9" in height. His cause of death was blunt force trauma to the head. Recovered with the remains was a 14-carat gold ring with engraved letters. Authorities had no leads for identification of the remains.

A ViCAP crime analyst searched the database using the physical description of the victim and then made an additional search, thinking that the letters engraved in the ring might be the initials of a name. A possible match was made with a July 1998 case where three people were reported missing from a midwestern state. The report was made by a fourth member of the family, a son, who waited a week before reporting his mother, father, and sibling as missing persons. Personnel had exhausted all investigative leads.

Authorities in the eastern and midwestern states contacted each other. In January 2001, ViCAP learned that forensic odontology had identified the bones in the bag as those of the father missing from the midwestern state. The letters in the recovered ring represented the maiden name of the missing mother and the name of the missing father.

ViCAP learned later that a suspect was identified and charged with the murder—the oldest son, who made the report in the Midwest.

ViCAP Alert

The monthly *FBI Law Enforcement Bulletin* publishes this feature to alert law enforcement agencies of solved and unsolved homicides and other cases inclusive within the ViCAP system. This alert is prepared at the request of the law enforcement agency and provides the agency name, location, and telephone number of a contact person. Information is further disseminated through the *Law Enforcement On-line Newsletter* and other media. These notices typically address (1) offender descriptive data, (2) crime(s), (3) background, (4) MO, and (5) maps showing travel. In addition, photographs or composites of the offender and vehicles are broadcast when possible.

The Homicide Investigation and Tracking System (HITS)

Detectives conducting investigations need methods and tools that will help them do their jobs as effectively and efficiently as possible. Ready access to information about the crimes being investigated is one of their needs. This information is crucial in order to develop good leads and, in turn, to solve the case. Collected information appropriately analyzed facilitates investigation success and public safety.

Washington State's HITS is an example of a regional system that relies on law enforcement agencies in the Pacific Northwest, primarily Washington and Oregon, to voluntarily submit information to it on murders, attempted murders, missing-persons cases in which foul play is suspected, unidentified persons believed to be murder victims, and predatory sex offenses in the Pacific Northwest.

HITS was originally developed by Robert D. Keppel, PhD, who started the program in Washington State in 1987. High-profile cases such as Ted Bundy and the Green River Killer emphasized the need for such a program due to the multijurisdictional offenses so often committed by serial offenders. The National Institute of Justice (NIJ), the research arm of the Department of Justice, played a key role in the development of this project. This same organization encouraged Pierce Brooks in the 1970s to pursue ViCAP, which was originally designed to provide local law enforcement access. From the start, it was such a success that the state legislature mandated it also track all violent crimes, including sex crimes. HITS helps investigators by allowing them access via computer to a wide range of information about serious crimes and to resources that can help solve them.

HITS collects, collates, and analyzes the noticeable characteristics of all murders and predacious sexual offenses in the states of Washington and Oregon. HITS complements federal research and programs against violent crime because the system generates a ViCAP report, which is sent to the National Center for Analysis of Violent Crime (NCAVC). ViCAP staff can then determine if the similar pattern characteristics exist among the individual cases in the ViCAP system.

HITS provides three major services to law enforcement agencies. First, it supplies information related to a murder or predatory sexual assault case, including the following:

- Incidents with similar characteristics involving murder, attempted murder, suspected murder, or predatory sexual assault and persons missing as a result of suspected foul play
- Evidence, victimology, offender characteristics, offender's method of operation, associates, geographical location of the case, weapons, and vehicles
- Identification of known murderers and sex offenders living in a particular community

Second, HITS permits analysis of murder cases to identify the following:

- Factors that may help solve a particular murder case
- Possible links between a single victim, offender, or case and other incidents of violence
- Verification of statements provided by informants, offenders, or both, in which the information relating to an alleged murder is incomplete or questionable

Third, HITS provides investigators with the following resources:

- Names of experts who can assist with a murder or sexual assault investigation
- Advice and technical assistance on the various steps to be followed in a murder or sexual assault investigation

Prior to HITS use in Washington, the only way to obtain this type of crime information was through time-consuming, labor-intensive personal visits, interviews, telephone calls, teletypes, and mail. By filling out a simple form that takes less than 30 minutes, investigators save countless hours on the phone or on their feet searching for information that the HITS system locates for them. More importantly, HITS provides investigators with that important two-way communication.

As with ViCAP and TracKRS, HITS was founded on the premise that information plays a critical role in solving homicides. The key to solving crimes and making arrests is to understand how much and what kind of information is available and how to organize it to make it more accessible and useful. Because of the need to collect and collate violent crime information, HITS investigator/analysts work very closely with police detectives to provide assistance in their cases.

In the opinion of expert homicide investigator Vernon Geberth, the most viable alternative to ViCAP is a series of statewide or regional systems that compile all serious crimes such as rape, murder, and gang-related crime into integrated databases that provide ready access to local law enforcement. In addition, any missing-persons cases where the circumstances indicate that they are missing under suspicious circumstances as well as unidentified bodies where the manner of death is known or suspected to be homicidal in nature should be entered into the system.

Taskforce Aimed at Catching Killers, Rapists and Sexual Offenders (TracKRS)

In 1996, the Orange County, California, District Attorney's Office recognized that there were approximately 1000 unsolved murders in the county and that efforts to link cases were fragmented due to rotations, retirements, promotions, and a lack of central information. The office believed that legislation, DNA science, and technology existed that could be better utilized if local law enforcement united to organize those resources. The district attorney (DA) accepted that leadership role and responsibility.

In March 1997, the DA proposed the TracKRS Project to the Orange County Chiefs of Police and Sheriff's Association, and it was adopted unanimously.

The DA's office TracKRS Unit would provide investigators access to a central database of homicide and sexual assault cases and offer a problem-solving team to assist local investigators (Figure 7.10).

Purpose of TracKRS

Committed to helping protect the community by providing the best available resources for investigators to obtain the highest yield from their efforts, the agency operated on the premise that "if you give good investigators good resources, they will get good results."

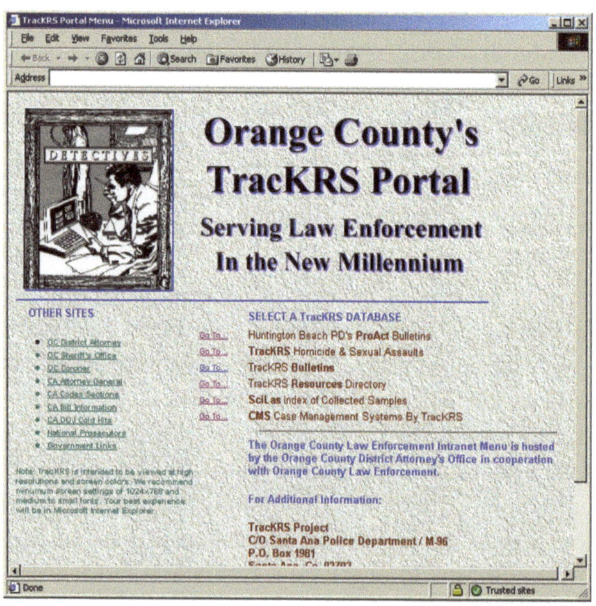

Figure 7.10 Orange County TracKRS Portal. (Courtesy of Investigator Ron Shave, Orange County District Attorney's Office [ret'd].)

The Scope of TracKRS

The heart of TracKRS is an information system available to investigators from their desktop computer via a secure Internet site maintained by the DA. The TracKRS Unit has focused on providing resources to help in the investigation of our community's worst crimes, homicides, and sexual assaults. The unit identifies what investigators need, establishes a plan, and seeks to provide the solutions. The unit is flexible and responsive.

The TracKRS Review Committee is the team that helps the TracKRS Unit identify the problems and set priorities. The committee consists of police investigators, crime analysts, criminalists, forensic technicians, fingerprint experts, deputy DAs, DA's investigators, and other experts willing to help TracKRS identify the roadblocks that interfere with homicide and sexual assault investigations. Solutions, in light of available resources, are recommended. The TracKRS Unit implements the solution.

The team meets quarterly, and any law enforcement person is welcome to attend.

Why Homicides and Sexual Assaults?

There are several reasons TracKRS has targeted homicide and sexual assault cases. The obvious is that these crimes exact a huge toll on the victims and their families, and the implications to the community are enormous. But there are also very sound statistics, technologies, and legislation that have prompted their focus.

As many experienced investigators know, most sexual offenders repeat their crimes. For instance, if you have an unsolved sexual murder, there is strong likelihood your suspect has prior conviction(s) in cases with similarities to yours. This knowledge has helped law enforcement to better focus their work on cases that will improve results. However, the necessary computer technology and data must be available to the investigator to achieve better results. Fortunately, TracKRS has the technology and has made it available to local investigators. It enables investigators to link evidence, characteristics of the crime, offender's MO, and signature of the offender.

DNA technology has improved dramatically since the inception of the TracKRS Unit. DNA examinations that once took weeks can now be performed in days, if not hours. Examinations that once required a substantial amount of sample can now be performed on microscopic cells. Also, the federal, state, and sheriff's crime labs are now using compatible DNA standards for comparison. In addition, new legislation permits law enforcement to collect samples from previous offenders. Each new component alone does not solve cases. They are additional tools available to Orange County investigators, and cooperation and coordination can dramatically improve their results.

On April 16, 2001, the *Los Angeles Times* reported, "A string of arrests in old murder cases has catapulted Orange County from worst to first when it comes to solving homicides in Southern California…." "Wheelock's case also underscores a dramatic improvement by investigators in Orange County, which a decade ago posted the regions worst record in clearing homicides" (Leonard 2001).

This "dramatic turnaround" since TracKRS was implemented in 1997 was a direct result of an overwhelming team effort supported by Orange County administrators. The sheriff's crime lab committed extensive resources, as well as their cold case unit. Many cities supported the reviews of cold cases, and Santa Ana, Garden Grove, Anaheim, Costa Mesa, and Newport Beach, among others, committed investigators solely to cold case investigations.

TracKRS Development

The effort to develop the TracKRS Unit was to provide local investigators a database of homicides and sexual assault cases that they could research themselves. In March of 1997, every Orange County chief and the Orange County sheriff agreed to support the project by providing their cases for input into the TracKRS MO database. The DA's office began entering the descriptions of previously prosecuted offenders to support the premise that those offenders were likely responsible for unsolved cases. The database was designed with the investigator in mind. Queries are simple, and the response is immediate.

TracKRS has also provided a more efficient means to share information. The Bulletins database provides investigators the ability to immediately post online any information they believe will be able to help other investigators. This information remains available and will not be deleted. Think of it as a permanent teletype (Figure 7.11).

The Resource Directory is similar to an online phone book of investigators and other experts in the law enforcement community (Figure 7.12).

TracKRS authorized investigators have access to data 24 hours a day, 7 days a week, from their desktop computer over a secure Internet connection.

Projects Involving TracKRS

Cold Case Reviews

Cold case reviews and collecting the case information for the database were among the most difficult challenges of TracKRS. Investigators often have too much responsibility on current caseloads to take time out to review cold cases. In response, TracKRS employed retired investigators to help review cold cases and get the information online. During those reviews, observations are made as to what evidence may benefit from new technology. Since its inception, many murder cases were identified with what is likely suspect DNA and others through Cal-ID (an automated fingerprint identification system) fingerprint hits on prints previously entered into Cal-ID. TracKRS does the data entry, and the local investigator gets an online case summary that is available to all new investigators and supervisors who may rotate through the office.

To help with the collection of current case information, most agencies have provided TracKRS with a liaison officer. That person ensures that TracKRS is provided with copies of the appropriate cases. Without a complete set of cases, offenders may slip through the cracks.

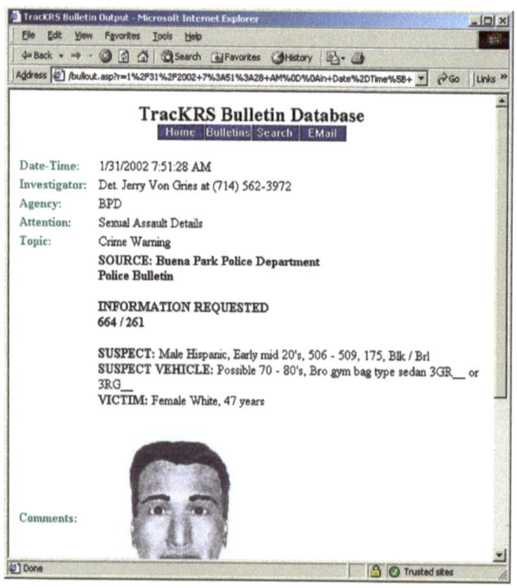

Figure 7.11 TracKRS Bulletin Database. (Courtesy of Investigator Ron Shave, Orange County District Attorney's Office [ret'd].)

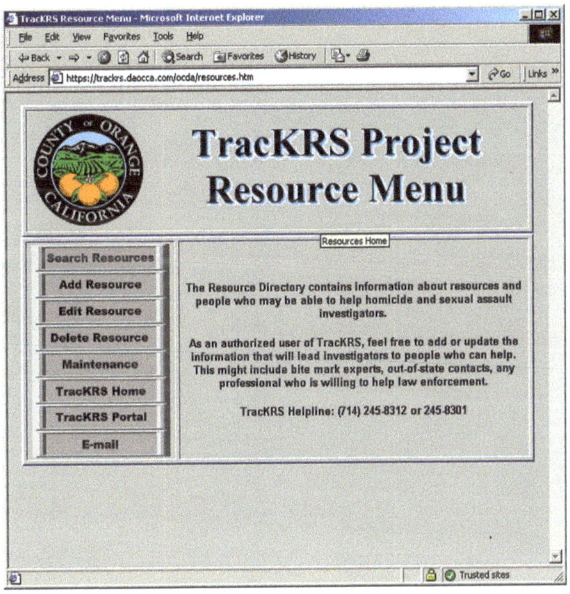

Figure 7.12 TracKRS Project Resource Menu. (Courtesy of Investigator Ron Shave, Orange County District Attorney's Office [ret'd].)

Cold Case Investigations

The *Los Angeles Times* reference to the murder of Larry Wheelock in 1975 is an example of a TracKRS cold case investigation. TracKRS investigators actually investigated the case with the consent of the responsible agency. In this example, TracKRS had submitted fingerprint evidence for resubmission to Cal-ID as part of the case review process even though it had been previously entered into Cal-ID. As a result, a suspect, Larry Paige, was identified and later convicted. Although TracKRS investigated the case, TracKRS does not take over a case without consent. TracKRS will only work within the boundaries agreed upon by the agency "owning" the investigation.

The Samples Collected Index—Location, Activity, and Status Database (SciLas)

The TracKRS Review Committee recognized that although state law authorized the collection of blood samples from certain mandated offenders and even provided reimbursement for the effort, local law enforcement was not collecting the samples from out-of-custody offenders. Translated, this meant that law enforcement might miss connecting suspects to DNA collected from crime scenes. In response, the TracKRS Review Committee determined that Orange County investigators needed assistance in getting the samples collected.

TracKRS created a database, now known as the Samples Collected Index—Location, Activity, and Status Database (SciLas), to help track the collection effort and established an efficient system for the collection of the samples (Figures 7.13 and 7.14).

The SciLas program at TracKRS provides investigators access to the SciLas database, a blood collection site at a local police department, and training to assure that the offenders in every jurisdiction have provided samples.

The Sexual Assault Backlog Reduction Effort (SABRE)

Sexual Assault Backlog Reduction Effort (SABRE) is hosted by the sheriff's office. It is a project that aims to identify and collect rape kits requiring DNA examination going back to January 1995. TracKRS assists the

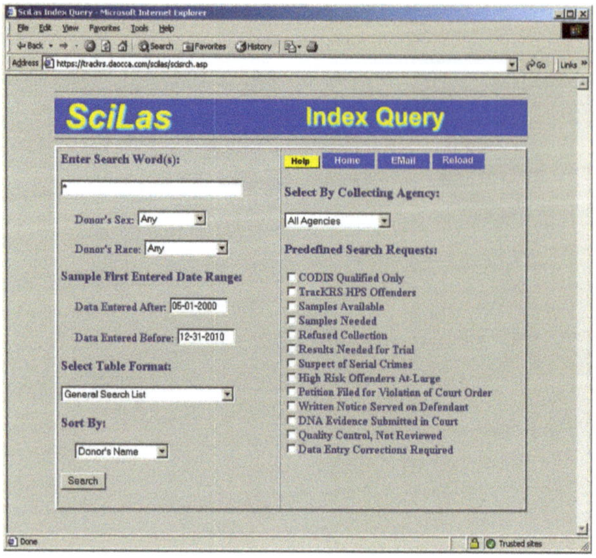

Figure 7.13 SciLas Index Query. (Courtesy of Investigator Ron Shave, Orange County District Attorney's Office [ret'd].)

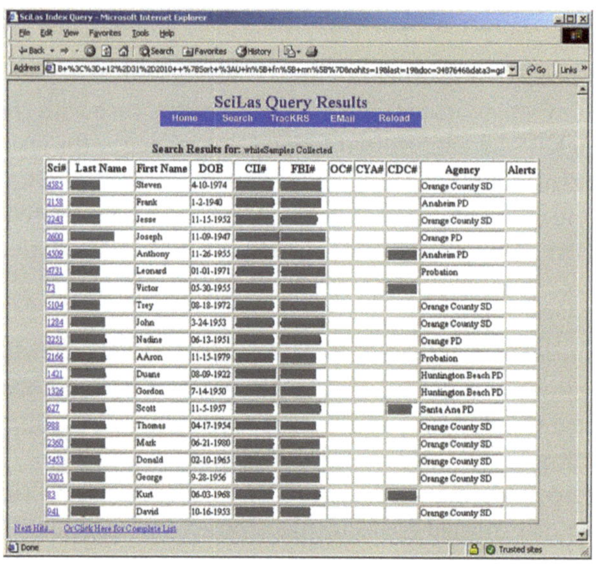

Sci#	Last Name	First Name	DOB	CII#	FBI#	OC#	CYA#	CDC#	Agency	Alerts
4585	[redacted]	Steven	4-10-1974	[redacted]	[redacted]				Orange County SD	
2138	[redacted]	Frank	1-2-1940	[redacted]	[redacted]				Anaheim PD	
2243	[redacted]	Jesse	11-15-1952	[redacted]	[redacted]				Orange County SD	
2600	[redacted]	Joseph	11-09-1947	[redacted]	[redacted]				Orange PD	
4509	[redacted]	Anthony	11-26-1955	[redacted]	[redacted]			[redacted]	Anaheim PD	
4731	[redacted]	Leonard	01-01-1971	[redacted]	[redacted]				Probation	
73	[redacted]	Victor	05-30-1955	[redacted]	[redacted]			[redacted]		
5104	[redacted]	Trey	08-18-1972	[redacted]	[redacted]				Orange County SD	
1284	[redacted]	John	3-24-1953	[redacted]	[redacted]				Orange County SD	
3251	[redacted]	Nadine	06-13-1951	[redacted]	[redacted]				Orange PD	
2166	[redacted]	AAron	11-15-1979	[redacted]	[redacted]				Probation	
1421	[redacted]	Duane	08-09-1922	[redacted]	[redacted]				Huntington Beach PD	
1326	[redacted]	Gordon	7-14-1950	[redacted]	[redacted]				Huntington Beach PD	
627	[redacted]	Scott	11-5-1957	[redacted]	[redacted]			[redacted]	Santa Ana PD	
988	[redacted]	Thomas	04-17-1954	[redacted]	[redacted]				Orange County SD	
2360	[redacted]	Mark	06-21-1980	[redacted]	[redacted]				Orange County SD	
5453	[redacted]	Donald	02-10-1965	[redacted]	[redacted]				Orange County SD	
5005	[redacted]	George	9-28-1956	[redacted]	[redacted]				Orange County SD	
83	[redacted]	Kurt	06-03-1968	[redacted]	[redacted]			[redacted]		
941	[redacted]	David	10-16-1953	[redacted]	[redacted]				Orange County SD	

Figure 7.14 SciLas Query Results. (Courtesy of Investigator Ron Shave, Orange County District Attorney's Office [ret'd].)

sheriff's office in that effort. The cases are entered into the TracKRS database and enable the DA's office to guarantee that the cases with DNA can be prosecuted at any later date (Figure 7.15).

Prefiling Case Reviews of DNA Cases In January 2001, the statute of limitations for certain sex crimes was extended from 6 years to 10 years, and if suspect DNA was identified, there was no statute of limitations on the crime. It could be prosecuted at any later date, with few restrictions. The DA's office established

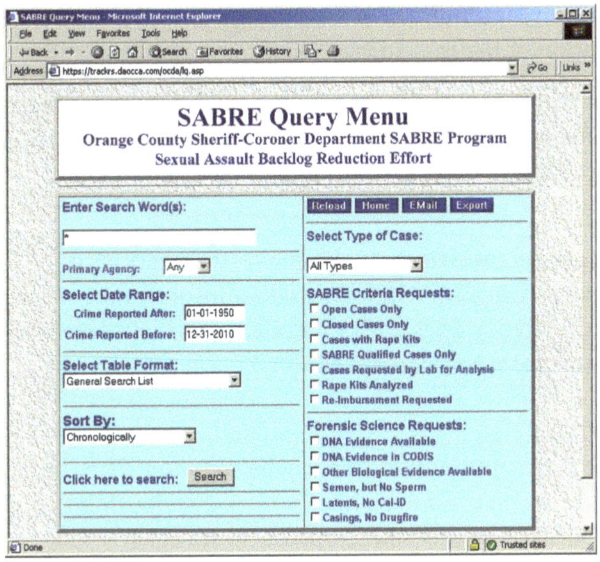

Figure 7.15 SABRE Query Menu. (Courtesy of Investigator Ron Shave, Orange County District Attorney's Office [ret'd].)

a procedure to protect those cases from the consequences of time. Since the TracKRS database is able to track the unsolved cases that have DNA, the unit will request certain qualifying cases to be submitted to the deputy DA assigned to review cases for critical evidence that can only be gathered at, or about, the time of the crime. The review will assure each agency that the case will not be forfeited at some later date on a technicality.

Inmates Refusing to Give Blood Samples TracKRS discovered that California law did not authorize the collection of blood from inmates with reasonable force when they refuse to provide a mandated sample. Therefore, the California Department of Corrections had ceased blood collections from nearly 16,000 mandated inmates, a group certainly more likely to be connected to DNA crime scene samples than any other group. TracKRS prompted the involvement of the DA's office and helped propose new legislation.

Evidence Retention Guidelines In meetings with property and evidence persons in Orange County, TracKRS was advised that every agency has difficult decisions to make when it came to the retention of evidence. The problem has been exacerbated because of the new statute of limitations on sex crimes and legislation on postconviction DNA testing of evidence. Even the moral implications of destroying evidence that now may be able to identify dangerous predators, or exonerate the innocent, are a consideration.

Streamlining Failure to Register Violation Filings Investigators complained to TracKRS that the filing process for registration violations by sex offenders was difficult and inconvenient. In response, the DA's office established guidelines for filing violations and has assigned attorneys to assist investigators with filing the cases. The same guidelines may be used for offenders who refuse to give blood samples, when required to do so pursuant to law.

The FBI's Violent Criminal Apprehension Program (ViCAP) The FBI hosts a national database of significant homicide cases, ViCAP. Orange County entered into an agreement with the FBI to provide homicide case information to the national database. TracKRS is required to collect all Orange County homicide information and put that information into the ViCAP computer. TracKRS has the ViCAP forms available and can assist in the preparation of the case information upon request.

The State Department of Justice Sexual Predator Apprehension Team (SPAT) The California Department of Justice implemented the Sexual Predator Apprehension Team (SPAT). The team is available to assist local law enforcement locate Orange County's worst offenders. TracKRS maintains a liaison with those investigators.

Referrals Occasionally, TracKRS investigators will make observations or obtain information that may be able to assist local investigations. TracKRS will forward that information to a supervisor for evaluation. The referral is a courtesy. What the agency does with that referral is their decision; however, TracKRS appreciates feedback, especially in an effort to update case information.

Murder Case Due Diligence

The DA's office entered into agreements with local agencies to better share murder case due-diligence information. The program aims to eliminate duplicated efforts by distributing the work between the originating agency that has obtained a murder warrant and the prosecuting agency. The details of the distribution were described in a memorandum of agreement signed by each of the chiefs of police and the DA.

The due-diligence work performed is summarized on the TracKRS database. This ensures that cases are not neglected due to transfers, promotions, retirements, workload, or misunderstandings between agencies.

The DA acknowledged that the originating agency owns the case and has the right to continue the investigation when the defendant is arrested. However, case law requires the prosecutor to provide the court with justification to proceed with the prosecution. The prosecutor needs sufficient written documentation and witnesses to prove that an adequate ongoing effort was made to arrest the defendant since the warrant was issued (Figures 7.16 and 7.17).

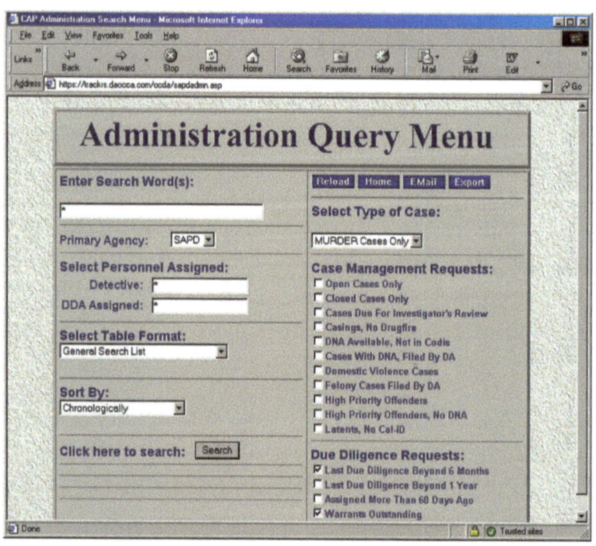

Figure 7.16 Administration Query Menu. The DA's office and the primary investigating agency will be able to log on to TracKRS and determine what cases need attention. The queries are simple. Just make the menu selections for the conditions of interest. (Courtesy of Investigator Ron Shave, Orange County District Attorney's Office [ret'd].)

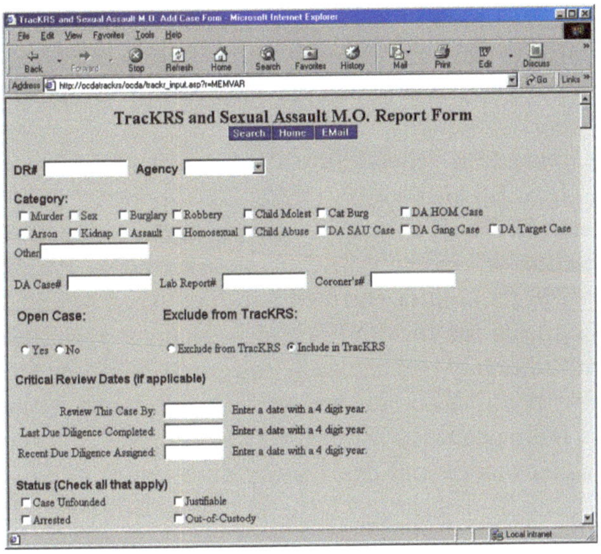

Figure 7.17 TracKRS and Sexual Assault MO Report Form. TracKRS will update case summaries and the dates relevant to due diligence. (Courtesy of Investigator Ron Shave, Orange County District Attorney's Office [ret'd].)

Conclusion

TracKRS has focused on the provision of an MO database of homicide and sexual assaults, a means to manage the collection of DNA samples, and a system to address the backlog of casework examinations. Together, the project addresses the three components required to get the best results from DNA. The three components are

- An MO database to identify cases linked by leads other than DNA
- A DNA collection process that helps ensure that required offenders are in the CODIS database
- An examination process to get as much casework evidence examined as possible to connect to other cases and offender DNA

The TracKRS Review Committee constantly evaluates the investigators' needs and works to remove obstacles and provide the coordinated efforts the community deserves. The Orange County District Attorney's Office believes that by taking regional responsibility for integrating law, science, and technology, they are continually providing good investigators with better resources.

Acknowledgments

I wish to thank the Federal Bureau of Investigation and to acknowledge its leadership role in enhancing law enforcement and its proactive efforts to protect citizens from violent, predatory, and often serial offenders. Through programs such as ViCAP and the HSK, the bureau has facilitated law enforcement and communication and public safety.

I wish to acknowledge Eric Witzig, major case specialist, and former crime analyst Jane Whitmore for their contributions to the initial chapter section in the first edition.

This updated edition has drawn heavily upon materials and documents furnished to the author from FBI ViCAP. Specifically, I wish to acknowledge my deepest appreciation to Glen "Gunny" Wildey of ViCAP for his support and assistance, as well as Lesa Marcolini, FBI ViCAP program manager, and all who assisted them.

For further information, contact the Federal Bureau of Investigation Critical Incident Response Group, FBI Academy, Quantico, Virginia, 22135.

This basics of the discussion on the HITS program are reprinted with permission from Vernon Geberth and are taken from his benchmark homicide investigation textbook, *Practical Homicide Investigation: Tactics, Procedures, and Forensic Techniques*, third edition (published by CRC Press). Geberth is a retired lieutenant commander of homicide for the NYPD and is renowned worldwide for his experience and expertise in this field. The first edition of this textbook was proclaimed "the Bible" by experts in the field of homicide investigations. Geberth is an accomplished writer and lecturer on the myriad of subjects encompassed under the umbrella of homicide investigation.

In addition, I wish to acknowledge and express my deep gratitude to Chief Criminal Investigator Marvin Skeen of the Washington State Attorney General's Office HITS program, and his salient wisdom over the years.

I wish to acknowledge and extend my gratitude to Investigator Ronald Shave (ret'd) of the Orange County District Attorney's Office for the initial authorship of the TracKRS segment and to recognize and extend my deepest appreciation also to Senior Agent Carlos Field of the Orange County District Attorney's Office for his review of this chapter for updating.

Suggested Readings and Bibliography

Attorney General's Office. Washington State. http://www.atg.wa.gov/hits-overview.

FBI. (2016). Handbook of Forensic Services. U.S. Department of Justice, Federal Bureau of Investigation. Government Printing Office, Supt. of Documents.

Geberth, V. (1996). *Practical Homicide Investigation: Tactics, Procedures and Forensic Techniques* (3rd ed.). Boca Raton, FL: CRC Press.

Glover, S. (2009). "FBI links truckers, serial killings." *Los Angeles Times*. April 8, 2009.

Howlett, J.B., Hanfland, K.A., and Ressler, R.K. (1986). The Violent Criminal Apprehension Program-VICAP: A Progress Report. *Law Enforcement Bulletin* (December).

Leonard, J. (2006). "Solving Old Murder Brings New Anguish." *Los Angeles Times*. April 16, 2001. Originally cited in Walton, R.H. *Cold Case Homicides: Practical Investigative Techniques*. CRC Press.

Witzig, E.W. (2003). The New ViCAP: More User Friendly and Used by More Agencies. *FBI Law Enforcement Bulletin*, June 2003, 72/6. 1–7.

FBI Criminal Justice Information Services and the National Crime Information Center

8

R. H. WALTON

Contents

Operated by the Federal Bureau of Investigation (FBI), the Criminal Justice Information Services Division (CJIS) is tasked to "reduce terrorist and criminal activities by maximizing the ability to provide timely and relevant criminal justice information to the FBI and to qualified law enforcement, criminal justice, civilian, academic, employment, and licensing agencies concerning individuals, stolen property, criminal organizations and activities, and other law enforcement related data" (FBI). This division is now a consolidation of previously separate programs. Services within this division may be of benefit to cold case homicide investigators.

Background and History

The CJIS Division was established in February, 1992, to serve as a central repository for criminal justice information services in the FBI. Now the largest division within the FBI, CJIS consolidated the National Crime Information Center (NCIC), Uniform Crime Reporting (UCR), and Fingerprint Identification into a single facility at Clarksburg, West Virginia. This consolidation became effective in June 1992. Several ongoing technical programs were also transferred to the CJIS Division. Among these were

- Integrated Automated Fingerprint Identification System (IAFIS)
- NCIC
- National Incident-Based Reporting System (NIBRS)

National Crime Information Center

The NCIC became operational in January, 1967, as a computerized, nationwide information system serving and supporting criminal justice agencies at the local, state, and federal levels. The initial goal was to assist law enforcement in apprehending fugitives and locating stolen property. The goal has been expanded since this time to include locating missing persons, fighting terrorism, and further protecting law enforcement personnel and the public.

The structure and basic procedures of the NCIC were approved by resolution of the full membership of the International Association of Chiefs of Police (IACP) in Philadelphia, Pennsylvania, in October, 1966. The previous year, a small number of local and state agencies were implementing electronic law enforcement information systems. To enable the sharing of criminal justice information across these jurisdictions, a national system was needed. The FBI conducted a feasibility and developmental study concerning the establishment of a national crime information system. The purpose of the study was to develop a system that made available to all local, state, and federal law enforcement agencies needed information on crime and criminals with data to transcend statewide and metropolitan area boundaries.

The NCIC has operated under a shared-management concept between the FBI and state users with telecommunication lines to the CJIS Systems Agency (CSA) in each of the 50 states, the District of Columbia, Guam, Puerto Rico, the U.S. Virgin Islands, and Canada. Those jurisdictions, in turn, operate their own computer systems, providing NCIC access to local criminal justice agencies. The CSAs are responsible for monitoring system use, enforcing system discipline, and assuring that the NCIC operating procedures are followed by all users within their jurisdiction. Through this cooperative network, more than 94,000 law enforcement and other criminal justice agencies have direct online access to an ever-expanding volume of millions of records. General policies concerning the philosophy, concept, and operational principles of the NCIC are based upon the recommendation of the CJIS Advisory Policy Board (APB). The APB is composed of top administrators from local, state, and federal criminal justice agencies throughout the county.

NCIC contains records entered by participating criminal justice agencies, and the individual agency is responsible for their accuracy, timeliness, and completeness. Access and input information was provided through terminals authorized by NCIC. Those authorized terminals were given an individual identifier and are known as the Originating Agency Identifier (ORI). In its initial stages, NCIC contained information on wanted persons, missing persons, and stolen property. In subsequent decades, the system has evolved to include a wide array of files pertaining to other matters, individuals, and identifications. The NCIC computer stores vast amounts of criminal justice information that can be instantly retrieved and furnished to any authorized terminal. Access to the NCIC system is through a regional and/or state computer system. NCIC standards require responses to be returned within specified time limits.

NCIC also provides inquiry-only capability to more than 30 foreign countries for access to records maintained in the Vehicle, License Plate, and Boat Files. In 1999, the system had a complete upgrade known as *NCIC 2000*. This was a major upgrade to those services previously offered by NCIC and extends services to patrol cars and mobile officers. The NCIC computer receives millions of inquiries each day, the majority of which contain subject and/or vehicle information.

Although there is no specific documentation addressing this issue, it is reasonable to assume that some small amount of data was lost over the years, as with any computer system operated in the 1960s and 1970s. Currently, the NCIC has a real-time backup system located at a disaster recovery site. Previously, all data in the NCIC were routinely copied to electronic media and stored off site. Additionally, a system log is maintained. If the system crashes, the NCIC would be restored using the backup data and the system log.

NCIC Files: Property

NCIC computer files and their initial dates of operation include the following:

- *Article File (1967).* Contains items of property with unique serial numbers. This file contains records for stolen articles in which a theft report has been made. It also includes records for lost Public Safety, Homeland Security, or Critical Infrastructure items of identification. This file also includes information relating to livestock and toxic chemicals. Records remain in file for the balance of the year entered, plus one year, with the exception of lost Public Safety, Homeland Security, or Critical Infrastructure items of identification, which stay active indefinitely.

  Criteria at outset and evolution of entry:
  - Individual serially numbered property items valued at $1000 or more.
  - Multiple serially numbered property items totaling $5000 or more in one theft.
  - Other serially numbered property items may be entered at the discretion of the reporting agency (1) if the circumstances of the theft indicate that there is a probability of interstate movement or (2) where the seriousness of the crime indicates that such an entry should be made for investigative purposes.
  - Value reduced from $1000 to $500 sometime pre-1975.
  - Ability to enter records for office equipment, television sets, and bicycles regardless of value occurred sometime pre-1975.
  - Stolen property about June 1996.
- *Boat File (1969).* Records for stolen boats. Entry requires an unrecovered stolen boat that has a registration number, document number, permanently attached Boat Hull Serial Number (BHN), or owner-applied number (OAN) with a filed theft report or a loaned, rented, or leased boat with a theft report or a filed complaint that results in the issuance of a warrant charging embezzlement, theft, etc. Records remain in file for the balance of the year plus four years. Records without a BHN or OAN remain in file for 90 days after entry.
- *Gun File (1967).* Records for serially numbered stolen, lost, felony, and recovered firearms. A record for a lost or missing firearm if the agency has supporting documentation. Records for stolen, felony, and lost records remain in file indefinitely or until the originating agency removes the record. Records for recovered weapons will remain for the balance of the year entered plus two years.
- *License Plate File (1967).* Records for uniquely numbered stolen license plates. This includes standard passenger automobile plates and special plates that have a theft report on file. License Plate File records remain active for balance of the year of entry plus four years.
- *Vehicle File (1967).* Records for stolen vehicles, including aircraft and trailers, as well as vehicles involved in the commission of a felony crime. The file contains information about the following:
  - Recovery of stolen vehicles or loaned, rented, or leased vehicles that have not been returned (providing an official police theft report has been made or a filed complaint results in the issuance of a warrant charging theft or embezzlement)
  - Location of vehicles used in the commission of a felony
  - Recovery of vehicles subject to seizure based on a federally issued court order

Criteria at outset and evolution of entry:
- Some states initially mandated a 24-hour period before entry of the report made to NCIC. For motor vehicles, no documentation exists indicating why there was a delay for entry of vehicle records, but it appears that sometime prior to 1975, this waiting period was dropped.
- Unrecovered stolen engines and transmissions identified by all or a part of the vehicle identification number (VIN) will be entered in the file on the same basis as stolen vehicles.
- In 1996, the entry criterion was expanded to include vehicles subject to seizure based on a federally issued court order.
- In 1999, the Vehicle/Boat Part File was implemented. Previously, part records were included in the NCIC Vehicle File.

- *Vehicle/Boat Part File (1999).* Records for serially numbered stolen vehicle or boat parts. Previously, part records were included in the NCIC Vehicle File. If a stolen vehicle/boat part records remains on file for 90 days and it does not contain a serial number (SER) or OAN, the record is retired. Stolen Vehicle/Boat Part File records that contain an SER or OAN will remain on file for the balance of the year plus four years.
- *Securities File (1968).* Contains serially numbered identifiable securities that have been stolen, embezzled, our counterfeited for which a report has been made. In addition, records for currency that have been stolen, used as bait money, or paid as ransom can be entered. The following do *not* meet the definition for entry in the NCIC Securities File:
  - Personal notes
  - Bank drafts
  - Bank officer's checks
  - Cashier's checks
  - Certified checks
  - Company checks
  - Lost or stolen credit cards
  - Gift certificates
  - Personal checks
  - Savings and checking account passbooks
  - U.S. treasury checks
  - Gold or silver coins
  - Other types of government checks

  Pre-1975, the entry criterion was expanded to include securities used for ransom.

NCIC Files: Persons

- *Wanted Person File (1967).* Contains records on individuals who have outstanding warrants for their arrest. It also includes the following:
  - Parole and probation violators.
  - Juveniles who were charged with committing an act of delinquency but will be tried as adults, have been adjudged delinquent and have absconded while on probation or parole, or have escaped from an institution or agency vested with legal custody or supervision, or where the Rendition Amendment to the Interstate Compact on Juveniles has been executed.
  - Agencies may also enter temporary felony want records in this file. Temporary felony want records allow a law enforcement agency to take prompt action to apprehend a person suspected of committing a felony when circumstances prevent the agency from immediately obtaining

a warrant. Except for temporary felony want records, which are active for 48 hours, wanted-persons records remain in file indefinitely.

Criteria at outset and evolution of entry:

- Inclusion of warrants for serious misdemeanors occurred sometime pre-1975. In 1984, the Wanted Person File was expanded to include records on juvenile offenders, and in 1998, the policy was changed to permit the entry of wanted-persons records wherein extradition was not anticipated.

- *Missing Persons File (1975).* Contains records for persons meeting any of the following criteria:
  - *Juvenile.* A person (child) under 21 years of age who is missing and not declared emancipated as defined by the laws of his/her state of residence under the age of 21 years.
  - *Endangered.* A person of any age who is missing under circumstances indicating that his/her physical safety may be in danger.
  - *Disabled.* A person of any age who is missing and under proven physical/mental disability or is senile, thereby subjecting himself/herself or others to personal and immediate danger.
  - *Involuntary.* A person of any age who is missing under circumstances indicating that the disappearance may not have been voluntary (abduction or kidnapping).
  - *Catastrophe victim.* A person of any age who is missing after a presumed or known catastrophe.
  - *Other.* A person not meeting the criteria for entry into any other category who is missing (1) for whom there is a reasonable concern for his/her safety and (2) who is under 21 and declared emancipated by the laws of his/her state of residence.

  More than 75% of NCIC Missing Persons File entries pertain to juveniles. The National Child Search Assistance Act of 1990 ("Child Act") requires law enforcement agencies to make entries for all missing juveniles *without observing any waiting period.* Agencies may formulate an inquiry using nonunique identifiers, including approximate age, sex, race, height, weight, and eye and hair color. While such an inquiry may generate more than one missing-persons record, investigators may review to ascertain if any such has occurred. This file compliments the Unidentified Person File. Records entered into the NCIC Missing Persons File are automatically searched against records in the Unidentified Person File to seek possible matches (Figure 8.1).

  Records remain on file indefinitely or until the agency removes the record.

  When reviewing long-term missing-persons cases or recovered human remains, see Chapters 5 and 17.

- *Unidentified Person File (1983).* This file compliments the Missing Persons File. Records entered into the NCIC Missing Persons File are automatically searched against records in this file to seek possible matches. This file assists law enforcement in the identification of unidentified persons and body parts. There are three different categories for entry of records into this file. These are as follows:
  - *Unidentified deceased persons.* A person who is no longer living whose identity cannot be ascertained (includes recovered body parts when the body has been dismembered).
  - *Unidentified living persons.* Persons who are unaware of their identities (i.e., amnesia victims, small children, persons with Alzheimer's disease, etc.).
  - *Catastrophe victim.* A person who is the victim of a catastrophe whose identity cannot be ascertained or body parts when the body has been dismembered as a result of a catastrophe. These records may provide an investigative link between agencies that have recovered body parts. An agency that recovers an unidentified, partial body can make an inquiry by identifying the specific body part(s) that has been recovered. The system will search for other records of incomplete bodies and transmit any matches that have that part missing. As with the Missing Persons File, nonunique identifiers can be used when inquiring for unidentified-person records, including approximate height, weight, age, sex, race, and eye and hair color.

Comparison of Missing Person and Unidentified Person Identifiers

The NCIC Cross-Match is an automatic comparison based upon personal descriptors and dental characteristics. The personal descriptor comparison returns up to 100 potential candidates and the dental characteristic comparison returns up to 35 candidates. If either comparison exceeds the number of potential candidates, then the entire list is available by contacting the FBI CJIS Division. The following Missing and Unidentified personal descriptor fields are used for the comparison when they are either entered of modified:

Date of Birth	-	Estimated Year of Birth
Sex	-	Sex
Race	-	Race
Eye	-	Eye
Hair	-	Hair
Height	-	Estimated Height
Weight	-	Estimated Weight
Date of Last Contact	-	Estimated Date of Death
Date of Last Contact	-	Date Body Found
Scars, Marks, Tattoos	-	Scars, Marks, Tattoos
Fingerprint Classification	-	Fingerprint Classification
Jewelry Type	-	Jewelry Type
ORI State Code	-	ORI State Code
Blood Type	-	Blood Type

Figure 8.1 Comparison of missing persons and unidentified person identifiers.

Records remain in file indefinitely or until the agency removes the record.

The basic criteria for entry has not changed since 1983.

- *Protection Order File. (POF, 1997).* Records of individuals who are subject to court-issued orders to prevent violent or threatening acts and harassment against, contact or communications with, or physical proximity to another person(s).

  The Violent Crime Control and Law Enforcement Act of 1994 contained provisions that necessitated development of the NCIC POF. The CJIS APB approved the design of the program in December 1995, and the POF was implemented on May 4, 1997. Court-issued protection orders are intended to prevent acts of domestic violence against a person or to prevent a person from stalking, intimidating, or harassing another person. The types of protection orders issued and the information contained within vary from state to state. In order for these to be entered into this file, it *must* meet the following criteria under 18 U.S.C. §2266(5).

  PROTECTION ORDER.*—The term "protection order" includes any injunction or other order issued for the purpose of preventing violent or threatening acts or harassment against, or contact or communication with or physical proximity to, another person, including any temporary or final order* *issued by a civil and criminal court (other than a support or child custody order issued pursuant to State divorce and child custody laws, except to the extent that such an order is entitled to full faith and credit under other Federal law) whether obtained by filing an independent action or as a pendent elite order in another proceeding so long as any civil order was issued in response to a complaint, petition or motion filed by or on behalf of a person seeking protection.*

And under 18 U.S.C. §2266(6):

Reasonable notice and opportunity to be heard must be given to the person against whom the order is sought sufficient to protect that person's right to due process. In the case of ex parte orders, notice and opportunity to be heard must be provided within the time required by State or tribal laws, and in any event within reasonable time after the order is issued, sufficient to protect the respondent's due process rights.

Active records will be retained until cancelled by the entering agency or expiration date of the order is reached. Inactive records will be retained online for the remainder of the year in which cleared/expired plus five years. Inquiry of the Wanted Person and/or Vehicle Files will result in an automatic cross-search of the POF. Active records will be returned in a positive response, and inactive records will not.

Criteria at outset and evolution of entry:

The entry criterion was modified by the Violence Against Women Act of 2000, which took effect on October 28, 2000.

- *National Sex Offender Registry File (1999).* Records of sex offenders or other persons required to register under a jurisdiction's sex offender registry program. Added with implementation of NCIC 2000. This file contains information records for a person who has been convicted of a criminal offense against a minor. This is defined as any criminal offense in a range of offenses specified by state law that is comparable to or exceeds the following range of offenses:
  - Kidnapping of a minor except by a parent
  - False imprisonment of a minor except by a parent
  - Criminal sexual conduct toward a minor
  - Solicitation of a minor to engage in sexual conduct
  - Use of a minor in a sexual performance
  - Solicitation of a minor to practice prostitution
  - Any conduct that by its nature is a sexual offense against a minor
- *Supervised Release File (1999).* Added with implementation of NCIC 2000. Local, state, and federal supervision officers may enter records in NCIC for subjects under specific restrictions during their probation, parole, or supervised-release sentence following imprisonment. Records have the same unlimited retention period as wanted-persons records. The agency is responsible for clearing a record when the terms of the probation or parole have expired.
- *Protective Interest File (2011).* Records for individuals who an authorized agency reasonably believes, based on its law enforcement investigation, might pose a threat to the physical safety of protectees or their immediate families. Only law enforcement agencies with a protective mission as specified within municipal, state, or federal statutes, regulations, or other appropriate legal authority may enter records into this file. The Protective Interest File expands upon the U.S. Secret Service Protective File. Records remain in this file indefinitely.
- *U.S. Secret Service Protective File.* Records for individuals who may pose a threat to the President of the United States or others afforded protection as authorized by law.
- *Gang File (2009).* Records for violent gangs and their members. Records of gangs remain in file indefinitely. Records of gang members are retained until the record reaches the date in the Date of Purge (DOP) field. Records with a nonexpiring DOP are retained indefinitely.

- *Immigration Violators File (1996).* Includes records for criminal aliens who have been deported for drugs or firearms trafficking and/or serious violent crimes. Reentry of these criminal aliens into the United States violates 8 U.S.C. §1326.
  Records remain indefinitely or until removed by the authorizing agency.
- *Foreign Fugitive File (1987).* Records for persons wanted by another country for a crime that would be a felony if it were committed in the United States. Wanting country must be a signatory to an extradition treaty or convention with the United States. Generally, U.S. law enforcement officers cannot execute foreign-issued arrest warrants. However, 18 U.S.C. §3184, states that a U.S. extradition warrant (federal arrest warrant) may be issued for the apprehension of a foreign fugitive who is found in the United States. This holds true only if a treaty or convention for extradition exists between the United States and the wanting foreign country.
  Records remain in file indefinitely or until the agency removes the record.
- *Known or Appropriately Suspected Terrorist (KST) File (2009).* The FBI's Terrorist Screening Center (TSC) is the only entity that can enter records in this file. The file contains information on persons who have been nominated as a known or suspected terrorist to the TSC.
  The records remain in the file indefinitely or until the TSC staff removes them.
- *Violent Person File (2012).* This file was created exclusively to enhance officer safety. The file provides law enforcement officers with a direct warning of individuals who may have the propensity to be violent against law enforcement. Records remain in the violent person file indefinitely.
  - This file should not be confused with the now-discontinued Violent Felon File (VFF). This file was established in 1992 and discontinued in 1998. The ATF was the only agency authorized to make entries into this file, and the criteria were based on prior violent felony convictions including but not limited to involvement with firearms.
- *National Instant Criminal Background Check System (NICS) Denied Transaction File (2012).* Records on individuals who have been determined to be prohibited persons according to the Brady Handgun Violence Prevention Act of 1993 and thus denied as a result of the NICS background check.
- *Identity Theft File (2005).* Records of victims of identity theft with descriptive and other information that law enforcement personnel can use to determine if an individual is a victim of identity theft or if the individual might be using a false identity. The NCIC system retains records in this file until the record reaches the date in the DOP field. The maximum retention is five years.

Other CJIS/NCIC Systems and Files

- *Interstate Identification Index (III) (1983).* This is an automated system, accessed through NCIC, that facilitates the interstate exchange of online criminal history record information among criminal justice agencies. It consists of an index containing identifying data, including
  - Individual's name
  - Aliases
  - Physical descriptors
  - Identifying numbers
  - Fingerprint classifications
  - Names of the agency maintaining the criminal history information

  Records remain on file until the individual reaches the age of 99 years. Records can be removed due to expungement or seven years after death.

- *Image File (1999).* Images may be of a person, property, or reference. Images may be entered for convicted persons on the Supervised Release, Protective Interest, Missing Persons, Deported Felon, Immigration Violators, Gang, Known or Appropriately Suspected Terrorist, Unidentified Person, Wanted Person, National Sexual Offender Registry, Article, Vehicle, Boat or Vehicle/Boat Part, and Violent Person File. Images associated with records are subject to the same retention periods as those records. The types of images that may be stored for a person are
  - Fingerprint
  - Mug shot
  - Signature
  - Identifying images such as scars or tattoos
- *Originating Agency Identifier (ORI) File (1985).* An ORI is a nine-character identifier assigned by NCIC to an agency in order to identify the agency in transactions on the NCIC system. This file addresses those records for agency information that has been assigned an NCIC ORI for purposes of accessing the NCIC system. Through this file, authorized users may identify other agencies revealed through an ORI number. The ORI File maintains pertinent information on virtually every criminal justice agency in the United States, Commonwealth of Puerto Rico, U.S. Virgin Islands, and Canada, as well as certain foreign criminal justice agencies.

  In some cold case homicide investigations, this may be useful in identifying agency source documents that contain an ORI number but no other identifying information. In addition, this file may assist to identify law enforcement agencies that may no longer exist as separate entities due to merging with another agency or termination with police services contracted to another agency.

  Records remain indefinitely. If an agency no longer qualifies for NCIC access, the ORI record is retired but kept in an inactive status.

Next Generation Identification (September 2014)

The Integrated Automated Fingerprint Identification System, commonly known as IAFIS, was replaced with the Next Generation Identification (NGI) on September 7, 2014. NGI is a national fingerprint and criminal history system maintained by the FBI's CJIS Division.

With a database containing criminal and civil fingerprints going back over 110 years, the NGI system operates 24 hours a day, year round. NGI utilizes two primary repositories:

- *The Criminal Master Repository.* The Criminal Master Repository contains fingerprints acquired as a result of an arrest at a local, state, or federal level. Fingerprint and corresponding criminal history information are voluntarily submitted by local, state, and federal law enforcement agencies. This file contains fingerprint information and corresponding criminal history data for more than 69 million persons. The fingerprints are processed at the local level, forwarded electronically to a state or other federal agency system for processing, and then transmitted electronically through the CJIS Wide Area Network (WAN) to the FBI's IAFIS for processing.
- *The Civil Repository.* Fingerprints are acquired as a result of submission from background checks for employment, licensing, and other noncriminal justice purposes where authorized by state and federal law and in compliance with appropriate regulations. Similar to criminal fingerprints, civil fingerprints are processed by local, state, or federal agencies prior to being submitted to the IAFIS for processing. Civil tenprint cards are submitted electronically or by mail. An identification or a nonidentification response may be generated. For submissions that require payment, a billing record is created. This file contains approximately 37 million subjects.

The NGI offers integrated state-of-the-art biometric identification services and the capability for multimodal functionality. The NGI was delivered in four increments and provides six categories of services to CJIS users: identification, verification, information, investigation, data management, and notification.

The Advanced Fingerprint Identification Technology (AFIT) was deployed with Increment 1 on February 25, 2011, providing enhanced fingerprint and latent search capabilities. This component provided a new algorithm that provides more efficient processing of flat fingerprint impressions, improves latent processing, and increases the lights-out processing, resulting in faster response times, and has improved the matching accuracy to 99.6%.

The *Repository for Individuals of Special Concern (RISC)* deployed on August 25, 2011, Increment 2, enables law enforcement officers to perform a rapid search against a repository of wanted persons, sex offender registry subjects, known or suspected terrorists, and other individuals of special interest to screen detainees and criminal suspects. From a mobile fingerprint device, law enforcement officers submit a minimum of two rolled or flat images, which are routed to the RISC repository. A *red*, *yellow*, or *green* response is provided within seconds. A red response is a hit, yellow indicates a possible candidate, and green is returned when no candidate is located. This service is available to authorized criminal justice personnel for criminal justice purposes; there are currently 21 agencies using this capability with a red hit rate between 3% and 6%.

On May 5, 2013, Increment 3 delivered the *Latent and National Palm Print System* (NPPS), resulting in a centralized repository containing millions of searchable palm prints on a nationwide basis. NGI has expanded search capabilities of latent users to include the criminal, civil, and Universal Latent File (ULF) repositories. Incoming criminal and civil submissions are cascaded against the ULF. IAFIS was responsible for the identification of cold case homicide perpetrators going back many decades, allowing for the resolution of these cases. With the expanded investigative opportunities afforded by NGI's increased latent fingerprint search capabilities, it is expected that new leads will be generated in unsolved and/or cold cases.

On September 9, 2014, the final increment, Increment 4, delivered two new services: *Rap Back* and *Facial Recognition*.

The *Interstate Photo System* is a national repository that holds over 23 million front-facing photos. These photos are a collection of all photos received with a tenprint transaction. Authorized law enforcement agencies may submit a photo image for a face recognition search; the results are processed lights-out with the response being a ranked candidate list. These results are considered investigative leads only and should not be considered a positive identification.

The *Rap Back* service provides notifications to authorized agencies of criminal and, in limited cases, civil activity on an individual for whom a subscription has been set. Law enforcement agencies can set subscriptions on fingerprints of probationers, parolees, sex offenders, persons under court supervision, as well as suspects and other persons involved in investigation.

For further information regarding connectivity to NGI or any of the services available, contact the CJIS Division at 304-625-2000.

A Note on NCIC Record Retention

Upon its start-up in 1967, NCIC provided a means to check items possessing serial numbers or license plates for wanted, stolen, or other status. Records entered into NCIC were retained for a specific period of time, and some of these periods have changed over the years. Computer systems and file designations and designs have been constantly revised or upgraded, and record retention depends upon the NCIC file into which the record was entered, as well as the type of record that was entered.

Cold case investigators are cautioned that information entered decades ago may not now be in the active NCIC computer data banks. Investigators who handle cases that continue for extended periods of time should be aware that their NCIC entries may automatically be retrieved. Records may be reentered if the circumstances surrounding the case warrant such an action. NCIC can retrieve old records through a process known as an *off-line search*.

During the review of cold case homicide files, investigators may look for copies of older forms indicating that related crime items, such as firearms, were entered into the original NCIC data bank, or local or state systems. The presence, or absence, of such indicators should not mean the property was entered or was not entered, or that it still remains accessible in these systems. An archive of entries is kept in an off-line system. Record-keeping practices or lost or misfiled forms may create an erroneous impression. When evidence that an item capable of being entered into NCIC is found in file, cold case investigators are urged to check the item for previous entry and inquiries from other law enforcement agencies. It is recommended that input items be updated when appropriate.

IF in doubt, contact CJIS/NCIC and work with appropriate personnel to determine what is or is not available.

NCIC 2000

Recognizing the need to update and improve operations, the FBI completed a new project called NCIC 2000. This system went into effect July 11, 1999. NCIC 2000 provided a major upgrade to those services provided by the older version of NCIC, termed *Legacy NCIC*, and extends these services to those serving in patrol cars as well as mobile officers. This system enhances the base capabilities of the Legacy NCIC system and added new files. The additional capabilities of NCIC 2000 include the following:

- *Enhanced name search.* Uses the New York State Identification and Intelligence System (NYSIIS). Returns phonetically similar names (e.g., Marko/Marco, Knowles/Nowles, or derivatives of names such as William/Willie/Bill).
- *Fingerprint searches.* Stores and searches the right index fingerprint. Search inquiries compare the print to all fingerprint data on file (wanted persons and missing persons).
- *Probation/parole.* Convicted Persons or Supervised Release File contains records of subjects under supervised release.
- *Information linking.* Connects two or more records so that an inquiry on one retrieves the other record(s).
- *Mug shots.* One mug shot per person record may be entered into NCIC 2000. One fingerprint, one signature, and up to 10 other identifying images (scars, marks, and tattoos) may also be entered.
- *Other images.* One identifying image for each entry in the following files: Article, Vehicle, Boat, Vehicle/Boat Part. A file of generic images (i.e., picture of a 1989 Ford Mustang) is maintained in the system.
- *Convicted sex offender registry.* Contains records of individuals who are convicted sexual offenders or violent sexual predators.
- *SENTRY File.* An index of persons incarcerated in the federal prison system. Response provides descriptive information and location of prison.
- *Delayed inquiry.* Every record entered or modified is checked against the inquiry log. Provides the entering and inquiring agency with a response if any other agency inquired on the subject in the last five days.
- *Online ad hoc inquiry.* A flexible technique that allows users to search the active databases and access the system's historical data.

Special Capabilities of NCIC

Off-Line Search

Online inquiries conducted by law enforcement can quickly retrieve accurate information. Frequently, however, an investigator will not have all the information necessary to perform an online inquiry of NCIC and lacks required parameters such as date of birth, license plate number, or VIN. In these and other investigative situations, online inquiries alone may not be adequate. This may be especially true in cold case investigations in which a number of years have passed. In such cases, investigators and their agencies may need to request off-line searches of the NCIC database. In addition, state agencies also have off-line search capabilities. Agencies can contact their state organization for further details.

An *off-line search* is a special technique that can be used in a variety of situations to obtain information not available through online channels. The results may provide an investigator with information to

- Determine if any other agency(s) has made an inquiry on a particular individual or item of property
- Place an individual at the scene of a crime or miles away from the scene
- Substantiate or discredit an alibi
- Determine if a record for a person or item of property was previously entered into NCIC and subsequently removed
- Track the route of witnesses, suspects, or other persons of interest

Information obtained through the off-line search process can be retrieved from three different sources:

- The NCIC *active record database*, which is maintained in an online mode for 24 hours a day, 7 days a week.
- The NCIC *historical database*, which includes records that have been removed from the active database as a result of cancellation, clearance, or retention expiration. From an off-line search of purged records, it can be determined if a property item was entered and subsequently removed due to its retention expiration, even though an online inquiry produces a "no record" response.
- The *transaction log* that contains historic NCIC transactions. An off-line search of the NCIC transaction log will reveal whether inquiries were made on a particular individual or property item (i.e., during a traffic stop) for a specified time frame. This type of information can assist in determining if a subject was near the scene of a crime or miles away. These log searches are normally limited to a six-month time frame, for example, a certain month(s), day(s), or hour(s). NCIC transaction log tapes are maintained for 10 years.

Off-line searches may be tailored to the unique needs of the individual case. An off-line search can be made with a minimum of one search parameter, but as with other aspects of investigation, having more information available to assist may produce more effective results.

- *Persons.* In order to identify a wanted, missing, or deceased person, searches can be made on non-unique personal descriptors such as sex, hair color, approximate height, approximate weight, and estimated age.
- *Vehicle identification.* May be made on
  - Partial license plate number
  - Partial VIN

Even in cases in which all VINs and serial numbers have been obliterated beyond restoration, the off-line search has been of value. In some cases, off-line searches have provided identifying data on suspect(s). In addition, gun make, article type, securities descriptors, date of theft, and date of warrant can also be used as off-line parameters.

Name-Only Off-Line Inquiry

NCIC has a specialized program that enables inquiries of the Wanted Person and Missing Persons Files by *name only* when a date of birth or other numeric identifier is unavailable for an online inquiry. The name-only inquiry can be requested by contacting the staff of the Investigative and Operational Assistance Unit (IOAU) or by forwarding an administrative message via the National Law Enforcement Telecommunications System (NLETS). The results of the search will be furnished on a computer printout or, if circumstances require, a magnetic tape. A survey is included with the results of each survey, and participants are urged to complete and return the form as soon as practical to assist the FBI in evaluating the usefulness of the NCIC off-line search program.

Delayed-Inquiry Program

User inquiries are stored in NCIC for five days. Subsequent entry or modified transactions received by NCIC are checked against the file of inquiries. If any match occurs, both the user entering or modifying a record and the user who made the initial inquiry are respectively advised by way of a delayed-inquiry notification and a delayed-inquiry hit response. Agencies should contact each other to obtain additional information.

One-Crime Inquiry

This transaction enables the user to submit an inquiry for all information related to a crime based on ORI and date of entry and/or case number. The inquiry can be directed to one, more than one, or all file types. If not specified, the inquiry will search all files. The inquiry will return up to 20 hits online. If the hit response contains more than 20 responses, a notification will be included to indicate that a file is being created with the additional hits.

Date and Time of Entry

This inquiry is used to inquire upon the date and time of entry of a record and is available to all users. If a record was entered prior to NCIC 2000 implementation (July 11, 1999), then the inquiry result will feature a date of entry only. If a record was entered subsequently, then the response returned will include the date and time the record was entered.

Double Query Match

In October 2002, the Beltway Sniper terrorized the Washington, District of Columbia, area. FBI staff conducted numerous off-line searches of NCIC transaction logs based upon various reporting by persons who suspected neighbors, coworkers, and even family members. These searches attempted to place the person near one of the crime scenes. These searches generated volumes of printouts but little useful information. On October 18, FBI staff discussed a new search strategy that would be called the *double query match* technique. This was a data mining application that would search the NCIC transaction log twice. The first search would be to extract license plate number inquiries made by law enforcement agencies in the immediate area of each shooting limited to five hours before through five hours after each incident. The second search would list only those inquiries that contained a license plate number that had been queried by more than one agency.

By the morning of October 21, NCIC generated a printout containing 92 sets of inquiries on different license plates. Included within the printout was the license plate registered to a blue 1990 Chevrolet belonging to John A. Muhammad. Later that night, FBI latent fingerprint examiners working on the case received four latent prints taken from a weapon's magazine found at the scene of a previous murder in Alabama. The recovered prints were searched against IAFIS. The four prints were identified as belonging to John Lee Malvo. His criminal history revealed that he was a Jamaican citizen who had been arrested by the U.S. Immigration and Naturalization Service (INS) in December 2001. The INS, now called Immigration and Custom Enforcement (ICE), was in the process of removing him from the country. Further investigation turned up his connection to Muhammad. Before the Sniper Task Force had an opportunity to review the NCIC information, however, the latent print examiner had identified Malvo as a suspect. The reign of terror was coming to an end, and one can speculate that perhaps within a few days of further investigation to eliminate the others, the double query match lead could have pointed to these suspects, who were later convicted for the crimes.

Since the Beltway Sniper case, the double query match technique has been used in additional cases involving serial criminals. In each case, the double match returned a relatively small number of names and/or license plate numbers as lead information. In one case spanning a 10-year search for a serial sex offender, a single name was returned. The subject had not previously been identified or linked to the crimes, although the man had a significant criminal history of similar crimes.

The NCIC double query match has proven to be a powerful investigative tool. Matching identical inquiries made by different law enforcement agencies on vehicles or subjects within the circumscribed areas and approximate times of crime occurrences can generate more specific investigative leads. The CJIS Division encourages investigators to contact the IOAU for assistance in using this new technique for cases in which *a minimum of four to six incidents are involved and no suspects have been developed.*

Global Transaction Inquiry

This is the same as an off-line search. This is a request for records that cannot be retrieved by way of a standard inquiry transaction. The use of the global transaction inquiry is restricted to authorized terminals. Searches can be made of active or retired (purged) NCIC records.

Case History

In the fall of 1946, the victim, a white female in her early 50s, was found in the garage of her bungalow in a small blue-collar town on the West Coast. The victim had been struck in the forehead with an axe kept in the garage for splitting kindling. She was subsequently dragged from the interior of the residence down a flight of stairs to the basement. The axe was recovered and processed for latent prints at the time with negative results. Approximately a dozen black-and-white photos of the victim and the blood spatter near the wall telephone and in the hallway leading to the garage were taken at the time (Figure 8.2).

There were no photos of the exterior of the house or of other rooms in the residence present in the case file when I reviewed it in 2001. The original case file is approximately one inch thick, and most reports are more synopsis oriented than detail specific. Such a style of reporting is not uncommon in homicide investigation reports from this and subsequent decades.

Remaining physical evidence consisted of a portion of the skullcap and the axe. The axe head was loosely wrapped in paper and had obviously been handled without thought to potentially preserving it for future evidence. Indeed, the captain of the detective bureau took it out of the remaining paper wrapper, handled it, and attempted to give it to me (Figure 8.3).

Figure 8.2 Pre-NCIC homicide scene. This unsolved 1946 homicide occurred almost 20 years before NCIC became operational in 1967. During case file review, any information from crimes predating this data bank may, and should be entered. Note the measuring instrument. (Author's collection.)

Figure 8.3 Axe found at scene. The murder weapon with blood spatter is still in evidence. It has been handled an unknown number of times. (Author's collection.)

Investigation at the time indicated that the victim operated a successful small business and was married. There was a significant age difference between the younger husband and his wife. They slept in separate bedrooms, however, and the husband had an alibi for the time of the homicide. Investigators surmised that the intruder entered through a side garage door and may have interrupted the victim while she was talking on the telephone. Original investigators discovered that the victim's bedroom was ransacked. The husband's bedroom was reportedly undisturbed. A substantial sum of cash kept by the victim was missing. Also missing were two handguns. The makes, models, caliber, and serial numbers of the guns were recorded in the file (Figure 8.4).

The description of the weapons had been mailed by letter to several other law enforcement agencies, but there was no indication they had ever been submitted to any modern databases.

The primary investigation appeared to last about six months. Periodic inquiry into the husband's activities and whereabouts was randomly made. The last report in the file was dated 1963 and reported the husband's location in another distant county. The town is still relatively small, and the case was well known among the surviving generation from this period. The local rumor mill among survivors of the period suggested that "the husband did it."

In 1997, an experienced homicide detective reviewed the case evidence to ascertain that it still existed and to check its condition. As is frequently encountered in older cases, review of the reports showed that personal identifying information of those interviewed was lacking. Although there were lists of persons interviewed, there was little or no identifier information such as date of birth; many were recorded by nicknames or similar incomplete information. This is not uncommon in older cases. Present in the case, however, was a case synopsis and a list of those persons who had been interviewed.

During my later discussion, the detective advised he had no way to identify these persons, and no further investigative action was taken. Subsequently, the news media broadcast a short story on the unsolved case. A local judge angrily called the police department to denounce the publicity and to demand that no further such efforts be made as his wife had been the little girl who found the body and this was distressing to her.

I inquired of the captain of the detective bureau regarding the guns, and he assured me they were "...entered into NCIC at the time." He further advised me that they would expend no further energy to investigate this case as there were no leads and no evidence. At my request, he did reenter the weapons into NCIC after running the serial numbers through this system to ascertain if the weapons had been already previously entered.

Figure 8.4 Missing weapon. Review of the case file indicated that at the time of the murder, the victim's bedroom was ransacked, and a large amount of cash was stolen. In addition, two pistols were also taken, including a Colt .25 similar to this pistol. The makes, models, and serial numbers of both were known and recorded in the report. In such instances, these serial numbers should be entered into NCIC, even if the crime predates NCIC's operation. (Author's collection.)

There are investigative leads that offer potential for this case, despite its age. Among these are the following:

- Run an off-line NCIC check for any record of the gun.
- Contact the manufacturers with the serial numbers and ascertain if either gun has ever been returned to the factory for repair or other work.
- Utilize resources of BATF regarding any history for the weapons.
- Review remaining physical evidence with criminalist.
- Obtain a death certificate and review it for relative information.
- Obtain the newspaper obituary and review for known names and relationships.
- Contact the initial reporting party and reinterview.
- Review the names of subjects found in the case file with this witness and attempt to identify them further, who they might be related to, known associates or friends, and others who might have knowledge at this later date.
- Review newspaper accounts at the time for details and names.
- Contact retired officers, investigators, and other personnel to ascertain if they have any records, photos, knowledge of the case, etc.
- Consider further use of the news media as a source of eliciting further information.
- Attempt to identify relatives of the victim for interview.
- Attempt to learn the status of the husband and police record, and if he is still alive.

Acknowledgments

I wish to acknowledge the gracious assistance and contributions of Stephen Fischer, unit chief of the Multimedia Productions Group, Criminal Justice Information Services, and his staff; Travis Olson and Patsy Sabatelli of the NCIC Operations and Policy Unit (NOPOU) in the Law Enforcement Support Section; and acting section chief Jamie Sigler McDevitt of the Global Operations Section (GOS) for their extensive assistance and contribution in compiling the material used as a basis for this chapter. In addition to providing updated material, Fischer further gave freely of his time to review and fact-check this material. Material that addressed the double query match was taken extensively from "Double Query Match Can Help Catch Serial Offenders" printed in the Winter 2002–2003 issue of the *CJIS Link*.

Suggested Readings and Bibliography

Federal Bureau of Investigation. "NCIC's Double Query Match can help catch serial offenders." *The CJIS Link*, Vol. 6, No. 4/Winter, 2002–2003.

Federal Bureau of Investigation. The Investigative Tool. NCIC: National Crime Information Center. Booklet. Revised, April 2001.

Federal Bureau of Investigation. "The off-line search." National Crime Information Center. Revised, October 2000.

Federal Bureau of Investigation. National Crime Information Center (NCIC): NCIC File Reference Card. Revised, July 2000.

Walton, R.H. (2013). *Practical Cold Case Homicide Investigations Procedural Manual*. CRC Press, Boca Raton, FL.

Interviewing Senior Citizens

9

R. H. WALTON

Contents

Introduction

Interviewing senior citizens and eliciting useful information in the conduct of a criminal investigation is a form of police procedure not taught in normal training channels. Yet it is one that police officers and investigators frequently encounter. Elder abuse is a national problem, and senior citizens—those above 65 years of age—are often encountered as victims of burglary, violent crimes, and especially fraud and white collar crimes. They are also encountered as victims of sexual assault, homicide, and attempted homicide. In the course of cold case homicide investigations, investigators revisiting older cases may encounter now older witnesses during the course of the reinterview process, or in the course of developing heretofore unknown witnesses. Successful interviews and processing of information furnished by senior citizens can often lead to arrest and successful prosecution in cold case homicides.

For a variety of reasons, senior citizens present unusual challenges to investigators. Social, health, and family considerations may govern the nature and extent to which they cooperate, or appear to cooperate, with law enforcement. In general, the passage of time is often friendly to cold case investigators in the course of these investigations. Family considerations, however, may significantly contribute to a lack of cooperation by some in this age group.

- *Family secrets*. Rejuvenation of a cold case homicide may resurrect actions or activities on their part that they do not wish their family to learn. This applies to other than direct suspects or perpetrators, including family members of the homicide victim in some instances. Events thought long past and buried resurface when investigators begin asking questions. As investigators ask questions, family members may begin asking questions also.
- *Enhanced relationships*. It is important to keep in mind during this phase of investigation and interview that with time, relationships may change. These changes may have, in some cases, enhanced relationships that investigators are not aware of. We normally tend to believe that relationships between the offender and those with knowledge will deteriorate with the passage of time, and that those with information of the crime and events may now be more forthcoming to investigators. However, in our efforts to learn that which investigators could not in decades past, relationships may have developed over the succeeding years, and these may be hidden from all but those closest to these parties.

DON'T ASSUME ANYTHING

Unfortunately, investigators may sometimes be disinclined to press beyond initial statements when faced with an apparent or perceived reluctance on the part of these persons to cooperate. This may include statements disclaiming any knowledge of the persons or events. The result is that less than an optimum exchange of information occurs. It is the purpose of this section to assist the investigators in overcoming these shortcomings and to further their abilities in the course of the interview process during cold case homicide investigations. This information derives from literature on the aging and memory process, and my experiences and those of other investigators in working with senior citizens in fraud, elder abuse cases, and cold case homicide investigations.

Memory

The *Merriam-Webster Medical Dictionary* defines memory as "the power or process of reproducing or recalling what has been learned and retained especially through associative mechanisms...the store of things learned and retained from an organism's activity or experience as evidenced by modification of structure or behavior or by recall and recognition." In less formal terms, it is the retention and retrieval in the human mind of past experiences. Learning cannot occur without the function of memory. Memory, however, is not the result of a single system, but encompasses a number of functions and components within the human body. Exactly how memory works, however, is still poorly understood, and it is one of the puzzles of neurology.

Human memory utilizes systems that store and retrieve information gleaned from our senses. These include sight, sound, smell, or other tactile impressions. Noted eyewitness researcher and author, Dr. Elizabeth Loftus, writes that memory is less like a video recorder that captures an event for repeated playback than it is an interpretive process of putting together information when it is called for. According to Loftus (1996), "When we experience an important event, we do not simply record that event in memory as a videotape recorder would. The situation is much more complex." Memory is a physiological process. There are three stages theoretically attributed to memory by researchers and those who specialize in the memory process. Understanding these may be noteworthy for the cold case investigator:

1. The *acquisition stage*—To recognize and absorb an event. Information is encoded and entered into a person's memory system. It is here the witness decides which aspect of the visual environment should be attended to and encoded or stored in memory. Not everything perceived is absorbed and stored evenly, however.
2. The *retention stage*—This is the period of time that passes between the event and the eventual recollection of some particular item of information. The information is physiologically committed to the brain. During this period, some information may remain here unchanged and some may not. The witness may subsequently be subjected to post-event conversations, media stories, or other secondary sources of input.
3. The *retrieval stage*—This is the period during which a person recalls stored information. It is upon this occasion when the acquisition and retention stages are crucial. Any answer that a person may pose to one asking a question is based upon these first two stages. A failure in the acquisition stage can be a cause for failure in the retrieval stage. If it was accurately perceived in the acquisition stage, it may have been interfered with or contaminated during the retention stage.

According to Loftus (1996), this three-stage analysis is central to the concept of human memory and is "...virtually universally accepted among psychologists." With the passage of time, these stages may be of significant importance to cold case investigators. Loftus attributes two groups of variables (Event Factors and Witness Factors) during the acquisition stage that may affect the ability of a witness to perceive events accurately.

Event Factors

- *Exposure time.* This is the amount of time a witness has to observe that which is going to be later remembered.
- *Frequency.* This is the number of opportunities an individual has to observe and perceive particular details to be remembered.
- *Detail salience.* Many events consist of a number of sub-events, and not all the details within that event are equally salient or memorable to the witness. According to Loftus (1996), a salient detail is "one that has a high probability of being spontaneously mentioned by individuals who witness a particular event."
- *Type of fact.* This may include the length of time for the crime to occur or the height and weight of suspect, and these are facts not equally easy to perceive or recall.
- *Violence of the event.* The brutality and violence of the act. While the immediate effects of bearing witness to unaccustomed violence may outwardly appear to diminish with the passing of years, the cold case investigator is cautioned not to automatically assume that they have vanished and that the witness can now speak accurately and devoid of the effects of emotional impact of the event. As with friends and family of the victims of homicide, the pain may be just below the surface.

Of importance to cold case investigators are *situational factors*, which may include factors associated with

- Physical location and obstacles. In this category, the cold case investigator would seek to determine whether the witness's line of sight was inhibited by any physical barriers or obstacles. Included among these might be trees and vegetation or other hindrances.

- Environmental obstacles.
- Lighting conditions.
- Distance from the subject.

Witness Factors

- *Stress.* The amount and nature of stress an individual endures at the time of perception. According to the Yerkes–Dodson law, strong motivational states such as stress or other forms of emotional arousal facilitate performance and learning "up to a point." After this point, there is a decline in the ability to perform.
- *Expectations.* Perceptions may be influenced by expectations; what they expect to see, feel, etc.
- *Cultural expectations.* A belief held by a large number of people within a certain culture. These are sometimes referred to as stereotyping and may be widely held and accepted within certain populations. According to Loftus, cultural expectations can affect perception, and are "…highly inaccurate." It is not uncommon in the course of police investigations to encounter persons who personify such stereotyping, and may be encountered in cold case homicide investigation as well.
- *Expectations from past experience.* This is the role that prior experience may play in the ability of a witness to perceive an event. That perception then becomes embedded and subject to retrieval at a later date.
- *Personal prejudices.* These are individual stereotypic beliefs that affect perception.
- *Temporary bias.* Momentary bias that may affect perception.
- *Perceptual activity.* The activity the witness was engaged in at the time of being a witness. This activity may be important in attempting to determine how well aspects of the event may be remembered.

Additionally, the cold case investigator may seek to determine the nature of involvement in the event to which they are a witness. These include whether they are

- *Active witness.* These are witnesses who may be included as victims of the crime or those who were close enough to the crime to feel threatened.
- *Passive witness.* These are witnesses who may be more impartial and who may have had occasion to view the event from a safe distance with no feeling of personal threat.
- *Inactive witness.* These are those witnesses who may not have realized something they saw was significant and/or may not have realized a crime was taking place.

Information Retention

Cold case investigators should be cognizant that researchers have theorized that post-event information may factor into the ability of a witness to provide information after a long interval between acquisition and recalling events to an investigator. Time in itself does not cause a loss or slippage of memory. Such a loss may occur due to other events in the intervening process.

What a witness sees or hears after the event may contaminate his or her original perception and subsequent retention. This post-event information can not only augment an existing memory but also change the memory. In some instances, it may even cause nonexistent information to become incorporated into the previously acquired memory. It is suggested that the cold case investigator design the interview questions in an attempt to distinguish between the actual firsthand perception of the event and post-event contamination. Avoidance of leading questions is suggested, and perhaps utilize more open-ended questions that cause the witness to think to respond and not offer avoidance answers. Such was the experience with Russell Hunt in the following case history.

Forms of post-event information may include

- *Enhanced memory.* Memory enhanced by suggestion of another.
- *Compromised memory.* This may occur when a witness to an event later learns information that potentially conflicts with that which was previously seen and may compromise the original perception with the later information. This is a compromise between what a witness saw and what he or she was later told. During review of the case reports, investigators may seek to determine when/if witnesses were separated prior to giving statements to investigators. In addition, investigators may seek to determine if the witnesses wrote individual statements before contact with investigators or others. The cold case investigator may seek to compare these with later statements to investigators or, in some situations, defense investigators.
- *Timing of post-event information.* When potential post-event information is introduced to the witness, the cold case investigator may seek to determine the following:
  - How long after the event the information was introduced?
  - By who was the information introduced?
  - Under what circumstances was the information introduced?
  - Does the information introduced subsequent to the event have a different impact depending upon whether it was introduced immediately after the event or just prior to recall of the event?
- *Nonverbal influences.* In addition to spoken influences in the post-event setting, the cold case investigator may seek to determine whether the witness's memory of events may have been subjected to nonverbal influences. These may include
  - Tone of voice by original officers, investigators, or others whom the witness encountered.
  - Movement of body parts such as head and eyes to convey ideas to others. This could occur in the immediate post-event circumstances or, indeed, even during interview by cold case investigators. As a result, it is important for cold case investigators to maintain a sense or tone of neutrality during their contact with the witness.

As a result of post-event information, the cold case investigator may seek to determine the following:

- Whether facts and events have been added to the circumstances perceived at the time of the event, or subtracted or altered in the memory of the witness.
- Has the passage of time significantly affected the accuracy of recall? Included within this category may be perceptions of the noise associated with the event and/or violence of the event.

Loftus has further suggested other factors that may affect retention of information in the memory. These include

- *Intervening thoughts of a witness.* During the intervening time period, the witness's thoughts may tend to bend toward self-serving purposes.
- *Labeling.* How a witness labels a given situation may affect the way in which the situation is remembered. The cold case investigator may seek to determine whether the witness views the

situation as serious, and thus is potentially more liable to recall the circumstances with less potential for bias. If the witness labels the event as less serious, the witness may downplay those circumstances relayed to the investigator and potentially be less forthcoming and descriptive.

In addition, the cold case investigator may attempt to learn whether the potential witness is *guessing* when recalling certain aspects of the event.

Age and Memory

There are many misconceptions about regarding age and memory. Among these are the following:

- Old age automatically triggers memory loss.
- Forgetfulness is a symptom of old age.
- Most old people will develop Alzheimer's disease.
- A person can kill or hurt another person and never remember it.
- Each of us is born with the same memory abilities; some use it and others lose it.

Research has shown that aging does not automatically cause memory loss, and the investigator faced with the task of interviewing people in their late 60s and beyond should not fall prey to common societal misconceptions concerning the aging process and memory. Memory can be likened to a muscle. If it is not exercised and used, you lose it. It improves with exercise and the investigator interviewing elderly persons should take this into account during the interview.

Reactions slow with age and so does memory. With increasing age, thinking slows and paying attention becomes more difficult. Distractions may become harder to ignore, and interruptions may cause older people to forget more easily. However, many memory difficulties are problems of *attention* and not necessarily retention. The investigator interviewing elderly persons must be aware of this and recognize that the period between the time the question is asked and answered is not necessarily indicative of the subject's inability to understand or that of formulating alternative responses to the truth. Nor is it necessarily an indication of their ability to retrieve the desired information.

Attempts to understand memory have suggested that life may be categorized as a time for (1) childhood; (2) Adolescence; (3) Adulthood; and (4) Old age.

The age of witnesses involved in a cold case homicide investigation may derive from any of these groupings, and so may memory and the ability to recall. Memory is directly related to interest level. Those events that one cared about and paid attention to are more rapidly recalled than events in which there was little or no interest. As age progresses, interests change and with these changes comes the ability to retrieve. *Concentration* is a key factor in the quality of storage, and subsequently, memory and recall. Researchers have found that people tend to remember what at the time seemed most important or influential. Some believe fear and anxiety are linked to the ability to forget or repress a consideration of note to the investigator. These factors are influential elements in witness perception of events. Although such emotions may dim with age, they do not disappear.

One of the more erroneous assumptions that an investigator can make is that interviewing elderly or senior citizens will result in a *lesser* quality product than interviews of much younger persons. Memory is one of the most important considerations to be competently recognized and understood while interviewing senior citizens and evaluating the quality and worth of their statements. A variety of influences affect the memory of people at all ages, and these influences are also applicable to the memories of senior citizens. Among these are

- Fear. This fear may stem from the event or its aftermath.
- Anxiety. This may result from the event, its aftermath, or the renewed interest on the part of law enforcement and subsequent contact with the witness.
- Physiological conditions.

Memory Types

Speculation and theories about how memory works have been evolving for at least 2000 years. Greek philosopher Aristotle reportedly believed that while thinking took place in the head, memory was stored in the heart. Scientific investigation into this process, however, began approximately 100 years ago. Prior to the 1950s, many believed that memory was thought to be a unitary system. This thought gave way to the belief that memory was composed of a short-term memory for immediate functioning and a long-term memory for life skills, including language, mathematics, and similar abilities. Further research evolved during the 1960s and 1970s, suggesting that memory was a storage system, and later a part of a larger, more elaborate information processing system. The latter included the ability to reason, perception, and comprehension. In the 1980s, renewed interest focused on nonverbal aspects of memory, including more than one system that was involved in this process. Experts in this area of research and study do not necessarily agree on all aspects of this function, although a basic concept of memory is that it is based on practice.

Memory may be generally categorized as *short term* or *long term*. Some researchers have attributed a third category to this function, *sensory memory*. Awareness of these categories may be of importance to the interviewers in cold case homicide investigation.

Short-Term Memory

Short-term memory is a system to retrieve information of a recent duration, or "in use." The definition is considered by some to be of less than one month or so, and is memory most common in more current day-to-day activities. Unlike long-term memory, the ability to store information in this form is of a limited capacity, and short-term memory decays rapidly. An example would be remembering a telephone number. Unless it is rehearsed, it is forgotten within seconds. The very act of reading involves holding in memory the beginning of the sentence while reading to the end.

If it is rehearsed, the information is maintained and transferred to the next stage, *long-term* memory. While this form of memory often takes longer to function with increasing age, it does not necessarily deteriorate with age, although it may become increasingly susceptible to *interference*. For this reason, we may seek to complete a task stored in short-term memory as quickly as possible. The cold case investigator should be aware that short-term memory is directly affected by a number of factors. Among these are

- Neuron breakdown
- Medical condition
- Dietetic considerations

Long-Term Memory

Long-term memory is the form of memory usually addressed during cold case homicide investigations. It is that memory associated with events long past (commonly considered to be in excess of a month or more). It is a form of memory that reportedly appears limitless, although not all the stored information may ultimately be subject to retrieval. This form of memory retains strongly during the aging process, and is one in which there is little decay. This is the form of memory formulated and activated during the younger, usually more chemically and nutritionally balanced years. It is memory formed when the body and brain are growing in physical and mental condition. Many consider it to be a *learned process* that develops as a result of social stimulus.

There are two types of long-term memory:

- *Episodic memory.* This type of memory represents our memory of experiences and events in serial form. From this memory, we are able to reconstruct the actual event(s) that occurred at a specific time in our life. It may be thought of as the *how–when–where* file for an event occurrence.
- *Semantic memory.* This form of memory is more structured and encompasses the facts, skills, and concepts that have been acquired in life. It involves our organized knowledge about words, meanings, relations, concepts, symbols and rules, etc. This information is derived from episodic memory and enables us to learn new facts or concepts from our life's experiences.

There are reportedly three primary activities related to long-term memory:

- *Storage.* Repeated information from a stimulus is stored in the short-term memory and transferred to storage in the long-term memory.
- *Retrieval.* Some researchers have debated whether we actually ever forget, or whether it just becomes increasingly more difficult to retrieve certain information from memory. Of importance to cold case homicide investigators, forgetting something may be a matter of retrieval. Information may not be immediately recalled but may be recognized or may be recalled by prompting. Two primary types of information have been suggested. These are
  - *Recall.* By this process, information is reproduced from memory. Recall may be assisted with retrieval cues, which assist in the ability of the witness to more quickly access the information.
  - *Recognition.* This is a lesser complex process as information is provided in response to a cue. In this process, the presence of the information stimulates knowledge that this information has previously been seen.
- *Deletion.* This may be caused by decay or interference.

Long-term memory is *organized* memory. It is memory that often is retrieved by *association* with other events, times, and places. *Association* is the ability to associate the event or material to information learned and stored through correlation to another. Long-term memory is affected by *attention* and *association.* These factors influence the ability to *recall*—to retrieve—information stored in the long-term memory. If the information was learned and stored, the ability to retrieve is directly linked not only to the attention given at the time in order to learn and store the information but also to the attention required in order to retrieve this information at a later date.

Strategies such as association and *visualization* help people remember. Such time sequences, however, may be very relative and long-term memory can remain strong with increasing years. The significance of this to the cold case investigator cannot be underestimated. Often while interviewing senior citizens, especially regarding events stored in long-term memory, the subject may appear to be talking incoherently or in a disorganized fashion. What they may be doing, however, is *associating* the event under discussion with other events, times, or people in order to facilitate their response to the question at hand.

This process may also work in tandem with the process of *reminiscing*. The investigator is cautioned to not misinterpret this as a sign of mental incompetence or the inability to understand and to communicate. *Reminiscing* involves the recall of persons and sequences of events associated with particular areas of attention. According to the *Merriam Webster Dictionary*, reminiscing is the "recall to mind of a long-forgotten experience or fact…the process or practice of thinking or telling about past experiences…a remembered experience…an account of a memorable experience…something so like another as to be regarded as an unconscious repetition, imitation, or survival." This process helps people to remember names, events, and places, and enhances self-confidence and esteem.

While the investigator may question a subject with the desired purpose of eliciting specific information about a specific person or event, such stimulation may trigger what might seem to be unrelated bits and pieces of information about other people and events. Reminiscing allows the subject to activate the recall process, associating other information with the information desired by the investigator. Depending upon the (amount of) information sought by the investigator, and the ability of those interviewed to furnish it, the amount of reminiscing undertaken may vary considerably. The interview may thus become an extended session, and the interviewer is cautioned not to rush the interview. It is a good idea for the cold case investigator intent on interviewing senior citizens to allow extra time.

Reminiscing further allows the subject to cover a variety of subjects, thus activating the mind to the time period under discussion and opening avenues of thought perhaps long retired. The investigator must take extra care to remain focused upon the information desired and the efforts to elicit such, while also listening carefully for indicators of other relevant information offered unintentionally or in passing. Such may be only a word or two, a thought or short utterance. Care and attention must thus be directed not only to what the investigator is searching for while remaining focused on the responses desired but also to what else the subject may intentionally—or unintentionally—offer. Such offerings may be lead material for future or follow-up investigation.

To the unknowing, reminiscing can be likened to *wandering*. This is a different mechanism. While reminiscing is usually associated with events brought about by the thought processes involved in recalling certain event(s), wandering is a less organized situation wherein there is little or no cohesion to the thought process. This is more often associated with difficulty in the ability to *retrieve* and is influenced or affected by areas noted below in the discussion of short-term memory. An investigator should not assume that the information is not there, but the ability to recall may present formidable obstacles to the investigator. Such condition should be recorded in the course of the investigation so that follow-up investigators and prosecutors are aware of the situation. While the investigator would like to keep subjects being interviewed on track of the subject under discussion, allowances and tolerances must be given to aging citizens.

Sensory Memory

These memories are acknowledged to act as a buffer for stimuli that are received through the senses. These are further categorized as *iconic memory* (visual stimuli), *echoic memory* (aural stimuli), and *haptic memory* (touch). Information from these memories is transmitted to the short-term memory through attention and thus acts as a filter for what is of interest at the moment.

During the aging process, a variety of factors can cause memory failure or loss. These can act together or independently of each other. During the course of cold case interviews, it is suggested that the investigator look for indications of these characters and document this for future investigators and prosecutors. These include

- Reaction time
- Attention
- Diet
- Medications
- Emotions and other emotional factors
- Inactivity
- Isolation
- Lost confidence
- Vision and hearing problems
- Alcohol abuse

Impaired Memory

Forgetting. Those experienced with interviewing the elderly often encounter the "I forget" factor. Every investigator is aware that suspects and witnesses may overuse the "I forget" phrase. Some are truthful, while others are not. In the course of interviewing senior citizens, the reality of this element is more often than not innocent in scope and not one of intent to mislead or deceive. *Forgetting* is a process whereby information in memory becomes inaccessible. Such memory lapses can happen at any time, especially if a person is distracted, overloaded, or busy.

Simplicity in asking the question and allowing the subject time to answer is suggested during these interviews. Rushing another question while the person is attempting to answer the preceding question may cause overload and confusion in some instances. The ability to retrieve is affected by factors that preclude instant or quick recall. Careful questioning can elicit information that may tend to substantiate or otherwise indicate that the subjects being interviewed truthfully do not know, or may think they do not know because they cannot *retrieve* the information.

Forgetting may be influenced by a number of factors. Among these may be interference from other material learned before and after the time sequence. The amount of material forgotten increases with the amount of other distractions or other material that interferes with the smooth retrieval of the information. Occasional moments of forgetfulness or memory loss are not uncommon in many age groups. In more senior age groups, however, these may be indicative of senility, stroke, or diseases such as Alzheimer's disease, although this is not necessarily so.

Symptomatic of this is *panic* on the part of the senior citizen. In addition to verbal statements, this may be demonstrated by outward signs of alarm that include shaking or a visible look of fear or panic. This panic is a manifestation of their self-perceived deteriorating condition, which in fact may not be the case. Forgetfulness can afflict persons of any age, including those in their 30s and 40s. The interviewer is advised to downplay this during the course of the interview, attempting to put the subject at ease to diminish self-induced notions of declining mental ability and self-worth. When this occurs, the investigator may respond to their feelings, explaining that it is "OK" and downplay the significance and importance of their visit, reassuring the potential witness. Do not remind them they are forgetting, use slang, or argue.

Amnesia. Amnesia is a form of impaired memory. This form of impaired memory is reported as one of the most common symptoms following brain damage. This damage may arise from physical trauma, disease, or a stroke, or may be attributed to the aging process. Amnesia does not affect other workings of the brain but interferes with, and blocks, elements of the memory process. There are a number of forms of amnesia, and among these are

- *Pure amnesia.* This is a quite rare form. It affects those memories acquired within the past few months or few years prior to the onset of amnesia. Access to older, more deeply embedded memories is normal.
- *Post-traumatic amnesia.* A stage of amnesia resulting from a head injury in which the victim emerges from a relatively confused period and encounters difficulty keeping track of ongoing activities and exhibits other degrees of confusion.
- *Retrograde amnesia.* This amnesia reflects difficulty in recalling events and information from the distant past. After a head injury, the victim may have trouble recalling events that occurred before the injury. The degree of this form of amnesia may be correlated to the extent of the head injury and its impact upon short-term and long-term memory.
- *Anterograde amnesia.* This form of amnesia refers to problems in new learning and in ongoing memory.

Dementia. (Psychiatrists now refer to *dementia* as "major neurocognitive disorder" per DSM-5. This segment will utilize the publicly associated term.) According to the National Institute on Aging, *dementia* is a term for a group of symptoms that are usually caused by changes in the normal activity of very sensitive brain cells. The name means "without mentation." The brain suffers a breakdown in the ability to pass electrical messages. As a result, the ability to learn, remember, or retrieve is affected. This seriously interferes with a person's ability to carry out daily activities. Dementia is a progressive deterioration of the brain and is irreversible; it cannot be cured. Dementia is a syndrome in which a person suffers from impaired memory, and also at least one of the following conditions:

- Problems with executive functions such as planning, thinking abstractly, appropriately starting or stopping behavior, switching focus, or considering consequences
- Inability to recognize people or objects
- Inability to use language in an appropriate manner for time and place
- Inability to perform overlearned tasks such as brushing one's teeth

It should be noted that dementia is not in itself a disease. Rather, it is a group of symptoms that may accompany certain diseases or physical conditions.

Alzheimer's disease is the most common cause of dementia. This progressive disease frequently starts with short-term memory impairment but may also include impairment in the ability to recall faces, sequences of events, distances and shapes, etc. Although Alzheimer's disease is not curable, diagnosis and early treatment may slow the progression of cognitive losses.

Vascular disease is the second most common cause of dementia. This is a condition in which blood flow in the brain is impaired because the blood vessels become blocked or damaged, as in a stroke. This is not the same as Alzheimer's disease, although similarly the afflicted person becomes progressively worse and eventually incapable of caring for himself or herself. Alzheimer's disease and vascular disease account for approximately 85% of all dementias. However, dementias may also be caused by treatable conditions such as depression, certain nutritional deficiencies, and some endocrine disorders. In these cases, the cognitive problems may resolve when the underlying medical issue is addressed.

The onset of dementia may be noted by

- A decline in reasoning and judgment
- Changes in memory, including the ability to perform word problems or getting lost
- Changes in ability to handle life's functions

- Potential personality and mood changes
- Behavioral changes

There are many conditions with symptoms that resemble dementia, but which are not. Among these are loneliness, anxiety, sadness, and boredom.

Alzheimer's Disease

This is a kind of memory deficit in the form of progressive dementia. Alzheimer's disease is one of a group of diseases called the *dementias*. This disease appears to damage, and ultimately kill, many of the nerve cells in the brain. In this process, it also weakens and damages the connections between them. As a result, the patient shows increasingly pronounced symptoms affecting language, perceptual, and emotional problems and ultimately results in a terminal stage.

The beginnings of Alzheimer's disease may be almost imperceptible at the start, but memory loss becomes more severe with increasing time. Old memories may tend to be substituted for new ones; thus the victim of this disease repeats events from the past. As the disease progresses, old memories suffer and ultimately the damage to nerve cells and connections results in knowledge being erased. As old knowledge and information occur, the ability to learn anything new also suffers. In addition, damage occurs in other parts of the brain as well, resulting in further alteration of behavior and ability to function normally. Alzheimer's disease is uncommon before age 65, but the percentage of people afflicted rises rapidly between this period and age 80–85.

Physicians typically use some of the following criteria to diagnose Alzheimer's disease:

- Age of onset is between 40 and 90.
- Lack of disturbance of consciousness.
- Problems in two or more areas of mental function, such as speech, memory, or ability to draw.
- Progressive worsening of these mental problems.
- Lack of evidence of other disease to explain these conditions.

Stroke

A *stroke* is a sudden disruption in the flow of blood to an area of the brain. Thus deprived, the affected brain cells are damaged or die. Cell damage can be repaired, but the death of brain cells is permanent and results in disability.

Stroke victims, depending upon the severity and number of strokes, may/will not audio-record as clearly as the interview may have seemed in person. They do not necessarily transcribe clearly, depending upon the medical condition and medication. This does not necessarily mean, however, that they cannot understand what the investigator has to say nor that they are unable to accurately communicate in response. These victims require additional time for the investigator to attempt to understand the individual's degree of impairment, and the ability to clearly receive and understand what the victim may be communicating. While each affected individual must be measured and weighed upon their individual merits, they should not necessarily be discarded as potential sources of information. The following example illustrates this point.

Case History

During the reinvestigation of the series of murders and alleged rapes that occurred in a rural mountain region during the mid-1920s, I had occasion to interview Russ in the mid-1980s.

I initially contacted Russ in a face-to-face interview at his home and told him that I wished to speak to him about events that had occurred in the period 1925–1930. At the time of the interviews, Russ was in his late 80s. I had been told by others that Russ possibly had critical information pertaining to the case. I was advised by his family that he had recently suffered two small strokes, however. Russ spoke with difficulty and his words were garbled. To ascertain if he understood my questions, I asked him the same question on three different occasions, slightly rephrasing it each time so that it did not appear to be the same question yet solicited the same answer. Each time, however, he responded with the same answer.

Frequently during the interview, after asking a question and receiving an answer, I would pause before asking another question. This served to downplay any stress from the interview brought up by revisiting the events that had occurred 60 years before. Despite the passage of time and the death of one of the killers in the mid-1960s, Russ was still afraid of this man and would not mention his name. At one point during the interview, Russ paused, and then asked me if I knew that another principal figure in the case, the corrupt district attorney who convicted the innocent man, had visited him at his ranch during the period surrounding the conviction? I did not.

Russ then told me that the prosecutor had come to the ranch to go deer hunting. While present, he had told Russ and a group of other men present how he had forced a confession to murder, under fear of death, from the Indian cowboy. This information was significant as it corroborated documentary evidence with a living, eye-witness account. I subsequently reviewed Russ's family photo album. I observed two photographs of interest. One photograph depicted Russ and a group of men (Figure 9.1), and the other photo depicted the corrupt prosecutor at the ranch (Figure 9.2).

I showed the photos to Russ. Russ identified the prosecutor and stated that the man had visited the ranch on only *one* occasion, in 1929. He then identified each of the other men in the group photo. All the others were deceased now. However, his memory of the event was very clear and he was able to communicate this to me, although the tape recording was very difficult to understand if one was not familiar with listening to, and understanding, Russ.

Figure 9.1 1929 witness interviewed in 1988. In the 1980s, Russ, back row second from left, was the only surviving member of this group photo taken in 1929. This photo was taken when the corrupt district attorney, Figure 9.2, visited the ranch. At this time, he brought illegal alcohol to the gathering. It was later shown that he was also running the biggest bootlegging ring in the county from the DA's office, and he was convicted in federal court. The DA told these men how he forced a confession from the Indian cowboy by fear of death, and bribed witnesses. Despite his age and strokes, Russ provided myself and follow-up reviewers credible, firsthand account of an event he witnessed. (Courtesy of the Harold Hunt Family.)

Figure 9.2 This photo was taken when the corrupt district attorney visited the ranch. (Courtesy of the Harold Hunt Family.)

Russ's information was very significant, and I returned in two weeks, accompanied by the chief investigator for the district attorney's office. The purpose of this follow-up interview was to seek a second opinion about his credibility and clarity. I again asked Russ the series of questions from my first visit, and he answered just as he had two weeks before. His memory was clear and concise. Russ ultimately became a cornerstone witness in subsequent legal proceedings that identified two killers from the period, and contributed toward a pardon for a man who was wrongfully convicted for the murders almost 60 years before.

The interview process during cold case homicide investigations builds upon the experience and training of the homicide investigator and is not separate and detached. Recognition of such symptoms, and the ability to distinguish between real and artificial memory loss, is a skill that enhances the proficiencies of the cold case investigator during interviews with senior citizens and the elderly. With age, distractions are often harder to ignore and interruptions can cause older people to forget more easily. This can be a positive assurance to the investigator trained to recognize such. During the course of an interview in the cold case process, I have found that it is a useful technique to ask the same question several times, altering the wording while designing the question to elicit the same response. If the subject recognizes this tactic, it is indicative of short-term memory retention (and with such, potential clarity of memory). If they do not recognize this tactic, yet furnish the same answer, it is suggestive that they are truthful.

Interviewing some senior citizens may be time consuming and delicate in nature. Occasionally in the course of the interview, the investigator may point out seemingly areas of conflict in the statement. Care must be given to do this in a non-accusatory tone or suggestion that the investigator is belittling the witness. A natural tendency may be to give deference to senior citizens, even perhaps extending sympathy, compassion, and courtesy during the interview. Do not let sympathy and a false sense of respect for the elderly overcome your investigative skills and abilities. It could get you killed.

Capacity

According to Dr. Bennett Blum, a psychiatrist considered by many to be the nation's top expert on geriatric forensic work, there is much more to assessing the competency of a potential elderly witness than "memory." While a battery of examinations, interviews, and observations may be needed for a complete forensic psychiatric assessment, this is not necessarily so during the witness interview process in cold case investigations. One of the components used to assess competency, observation, may be utilized by cold case investigators.

Investigator observation of the subjects' behavior during the course of an interview may assist in assessing the capacity of a potential elderly witness. In addition to memory, observations may include

- Daily living activities, including bathing, grooming, dressing, and eating
- Concentration and orientation
- Subject's ability to plan and strategize (including ability to understand the probable outcome of decisions)
- Speech and language
- Thought processes
- Emotional control
- Insight and judgment
- Anticipation, anxiety, irritability
- Impaired recall of recent or more remote information

Interview Techniques and Considerations

Contact and interview with a senior citizen, or other witnesses for that matter, may occur in the course of a cold case homicide investigation in any of the following occasions or combinations:

- Reinterview of the witness due to reactivation of the case after an extended period of time
- Change in investigators
- Clarification and follow-up of information in a previous statement(s)
- Identification of the new witness

While preparing for an interview and during the interview process, I have found the following considerations to be helpful:

- Formative years
  - During what era or decade(s) did the witness begin to experience life and to form opinions?
  - What effect did this period have on their mindset?
  - How much effect and impact do those experiences carry over to today?
  - What is their geographical, demographic, or cultural history? This may be important to the interview process. Those who have immigrated from other countries and Third World nations may have an impression of law enforcement based upon their early history and law enforcement standards and tactics far removed from those in the United States, or media accounts. This may impact their willingness to cooperate with law enforcement.
  - Do they have a criminal record during these years?

Past Law Enforcement Practices

In the United States, wide-ranging law enforcement practices and procedures marked the period from the 1930s to the 1970s. Different regions within the country witnessed a mixture of police styles and practices that were not necessarily in agreement with the standards and styles uniformly practiced in other regions of the country. Since this period, law enforcement standards and ethics of conduct have progressed significantly. However, bribery and corruption were not uncommon during the middle half of the twentieth century, especially in some jurisdictions. Those raised in an inner-city environment may have different exposure and concepts of law enforcement than those in a more rural environment, and media exploitation or coverage of incidents in recent years may have contributed to their perceptions. Either may be more positive than the other, and each must be appraised on an individual basis. The cold case investigator is advised not to generalize that, due to a witness's upbringing or environment, he or she is automatically inclined to not be truthful, however.

The perception of law enforcement by a senior citizen is important to a cold case investigator. The style of cop portrayed in old Jimmy Cagney gangster movies is not far removed from fact in decades past, and media portrayal may be a factor in their willingness to speak. The *Third Degree* stuff was very real and, on rare occasions, has carried over to the present. This may be conscious or unconscious on the part of the interviewee.

Conversely, however, prior experiences with law enforcement may have been positive and engendered a respect for the "system."

- The senior citizen of today may have been raised in an atmosphere where you did not question government officials, or "buck the system."
- In preceding eras, there was a more blind respect for authority of the courts and law. In decades past, few might question the actions of a judge, and did not argue with his or her authority or that of detectives. Investigative reporters were not as prevalent as today, and society was not as open. Policy was what one person said it was.

The Approach and Introduction

The significance of the initial meeting and rapport building period of the interview cannot be underestimated. It sets the tone for the subsequent interview and post-interview relationships between law enforcement and the witness. When conducting an interview with senior citizens, it has been my experience to be especially observant and intuitive during the approach to the interview. Although it is dependent upon the style of the investigator and circumstances of the case, I have found that interviews of senior citizens as witnesses are most effective when accomplished in a face-to-face environment. This format is most effective because it

- Establishes, builds, and enhances a relationship between the witness and the investigator
- Allows the investigator to observe and evaluate a number of factors that may affect the reliability and quality of the interview and the information sought and received
- Diminishes the potential for miscommunication and misunderstanding
- Facilitates identification of additional information

This phase includes both verbal and nonverbal communications, as well as observation of the individual and surroundings.

- They may be distrustful of your purposes/motives.
- Make them feel relaxed and comfortable.
- Don't rush.
- Do a short explanation of your presence at this time.

- Be casual yet professional.
- Attempt to establish common interests.
- Spend time "warming up" with witness. Talk about a variety of matters. Some senior citizens are often lonely and welcome the visit and desire conversation.
- Use initial conversation to feel out their background, attitude, and potential for cooperation.
- Be honest. Senior citizens have a good capacity to "see through" or evaluate.
- Note their concerns for future publicity or family awareness.

Spouse/relationships. Learn as much as possible about your witness as it may lead to other sources of information that may be unknown to the investigator or who may substantiate the credibility and accuracy of the witness.

- Any/number of prior spouses/relationships?
- Period of relationship
- Statements to witness by former spouse or others
- Time of separation
  - Why? (Potential for additional witness or source of information)
  - Number of children (identify as potential source of information)
  - When?
  - Where?
  - How?
  - Violence in background?
- Background of their relationship with spouse's family?
- Other leads, contacts, or referrals?

Friends. The cold case investigator may seek to identify friends of the witness as these persons may become additional witnesses or corroborate the witness or provide further follow-up information.

- Speak of?
- Long term/short term (identify)?
- Nearby/distant?
- Number/relationship?

Physical condition. During the approach and subsequent interview, the cold case investigator should note the physical condition of the witness as it may suggest the ability of the witness to see, hear, and perceive the events of the interview. These may also impact the ability of the witness for future court appearances. Among these observations might be

- Physical appearance
- Presence of eyeglasses
- Presence of hearing aid
- Medical bracelets or necklaces
- Presence of prescription drugs or other medications

Mental condition. During the interview, the cold case investigator should take note of the apparent mental condition of the witness. This may tend to enhance or diminish the reliability and veracity of the witness.

- Do they appear "all together?"
- Observe physical appearance.

- Self-concern about appearance?
- Stated medical background. What medical conditions may affect the ability of the witness to hear, understand, and communicate with the investigator? In addition, the cold case investigator seeks to identify any medical conditions that may affect the reliability and consistency of the witness.
  - Medication
  - Strokes
    - May/may not affect reliability of memory
    - May influence response time from question to answer
    - May affect ability to verbally communicate with interviewer

Outlook on life

- Desire to live?
- Desire to die?
- Live in the past?
- Live in the present?
- Live for the future?

Observation at residence/location of witness. These may provide subjective insight into the ability of the witness to present a credible presence and consistency.

- Standard of living
- Self-sufficiency
- Economic status
- Style/maintenance and care of residence
- Neighborhood

Physical surroundings. What does the physical setting of the witness suggest about their potential credibility and reliability?

- Clean and neat
- Cluttered and dirty
- Living in the past vs. present
- Furniture
- Age of furnishings and condition
- Style ("Chesterfield")
- Age of appliances/condition
- Pictures and decorations
- Type and age
- Reflect interest of witness
- Family
- Locations
- Artwork

Pets. Subjectively, what does this suggest regarding the ability of the witness to present a credible and reliable presence and ability to communicate? Of their ability to focus?

- Dogs
  - Noisy/yappy
  - Big/small
  - Attention paid to by witness during interview
- Cats
  - Number
  - Type (domestic/alley)

Family. Does the witness have other family that may provide further information, provide support to the witness, or potentially be a cause of concern or embarrassment to the witness?

- Children and grandchildren.
- Are pictures abundant/sparse/lacking?
- Attentive to or reference by witness.
- Surviving.
- Near/far/identify.
- Amount of contact.

Audio Recording

The use of an audio recorder may be desirable while conducting an interview with a senior citizen. However, the display and use may warrant additional considerations other than those perhaps found with younger individuals contacted during the course of investigations.

- Do *not* walk in and immediately pull out a recorder.
- Do not let them see it immediately.
- Use a warm-up period of conversation and ask if they would mind if you use it. "It's easier for me" or similar phrases to downplay its presence and use.
- Recording may be an object of distrust or uncertainty by the senior citizen. It may be too formal a technique for them.
- The recorder may elevate any anxiety level felt by the senior witness.
- If used, try to do so unobtrusively and don't continually look at it or allow them to focus on the object instead of you.
- Keep in mind that the voice characteristics of senior citizens in some interviews may pose additional problems for those who later listen to the recording or attempt to transcribe it. It is suggested that specific points of interest be clarified by the investigator repeating the conversation and eliciting a "yes" or "no" answer.

Documents, Pictures, and Props

Documents. The elderly usually need greater visual contrast to read documents than younger adults. In addition, the elderly may need larger print than younger adults. Printing should be at least 14-point.

Documents should be in black ink, printed on white paper. Dr. Blum reported of having once seen a series of bank brochures that had red-colored writing on a black background. The creators thought this would emphasize key points for their elderly customers. Instead, most customers could not see those sections at all.

Photos. If the purpose of the interview entails showing crime scene or other photographs to the witness, the investigator may consider using enlarged photographs, perhaps 8 × 10 inches in lieu of smaller photographs. In reactivating older cold case files, the investigator may encounter black and white photos approximately 4 inches × 4 inches. Whether the case file photos are in this format or later 4 × 6 inch or other format, the investigator may consider using enlarged photographs for witness review and identification.

Witnesses may be too embarrassed to admit that they cannot see as clearly as they once did. In this instance, the investigator may run the chance of a well-meaning witness making an erroneous or mistaken identification based upon embarrassment of visual acuity.

Enlarged photos may enable the witness to identify or reveal information not previously known to the investigator but recognized in the photograph by the witness. Viewing photos might stimulate recall of other information by the witness. Note during interview/observations whether the witness normally wears glasses and/or if glasses are worn at the time of the witness review.

Photo lineup. If the purpose of the interview entails the investigator showing a photo lineup, it is suggested that the investigator consider

- Use of enlarged photographs in an 8 × 10 inch format. This is for the same reasons noted above.
- Using a sequential lineup instead of the traditional six-pack. While this style of photo lineup has been espoused by some to reflect a more fair and balanced format, there may be an additional advantage in this style of lineup when used with senior citizens. This format may appear less intimidating, thus reducing stress and anxiety felt by the elderly witness.

In all cases, these photos should be marked and retained per department procedure for their evidentiary value in future court proceedings.

Calendars. When conducting an interview with a senior citizen regarding past events, a calendar of the month as well as those preceding and following that in which the crime occurred may serve as an investigative aid. The investigator may also want to include a calendar of the year also. It has been my experience that witnesses in cold cases, as well as current, may identify or associate other events with the date/time under discussion. In doing so, they may recall the day, but not the date. Or, they may recall the date and not the day. It is important that these be in sync. Showing a witness a calendar may elicit further information not known to the investigator by stimulating recall of case or other period events.

For example, a senior citizen may inform the investigator that he or she found the victim dead on the afternoon of October 11. This may be contrary to the statements of others who last saw the victim alive in the morning on October 12. During the course of the interview, the investigator may elicit from the witness that the witness was coming home from church when he or she last saw the victim. A check of a period calendar may reveal that October 12 was a Sunday, and that the witness was in error on the date but not the day due to association with church activity that same day. Thus, the calendar serves as an investigative aid for the investigator and the witness. The object of investigation is to obtain the facts, and with the passage of time, the use of props such as calendars enhances the investigator's ability to seek the truth.

The Interview

The traditional police interview has often utilized a "just the facts ma'am, just the facts," question and answer approach. In this manner, the investigator asks questions that seek to answer the question "who, what, when, where, why, and how?" Depending upon the circumstances and available location, the investigator seeking to interview a senior citizen may seek to do so in a physical setting most accommodating to the interviewees. Most often this may be their home or other zone in which they feel most comfortable. The goal of the investigator in this regard should be to make the witness physically and emotionally comfortable, and to enhance witness cooperation.

When interviewing, all other distractions should be removed or turned off, especially radios and televisions. If someone has even a mild cognitive impairment, any distraction could significantly reduce the quality of information provided to investigators. Dr. Blum reports of one interview of a man who could not answer any questions while the door to his hospital room was open. The hallway noise distracted him so much that he became, literally, incoherent. When the door was closed, however, he was able to hold a reasonable conversation and provided information that turned out to be essential.

On occasion, the senior may wish to have a relative present during the interview. The cold case investigator must make the decision to allow such a visitor depending upon the perceived importance of the witness, the information they may have to offer, and the anticipated or perceived assistance or interference the visitor may pose.

Make sure the witness heard the question and that they understand the question. Allow adequate time to respond, and if necessary, ask if they understand the question. Repeat and clarify the question if they indicate they do not, or if you are not sure. During the interview, the investigator should seek to avoid a confrontational atmosphere. If the witness exhibits initial anxiety, consider changing the subject to a more neutral topic, such as "Did you paint that picture yourself?" When appropriate, slowly come back around to the investigation. If they appear to become upset over little things, respond positively and do not hesitate to accept blame and move forward. Let the witness wander off the topic on occasion, guiding them back on track as necessary. During the interview, a cold case investigator may consider the following:

- Formulate and ask as few good questions. Look for areas they may be avoiding.
- Don't use an accusatory tone.
- Let them know that it is ok now to tell what they know.
- Ask leading questions to stimulate other thoughts, questions, and answers.
- If they have given previous statements, use previous questions and answers and statement as guide to ascertain if their statement now is in agreement or not. The investigator must use judgment in advising the witness if or when it is not to stimulate recall and to correct any earlier or subsequent statements. Know their statements in advance so you do not have to keep referring to the statement.
- Avoid physical barrier between the investigator and the witness, such as desk, table, etc.
- Avoid distractions such as radio, television, etc.
- Avoid sarcasm, "police humor," or comments they may interpret in different context.
- Observe how they react to questions: note their body language at the time of question and the time of answer.
- Note unsolicited statements.

Once you have completed the interview, review the high points or critical areas in a "yes/no" answer format. If necessary, ask the same question a few minutes apart.

A Word of Caution

The experienced investigator should *not* fall prey to thinking that senior citizens are like small children; that they are simple and will always be truthful. They have a whole life experience to draw upon, a life configured by circumstances unknown to the investigator. It has not been uncommon for cold case investigators to interview witnesses and suspects in cold case homicides that occurred before the investigator was born. Like some children, some elderly people possess an ability to lie and deceive, which may fool even veteran, experienced investigators. Treat them courteously and as professionally as any other victim or witness. Keep in mind that while you are interviewing them, they may be interviewing you. They may be attempting to learn how much you know (about them). In the arena of cold case homicide investigation, those with something to hide may turn deadly at any moment.

Always think and practice officer safety!

Conclusion

Senior citizens may offer cold case investigators valuable information. As with the interview process for others, each must be accomplished given the experience and best judgment of the investigator. Understanding what researchers believe about the memory process and how it functions may assist in the interview and evaluation by the investigator when interacting with a senior citizen as a witness. Memory lapses can be completely normal, especially during the aging process. Forgetting, blurring, or invention of events is a part of the normal memory process. Knowledge and understanding of their physical, emotional, and mental states, as well as familial relationships and pressures, may contribute to the ability of the investigator to elicit important information. Keep in mind the life experiences these people possess, and

Be patient!

Acknowledgments

I wish to gratefully acknowledge the significant material contributed to this topic by Dr. Bennett Blum. Dr. Blum has reported nationally upon the dementia syndrome and Alzheimer's disease. Dr. Blum's research and writing on forensic issues in geriatric psychiatry are widely acclaimed, and his works have been utilized by lawyers, law enforcement, and social service personnel. In addition, I wish to extend my deepest gratitude and appreciation for the review and input into this topic by Dan Martell, PhD, and Richard Walter, MA.

Suggested Readings and Bibliography

Anonymous. (1991). *Confusion and Memory Loss in Old Age: It's Not What You Think*. National Institute on Aging. Gaithersburg, MD.

Anonymous. (2003). Information from Your Family Doctor: Memory Loss. *American Family Physician*. Kansas City, V67, I5. March 1, 2003.

Baddeley, A. (1998). *Human Memory: Theory and Practice* (Revised edition). Allyn and Bacon. London.

Blum, B. (2005). *Geriatric Psychiatry-Forensic Issues. Kaplan and Sadock's Comprehensive Textbook of Psychiatry* (8th edition). Lippincott, Williams, and Wilkins. Philadelphia, PA.

Blum, B. Texas Lawyer E-Alerts/Litigation, http://www.tlealerts.com/litigation/18.htm.

Blum, B. and Richards, D. (2013). "Assessing Mental Capacity," in *The Encyclopedia of Elder Care:* (3rd edition). Capezuti, E., Malone, M., Katz, P., Mezey, M. (editors). Springer Publishing Company. New York.

Fitch, B. (2015). *Memory Puzzle: What Every Investigator Should Know*. FBI Law Enforcement Bulletin. January.

Gordon, B. (1995). *Memory: Remembering and Forgetting in Everyday Life*. Mastermedia Limited. New York.

Haberlandt, K. (1999). *Human Memory: Exploration and Application*. Allyn and Bacon. Boston.
Loftus, E.F. (1996). *Eyewitness Testimony*. Harvard University Press. Cambridge, MA.
Lovden, M., Ronnlund, M., Washlin, A., Backman, L. et al. (2004). *The Journals of Gerontology: Series B: Psychological Science and Social Sciences*. Washington, DC. V59B, I3. May 2004.
Memon, A., Barblett, J., Rose, R., and Gray, C. (2003). *The Journals of Gerontology: Series B: Psychological Sciences and Social Sciences*. Washington, DC. V. 58B, I6. November 2003.
Parkin, A.J. (1993). *Memory: Phenomena, Experiment and Theory*. Blackwell Publishers. United Kingdom.
Taylor, K.T. (2001). *Forensic Art and Illustration*. CRC Press. New York.

Death Certificate, Obituary, and Coroner's Inquest

10

R. H. WALTON

Contents

A number of documents not normally encountered in the unsolved homicide investigation case file may provide investigative direction to cold case homicide investigators. These documents may be especially valuable when, in the perception of the investigator(s), the case file is incomplete or lacking in some material areas, or as a guide for investigating and determining relationships. Among these documents are

- Certificate of death
- Application and permit for disposition of human remains
- Physician/coroner's amendment
- Obituary
- Coroner's inquest

This section examines the foregoing and their relevance during the course of a cold case homicide investigation.

Death Certificate

Interestingly enough, in my experience, it is not uncommon or unusual to find the certificate of death, also called the *death certificate*, absent when reviewing a case file that has been inactive. During the course of the initial homicide investigation, obtaining this document for the file may not have been a high priority due to the course of the investigation and other duties encountered by the original investigators. As the case was not forwarded to the district attorney for prosecution, obtaining this document for the murder book, as it was, did not get done.

With the reactivation of a cold case, obtaining and reviewing this document is an important course of action. The information in the certificate of death is compiled and constructed by officials involved in the course of establishing death and disposition of the remains. Unlike the obituary, this document is not directly compiled by family members, although some information on the death certificate may originate with a family member or close friends.

There is no national system of death investigation in the United States, nor is there a uniform system for recording the information on a certificate of death. There is, however, some information that is consistent across the nation. This includes basic information identifying the deceased and other individuals, and information surrounding the cause and manner of death. All states provide for a permanent and compulsory vital registration system. This system, however, depends upon the willingness and cooperation of those involved with the decedent, including physicians, hospitals, coroners or medical examiners, and funeral directors, to prepare and certify necessary information.

In some states, vital statistic information relating to births, deaths, or fetal deaths may be mandated for direct reporting to the state vital statistics unit by the primary source. This may include hospitals, coroners and/or medical examiners, and funeral directors. Some, but not all, states are divided into registration districts in furtherance of collecting vital statistic information and utilize a local registrar system. These districts may be a county, city, or other geographical or political subdivision, or a combination of these. In these states, this office collects the necessary information for transmittal to the state bureau or office of vital statistics. The local registrar is required to ensure that that a complete certificate for each of these events is filed. In some states, this official also issues burial and transportation permits for deceased persons.

Not uncommonly, the certificate of death is initiated by the mortuary. The mortuary obtains vital information from the family (as the legal representative) as well as the attending physician. It prepares the document and forwards it to the physician for signature. After this signing, the document is returned to the mortuary and then forwarded to the registrar for assignment of a file number and permit for disposition. A sign of the times—in some locales, mortuaries are now prohibited from keeping copies of death certificates in their case files due to identity theft concerns and post-9/11 concerns (Figure 10.1).

It is suggested that review of the death certificate be completed in the earliest stages of the reinvestigation of a cold case homicide. In those cases in which the identity of the victim is known yet the case must be reconstructed from scratch, that is, with little or no information in file, this document provides a jump-off point for numerous avenues of investigation. These include

- Identification of dates for newspaper review and subsequent identification of persons and reported events
- Dates and time frames for review of agency archives and document search
- Names of relatives
- Mortuary records or other disposition information, which may contain more detailed information

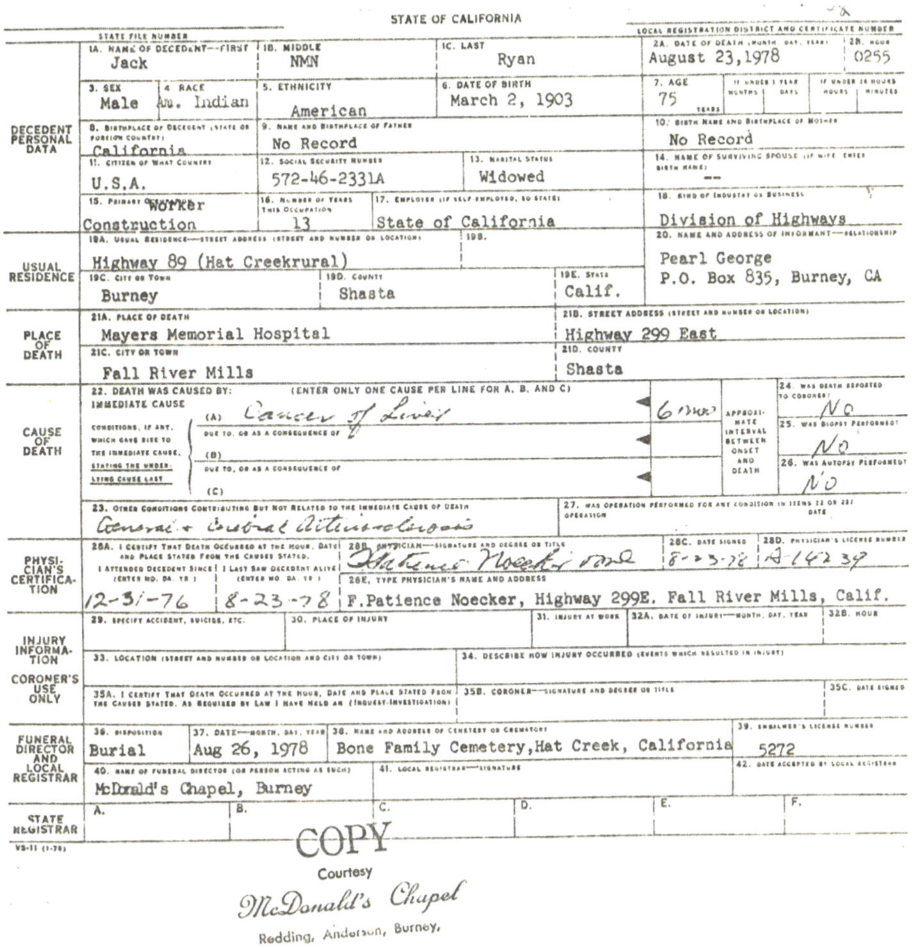
STATE OF CALIFORNIA

STATE FILE NUMBER

LOCAL REGISTRATION DISTRICT AND CERTIFICATE NUMBER

DECEDENT PERSONAL DATA

1A. NAME OF DECEDENT—FIRST: Jack
1B. MIDDLE: NMN
1C. LAST: Ryan
2A. DATE OF DEATH (MONTH, DAY, YEAR): August 23, 1978
2B. HOUR: 0255
3. SEX: Male
4. RACE: Am. Indian
5. ETHNICITY: American
6. DATE OF BIRTH: March 2, 1903
7. AGE: 75 YEARS
8. BIRTHPLACE OF DECEDENT (STATE OR FOREIGN COUNTRY): California
9. NAME AND BIRTHPLACE OF FATHER: No Record
10. BIRTH NAME AND BIRTHPLACE OF MOTHER: No Record
11. CITIZEN OF WHAT COUNTRY: U.S.A.
12. SOCIAL SECURITY NUMBER: 572-46-2331A
13. MARITAL STATUS: Widowed
14. NAME OF SURVIVING SPOUSE (IF WIFE, ENTER BIRTH NAME): ---
15. PRIMARY OCCUPATION: Worker Construction
16. NUMBER OF YEARS THIS OCCUPATION: 13
17. EMPLOYER (IF SELF-EMPLOYED, SO STATE): State of California
18. KIND OF INDUSTRY OR BUSINESS: Division of Highways

USUAL RESIDENCE

19A. USUAL RESIDENCE—STREET ADDRESS (STREET AND NUMBER OR LOCATION): Highway 89 (Hat Creekrural)
19B.
19C. CITY OR TOWN: Burney
19D. COUNTY: Shasta
19E. STATE: Calif.
20. NAME AND ADDRESS OF INFORMANT—RELATIONSHIP: Pearl George P.O. Box 835, Burney, CA

PLACE OF DEATH

21A. PLACE OF DEATH: Mayers Memorial Hospital
21B. STREET ADDRESS (STREET AND NUMBER OR LOCATION): Highway 299 East
21C. CITY OR TOWN: Fall River Mills
21D. COUNTY: Shasta

CAUSE OF DEATH

22. DEATH WAS CAUSED BY: (ENTER ONLY ONE CAUSE PER LINE FOR A, B, AND C)
IMMEDIATE CAUSE (A) Cancer of Liver — 6 mos — APPROXIMATE INTERVAL BETWEEN ONSET AND DEATH
CONDITIONS, IF ANY, WHICH GAVE RISE TO THE IMMEDIATE CAUSE, STATING THE UNDERLYING CAUSE LAST
DUE TO, OR AS A CONSEQUENCE OF (B)
DUE TO, OR AS A CONSEQUENCE OF (C)
24. WAS DEATH REPORTED TO CORONER? No
25. WAS BIOPSY PERFORMED? No
26. WAS AUTOPSY PERFORMED? No
23. OTHER CONDITIONS CONTRIBUTING BUT NOT RELATED TO THE IMMEDIATE CAUSE OF DEATH: General + Cerebral Arteriosclerosis
27. WAS OPERATION PERFORMED FOR ANY CONDITION IN ITEMS 22 OR 23? OPERATION — DATE

PHYSICIAN'S CERTIFICATION

28A. I CERTIFY THAT DEATH OCCURRED AT THE HOUR, DATE AND PLACE STATED FROM THE CAUSES STATED. I ATTENDED DECEDENT SINCE (ENTER MO, DA, YR): 12-31-76 I LAST SAW DECEDENT ALIVE (ENTER MO, DA, YR): 8-23-78
28B. PHYSICIAN—SIGNATURE AND DEGREE OR TITLE: F. Patience Noecker MD
28C. DATE SIGNED: 8-23-78
28D. PHYSICIAN'S LICENSE NUMBER: A-14239
28E. TYPE PHYSICIAN'S NAME AND ADDRESS: F.Patience Noecker, Highway 299E. Fall River Mills, Calif.

INJURY INFORMATION

29. SPECIFY ACCIDENT, SUICIDE, ETC.
30. PLACE OF INJURY
31. INJURY AT WORK
32A. DATE OF INJURY—MONTH, DAY, YEAR
32B. HOUR
33. LOCATION (STREET AND NUMBER OR LOCATION AND CITY OR TOWN)
34. DESCRIBE HOW INJURY OCCURRED (EVENTS WHICH RESULTED IN INJURY)

CORONER'S USE ONLY

35A. I CERTIFY THAT DEATH OCCURRED AT THE HOUR, DATE AND PLACE STATED FROM THE CAUSES STATED. AS REQUIRED BY LAW I HAVE HELD AN (INQUEST-INVESTIGATION)
35B. CORONER—SIGNATURE AND DEGREE OR TITLE
35C. DATE SIGNED

FUNERAL DIRECTOR AND LOCAL REGISTRAR

36. DISPOSITION: Burial
37. DATE—MONTH, DAY, YEAR: Aug 26, 1978
38. NAME AND ADDRESS OF CEMETERY OR CREMATORY: Bone Family Cemetery,Hat Creek, California
39. EMBALMER'S LICENSE NUMBER: 5272
40. NAME OF FUNERAL DIRECTOR (OR PERSON ACTING AS SUCH): McDonald's Chapel, Burney
41. LOCAL REGISTRAR—SIGNATURE
42. DATE ACCEPTED BY LOCAL REGISTRAR

STATE REGISTRAR A. B. C. D. E. F.

VS-11 (1-76)

COPY

Courtesy
McDonald's Chapel
Redding, Anderson, Burney,

Figure 10.1 Ryan death certificate (1978). The format of death certificates has changed over the years, but the core information has not. (Author's file.)

At the outset of the cold case investigation, the certificate of death identifies significant information about the deceased as well as time and circumstances surrounding death, informant information, as well as physician and coroner/medical examiner certifications and mortuary/disposition information.

As a result, this document provides specific information as officially recorded. This information, or portions of this information, may be lacking in the present case file, and this document offers investigators potential sources for investigative information as well as, in some circumstances, potential sources to recover missing or uncollected evidence. That the death was ruled a homicide is important for investigation and prosecution, although cold case investigations can, and have, gone forward when the death certificate has initially ruled the case as accidental, suicide, or undetermined (Figure 10.2).

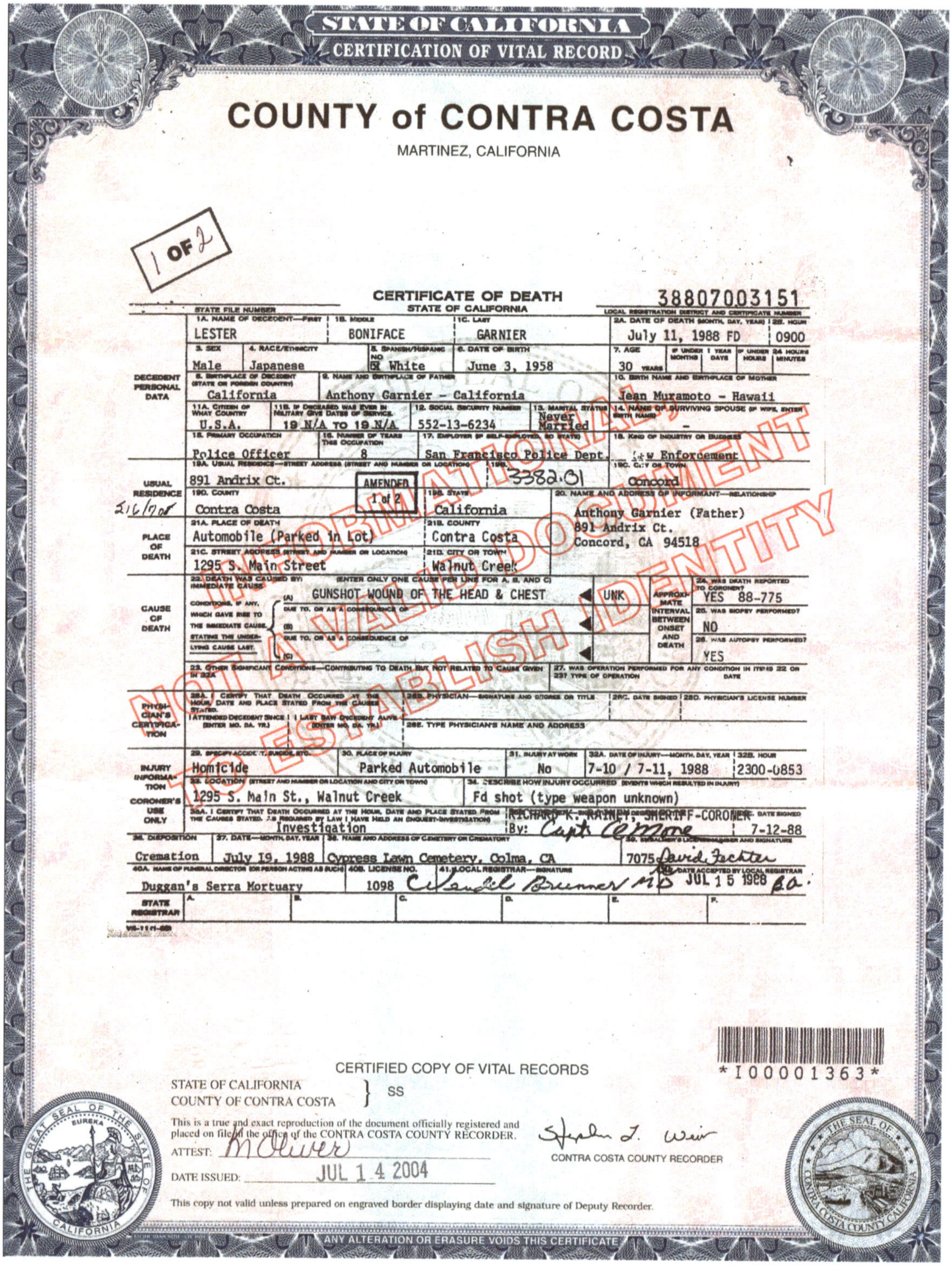

STATE OF CALIFORNIA
CERTIFICATION OF VITAL RECORD

COUNTY of CONTRA COSTA
MARTINEZ, CALIFORNIA

1 OF 2

CERTIFICATE OF DEATH
STATE OF CALIFORNIA
38807003151

INFORMATIONAL, NOT A VALID DOCUMENT TO ESTABLISH IDENTITY

1A. Name of decedent—first	LESTER
1B. Middle	BONIFACE
1C. Last	GARNIER
2A. Date of death	July 11, 1988 FD
2B. Hour	0900
3. Sex	Male
4. Race/Ethnicity	Japanese
5. Spanish/Hispanic	NO White
6. Date of birth	June 3, 1958
7. Age	30 years
8. Birthplace of decedent	California
9. Name and birthplace of father	Anthony Garnier - California
10. Birth name and birthplace of mother	Jean Muramoto - Hawaii
11A. Citizen of what country	U.S.A.
11B. If deceased was ever in military give dates of service	19 N/A to 19 N/A
12. Social security number	552-13-6234
13. Marital status	Never Married
14. Name of surviving spouse	-
15. Primary occupation	Police Officer
16. Number of years this occupation	8
17. Employer	San Francisco Police Dept.
18. Kind of industry or business	Law Enforcement
19A. Usual residence	891 Andrix Ct.
19B.	3382.01
19C. City or town	Concord
19D. County	Contra Costa
19E. State	California
20. Name and address of informant—relationship	Anthony Garnier (Father) 891 Andrix Ct. Concord, CA 94518
21A. Place of death	Automobile (Parked in Lot)
21B. County	Contra Costa
21C. Street address	1295 S. Main Street
21D. City or town	Walnut Creek
22. Death was caused by: (A) Immediate cause	GUNSHOT WOUND OF THE HEAD & CHEST
Approximate interval between onset and death	UNK
24. Was death reported to coroner?	YES 88-775
25. Was biopsy performed?	NO
26. Was autopsy performed?	YES
29. Specify accident, suicide, etc.	Homicide
30. Place of injury	Parked Automobile
31. Injury at work	No
32A. Date of injury	7-10 / 7-11, 1988
32B. Hour	2300-0853
33. Location	1295 S. Main St., Walnut Creek
34. Describe how injury occurred	Fd shot (type weapon unknown)
35A. Coroner's certification	Investigation
35B. Signature	RICHARD K. RAINEY, SHERIFF-CORONER By: Capt. [signature]
35C. Date signed	7-12-88
36. Disposition	Cremation
37. Date	July 19, 1988
38. Name and address of cemetery or crematory	Cypress Lawn Cemetery, Colma, CA
39. Embalmer's license number and signature	7075 [signature]
40A. Name of funeral director	Duggan's Serra Mortuary
40B. License no.	1098
41. Local registrar—signature	[signature] MD
42. Date accepted by local registrar	JUL 15 1988

AMENDED 1 of 2

I00001363

CERTIFIED COPY OF VITAL RECORDS

STATE OF CALIFORNIA
COUNTY OF CONTRA COSTA } SS

This is a true and exact reproduction of the document officially registered and placed on file in the office of the CONTRA COSTA COUNTY RECORDER.

ATTEST: [signature]

DATE ISSUED: JUL 14 2004

CONTRA COSTA COUNTY RECORDER

This copy not valid unless prepared on engraved border displaying date and signature of Deputy Recorder.

ANY ALTERATION OR ERASURE VOIDS THIS CERTIFICATE

Figure 10.2 Informational death certificate (Garnier 2005). Due to increasing concerns for identity theft and terrorism, access to copies of death certificates is increasingly more restricted. For non–family members or other nonofficial purposes, copies of more recent death certificates may be marked as "informational" so as to identify them as being issued to third parties. (Author's file.)

At the forefront of the investigation, the death certificate informs the cold case investigators as to the medical opinion rendered at the time of the autopsy (if there was an autopsy). While required in homicide cases, they may not have been performed, depending upon the medical, legal, or—sadly—political climate at the time.

According to the National Center for Disease Control and Prevention (CDC), two types of autopsies are performed in the United States. These are either "(a) hospital or clinical autopsy which family or physicians request to clarify cause of death or assess care, or (b) medicolegal autopsies which legal officials order to further investigate the circumstances surrounding a death." The CDC has also reported, "Autopsy rates declined more than 50 percent from 1972 through 2007…In 1972, almost 1 out of 5 deaths were autopsied. From 1972 through 2003, however, the autopsy rate dropped 58 percent from 19.3 percent to 8.1 percent" (CDC). The agency noted that "while the autopsy rate increased slightly since 2003, …fewer than 1 out of 10 deaths, were autopsied in 2007" (CDC). It is important for cold case investigators to be aware that cases exhibiting external causes were more likely to be determined by autopsy than deaths due to diseases or ill-defined conditions, according to the CDC, and autopsy rates declined with increasing age after ages 15–24 years (CDC). This raises the serious issue of how many criminal homicides went undetected due to lack of autopsy.

Death certificates are issued for the known death of any human being. Death certificates are normally issued only in the county and state in which the death occurred, excluding a death at sea. A *regular* state death certificate is issued for any person who has breathed on his/her own. A *fetal* death certificate may be issued for the death of a fetus. If a fetus took one breath of air on his/her own, a birth certificate would be issued and then a death certificate.

A legal document, the certificate of death is a certification of vital record and is issued in the name of the state. It may indicate the manner of death as natural, accidental, suicide, homicide, or undetermined.

Death certificates may be *amended* when erroneous information has been found to have been included on the original death certificate (Figure 10.3). Normally, this change is at the behest of the physician or coroner. In this case, an affidavit to amend a record or similar procedure may be filed to correct the error, and the certificate of death will subsequently reflect these changes as well as noting that this change process occurred. Only a physician can amend those portions of the certificate of death pertaining to medical aspects of the document. If a typo or other change needs to be made, the mortuary may process the amendment. When obtaining a certificate of death for a cold case homicide, investigators may seek to determine whether any subsequent corrections and amendments had occurred.

Information Found on the Death Certificate

In addition to the autopsy report, inspection of the death certificate may reflect detailed information that includes

- Decedent personal data
    - First, middle, last name
    - Date of death (month/day/year)
    - Estimated hour of death
    - Sex
    - Race/ethnicity
    - Date of birth
    - Age at time of death
    - Birthplace
    - Name and birthplace of father

STATE OF CALIFORNIA
CERTIFICATION OF VITAL RECORD

COUNTY of CONTRA COSTA
MARTINEZ, CALIFORNIA

AFFIDAVIT TO AMEND A RECORD

STATE CERTIFICATE NUMBER

☐ BIRTH ☒ DEATH ☐ FETAL DEATH ☐ MARRIAGE

38807003151
LOCAL REGISTRATION DISTRICT AND CERTIFICATE NUMBER

PART I INFORMATION AS REPORTED ON THE ORIGINAL REGISTERED CERTIFICATE

TYPE OR PRINT IN BLACK INK ONLY

1A. FIRST NAME	1B. MIDDLE NAME	1C. LAST NAME
Lester	Boniface	Garnier

2. SEX	3. DATE OF EVENT	4. PLACE OF OCCURRENCE—CITY AND COUNTY
Male	July 11, 1988	Walnut Creek - Contra Costa

5. NAME OF FATHER	6. BIRTH NAME OF MOTHER
Anthony Garnier	Jean Muramoto

2 of 2

PART II STATEMENT OF CORRECTIONS

216/709

LIST ONE ITEM PER LINE

7. ITEM NUMBER	8A. ERRONEOUS INFORMATION AS STATED ON THE ORIGINAL RECORD	8B. CORRECT INFORMATION THAT SHOULD HAVE BEEN STATED ON THE ORIGINAL RECORD AT THE TIME OF OCCURRENCE
5	X - White	No

REASON FOR CORRECTION: 9. to correct the record

PART III SUPPORTING AFFIDAVITS

FIRST SUPPORTING AFFIDAVIT

I hereby certify under penalty of perjury that I have personal knowledge of the above facts and that the information given above is true and correct.

10. SIGNATURE OF PERSON COMPLETING THE AFFIDAVIT	11. RELATIONSHIP TO PERSON WHOSE NAME IS ENTERED IN ITEM 1.	12. AGE OF PERSON COMPLETING THE AFFIDAVIT
Billie Jo Ecker	Funeral Director	28

13. DATE SIGNED	14. ADDRESS OF PERSON COMPLETING THE AFFIDAVIT (STREET, CITY, STATE)
July 27, 1988	500 Westlake Ave., Daly City, CA 94014

SECOND SUPPORTING AFFIDAVIT

I hereby certify under penalty of perjury that I have personal knowledge of the above facts and that the information given above is true and correct.

15. SIGNATURE OF PERSON COMPLETING THE AFFIDAVIT	16. RELATIONSHIP TO PERSON WHOSE NAME IS ENTERED IN ITEM 1.	17. AGE OF PERSON COMPLETING THE AFFIDAVIT
[signature]	Funeral Director	51

18. DATE SIGNED	19. ADDRESS OF PERSON COMPLETING THE AFFIDAVIT (STREET, CITY, STATE)
July 27, 1988	500 Westlake Ave. Daly City, CA 94014

STATE OR LOCAL REGISTRAR USE ONLY

20. DATE ACCEPTED	21. OFFICE OF THE STATE OR LOCAL REGISTRAR
JUL 28 1988	Wendel Brunner MD

STATE OF CALIFORNIA, DEPARTMENT OF HEALTH SERVICES, OFFICE OF THE STATE REGISTRAR OF VITAL STATISTICS (REV. 7-85) FORM VR-24

INFORMATIONAL, NOT A VALID DOCUMENT TO ESTABLISH IDENTITY

CERTIFIED COPY OF VITAL RECORDS

I00001364

STATE OF CALIFORNIA
COUNTY OF CONTRA COSTA } SS

This is a true and exact reproduction of the document officially registered and placed on file in the office of the CONTRA COSTA COUNTY RECORDER.

ATTEST: M Oliver

DATE ISSUED: JUL 14 2004

Stephen L. Weir
CONTRA COSTA COUNTY RECORDER

This copy not valid unless prepared on engraved border displaying date and signature of Deputy Recorder.

ANY ALTERATION OR ERASURE VOIDS THIS CERTIFICATE

Figure 10.3 Amendment to death certificate. (Author's file.)

    - Birth name and birthplace of mother
    - Country of citizenship
    - Dates of military service
    - Social Security number
    - Marital status
    - Name of surviving spouse
    - Occupation
    - Number of years in occupation
    - Employer
    - Nature of business or industry
- Residence information
    - Usual residence (street and address or location)
    - Town or city
    - County
    - State
- Place of death
    - Physical location of death (inside automobile in a parking lot, etc.)
    - Nearest street address
    - City
    - County
- Name and address of informant (and relationship)
    - Normally the legal next of kin (which goes in order from wife, adult children, parents, etc.) who provides needed information for the certificate. An exception could be a person with a medical durable power of attorney or the public administrator.
- Cause of death
    - That which caused *immediate* death
    - Conditions, if any, that gave rise to the immediate cause of death
    - Underlying cause of death
    - Other significant conditions contributing to death but not related to cause given
- Approximate interval between onset and death
    - Was death reported to the coroner/medical examiner (and case number)?
    - Was biopsy performed?
    - Was autopsy performed?
- Physician's certification
    - Certification by physician that death occurred as described
    - Certification of attending physician, if applicable, for time period prior to death
    - Physician signature and title
    - Date signed
    - Physician's name and address (typed)
    - Physician's license number
- Injury information
    - Specific injury type (accident, suicide, etc.)
    - Place of injury (parked automobile, etc.)
    - Location of injury (street or other address)
    - Description of how injury occurred or events resulting in injury ("found shot, type of weapon unknown")
    - Whether work related

    - Date of injury (month/day/year)
    - Hour of death
- Disposition of remains
    - Type of disposition
    - Date (month/day/year)
    - Name and address of cemetery
    - Embalmer's name and license number
    - Name of funeral director or person acting as such
    - License number
- Other information
    - Coroner's investigation
    - Coroner's inquest
    - Signature of coroner or medical examiner certifying the document and events
    - Date of signature

Certificate of Fetal Death

When the deceased is a fetus, a certificate of fetal death may be substituted for a regular state certificate of death. While the specific definition for this purpose may vary, for example, in California, a fetus for this purpose would be defined as one 21 weeks of age or older and who has not breathed air on his/her own. In this state, if the fetus is less than 21 weeks of age, no death certificate is required. In some circumstances, if the fetus is less than 21 weeks, a letter from an attending physician attesting to gestation may only be necessary, and the fetus may be buried or otherwise disposed of with no formal certificate or permit. Due to the nature of the victim in these cases, and apparent statistical reporting purposes, additional information is required on the certificate (see Figure 10.4).

This certificate may indicate information relative to

- This fetus
    - First (given), middle, last (family) name
    - Sex
    - Single, twin, etc.
    - If multiple birth, whether this fetus is first, second, etc.
    - Date of event (month/day/year)
    - Hour
- Place of delivery
    - Place of event
    - Address
    - City
    - County
    - Planned place of delivery
- Father
    - Full name
    - State of birth
    - Date of birth

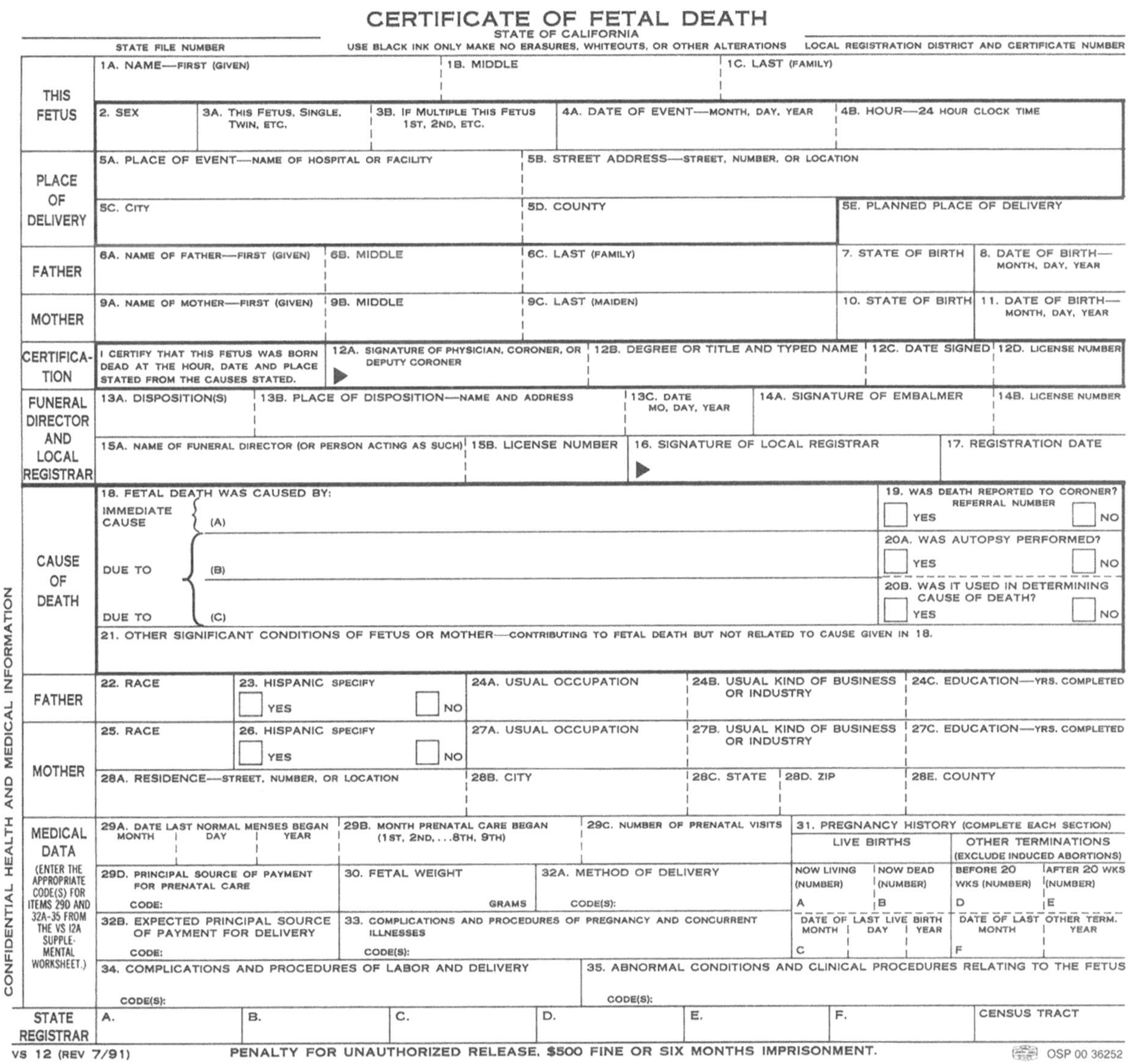

CERTIFICATE OF FETAL DEATH
STATE OF CALIFORNIA
USE BLACK INK ONLY MAKE NO ERASURES, WHITEOUTS, OR OTHER ALTERATIONS
STATE FILE NUMBER
LOCAL REGISTRATION DISTRICT AND CERTIFICATE NUMBER

THIS FETUS
1A. NAME—FIRST (GIVEN) | 1B. MIDDLE | 1C. LAST (FAMILY)
2. SEX | 3A. THIS FETUS, SINGLE, TWIN, ETC. | 3B. IF MULTIPLE THIS FETUS 1ST, 2ND, ETC. | 4A. DATE OF EVENT—MONTH, DAY, YEAR | 4B. HOUR—24 HOUR CLOCK TIME

PLACE OF DELIVERY
5A. PLACE OF EVENT—NAME OF HOSPITAL OR FACILITY | 5B. STREET ADDRESS—STREET, NUMBER, OR LOCATION
5C. CITY | 5D. COUNTY | 5E. PLANNED PLACE OF DELIVERY

FATHER
6A. NAME OF FATHER—FIRST (GIVEN) | 6B. MIDDLE | 6C. LAST (FAMILY) | 7. STATE OF BIRTH | 8. DATE OF BIRTH—MONTH, DAY, YEAR

MOTHER
9A. NAME OF MOTHER—FIRST (GIVEN) | 9B. MIDDLE | 9C. LAST (MAIDEN) | 10. STATE OF BIRTH | 11. DATE OF BIRTH—MONTH, DAY, YEAR

CERTIFICATION
I CERTIFY THAT THIS FETUS WAS BORN DEAD AT THE HOUR, DATE AND PLACE STATED FROM THE CAUSES STATED. | 12A. SIGNATURE OF PHYSICIAN, CORONER, OR DEPUTY CORONER | 12B. DEGREE OR TITLE AND TYPED NAME | 12C. DATE SIGNED | 12D. LICENSE NUMBER

FUNERAL DIRECTOR AND LOCAL REGISTRAR
13A. DISPOSITION(S) | 13B. PLACE OF DISPOSITION—NAME AND ADDRESS | 13C. DATE MO, DAY, YEAR | 14A. SIGNATURE OF EMBALMER | 14B. LICENSE NUMBER
15A. NAME OF FUNERAL DIRECTOR (OR PERSON ACTING AS SUCH) | 15B. LICENSE NUMBER | 16. SIGNATURE OF LOCAL REGISTRAR | 17. REGISTRATION DATE

CAUSE OF DEATH
18. FETAL DEATH WAS CAUSED BY:
IMMEDIATE CAUSE (A)
DUE TO (B)
DUE TO (C)
19. WAS DEATH REPORTED TO CORONER? REFERRAL NUMBER YES NO
20A. WAS AUTOPSY PERFORMED? YES NO
20B. WAS IT USED IN DETERMINING CAUSE OF DEATH? YES NO
21. OTHER SIGNIFICANT CONDITIONS OF FETUS OR MOTHER—CONTRIBUTING TO FETAL DEATH BUT NOT RELATED TO CAUSE GIVEN IN 18.

CONFIDENTIAL HEALTH AND MEDICAL INFORMATION

FATHER
22. RACE | 23. HISPANIC SPECIFY YES NO | 24A. USUAL OCCUPATION | 24B. USUAL KIND OF BUSINESS OR INDUSTRY | 24C. EDUCATION—YRS. COMPLETED

MOTHER
25. RACE | 26. HISPANIC SPECIFY YES NO | 27A. USUAL OCCUPATION | 27B. USUAL KIND OF BUSINESS OR INDUSTRY | 27C. EDUCATION—YRS. COMPLETED
28A. RESIDENCE—STREET, NUMBER, OR LOCATION | 28B. CITY | 28C. STATE | 28D. ZIP | 28E. COUNTY

MEDICAL DATA (ENTER THE APPROPRIATE CODE(S) FOR ITEMS 29D AND 32A-35 FROM THE VS 12A SUPPLEMENTAL WORKSHEET.)
29A. DATE LAST NORMAL MENSES BEGAN MONTH DAY YEAR | 29B. MONTH PRENATAL CARE BEGAN (1ST, 2ND, ...8TH, 9TH) | 29C. NUMBER OF PRENATAL VISITS | 31. PREGNANCY HISTORY (COMPLETE EACH SECTION)
LIVE BIRTHS: NOW LIVING (NUMBER) A | NOW DEAD (NUMBER) B | DATE OF LAST LIVE BIRTH MONTH DAY YEAR C
OTHER TERMINATIONS (EXCLUDE INDUCED ABORTIONS): BEFORE 20 WKS (NUMBER) D | AFTER 20 WKS (NUMBER) E | DATE OF LAST OTHER TERM. MONTH YEAR F
29D. PRINCIPAL SOURCE OF PAYMENT FOR PRENATAL CARE CODE: | 30. FETAL WEIGHT GRAMS | 32A. METHOD OF DELIVERY CODE(S):
32B. EXPECTED PRINCIPAL SOURCE OF PAYMENT FOR DELIVERY CODE: | 33. COMPLICATIONS AND PROCEDURES OF PREGNANCY AND CONCURRENT ILLNESSES CODE(S):
34. COMPLICATIONS AND PROCEDURES OF LABOR AND DELIVERY CODE(S): | 35. ABNORMAL CONDITIONS AND CLINICAL PROCEDURES RELATING TO THE FETUS CODE(S):

STATE REGISTRAR
A. | B. | C. | D. | E. | F. | CENSUS TRACT

VS 12 (REV 7/91) PENALTY FOR UNAUTHORIZED RELEASE, $500 FINE OR SIX MONTHS IMPRISONMENT. OSP 00 36252

Figure 10.4 Certificate of fetal death. This form of death certificate reveals more information about mother, father, and other births. (Author's file.)

- Mother
  - First, middle, last (maiden) name
  - State of birth
  - Date of birth
- Certification by physician, coroner, or deputy coroner
  - Degree or title and typed name
  - Date signed
  - License number

- Funeral director and local registrar
  - Disposition
  - Place of disposition
  - Date
  - Signature of embalmer
  - License number
  - Name of funeral director or person acting as such
  - License number
  - Signature of local registrar
  - Registration date
- Cause of death
  - Immediate cause
  - Whether death was reported to coroner and referral number
  - Was autopsy performed
  - Whether it was used in determining cause of death
  - Other significant conditions of fetus or mother contributing to fetal death but not previously given
- Father
  - Race
  - Ethnicity
  - Usual occupation
  - Usual kind of business
  - Education
- Mother
  - Race
  - Ethnicity
  - Usual occupation
  - Usual kind of business
  - Education
  - Residence address
  - City, state, and zip code
  - Country
- Medical data
  - Date last normal menses began
  - Month prenatal care began
  - Number of prenatal visits
  - Principal source of payment for prenatal care
  - Expected principal source of payment for delivery
  - Complications and procedures of pregnancy and concurrent illnesses
  - Complications and procedures of labor and delivery
  - Abnormal conditions and clinical procedures relating to the fetus
  - Fetal weight
  - Method of delivery
  - Pregnancy history
    - Live births
      - Now living (number)
      - Now dead (number)
      - Date of last live birth

  - Other terminations
    - Before 20 weeks
    - After 20 weeks
    - Date of last other term

Application and Permit for Disposition of Human Remains

Normally, a permit from local health authorities is required to transport human remains. This permit may offer additional information to cold case investigators regarding the decedent, death, and disposition of the remains. This permit may be required at all stages of the handling of human remains, including the forensic exhumation (see Chapter 22). This application and permit may be issued by the city or county registrar or other designated official, including the health department. Among the information to be found on this document may be found

- Decedent's full name
- Date of birth
- Date of death
- Sex
- City of death
- County of death
- Name, relationship, and address of informant
- Name and address of funeral director or those acting on his/her behalf
- Signature and date of applicant for permit

Types of Disposition of Human Remains

There are a number of options available for the disposition of human remains.

- Burial (including entombment)
- Temporary envaultment
- Cremation
- Disposition of cremated remains other than in a cemetery
- Scientific use
- Transit
- Scattering or burial at sea or disposition other than in a cemetery

While a review of this application and permit denotes the disposition of the remains, it may also indicate

- Name and address of the cemetery of burial, including
  - Date buried
  - Signature of person in charge of burial
- Cremation
  - Name and address of crematory
  - Date cremated
  - Signature of person in charge of cremation

- Scientific use
  - Name and address of facility receiving remains
  - Date received
  - Signature of person in charge of facility
- Transit
  - Name and address in receiving state or country where remains or cremated remains are to be shipped
  - Date shipped
  - Address and signature of person in charge of placing with the carrier
- Scattering, including burial at sea or disposition other than in a cemetery
  - Address, nearest point on shoreline, or other description sufficient to identify final place. If burial at sea, latitude and longitude.
  - If a full-body burial at sea by a military service, the name of the branch of service is given.

Other Mortuary and Funeral Home Resources

Although local and regional customs may vary, cold case investigators may consider visiting the funeral home or mortuary to seek further information. Among those records that may be of interest is the *case file*. Review or copying of such records may require a search warrant or subpoena. This contains most of the records pertinent to the individual deceased's case. It may include

- Cemetery records.
- Copies of any checks written for funeral and internment expenses.
- Work sheets.
- Burial record or record of funeral.
- Logs of family conversations, or any problems experienced during the handling and internment or disposition of the remains.
- Embalming report. (The embalming process tends to bring out bruises that may have not been previously noticed, especially with children.)
- *Removal sheet.* This is the document(s) that cemetery personnel fill out when picking up a body for transport. It will note the date, times, and vital information of the decedent such as Social Security numbers, when the deceased last seen by a physician, time of death, next of kin, and list of personal effects on the body.
- *Hospital sheet.* Similar to the removal sheet, vital information, Social Security numbers, date of birth, etc.
- *Clothing sheet.* Clothing brought in by the family for dressing the decedent.

Mortuary or funeral home personnel that who possess information of interest to the investigation may include

- *Case arranger.* This is generally the person responsible for overseeing the process.
- *Funeral director.* Handles the funeral as set up by the arranger. On the mortuary side, handles the arrangement, and on the cemetery side, handles markers, internment, etc.
- *Super director.* In some locales, this person handles both mortuary and cemetery sides, but this practice varies from place to place.

Visitor's Log

A visitor's log is often present at the time of viewing of the deceased through the internment. These names may be of interest to cold case investigators in some situations. These are normally returned to the family at the conclusion of the service. The case file may reflect to whom the log was given after the service.

Obituary

The obituary is a voluntary, unofficial public announcement by the family or friends of the deceased pronouncing their passing. It is published in the local newspaper, typically in a dedicated "Notices" section of the paper, pursuant to that media's rules and policies. In most cases, it is published within a week and runs for a number of days, depending upon the arrangement between the family or author and newspaper.

The obituary often attests to the deceased's birth, youth, career, hobbies, military or other service, and other interests. It commonly closes by listing the names of relatives—to the grandchild level—and friends, as well as to where contributions in their memory may be sent. In cold case investigations, these obituaries may offer information of interest that includes

- Date of death
- Age at death
- Residence community
- Names of parents, siblings, and other relatives
- Names of close friends and associates
- Relationships
- Deceased children or siblings
- Residence locations and history
- Employment and military history
- Other biographical information and hobbies or interests
- Mortuary or funeral home
- Dates and location of services
- Location of internment
- Casket bearers

Coroner and Medical Examiner Operations

The American medicolegal system of death investigation was founded in the English coroner system and was brought to the United States by the early colonists. In this founding period, the positions of sheriff and coroner were usually combined in one office and person, and the earliest reported coroner's inquest was held in the colony of New Plymouth, New England, in 1635. In the late 1800s, pathology began to become an important role in death investigation, and in 1915, New York City eliminated the coroner's office and instituted a medical examiner's system. The first statewide medical examiner system was instituted in Maryland in 1939. This system has grown and expanded in the ensuing decades (Westvear).

Three primary systems are in use today. These systems may vary from county to county within a state, and understanding the type and background of their system may be of value to cold case investigators. These are the county coroner, the sheriff–coroner, and the medical examiner.

The roles and duties of these offices may often be found in the government code or other codified sources of agency authority. Cold case investigators, when seeking to identify what material may be, or has been, present in coroner's inquest files, may attempt to find the appropriate codes from the time of the homicide under investigation in an attempt to learn what may or may not have been done. A coroner's inquest record may be a very informative resource during a cold case homicide investigation.

County Coroner

The county coroner is usually an elected official and normally does *not* need to be a licensed and trained physician. As such, he/she is not authorized or permitted to physically open human remains. Not infrequently, the minimum qualifications are to be 18 years of age or over and a resident of the county or district. There is no minimum qualification for education and training in the forensic sciences. These persons usually have primary jurisdiction within their county or district. An additional qualification is, and has always been, that they need to win a popular vote. In some jurisdictions, the coroner may have additional duties, such as acting as the public administrator. This office may be part time, full time, or on an as-needed basis. In the past, coroner's fee schedules may have been based upon the findings they officially rendered.

In my experience, especially in smaller, more rural counties, record-keeping systems varied, and record retention for periods dating to the 1980s and before may be hit or miss. The writing of reports and file organization and maintenance were at the discretion of the office holder. A search for coroner's records by investigators in older cold cases may entail identifying previous coroners and their assistant coroners and attempting to locate these individuals and make inquiry into possible retention of records from their tenure. Similarly, identifying their secretaries or other clerical personnel may yield helpful information. Smaller agencies are not alone in this, however, and larger coroner's offices have been known to lose files, bones, and other remains, property, or evidence.

During the course of their duties, the coroner or staff may have consulted with local medical personnel or have employed qualified forensic pathologists to conduct autopsies. In decades past, in some instances, autopsies were not always conducted by the most qualified of medical personnel. Their education in forensic matters may have been minimal, and ultimately, however, the coroner made the conclusion reflected upon the death certificate regarding cause and manner of death. I recall one report decades ago in which the part-time coroner, a hotel owner, held a .25-caliber rifle bullet to an entrance wound and proclaimed it as the fatal projectile as opposed to a .32 pistol bullet as it most closely matched the entrance wound!

Investigators may consider conducting a forensic exhumation for a secondary autopsy. See Chapter 22.

Coroners may be required by law to keep a coroner's register. This record contains

- Name or alias of the deceased
- Description necessary for identification
- Property taken from person or premises
- Disposition of money or property
- Cause of death
- Information as to disposition of remains
- Persons notified of the death as well as notations of any unsuccessful attempts at notification

Sheriff–Coroner

A variation of the coroner system is the office of sheriff–coroner. This practice is less common but still in use today in some areas. In addition to other prescribed law enforcement duties, the sheriff of the county is also mandated to perform the duties of the coroner. As such, deputy sheriffs may also be empowered as deputy coroners. In these jurisdictions, a search for records may begin within the county sheriff's office.

Medical Examiner

The medical examiner may have county, district, or statewide jurisdiction. These persons must be licensed physicians and are generally forensically trained pathologists. They are usually appointed and serve at the discretion of the appointing authority, and traditionally have been encountered in more metropolitan areas or larger population bases.

For the purposes of this segment, the term *coroner* is used synonymously as reference to the medicolegal authority responsible for conducting the death investigation.

Despite the variations in these systems, their responsibility was, and is, to take charge of the body when notified of the death; make identification; and inquire into circumstances, manner, and means of death. Classification of deaths requiring inquiry was mandated by the state in which the jurisdiction rested. Not uncommonly, the duty of the coroner, past and present, would include inquiry and determination into the circumstances and manner of

- All violent, sudden, or unusual deaths, unattended deaths, or deceased not attended by physician within the past 20 days before death and deaths related to or suspected to be self-induced or resulting from criminal abortion
- Deaths known or suspect homicide, suicide, or accidental poisoning
- Deaths due to accident, injury, drowning, fire, hanging, gunshot, stabbing, cutting, exposure, starvation, acute alcoholism, drug addiction, strangulation, aspiration
- Death in whole or in part occasioned by criminal means; deaths associated with a known or alleged rape or crime against nature; deaths in prison or while under sentence
- Deaths under such circumstances as to afford a reasonable ground to suspect that the death was caused by the criminal act of another

These duties were separate from those performed by other law enforcement agencies. Review of older unsolved cases has shown a joint coroner–law enforcement participation in those cases that ultimately became cold cases. Other qualifying deaths may include those situations in which there is a possible threat to public health. In all events, the medicolegal investigation sought to learn the following:

- Who died?
- How and why?
- Who did it (when applicable)?

Coroner's Inquest

To answer these questions, coroner officials in past decades, as well as medical examiners, have utilized a process called the coroner's inquest. This centuries-old system was once more prevalent than it is today, although it is still in occasional use. Documentation that this inquest occurred may or may not be found in the cold case file but, rather, in review of coroner's or newspaper files.

A primary purpose of a coroner's inquest was to provide a means for the prompt securing of information for the use of those charged with the detection and prosecution of crime. In this manner, people were subpoenaed to the inquest and questioned under oath, and a transcript was made of the proceedings. Knowledge of this process and the record systems it produced may provide investigators with information in those cold cases in which this process was utilized.

These may be valuable investigative sources. While variations may occur in different states, this synopsis provides an overview of the manners and methods of coroner's inquests as may be encountered in practical cold case investigation. Issues identified with the coroner's inquest include

- Discretion of the coroner or medical examiner to hold an inquest
- Jurisdiction and venue of the inquest
- Juror qualifications to serve on a coroner's inquest
- Oath and duties of the juror
- Inquest process
- Verdict or decision and findings

Unlike a grand jury process, there was and is no confidentiality or secrecy barrier.

For cold case investigators, decades after a coroner's inquest, there is no legal barrier to identifying and attempting to contact former members of the coroner's inquest, or coroner's jury, when and where possible. As in any other cold case interview, ask about any notes or other documents or photos. Until you ask the question, you never know what might turn up.

Discretion

The decision to hold a coroner's inquest rested with the coroner or medical examiner and was *discretionary* at their pleasure and if circumstances warranted it. These circumstances could range from mystery surrounding the death to political considerations. An inquest could be held using a coroner's jury or with the coroner acting as the sole inquisitor and official, at the discretion of the coroner. The coroner only needed a reasonable ground to suspect the possibility of death at the hands of another or through the instrumentality of some other person. The coroner did not need the consent or permission of the family to hold an inquest. These inquests were open to the public and, especially in more sensational investigations, attended and reported by the local media.

Such an inquest may have been mandatory, however, when requested by the sheriff or chief of police, district attorney, or attorney general. In those circumstances in which the coroner conducted the inquiry, the coroner or a deputy would personally sign the certificate of death. If the death appeared to have occurred under natural circumstances, and the inquiry determined that the physician of record possessed sufficient knowledge to state that death occurred under natural circumstances, a coroner could authorize that physician to sign the certificate of death.

Jurisdiction and Venue

The inquest was limited to conduct inquiry into death in the county where the death occurred (rather than the county where the deceased may have resided). The coroner or his/her authorized deputy or a hearing officer would conduct the inquest. In addition, the coroner had the right to exhume the body of a deceased person when necessary to discharge his/her duties as prescribed by law. Depending upon authority and location, the coroner or his/her deputy may have exercised peace officer power. Although coroners usually did not have power to subpoena witnesses from outside their county, they have had authority to travel outside the jurisdiction to obtain information.

Juror Qualifications

No one was exempt for jury service except at the discretion of the coroner. Inquest jurors were not subject to challenge by any party. Exemptions were noted, however, and included those persons

- Related to the decedent
- Charged or suspected with the killing of the decedent
- Prejudiced for or against the deceased

Oath and Duties

Upon selection, the jurors participating in a coroner's inquest took an oath in which they were sworn to inquire into who the person was; when, where, and by what means the person came to his/her death; and circumstances attending his/her death; and render a verdict according to the evidence offered or arising from inspection of the body.

Inquest Process

Upon notification that a death had occurred and the coroner determined that an inquest was to be conducted, the coroner decided whether to conduct the inquest himself/herself or to use a coroner's inquest jury. The coroner was authorized by law to summon a number of jurors to serve as coroner's inquest jurors, and the number varied among different jurisdictions. For instance in California, the coroner

> ...shall summon, or cause to be summoned by any sheriff, constable, or policeman, not less than nine nor more than 15 persons qualified by law to serve as jurors, to appear before him forthwith, either at the place where the body of the deceased is or at some other convenient place within the county designated by him, or at the request of the district attorney, to inquire into the cause of the death.

In the "Boulder Jane Doe" case cited in Chapter 22, the recovered records indicated that the coroner's inquest jury numbered six persons. The inquest did not have to be held at the coroner's office or in a government facility. Such inquests could be, and have been, held at the site where the deceased died or other locations.

Jurors could be summoned orally or in writing. A summons was that, a command to a person to appear at a given time and place to meet. Coroner's inquest jurors were residents of the county in which the inquest was to be held. Coroner's jury members were compensated at a schedule set by the county.

During the proceedings, coroner's inquest jurors were often required to view the body as a necessary part of the identification process.

Witnesses were subpoenaed to attend a coroner's inquest in a manner similar to being summoned to appear in a regular court. Upon being called, a witness would step forward and be administered an oath. Questions would be directed toward the witness by the coroner, or in some instances, by members of the coroner's jury. In some situations, witnesses also viewed the body (most often to establish the identity of the deceased). Among those summoned to a coroner's inquest would include

- Person who discovered the body
- Law enforcement personnel
- Medical personnel
- Expert witnesses (who may provide opinion as to cause of death)
- Family members of the victim
- Friends, associates, and coworkers of the victim
- Spouse, boyfriend, or girlfriend of the victim
- Others thought to have knowledge pertinent to the investigation

Transcripts and Records

A court reporter or stenographer made a transcript of testimony taken at coroner's inquests. Beginning around the late 1940s, a mechanical device could be used to make a recording of the inquest process in lieu of a written record in some locales. Upon completion of the proceedings, the transcript or tape recording was filed with the coroner, or county clerk, usually within a specified time period. I have seen coroner inquest files that include original stenographic notepads. Transcriptions may or may not have been made.

Verdict or Finding

Upon completion of their duty, coroner's inquest jurors were to render a verdict or finding based upon what they heard and saw. This verdict, ***inadmissible*** as evidence in civil or criminal proceedings, was set forth without regard to civil or criminal responsibility

- Name of the deceased
- Time and place of death
- Medical cause of death and whether by
  - Natural causes
  - Suicide
  - Accident
  - Hands of another other than by accident
  - Undetermined

When the findings of the coroner's jury suggested that death came at the hands of another, the coroner would also transmit his written findings to the district attorney and/or police agency for the jurisdiction in which the body was recovered.

In addition, I have viewed a number of coroner's inquest verdicts in which the jurors provided additional detail, including

- State or country of origin (birth)
- Age
- Occupation
- Marital status
- The name of the person who inflicted the fatal injuries upon the victim

Suggested Readings and Bibliography

Center for Disease Control. http://www.cdc.gov/nchs/data/databriefs/db67.htm. Retrieved June 11, 2015.

Hoyert D. (2001). The autopsy, medicine, and mortality statistics. National Center for Health Statistics. *Vital Health Stat* 3(32).

Cold Case Investigation Units

11

R. H. WALTON

Contents

Introduction

Rising crime rates, declining clearance rates, staff shortages, and budget restrictions in the last decades of the twentieth century taxed American law enforcement. This was felt across a wide spectrum of the public safety arena, including within homicide investigation and the medical examiner/coroner arena. More crime and fewer resources were coupled with organizational issues within these departments, including retirements, transfers, and other personnel changes. Younger, less experienced detectives were thrust into positions for which their predecessors had heretofore been groomed and prepared for—investigation of criminal homicide. With the decline in murder rates, agencies began to explore various options to revisit unsolved homicides. One of these methods was the *cold case squad.*

Cold case squads are specialized units of investigators within a law enforcement agency tasked to review and investigate unsolved homicides. Such units may also be formed for proactive review and investigation of unsolved sexual assaults. This chapter presents a background on the origin and development of these units and how they may be formed, and presents guidelines and protocols that have been found to work. History

Figure 11.1 "Iceman": unofficial Los Angeles Police Department (LAPD) Cold Case Squad logo. (Courtesy of Mary Ann Hunt.)

has shown us, however, that these units may come and go, and these units or the forms, policies, and procedures that they utilize may be significantly modified or revised at any time. Similarly, many prosecutors' offices have established specific integrity units with their agencies tasked to review and reinvestigate claims of innocence (Figure 11.1). This chapter offers the reader examples of what has been shown to *work*.

Why Form a Cold Case Squad?

According to the National Institute of Justice (NIJ), cold case squads have been found to be a practical means for jurisdictions faced with a significant number of unsolved murders. Police agencies of all sizes can organize cold case squads. Smaller agencies usually have a lesser amount of unsolved homicides, however, and a detective or two dedicated to these investigations may be a realistic solution while larger departments may assign proportionately more personnel to their higher number of cases.

This concept provides a practical opportunity to identify and solve some of these cases. Some cold case squads have been formed because the volume of fresh cases or other responsibilities prevents detectives from going back and revisiting unsolved cases. In other instances, cold case squads have been formed due to a decline in the number of new murder cases and the resultant availability of personnel and other resources. In either circumstance, these provide a mechanism to identify and investigate unsolved murders. These systems offer the agency, and individual investigators, a potential win–win arrangement for maximum utilization of departmental and human resources in the investigation of unsolved murders.

For the agency, cold case squads offer a mechanism to continue the investigation of unsolved or suspected homicides long after the lead detectives have departed from the case. In doing this, they provide a means to reduce the backlog of unsolved cases. Experience has shown also that success in one case may solve other cases. These investigative units can help bring some sense of justice to the families of victims with the successful solution or resolution of a case. Further, through developed resources, these units can be very useful in locating and working with witnesses in past or potential cases as well as reviewing evidence.

In addition, specialized cold case victim–witness unit/personnel may render great assistance and support to the investigators within these units. See Chapter 31.

What's in a Name?

Some investigators and agencies dislike the term *cold case*. Why? Because it sends a negative message to the family and friends of victims—as well as the public—that their cases are old, cold, and forgotten. Unsolved homicides cases are those that were investigated as thoroughly as possible and then shelved, suspended, or otherwise reflected in noninvestigative or inactive status in department records, pending further leads and investigation, while in some instances, cases have been lost, misfiled, misplaced, or otherwise consistently relegated behind more active investigations, they are still open. In this regard, cases are solved or unsolved. They are open or closed. There is no legal category or definition of a cold case.

The name *cold case squad* is one that has apparently originated as a media term. It has become prevalent in media and literature, however, as well as police agency protocols and jargon. In addition to this term, however, agencies have utilized other names to define their investigative bodies dedicated to the investigation of older, unsolved murder cases. Among these are

- Unsolved Unit.
- Unsolved Homicide Unit.
- Old Mysteries Homicide Unit.
- Historical Homicide Section.
- Archive Unit.
- Cold Case Team.
- Cold Case Unit.
- Homicide Evidence Assessment Team (H.E.A.T.).
- The Gray Squad. Interestingly enough, this term has been used by a volunteer cold case review group in the Tulsa Police Department, Oklahoma. It refers to cases in a gray area, not active, not solved. It does not reflect upon the hair color of the detectives.

In addition, while some agencies may not have a formally recognized cold case unit yet have unsolved cases, they may consider having a detective or investigator assigned to monitor or coordinate these older cases and their investigation. Such a designation provides a single contact point when agencies or citizens call in with information. This individual is familiar with all unsolved cases and serves as a specific point of contact for receiving information and coordinating inquiries from other agencies. The designation of a specific individual contributes to lessening the chance that when a tip or information comes in, it gets lost, misplaced, or misfiled, or worse, that it is not reviewed in context with the case and no action is taken (Figure 11.2).

Figure 11.2 Units that specialize in the investigation use a variety of names, but *cold case squad or team* is a commonly used term. *Team* implies just that, that the unit works together as a team to solve unsolved homicides. (Author's file.)

Forming the Cold Case Squad

Cold case investigation units can be a resounding success for an agency or a costly failure (in terms of money, morale, and press exposure). Chief among contributing factors that make these units a success are (1) organizational leadership and administration and (2) selection of personnel.

Administration

Administrative commitment and support are critical to the design and implementation of a cold case squad. The concept of a cold case, and that of a cold case squad, is relatively recent in origin. Members of these units must perceive that they have the support and backing of the department administration, both in fiscal and other necessary resources, and also in the flexibility required to do their job. This flexibility may involve the authority and ability to exercise independent judgment when and as required, based upon experience and case needs, and to not be hamstrung in their efforts by needless or unnecessary barriers. Micromanagement does not fit here.

In many cases, everyone identified in the initial investigation may need to be reinterviewed. Investigators will often need to travel, sometimes long distances, to conduct these interviews. Previously unknown persons may similarly have to be located and interviewed. The greater the number of cases investigated, the greater the cost. They will need to have evidence examined, or reexamined. They will incur overtime. They may require the assistance of outside experts. Cold case investigators can work most effectively, and efficiently, when provided the resources necessary to do their jobs.

If cold cases were easy to solve, they would have been solved before. As one cold case team leader once told me, "I'd be thrilled if my people could solve 5% of our unsolved cases." Cold case investigation requires concentration and *focus*. Those assigned to cold case investigation must be allowed to work exclusively on designated unsolved cases. When cold case investigators are assigned to rotating shifts, assigned hot calls as backfill to regular homicide investigators, or assigned to dignitary protection or other non–cold case activities, their effectiveness is greatly reduced. This translates to fewer cases solved. Administration support in providing all necessary resources and flexibility to investigate cold cases is very important to the success of the program.

It is suggested that one case at a time is a highly desirable case load for cold case investigators.

Selection of Personnel

Selection of the most qualified personnel is critical for the success of a cold case squad. This is not the place for repayment of political favors or cronyism. Nor is it a place to put someone who is looking to coast before retirement. Cold cases require detailed review and analysis of the previously investigated case, coupled with the instinct of an experienced homicide detective, to identify perhaps a single avenue that may lead to a successful conclusion.

Ideally, those selected for these positions in cold case squads should be experienced homicide investigators with traits that include

- Strong communication and interpersonal skills (interview and interrogation)
- Strong research skills and cerebral skills
- Patience and creativity
- High motivation and enthusiasm
- Experience with informants and undercover operations
- Tenacity

These desired qualities for cold case investigators have been explored in previous chapters in more detail. While many agencies employ the *team* concept for investigation of homicide, cold case investigators may approach a case with a preference for working a more *individualistic* approach. Some investigators prefer to work alone. By this time in their careers, they have demonstrated an ability for productivity in this capacity, and this is a flexibility that works well in many cases. In either method, investigators selected for cold case squad investigation may draw upon knowledge and experience in areas including

- Firearms examination
- Medical examination
- Behavioral analysis
- Blood pattern analysis
- Crime scene identification and reconstruction
- Forensic anthropology and odontology
- Forensic botany and entomology
- Current investigative methods including wiretaps

It has been demonstrated, however, that a cold case squad can successfully utilize otherwise qualified and experienced personnel who may have incurred some forms of injury or light-duty status. This offers the investigator the ability to continue to ply his/her talent and expertise, and the department continues to benefit from his/her experience and capabilities. Neither suffers an unwanted separation. Depending upon circumstances, investigators so assigned may

- Review cases and write case summaries
- Review evidence and facilitate evidence processing and reprocessing
- Compile and construct witness lists
- Utilize computer resources for case-related tasks, including constructing time lines
- Perform witness and suspect background checks and information gathering

This offers a win–win for both and reaffirms commitment by the agency to its personnel as well as contributing to higher morale by personnel who see, feel, and appreciate this commitment.

Supervisors and Investigators

A proper blend of supervisory and investigative talent optimizes the work of a cold case squad. In agencies with dedicated homicide investigation units, personnel for cold case investigation are normally drawn from this investigative pool. Smaller agencies, however, have drawn on personnel who investigate a wide variety of crimes, in addition to homicide. Regardless, how these units are staffed is dependent upon the organization and makeup of the cold case squad.

Unfortunately, in some instances, personnel have been assigned to supervisory duties in areas in which they have minimal or no experience and expertise. Homicide supervision has not been exempt in this area. Supervision of a cold case squad is optimized by selecting as supervisors those who have experience in homicide *and* cold case homicide as well as supervisory experience.

Where conditions allow, supervisors may carry a minimal investigatory load as well as their supervisory duties. As an example, the Los Angeles County Sheriff's Department, California, utilizes a single homicide bureau facility. This bureau of the department is physically separate from other components within the department. Cold case calls or inquiries from citizens or law enforcement to the Homicide Bureau are routed to the supervisor in the Unsolved Unit of the Homicide Bureau. The supervisor, an experienced homicide investigator and cold case investigator, evaluates the information and assigns the follow-up to an investigator. The supervisor also carries a minimum load of cold case investigations. In this manner, supervisorial and investigative roles allow the individual to maintain professional expertise in the field as well as supervisory duties of other investigators.

Not uncommonly, cold case squads usually include the following, or a variation thereof:

- *Supervisor or administrator.* Usually a lieutenant or other ranking member from the homicide division who oversees police management and serves as liaison between administration, participating law enforcement agencies, the community, and the media.
- *Immediate supervisor.* Usually a sergeant who coordinates and oversees daily operations of the team. The sergeant is there to make day-to-day decisions, to supervise assignment of cases, and to monitor investigation progress.
- *Investigators.* Those assigned as *investigators* within cold case squads may have previous supervisory experience from other assignments in the agency. Their service within the organization has fostered their abilities and experiences in a manner not shared by those who do not share this wider background. As such, they possess a different perspective and thus do not always take "no" for an answer. They have the experience to know where to go, what to do, and how to go about doing it in homicide investigation. Through their experiences and seniority, they may have the ability to communicate directly with upper echelons of the department, who may have, earlier in their careers, worked under or been mentored by the cold case investigator. These investigators have contacts, know whom to call, are versed in the latest in forensic technology, and are up to date on the law. These should be the best of the best. Above all, they are *tenacious*!

Additional Staffing

Similar to other investigative units, cold case squads may benefit from the skills and abilities of other support personnel. These support personnel may be assigned full or part time to the cold case squad, depending upon organizational circumstances. These include:

- Clerical and secretarial, the backbone of many organizational units
- Analysis and specialized computer skills such as database research

- Information technology (computer persons)
- Forensic specialists
- Behavioral science resources

Assignment to a Cold Case Squad

Assignment to a cold case squad may offer a variety of benefits. This may include (1) ability to work regular Monday–Friday daytime shifts (in theory, anyway); (2) increase in rank; (3) pay incentive; (4) lack of nighttime callouts; (5) lack of shift rotation; and (6) use of separate office and equipment, including assigned automobile. Given agency resources, it is highly desirable that those assigned to cold case squads work out of facilities separate from the main homicide or detective division or central agency facility. This separation not only facilitates their focus on cold cases; it may serve to keep them from being drawn as resources into other "temporary" assignments or high-profile cases. In addition, this *distancing* serves to remove them from day-to-day, mainstream petty politics and unconstructive activities.

This assignment, however, should not be perceived as a "gravy" assignment. It *will* entail night work, weekends, and holidays. Nor should assignment to a cold case squad be perceived as a "retirement" position. When informants call or someone wants to talk, the opportunity must not be wasted. It is not unusual that a break on one cold case may offer up leads in other cold cases, the snowball or domino effect. The stress of working a regular homicide beat may transfer to the cold unit as well. This stress, conversely, may diminish in many cases, however.

There may be a perception by other detectives, in some instances, that cold case detectives are receiving a "plum" assignment. They may resent the working conditions and assignments enjoyed by the cold case detectives. Keep in mind, however, that cold case detectives are usually the most senior personnel. They have paid their dues, and while they may, in some cases, not be far from retirement, they represent the most experience and ability available within the department. In addition, by handling the cold cases, they relieve their brethren of having these cases added to their case load.

Case Identification and Selection

Rule number 1: pick the easiest cases first. When a cold case squad is formed, there may be media attention. The agency administration has committed personnel and resources. The reality is that people like to see results. In this case, they wish to see arrests and convictions in cold cases. As cases are solved, the media reports favorably on this innovative concept, and others may come forward with information on other cases. As a result, the agency may strengthen its commitment and provide more financial and personnel resources.

Cold case homicides are not investigated in the same manner as a hot case. This presents a difficulty to those assigned to initial cold case squad investigations, one that is not really portrayed in the media: (1) the nature of these cases is that they are the most difficult to solve; (2) they entail additional resources and expenditures; and (3) they are *time consuming.* The dilemma facing the establishment of these units is that they must quickly show results or face the threat of disbanding of their squad. Perception is reality, and this has happened.

Common agency guidelines utilized to select cases for cold case squad reinvestigation seek to identify those in which time has now become an ally to solving the case. The most common considerations in selecting these cases have been discussed in other chapters and are

1. Changes in relationships
2. Advances in technology

Those cases in which advances in technology can utilize remaining evidence may offer cases with a stronger possibility for a more ready solution. Among these would be cases that can take advantage of the following:

- *Combined DNA Index System (CODIS).* This DNA-based tool would take in cases in which remaining evidence would include blood, saliva, and other biological material (Chapter 18).
- *Next Generation Identification (NGI)/automated fingerprint identification system (AFIS).* This fingerprint technology may maximize identification of unidentified fingerprints (Chapter 14).
- National Integrated Ballistic Information Network (NIBIN) Computer database of firearms identification related evidence (Chapter 19).
- *National Missing and Unidentified Persons System (NamUs).* This national data bank includes information on missing and unidentified persons and unclaimed bodies. Part of it is accessible by private citizens (Chapter 17).

Unfortunately, some cases, when given full review, offer strong potential for solution based upon time and relationship changes but are bypassed in favor of those with a quicker resolution based upon technology.

A possible prioritization of a cold case squad review in these circumstances might be those with evidence that may utilize or take advantage of

1. CODIS
2. NGI/AFIS
3. NIBIN/DRUGFIRE where applicable
4. Identified changes in relationships

These data banks are expanding daily and present a growing opportunity for solving cold cases.

If cases have been previously identified and systematically reviewed and prioritized, case investigation may begin with selection from this list. Case review and prioritization schedules were addressed in more depth in Chapter 2. Additionally, investigator expertise and experience may refine this list and identify cases that, in their view, offer more hope for resolution as opposed to others. This is subjective but further maximizes the cold case effort. The ability for experienced investigators to handpick their cases may contribute to an increased potential to solve cold cases.

Additional steps to be utilized in the identification and selection of cases may include

- Review of all open and closed files in agency archives and records
- Assimilate case information from surrounding law enforcement agencies
- Input from senior detectives assigned to homicide or those previously assigned or retired

Cold Case Squad Design

Experience has shown that there is no one-size-fits-all method of constructing a cold case squad. How these squads are formed depends upon a number of variables, including

- Financial resources
- Availability of personnel
- Size and scope of the unsolved problem

Cold case units may be constructed within local agencies, a state agency, a federal law enforcement agency, or a combination of these.

Regardless, experience has shown that agencies aspiring to construct a cold case squad most commonly contact *other* law enforcement agencies that have successfully implemented such a unit. There is nothing like experience. In this attempt, agencies may identify other jurisdictions that appear similar to theirs and contact or visit them. In doing so, the agency seeking to set up a cold case squad may seek to identify the following from their target agency:

- How did they go about setting up their unit?
- Whom did *they* contact for assistance and information?
- What have they found to work best?
- What did not work?
- What advice and recommendations would they make?

Differences in population bases, demographics, economics, resources, the nature and extent of the unsolved homicide problem, and other factors all contribute to each agency's need to tailor a design to fit its own needs. Certain styles and forms of cold case squads have been successfully implemented, however. These are as follows:

- *Single full-time investigator.* This form of a cold case squad utilizes one person assigned and dedicated full time to the investigation of cold case homicides. This style may operate on a one-case one-time basis.
- *Two or more full-time investigators.* This form of a cold case squad utilizes two or more full-time, qualified investigators dedicated to cold case investigations. Supervision may be among the membership or may be the responsibility of the supervisor or commander of a larger unit under which they operate.
- *Other investigative duties that include cold case investigation.* This form of a cold case squad recognizes the cold case problem and assigns personnel with responsibility for investigating these cases. This responsibility, however, occurs in addition to other investigative assignments not related to cold case homicide.
- *Hired-back squad.* This form of a cold case squad utilizes the experience of former homicide detectives hired back by the agency to review and/or investigate cold cases. These detectives may participate on a part-time basis, full-time basis, or volunteer basis, or combination thereof.
- *One-time squad.* This form of a cold case squad is utilized for a single case, often high profile. The number of personnel in the complement may vary.
- *Occasional squads.* This form of squad operates on an as-needed basis or when time allows from other duties.
- *Volunteer squad.* This form uses civilian volunteers with or without law enforcement experience to review unsolved cases, identify potential leads and investigative avenues, and prepare written summaries for follow-up investigation by an assigned detective or investigator. Volunteers have included college interns or students, internal or external forensic specialists (firearms, fingerprints, etc.), and others retired from the criminal justice system. See Chapter 31.
- *Interagency cold case squad.* This form of cold case squad incorporates multijurisdictional agencies. Unlike a *task force* composed of representatives of various agencies to solve a particular crime or series of crimes, this form of unit may be made up of local, county, state, and/or federal agencies participating in an effort to identify, review, and solve cold cases. As an example, the San Diego Police Department, California, Homicide Evidence Assessment Team (H.E.A.T.) utilizes full-time personnel assigned from the district attorney's office, the Federal Bureau of Investigation (FBI), and the U.S. Marshals office. Similarly, the Washington Metro Police Department, District of Columbia (MPD), has utilized a cold case team concept incorporating representatives from the FBI and the MPD, as well as a Assistant U.S. Attorney (AUSA) assigned full time to the unit.

- *District Attorney cold case squad.* A variation in the concept of cold case investigation has been the design and implementation of a cold case squad operated by the district attorney's or county prosecutor's office. These have been exemplified by the San Diego County District Attorney's Office, California, and the Morris County Prosecutor's Office, New Jersey.
- *DNA cold case squad (aka CODIS team or CODIS squad).* This is a concept designed to implement focused review and investigation into unsolved sexual assaults in which suspects have been identified by CODIS. These combine cold case homicide investigation methodologies with an initial focus on the DNA/biological material component of the unsolved case. In recent years, however, we have seen experienced cold case investigators reassigned from cold case homicides to these units due to increasing numbers of "cold hits" from CODIS.

Charlotte-Mecklenburg Cold Case Unit Experience

Faced with over 600 unsolved homicides dating to the early 1960s, the Charlotte-Mecklenburg Police Department created a cold case unit in 2003. Organizationally situated in the violent crimes division, the sergeant in charge today supervises detectives and volunteers to work unsolved homicides and 3000 unsolved sexual assaults. In addition, this unit utilizes a civilian review team, as shown in the section titled "Volunteers" in Chapter 31.

Defining Responsibilities of the Cold Case Unit

Once a cold case squad has been designed, it must have parameters that define its mission, means, and goals. These include

- Identification of the organizational unit in which the cold case squad will operate
- Date of operationalization
- Authority of the unit
- Staffing of the unit
- Facilities
- Investigative priorities/direction of the unit
- Case review and investigation parameters
- Organization/administration

Example of a Cold Case Squad Setup

The following example is extracted from the fact sheet establishing the cold case squad of the Los Angeles, California, Police Department, in 2011, and serves as a model to illustrate the foregoing:

> To: All Operation Support Division Commanders
> From: Commanding Officer, Detective Services Group
> Subject: Robbery–Homicide Division, Cold Case Homicide Unit
> At the direction of the Chief of Police, a cold case homicide unit is being formed within the Robbery–Homicide Division. This unit will be operational as of November 15, 2001. This Unit has the authority to reopen any homicide case in the City. However, due to available grant funding and advances in DNA technology, this Unit will initially focus on unsolved sexually motivated homicides.

The Cold Case Homicide Unit will systematically review all unsolved homicides and reopen cases based on solvability factors. These include: (1) Cases with suspect DNA that can be submitted to the Combined Offender DNA Information Systems (CODIS); (2) Cases with latent print evidence that can be submitted to Cal-ID, Western States, or the FBI's automated fingerprint systems; (3) Cases with ballistic evidence that can be submitted to DRUGFIRE and/or National Integrated Ballistics Information Network (NIBIN); (4) Cases with modus operandi and/or signature aspects that are sufficiently unique for matching to other cases captured in through the FBI's Violent Crime Apprehension Program (ViCAP); (5) Cases that could not be filed because identified suspects and/or witnesses could not be located or were uncooperative at the time of the original crime; and, (6) Cases that originally lacked evidence for a criminal filing, but could now be proven through the application of new evidence processing techniques.

The memorandum fact sheet further specifies the following:

- The Cold Case Homicide Unit will concentrate its efforts on unsolved homicides that occurred between 1960 and 1995. If a case is reopened and the original investigating officer is still on the department, a request will be made for that officer to work with the Cold Case Homicide Unit to the degree necessary for the successful resolution of the case.
- Staffing
    - This Unit will be under the auspices of…
    - Detective XXX will have functional responsibility for the Unit as the OIC.
    - Detective XXX and six additional detectives will staff the Unit. [Source of origin from which these detectives will participate is delineated.]
    - The selection criteria for the Unit is based on prior or current homicide experience, a commitment to the mission of the taskforce, and specialized skills including bilingual abilities (at least one Spanish speaker will be required) and "cold case" experience.
- Facilities
    - This Unit will require a secure office with sufficient space for the assigned detectives, plus storage space for the numerous casebooks that will be in constant transit between City and Divisional archives and the Unit's office. This office will require telephones, computers, fax, and a copy machine.
    - Sufficient vehicles will have to be provided. The investigation of unsolved cases generally requires a greater amount of travel than newly occurring investigations because it is common for witnesses and suspects to move out of the area since the time of the crime. Therefore, the provided vehicles will have to be of sufficient quality to provide reliable transportation to various locales across the State.
- Investigative priorities
    - This Unit will have the authority to reopen any unsolved homicide case in the City. However, in light of the $50 million in State grants for DNA processing in sexually motivated homicide cases, these cases will have the top priority.
    - Cases will be reopened based on solvability factors. The Unit will focus on cases with suspect DNA that can be submitted to the Combined Offender DNA Information System (CODIS); cases with latent print evidence that can be submitted to Cal-ID, Western States, or the FBI's automated fingerprint systems; cases with ballistic evidence (shell casings) that can be submitted to DRUGFIRE; cases with modus operandi and/or signature aspects that are sufficiently unique to be submitted to the FBI's Violent Crime Apprehension Program (ViCAP); cases with identified suspects and/or witnesses that could not be located or who were uncooperative at the time of the original crime; and, cases where suspects were identified and located, but filings

weren't obtained due to the unavailability of evidence processing techniques that have been developed since the time of these crimes.

- Organization/administration
  - This Unit will establish and maintain a close working relationship with the Scientific Investigation Division (SID) and the Forensic Science Section of the District Attorney's Office. The Scientific Investigation Division will designate a criminalist for evidence evaluation and processing; the District Attorney's Office will provide legal advice and support to the taskforce throughout the investigative and prosecution phases.
  - A reporting schedule will be instituted to keep the Department apprised of the efforts of the Unit. It is expected that the first several months will be strictly devoted to research and the identification of those cases with the highest solvability factors. As these cases are identified, the appropriate requests for evidence processing will be submitted. As stated earlier, there will be a priority placed on sexual assault homicides so that full advantage can be taken of the $50 million grant (this grant is only in effect for two more years). It is expected that the application of new forensic techniques will result in numerous cases being solved, however, due to processing delays, it is estimated that suspects will not begin to be identified via the use of these techniques for approximately six months after evidence submissions.
  - This Unit will have the authority to investigate any case no longer being actively pursued by divisional homicide units. If the detective who originally investigated the case is still working for the department, (s)he will be involved in the investigation to the degree necessary for the successful resolution of the case. Any clearances obtained by the taskforce will be credited to the Division who holds the investigative responsibility for the case. Therefore, the official case responsibility for statistical purposes will remain with the division assigned the case at the time the Unit initiates its investigation.
  - The Unit will be the primary duty assignment for the assigned detectives. The Unit will be under the command and control of the Robbery–Homicide Division, and its sole mission will be the investigation of cold-case homicides (Figure 11.3).

Figure 11.3 Cold case Detective Rick Jackson (ret'd) of the Los Angeles Police Department, California, with some of the unsolved homicide cases he currently carries in his caseload. The LAPD instituted a cold case homicide investigation unit in November 2001, to address over 8000 unsolved homicides between the 1960s and 1996. (Author's file.)

Case Tracking and Clue Management Systems

The decision to implement a cold case squad, and to proactively address cold cases, necessitates a records system to keep track of the cases and their status. Will you continue to use written or computerized forms currently in use? Is there a need to design new forms? The records system should be able to give an overview of the case such that a supervisor, or investigator, can see at a glance necessary particulars of the case as well as its status. As cases are solved, the records must indicate their closure so that needless time and effort are not later spent pulling the case from archives only to find that it has been investigated and solved. In addition, the ability to retrieve this information and to show the squad's successes may be a significant factor in obtaining additional financial and investigative resources.

In one systematic review of cold cases, a large agency discovered that faulty record keeping in old paper binders had erroneously neglected to record hundreds of solved cases, which were still carried on the books as unsolved. Hundreds of investigator hours were necessitated to separate these cases before they could begin to systematically review unsolved cases. Subsequently, however, and after many investigative successes, the records system was not constructed so as to allow retrieval of these successfully solved cold case records.

Numerous computer database programs are available. These may be implemented on a computerized system linked within the agency computer network, or stand-alone systems. Specificity of who is responsible to enter data and to monitor data entry and case status will assist in timely and efficient cold case identification, review, assignment, and updating.

Identifying data, computerized alphabetically and in an accessible and easy-to-use database, may include (when known) the following:

- Victim name and related information
- Date/time of offense
- Date/time of finding of body
- Suspect name and related information
- Names of original investigators
- Case summary of known facts
- Record tracking information by supervisor or investigator on timely basis

Example Protocol—Cold Case Squad

The operational protocols vary among agencies. The following protocol is utilized by the San Diego, California, Police Department Homicide Evidence Assessment Team (H.E.A.T.).

H.E.A.T

Open Case Review Protocol

The Homicide Evidence Assessment Team (H.E.A.T.) has been formed to reinvestigate homicide cases that have been inactivated by the original investigative team. Additionally, we will review cases brought to our attention by investigators who believe that a case is workable and solvable. Our course of action in reviewing a case should be as follows:

The case is logged out of the records division by the H.E.A.T. custodian of records.
The case is logged into the H.E.A.T. case review log.

The case is assigned to a detective for review. After the case is reviewed by a detective, an open case evaluation form is to be completed and attached to the case (Figure 11.4). The entire case will be returned to the H.E.A.T. sergeant after the review is completed. Each investigator should keep in mind that evaluating the case for eventual reinvestigation does not equate to immediately investigating the case. A case should not be reopened unless there is ample time to pursue the investigation.

If the case is to be reopened, the reviewing detective may elect to reinvestigate the case. The reinvestigation will be conducted by one or two pairs of investigators, after the case is reviewed by each person participating in the investigation.

If the case is not to be opened for reinvestigation, it will be reviewed by the sergeant. If the sergeant and the investigator agree that there is no possibility of resolving the case, a summary will be

HOMICIDE

OPEN CASE EVALUATION FORM

CASE # ____________

TEAM # ________ TYPE ________

VICTIM(S) ____________

DATE/TIME OCCURRED ____________ LOCATION OF OCCURRENCE ____________

SUSPECT(S):

☐ SUSPECT PREVIOUSLY IDENTIFIED NAME(S): ____________
☐ SUSPECT IDENTIFIED BY FORENSIC METHODS
☐ SUSPECT INFORMATION RECEIVED FROM CRIME STOPPERS, ETC.
☐ WARRANT OUTSTANDING
☐ SUSPECT INFORMATION RECEIVED FROM WITNESS

WITNESSES:

☐ WITNESS NEVER CONTACTED NAME(S): ____________
☐ WITNESS NEEDED TO BE RE-INTERVIEWED NAME(S): ____________
☐ PHOTO LINE-UP NEEDED TO BE SHOWN
☐ OTHER ____________

FORENSIC EVIDENCE:

☐ LATENT PRINTS TO BE EXAMINED
☐ CAL ID PRINTS ON FILE TO BE CHECKED
☐ DNA EVIDENCE TO BE ANALYZED
☐ DRUGFIRE
☐ PROCESS / ANALYZE EVIDENCE
☐ OTHER ____________

CASE SUMMARY: ____________

IN THE OPINION OF THIS EVALUATOR, THIS CASE WARRANTS RE-INVESTIGATION

☐ YES PRIORITY # ________
☐ NO

NAME: ____________ DATE: ____________

APPROVED: ____________

Figure 11.4 H.E.A.T. open case evaluation form.

written by the sergeant, and the case will be returned to the records division via the H.E.A.T. custodian of records (Figure 11.5).

H.E.A.T. is made up of one San Diego Police Department sergeant and three San Diego Police Department detectives. One district attorney investigator is assigned to the team. Each pair of investigators will work together while reinvestigating the case. The objective of the investigation is to resolve the case through an arrest and prosecution of the suspect or the identification of the suspect, even if there is not enough evidence to support a prosecution.

All investigative efforts will be documented on a Police Department Investigator's Report. The reports will be individually prepared by the investigator, or they can be recorded and submitted to the support staff for typing.

SAN DIEGO POLICE DEPARTMENT
HOMICIDE EVIDENCE ASSESSMENT TEAM
CASE SUMMARY

INVESTIGATOR:__________ DATE ASSIGNED:__________

CASE NUMBER: __________ DATE:__________ TIME:__________

LOCATION: __________

VICTIM: __________ SUSPECT: __________

WEAPON: __________

EVIDENCE SUMMARY: __________

CASE
SUMMARY:__________

Figure 11.5 H.E.A.T. case summary form.

Team Members

The team will be made up of members of the San Diego Police Department Homicide Unit and the San Diego County District Attorney's investigative staff.

- *Lieutenant.* One of the lieutenants assigned to the homicide unit will manage the team. The lieutenant will coordinate liaison with the press and the participating agencies.
- *Sergeant.* One homicide sergeant will supervise the daily operations of the team.
- *Investigators.* The investigators will consist of three San Diego Police Department detectives and one district attorney investigator.

Unsolved Homicide Evaluations

Unsolved homicide cases will be reviewed in their entirety, including viewing all evidence. Following the review, the case will be given a priority number using the below criteria. This process will be used to determine if the case warrants reinvestigation.

Priority 1. Suspect(s) have previously been identified. A warrant of arrest has previously been issued. A suspect has been identified by forensic methods. The cases will be given the highest priority for reinvestigation.

Priority 2. There are witnesses who can assist in identifying the suspect(s). Information has developed that identifies possible suspect(s). Evidence has been developed that can assist in identifying suspect(s). Initial investigation identifies witnesses who could not be located and/or need to be reinterviewed. These cases will be reinvestigated.

Priority 3. Evidence has been preserved and modern technology, i.e., AFIS, DNA, DRUGFIRE, and vacuum metal deposition, can be utilized to process and analyze evidence. These cases will be reclassified depending on the results of the additional laboratory analysis.

Priority 4. There are no known witnesses who can assist in identifying the suspect(s). There is no physical evidence that can assist in identifying the suspect(s). There is no physical evidence that can assist in identifying the suspect(s). These cases will not be reinvestigated.

State Agency—Cold Case Squad Protocol

The following operating protocol outlines the selection of team members and procedure used in assigning cases to the cold case teams of the Indiana State Police (ISP) when the agency implemented two investigative teams in 1998. At that time, the teams comprised two very experienced detectives, with each team operating on opposite ends of the state. The system has since been modified such that the detective in charge at each of the 14 state police posts is now responsible to ensure that cold cases that occurred within their district boundaries and for which the ISP is the lead agency are assigned and any new leads or tips are investigated and documented. This protocol, however, is an example of such a state method and may serve as an example of this format.

I. PURPOSE

Establishes guidelines for the selection and utilization of the cold case tam personnel.

II. POLICY

The unlawful taking of a human life should not go unresolved just because of the passage of time. The selection, training, and utilization of detectives assigned to investigate unresolved homicides (cold cases) are outlined in this procedure.

III. PROCEDURE

A. The investigation of an unresolved homicide could be considered when the investigation has been closed or suspended and enough time has elapsed to assume that new leads will be forthcoming. The term *cold case* should only be used on investigations that have fallen into that category, ideally, when enough time has passed that the perpetrator begins to feel confident enough to talk freely about his/her involvement. This length of time can be anywhere from five years or more.
B. The careful selection for investigation of an unresolved homicide case is paramount in the team's ability to successfully resolve the case. The following factors shall be considered before a case selection is made:
   1. *Known cause of death.* A thorough, well-documented, and photographed autopsy is essential.
   2. *Witnesses.* Witnesses, who may, over a period of time, begin to relax their fear or loyalty to the perpetrator. The reverse is true when considering a case selection. As an example, if all of the witnesses have died or cannot be found, the chances for a successful conclusion will be greatly diminished.
   3. *Suspects.* Known suspect or suspects, who had motive or evidence linking them to a homicide, is an additional factor that increases the probabilities for successful conclusion. The former friends or relatives of these suspects may no longer be loyal to them and may be willing to share information now that they would not have at the time of the crime.
   4. *Informants.* The use of informants in the investigation of any crime is important. In the investigation of cold cases, informants are invaluable. It is a rare person who can remain silent forever. Almost without exception, perpetrators will talk during a weak moment. While under the influence of alcohol or during a moment of anger, they will talk; and someone will be listening. Finding these people can make or break investigations.
   5. *Evidence.* The amount and type of evidence is extremely important in the probability of resolution of a cold case. The proper collection and storage of evidence is essential, without which the potential for successful conclusion will be limited.
   6. *Forensic technologies.* New technologies in the identification of human tissues and fluids have made great strides in recent times. If the collection and storage of these types of evidence have been done properly, the use of this type of technology, which was not available when these homicides were committed, greatly increase the chances of successful resolution of the cases.
C. Case selection process.
   1. Priority will be given to cases contained in the files of the ISP; however, consideration shall be given to homicide cases from other law enforcement agencies, if asked to do so and the case meets the selection criteria.
   2. Appropriate cold case team/detectives shall review the case files for cases with solvability factors. The selection and review shall be accomplished under the direction and supervision of the regional investigative commander.
   3. During the selection process, consultation with laboratory and evidence personnel is extremely important. The physical evidence is a very important solvability factor. The team must be sure that the evidence collected at the time of the homicide has been properly stored; the chain of custody is still intact; and, in cases where there is trace evidence, there is enough for modern laboratory techniques to be utilized.
   4. Case selection requires approval by both the applicable regional investigative commander and the appropriate BCI North/South Operations commander.

D. Organization and team selection.
   1. Cold case detectives shall be supervised by their respective regional investigative commander. The appropriate BCI North/South Operations commander shall have secondary supervision and shall place cold case detectives into a team concept, wherever appropriate.
   2. When a vacancy exists, the appropriate BCI North/South Operations commander shall notify the appropriate regional investigative commander and shall advertise the vacancy statewide for a minimum of 21 days. Interested personnel shall submit a memorandum, with appropriate endorsements and recommendations, through channels, to the appropriate BCI North/South Operations commander. The appropriate BCI North/South Operations commander shall, with the approval of the commander of the BCI, accept requests for TDY assignments to each cold case team.
   3. Detectives wanting to be assigned to a cold case team must
      a. Be a detective assigned to BCI
      b. Have extensive experience, training, ability, and interest in homicide investigations
      c. Be a volunteer
      d. Have excellent interview techniques
      e. Have excellent writing and verbal skills
      f. Have patience, diplomacy, and an open mind

E. The recommendations of a detective for a cold case team shall be made by the regional investigative commander, the appropriate BCI North/South Operations commander, and current members of the cold case team having the vacancy, per approval by the BCI commander.

F. The TCY assignment may be terminated, at any time, upon either of the following:
   1. Request, in writing, by the assigned detective and approval by the appropriate BCI North/South Operations commander
   2. Request by the appropriate BCI North/South Operations commander, CID commander, or BCI commander

G. Each TDY assignment shall be reviewed on an annual basis, dependent on the date each cold case detective began a TDY assignment. Requests for extensions of assignments to a cold case team may be made by the detective assigned to the team. Extensions of assignment may be granted only with the approval of the appropriate BCI North/South Operations commander.

H. This procedure is to be used in conjunction with all relevant department regulations, rules, policies, and procedures.

Media and Cold Case Squads

Despite the uneasy relationship that has existed on some occasions between the news media and law enforcement, the relationship between news media and cold case squads may be positive for both. When cold cases are solved, the media reports these with favorable publicity for the law enforcement agency. The public *is* interested in these cases. This in turn may bring forth witnesses or information for other unsolved cases. In addition, the media may assist by reaching out to reluctant or uncooperative witnesses, or serve as a medium to seek information or offer rewards (Figure 11.6). In some circumstances, the media has assisted cold case investigations by running stories on anniversaries or other significant dates of cold case homicides.

$10,000 Reward

for any information leading to the arrest and conviction of person or persons related to this 40-year-old cold case file.

The Carbon County Sheriff's Office is reopening a 40-year-old fatal shooting investigation and is asking for help from the public in unraveling the mystery.

The case involves the death of Boyd Kimber Harvey of Cleveland, Utah, the 34-year-old father of eight who was shot in the abdomen near Clear Creek on Oct 18, 1975. It was the opening day of the general deer season.

According to Detective Sgt. David Brewer and Wally Hendricks, Harvey had left his camp on horseback at about 4 p.m. and was found with a severe wound about 45 minutes later by other hunters. The Sun Advocate had reported that about 15 hunters gathered at the scene and helped move the victim several hundred yards through mud to bring him to a waiting ambulance.

The ambulance arrived at the county hospital at 8:10 p.m., but Harvey had died en route. "It was not an accidental shooting with his own gun and it was not a suicide," Brewer noted that there was hundreds of people in the field during that hunt and the shot most likely came from another hunter. The mystery is whether the shot was accidental or intentional.

"Somebody had to hear something, somebody had to see something, maybe the victim himself said something before he died," Hendricks said. Sheriff Jeff Wood has directed the case to be reopened.

Brewer and Hendricks said that anyone who was in the area at the time or has talked to anyone who was there should contact the Carbon County Sheriff's Office. "It doesn't matter if they think it's too far fetched," Brewer said. Any information is welcome and the number to call is (435) 636-3281.

"Even though it happened a long time ago, a human being died tragically in our county and I feel strongly that there is information available that would prove useful," Sheriff Wood said.

Figure 11.6 Media request for information and offering $10,000 reward. (Courtesy of Detective David Brewer, Carbon County Sheriff's Office, Utah.)

Additional Training and Resources for Cold Case Squads

Cold case homicide investigative techniques and tactics build upon the experience and expertise of those involved in homicide investigation and the training they have incurred over the years, or decades. Specialized instruction for investigating cold case homicides has been conducted by the Naval Criminal Investigative Service (NCIS), Army Criminal Investigation Division, and Air Force Office of Special Investigations. These military-related organizations may be able to assist municipal or other local/state cold case squads when there is a nexus to a military involvement, such as involvement of military personnel as victims or suspects. In addition, local task forces or cold case units often have representatives from the U.S. Marshals Service and the FBI. Other assistance may be available from the FBI, through utilization of its laboratory resources, as well as the Violent Criminal Apprehension Program (ViCAP), or direct investigative assistance in some circumstances.

The Vidocq Society is a potential alternative to those involved in cold case investigation, whether it be a formal cold case squad or a single cold case investigation. The services and work of this organization as well as other resources will be addressed in Chapter 31.

Acknowledgments

I wish to extend my deepest gratitude to former Director Larry Welch of the Kansas Bureau of Investigation (KBI) for his assistance in providing material for the original preparation of this chapter. In 2005, the KBI and other team members participated in the solution of the notorious "BTK" cold cases from the 1970s in the Wichita, Kansas, area. In addition, I wish to recognize and extend my appreciation to Senior Special Agent Ray Lundin and Katie Schuetz of the KBI for their assistance and participation in the preparation of this original chapter, as well as to acknowledge their role in the solution of this notorious case.

Further, I wish to extend my deepest gratitude to Detective Rick Jackson (ret'd) and Officer-In-Charge Tim Marcia, Los Angeles Police Department Cold Case Squad; Capt. Jorge Duran and Sgt. Bruce Bennett of the San Diego Police Department; and Sgt. Darrell Price of the Charlotte-Mecklenburg Police Department for providing the material and taking the time and effort to assist in presenting their experiences for all of us to learn from. In addition, I wish to acknowledge the ready interest and assistance of Col. Larry C. Turner of the Indiana State Police for his professionalism and assistance in updating this segment. Each of these persons has exemplified American law enforcement at its best, and I am extremely grateful to each for their efforts.

Suggested Readings and Bibliography

Adams, M. (2003). Cold case squad: Partnering with volunteers to solve old homicide cases. Subject to debate (Vol. 17, pp. 1, 7). Washington, DC: Police Executive Research Forum.

Anonymous. (2003). Los Angeles sheriff's cold case unit uses old fingerprints in new ways. (February 14, 2003). *Crime Control Digest.* 37, 6, p. 6.

Blankstein, A. (2002). When trail goes cold, homicide unit turns up heat. *Los Angeles Times.* p. B-3.

Eliopulos, L.N. (2003). *Death Investigator's Handbook: Expanded and Updated Edition.* Boulder, CO. Paladin Press.

Ellis, K. (2004). Kansas City cold case squad solves string of murders. *Subject to debate.* 18(7), pp. 1, 7.

Gore, W.D. (Winter 2003–2004). A new look at the DA's bureau of investigations. *Law Enforcement Quarterly.* 32, pp. 16–17.

Innocence Project. http://www.innocenceproject.org/

Lord, V. (2005). Implementing a cold case homicide unit. *FBI Law Enforcement Bulletin.* 74(2), February 2005, pp. 1–6.

Markey. J. (2003). New technology and old police work. *FBI Law Enforcement Bulletin.* 72(9), September 2003.

NIJ. (2002). Using DNA to solve cold cases. (Commission report no. ncj 194197). Washington, DC. National Institute of Justice.

North Carolina Innocence Inquiry Commission. Annual Report. (2015). http://www.innocencecommission-nc.gov/gar.html. Retrieved May 26, 2016.

Nyberg, R. (1999). Investigations: Cold case squads re-activate old investigations. *Law and Order,* 47(10), pp. 127–130.

Nyberg, R. (2004). Justice served cold. *Police: The Law Enforcement Magazine.* 28(10), pp. 44–52.

Poole, H. & Jurovics, S. (1993). MUST: A team for unsolved homicides. *FBI Law Enforcement Bulletin.* 63(3), (March 1993), p. 2.

Regini, C.L. (1997). The cold case concept. *FBI Law Enforcement Bulletin.* 66(8), (August 1997). pp. 1, 6.

Smith, C.A. (1999). Tulsa's gray squad solves cold cases. (November 1999). *Law and Order.* 47(11), pp. 48, 49.

Spraggs, D. (2003). How to open a cold case. *Police Magazine.* (May 2003). pp. 28–31.

Turner, R. & Kosa, R. (2003). Cold case squads: Leaving no stone unturned. (Report ncj 199781). (July 2003). Washington, DC. Bureau of Justice Statistics.

Fromson, N. *Conviction Integrity Units Expand Beyond Texas Roots. Texas Tribune.* March 12, 2016.

The Media in Cold Case Investigation

12

R. H. WALTON

Contents

Introduction

Despite the sometimes rancorous relationship between members of law enforcement and the media—misunderstanding on both sides—the news media plays an integral role in the function of a free society. The media, through print mediums such as newspaper and magazines and through video and the Internet, informs the public of local, regional, and national news and events. In this manner, they serve to inform, and to help safeguard, the public. Agency news releases, publication of the FBI's Top Ten wanted fugitive list, and television shows such as *America's Most Wanted* utilize different forms of media to alert the public to wanted persons, and regularly result in their apprehension as a direct outcome of public involvement.

Crime and politics are chief among those events that have been regularly reported since news reporting began. The public is fascinated with crime, and this interest has long been noticed by those who report crime, those who investigate crime, and those who study various aspects of crime and public interest. In the investigation of cold case homicides, the media has taken on a new, and valuable, role in its mission to inform and safeguard the public. The media serves as an *information resource* for cold case homicide investigation, and in some instances, may be the only repository of information cold case investigators have when they seek to build a case from scratch. In addition, the media at times may assist in the furtherance of a cold case investigation. The role of social media is addressed elsewhere in Chapters 4 and 5.

This chapter presents the role of the media in cold case investigation. This role is presented in three major categories: (1) information base, (2) generating public interest and assistance, and (3) reporting successful conclusion and resulting public perception and increased affirmation of agency mission: positive public relations.

The Media as Information Resource

During the initial review of a cold case file, and subsequent in-depth familiarization with the case, investigators become immersed in the facts of the case. These facts encompass people, places, dates and times, relationships, and more. Media records with potential information about the crime may include

- Newspaper reporting at the time of the crime and thereafter
- "Sunday Supplement" and other reviews in subsequent years and decades
- Magazine articles, books, or other literary publications
- Old video clips and sometimes movies

Review of available newspaper and other media reports of the cold case under investigation is suggested during the early stages of a cold case investigation. These accounts may yield information not necessarily found in the case reports. Of importance in this review is to determine what facts and information regarding the case are to be found in the media sources. Among these may be

- Nature and location of injuries
- Weapon used
- Property taken
- Ingress and egress to the crime scene
- Other information known only to the killer

This may become an issue later during suspect development or at defense when someone says "Well, I read about it in the papers."

This source may be especially more valuable in older, more sketchy, and seemingly uninformative or incomplete case files. In my experience, the older the homicide case becomes, the more detailed, and voluminous, the written media reporting *may* be. This reporting, however, may have been influenced by a number of other factors at the time, including

- Victim status. Prostitute versus young child of prominent citizen
- Other newsworthy events at the time
- Bizarre or more unusual elements of the crime
- Mystery surrounding the crime or lack thereof
- Political links or ramifications
- Relationship to other crimes
- Personal or professional interest of the editor
- "Newsworthiness"

Keep in mind that while the media serves as an unofficial record of events, it does serve as a record. In this regard, the media may serve as a basis to turn a once unofficial record into the official record. These issues may become a major source of information in those cases in which files are missing, or nonexistent, and provide the basis for crime scene reconstruction and identification of those involved in the case as victims, suspects, investigators, etc. However, the information in media accounts is only as reliable as the sources of information, the interpretation and repetition of the information, and any self-serving motives of those providing information. Just like in a police investigation.

Newspapers

Print media was the standard for decades of how Americans received their news. In the age before radio, and later television, it was *the* primary news medium. Newspapers were the daily format for news, and magazines and short story booklets or magazine articles also recorded people, stories, and events. In prior decades, it was not unusual for towns and cities to have multiple, competing print news media. These may have operated on a morning daily schedule, an afternoon basis, sometimes a semiweekly or weekly schedule, or variations of these. When newspapers competed with one another, it might not be unusual to find one paper hitting the streets in the morning hours, while the competition came out in the afternoon. Over the past two decades, however, many major dailies have closed their doors. In addition to closing, some have been bought out by other news organizations or merged with other media interests.

For cold case investigators, this is relevant as a review of both editions may be valuable, as well as the awareness of potential other sources of news reporting. Due to deadlines for reporters' stories, what one newspaper printed in detail may have been only lightly touched by the competitor, which instead perhaps concentrated on an aspect of the story totally neglected by the competition. And that's what reporting was: *competition.*

Then, like now, the media sought to solicit readership and to sell advertising. Crime stories could mean additional sales. On occasions, and in response to intense public interest, newspapers would rush to press urgent breaking news stories—often to "scoop" the competition—known as "extras." These might be exemplified by the word "EXTRA" in color at the top of the first page. The addition of this color, and an extra edition, often were more expensive to produce and are found usually in the most sensational of cases (see Figure 12.1).

Where to Find Newspapers

Historically, the newspaper companies themselves kept back copies of their editions. This served not only as a record of their business but also, in the pre-computer age, as an in-house source of background information on persons, events, places, and other items of report. These repositories of back issues were called the newspaper *morgue.* This is *not* to be confused with the coroner's repository of the deceased by the same name.

In the past quarter century, however, some newspapers have eliminated the storage costs and other accompanying problems and issues by getting rid of their original hard copies of back editions. Computerized data systems and other techno-advances have eliminated the need to maintain hard copies of daily editions. Decades of back issues took up a lot of space. After copying these to microfilm, many news organizations have simply destroyed the original copies or donated them to universities or research facilities that have room to store them (see Figure 12.2). In some instances, media companies may retain hard copies for a set period of time before copying them to microfilm and destroying or otherwise discarding these.

EXTRA

Humboldt Standard

FIND CARMEN DEAD

HEARING IS DATED FOR NEXT WEEK

BULGARIA STILL HOT FOR BLOWS

Two Members Of Posse Locate Bodies Of Girl And Her Pet Dog "Pronto"

BODY IS DISCOVERED BURIED IN SHALLOW GRAVE ALONG CREEK NEAR FORT BAKER

COYOTE FLAT, Oct. 23. (Via Standard's Wireless) – Carmen Wagner was found dead today a few feet from Baker Creek near Fort Baker, buried in a shallow grave. Fifteen feet away lay her dog Pronto, shot to death.

The discovery was made by Sidney Pixton and Kenneth Buck who first discovered the dog Pronto. Led on by the finding of the body of the dog, the men searched the neighborhood carefully, and soon came upon a human arm projecting from a shallow grave. A little exhuming soon uncovered the body of Carmen.

The body was lying in a piece of ground between a large rock and the river bank, where it had been carefully covered with loose earth, driftwood and rock.

The right arm was lying on the breast, and the left elbow was crooked and sticking above the surface. This led to the discovery. It had not been ascertained yet if she was shot, but the condition of the dog has pretty well demonstrated that she was killed in that way.

KELLOGG HAS AROUSED NEW RUMPUS OVER COMMUNISTS

BITTER LEGAL BATTLE IS ON OVER RAILWAY BOOZE MOVING

SEAPLANE SHATTERED BY TUMBLE

SAVE with SAFETY at your Rexall DRUG STORE

LODGE SAYS LEAGUE HAS NO POWER TO END CONFLICT

Convicts Moved To Another Sanctuary

STOP

GEORGIA ROSE BODY POWDER

Atkinson & Woods

HEMSTITCHING STAMPING ART NEEDLEWORK SUPPLIES

Figure 12.1 Humboldt Standard EXTRA newspaper 1925. Review of newspapers is necessary to identify witnesses and information not found in the file as well as what information is found in the public domain. Older newspapers may furnish more detail than more recent. (Author's file.)

For cold case investigators seeking to locate back issues of local newspapers, whether original hard copy or microfilm style copies, there are a number of places to explore. Among these are

- The local newspaper publishing company (if still in business locally). When this source is contacted, however, keep in mind that good reporter's sense stories. If known detectives start asking questions about cold cases, so might a reporter.

Figure 12.2 Photo of microfilm reader. Cold case investigators may spend hours reading microfilm, a tactic not encountered in normal homicide investigations. (Author's file.)

- Local library. May possess original or microfilm copies.
- Local college or university. Most often possesses microfilm copies (see Figures 12.3 and 12.4), but may have originals.
- Other college- or university-operated libraries or research facilities.
- Local historical society. May possess older, original newspapers as a result of donation by the newspaper publisher.
- State archives or repositories.

Figure 12.3 Photo of San Diego Public Library building. Libraries may be a source of a number of investigative aids in cold case investigation, including newspapers, city directories, and telephone books. (Author's file.)

WOMEN'S NEWS
MEXICO ROUNDUP
SAN DIEGO COUNTY

The San Diego Union

LOCAL NEWS

SAN DIEGO, CALIFORNIA, MONDAY MORNING, JUNE 7, 1965

PAGE A-19

Ferryboats Whistling A Parting Tune

OF THE SEA

Short Trip Is Lure To Thousands Daily

23 Receive Law Degrees In Colorful Rite

By DAVID FARMER

POLITICAL SNARL

Love Out Of Reach For Giraffe

Teen Divorcee Is Found Slain

An attractive, 19-year-old divorcee was found strangled in her El Cajon apartment yesterday.

CHERYL BURNETT . . . called "Cinderella"

Figure 12.4 Microfilm homicide report San Diego Union front page June 7, 1965. (Courtesy of El Cajon Police Department.)

What May Be Found in the Newspapers

"Killed by two savage blows on the forehead, the lifeless body of Mrs. Pearl Martin, 55, was discovered yesterday afternoon lying at the bottom of steps, which connected the Martin garage with the family living quarters at 2926 E Street…Mrs. Hazel Skipper, 16 West Trinity St., on her way to an appointment with Mrs. Martin, discovered the crime and notified police at about 2 p.m. when she looked through the half-open garage doors at the Martin residence."

This was the lead story reporting a homicide in the Eureka, California *Humboldt Times* newspaper on December 11, 1946, and reported in a story on cold case homicides in the *Times-Standard* newspaper in Eureka, California, 58 years later. The information revealed in these few passages is not untypical reporting, even today. Cold case investigators reviewing this case would immediately note that in just these few sentences, information is found.

- Identifying the name of the victim
- Identifying the age of the victim
- Identifying the victim's address
- Identifying the location where the body was found
- Identifying the name of the person who discovered the crime
- Identifying the name of the person reporting the crime
- Reporting the manner of death
- Reporting the location of potential fatal wounds to the victim
- Describing the scene of the crime
- Reporting the date and time the crime was reported to police
- Reporting the circumstances by which the victim was discovered

In this and subsequent reports, the newspaper reported that she was a victim of a robbery and that approximately $300 in cash, jewelry, and a handgun were reported missing. Thus, information perhaps known to the suspect is now in the public domain.

Initial and subsequent newspaper reports regularly report information of interest in a cold case investigation. In addition to the aforementioned topics, newspaper reports not uncommonly provide information including

- Names and addresses of witnesses
- Names and addresses of friends and associates of the victim
- Names and addresses of relatives and coworkers of the victim
- Employment information regarding the victim
- Victim marital status
- Victim's past or ongoing relationships
- Identities of those last known to have seen the victim
- Names of responding law enforcement officers and investigators
- Identities of initial coroner/medical examiner personnel
- Identity as to where the remains were transported
- Other circumstances surrounding discovery of the body
- The victim's activities prior to disappearance and/or commission of crime
- Reported relationships of the victim, including possible suspects
- Suppositions and theories of those who knew the victim
- Other similar crimes in the neighborhood or time span
- Political or time and circumstances potentially relevant to the crime
- Identities of persons of interest
- Statements by friends, associates, and others
- Name of the author of the article
- Description or discussion of the weapon used
- Description of victim injuries
- Description of evidence seen by others

- Discussion of evidence or property seized by law enforcement investigators
- Coroner or medical examiner findings

In some, especially more notorious or sensational cases, suspects have mailed letters or items belonging to the victim to local news media. In most cases, these have been turned over to the police. Cold case investigators may keep the possibility of this in mind during interviews and conversations with media representatives. If so, do they *still* possess any of these items?

Searching the Newspapers

Depending upon the source location, newspaper contents may be indexed or catalogued as to allow searching for specific news stories, or they may not be catalogued. In either case, investigators should query the custodian of these newspapers or files to ascertain what retrieval options exist.

- Catalog systems may be indexed by card index files in which articles between a given time period are referenced by type, i.e., "crime" or "murder," by individual names, or a variety of other methods (see Figure 12.5). Investigators will need to identify what, if any, information retrieval systems exist and work with the custodian of the newspapers to maximize efforts to retrieve all relevant items. In other instances, they may be computerized back to a certain date, and these systems may more readily facilitate item retrieval.
- Noncatalogued. In this situation, the newspapers are usually filed and maintained by year on shelves or stacks, or on microfilm. Investigators will need to know a starting date or period to being a review. In my experience, homicide cases are usually found within the first few pages, if not the first page, depending upon the time period, size of the newspaper, perceived public interest, and other editing factors. If the date of the homicide is not known, and the identity of the victim is, the death certificate may provide a starting date for a newspaper search. These searches will be very time consuming.

Keep in mind that as the case grew "cold," so did media interest. Stories that once occupied front page, consecutive issues became smaller references, often weeks or months later, and ultimately nothing more than

Figure 12.5 Library newspaper file index system. Not all libraries have index systems, and the only way to research information about cold cases is to begin with the initial reporting and review subsequent issues. (Author's file.)

brief mention that detectives were still following up on leads. As fresh cases overtake ongoing investigations and consume law enforcement resources, the news media experiences a similar situation. Their business is to report the news and, for the most part, they do not go back on a story unless there is a "newsy" element. As a consequence, media reporting of a homicide may trail off after a day or two, a week, or a month.

In either case, however, it may be prudent to check newspaper accounts on anniversaries of crimes and for a month or two afterward for any mention.

- Internet. Investigators may search online for newspaper articles, and some search engines may allow searching for specific news items. My experience in doing this has suggested that searching the local newspaper as well as searching the nearest large city newspaper may prove beneficial. In some instances, expand your search for other large newspapers of national scale. These may include the *Los Angeles Times*, the *Washington Post, New York Times*, and others. Some newspapers, however, do not put stories prior to 2000 on the World Wide Web due to legal concerns addressing copyright and royalty issues for authors of articles. I have not found this to be a uniform practice, however. In addition, local universities or colleges may have research facilities that may assist investigator efforts in this regard.

The Photographic Record

Newspaper reports were, and are, often illustrated with photographs and diagrams or sketches of the scene of the crime (see Figure 12.6). These photos may be of the exterior of the building of a crime scene, interior

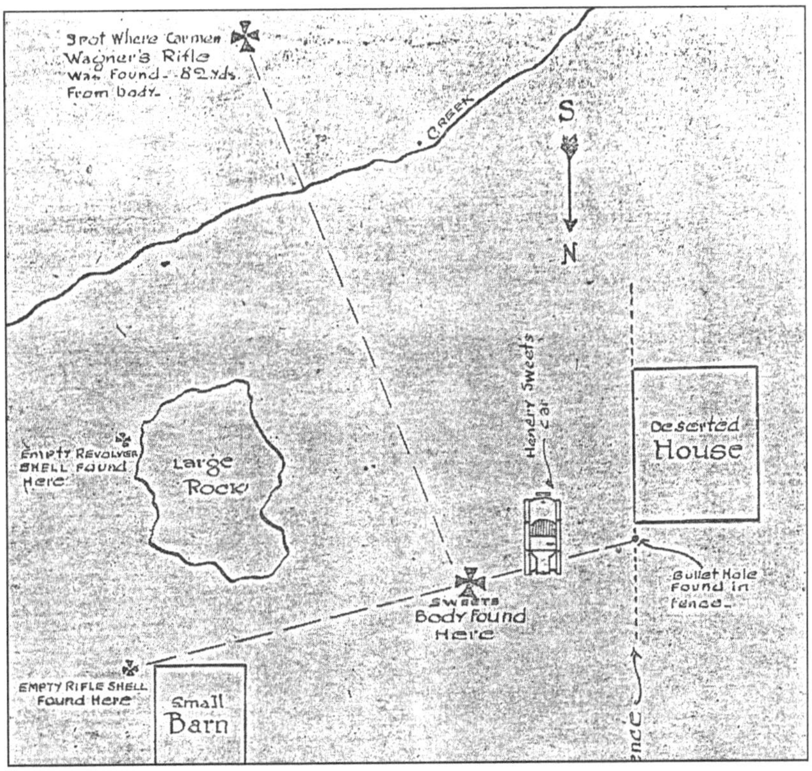

Figure 12.6 Sketch of crime scene 1925. While perhaps more common many decades ago, media crime scene sketches are to be found in reporting today as well. They can serve to orient the reader. Not the specific distance and orientation of evidence. (Courtesy of Humboldt Standard Newspaper.)

shots, neighborhood shots, or a combination of these. Additional photos to be found in review of newspapers in the course of a cold case investigation may be of

- Other persons connected to the victim or the crime, often identifying them by name and occupation, and address
- Weapons
- Scene of the crime
- Persons present *within* the crime scene
- Surroundings of the crime scene
- Potential witnesses or suspects (in crowd scenes)

In the past, in some jurisdictions, *private photographers* responded to crime scenes to take the pictures for the law enforcement agencies. For other purposes, including financial gain, other persons may also have taken photos of the crime scene or related locations or persons or items and sold or otherwise furnished these to the media. During the review of the newspaper photos, cold case investigators may seek to ascertain *who* took the photographs. This source information is often noted at the bottom of the picture. In cases of private photographers, cold case investigators may seek to locate them to ascertain if they have other photographs remaining of the case and to attempt to obtain copies. In those instances in which the photographer is determined to be deceased, attempts may be made to

- Identify the descendants of the photographer or
- Determine the disposition of photographs remaining in the individual's estate

In situations where the local photographer was a professional and operated a business, inquiry to determine who bought the business may seek to learn whether they also bought any photographic collections as well. Other sources of potential photographs may be

- Local private photograph collections
- Historical society photograph collections
- Local or state archives
- Colleges or university libraries or photo collections

When reviewing newspaper accounts, it was not uncommon to see a photograph of the victim's face with the article. *Who* furnished the picture? *Where* did it come from?

Keep in mind that a reporter's information was only as good as their sources.

Film and Audio Media

With the growth of television in the 1950s, and later cable news networks in the early 1980s, written media began to be usurped by these mediums. In decades past, many stations were individually owned and affiliated with major news organizations, ABC, NBC, or CBS. In later periods, many of these stations began to be bought by other media concerns, and it would not be uncommon to find a station in one city owned by a company that owns similar media in other cities and states. Newspaper and film stories and photographs were carried and transmitted nationally and internationally by the Associated Press (AP) and United Press International (UPI), including photos. These two organizations also transmitted photos for the newspaper media for many decades.

Local camera crews (not uncommonly one person) recorded information in the field for nightly broadcast. After shooting the event, the camera crew brought the film back to the studio where it was edited for broadcast. It was up to the discretion of the editor to preserve and broadcast what suited their purpose. Material that was not broadcast often wound up on the proverbial "cutting room floor" and was discarded.

Film and video taken in the field are described in the media jargon as "raw material" or "raw footage." The material that is broadcast is "aired material" or "air cuts." This distinction is important for cold case investigators to understand. Raw material is all the film or footage that was shot, including the snippets that found their way onto the air. This material was normally discarded, unless, perhaps, the case was high profile. Investigators should ask if the station retains any raw footage. However, news media will *only* release to law enforcement, even under subpoena, that material that was aired and will not normally release unaired footage. This material may be protected under the shield laws that govern media disclosure of sources or other material.

Aired material is that portion of the raw material that was broadcast by the medium. This is the material normally retained by the news facility. For cold case investigators, it may be significant to understand that, in older cases, it was not uncommon for news cameras and reporters to conduct an interview with a witness or other person at length and shoot perhaps 20 minutes of footage. However, by the time editing was complete, perhaps two-minutes was aired, and partial statements—*sound bites*—were broadcast. It would not be unusual for a reporter's three-minute interview to be reduced to a 15-second sound bite. In older broadcasts, it might not be uncommon to view a lengthier interview than later, or present, practices and constraints allow.

As a consequence for cold case investigators, ease of media review and access to this material is somewhat more difficult. In my opinion, written media no longer reports in detail to the degree as was once common. One of the many advantages of assigning senior, veteran investigators to cold case homicide investigation is their grounding in the local community. This experience includes knowledge of media, newspapers and audio-video, and changes in media ownership or broadcast initials as well as potential personal contacts.

When reviewing and investigating cold cases, do not *assume* anything! This includes the assumption that the film media has nothing remaining decades later. You don't know until you inquire, and it is not to be unexpected that local media may still possess film footage many decades old. This was the experience of El Cajon, California, cold case investigators Robert Anderson and Jon Wooddell during their investigation of the 1965 homicide and other crimes committed by serial killer Clyde Wilkerson (discussed in Chapter 4). Investigators determined that San Diego television channel KFMB had retained footage of their coverage of the case, which the station converted to videotape and provided to detectives.

Not uncommonly, news stations have video footage dating to their origins. In the case of KFMB, they retain film video dating to the late 1950s and early 1960s. The earliest format was 16 mm film, and a transition from film to video began in the 1970s. This format was originally a three-quarter inch Sony Betta formatted tape with a different encoding from the Home Betta format. The three-quarter inch format later changed to a one-half inch format and to a mix of one-half inch Betta and digital. The current trend is to all digital format.

Elements of a Newscast

Depending upon the time period and type of newscast, these elements made up the dissemination of the news event:

- Film or videotape of the event
- Written script of what was aired in the media
- Anchor's script of what was aired regarding the story

Depending upon age, film footage may not have had sound on the same reel. Sound came later with the addition of a sound stripe. Film with audio was sometimes accompanied by a separate sound track containing the reporter's narration of the story. In addition, the media had a "reporter package" where the narration is put on the story and the anchor would make reference to the reporter, whose narration is on one track and field footage is on another track.

Further, in stories where there was no reporter in the footage and the anchor speaks over it, there might have been an original reporter, but three to four days later, they may have pulled the footage from the crime scene or topic and the anchor would now say "Now for an update…" and reuse this footage, imposing later dialogue over earlier footage as the anchor narrated it on air.

Contacting the Media

Any contact with the media offers a potential for making law enforcement's cold case effort public. As with some prosecutors and judges, there are misconceptions about what cold case investigation is and how it is conducted. Cold case investigators can go a long way by educating those in the media of some of the aspects of cold case investigation and how it differs from hot case investigation. Among these differences is maintaining a lack of publicity until the right time. Responsible journalists may understand this, but ask that they be notified when the case breaks. This is not unreasonable and may facilitate obtaining the desired footage and information, as well as promoting relations for future cooperation.

When seeking this information, it is suggested that investigators first approach the station management. Contact may be made with the manager or a "special projects" person. In some instances, the station may request a subpoena. This is one reason why a prosecutor should be brought on board as early as possible in the investigation. Keep in mind that the degree of cooperation and speed of cooperation varies on a case by case basis, depending upon station personnel, resources, and policies.

Media Retrieval

Media stations have different filing systems, and like those in law enforcement, these have changed and evolved over the years and decades. Once common card files have been replaced by computerized databases, and on occasions, some stations still maintain both. Card index files were common pre-computer, and this requires a manual search. In some instances, these were later transferred to a computer program, but that program may have become history with software advances and the data may no longer be retrievable. Many stations, as do some law enforcement agencies, maintain off-site storage facilities, and it may require some time and effort on the part of station personnel for them to cross-check records in available databases. Remember: the information on card files was only as good as the person who filled it out, and information retrieval may well depend upon the ability to cross-check information between cards.

When contacting media, date of the crime, discovery of the body, or when the story aired is important for their search. Knowing this date allows them to more quickly identify and retrieve the film. Since the advant of computers, however, software for newsrooms allows them to search national as well as local stories.

When attempting to locate the film, also attempt to locate the written script. The *written script* is what is said on the air; it may also include what the reporter *did* during the broadcast of the story and may include narration and text of the sound bite. The written script is not uncommonly transcribed and filed. If it is one read by an anchor, what the anchor says is also in the script. Names in sound bites and scripts may be searchable in databases and, in older instances, card files, depending upon how the story was catalogued by the local station.

Maintenance of scripts may vary from station to station, depending upon their policies, and may be searchable depending upon their filing systems or databases. Usually, however, what is saved is only that which was aired. Also ask if they have still pictures, "stills," from old interviews.

When reviewing older footage, do not be surprised to see camera crews in the heart of the crime scene, or officers handling evidence in front of the camera. It happened.

During review of footage, investigators should note what is revealed about people, the scene, and other revelations by the footage, in particular

- Names. Cold case investigators should cross-check to be sure that persons interviewed by the media had been interviewed by law enforcement. These investigative statements should be cross-checked to their media accounts.
- Dates and times. These should be compared to the case file and may assist in timeline preparation and/or enhance or discredit statements of concerned persons.
- Scene and analysis of what the footage shows and compared to case photos.

Film Degradation and Acuity

Film is subject to degradation, depending upon storage conditions and exposure to heat and humidity. Normally, film does not readily show detail like blood spatter and holes unless a zoom lens was used. In addition, film footage is usually not of the quality of later videotape. In certain cases, cold case investigators may wish to have a forensic specialist examine the film for possible enhancement of frames or images. Investigators may consider consultation with local law enforcement or state laboratory personnel or other specialists.

Magazines and Other Literature

When reviewing cold cases, keep in mind that these may have been written up in magazines or books. During the course of investigation, officers from the time period of the case, friends or family of the victim, or other witnesses may have knowledge whether, and when, the story was reported in news magazines or literary magazines or books.

In previous decades, magazines such as *True Detective* and similar works regularly published true-crime stories submitted by law enforcement authors (see Figure 12.7). These reports may detail names, events, and other matters concerning the crime, as well as photographs. It may be prudent to ascertain if any such publication occurred. Keep in mind that many of these accounts may or may not be "enhanced" or embellished. When direct knowledge of the existence of a specific article or crime report is not known, cold case investigators may attempt to use Internet resources such as http://www.e-bay.com to identify and locate these articles.

During the course of a cold case investigation, it may prove valuable to ascertain if any persons connected to, or known to, the original or subsequent investigation authored any published material or unpublished manuscripts. Comparison of what is revealed in this material to the case file may be of interest in the cold case investigation.

In one extreme example, a fire of suspicious origin in South Pasadena, California, in 1984 claimed the lives of four persons, including a 2 1/2-year-old boy. It was initially ruled "accidental," although some fire investigators did not agree with this conclusion by law enforcement investigators. The fire case was closed and remained this way for over a decade.

Among those involved in the earliest stages of the investigation was Glendale, California, fire department arson investigator John Orr. Orr was considered an expert arson investigator by his peers and highly respected. In 1998, Orr was convicted of setting the fatal fire, one in a series the esteemed fire marshal had set over the years. During the course of their investigation, investigators discovered that Orr had authored an *unpublished manuscript* detailing people and events in a fatal arson. The revelations contained in this document became a pivotal point during the investigation and ultimate conviction of Orr for the murders. This is represented in Figure 12.8.

Figure 12.7 *True Detective* 1958. This issue carried detailed reporting and pictures to be found nowhere else when cold case investigators revisited the 1957 murders of two El Segundo Police officers in 2003. (Courtesy of El Segundo Police Department.)

POINTS OF ORIGIN

by

John L. Orr

It flared up much quicker than he expected. He had planted the device only seven minutes earlier and already the paper bag was on fire. The blossoming flames quickly spread to a weathered cardboard box, then began eating away at the side of a discarded sofa next to it. He lowered himself in the driver's seat and squinted through binoculars for a better view. It was a moonless night and the flickering light from the fire looked obscenely out of place, scarring the otherwise serene August evening. Beyond the carport where the fire was burning, he saw the HOLLYWOOD sign lighting up the horizon above the deteriorating city.

Figure 12.8 Manuscript of John Orr paper. Cold case investigators should inquire if anyone connected with a cold case authored any papers, stories, or other literature on the case. This front page of a text authored by former Glendale, California, arson investigator John Orr helped to convict him for setting a series of fires, including one that killed four people. His descriptions of "fictional" events were too close to factual to be considered fictional by investigators, and the jury agreed. (Courtesy of Special Agent Mike Matassa, ATF.)

Other Media Sources for Information

Ever wonder how or where the media obtains information for broadcast today on something that happened years, or decades, ago? Complete with footage and pictures? Go to http://www.footage.net. This website links numerous archives of footage dating to 1896, including dash cam or caught on tape, amateur surveillance videos, and more. This news footage network offers the media the ability to rapidly find previous news reports and archival footage. This site links to stock footage houses with access to footage, news reports, and more. After checking with your local media, this may be a good place to start when searching for footage and pictures. Links are provided to numerous sources of historical clips, images, and footage. And don't forget to check "Youtube."

Case Study

The following case history is drawn only from four newspaper accounts and the death certificate. The information presented is retrieved from post-initial reporting articles in the *Los Angeles Times* newspaper, January 5, 1989, and the *San Francisco Chronicle* newspaper from July 9, 1991 and May 20 and 21, 1998. The subject was the unsolved murder of San Francisco police officer Lester Garnier (Figure 12.9). The purpose of this is to illustrate the *detailed* information that *may* be uncovered in a cold case newspaper review and to explore possible avenues of investigation due to the passage of time in light of changes in relationships and technology.

It will appear that there is information in these reports that many investigators would prefer not to see in the press. These reports reflect the depths of investigation and variety of sources utilized in news reporting. By use of this case example, I intend in no manner or design to criticize, demean, or impugn the character or reputations of the victim or of any personnel involved in the investigation, nor of the law enforcement agencies. In cold case investigation, best results are obtained not by looking back and saying "why didn't they do this?" or "why did they do this?" but rather by objective, systematic study of the facts and evidence and moving forward in a cooperative manner with the objective of solving the case.

What happened in the past is in the past...move forward.

Figure 12.9 San Francisco Police Officer Lester Garnier was murdered in Walnut Creek, California, in 1988. His murder remains unsolved. (Courtesy of Lt. John Hennessey, San Francisco Police Department.)

The Initial Investigation

The Crime Scene

Police Officer Lester Garnier was found shot to death, slumped behind the wheel of his blue 1984 Corvette, in a parking lot of a shopping mall in Walnut Creek, California, on July 11, 1998. The general location is a suburb of homes and office complexes on the east side of San Francisco Bay.

The vehicle was angled across three spaces near a group of upscale department stores. This was a position a police lieutenant would later state indicated that he was making a "meet." The same lieutenant stated that the murder had to be work related, as his car was placed so that no one could surprise him.

Garnier was found by workers approximately 7:30 a.m., the vehicle being reported as having been there all night. The car still had its parking lights on, the doors were unlocked, and the driver's window was down. He apparently had no gun or any money with him at the time of his death.

The victim's face was streaked with dry blood, and blood stained his long-sleeved white sweatshirt and Levi pants. The victim's badge was inside one of the car's storage compartments.

Upon report of the crime, eight officers from the 78-member Walnut Creek police department, which usually experienced perhaps one murder a year, responded to the scene.

Reported Witness Statements

1. A workman in the shopping center reported hearing several gunfire-like noises approximately 11:30 p.m. but paid no attention as it was near July 4. This witness later observed two women walking in the parking lot area. This may be the same witness as #3 reported below.
2. Another witness told of seeing a woman exit the passenger's side of Garnier's vehicle. Police used a hypnotist with this witness in an attempt to create a composite drawing of the woman. The woman was described as being approximately 28 years old, blonde, 5 feet 6 inches to 5 feet 8 inches, weight approximately 110 pounds. Neither woman had been identified as of July 9, 1991, despite repeated requests by police to the public for information. This may be the same as #4 below.
3. Approximately 11:15 p.m., a man laying carpet at a store near the Ross Dress for Less Parking lot heard what appeared to be two or three gunshots coming from the vicinity of the parking lot. A few minutes later, he saw two women walking through the lot. One woman was described as in "…her mid-30s, tall and slender with blond hair below her shoulders." The other was described as being in her 20s and had shoulder-length blond hair and a medium build. The witness stated he observed the taller woman drive away in a faded blue Toyota, while the other drove away in a Toyota or Datsun with white or gray oxidized paint.
4. Another witness reported driving through the parking lot around 11:30 p.m. and observed a "slim, blond woman get out of the passenger's door of Garnier's Corvette. The witness said the woman circled the car and appeared to look in the driver's window before she walked away. None of the women was ever located."

The Investigation

These news accounts further reported that within approximately three years of the homicide, the Walnut Creek Police Department had "…interviewed more than 600 persons and traveled hundreds of miles in search of clues." During this, they had used hypnosis on a key witness and also consulted a psychic. In addition, "…every time a similar gun was used in a crime elsewhere," investigators "discussed it" with law enforcement representatives of that agency.

The investigation into Garnier's personal and professional life is reported in the news accounts. The media also stated that investigators had spoken to "several hundred prostitutes" Garnier had arrested in the course of his undercover work. Other information found in these reports includes the following.

1. **Evidence**

According to media reports, little physical evidence was recovered at the scene. However, the reporting in these articles indicates that fingerprints and a spent bullet were recovered. According to the media, "Fingerprints in the car didn't produce a suspect."

The news reports further stated that "...police recovered one copper jacketed bullet from inside Garnier's sweatshirt and tested it against similar guns owned by eight San Francisco police officers, finding no matches." In a report by the *Los Angeles Times* in 1989, the media review suggested deeper elements of the investigation, noting that the "revolvers" of 10 San Francisco police officers had been reportedly checked by Walnut Creek detectives.

In my experience, the media and others have not, infrequently in the past, lumped the term "revolver" as identifying *all* handguns, including semiautomatics, which is not correct. According to the chief of SFPD, this was done "merely to cover all the bases." The chief is further reported as saying he had no knowledge of a police officer as a suspect in this case. By this and other news reports, it was suggested that a strong rift had occurred between the SFPD and the agency of primary jurisdiction, the Walnut Creek Police Department. Senior officers and investigators of the SFPD are identified and quoted at length in these accounts regarding their lack of participation in the initial investigation.

The *San Francisco Chronicle* in 1991 further reported similarly that, "In addition, they ran innumerable fingerprint checks and test-fired the weapons of eight officers in the San Francisco Police Department who owned guns similar to the murder weapon. In at least one instance, a San Francisco officer submitted to a lie detector test." This brings to mind the question, why were the guns and fingerprints of fellow officers examined? The answer to this would be found in the review of later news reports.

"Within the San Francisco department, rumors have circulated that an officer killed Garnier and that Walnut Creek did not trust San Francisco police to help find the killer. Some San Francisco officers are angry that their detectives were not summoned to the murder scene immediately." Senior SFPD officers are quoted regarding their perception of the Walnut Creek investigation. In response, Walnut Creek police are reported as responding that they tested the officers' weapons "'to cover potential defense issues at a later time' and that they came up with no ballistic matches." Walnut Creek police were reported as saying the suspect could be, or could not be, a police officer. This area of investigation had not been eliminated.

2. **The Victim**

Garnier's life was reportedly examined in detail by investigating detectives, and published in the press. He was held in high esteem by his colleagues and known as a very cautious man. According to the press, Garnier "...was extremely particular about who he let into his car, but apparently allowed his assailant to get into his vehicle and sit next to him without evidence of a struggle." On the night of the homicide, he apparently left his 9mm and .357 caliber handguns at home.

The media, and investigation, explored his past. Garnier was born in the local Mission District of San Francisco and attended Mission Dolores Elementary School and Riordan High School. Described by a classmate as a "solid B student," the victim was further described as "street smart." After school he would stay around the Boys and Girls Club. Garnier was named Boy of the Year and Regional Boy of the year, and earned a trip to Washington, District of Columbia, to meet President Gerald Ford. Those who knew him advised they had never heard anyone say anything bad about him.

Beginning in 1980, Garnier worked for the Broodmoor Police Department, a suburb near San Francisco. He joined the SFPD that same year and spent four years as a patrol officer at the Northern Station in the Fillmore District. He arrested three gunmen holding up a restaurant on a main city street in 1981, and in 1983, helped capture an attempted murderer. He was twice decorated for bravery. In 1984, he transferred to the vice unit and worked there until his own murder. During this time, he had arrested hundreds of prostitutes. Prior to his assignment to the unit, a series of scandals and allegations of corruption had been levied against the SFPD. These were reported in the media as centering on the vice unit amid allegations of officers using and selling drugs, hiring prostitutes, and providing favors for bookies, drug dealers, and pimps.

When he was off-duty, Garnier worked three part-time jobs (other accounts state four part-time jobs), and reports indicated that he was further thinking of opening up a small business—a hot dog stand. He bought the Corvette and had a cell phone. The latter was not yet common at that time. Garnier liked nice clothes, worked out, and had dated a number of women.

According to these reports, Garnier purchased a home with a pool in nearby Concord and lived there with his parents shortly before his death. Other reports say he helped his parents purchase the home.

Garnier was reportedly a quiet person and did not often speak about his job with his family. He did, as was reported, once say that "There are good policemen and bad policemen, just like anything else."

3. **Victim's Movements on the Night of the Homicide**

   On the night of the homicide, Garnier ate a roast beef dinner with his family and left his home at approximately 8:45 p.m. At approximately 9 p.m., he called his "best friend," the owner of a San Francisco gas station. The two had spoken of going to see the movie *Bull Durham*, but Garnier said he was behind schedule and could not make it. His best friend later reported that he tried to call Garnier back but that the phone just kept ringing.

4. **The Weapon**

   The weapon used in the slaying was an AMT .380 caliber semiautomatic pistol. It has never been recovered.

5. **Motive**

   No motive has been identified in this crime.

6. **Suspect**

   No suspect has been identified in this crime.

7. **The Wounds**

   The victim was shot twice at close range, once in the right temple and once in the right side.

8. **The Political and Investigative Environment**

   Not unheard of in hot homicide cases, political and other elements are thrust into homicide investigations. Cold case investigations are no different. By 1991, according to press reports, police had no reported motive or suspect. The two lead detectives on the case are identified and quoted during the news reports. Detectives reportedly had eliminated motives that included robbery, revenge, a casual pick-up, girlfriend, or prostitutes that Garnier had arrested. At this time, police discounted any relationship of this crime to a series of political scandals within San Francisco City Hall. Press reports offer insight into elements that cold case investigators may need to examine in depth for relevance to the murder of Officer Garnier.

Not long before his murder, Officer Garnier was assigned to surveillance duty on a brothel that reportedly specialized in underage girls. This was part of an investigation into the activities of the brothel and that led to the indictment of the city's chief administrative officer, a San Francisco police officer, and numerous others for patronizing the brothel. The investigation stemmed from an informant's letter, and a follow-up letter advising of the brothel, and a second letter notifying the SFPD of possible officer patronage of the brothel. Later reports of a friend of Office Garnier note that Garnier told his friend he was working on a case that had high-level political ramifications. Subsequently the brothel was raided on April 30, 1988, but the two named "ringleaders" got away. Officials were later reported as saying the suspects were tipped off in advance of the raid. When one *timelines* the events reflected in news accounts, this was almost a year after the initial reports of the existence of the brothel yet slightly over two months *before* Officer Garnier's murder.

Garnier's surveillance activities were reportedly documented in his logs. The newspaper reports detail statements of other "authorities" relating to past "police bachelor parties" attended by officers from other jurisdictions in which young prostitutes were alleged to have attended by invitation of the indicted officer. The indicted officer's lawyer is quoted in the articles suggesting that Garnier may have attended one of these "stag parties" while a reserve officer, and perhaps known some of the girls in the brothel he was staking out. In addition, the indicted officer had previously served as a reserve officer in the same agency as Officer Garnier. According to the press accounts, the SFPD could not verify this information and the former officer "could not be reached for comment." According to the news accounts, the SFPD officer was fired from the force after pleading to one count of unlawful sex with a minor in which he received a suspended sentence, fine, and probation. The city official also pleaded guilty to patronizing the brothel, was fined $100,000, and "performed six months of community service picking up trash in the city." The chief of police at the time of the murder was reported as saying Officer Garnier's murder was not connected to the prostitution ring and in 1998 reportedly said that while he could not recall saying this, assumed it was the result of information from subordinate officers.

The news media often timelines events in accounts of reporting of events and, in this instance, provided summaries detailing, in part, the careers of the dismissed officer and murder victim Garnier as well as other events:

- Garnier served as a reserve officer in 1980. During this period, the dismissed officer was employed for a private security service at an apartment complex near Broadmoor, had friends on that force, and may have known Garnier.
- Garnier joined the SFPD in 1980 and the dismissed officer in mid-1982.
- One of the brothel ringleaders attended bachelor parties also attended by members of the Broadmoor Police Department and other agencies. The dismissed officer allegedly invited prostitutes to these parties.
- In May 1987, SFPD receives an anonymous letter regarding the brothel. A second letter follows two months later.
- On April 30, 1988, the brothel is raided.
- Capture of one of the brothel owner suspects in Oklahoma on July 9, 1988.
- Officer Garnier was murdered the next day.
- Presence of a grand jury investigation of a prostitution ring specializing in underage girls.
- Capture of the second brothel owner suspect in South Carolina on July 19, 1989, after the case is aired on the television show *America's Most Wanted*.

- Walnut Creek police were reported as interviewing an SFPD narcotics officer who had filed an unsuccessful lawsuit alleging that he had been punished for "blowing the whistle" on corruption within the department.
- Early 1998, SFPD reopens a new investigation as a result of discovery of an internal memorandum in a vice unit file suggesting the presence of a corrupt officer within the unit about the time Garnier was murdered. The SFPD pledges to follow this investigation to wherever it leads.

According to newspaper reports, police were unable to find any link between the death of Officer Garnier and the prostitution ring. In addition, the news reports announce that the San Francisco Police Department had launched a new investigation in early 1998 into the murder of Officer Garnier. Interestingly enough, the news accounts do not report how well Garnier and the dismissed officer knew each other, and noted that this relationship was one that was being investigated.

These accounts reflect concern and anger by SFPD police officials and investigators about their lack of participation in the initial homicide investigation. This decision not to conduct a formal investigation into the death of one of their "own" is reported as a decision that "…still rankles officers in the department," although it occurred in another agency's jurisdiction. These accounts further suggest that Walnut Creek police "…tried with little success" to establish a link between the murder and allegations of corruption or scandals within the SFPD of the period.

According to press reports in 1998, the FBI confirmed that Walnut Creek investigators had requested the Bureau to reopen an investigation into allegations of corruption involving SFPD officers that had been conducted in the mid-1980s. An FBI agent is quoted as saying that Walnut Creek police were interested in knowing if someone from within the SFPD was involved in the murder of Officer Garnier. The request had been denied due to lack of new information.

Based upon review of these four newspaper reports only, and assuming the validity as written, cold case investigators would seek to apply the advantages to be gained from exploiting (1) advanced technology and (2) changes in relationships.

- Changes in technology
    - Automated fingerprint identification system (*AFIS*). Rerun all fingerprints and utilize updated databanks and techniques. Also run them in other local, state, and national databanks.
    - National Integrated Ballistic Information Network (*NIBIN*). Input and run the bullet through updated data banks, despite the age of the case. In addition, due to the growth of laboratories in the region, update publicizing this bullet to local crime laboratories and police agencies. The news reports do not indicate that the shell casings were recovered; however, this avenue would be explored also.
- Changes in relationships
    - It appears from the news media reports that hundreds of persons, including those arrested by the victim, were interviewed against a possible background of corruption and a prostitution ring. These included suspects in the brothel investigation as well as friends and coworkers of the victim. Cold case investigators may seek to identify those for re-contact and interview in light of the intervening years and changes in relationships, as well as to update information they may have "heard" over the years. Among these would be those close to or associated with named principals, and personal or professional relationships.
    - Reinterview those close to the victim for additional statements after passage of time.

The news accounts further suggest exploration and a review of

- Cell phone records (if existent and obtained) and residence or work telephone records of the victim and others. Cell phones were coming of age at this time and were not the compact devices we have today. The carriers have changed many times since this time period, and if these records were not obtained during the initial investigation, they may or may not be available now. How he came to be where he was when reportedly going to a movie with a friend is of interest. In addition
  - Phone records of the two fugitives and communications before the murder
  - Known associates of the two fugitives just before and after the murder
- Parallel duty assignments that might have brought the victim and the deceased officer into possible frequent contacts. Reinterview of coworkers, friends, and associates of each.

These ideas are but a few that may be suggested from review of these media reports. A full, in-depth identification and review of all media accounts may provide further detail for possible exploration. This example is used for illustrative purposes only.

Media Assistance in Cold Case Investigation

Unlike hot homicide investigation, there is no fresh crime scene to which the media responds and begins to take pictures and conduct interviews. In cold cases, the press doesn't know when a cold case is reactivated, and does not learn of it until the case is solved and a news conference is called or a news release is generated by the agency. In the course of cold case investigations, investigators may seek to maintain a low profile to further their efforts until the suspect has been identified and taken into custody. The element of surprise may be a consideration in many of these cases.

In some instances, however, and as an investigation progresses, investigators may decide whether to release information to the public. These situations may include

- Law enforcement efforts to seek new witnesses and tips
- Publishing or running stories on anniversaries of a crime or other significant dates
- Law enforcement attempts to identify property associated with unknown or known victims
- Law enforcement attempts to locate suspects or others

Law enforcement efforts may utilize more proactive methods, depending upon the circumstances of the case. These may include

- National media or special reenactments of crimes and information wanted such as *America's Most Wanted*
- National law enforcement media resources such as the FBI *Law Enforcement Bulletin*
- Written flyers and posters, widespread or localized
- Local televised or radio broadcasts
- Newspaper announcements
- Local magazine or other publications

Figure 12.10 Billboard—Use of media to solicit public information. On June 19, 1991, this young girl apparently answered the doorbell at her family residence in a condominium complex shortly after 9 p.m. A short time later, her family noticed her missing, and her shoes by the door. The next morning, her body was found by workers at a nearby business complex, still wearing the pajamas she had worn when she disappeared. She had been hacked to death. A billboard was utilized to seek information about the case. The murder went unsolved. In October 2003, the DNA Laboratory of the San Diego (California) Police Department discovered a perfect DNA profile match between oral swabs and fingernail material collected from the victim, and the DNA profile of a neighbor, a convicted felon. (Courtesy of Detective Bob Conrad, Chula Vista Police Department.)

Consideration of media resources in furtherance of cold case investigation should not be limited to just newspapers, radio, or television (see Figure 12.10). Seeking information through other forms of media may include Internet websites such as

- Agency World Wide Web site
- Social media
- Special focus websites such as http://doenetwork.org. This volunteer organization assists law enforcement concerning unexplained disappearances and unidentified victims from North America, Australia, and Europe (see Chapter 31).

Case Study

On May 28, 1982, 16-year-old Los Gatos, California, high school student Russell Jordan vanished without a trace. A missing persons report was taken by the Santa Cruz County Sheriff's Office, Jordan's official county of residence. The student disappeared, however, in neighboring Santa Clara County, where he attended school. During the investigation, it was discovered that he had cleaned out his high school locker a month before he disappeared and many presumed the youth was a runaway juvenile. In April 1995, a transient found some bones in Los Gatos Creek not far from the boy's high school. Determined to assist police, the homeless person picked up some bones and carried them to the front counter of the police department.

Responding officers returned to the scene and conducted a detailed search in which they applied anthropological recovery techniques and recovered more remains. Winter rains and wildlife activity had affected the site, however. The skull and other parts were missing and could not be located. Among the items recovered, however, was a distinctive belt buckle. Investigators were aware of the missing juvenile from 13 years before, and believed that this might be the missing boy. The belt buckle was identified as very similar to the one he was last known to be wearing, but could not be considered conclusive proof of identity, however. The remains were turned over to the county coroner. Although the case was treated as a homicide by the police department, they were unable to identify the remains. *Forensic anthropology* examination suggested that the remains were of the same description as the missing boy, but identification was inconclusive.

In late 1999, advances in DNA technology presented the Los Gatos Police Department with the opportunity for further investigative possibility. The remains were sent to the FBI mitochondrial DNA unit. In 2003, this specialized unit of the FBI Laboratory affirmed the identity through *mitochondrial DNA* comparison to the victim's mother.

In March of 2003, the results of the DNA examination were published in the newspapers with a request for information. As a result of this newspaper story, a former classmate of the youth came forward to admit that the missing boy was not a runaway juvenile but in fact had been murdered by another classmate.

Sergeant Tim Morgan and Officer Randy Bishop of the Los Gatos Police Department moved quickly on the investigation. The investigators learned that after Jordan was reported as a runaway, Jordan's friend, Sean Viehweg, had told others that he was not a runaway and admitted that he had killed the boy. Thus, other *classmates* knew but had kept quiet over the decades. Investigators began to interview others in Jordan's close circle of friends, and as a result, obtained the names of two other classmates with knowledge of the murder. In the course of this investigation, officers of this smaller police agency encountered what many in cold case investigation have discovered is not unusual—the need to travel and the extra unbudgeted expense of this particular investigation.

One of the witnesses to the admission still lived locally, but another now lived many miles away in Eureka, in northern California. Morgan and Bishop located and interviewed the second witness, who admitted to helping Viehweg dispose of the body the day after the murder. As a result, investigators obtained an arrest warrant for Viehweg.

Investigation revealed that Viehweg, now 38 years old, lived near Klamath Falls, a small farming community in southern Oregon. In my experience, it is not unusual that suspects in cold case homicides have often moved out of the state in which they committed their crimes. Viehweg was now married and had a family. In the course of planning their strategy for the investigation, the investigators contacted detectives in the Los Angeles Police Department to draw upon their experiences and expertise in this phase of the investigation. This was an excellent tactic on the part of the Los Gatos investigators.

The investigators contacted law enforcement in the jurisdiction where Viehweg now lived, and strategized their investigative plan. In this phase of the investigation, there are no clear-cut rules to define what cold case investigators should do or not do. Each case, and circumstance, is different. Investigators consider the suspect's background and the life he or she has led in the period since the homicide. *Is the suspect a career criminal? Is the suspect a serial killer? Is this the suspect's only crime?* The investigators had checked Viehweg's background. Viehweg had served honorably in the military, including duty in Somalia, Panama, the Persian Gulf, and elsewhere for eight years. Nothing suggested a serious criminal history. Officers were aware, however, that at this phase of the investigation, suspect contact offers a number of options. These may be (1) fight, (2) flight, or (3) admission and/or confession.

Individual investigators have different methods that have worked for them, and here is where experience and training pay off. Sgt. Morgan and Officer Bishop, assisted by officers from the local jurisdiction, contacted Viehweg, in a low-key approach at home. At this initial contact, cold case investigators should note, and record, the *immediate* reaction of a suspect when confronted about the past crime or advised of the investigator's jurisdiction. Observe their *immediate* reaction and record their *exact* words at this initial confrontation with their past. Viehweg turned "white." He agreed to accompany officers to the local law enforcement facility for an interview and Viehweg was arrested on May 17, 2003. He ultimately waived extradition to return to California, and offered a defense that he killed the victim when the victim assaulted him with a knife. The suspect subsequently pleaded no contest on December 18, 2003, to one count of voluntary manslaughter.

Identified cold case issues

- Initial report as missing juvenile
- Knowledge, and silence, by peer group (classmates)
- Recovery of suspected remains but inability to confirm identity
- DNA advances that allow for positive identification of the remains
- News media information and request for information from the public
- Previously silent witness coming forward
- Identification of other witnesses and accomplices
- Suspect out-of-state residence and arrest by local law enforcement agency from another jurisdiction
- Legal considerations of prosecution as juvenile or adult
- Suspect's life style and law-abiding status since the murder
- Age of the case and lack of witnesses to the act

Media and Reporting of Solved Cold Cases

Announcement to the public via the news media of the successful conclusion of a cold case investigation serves a number of purposes. Among these are as follows:

- Announces the identification and arrest of an alleged murderer
- Advises the public that law enforcement has not forgotten these cases, as exemplified by this case solution
- May stimulate others with knowledge of unsolved homicides to come forward with information
- Recognizes the role of the dedicated persons and investigators who made this possible
- Reaffirms the commitment of the police agency to serve and protect the community

Other Guidelines

Prior to the news release or new conference, the victim's family or other concerned persons should be notified. It would not be unusual for the media to locate and contact relatives of the victim and the suspect after the announcement. Efforts to provide victim assistance resources should be made available to the victim's family members as soon as possible upon arrest of the suspect and prior to news release (see Chapter 31).

In cold cases where the victim was a member of a minority community, the agency may consider news or press release to be disseminated to any media groups that focus or are dedicated to that community. As an example, if the victim was a member of a Korean community and that community has a community newspaper or radio or television station, be sure that these entities are notified of the arrest and case developments (see Figure 12.11).

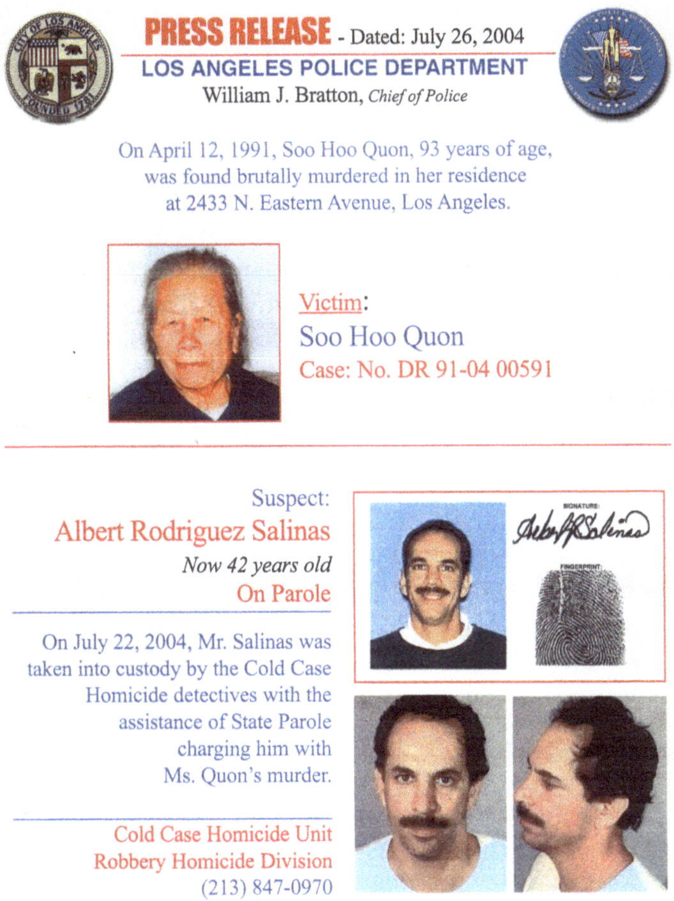

Figure 12.11 Press release to announce a solved cold case homicide. Cold case homicides are the most difficult to solve. When they are, it is incumbent that law enforcement blow its own horn. There can be no better use of resources than to clear an old, unsolved murder. This reassures the public that these victims are not forgotten, and that the law enforcement agency is committed to solving these crimes. In cases involving the member of a minority community and that community has local media, press releases should be brought to their attention in addition to regular press outlets. In this case, the LAPD solved a 13-year-old homicide of an elderly woman. It is no surprise that the offender was a parolee. (Courtesy of Detective Rick Jackson, Los Angeles Police Department Robbery-Homicide, Cold Case Unit.)

Conclusion

Freedom of the press is a hallmark of democracy and a necessary component of our society. The press, like law enforcement, helps to safeguard the public and to expose wrongdoing. For cold case homicide investigations, the press may serve as an information base, providing a record of persons and events sometimes not retained, or found, in the original case file. These records may offer additional avenues of investigation for cold case investigators through reporting of persons, events, and other information pertaining to the crime and related events. In addition, the media may serve to generate public interest and assistance for cold case investigations, and ultimately serve to broadcast the successes of cold case investigations. These successes reflect positively on the law enforcement agency and serve to remind the public, and those who have killed and not yet been caught, that law enforcement does not forget.

Acknowledgments

I wish to recognize and extend my deepest gratitude and appreciation to David Gotfredson of KFMB in San Diego, California. Gotfredson is a veteran newsman and editor and contributed much of the material used as a basis in this chapter. In addition, I wish to also acknowledge and express my deepest gratitude to David Browning for his material, input, and thoughtful review of this chapter. Browning is a veteran producer of news and documentaries for CBS News, covering stories such as the RFK assassination, the Manson murders, the Patty Hearst kidnapping and trial, as well as natural disasters, political conventions, and Hollywood frivolities. In the 1990s, he served in the *CBS Reports* documentary unit, writing and producing the television memoirs of Walter Cronkite and Mike Wallace, and has worked in recent years primarily for *60 Minutes* as well as occasional production duties for *48 Hours*.

Suggested Readings and Bibliography

Anonymous. (1989). The state: Metro desk. *Los Angeles Times*, p. 2 (January 5, 1989). Los Angeles, CA.

Durant, C. (2005). Humboldt County's cold cases: Can these crimes be solved? *Times-Standard* (May 29, 2005). Eureka, CA.

Gathright, A. (2003). Others knew of killing, D.A. says: Los Gatos students remained silent about 1982 death. *San Francisco Chronicle*, (May 10, 2003). San Francisco.

Ryan, K. (2003). No contest plea in '82 killing of teen. *San Francisco Chronicle*, (December 19, 2003). San Francisco.

Stannard, M. (2003). Arrest in 1982 Los Gatos Killing: Oregon man accused in death of classmate in high school years. *San Francisco Chronicle*, (May 9, 2002). San Francisco.

Stannard, M.B. (2003). Dad says his son admitted to killing: Self-defense claim in 1982 death of Los Gatos classmate. *San Francisco Chronicle*, (May 12, 2003). San Francisco.

Sward, S. and Wallace, B. (1998). Still no suspect, motive in '88 killing of sf cop: '88 slaying stumps Walnut Creek police. *San Francisco Chronicle*, (July 9, 1991 Final Edition). San Francisco.

Sward, S. and Wallace, B. (1991). New probe of s.f. cop's '88 slaying. *San Francisco Chronicle*, (May 20, 1998 Final Edition). San Francisco.

Sward, S. and Wallace, B. (1991). How trail grew cold in '88 s.f. cop killing. *San Francisco Chronicle*, (May 21, 1998 Final Edition). San Francisco.

Wambaugh, J. (2002). *Fire Lover: A True Story*. New York: Avon Books.

Technology

II

Friction Skin Impressions

13

EDWARDO PALMA

Contents

Introduction

On the surface, fingerprint collection and identification might seem easy and simple, but it should be left up to properly trained specialists qualified to collect, develop, and individualize fingerprint evidence. Fingerprint evidence has a long history and is an efficient method of identification if used properly. It has been used successfully to solve many crimes from burglaries to homicides. In some cases, fingerprint evidence is the only evidence connecting the perpetrator to the crime. In other cases, fingerprint evidence is helpful to investigators when it corroborates eyewitness statements or other evidence. Take, for instance, a case in which an eyewitness accuses a certain person of a crime but that suspect adamantly denies involvement. The exclusion of alleged suspects as donors of the fingerprint evidence is just as valuable as identifying the donor. When suspects are eliminated based on fingerprint evidence early in the investigation, the investigators are able to focus their attention and resources elsewhere.

This chapter will enhance the investigator's knowledge of fingerprint evidence from the earliest years of detection methods to the most modern detection methods. The information contained will help investigators appreciate the significant advances made in the past two decades, from 1980 to 2000, in the area of fingerprint detection. In addition, the more recent use of a valid scientific methodology of fingerprint identification/individualization known as *ridgeology*[1] will be presented. Ridgeology uses biology, histology, genetics, and embryology as the basis for establishing the individuality/identification of fingerprints.

In order for this chapter to accomplish the goals set out by the author, we as investigators need to educate ourselves about advances made in the field of fingerprint evidence. For this to be effective, one must appreciate the rich history of fingerprints and the research and development that has pushed the science of fingerprints into the modern era. The science of DNA has held the limelight in forensic science in recent years. However, fingerprints can be differentiated between monozygotic twins, while their DNA profiles cannot be differentiated. In return, fingerprints that lack qualitative and quantitative detail for individualization can be analyzed for DNA content, to obtain a genetic profile of the subject.

Man's Knowledge and Uses of Fingerprints

China would have to be regarded as the birthplace of man's use of fingerprints. In China, the intentional use of fingerprints dates back centuries from the first use of clay seals to the unmistakable use of ink impressions on legal documents. During the Han dynasty, 202–220 BC, the use of clay fingerprint seals to sign official documents was common among officials. In approximately 650 AD, a law book of Yung-Hwui described the use of fingerprints to officially sign divorce matters between a man and a woman. From this, we can surmise that authentication of the seal had to come from a skilled individual who could read the fingerprint by comparing it to an identical matching impression made in either clay or ink.

From China, use of fingerprints spread east to Japan and west to India. The use of fingerprints as a signature is proof that the Chinese understood the significance of fingerprints long before the Englishman Sir William Hershel (1858) collected handprints of natives in India and attempted to claim he was the inventor of modern fingerprinting.[2] The Chinese use of clay fingerprint seals showed that the Chinese understood the significance of fingerprints to establish individuality.

A Chinese crime novel written in the twelfth century by a Chinese author, Shinaingan, entitled *The Story of the River Bank*, says, "Wu Sung captured two women who had killed his brother...He compelled them to ink their fingers and to record their fingerprints" (Farelo 2009, p. 4). Undoubtedly, the Chinese had advanced fingerprinting to a level of acceptance in criminal matters. This, however, appears to be more a coercion of the two women into a confession rather than a comparison of fingerprints to bloody fingerprints at a murder scene. This is significant, because the West did not see a crime novel with a fingerprint connection written until the nineteenth century, by well-known American novelist Mark Twain.

Mark Twain's novel *Pudd'nhead Wilson* (1893) tells about a fictional detective who makes use of fingerprints in a criminal proceeding. Pudd'nhead, an attorney, identifies two twins by their fingerprints and assures the jury he will use them to convict the murderer. This Mark Twain novel was written two years after Vucetich's fingerprint classification system was proven practical enough to be placed in service. Juan Vucetich (born Josip Vucetic) (1858–1925), a Croatian-born Argentinean schooled in anthropology,

[1] 1983, new word coined by David R. Ashbaugh of the Royal Canadian Mounted Police used to describe a scientific method of analysis, comparison, and evaluation of friction skin incorporating friction ridge detail viewed in three levels of detail for individualization.

[2] It is documented in the late nineteenth century that both Henry Faulds and Juan Vucetich knew fingerprints were used in China and that Vucetich traveled to China and India to further educate himself on the subject of fingerprints.

became a police official with the Central Police Department, La Plata, Argentina, where he pioneered the use of fingerprints. Vucetich acknowledged reading about the research of another fingerprint pioneer, Sir Francis Galton (1822–1911), in the journal *Revue Scientific*. Vucetich took that research and expanded Galton's ideas to form a working classification system for filing and retrieving fingerprints. He also used the same crime-solving ideas put forward by still another fingerprint pioneer, Henry Faulds (1843–1930). Faulds is given credit for first suggesting the use of fingerprints in a criminal case and writing about it in a letter published in the British scientific journal *Nature* on October 28, 1880.

Dr. Henry Faulds, who studied medicine in Scotland, was sent to Japan as a doctor and evangelist. He became surgeon superintendent and opened the Tuskiji Hospital in Tokyo. While studying prehistoric pottery shards, he saw that finger marks were made before the clay had hardened and remained after firing. Later, he observed that bloody finger marks might lead to the scientific identification of criminals by comparison of the papillary ridges, especially if a previous record of all 10 finger marks had been taken. He suggested that fingerprints could be used in investigations to eliminate an accused individual, and also to prove identity by comparison of finger marks left at scenes of crimes by the criminal.

Faulds states in his letter published in the scientific journal of that day,

> I have had experience in two such cases, and found useful evidence in these marks. In one case greasy finger marks revealed who had been drinking some rectified spirits. The pattern was unique, and fortunately I had had previously obtained a copy of it. They agreed with microscopic fidelity. In the other case sooty finger marks of a person climbing a white wall were of great use as negative evidence. Other cases might occur in medicolegal investigations, as when only the hands of some mutilated victim were found.

To accomplish this comparison Faulds suggested that a very small dab of printer's ink could be spread thinly over the surface of a slate or smooth board to record the pattern of the papillary lines of a finger (Figure 13.1). Although it is now known that China had practiced what Faulds had suggested in his letter for centuries, he states in his letter, "I have heard since coming to these general conclusions…that the Chinese

Figure 13.1 The black lines represent the friction ridges of the fingerprint. The white spaces between the lines are furrows. The print was recorded with black printer's ink.

criminals from early times have been made to give the impressions of their fingers just as we make ours yield their photographs" (Faulds 1880, p. 605).

Faulds, through his own curiosity while studying ancient pottery, rediscovered this practice and became the first European to suggest the practice to the West.

By 1891, Vucetich's fingerprint classification system was proven practical enough to be placed in service in the La Plata Police Department. In 1892, Vucetich made the first positive fingerprint identification in a murder case. The case was the bloody murder of two young brothers. The mother maintained that an outsider had committed the murders. Vucetich, nonetheless, committed to his ideas about the possibility of identifying a bloody fingerprint, continued to investigate. He discovered that the bloody fingerprint belonged to the mother of the murdered boys, which ultimately led to her confession.

The Argentinean police adopted Vucetich's method of fingerprint classification, which spread to police forces of Spanish-speaking countries around the world. Vucetich personally classified 101 different types of fingerprints based on Sir Francis Galton's incomplete taxonomy of fingerprint patterns. Vucetich went on to identify 23 more felons with his method of classification. On September 1, 1891, his system of fingerprint classification was adopted. However, a decade would pass before Henry De Forrest at the New York Civil Service Commission introduced fingerprints into the United States. Today, there are many millions of sets of computerized fingerprint records in the Federal Bureau of Investigation's (FBI's) Next Generation Identification (NGI) and automated fingerprint identification system (AFIS).

Fingerprint Identification: Then and Now

On May 25, 1995, crime scene investigators (CSI) arrived at the house of a prominent Pasadena, California, resident to investigate the murder of an 82-year-old female who lived at that residence. The Pasadena Police Department suspected that she was murdered during the commission of a burglary. At the request of the Pasadena Police Department, three Los Angeles County Sheriff's Department CSI investigators responded to the murder scene and proceeded to brush black fingerprint powder over all likely surfaces that could possibly retain fingerprints.

Fingerprints recovered from crime scenes in police circles are known as *latent prints*. The word *latent* is derived from the Latin word *latent*, which means "to lie hidden." Black fingerprint powder has a long history of successful use in bringing out or making a latent print visible when brushed with a carbon, fiberglass, or camel-hair brush to reveal the hidden fingerprints. Black fingerprint powder is commonly used on nonporous surfaces such as glass, metal, finished, or painted wood surfaces. Other colors have been employed to provide appropriate contrast on particular surfaces.

Shortly after their arrival, the sheriff's department personnel were able to recover fingerprints from the suspected entry point. The CSI team, being expert fingerprint examiners themselves, recognized that the fingerprint impressions were not from the victim. They saw that the prints recovered showed no signs of skin creases or flattening of fingerprint ridges that the 82-year-old victim would have. The recovered latent prints were crisp and clear, so clear that that the fingerprints warranted a rush to the nearest bureau that operated a computer terminal specifically designed to read fingerprints.

The input into an AFIS would require preparation in the form of photography and other specialized techniques devised in Japan that were introduced into the United States in 1983. The fingerprint was photographed with Polaroid film to produce an enlarged 5:1 image of the fingerprint. The technician placed a semiclear Mylar foil over the fingerprint image, tracing with a pencil the ridgelines of the fingerprint. The purpose of this tracing is to remove unwanted background noise and provide high-contrast ridgelines for the computer fingerprint scanner. The scanner then converts the image into a digitized signal. Computer software then converts the unique fingerprint characteristics into a string of numbers. AFIS provides a rapid search of these known fingerprint number strings that are unique to that particular fingerprint. However, because of possible distortion in fingerprint characteristics,[3] the number strings may vary. Consequently, fingerprint experts are required to review and verify all possible fingerprint hits suspected to correspond.

In this case, CSI Bill Leo did a fingerprint comparison to verify the AFIS hit and identified suspect James Edgar Williamson Jr., a step-grandson of the victim. An arrest warrant was obtained based on the fingerprint evidence found in the vicinity of the point of entry that strongly implicated the step-grandson. Williamson, upon hearing the news media broadcast, decided to turn himself in at a nearby Orange County fire station.

Without the technology of an AFIS, the aforementioned case could have easily gone unsolved for many years. When the perpetrator of a crime is not a relative or acquaintance and the death is the outcome of a chance encounter, the chances are increased that the case will eventually turn into a cold case. Fingerprint evidence properly collected and preserved, either by fingerprint powder and lifting tape or by photography, will be available for review for decades.

Millions of fingerprint cards maintained by the FBI have been submitted since 1924, when Congress established the Bureau of Identification to fill the need for a national repository of fingerprint cards, which were then stored and searched using the Henry classification system that originated in England in 1901. Up until that time, fingerprint cards were classified, stored, and searched by fingerprint classifiers that require all 10 fingerprints to obtain a classification formula to file the card. Searching a single or partial fingerprint like a latent print was next to impossible. Single-fingerprint systems like the Battley single-fingerprint system were devised and employed using a 3 × 5–inch card whereupon a rolled and plain impression was placed and then classified. The Battley system used a separate classification glass from the one used for the Henry classification system. The Henry system used a reticle glass with the straight classification line placed over the fingerprint, whereas the Battley system employed a reticle glass with seven concentric rings that was used to obtain the necessary information about each single print. The FBI modified the classification ring so both Henry and Battley classifications could be done with one reticle. The fingerprint information was gleaned from two focal points—the core (center) and the delta. Once the latent print information was classified, the print could be searched through the Battley single-fingerprint files.

The FBI gave up on the Battley system and then used the five-finger classification. The left and right hands from a separate fingerprint card were filed separately. A latent fingerprint developed at a crime scene had potential as evidence, but that rested on being able to identify a suspect to compare his/her fingerprints or classify the latent print with a Battley-classifying ring and manually search a single–fingerprint file. This action proved to be an expensive task with long hours of searching fingerprint files only to find that many prints were never identified.

Two decades of research and development in America, Japan, and Europe and the resulting computer hardware and software were needed to handle the millions of fingerprints stored in static file cabinets. The biggest technological leap forward came when development of computer technology and optical image storage became sophisticated enough in mid-1980 that a computer could handle large volumes of fingerprint data. In fact, some computer processors and storage devices were specifically built to handle fingerprint data. The only task remaining was to convert fingerprint cards containing inked fingerprints into a digitized format that computers could analyze.

The FBI database is a collection of fingerprint records, many of which are electronically submitted to the FBI from state identification bureaus, which in turn have received prints from local law enforcement

3 Distortions to characteristics of fingerprint ridges are caused by many factors, primarily surface-to-skin deposition pressure and lateral pressure when the skin of the finger makes contact with a receiving surface. Distortions can change the appearance of the print, making it unrecognizable when compared to the original. Distortion is more likely to be a cause for failure to individualize fingerprints to the original creator of the fingerprint as opposed to being falsely individualized to another person.

agencies. Law enforcement agencies employing latent print examiners have begun to electronically search latent fingerprints against this national fingerprint database, and many cold fingerprint identifications such as the one cited previously have resulted.

Investigators in cold cases should not assume that just because a previous request for a fingerprint check was unproductive, the same results would be obtained today. The accessibility to larger fingerprint databases has improved, so investigators should re-request fingerprint checks. Investigators should not assume that laboratories have checked every possible file. Investigators should insist on receiving documentation as to which databases their case prints were checked against, i.e., local city and county, regional or neighboring counties, state and regional or neighboring states, and federal. See Chapter 14.

Dermal Friction Skin Ridges: The Living Skin behind the Fingerprint

The skin that is responsible for leaving finger marks is referred to as friction skin. It is found on the palmar side of the hands and plantar side or soles of the feet, including the phalangeal surfaces of the fingers and the toes of the feet. The first person responsible for calling this dermal skin "friction ridges" was David Hepburn (1895) of Scotland. He recognized that the dermal ridges assisted grasping by creating friction. He named the two larger cushion pads of the palm the *thenar* (the cushion pad directly under the thumb) and the *hypothenar* (the cushion pad directly under the little finger). The third area in the palm is called the interdigital area, which lies just below the area where the fingers attach to the palm (Figure 13.2)

Interdigital patterns many times are mistaken for fingerprints. A police officer trained as a fingerprint examiner may not have had formal training on identifying partial palm print impressions. Many partial interdigital loop impressions have been mistaken for fingerprints and thus remain unidentified. A qualified friction skin examiner trained on the orientation and recognition of palm prints should reexamine unidentified fingerprints in cold cases. Partial palm prints, especially from the thenar, hypothenar, and

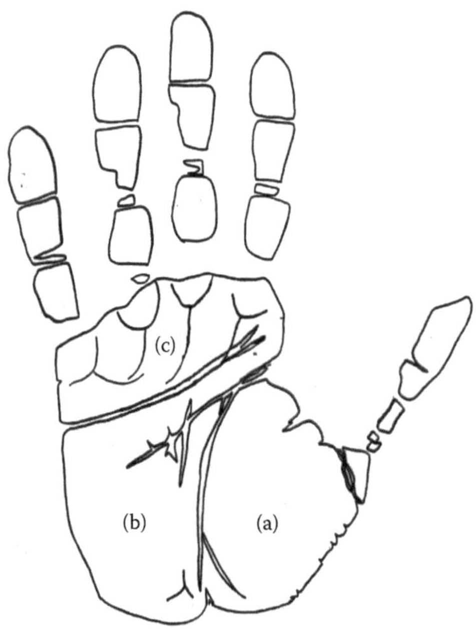

Figure 13.2 Outline of the palmar surface of the right hand. (a) *Thenar* cushion area. (b) *Hypothenar* cushion area. (c) *Interdigital* area containing fingerlike patterns.

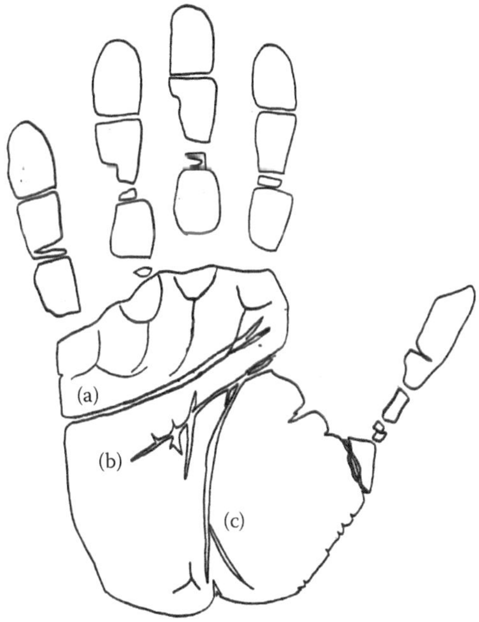

Figure 13.3 (a) Distal transverse crease. (b) Proximal transverse crease. (c) Radial longitudinal crease.

interdigital areas, are found in as many as 30% to 45% of crime scenes. Therefore, manufacturers of automated fingerprint systems have incorporated palm print databases. In many police agencies, the practice of palm print collection has not been customary at the time of booking. Recent legislation has been enacted in some states authorizing collection of palm prints along with DNA samples from convicted felons.

In addition to the pads in the palm, other features are visible. When looking at the palm of the hand, flexion creases are noticeable. These are the folds associated with the joints in the hand that permit it to bend or flex when grasping. Most people have three main flexion creases in the palm (Figure 13.3). The *radial longitudinal crease* separates the thenar and hypothenar. The *proximal transverse crease* and the *distal transverse crease* split the palm horizontally and can be seen when the fingers are drawn to touch the palm nearest the wrist. Although the palm surface contains patterns similar to fingerprint patterns, it has large areas of ridges with no patterns. This friction skin is just as identifiable as finger patterns.

Biology Aspect of Friction Ridge Skin

A specific group of cells, called basal cells, found on the underside top layer of skin called the *epidermis* is responsible for friction skin *uniqueness* and *persistence.* Uniqueness is due to the particular pattern of features in a given area of the friction skin. Distinct ridge features of the skin are randomly created by a burst of basal cells that reach maturity in a fetus at about 24 weeks. Persistency implies that those peculiar features remain the same throughout one's life and are persistent even after death until decomposition totally destroys the skin. The dermis skin is the lower layer of skin that contains blood vessels, nerve endings, and perspiration glands. One can get an understanding of the persistency feature of this very important cell layer made up of basal cells by observing what happens when our skin is cut or abraded. Some injuries to the skin do not penetrate the basal layer. A surface injury is noticeable only for about two weeks. The area of the skin that was affected by the injury will heal and return to its original appearance. However, when the skin is cut more deeply and bleeds, basal cells are destroyed. When the skin heals, it heals with a scar,

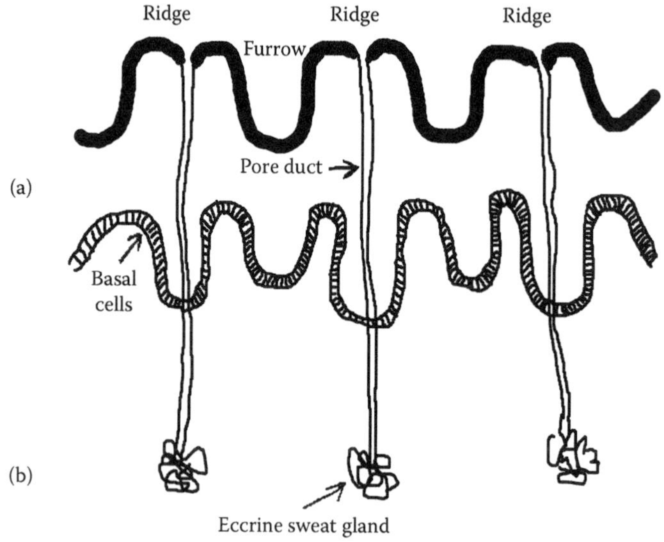

Figure 13.4 Friction ridge skin cross-section view. (a) Epidermis, or upper layer of skin. (b) Dermis, or lower layer of skin.

especially noticeable in the friction skin. Scars in the friction skin lend additional individualizing characteristics to the skin.

In 1684, Nehemiah Grew described sweat pores, epidermal ridges, and their various arrangements in a scientific paper on the subject. Scientists over the years have used developments in biology, embryology, genetics, mathematics, and physics to help describe friction skin and further the science of fingerprints. Recently, a *holistic* approach has been used in examination of fingerprints. No longer is the fingerprint identification determined by a threshold number of *points of identity.* The holistic approach incorporates a scientific method called ridgeology wherein the fingerprint specialist makes a complete study of the ridgeline structure and shape, down to near-microscopic level, for agreement of detail between the latent and known impressions.

Skin gland activity is a natural biological phenomenon where water and salt along with other organic mixtures of amino acids, semisolid fatty acids, and proteins are secreted to the skin surface. The *eccrine* gland is the gland found in the tissues of the hands and feet, and it dispenses moisture (>98%) over the entire skin surface and, most importantly, to the underside of hands and feet. This distribution of moisture is through a series of pore ducts found on the top of friction ridge skin. Through a simple touch of a surface, this moisture can deposit an outline or pattern of the friction skin on the surface touched (Figures 13.4 and 13.5) The raised skin can also transfer oils and moisture from one's own body to another surface by touching other areas of the body before touching a surface. *Sebaceous* and *apocrine* glands, associated with hair follicles, secrete oily secretions that contain proteins, carbohydrates, sterols, glycerides, fatty acids, wax ester, and squalene. These secretions are easily picked up and transferred by the friction ridge skin of the fingers.

When one looks closely at the friction skin of the hand, what are seen are two distinct shades of color in the skin. The darker of the two, providing the skin is clean and not contaminated, is actually the furrow. This is the space between the raised ridges. The actual raised ridge is between the darker furrow lines and is more translucent because of the mammalian *epithelium skin*, which is made up of cornified (keratinized) cells that are stratified to make up the *epidermis* layer that forms the ridge structure.[4]

[4] The outer nonsensitive and nonvascular epithelial layer of the skin that overlies the dermis layer.

Figure 13.5 Fingerprint on newspaper that was digitally enhanced to suppress the black type letters.

In Figure 13.1, the black lines represent the friction ridges of the fingerprint. The white spaces between the black lines are furrows. The print was recorded with black printer's ink.

The basal layer of epithelial stem cells is responsible for the proliferation of epidermal cells, referred to as keratinocytes, which appear as stratified tissue that forms the upper epidermis layer of skin. These cornified (keratinized) bundles of cells are being pushed, up forming the strata layers of the epidermis. Friction ridge skin forms by the 16th week of gestation. The proliferation of cells continues after birth to sustain the permanence of friction ridge structure, and that permanence is one of the bases for friction ridge identification of fingerprint patterns.

The actual individualization of *latent* prints is made possible because of two biological factors. First, as basal stem cells divide proliferating keratinocytes, they move in tandem toward the skin surface by resilient bundles or cables that anchor to cell–cell junctions called *desmosomes*. Thus, desmosomes and basal cells provide the basis for permanence of the friction ridge structure. Second, the eccrine sweat gland distributed over the entire friction skin area exudes perspiration that is 98% water but also contains organic and inorganic compounds.

The perspiration helps maintain pliable skin that enables precision gripping or power grasping by the hand. Friction ridges are coated with continuous perspiration that is exuding from the pore openings located on the top of the ridges. When these ridges contact a surface, either porous (e.g., paper, wood, or cardboard) or nonporous (e.g., glass, metal, or plastic), an outline of the friction ridge design is transferred to that surface, which is typically a partial image of the finger, palm, or both. The same holds true with a bare foot and an impression of a bare foot.

Sebum is waxy oil from the *sebaceous* gland. Sebaceous and apocrine glands are not found on the papillary skin but, rather, are associated with hair follicles on other areas of the body. Therefore, the waxy oil found on the friction ridges is considered a natural contaminant from other areas of the body.

Knowing what the constituents are that are found on friction ridges from eccrine secretions or from the sebaceous and apocrine glands assists CSIs in approaching latent print sequential chemical processing of the impressions at crime scenes. After determining which constituents may be present on the item, the next step is selecting the type or types of latent print developments to employ. Table 13.1 combines in one easy view (surface + (source) + process) to aid in selecting a development process. For further clarification of the table, the source indicates (1) sebaceous or fatty acids; (2) eccrine or water and amino acids—amines; and (3) dried blood, which is made up of amines and proteins. Photograph all bloody fingerprints before applying fingerprint powder, and, at this point, determine if protein stains are needed.

Fingerprint Processes

In the past few decades, techniques for developing latent fingerprints[5] have rapidly expanded from the traditional black powder method to more sophisticated fluorescent powders and cyanoacrylate (CA) or superglue fuming techniques. The old iodine fuming method has taken a backseat to the CA common superglue method because of the versatility of CA to be stained or powdered for visualization. We have also seen a shift from the use of silver nitrate for detecting salt residue from fingerprints to a more refined mixture called physical developer (PD).

The traditional ninhydrin reagent (NIN) for staining amino acids found in latent fingerprints is still the workhorse for processing porous surfaces such as paper; however, chemical advances with amino acid–specific reagents called *ninhydrin analogs* are better suited because of their luminescent selectivity where surface background interference is an issue on porous surfaces.

Lasers and alternate light sources (ALSs) or forensic light sources (FLSs) capable of delivering monochromatic light are useful as forensic tools. These instruments help extend the visual capability of the human eye to see and record fingerprints that might otherwise be considered to be of no value for identification. Now investigators are routinely developing fingerprints on surfaces previously thought to be incapable of yielding fingerprints. This is significant for cold case investigators.

Investigators can no longer ignore surfaces that have been wet or are wet when encountered. Development of fingerprints exposed to water through condensation or rain can be achieved using small-particle reagent (SPR), which uses molybdenum disulfide powder in a detergent solution, or PD, a salt-silver developer that is used for the detection of fingerprints on paper even if the paper had been wet.

Two Types of Fingerprint Evidence

Before continuing a discussion about fingerprint evidence, we must have an understanding of the two types of fingerprint evidence encountered at crime scenes: *visible impressions* and *nonvisible impressions*.

1. Visible (patent) print impressions.
   a. Friction ridges from the fingers, palms, soles, or toes made deliberate with ink or live scan for recording known impressions
   b. Nondeliberate fingers, palms, soles, or toes contaminated with, i.e., blood, paint, grease, grime, etc.

[5] Latent fingerprint is a common term for all unseen finger and palm print impressions made from body perspiration and oils deposited on objects.

Table 13.1 Fingerprint Processing Table

Nonporous Surface	(Source) Process	Semiporous Surface	(Source) Process	Porous Surface	(Source) Process
Glass: **Ceramic** **Tile** **Pottery** **Eyeglass lens**	(1)(2)(3) Cyanoacrylate fuming and fingerprint powder (3) Photograph (Triplett, 2006)	**Glossy (multicolored) paper:** **Magazines** **Book covers** **Mail flier inserts** **Photographs**	(1)(2) Cyanoacrylate fuming and florescent powder (2) Indanedione (3) Photograph (Triplett, 2006)	**Paper:** **Currency** **Newspaper** **Book pages** **Map** **Bag**	(1) Iodine vapor—photograph (2) DFO or ninhydrin reagent (Triplett, 2006)
Metal: **Aluminum** **Steel** **Brass** **Copper** **Lead**	(1)(2)(3) Cyanoacrylate fuming and fingerprint powder (3) Photograph	**Wallpaper** **Latex paint**	(1)(2) Ninhydrin reagent Black fingerprint powder or florescent fingerprint powder	**Cardboard:** **Ammunition box** **Shipping box**	(1) Iodine vapor (2) DFO or ninhydrin reagent
Plastic: **Polyvinyl chloride (PVC)** **Baggies** **Vinyl** **Film** **Eyeglass lens** **Purse** **Wallet**	(1)(2)(3) Cyanoacrylate fuming and fingerprint powder (3) Photograph			**Cloth:** **Bedsheets** **Pillowcases** **Shirt** **Blouse** **Pants** **Jacket**	(1) Iodine vapor (2) DFO or ninhydrin reagent
Finished wood: **Furniture** **Rifle stock** **Pistol grip**	(1)(2)(3) Cyanoacrylate fuming and fingerprint powder (3) Photograph	**Wood (treated)**	(1)(2) Ninhydrin reagent Cyanoacrylate fuming followed up with black fingerprint powder or florescent fingerprint powder	**Unfinished wood**	(2) Ninhydrin reagent

(*Continued*)

Table 13.1 (Continued) Fingerprint Processing Table

Nonporous Surface	(Source) Process	Semiporous Surface	(Source) Process	Porous Surface	(Source) Process
Leather (treated): **Wallet** **Holster** **Belt**	(1)(2)(3) Cyanoacrylate fuming and fingerprint powder (3) Photograph			**Cork:** **Wine bottle** **Bulletin board**	(2) Ninhydrin reagent
Smooth stone: **Polished rock** **Countertop**	(1)(2)(3) Fingerprint powder or cyanoacrylate fuming followed by fingerprint powder (3) Photograph			**Leather (nontreated)**	(1) Iodine vapor (2) DFO or ninhydrin reagent
Fruit and leafy plants	(1)(2) Fingerprint powder				
Wet surface (let it air-dry)	(1)(2)(3) Fingerprint powder or Cyanoacrylate fuming and fingerprint powder	**Wet surface (let air-dry)**	Process as above depending on surface	**Wet surface (let it air-dry)**	Process as above depending on surface or physical developer
Dried bloody fingerprints	(3) Photograph Fingerprint powder Protein stain	**Dried bloody fingerprints**	(3) Photograph Fingerprint powder Protein stain	**Dried bloody fingerprints**	(3) Photograph Fingerprint powder Protein stain

Source: Margot, P., and Lennard C. (1994). *Fingerprint Detection Techniques.* Lausanne, Switzerland: Universite De Luasanne; Triplett, M. (2006). *Fingerprint Dictionary.* Bellevue, Washington: Two Rings Publishing. Courtesy of Edwardo Palma.

   c. Nondeliberate fingers, palms, soles, or toes depressed or indented into malleable material, e.g., wet paint, chewing gum, grease, etc.; commonly called *molded* or *plastic* impressions
   d. Negative print impression where fingers, palms, soles, or toes, through touch, remove material from the surface
2. Nonvisible (latent) impressions—these require a physical or chemical development to make them visible.

Factors Affecting whether Fingerprints Are Deposited on or Recovered from a Surface

Not all fingerprints are transferred to a surface, and when there is a transfer, not all fingerprints are usable. Age, gender, occupation, and illnesses may affect whether a person may or may not leave a fingerprint when he/she touches a surface. The pressure involved in touching the surface and the amount of moisture on the finger also play a part in whether a usable fingerprint is left. If the receiving surface is dirty, rough, textured, or contoured, the chances are diminished that a usable fingerprint will be left. A fingerprint may appear smudged due to excess perspiration and pressure. It may be that too limited an area of the finger is transferred, such that there are insufficient characteristics to make it useful for individualization.

Environmental conditions after the fingerprint is deposited are critical for the recovery of a good usable fingerprint. Heat can affect the latent print constituents by evaporating moisture or hardening fats and waxes in the latent print, leaving the print dry and incapable of absorbing fingerprint powder. Wet conditions can wash away water-soluble constituents like chloride salts and amino acids, thus affecting the chemical reaction of reagents like ninhydrin, 1,8-diazafluoren-9-one (DFO), and silver nitrate. However, a wet condition may not affect a fingerprint that contains a significant amount of sebaceous secretions.

Fingerprints deposited on surfaces are delicate. Latent print impressions can easily be accidentally wiped off during processing or unintentionally damaged or lost by mishandling of evidence. Latent prints can be damaged by an improper processing technique or an improper chemical sequence during the recovery procedure. Latent prints developed without regard to chemical sequencing can limit the processing potential of a print, leaving the print faint or overdeveloped and difficult to examine. Following proper processing guidelines during the recovery mode is critical for the successful development of usable latent print impressions.

Surfaces

Whenever fingerprint detection is necessary, the first and foremost element to consider is the type of surface involved that contains the latent print impression. The type of surface dictates the type of process to use for the development and recovery of fingerprints. There are three types of surfaces that all fingerprint technicians recognize. Identifying the surface is the first step in choosing the proper sequences and types of processes to use to develop fingerprints.

1. Nonporous surfaces
2. Porous surfaces
3. Adhesive surfaces

Examples of *nonporous* surfaces:

a. Glass
b. Metal
c. Plastic
d. Fired ceramic
e. Glossy painted surfaces

Examples of *porous* surfaces:

a. Unfinished wood
b. Paper
c. Cardboard
d. Fabric
e. Unfired ceramic
f. Nongloss painted surfaces

Adhesive surfaces can be found on many commercial tapes—masking tape, duct tape, electrician's tape, etc. Tapes contain two surfaces: the sticky side and the backing material, which can be made of paper, plastic, cloth, or a combination.

Sequencing

A sequence in applying enhancement techniques must be considered to optimize fingerprint recovery. An improper application of a fingerprint development process can restrict or limit any further development techniques used later on. It was once thought that the use of powders excluded the use of chemicals, but advances in technology have changed that assumption. For example, an application of black powder on nonporous surfaces could lessen the chances of developing amino acids using ninhydrin, but vacuum metal deposition (VMD) can be used after black powder application because the powder may have not developed prints that the VMD possibly could. There are so many processes available today that processing manuals or guides should be considered before applying any detection method for developing fingerprints.

The suggested sequence for testing a nonporous surface thought to contain fingerprints is as follows:

1. Visual examination of the surface with a strong light in a darkened room.
2. Examination with laser or ALS for any inherent fingerprint fluorescence.
3. CA fuming the object to polymerize fingerprints called polycyanoacrylate (a white crystalline powder that hardens the print to the surface).
4. Reexamination with laser or ALS for any surface reflectance yielding fingerprints.
5. Dye staining of the polycyanoacrylate.
6. Reexamination with laser or ALS for any luminescence yielding fingerprints.
7. For small to medium objects, test surface with a VMD.
8. Visual surface examination with a strong light.
9. Test surface with fingerprint powder.[6]
10. With conventional powders, reexamination visually with light; utilize laser or ALS when fluorescent powders are employed.

[6] Conventional or magnetic black or gray powder, or fluorescent powders.

The suggested sequence for testing a porous surface is as follows:

1. Visual examination
2. Check for inherent fluorescence using laser or ALS
3. Iodine fuming
4. DFO
5. Laser or ALS
6. Ninhydrin
7. PD

Adhesive Surfaces

Adhesive surfaces in the past were mostly ignored as a viable surface for fingerprint recovery, so in many homicide cases, only the nonadhesive surface would have been tested for fingerprints. Today, fingerprints can be detected with the proper technique on both the adhesive side and the backing material. Developing fingerprints on tape is relatively simple. Moreover, the approach and selection of powder or chemical should be an experimental exercise on similar tape to learn and understand the kind of results possible. One thing that must be considered is the protection of the adhesive side of the tape while processing the backing, and vice versa. A product called Un-do found at local craft stores can be used to separate or unstick the tape adhesion when the condition is either adhesive to adhesive or adhesive to surface. As the Un-do solvent is applied, the tape can gently be pulled apart. Once separated, the adhesive is allowed to dry thoroughly before applying a fingerprint development technique. However, the two sides of the tape will require different processing techniques to visualize fingerprints.

Here are some suggestions for sequencing adhesive tape development.

Nonadhesive side of tape:

1. Visual examination
2. Inherent fluorescence, using laser or ALS
3. CA fuming
4. Laser or ALS
5. Dyeing of CA
6. Laser or ALS
7. VMD
8. Powder

Adhesive side of tape:

1. Visual
2. Inherent fluorescence by laser or ALS
3. Sticky-side powder (SSP); alternate black or white[7] powder; gentian violet
4. Laser or ALS

[7] Best on black electrical tape.

Bloody Fingerprints on Porous and Nonporous Surfaces

When testing bloodstained impressions on *nonporous* surfaces, the practice in the past was to photograph visible bloody fingerprint impressions and then dust with black fingerprint powder before lifting with tape. Today, powdering practices have shifted to chemicals that react with the protein in blood residue, generally producing a bright purple color. An advantage to chemical development over powder dusting is brighter development and finer detail enhancement of the friction skin pattern. In the past, ninhydrin was used (to react with the amino acids in the blood) for enhancing bloody prints. Blood detection chemicals were also used, but they were usually the carcinogenic benzidine-type chemicals that are not advisable for use. Investigators examining cold case evidence that may have been previously tested for blood should practice personal safety by utilizing latex gloves and other safety equipment when examining evidence in cold cases that may have been exposed to carcinogens.

To preserve and enhance friction ridge detail of bloody fingerprints, the following protein enhancement chemicals are suggested:

1. Amido black
2. Coomassie brilliant blue
3. Crowle's double stain
4. Aqueous leucocrystal violet (LCV)
5. Fuchsin red (Hungarian red)
6. Benzoxanthene yellow

These chemical reagents are excellent choices with advantages because bloody impressions can be fixed before staining. Detection is carried out in a lighted environment, and basic forensic photography techniques can be used in the collection and preservation (as opposed to the use of luminol or fluorescein in a darkened room). These stains provide an advantage over heme-reactive chemicals, in that the resulting friction ridge detail will be sharper. However, if the application is to detect traces of bloody fingerprints on *dark surfaces* and for subsequent DNA testing, Bergeron (2003) suggested using a methanol-based suspension of titanium dioxide. Other heme-reacting chemicals are

1. Fluorescein
2. Phenolphthalein
3. Leucomalachite
4. Tetramethybenzidine
5. Luminol

Keep in mind that other latent print impressions may have been deposited on the nonporous surface as well. CA preprocessing can preserve latent prints that might otherwise be destroyed by the protein-staining technique. Research has shown that CA preprocessing is best followed by amido black when applying a sequential technique for developing bloody fingerprint impressions and latent fingerprints on nonporous surfaces.

Standard Fingerprint Detection/Recovery Techniques

Visual technique enhanced with oblique light#[8]: Deposits of latent fingerprints reflect light. Visually looking at a surface with oblique light can reveal the location of fingerprints.

[8] Fingerprint detection techniques suffixed with # symbol have been used 25 or more years.

Photography#: Latent fingerprints can be photographed at times without any pretreatment of powders or chemicals.

Ultraviolet (UV) light#: UV light and some inexpensive LED blue lights are useful for observations of reflection or absorption of wet and dry bloody fingerprints. UV light also can be used to observe fluorescence of special powders and chemicals used to treat fingerprints.

*CA**[9]: CA is the active ingredient in superglue, and the fumes are attracted to the moisture of fingerprints. Research has shown that various heating methods for fuming CA work well. However, CA fumes are irritating to the mucus membrane and must be contained in a fuming chamber or tank. The chamber must be aired out before retrieving objects containing fingerprints. Developed fingerprints can be dye stained and photographed, and then powdered for lifting.

Dye Stains

- *Rhodamine 6G**: Widely used dye for staining latent prints developed with CA. UV light can be used to visualize the fluorescence.
- *Ardox**: A yellow oily fluorescent chemical used to dye-stain CA-fumed fingerprints. Can be applied full strength or diluted, and then rinsed with tap water. The surface must be thoroughly dry before viewing with UV light or special blue lights.
- *Basic yellow**: A brilliant yellow dye stain applied after CA.

Powders

- *Fingerprint powders*#: Powders adhere to both water and fatty deposits of fingerprints. The choice of powder depends on the surface condition and color. Some specialized powders have fluorescent properties that can be used with UV light or special blue lights. Prints are photographed or lifted with tape.
- *SPR**: The active ingredient is molybdenum disulfide particles that adhere to fatty components of latent prints. This method is useful for detecting fingerprints on wet surfaces.

Adhesive Reagents

- *SSP**: This material adheres to the fingerprint on the adhesive side of tape. This is a wet process where the powder is painted on the adhesive side of tape and rinsed with tap water to reveal fingerprints. Various tapes respond differently to this process so testing should be carried out on similar tape before proceeding with actual evidence.
- *Gentian violet (crystal violet)**: This is a fat-soluble stain that can develop fingerprints on adhesive tape surfaces. The prints are stained dark purple against the light-background tape.
- *Iodine*#: Iodine is a temporary development process for fingerprints. Iodine fumes react with fatty deposits to produce a yellow-brown reaction that dissipates over time, making the prints no longer visible. Developed fingerprints must be photographed before they dissipate. Porous and nonporous surfaces can be fumed.
- *Ninhydrin*#: This is used to recover fingerprints on porous surfaces. Ninhydrin reacts with amino acids in a latent print. Depending on the composition of the print, the developing time could be from a few minutes to several days. Heat and humidity can be used to accelerate the process, so that developing time can be reduced to a few minutes. Prints must be photographed.

[9] Fingerprint detection techniques suffixed with * symbol were increasingly used for the observation, detection, or enhancement of fingerprint traces within the last 10 or more years.

- *Silver nitrate*#: This chemical reacts with sodium chloride in the skin secretions, developing fingerprints on porous surfaces. Reactions must be photographed to recover fingerprints before background discoloration occurs.

Blood Reagents

- *LCV**: This presumptive test for blood is highly sensitive for developing visible and invisible blood trace fingerprints. It is applied by spraying nonporous surfaces and some porous surfaces containing traces of bloody prints. Prints must be photographed to be recovered.
- *Ninhydrin*#: Ninhydrin reacts with amino acids in blood. The nonaccelerated method should be used. Fingerprints must be photographed to be recovered.
- *Ruthenium tetroxide (RTX)**: Modified RTX is a simple and rapid application. Surfaces can be fumed, dipped, or sprayed to reveal sebaceous fingerprints. Prints must be photographed to be recovered. However, on some surfaces, prints can be lifted with lifting tape and transferred to a backing card.

Prints from Human Skin

Human skin is a difficult surface for the development of fingerprints. Environmental conditions and body temperature are critical and must be controlled as soon as the body is discovered. Most attempts to develop fingerprints on human skin are not successful. However, it should be attempted. The following techniques are simple and rapid for the detection of latent print on human skin.

- *Iodine/silver-plate transfer*#: First iodine fumes are directed over the suspected area using a fuming wand, which requires blowing one's breath through the tube, warming the iodine crystals. The crystals sublime to a gaseous state. Fumes turn yellowish brown in contact with sebaceous latent prints. A silver-plated small metal sheet is then gently pressed against the surface for a few seconds. The plate is then exposed to UV light or sunlight. When conditions are right, a dark fingerprint image appears. The plate must immediately be removed from the light and the print image photographed.
- *CA*#: The body is tented and fumed with CA. Powder or a dye stain is applied to enhance fingerprints for viewing.
- *RTX**: The modified version described previously is fumed with a fuming apparatus that consists of a small glass jar with an inlet tube and an exit tube. Fumes are directed from the exit tube to the surface suspected of containing latent prints. Sebaceous prints present under the right conditions develop a light gray color. Fingerprints are recorded photographically. Lifting with fingerprint tape can sometimes be employed. However, background skin surface texture can interfere, making some lifts unacceptable for comparisons.

Sophisticated Fingerprint Detection/Recovery Techniques

Specialized Light Sources Designed for Forensic Use

- *Light amplification by stimulated emission of radiation (LASER)*: Since the late 1970s, lasers have been in limited use for the detection of forensic evidence. Four types of lasers have been employed: the argon ion, the Nd:YAG, the copper vapor, and the tunable dye laser. Those in the blue-green bandwidth are most popular. Some laser equipment requires dedicated electrical power and a cooling system to keep it within operating temperatures, so portability is eliminated. The Nd:YAG laser is a pulsating laser that has portability, but the pulse is annoying while examining fingerprints.

- *ALSs/FLSs*: High-intensity white-light lamps fitted with filters capable of selecting a monochromatic band of light in bandwidths from UV radiation through to the red end of the visible spectrum. These specialized light sources are well suited for crime scene use due to their portability. Although the ALS/FLS does not have the light intensity that a laser has, with proper use, it can be just as effective.

Digital Photography

Digital photography is rapidly replacing traditional silver-based film. Detailed image information not discernible to the human eye can be controlled by computer keyboard inputs to enhance its visibility. Developed latent fingerprints can be captured with digital cameras or flatbed scanners and then processed using digital enhancement software. Most popular among fingerprint specialists is Adobe software. Off-the-shelf software can mimic darkroom photography techniques that are common among fingerprint specialists. Some specialized routines like fast Fourier transform (FFT) are useful to remove repeating background patterns, thereby effectively bringing out the obscured detail of a fingerprint. In 1995, this technique was used in a murder case in the state of Washington to enhance a palm print in blood on a bedsheet that was processed with amido black. The technician suppressed the fabric background using FFT, enhancing the palm print. The palm print was later identified to the suspect (*State of Washington v. Eric Hayden*, 1998).

Figures 13.5 and 13.6 demonstrate an example of the sophistication of digital imaging. A fingerprint was detected using ninhydrin on a newspaper. The black ink type visually interfered with the analysis of the fingerprint. The black ink was suppressed using digital imaging, resulting in sufficient ridge detail for AFIS entry.

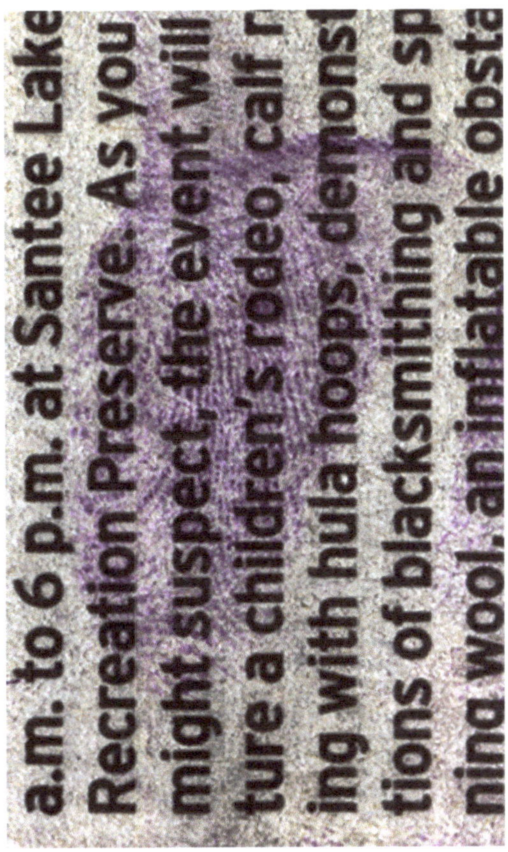

Figure 13.6 Original fingerprint on newspaper.

- *Liquid iodine*#: Iodine/benzoflavone can be used as a fine spray reagent at the crime scene on both porous and nonporous surfaces. Latent prints appear as dark blue impressions.
- *Vacuum CA**: Vacuum chambers develop fingerprints more evenly because the glue fumes distribute throughout the chamber. After fuming, luminescent stains are recommended. This technique is best for firearms. Plastic baggies are also processed in this way.
- *Special fluorescent powders requiring UV or FLS/ALS**: Fluorescent powders work well on dark or multicolored nonporous surfaces.
- *Fluorescent dyes requiring FLS/ALS**: Rhodamine 6G, basic yellow 40, basic red 28, RAM, 4-dicyanomethylene (DCM), NBD chloride, rose bengal, radiant orange, and Styryl 7. Many other luminescent dyes have been used experimentally as CA stains.
- *1,8-Diazafluorenone (DFO)**: This is a fluorescing ninhydrin analog that can develop more fingerprints than ninhydrin itself. This chemical is an excellent choice when reviewing porous evidence such as paper in cold cases.
- *PD**: This chemical is a silver-based developer that is excellent for processing items exposed to water. In the review of cold case homicide evidence, PD is another good choice for evidence previously exposed to iodine and ninhydrin.

*Blood Reagents**

- *Amido black*: A dye that stains proteins present in blood but will not detect normal residue of latent prints. Amido black may be used on porous and nonporous surfaces. It is useful on older bloody fingerprints that have been dry for some time. Amido black is not to be used on heavily blood-stained items. DNA analysis is possible even after application of Amido Black on both porous and nonporous surfaces.
- *Coomassie blue*: This is a dye that binds to protein in bloody fingerprints. The darker blue color is proportionate to the amount of protein found in the blood residue.
- *Crowle's double stain*: This reagent is sensitive to blood but is least effective for DNA recovery from porous items.
- *Multimetal deposition (MMD)**: (PD modified with colloidal gold.) This reagent has the ability to be used on many types of wet or dry porous and nonporous surfaces. Even fingerprints on older evidence items have been recovered with this technique, but on porous items such as paper, conventional ninhydrin and DFO are preferred, as is CA for nonporous surfaces.
- *VMD**: (At times can reveal fingerprints when other techniques have not.) This process deposits thin layers of gold and zinc through a process known as vacuum-coating technology to reveal prints either as positive or negative images. VMD has had success in developing prints on evidence that is several years old where other techniques failed to reveal any prints whatsoever.
- *Osmium tetroxide* (OsO_4)#: This reagent is similar to iodine in that it reacts with the oils and fatty substances in latent prints. Unlike iodine fuming, the coloration of the print is permanent when using OsO_4. OsO_4 has many disadvantages as a practical latent print development technique: it is expensive; it has explosive qualities; and the vapors are highly poisonous.
- *Autoradiography*#: This was an experimental technique. Latent print residues treated with radioactive aqueous solutions were placed in direct contact with photographic film or ordinary x-ray plates. This technique may have been used in highly specialized laboratories.
- *X-ray*#: Latent prints were dusted with lead powder and then x-rayed. This technique could have been used on currency and bank checks or porous surfaces that have multicolored designed backgrounds that made it difficult to see prints developed with conventional techniques.

Conclusion

In this chapter, the investigator working cold cases is given some background information on the history of fingerprints, the biology of friction ridge skin, and the myriad techniques that can be applied to develop fingerprints on various surfaces. Investigators should realize that fingerprint techniques are constantly changing and improving. New chemical formulations and instrumentation are being researched. Whatever the method or technique used to develop latent residues left behind by finger or palms in the past, cases can be reexamined with improved fingerprint applications such as VMD or PD.

When to use one method over another or in what sequence depends on the surface involved, and it depends on the environment the surface was exposed to. Each method or technique is capable of producing results; however, there may be one technique that is more suited than the others for a given surface and environmental conditions.

Acknowledgments

I wish to extend my deepest appreciation to Edwardo Palma, certified latent print examiner II, retired, San Diego Police Department (1986–2011). Certified by the International Association for Identification (IAI) in this field, his duties included analyzing, comparing, and individualizing friction skin—commonly known as fingerprints. Edwardo Palma began his career with the Laramie County Sheriff's Department in Cheyenne, Wyoming, in 1980 and served with three agencies including duties as a security police investigator with the U.S. Air Force. He is a life member of the IAI, of which he is past president of the California state division; past president of the Southern California Association of Fingerprint Officers; and a past fellow with the Fingerprint Society of the United Kingdom. He has taught advanced fingerprint identification courses at San Diego–area community colleges and police academies as well as trained many students in this area who are now employed with law enforcement agencies nationwide.

Suggested Readings and Bibliography

Alfonso, L. and Fuchs, E., Stem cells of the skin epithelium, *PNAS*, 2003, 100(1). [Online], http://www.pnas.org/cgi/content/full/100/suppl_1/11830.

Ashbaugh, D.R., Palmar flexion crease identification, *Journal of Forensic Identification, JFI*, 1991, 41(4): pp. 255–272.

Ashbaugh, D.R., *Quantitative-Qualitative Friction Ridge Analysis: An Introduction to Basic and Advanced Ridgeology*, 1999, CRC Press, Boca Raton, FL.

Baxes, G.A., *Digital Image Processing: Principles and Applications*, 1994, John Wiley & Sons, Inc., Hoboken, N.J.

Bridges, B.C., *Practical Fingerprinting*, 1942, Funk & Wagnalls Company, New York.

Champod, C., Lennard, C., Margot, P., and Stoilovic, M., *Fingerprints and Other Ridge Skin Impressions*, 2004, CRC Press LLC, Boca Raton, FL.

Cowger, J.F., *Friction Ridge Skin: Comparison and Identification of Fingerprints*, 1983, Elsevier Science Publishing Co. Inc., New York.

Everse, K.E. and Menzel, E.R., Blood Print Detection by Fluorescence, Center for Forensic Studies, Texas Tech University, National Science Foundation, Grant CHE 83 13527.

Farelo, A., A History of Fingerprints, *Interpol*, Operational Police Support. Directorate, I.C.P.O.—INTERPOL, General Secretariat, 2009, p. 4.

Faulds, H., On the skin—Furrows of the Hand, 1880, *Nature*, 1999 [reprinted], Minutia, pp. 8–9.

Faulds, H., On the Skin—Furrows of the Hand, *Nature*, Oct. 28, 1880, p. 605.

FBI Laboratory, Processing Guide for Developing Latent Prints, 2001, U.S. Department of Justice, Federal Bureau of Investigations, Washington, DC.

Fregeau, C.J., Germain, O., and Fourney, R.M., Fingerprint enhancement revisited and the effects of blood enhancement chemicals on subsequent profiler plus fluorescent short tandem repeat DNA analysis of fresh and aged bloody fingerprints, *Journal of Forensic Science*, 2000, Mar:45(2): pp. 354–380.

Lee, H.C. and Gaensslen, R.E., *Advances in Fingerprint Technology*, 1st ed., 1991, Elsevier, New York, p. 21.

Lee, H.C. and Gaensslen, R.E., *Advances in Fingerprint Technology*, 2nd ed., 2001, CRC Press, Boca Raton, FL.

Margot, P. and Lennard, C., *Fingerprint Detection Techniques*, 1994, Universite De Lausanne, Lausanne, Switzerland.

May, J., "Hand Across the Water: Hand Imagery in the Aboriginal Australian and Puebloan Artistic Traditions." Lecture presented at University of Virginia. *The Kluge-Ruhe Aboriginal Art Circular*, 2002, 5(1).

Media Cybernetics, *Media Cybernetics Reference Manual, Image Pro Plus*, 1993, Media Cybernetics, Inc.

Moenssens, A.A., *Fingerprint Techniques*, 1971, Chilton Book Company, pp. 174–193.

Olsen, R. Sr., *Scott's Fingerprint Mechanics*, 1978, Charles C Thomas.

Online. http:/encyclopedia.thefreedictionary.com/juan+vuceich

Online. http://www.reason.com/rb/rb022002.shtml

Russ, J.C., *The Image Processing Handbook*, 2nd ed., 1995, CRC Press, Inc., Boca Raton, FL.

SCAFO Publication, *The Print*, Nov/Dec;11(6): p. 11.

Scientific Research and Development Branch, Scene of Crime Handbook of Fingerprint Development Techniques [abridged from the Manual of Fingerprint Development Techniques]. Home Office, London 19888, Crown, Home Office London, United Kingdom.

Tillett, L.S., FBI fingerprints go digital, *Federal Computer Week* [Online], August 1999, http://www.few.com.

Wertheim, P., Inked major case prints, *Journal of Forensic Identification JFI*, 1999, 49(5): p. 468.

14

Automated Fingerprint Identification Systems

PETER D. KOMARINSKI

Contents

Introduction

Unsolved cases may not have been solved because of several reasons. The evidence collected at the crime scene did not point to a suspect; the crime outstripped the resources of the investigating agency; an avalanche of new cases prevented further development of leads on this case; or perhaps the physical evidence itself was not sufficiently complete to be of much use in making identification. As a result, the case went cold.

In addition to a review of the details of a cold case, there is a review of the physical evidence collected at the crime scene. Is that evidence still available? Is it still usable? Does it remain of value? In touching the crime scene, did the perpetrator leave a finger image that was captured by the evidence technicians? Is that latent finger image still available? This section addresses that latent print left at the crime scene by the perpetrator and the information that can be retrieved from it today, information that might not have been retrieved during the original investigation. The significant difference between then and now is the proliferation and generational improvement of automated fingerprint identification systems, i.e., AFIS systems.

Basic Latent Print Identification Practices

In the past, the primary method of making a latent print identification relied on the ability of a latent print examiner to physically compare a relatively short list of fingerprint cards (referred to as tenprint cards since they contain all 10 finger images as well as the plain impressions at the bottom of the card) against the latent print found at a crime scene (Figure 14.1).

This might involve a review of a few dozen cards of known felons. If there was no match, no identification was made. Another method of making identifications rested on the use of elimination prints, in which the finger images of the persons who had legitimate access to the crime scene (e.g., homeowner at a burglary) were compared against the latent print. This was a relatively simple process since the victim could be printed and the prints compared with the latent print. The third method was to compare suspect prints with the latent print

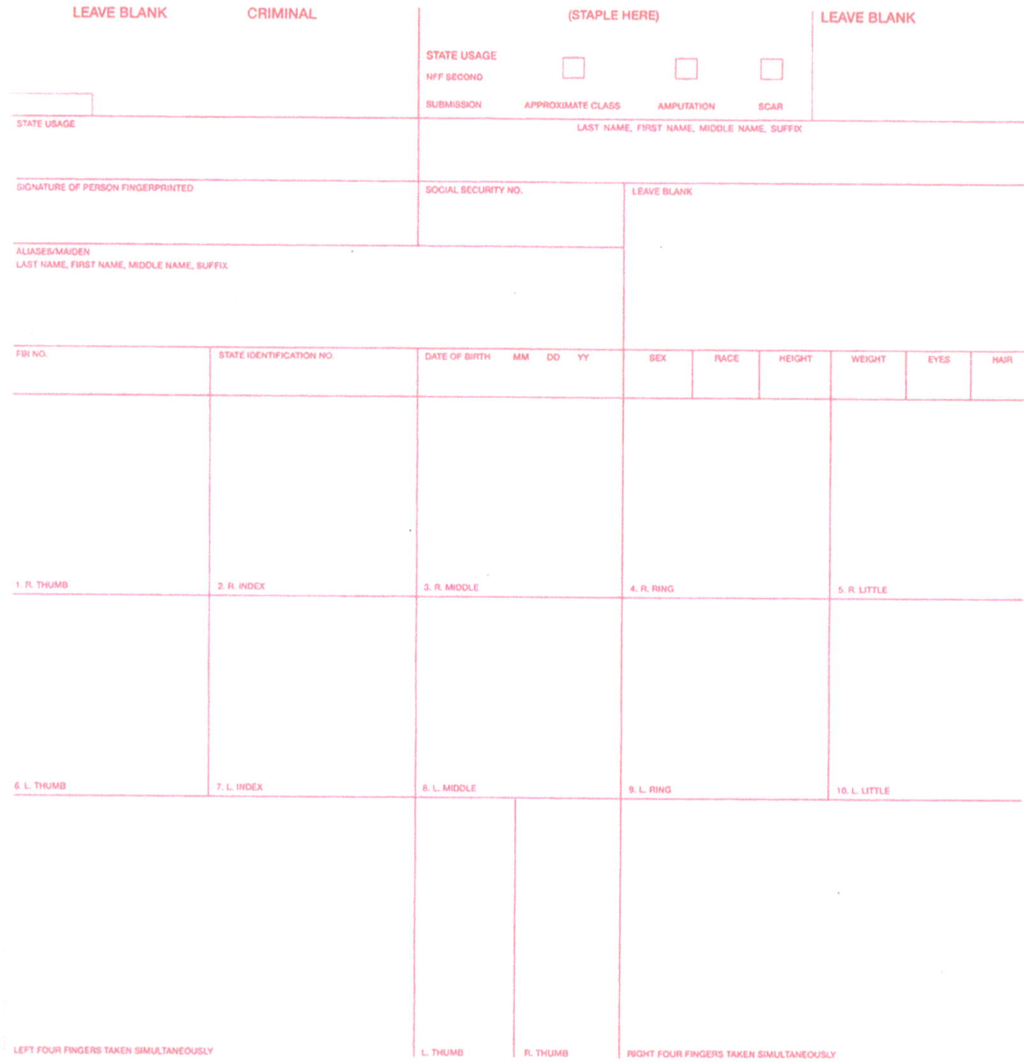
LEAVE BLANK CRIMINAL (STAPLE HERE) LEAVE BLANK
STATE USAGE NFF SECOND SUBMISSION APPROXIMATE CLASS AMPUTATION SCAR
STATE USAGE
LAST NAME, FIRST NAME, MIDDLE NAME, SUFFIX
SIGNATURE OF PERSON FINGERPRINTED
SOCIAL SECURITY NO.
LEAVE BLANK
ALIASES/MAIDEN
LAST NAME, FIRST NAME, MIDDLE NAME, SUFFIX
FBI NO. STATE IDENTIFICATION NO. DATE OF BIRTH MM DD YY SEX RACE HEIGHT WEIGHT EYES HAIR
1. R. THUMB 2. R. INDEX 3. R. MIDDLE 4. R. RING 5. R. LITTLE
6. L. THUMB 7. L. INDEX 8. L. MIDDLE 9. L. RING 10. L. LITTLE
LEFT FOUR FINGERS TAKEN SIMULTANEOUSLY L. THUMB R. THUMB RIGHT FOUR FINGERS TAKEN SIMULTANEOUSLY

Figure 14.1 Tenprint card. (Author's file.)

found at the crime scene. A suspect would be fingerprinted and the images on the tenprint card compared with the latent print image(s). Generally speaking, if they matched, there would be an arrest, case closed. All of this depends on the expertise and experience of the latent print examiner and the resources available.

This basic system worked, and continues to work, in many agencies. However, the process contains many assumptions and limitations. The first assumption is that the latent print found at the crime scene is of value, that it contains sufficient ridge detail and image characteristics to affect a positive identification. Second, it assumes that the perpetrator has previously been fingerprinted and that the tenprint record is in the identification area for comparison. Third, it assumes that the latent print examiner has sufficient time and expertise to review each finger image in the record file to make a reasonable comparison against the latent print from the crime scene. This is a manual system of latent print comparison. There is no automation required, and the most advanced piece of equipment is the examiner's loop or reticule. It is also a very limited application since it compares the latent print only against the images immediately available in the tenprint card file (Figure 14.2).

Figure 14.2 Fingerprint examiner's reticle. (Courtesy of Los Angeles County Sheriff's Department.)

Many agencies have moved forward in their identification processes and now use some form of AFIS.[1] Computer technology, advanced software, unparalleled reliability, and immense databases have combined to bring to the latent print examiner the ability to make identifications that were not possible before. The latent print examiner may now be able to bring to the investigator the identity of the person whose latent prints were found at the crime scene. This new information might close the case.

Fingerprint Identification Systems

Every investigative agency has a records section for storing information. These records include case files, fingerprint (i.e., tenprint) cards, and perhaps criminal histories. Many larger agencies and most states have a fingerprint identification system that has been operational for years. These agencies are the repositories for both the physical or digital tenprint cards as well as the criminal history associated with that record. Since there are so many variants of identification agencies, this discussion describes the operation through a single state agency that serves as the repository for all the criminal justice agencies within the state.

When a person was arrested and fingerprinted, the fingerprint card was sent to the identification agency to determine if the person had a criminal record and had any outstanding warrants or wants. The textual information along with the characteristics of the 10 finger images was searched against the existing list of records. If there was a match, the rap sheet containing the criminal history was sent to the inquiring agency. If there was no match, a record was created with a unique number (commonly referred to as a state identification number [SID]), and the information was returned to the inquiring agency.

Since identification agencies have been in operation for over 100 years, there have been many changes in the process and procedures. Prior to the age of electronics, this was an almost entirely manual process that required the arresting officer to ink the 10 fingers and roll them onto the tenprint card along with the slaps of four fingers and thumbs. Descriptive information was written into the boxes of the card and the card mailed to the state identification agency. Once at the state identification agency, the tenprint card would be given to an examiner, who would classify each of the finger images and assign pattern type and

[1] May also be referred to as an automated biometric identification system (ABIS) if more than one biometric is used.

classification based on prescribed rules, usually the Henry classification system. The card would then be taken though a lengthy process to visually compare the images against tenprint records that had the same pattern classification. The results of this search were mailed back to the inquiring agency (Figure 14.3).

This manual process, which required several days, if not weeks, from booking to response, remained relatively unchanged until the 1970s. The introduction of computers provided a better, faster, and less expensive method of retaining and retrieving textual information. Coupled with improvements in communications such as telephone systems and fax machines, the process for identifying an individual and providing a rap sheet improved in both quality and timeliness. While these improvements were underway, there was also an increase in the quantity of records being processed as the identifying agencies grew, provided background checks and rap sheets for increasingly greater numbers of people.

On the heels of the improvements to the tenprint or identification process, a secondary benefit to the investigator was the availability of more print images to search against. As part of the booking process, the arrestee was typically fingerprinted three times, with one card each sent to

- Federal Bureau of Investigation (FBI)
- State identification agency
- Local sheriff's office or police agency records section

This local record would be used by the latent print examiner at the police department to immediately compare against a latent print found at a crime scene.

This process of identification continued into the 1980s, when government leaders realized that the time to process the increasing volume of tenprint cards was no longer acceptable. Individuals were being released without the benefit of a complete background check because it took too long. As state agencies began to get bogged down, so did the FBI. The thousands of file cabinets housing millions of fingerprint cards continued to grow.

The solution to the problem was to automate the identification process. Wherever and whenever possible, manual steps in the process were to be replaced with automated electronic transactions. The federal government made millions of dollars available to states and units of local governments in a program called

Figure 14.3 FBI fingerprint examiners at work. Note the reticle on the desk in the left foreground. (Courtesy of FBI.)

the National Criminal History Improvement Project (NCHIP). The goal of these efforts was to automate the fingerprint identification process, to make an AFIS.

Automated Fingerprint Identification System

The AFIS system has provided an increasingly important tool for investigators. The number of tenprint identifications made with the assistance of AFIS technology is in the tens of millions. The number of latent print identifications is in the tens of thousands. The majority of identifications made with finger images are made with AFIS systems.

The AFIS system is commonly linked to a computerized criminal history or CCH. The CCH stores information about the subject's history such as previous arrests and/or finger-printable events such as a job application. The subject's CCH file information is increased with each new event. In its most simple form, an AFIS system has three elements:

1. Identification parameters (SID) linking the record to an individual
2. Image data
3. Minutiae that contain the friction ridge detail and image characteristics

A key element that distinguishes the AFIS system from previous identification systems is the ability to capture, store, and search on finger images. While the automation of textual information has been around for many years, it is only within the past 25 years that the finger image and characteristics have been converted into an electronic format useful for searching. Awareness of this time element is important to cold case investigators since this process and the data banks that support it are continually evolving.

AFIS systems incorporates many components that are common in every system. Among these components are *coders*, *matchers*, and *storage databases*. Coders are an element of the image capture process during which the finger image is digitized (think of it as digitally photographed). As part of this process, the coders examine the unique image characteristics such as a friction ridge ending, split or bifurcation, island, as well as the direction of the ridge flow and the finger pattern. These unique points are referred to as *minutiae*. It is these minutiae that are used in AFIS searches by another device called a matcher.

As its name implies, the matcher compares the minutiae from a recent submission against minutiae records in its database to determine if any record in the database matches. If a tenprint match occurs, there is a high degree of probability, now usually in excess of 99+%. This degree of accuracy is due to several factors, including the use of two or more finger images to affect the search.

Latent Print Applications of AFIS

With so many tenprint records on the AFIS database, it becomes apparent that there are many opportunities to exploit the powers of AFIS systems to make latent print identifications. The examiners are no longer limited by the physical space required to house the tenprint cards of known felons. The database with these records can be tens, hundreds, even thousands of miles away from the AFIS terminal and examiner. More importantly, these examiners can use the power of AFIS technology to search an entire database, millions of records, tens of millions of images, in just a few minutes.

Popular television shows that refer to the use of AFIS systems frequently, and mistakenly, state that the system made a "hit," i.e., the *system* made the latent print identification. AFIS merely produced a *list of candidates* in order of probability. The latent print examiner, with years of training and experience, made the identification. AFIS narrowed the list of candidates from several million to one, two, or none.

This example might help explain the AFIS concept. Think of all the tenprint cards stored in the cabinets in Figure 14.4. Multiply that number by 10 since there are 10 fingers per card. (Actually, there are usually 20 finger images since each finger is captured individually and then repeated in groups on the bottom of the card.)

If an examiner were to compare the latent print in question with every image on every card in every file cabinet, the process could take years. By searching the minutiae of these records, AFIS can complete the search in minutes and present a list of only the most likely candidates to the latent print examiner.

While it is convenient to think of AFIS processing as a completely automated process, it begins and ends with *people*. At the initial enrollment where the tenprint record is created, a person either rolled inked fingers onto a tenprint card or rolled the fingers onto a glass platen of a Livescan device. A Livescan device electronically captures finger images at a defined resolution, similar to a very high-end scanner. The data fields on either the paper or electronic tenprint records are completed by a person.

People are responsible for the care and maintenance of the AFIS system, and in the case of latent print identification practices, a person makes the final determination as to whether the latent print in question matches the image on the AFIS database. The latent print examiner, in addition to the skills required to make a comparison and identification/nonidentification decision, also has to know how to operate the AFIS system and how to launch a search, review candidate lists, and exercise the AFIS system to produce the most likely candidate. Unlike the tenprint examiner, who has 10 usually clear images to search with (actually 20 if the 10 plain or flat impressions are included), the latent print examiner has only the latent print found at a crime scene. The rolled tenprint finger images may contain up to 150 unique minutia points for the tenprint examiner to work with. The latent print examiner may have less than 10. Even with these constraints, both examiners are able to do their jobs with remarkable accuracy.

Figure 14.4 Cabinets of stored tenprint cards. (Courtesy of Peter Komarinski.)

AFIS Search Options

Many AFIS systems provide the latent print examiner with three opportunities for searching. These searches are as follows:

1. The latent to tenprint (LT/TP), in which the latent print is searched against all 10 finger images within a defined database. If there is no identification, the latent print image can be saved in the unsolved latent file for subsequent searching.
2. The tenprint to unsolved latent (TP/UL), in which the minutiae from new tenprint records are automatically matched against those latent prints that were not previously identified.
3. Unsolved latent to unsolved latent (LT/LT), in which no identification has been made but the unsolved database is searched to determine if prints from the same person have been found at another crime scene. This information can help detectives from different departments share information since they are looking for the same suspect.

In addition to these three types of searches, there are other databases that can be searched.

If the search of the local AFIS database does not result in a match, the state and/or FBI database can be searched. This can be somewhat time consuming but worth the investment of resources.

Given this background of how the latent print components of AFIS systems work, coupled with the myriad of choices for making a latent print search on the system and the various types of searches that can be made as well as the hierarchy of searches, cold case investigators can see the relevance and value of AFIS in cold cases that contain latent prints. With this understanding of how AFIS systems works, the cold case investigator is better equipped to use the power of AFIS to make an identification and perhaps close a case.

Further AFIS Application to Cold Cases

In reviewing the evidence, the investigator might inquire as to whether the latent print was searched on an AFIS system. If so,

- What system?
- When?
- By whom?
- What is the current status, i.e., is it in the unsolved latent (UL) print file?

The investigator might further ask if the print was searched on any other AFIS system, such as the FBI's Next Generation Identification (NGI).[2] If so, the same questions apply. If not, why not?

If the latent print has been searched in the past, *search it again*! And again. And again! As with any system that involves people and technology, there are always improvements. People get better at their jobs; systems get better with newer software and hardware. AFIS systems do not remain static. They get better, faster, bigger, and more accurate. Perhaps the reason no identification was made on the first search was because of the limitations of the earlier AFIS systems. The new systems have better coders that can extract minutiae more accurately and completely than before. A blurred minutia point on the latent print image that could not be identified a few years ago by the coder might be more apparent with newer technology. This crucial bit of data may lead to identification. Further, people become better at what they do as well. The skill set of the latent print examiner who originally searched the latent print on AFIS may have improved, along with a better understanding of how to get the most out of the system.

[2] The FBI announced full operational capability of the Next Generation Identification system in September 2014.

In addition to better coders, the matching algorithms have improved. Latent print examiners are presented with fewer but better candidates on their searches than in the past. Ask any latent print examiner who has searched latent prints on a new or upgraded system, and they will tell you that the results are impressive. It is not unusual to make an identification on a record that was present at the time of the original search but failed to hit. Better coders, better matchers, and a recoded and expanded database all contribute to making more identifications.

Cold case investigators should be aware that a search of the current database may produce an identification for a record that was *not* present at the time of the original search. Conversely, there may now be multiple image records of the same person. This may provide additional opportunities for identification that were not available at the time of the original search.

In addition to the processes within the AFIS environment, there are *imaging tools* that can aid the latent print examiner in teasing out the best latent print image possible. These tools do not enhance the latent print but, rather, may change the background so that the image and image characteristics are clearer. Think of two latent prints that overlay each other. Imaging technology can hide either of the two images, without enhancing or adding to either image. A latent print on a red background can be more apparent when the red is masked. The same applies to a latent on a pattern background.

While the earlier AFIS systems were limited to a single database, many agencies can now access millions of records on the NGI databases.[3] After completing a search of the local and state AFIS databases, the examiner can launch a search on another database(s) without the need to recapture or redigitize the latent print. This saves time and resources.

Unfortunately, not every latent print has been searched through an AFIS system. Many latent prints remain in jackets or in files, and are never searched on AFIS. The reasons for this are many but may include a lack of understanding of AFIS, and/or the skills required to be an AFIS operator or latent print examiner. There is always someone available at a local, state, or federal level who will assist, however. Another problem has been that many latent prints do not continue to be searched until all reasonable options are tried. In some cases, if no identification is made based upon the local database, no further searches are conducted.

Other Improvements

Testing by the National Institute of Standards and Technology (NIST), the FBI, research consortiums, and vendors have demonstrated the improved accuracy of newer AFIS systems. Latent images that produced no candidates in the past may now result in identifications when they are searched again. Since the latent search image may already reside in the system's unsolved latent file, there may be no need to reacquire the image before a new search.[4]

In addition to the technical advances, there are also procedural advances that will aid the examiner in improving the likelihood of identification. These include *Markup Instructions for Extended Friction Ridge Features, Evaluation of Latent Fingerprint Technologies: Extended Feature Sets, NISTIR 7859*, and *Latent Print Examination and Human Factors: Improving the Practice through a Systems Approach*.[5]

Does AFIS work on cold cases? Absolutely.

[3] For an example of an FBI NGI monthly fact sheet, see https://www.fbi.gov/about-us/cjis/fingerprints_biometrics/ngi/december-2015-ngi-fact-sheet.pdf.

[4] Further discussion of this can be found in *Automated Fingerprint Identification Systems* by Peter Komarinski.

[5] http://www.nist.gov/forensics/publications.cfm.

Conclusion

If the cold case contains a latent fingerprint, it must be searched on AFIS systems. Failure in the past to make an identification on this piece of evidence has little bearing on the likelihood of making an identification today. Better technology, better tools, and better trained-staff can all contribute to making the identification that can lead to an arrest, conviction, and closure. "Keep searching!"

For further information:

Komarinski & Associates, LLC
peter.komarinski@gmail.com

Acknowledgments

I wish to acknowledge and extend my gratitude to Peter Komarinski for his contribution of this chapter. Komarinski is the principal consultant of Komarinski & Associates, LLC. He is a subject matter expert on AFIS and identification technologies with more than 25 years' experience in the field of biometric identification. He served as an AFIS project manager for the New York State Division of Criminal Justice Services. His qualifications are summarized below:

- He was primary author of *NIST Writing Guide: Request for Proposals (NIST SP-1155)* and *Developing an MOU (NIST SP -1156).*
- He was member of the Noblis team on *Latent Interoperability Transmission Specifications (LITS), Terms and Metrics, Achieving Interoperability for Latent Print Identification in the United States* (draft).
- He has written extensively; is the author of *Automated Fingerprint Identification Systems* published by Elsevier/Academic Press; and is a contributor to *Cold Case Homicides* by Walton, the National Institute of Justice's (NIJ's) *The Fingerprint Sourcebook*, and FBI Biometric Center of Excellence's (BCOE's) State of the Art Biometric Excellence Roadmap (SABER) study.
- He is a regular presenter at the annual educational conferences of the International Association for Identification (IAI) and has lectured on topics such as Milestones in Identification; Terms and Measurements Quantifying Latent Identifications; Management Challenges to Interconnectivity; AFIS Upgrade Testing; Diamonds in the Rough: Re-Searching the Unsolved Latent File; and How to Get the AFIS You Want. He has served as the chair of the AFIS Committee of the IAI.

From Serology to DNA in Cold Case Investigations

15

MICHAEL J. GRUBB

Contents

Introduction

DNA is arguably the most valuable tool of the cold case investigator. Thousands of criminal cases have been solved across the country due to this powerful tool. DNA is the basis for genetic variation in all living things, and it is responsible for passing on genetic traits from generation to generation. Nearly all the cells in the human body have a nucleus, and the nucleus of each cell is packed with the full complement of chromosomes inherited from the individual's parents. The chromosomes are composed of DNA and protein. Different sequential combinations of four basic building blocks of DNA (the nucleotide bases guanine, adenine, thymine, and cytosine) result in the remarkable variation we see in humans, other animals, and plants. The variation is so great that each person's DNA is unique, with the exception of identical twins (Figure 15.1).

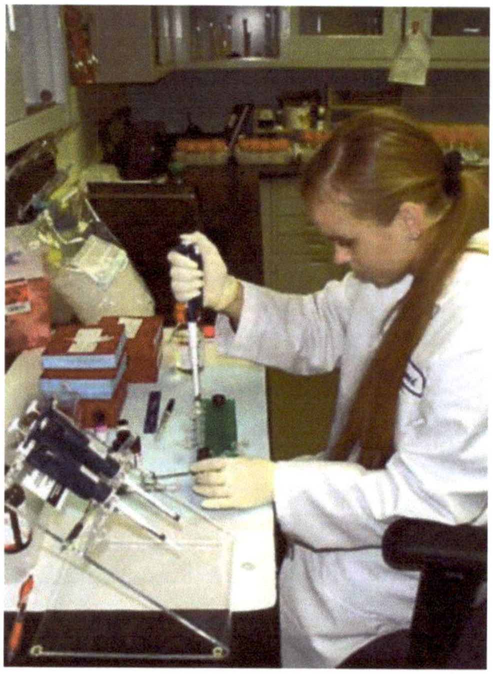

Figure 15.1 DNA laboratory. A criminalist prepares evidence samples for DNA analysis. (Courtesy of Mike Grubb, San Diego County Sheriff's Department Regional Crime Laboratory.)

Developments in DNA Science as Used in Forensic Science

DNA was first applied as an investigative tool in crime investigation in the United States in about 1986. Two different types of DNA analysis were available then, and which method was applied to the evidence depended on the sample size and the capabilities of the laboratory. *Restriction fragment length polymorphism (RFLP)* was a tremendously time-intensive method, and a full profile took as long as two months to develop. A bloodstain of approximately 1/4 inch in diameter was necessary to obtain a profile. In sex crime cases, thousands of sperm cells were necessary in the sample being tested in order to obtain an RFLP profile. Cases with only relatively few sperm recovered did not yield a result. Even with these limitations, some states began developing statewide felon DNA databases using RFLP, and dozens of cases were solved in this way. The advantage of RFLP was that it was very discriminating, typically giving DNA profile frequencies in the range of one in several million to one in several billion.

At the same time, *polymerase chain reaction (PCR)* DNA typing became available. The PCR method had an important advantage over RFLP. An amplification process was used to replicate certain parts of the DNA present, so that very small samples could be used to develop significant genetic information. However, when the PCR method was first applied, it was limited in its discriminating power, as it encompassed a single genetic locus, which was able to divide the population into approximately 20 subgroups. That locus was referred to as DQ alpha. It was very useful for those cases where the sample was limited or somewhat degraded. In about 1994, the value of PCR DNA typing was increased with the addition of *polymarker*, five additional DNA loci that increased the discriminating power of PCR-based DNA typing. With DQ alpha and polymarker, crime laboratories still had the advantage of being able to analyze very small samples but now had a typing result that would yield a DNA profile frequency of one in several thousand. This was extremely useful in casework with possible suspects, but the population frequency information with DQ alpha/polymarker was not sufficiently discriminating to make it useful for large-scale databasing (Figure 15.2).

In the late 1990s, the technology to analyze *short tandem repeat (STR)* DNA using PCR technology became available. Spaced along the strands of DNA that are coiled in the nucleus of the cell are sections that code for certain biological traits or functions—these areas are known as *genes*. There is also a considerable amount of DNA between the genes that doesn't appear to have a known purpose at this time (it doesn't code for any biological trait). It has been shown that much of this DNA between the genes has a repeating pattern of nucleotide bases. The number of repeats in a given stretch of DNA is an inherited trait, varies widely from person to person, and is the basis for STR DNA profiling. STR DNA testing gives the criminalist the ability to analyze up to 24 regions of DNA (called loci), resulting in statistical power far greater than was possible with RFLP. The advent of STRs gave the crime labs the ultimate tool—a PCR-based system (so very small samples having limited amounts of DNA can be analyzed), with the power of individualization necessary for nationwide databasing of DNA profiles of convicted felons and casework samples (and felony arrestees in some states). Using STRs, a typical laboratory report will provide frequency calculations in the septillions or octillions (a report might state, for example, "This DNA profile occurs on average in one person in every eight septillion"—*this number represents approximately a quadrillion times, in other words, a million billion times, the population of the planet!*). Because of the rarity of a given DNA profile, when a match is established between a casework sample and a person, many experts believe that it is now possible to state that the sample (bloodstain, semen stain, etc.) originated from that person, barring the existence of an identical twin (Figure 15.3).

The states in the late 1980s and 1990s with RFLP-based databases converted those databases to STRs by reanalyzing the samples. STRs are now the standard DNA analysis method accepted nationwide. An agreed-upon set of 22 DNA loci are uniformly tested and constitute the basis for local, state, and national databases. The databases are part of a system called the Combined DNA Index System (CODIS), which allows DNA profiles of convicted offenders and evidence samples from unsolved crimes to be entered into a computer and compared electronically.

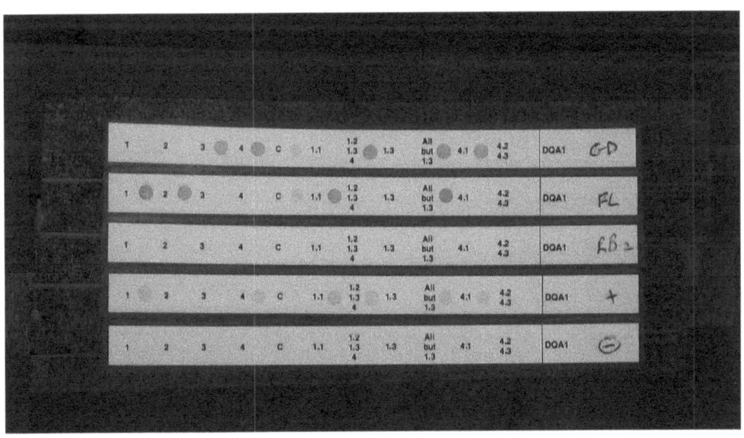

Figure 15.2 DQ alpha PCR DNA analysis. Between 1986 and 2000, the "dot blot" method pictured here was used for analysis of DNA. DQ alpha and polymarker PCR-based DNA analysis was performed using this technique. (Courtesy of Mike Grubb, San Diego County Sheriff's Department Regional Crime Laboratory.)

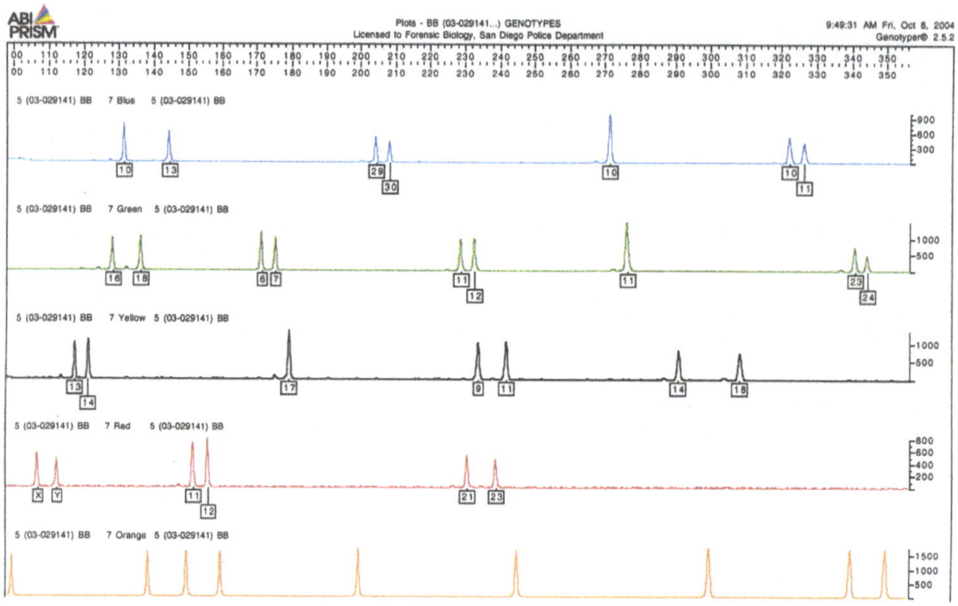

(a)

Identifiler Analysis of Crime Scene Sample	
Locus	**Profile Uploaded to CODIS Database**
D8S1179	10, 13
D21S11	29, 30
D7S820	10
CSF1PO	10, 11
D3S1358	16, 18
THO1	6, 7
D13S317	11, 12
D16S539	11
D2S1338	23, 24
D19S433	13, 14
vWA	17
TPOX	9, 11
D18S51	14, 18
Amelogenin	X, Y
D5S818	11, 12
FGA	21, 23

(b)

Figure 15.3 STR DNA profile. (a) The STR analysis of a sample using capillary electrophoresis results in a series of peaks on a printout, indicating the presence of certain DNA alleles. (b) This information is translated into a numerical sequence that is then uploaded as a DNA profile into CODIS. The CODIS software then searches the database for the same numerical sequence, indicating a match. (Courtesy of Mike Grubb, San Diego County Sheriff's Department Regional Crime Laboratory.)

The Combined DNA Index System

CODIS has three levels, local (LDIS), state (SDIS), and national (NDIS). At the local level, a crime laboratory will input DNA profiles obtained from evidence items. Only accredited government crime laboratories the meet the Federal Bureau of Investigation's (FBI's) published quality standards may input data into CODIS. Each state has an SDIS DNA database, which resides at a single laboratory. That laboratory will also receive uploaded case DNA profiles from local crime laboratories, which will be searched against all convicted offenders and arrestees who have been profiled and entered into the CODIS. The profiles will also be searched against all other case evidence DNA profiles (forensic unknowns) in the state CODIS. Three things may result: (1) The evidence DNA profile may match a convicted offender or arrestee in the state's database; (2) the evidence profile may match to another evidence profile, thereby linking two cases together; or (3) no matching profiles will be found.

The state uploads their convicted offender and forensic unknowns to NDIS weekly so that the searches are expanded to the national level. Many hits have been obtained with an evidence sample (forensic unknown) from one state matching a convicted offender in another state's database. By 2016, there were over 14 million DNA profiles of offenders and arrestees in the NDIS system, and over 600,000 forensic unknowns from casework samples. Over 325,000 cases have been solved or aided nationwide with the assistance of CODIS/NDIS.

Even though a forensic unknown may not hit against a known felon the first time it is searched, it remains in the system, so that if the assailant in the case is entered into the CODIS database at a later time, that felon's sample will hit against the forensic unknown entered previously.

There has been a general movement nationwide to increase the scope of the felon DNA databases. The classes of felonies that qualify for inclusion in the database vary from state to state. Most states are including all felons, and some include felony arrestees. The widening scope of felon DNA database statutes is driven by results from states that include burglars and drug offenders in CODIS. They are obtaining a remarkably high number of hits against sex crime evidence profiles. At the same time, legal challenges continue against the constitutionality of putting DNA profiles from arrestees into CODIS.

Crime laboratories also maintain a *local database* consisting of evidence profiles developed in their casework, and in some states, legally obtained DNA profiles of suspects are also kept in the local DNA database (LDIS). It is possible, then, that a laboratory could determine the perpetrator of a crime by use of this local database, even though the suspect has not been convicted of a felony. Suspect profiles, however, cannot be uploaded into SDIS without a written request by the case detective.

CODIS has value beyond matching a convicted felon with an evidence DNA profile. The sample may match with another evidence sample, or *forensic unknown*, previously loaded into the system. Thus, it is common to establish crime series based on DNA profiles, even though the MO may not have led the investigators to suspect the same perpetrator. This also alerts investigators from multiple jurisdictions that they are looking for the same individual, and they can compare investigative leads. Linking multiple offenses to the same perpetrator can have the potential of helping to identify a suspect, even when it would not be possible based upon any single case in the series. With the solution of any one of the cases in the series, the entire series of cases can be solved.

CODIS also has a missing-persons index containing both STR and mitochondrial DNA (mtDNA) types from unidentified human remains. In an attempt to identify the remains, these DNA profiles can be compared against relatives of missing persons.

Mitochondrial DNA

In some samples, such as bone, hair, teeth, or samples that have suffered environmental insult, sufficient nuclear DNA may not be available. *mtDNA* can be analyzed in these samples. The mitochondria of cells are structures found in the cytoplasm of the cells as opposed to in the nucleus. The mitochondria produce most of the energy needed by the cell to function. Many cells have only a single nucleus but contain a multitude of mitochondria, making mtDNA analysis more sensitive than STR typing. mtDNA types are different from and are not as discriminating as STR DNA profiling results, and cannot provide the rare DNA profile frequencies that we see in an STR report. mtDNA results are reported in terms of frequencies typically on the order of one in several thousand. An mtDNA type is searched against the mtDNA database maintained by the FBI, to determine the observed frequency of that type. mtDNA types are passed on to an offspring through the egg and not the sperm, so a person's mtDNA type will be the same as his/her mother's type.

Most public crime laboratories are currently using either the FBI laboratory or private consulting laboratories for mtDNA work. mtDNA typing is used less frequently than STR profiling, is technically challenging, and is a relatively expensive process. To date, it has been more cost effective for public crime laboratories to send this work out than to try to complete it themselves.

Y-Chromosome STR Analysis

Within the complement of 23 pairs of chromosomes in each nucleated cell, females possess two X chromosomes, and males possess an X and a Y chromosome. STR loci that are located on the Y chromosome are specific to males only. These are particularly useful when a mixture of male and female DNA is present on an evidence item. An example would be a small amount of male DNA under the fingernails of a female victim, where the victim's blood is also present. The victim's DNA will overwhelm in quantity the small amount of male DNA present. The male assailant's DNA will be specifically targeted in the Y-STR procedure. There will be no contribution from the female victim, as she possesses no Y chromosome. This technique allows the DNA laboratory to specifically amplify the genetic information from the Y chromosomes that were contributed by the male assailant, even when there is an overwhelming amount of DNA present from the female victim.

Sample Storage and Degradation

DNA in biological samples can be detected and profiled for many years on stains kept either frozen or in a dry, room-temperature condition. Evidence bearing biological stains kept at room temperature should be kept in paper packaging. If plastic packaging is used at room temperature, trapped moisture encourages the growth of bacteria, and problems may be encountered in DNA profiling. When biological samples are exposed to sunlight, heat, or moisture, it can rapidly lead to DNA degradation and the failure to obtain DNA profiles.

Importance of DNA to the Cold Case Investigator

The investigator will be wise to focus on the potential for the existence of probative biological evidence that may be DNA-profiled. It is also wise for the investigator to make use of crime laboratory personnel to discuss any physical evidence that exists and to develop a plan of attack regarding its analysis. The criminalist will often have insight into potential evidence value that the investigator overlooked.

When the cold case investigator encounters a case where RFLP or DQ alpha/polymarker technology was used in DNA analysis, the evidence may need to be reanalyzed using STRs. In addition, many samples that were insufficient for RFLP profiling years ago may now be sufficient for STR analysis.

It should also be realized that there has been a change in the way investigators think about biological evidence with the advent of STR DNA profiling. Samples that were never previously considered suitable are now being looked at more often as a possible source of DNA information. For example, a baseball cap can be tested for the DNA of the habitual wearer. A steering wheel can be swabbed, and a DNA profile can be obtained for a recent driver. A licked envelope, a cigarette butt, a chewed piece of gum, and saliva left on the rim of a drinking glass all are very suitable sources of DNA. Evidence that may have been originally overlooked when DNA was a newer science can still be revisited if the evidence items have been properly maintained (Figures 15.4 and 15.5).

DNA may also be used to establish a familial relationship, when necessary. If the investigator is faced with a bloodstain and there is no known DNA sample for comparison from the suspected source, it is possible to use DNA samples from the parents and/or children of the suspected source to solve the question. If in fact the stain originated from a parent or child of the person being tested, then the DNA laboratory will be able to show that with a very high degree of likelihood. One-half of the DNA characteristics found in a biological sample result from a maternal contribution, and the other half, from a paternal contribution. It is also possible to use known DNA samples from siblings of the suspected source to show a familial relationship when those are the only samples available.

Evidence	Possible Location of DNA on the Evidence	Source of DNA
Baseball bat or similar weapon	Handle, end	Sweat, skin, blood, tissue
Hat, bandanna, or mask	Inside	Sweat, hair, dandruff
Eyeglasses	Nose or ear pieces, lens	Sweat, skin
Facial tissue, cotton swab	Surface area	Mucus, blood, sweat, semen, ear wax
Dirty laundry	Surface area	Blood, sweat, semen
Toothpick	Tips	Saliva
Used cigarette	Cigarette butt	Saliva
Stamp or envelope	Licked area	Saliva
Tape or ligature	Inside/outside surface	Skin, sweat
Bottle, can, or glass	Sides, mouthpiece	Saliva, sweat
Used condom	Inside/outside surface	Semen, vaginal, or rectal cells
Blanket, pillow, sheet	Surface area	Sweat, hair, semen, urine, saliva
Through-and-through bullet	Outside surface	Blood, tissue
Bite mark	Person's skin or clothing	Saliva
Fingernail, partial fingernail	Scrapings	Blood, sweat, tissue

Figure 15.4 Identifying DNA evidence. Since only a few cells can be sufficient to obtain useful DNA information to help your case, the list above identifies some common items of evidence that may supply potential DNA evidence, and the biological source containing the cells. Remember, just because you cannot see a stain does not mean there are not enough cells for DNA typing. Further, DNA does more than just identify the source of the sample; it can place a known individual at a crime scene, in a home, or in a room where the suspect claimed not to have been. It can refute a claim of self-defense and put a weapon in the suspect's hand. It can change a story from an alibi to one of consent. The more investigators know how to use DNA, the more powerful a tool it becomes. The figure shows what may be revealed by a review of evidence/property sheets in a cold case file. (Reprinted from National Institute of Justice, "What Every Law Enforcement Officer Should Know About DNA Evidence" (brochure), 1999. With permission.)

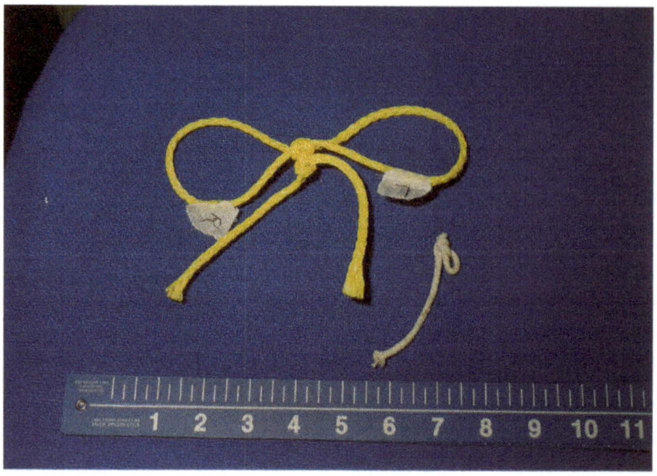

Figure 15.5 Ligature. Ligatures may offer a source of DNA from both suspect and victim. (Courtesy of Sgt. Bill Holmes, San Diego Police Department.)

Case Example of the Use of DNA on a Cold Case—The Keever and Sellers Homicides

Nine-year-old Jonathan Sellers and his friend, 13-year-old Charlie Keever, rode their bicycles on a path by a river in south San Diego in 1993. Their bodies were found the next day in a makeshift enclosure in some brush. Jonathan Sellers' body was hanging from a branch. Charlie Keever's body was close by. The usual biological samples were collected at autopsy, including oral and anal swabs. Samples of these swabs were extracted and searched for spermatozoa soon after the crime, but no spermatozoa were found. Other evidence collected from the crime scene included cigarette butts that had been stubbed out into the ground in the vicinity of the bodies (Figure 15.6).

In 2001, a reanalysis of the case was attempted, as the new STR DNA technology had been brought online, and it would now be possible to check any DNA profile obtained against a database of about 80,000 (at that time) felons in the California state felon DNA database. A more effective method of extraction of spermatozoa from swabs was used, resulting in the finding of spermatozoa in the oral swab from one of the boys. An STR profile was developed and matched a sex felon serving a 70-year term for a violent rape he had committed in San Diego several months after the Keever and Sellers homicides.

DNA profiles from the cigarette butts at the scene also matched the suspect, Scott Erskine. At trial, Erskine did not deny having killed the boys, and he was convicted of two counts of first-degree murder. This conviction resulted in large part from the tenacity of San Diego Police detective Sergeant Bill Holmes, enhanced by advances in technology and the teamwork with the crime lab.

Serology

Prior to the use of DNA to discriminate biological samples from different individuals, the science of identification of body fluids in the crime laboratory was known as *serology.* Serology units once existed in laboratories where the DNA units now stand. *Serology* now refers largely to the work done in *screening* evidence items for biological stains and identifying those stains as blood, semen, saliva, etc. Serology units in crime

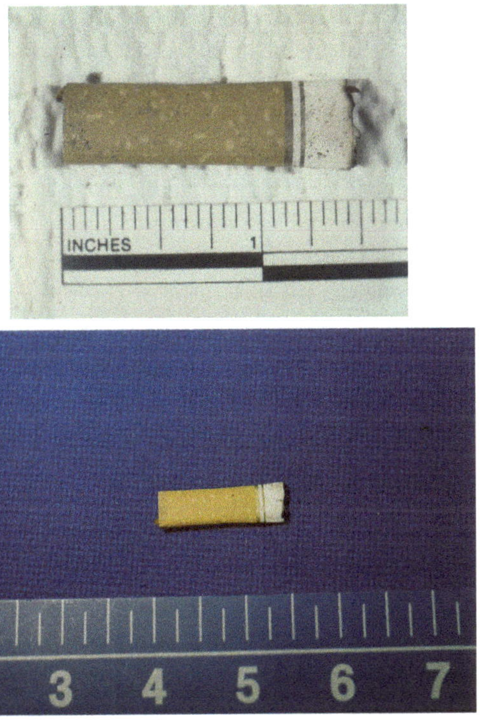

Figure 15.6 Cigarette butts as a source of DNA. Cigarette butts recovered at crime scenes may offer a source of suspect DNA. When found in the review of cold case homicide evidence, these should be profiled utilizing advanced DNA techniques. In 1993, at the time of this crime, older DNA technology led to a DQ alpha/polymarker DNA type, but that was insufficient for identification of a suspect using CODIS. Reanalysis of these recovered cigarette butts and other evidence using STR DNA technology in 2001 identified a suspect profile in the brutal murders of two young boys. (Courtesy of Sgt. Bill Holmes, San Diego Police Department.)

laboratories applied limited genetic marker testing of antigens, enzymes, and proteins as a means of distinguishing biological samples from different individuals. In the vast majority of crime laboratories now, serology refers to the steps prior to DNA extraction and profiling.

It is strongly recommended that the cold case investigator obtain the assistance of a criminalist when reviewing serology reports. It is difficult for an untrained investigator to discern all of the important information in these reports.

Identification of Biological Stains

Blood has been identified in stains via color tests for decades. Phenolphthalin, benzidine, tetramethyl benzidine (TMB), and ortho-tolidine are examples of some of these *presumptive* color tests. When a stain looks like a bloodstain and gives a positive presumptive test, the analyst may *presume* it is a bloodstain and (in the old serology days) would normally then undertake further analysis of the stain to determine species origin etc. Another presumptive test for blood sometimes used as a spray reagent is *leucomalachite green (LMG)*. LMG is used when blood is suspected to have been cleaned up from a surface, or to help develop faint bloody shoe prints on a light-colored carpet or floor. *Luminol* is also used as a presumptive test for blood, for example, on dark surfaces or dark carpets, where visualization of blood is very difficult. Luminol causes the faint bloodstains to *luminesce* in the dark when the reagent is sprayed onto the surface.

The next step would have been to identify the stain as of human origin or of some other species origin. This was accomplished by a *preciptin* test, reacting bloodstains against antihuman protein antiserum, as well as against *antisera* to other species. Several papers were published as early as 1901 regarding immunological differentiation of human blood from animal blood. The preciptin tests as used in crime laboratories were often performed by a *gel diffusion* or a *crossover electrophoresis* procedure.

Semen is identified by the microscopic identification of the presence of spermatozoa. In the absence of spermatozoa (for example, in cases involving vasectomized men), semen can still be identified through the identification of the semen-specific protein P30 in the stain. The enzyme acid phosphatase has also been used for decades as an indicator of the presence of semen. When a stain reacts positively for the presence of acid phosphatase, and the reaction is strong and relatively rapid, the analyst has good reason to suspect that the stain contains semen. The finding of acid phosphatase alone, however, in the absence of spermatozoa or P30 is not conclusive proof of the presence of semen. Semen is now commonly identified using a one-step *card* technique that detects trace amounts of the P30 protein.

Saliva is indicated by the presence of the enzyme amylase in the stain. Amylase is found in high concentrations in saliva and at lower concentrations in other body fluids. Old serology reports would refer to the "possible presence of saliva" or perhaps only an "elevated level of amylase" in a particular sample. These hints at the possible presence of saliva may be worth pursuing. This is represented in Figure 15.7.

Genetic Markers

The value of genetic markers is in their ability to provide information as to whether a bloodstain or semen stain *could have* originated from a particular individual. Prior to about 1973 (this year varies from lab to lab), most reports will describe the identification of stains as to the body fluid type. The only genetic marker (genetic characteristic that allows us to distinguish one person's biological material from another person's) in use in the crime laboratory prior to the early 1970s was the ABO system of blood grouping. Liquid blood and bloodstains were typed based on the detection of *antigens* on the red blood cell surfaces. The population could be subdivided into four groups: A, B, AB, and O. The typing of bloodstains in the ABO system extends as far back as the discovery of the existence of ABO blood groups in 1901.

Semen and saliva stains could also be typed in the ABO system, but only if the donor of the stain was a *secretor.* Approximately 75% of the general population are secretors. These individuals secrete their ABO blood type into their other body fluids, such as semen, saliva, and vaginal secretions. Those that do not secrete these substances are referred to as nonsecretors. ABO typing is generally not possible on a semen or saliva stain from a nonsecretor.

In the mid-1970s, crime laboratories were busily trying to add genetic markers to their repertoire. These genetic markers were protein and enzyme markers. For example, phosphoglucomutase (PGM), erythrocyte acid phosphatase (EAP), esterase D (EsD), and adenylate kinase (AK) are enzymes found in the blood, and those enzymes are polymorphic—that is, they are found in different forms in different people. They are referred to as genetic markers because they are inherited from one's parents and they are passed from generation to generation in predictable patterns.

Some of these enzyme markers were also of value for other biological materials. Semen could be typed in the ABO/secretor system, as well as for the commonly used polymorphic enzyme systems PGM/PGM subtyping, peptidase A, and rarely others. Hairs could be typed in the PGM and EsD systems.

In those cases where the laboratory was fortunate enough to obtain typing results in several genetic marker systems, the significance of the match between the evidence sample and the known sample of the

GEORGE B. TELLEVIK
Chief

STATE OF WASHINGTON
WASHINGTON STATE PATROL
2nd Floor Public Safety Bldg., 610 3rd Avenue • Seattle, Washington 98104-1820 • (206) 464-7038 • (SCAN) 576-7038

CRIME LABORATORY REPORT

Agency: Seattle Police Department — Laboratory No. 193-05823

Suspect: Not Listed — Agency Case No. 93-304200

Victim: Mia Zapata

Officer: Detective Allan R. Lima

Evidence Examined:

Item 20: Sealed envelope containing a liquid blood sample from "Mia Zapata."

Item 21: Sealed bag containing samples recovered from the body of "Mia Zapata", including oral, anal and vaginal swabs, vaginal wash, swabs from the right and left nipples, and a control swab from the breast.

Item 28: Sealed bag containing a pair of black cutoff jeans.

Item 29: Sealed bag containing a pair of black underpants.

Procedures and Results:

The blood sample from Mia Zapata was typed and was found to be ABO type O, and Lewis type Le^{a-b+}, which indicates that she is a secretor. A secretor is an individual whose ABO blood group is expressed in other body fluids such as saliva, vaginal secretions, etc.

The vaginal, oral and anal swabs were examined for spermatozoa and P30 (a semen-specific protein) with negative results. The vaginal wash was examined for spermatozoa, with negative results. Amylase (an enzyme found in high levels in saliva) was found to be elevated in the vaginal swabs. This indicates the possible presence of saliva in this sample.
Moderate levels of amylase were detected on the swabs from the nipples.

Secreted H(O) antigens were detected in the vaginal swab sample. No secreted ABO antigens were detected in the swabs from the nipples.

[signature] September 14, 1993
Michael J. Grubb, Supervising Forensic Scientist

JCM 1142

(a)

Figure 15.7 (a and b) Serology report. These reports may be found in pre-DNA unsolved cases. It is strongly recommended that investigators seek the assistance of qualified laboratory personnel to review these reports. It is difficult for an untrained investigator to discern all of the important information in these reports. (Courtesy of Mike Grubb, San Diego County Sheriff's Department Regional Crime Laboratory.) *(Continued)*

suspect or victim was determined by a frequency calculation. For example, a bloodstain on a suspect's shirt is typed as ABO type B, PGM type 2-1, EsD type 2-1, and EAP type BA. This combination of genetic markers would have significance if the victim's reference blood sample were shown to have the same genetic marker profile and the suspect's own blood was different. Beyond being able to say that the blood on the suspect's shirt is not the suspect's own blood, and could be from the victim, we can attach a significance to this by calculating the frequency with which this combination of genetic markers occurs in the population. ABO type B occurs in 11% of the population, PGM type 2-1 occurs in 36% of the population, EsD type 2-1 occurs in 19% of the population, and EAP type BA occurs in 42% of the population. To calculate the frequency of a person with this combination of genetic markers, we can multiply their individual frequencies ($0.11 \times 0.36 \times 0.19 \times 0.42 = 0.003$). Individuals with this combination of genetic markers constitute only 0.3% of the population, or three in a thousand. This would have been considered an outstanding result in the pre-DNA serology laboratory.

Laboratory Number:	193-05823
Agency:	Seattle Police Department
Agency Number:	93-304200
Suspect:	Not Listed
Victim:	Mia Zapata
Officer:	Detective Allan R. Lima

The underpants and cutoff jeans were examined for the presence of acid phosphatase, an enzyme found in high levels in semen and in lower levels in other body fluids. No acid phosphatase was detected on these garments. Three hairs were recovered from the cutoff jeans, and were repackaged with that garment.

Conclusions:

No semen was found on the vaginal, oral or anal swabs, vaginal wash, or on the underpants or cutoff jeans.

Saliva may be present in the vaginal swab, but no ABO antigens foreign to Mia Zapata were detected in that sample. No blood group substances were detected on the swabs from the nipples.

Michael J. Grubb, Supervising Forensic Scientist September 14, 1993

JCM 1143

2 of 2

(b)

Figure 15.7 (Continued) (a and b) Serology report. These reports may be found in pre-DNA unsolved cases. It is strongly recommended that investigators seek the assistance of qualified laboratory personnel to review these reports. It is difficult for an untrained investigator to discern all of the important information in these reports. (Courtesy of Mike Grubb, San Diego County Sheriff's Department Regional Crime Laboratory.)

Masking of Genetic Markers

A limiting factor in the serology lab's ability to give useful information to the investigator in the pre-DNA years was the phenomenon of *masking.* In sexual assault cases, the biological samples were usually mixed on swabs and clothing stains. When results were obtained for genetic markers on these swabs and stains, the victim's types would have to be subtracted out before stating any conclusions about the genetic markers contributed by the assailant. For example, the following is a typical set of case findings:

Vaginal swab: A and H[1]antigens found, PGM type 2-1 found.
Suspect: ABO type A, secretor, PGM type 2-1.
Victim: ABO type A, secretor, PGM type 1.

[1] An ABO type A secretor would normally secrete both A and H(O) antigens into his/her saliva, semen, vaginal secretions, etc.

Although the findings on the swab perfectly correspond to the suspect in the case (type A, secretor, PGM type 2-1, a combination found in about 11% of the population), the conclusion has to be couched in conservative terms. Some of the genetic markers could have come from the victim in this case, so the report would properly state, "The A and H antigens found in the vaginal swab may have been contributed by the victim herself. The victim could not, however, be the source of the PGM '2' band. Therefore, the semen is from an individual of either PGM type 2-1 or 2. This includes approximately 41% of the male population." This was a very common pre-DNA problem. The advent of DNA testing allowed the examiner to separate sperm DNA from nonsperm DNA.

The ABO, secretor, and protein and enzyme typing systems were what the crime labs had to work with until the advent of DNA typing in the late 1980s. Many crime labs continued to conduct non-DNA genetic markers into the 1990s.

What a Serology Report Says and Doesn't Say

A serology report is distinguished from a DNA report not only by the *methods* applied to the evidence but also by the *significance* of the findings. The most informative serology report will indicate whether and where blood, semen, or other biological materials were found on evidence items, and will indicate whether genetic marker testing of samples of that biological material *is indicative of* the stain originating from the victim or suspect. The percentage of the population that shares the particular genetic combination is often given in a serology report. For example, the conclusion of the serology report might state: "The bloodstain on the suspect's shirt has genetic markers indicating that the suspect could not be the source of the blood. Based on the genetic markers found, the victim could be the source of the blood on the suspect's shirt. This combination of types occurs in approximately 6% of the Caucasian population, 4% of the Black population, and 3% of the Hispanic population." The percentages in the report give the reader a sense of the significance of the match between the victim's known blood and the questioned stain on the suspect.

The report does not positively identify the source (victim, suspect, etc.) of the biological material. This is where a DNA report is significantly different. Some laboratories are now comfortable identifying an individual as the source of a sample (barring the existence of an identical twin) based on the astronomical population frequencies in DNA reports.

Cold Case Example of Use of a Dated Serology Report—The Mia Zapata Case

In July of 1993, a rising female rock star in Seattle was sexually assaulted, strangled, and left in the street. No semen was found in vaginal swabs or on the victim's clothing. The medical examiner, however, noted marks on the victim's breasts that appeared to be faint bite marks. Moistened swabs were used to collect any possible saliva that was present.

A subsequent crime laboratory report discussed "moderate levels of amylase" having been found on the breast swabs. Amylase was also found in the vaginal swab. ABO/secretor typing of the swabs at that time gave no result other than the victim's own ABO type.

Nine years later, cold case detectives in Seattle were reviewing the case and raised the question of attempting a DNA profile of the possible saliva present on the vaginal swab and breast swabs. The vaginal swab posed a technical problem, as there was no way to separate the cellular material from the victim's vaginal secretions from any cellular material from the saliva. However, the breast swabs gave a DNA profile foreign to the victim (Figure 15.8). The profile was searched against NDIS (the National DNA Index System), and a hit was obtained against Jesus Mezquia, a 48-year-old Cuban fisherman living in Florida. Further investigation showed that Mezquia was in Seattle at about the time of the Zapata murder. When questioned by detectives, he denied knowing or ever being in contact with the victim. This statement was

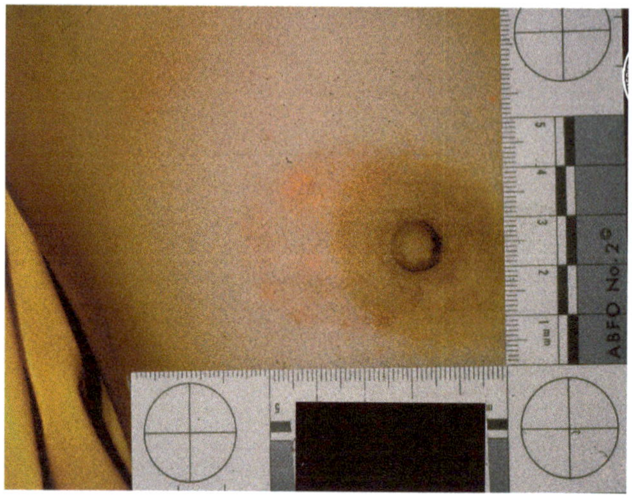

Figure 15.8 Bite mark DNA evidence. In older cases in which bite marks were evident or suspected during the investigation, cold case investigators should seek to determine if any swabs were taken of the suspected bite mark. While bite mark identification is more interpretive, DNA analysis of these is far more definitive for investigation and suspect identification purposes. (American Board of Forensic Odontology.)

useful to the prosecutors at trial, since Mezquia had removed any innocent means of his DNA being on the victim's body. The jury found him guilty of first-degree murder.

The Cold Case Investigator's Clues from a Serology Report

- The existence of a serology report in a cold case investigation indicates that biological evidence was an issue when the case was looked at previously, and the results or conclusions listed in the report will tell the investigator whether there are/were biological materials (blood, semen, saliva, etc.) present on evidence items in the case. There may also be an indication in the serology report as to how much of the stain sample was consumed in the previous analysis, and how much may still exist as evidence in the case.
- The existence of a serology report should encourage the cold case investigator to seek the assistance of a criminalist who can interpret the report(s).
- The serology report may cite other reports done in the case (e.g., by the FBI laboratory or a private consulting laboratory). Efforts should be made to obtain copies of these reports as well.
- If the serology report describes stains as bloodstains, or even if they are just referred to as "phenolphthalin positive," "TMB positive," etc., and information as to the origin of those stains may have value in the cold case investigation, then they should be DNA-profiled.
- If stains or swabs are described as containing semen, spermatozoa, P30, or acid phosphatase, and the stains are considered of possible value, the stains should be DNA-profiled.
- Stains or swabs that have been tested for saliva with positive results, or where the report states that the sample revealed an "elevated level of amylase," should be DNA-profiled if the results of the testing could be probative.
- Swabs of possible bite marks should be subjected to DNA typing.
- Hairs that are recovered in crime scene locations that suggest strongly that the hair is likely from the assailant should be subjected to DNA typing. In some instances, given enough hair root material, it

may be possible to obtain an STR DNA profile. Failing that, it should still be possible to obtain an mtDNA type from the hair shaft.

- The investigator needs to think in terms of many possible sources of DNA: licked stamps or envelopes, ski masks, hats, gloves, cigarette butts, chewing gum, or a used water glass.
- The investigator should realize that it might be prudent to follow up on apparent exclusions based on serology. What may have appeared to be an exclusion of an individual based on dated genetic marker testing should be followed up with DNA profiling. The now antiquated methods of genetic marker testing (such as ABO typing of bloodstains or semen stains) were more problematic and more likely to result in an error than DNA profiling.

Serology and DNA Advances with Time

Prior to the Early 1970s

- Bloodstains were typed in the ABO system only.
- Semen and saliva stains were typed in the ABO/secretor systems only.

Early 1970s through Late 1980s

- Bloodstains were typed in the ABO, PGM, PGMsubtype, EAP, EsD, AK, ADA (adenosine deaminase), and Hp (haptoglobin) systems (and occasionally others).
- Semen stains were typed in the ABO/secretor systems, as well as in some of the isoenzyme systems such as PGM, PGMsubtype, and EsD.
- Saliva stains were still typed in the ABO/secretor systems.

Late 1980s through 2000

- RFLP was introduced as a DNA analysis method.
- Bloodstains, semen stains, and other biological material were DNA-profiled using RFLP DNA technology.
- Relatively large stains were needed to achieve DNA profile results.
- RFLP results were very discriminating, resulting in frequency statistics commonly in the billions.
- PCR was introduced as a DNA analysis method suitable for small samples.
- Bloodstains, semen stains, and other biological materials were DNA-typed using PCR- based methods.
- The PCR systems in use were DQ alpha and polymarker.
- Using DQ alpha alone, the population was broken down into only about 20 different types.
- Adding polymarker made the results more discriminating.

Since 2000

- All forms of biological evidence have been DNA-profiled using a PCR-based method known as STRs. This is the current state of the art for DNA profiling.
- Using 13 or more genetic loci, this system distinguishes between all individuals other than identical twins.
- Results are reported in terms of frequencies typically on the order of one in septillions or octillions.

- For some evidence that doesn't lend itself to STR profiling (such as hair shafts and some bone evidence), mtDNA can be typed (see Chapter 16).
- For evidence that has a relatively small amount of male DNA in the presence of female DNA, Y-STR technology can be applied to look at only the male DNA.

Acknowledgments

I wish to express my deepest appreciation and gratitude to Michael J. Grubb, crime laboratory director for the San Diego County Sheriff's Regional Crime Laboratory, for his authorship of this chapter. In addition, Grubb has given much of his time and energy in reviewing and offering positive suggestions for other segments of this textbook. Grubb obtained his BS degree from the University of California at Berkeley in 1975 and began his forensic career at the Institute of Forensic Sciences in Oakland, California, that same year. In addition, Grubb wishes to acknowledge and express his gratitude to Patrick O'Donnell, Ph.D., and Brian Burritt of the San Diego Police Crime Laboratory's Forensic Biology Unit, and to Michelle Hassler and Shelley Webster of the San Diego Sheriff's Crime Laboratory's Forensic Biology Unit for their review and input.

Suggested Readings and Bibliography

Gaensslen, R. E., *Sourcebook in Forensic Serology, Immunology, and Biochemistry*, U.S. Dept. of Justice, National Institute of Justice, 1983, p. 222.

National Institute of Justice, "What Every Law Enforcement Officer Should Know About DNA Evidence" (brochure), 1999.

Trace Evidence in Cold Case Investigations

16

JAY W. HENRY

Contents

> Never give in, never give in, never, never, never, never—in nothing, great or small, large or petty—never give in except to convictions of honor and good sense.
>
> **—Winston Churchill**

Introduction

It was the week before Memorial Day 2005 when the investigator received the call. The laboratory had some unbelievable news. There was a Combined DNA Index System (CODIS) hit to some newly tested trace evidence. This "new" sample had previously been tested multiple times with older technology, but this was the first time that it would provide useful information. Originally, the item had been submitted in the 1980s as a bloodstain sample on U.S. currency; however, so much testing had been done that there was no longer anything visible. From everyone's perspective, further testing seemed bleak.

At the crime laboratory, the forensic scientist's quandary was, "Do I swab where the stain used to be or try another approach?" The many years of testing had consumed most of the visible blood sample. The evidence had essentially transitioned from a DNA to a trace submission, and a standard test didn't seem quite adequate. In a moment of inspiration, she decided to soak the sample, and that strategy produced enough DNA for a profile. The result: a critical first lead for the agency in over 20 years. The determination and perseverance of the investigator and laboratory had finally paid off.

Why the crime laboratory was performing another test on an otherwise overtested sample is interesting. For over two decades, many items on this case had already been tested and substantial resources expended. Discouraged, the case had even been closed by the agency until a motivated detective reopened it. Further, because of the constant resource drain of this one case, agency relations with the state crime laboratory were strained. However, the lead detective was undaunted. By using constant, personal communication supported with thoughtful probative logic, he managed to convince a poorly resourced laboratory to run one more test. That strategy ultimately tied a previously unknown individual to the scene.

The lab heard nothing more until a year later, when the agency and prosecutor requested additional testing due to a new theory, which, if proved true by the evidence, would strongly bolster their case. They believed that the suspect may have shed some hairs in an area of the crime scene referred to as the "fight area." This area of the scene was located on the floor of a dirty convenience store and probably had years of accumulated hairs and such. Additionally, the crime laboratory had already performed conventional DNA testing on the hair root of many of those same hairs, and that had yielded no results (Figure 16.1). Now, the agency wanted to send some of those hairs to a vendor laboratory for mitochondrial DNA (mtDNA) testing. Based on their many years of experience, the laboratory scientists felt that there was little chance of a positive result. In addition, outsourced DNA testing was expensive, and the lab could not and would not cover the cost. They advised the prosecutor to take the original trace results and move forward with the resolution of the case. The prosecutor felt otherwise.

The case was at an impasse until the legal team convinced local officials to provide funding to test nine of the evidence hairs. The laboratory, still believing it was a poor use of resources, nonetheless did their best to assist them in selecting samples. Using microscopy, the laboratory eliminated the candidate hairs that were least likely to give a result (e.g., hairs similar to the victim, animal hairs, etc.) and selected nine dissimilar hairs to send to the vendor laboratory.

The results that came back were significant. Much to the amazement of the investigative team, three of the hairs were associated back to the suspect, proving once again that a never-give-in attitude, coupled with a substantial resource investment, can make the difference in a case. The defendant was ultimately convicted and received a sentence of life without parole.

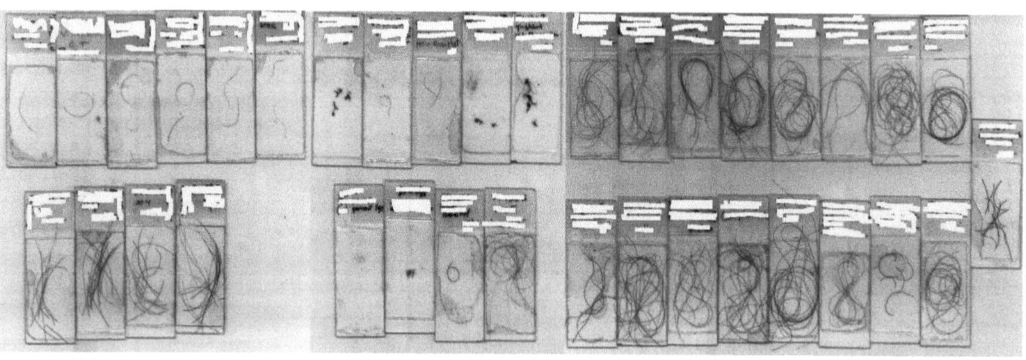

Figure 16.1 Fight scene and reference standard hair mounts. (Courtesy of Pilar Shortsleeve, Utah Department of Public Safety [DPS].)

Trace Evidence—The Last Resort for Physical Evidence?

Frequently, the person that finds himself/herself reading the chapter on trace evidence has exhausted all of the traditional forensic science choices (e.g., DNA, latent prints, etc.) and may be looking for anything trace related to provide a lead or establish an association.

Thus, the purpose of this chapter is to provide an overview of the concept of trace evidence:

- What is trace evidence?
- What is its *value* in a cold case criminal investigation?
- What are its *limitations* in cold case investigations?

As illustrated in the previous case example, it is not necessarily uncommon that investigators, prosecutors, and laboratory personnel have strong differences of opinion regarding case issues. Mutual understanding of these concepts, however, will enhance the teamwork aspect these cases require, as well as foster better communications and relations among all concerned.

While the glue that binds a successful cold case investigation together is the law enforcement investigator, it is critical that other team members understand these concepts involving trace evidence. The focus of this chapter is to provide a basic understanding to all involved in the investigation and prosecution of cold case homicides on the applicability of physical evidence and how to leverage it to provide case fact information.

Redefining Trace Evidence

The scope of what type of physical evidence constitutes "trace" is immense and does not fit a strict definition. Within the crime laboratory, the term trace has referred to evidence consisting of hair, fibers, paint, glass, soil, gunshot residue (GSR—primer residues), etc... However, the investigator should use a broader definition and think of it as "any evidence in small amounts," which includes DNA.

A principle of trace evidence is its mechanism of transference, and this is known as the Locard exchange principle. Locard was an early-twentieth-century French scientist who first proposed the idea of evidence moving back and forth across a contact boundary. This means evidence is transferred from the suspect to the victim or to the crime scene, and vice versa. In essence, a criminal brings something of himself/herself to the crime scene and takes something away, thus connecting each to the other.

Early crime laboratory technology methods could only detect evidence that fit into the traditional categories (e.g., hair, fibers, etc.). However, with scientific enhancements such as DNA, alternate light sources, and more, forensic scientists are now able to better study and find evidence that crosses that contact boundary. Scientists can do more with the traditional categories of trace evidence, such as expanding the analysis of hairs to include the root (e.g., short tandem repeat [STR] and Y-chromosomal short tandem repeat [Y-STR] DNA) and the shaft (e.g., mtDNA). (See Chapter 15.)

Technology has also made possible greater discrimination for fiber, paint, and glass evidence; however, a full description of those innovations is beyond the scope of this chapter. It is sufficient for the investigator and other cold case team members to understand that those technologies exist and for them to rely upon the laboratory to guide them through the various analytical options.

With regard to any forensic investigation, a concerted effort to maintain a spirit of teamwork cannot be overemphasized. Interpretation of forensic evidence can be complicated, and it is common for misunderstandings to occur among team members. Thus, all parties must work in conjunction with—not against—the laboratory.

Advantages and Challenges with Trace Evidence

The appeal of trace evidence is its pervasiveness. It has a wider range of applicability (compared to other disciplines) and can assume multiple forms (e.g., soil/dust to hairs/fibers). Because of its ubiquitous presence, it can be argued that trace evidence can be found in all crime scenes. No other physical evidence has this attribute; however, it does have some potential limitations.

One challenge with trace evidence can be determining its associative value. There is little debate about the significance of a DNA profile hit in the CODIS database. For instance, a comparison between a full DNA crime scene profile to a suspect's reference standard can result in a random-match probability in the quadrillions (1,000,000,000,000,000), which leaves little doubt with regard to whose sample was left at the scene. Contrasting against the strength and individuality of the DNA profile is the sample(s) recovered from trace evidence. What is the value or significance of a single fiber or glass fragment comparison? This question is difficult to answer since most of this type of evidence is based on class features.

Class characteristics are those aspects that a certain group of items have in common. An example would be two fibers that share the same color, cross-sectional shape, and chemical composition. Each of the listed physical properties (e.g., color, shape, etc.) is not in itself unique or, even if combined, sufficient to suggest they are unique to each other. This type of evidence is *associative* in manner but not normally sufficient to convey uniqueness. In layman's terms, a fiber "match" probably does not equate to a full DNA profile match, because currently, there is no commonly accepted manner in which to provide a statistical weight to a single fiber.

The associative power of trace evidence can be enhanced by evaluating additional physical properties of, for example, the examined fiber from above; looking for additional different types of fibers on the same evidence; or other searching for other types of trace such as glass, paint, building materials, etc. (Table 16.1). Furthermore, the forensic scientist is often able to offer an expert opinion regarding the rarity of class characteristics (e.g., orange automotive paint on victim's pants versus white) based on his/her case-working experience, training, and peer-reviewed published studies that address these issues.

Combining multiple types of associative evidence is a strategy that can be used to strengthen investigative facts. While it may not have the discriminating power of a fingerprint, DNA, or firearms identification, it can still provide powerful information. For instance, it would be a challenge for someone to explain how a homicide victim's body, which was discarded alongside the highway, came to "coincidentally" have five different carpet fiber types on his/her clothing that happen to be consistent with the flooring from the suspect's house. This is especially true if the suspect denies any involvement or knowledge of the victim.

Trace Evidence Types

Hair

Over the past 10–15 years, the discipline of hair comparison has been under considerable scientific and legal scrutiny, resulting in confusion and doubt about its evidentiary usefulness. For decades, forensic scientists

Table 16.1 Common Types and Properties of Trace Evidence

Types of Trace Evidence	Some Common Physical Associative Properties (Nonunique)	Some Potentially Individualizing Factors
Hair evaluation	Type: human versus animal/body origin/ presence or absence of root	Root = STR or Y-STR DNA Shaft (body) = mitochondrial DNA
Fiber	Type, color, shape	
Glass	Type, color, refractive index	Fracture match
Paint	Type, color, layer structure	Fracture match/layer structure
Soil	Type, color, composition	

used microscopic hair comparison techniques to compare physical hair attributes (e.g., color, texture, modulation, etc.). It was understood by most practicing forensic scientists that this process was not uniquely sufficient to provide individualization to the exclusion of all others. A laboratory report might read, "The hair from defendant X was found to be consistent in color, texture, and modulation to the hair recovered from the crime scene." Unfortunately, this approach probably left too much interpretation to nonscientists.

Perhaps the issue is not necessarily the comparative science of hair microscopy but a combination of factors. The wording of the laboratory report and the limitations of the technique combined with an adversarial legal system in which scientists are pressed to describe nonquantifiable similarities could easily create confusion, instead of clarity. Of more recent concern, regrettably, the testimony of some "experts" possibly went beyond the science involved, potentially contributing to wrongful convictions. Furthermore, when scientific reports are used without an adequate explanation of the limitations such as interpretation by law enforcement on the witness stand or use by attorneys in closing arguments, then misunderstandings can occur. Nevertheless, some laboratories still offer microscopic comparative hair analysis, a practice that is still acceptable; *however*, appropriate limitations to the technique must be understood by all entities evaluating that evidence. It is crucial that the investigator understand the difference between a microscopic hair comparison and a hair evaluation for potential DNA testing. The latter is the subject for this section's discussion.

Hair Evaluation for DNA

Most crime scenes contain too many hairs to practically test all of them. Indeed, depending on the collection method, hundreds to thousands of potential hairs can be collected. From a fiscal point of view, it is not possible to test each hair. There are not enough resources, and the math doesn't add up. Making a quick, conservative back-of-the-envelope calculation can show the sizeable financial obligation of a *test-all* policy: 50 hairs × $150 screening test per hair + 50 hairs × $400 DNA test per hair (average contracted standard STR test) = $27,500. No forensic provider could routinely afford to offer this level of service for testing on all potential hair roots for every crime scene. mtDNA testing of the hair shaft is even more costly, and with that same calculation and service, the cost approaches six figures.

An alternative to the test-all method is for the investigator and laboratory scientist to take a thoughtful, intelligent approach in assessing the crime scene hairs. Several steps are involved in this process.

- Step 1 is limiting the selection to the most useful, probative hairs that are most likely to provide investigative direction. Some examples are those hairs located in the victim's orifices, in areas of struggle, near defense wounds, or on the victim that are dissimilar to the victim's own hair.
- Step 2 is microscopic evaluation of the hair to determine suitability for further testing (Figure 16.2). Questions that the laboratory forensic scientist will attempt to determine in this screening assessment are as follows:
  - *Is the hair animal or human?*

    Depending on the crime scene, hair from multiple species may be collected. Thus, to find the probative hair for DNA analysis, the microscopist must determine the species of the compared hair. He/she does this by comparing the microscopic features within the hair itself (Figure 16.3).

    For most crime scenes, the probative value of analysis is the testing of human hair (e.g., associating a human to the crime scene). However, there have been cases that place value in associating an animal (e.g., cat or dog) to a person or crime scene. This is done by identifying the type of animal hair and then conducting the appropriate DNA test applicable to that species type. The majority of public crime laboratories are set up to perform human DNA testing only and do not have capability to test multiple species. As such, specialty laboratories such as the U.S. Fish and Wildlife Service Forensic Laboratory and other vendors have developed specialized DNA

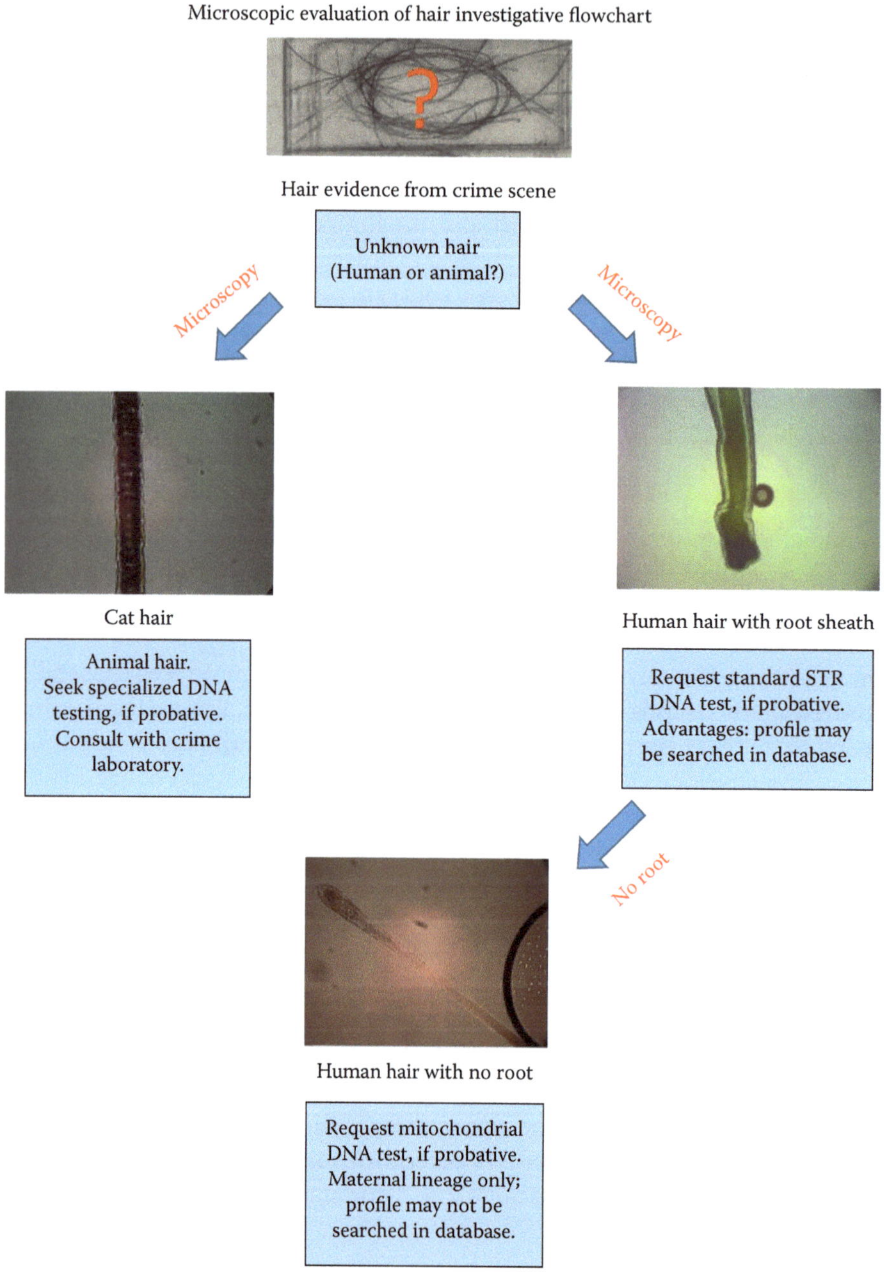

Figure 16.2 Hair flowchart. (Courtesy of Bryan Holden, Utah DPS.)

methods to individualize animals. If a cold case requires such analysis, the investigator should work closely with his/her crime laboratory to locate an appropriate vendor.

- *Does the hair contain a root tag of skin suitable for potential DNA testing?*

  The most crucial feature to maximize the value of a hair is the presence of a root sheath or tag of skin. This structure contains the nucleated cells that will provide the DNA for standard STR. (See Chapter 15.) If there is sufficient sample to develop a full DNA profile, then it may be eligible for entry into CODIS. This is the best solution for most cases.

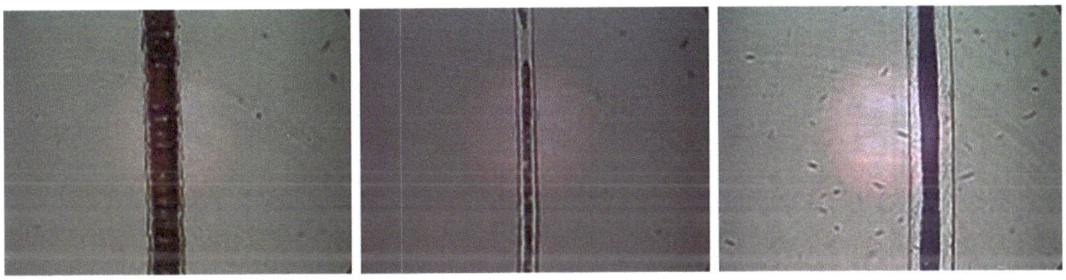

Figure 16.3 Cat, rabbit, and alpaca hair (left to right). (Courtesy of Bryan Holden, Utah DPS.)

- *Should mtDNA testing be considered?*
  Assuming that a hair was not amenable to STR testing, the next best option would be mtDNA testing. Mitochondria are cellular structures that are located within the shaft of the hair. While there are many more copies of this type of DNA available, which makes the test more sensitive with a greater likelihood of obtaining a result, it is less informative than the standard STR DNA test. Thus, it is not useful for a CODIS database search and can only be used as a direct comparison to a suspect or victim standard. Additionally, mitochondria are maternally inherited, which means that multiple individuals may have the same mitochondrial type, thus diminishing its uniqueness.

Reference Samples for Hair Evidence

For comparisons to distinguish between suspect and/or victim hair for the prioritization of DNA testing, reference hair must be collected and submitted to the laboratory along with the unknown hair. For head hair collections, representative hairs should be pulled from the parietal (sides), occipital (rear), and frontal areas of the scalp. For pubic hair, several representative groups of hair should be pulled from the pubic region. Be sure to consult with your laboratory for the number of samples to collect.

For DNA testing, a buccal (oral) swab or blood reference sample is sufficient.

Fibers

Often referred to synonymously with hairs, fibers are collected at the same time as hair evidence. Fibers do not have the potential for DNA testing; however, depending on case circumstances, they can provide very strong associative inference. The more like fibers found on the evidence, the stronger the association.

Similar to a hair analysis, the microscopist will evaluate trace evidence collections to determine the class characteristics of the recovered fibers to include type, color, shape, and chemical composition. (See examples of fiber shape in Figure 16.4.) These will then be compared to the submitted reference samples.

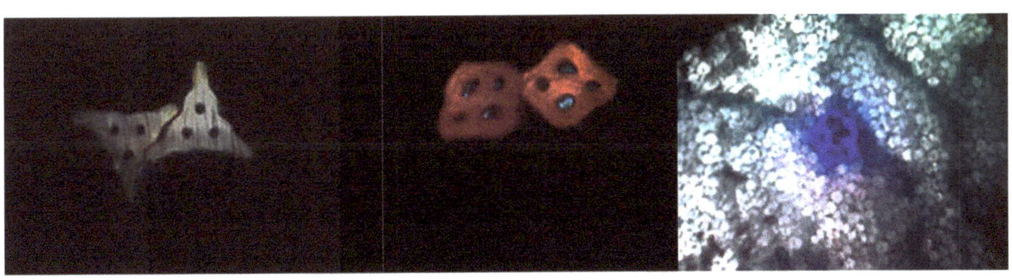

Figure 16.4 Cross sections of some common fibers. (Courtesy of Bryan Holden, Utah DPS.)

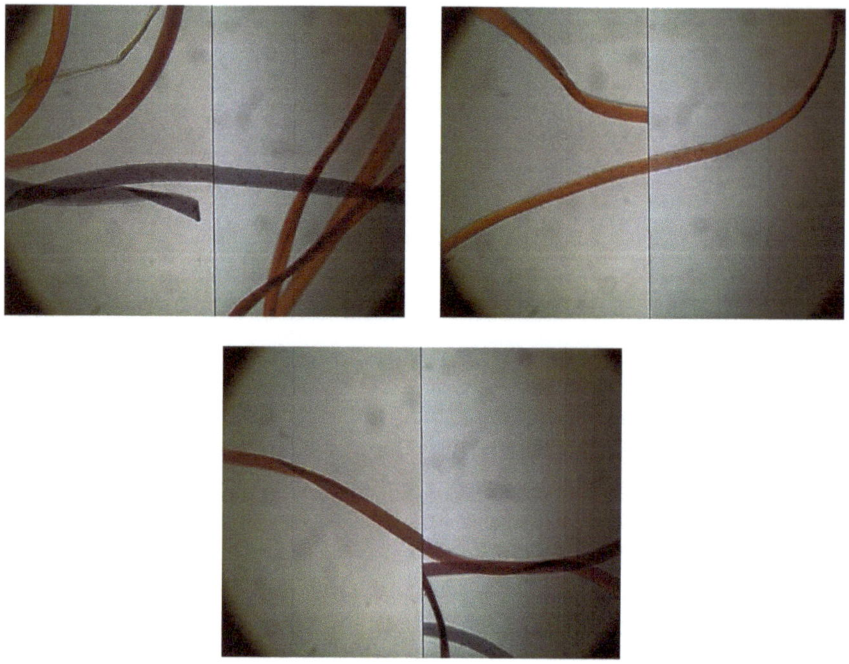

Fibers from residence on left, fibers from vehicle on right

Unusual fibers from residence linked to suspect's vehicle

At a local residence, investigators discovered many tufts of fibers. These tufts of fibers were collected (from the bedroom doorway and hallway). Upon searching the neighborhood, officers happened upon a vehicle. When officers made contact with the occupants, they noticed that there were tufts of fibers that were very similar to the ones found at the residence. The officers collected these fibers as well.

The fibers from the residence were compared to the ones recovered from the vehicle. Upon examination, the fiber analyst noted that these were fairly unique fibers in that they were half black and half red. The photos illustrate the red, the black (gray), and the transition areas of the compared evidence fibers.

The fibers from the vehicle and the fibers from the residence were found to be similar in all analyses. It was concluded that the fibers from the two locations could have come from a common source.

Figure 16.5 Unusual fibers from residence linked to suspect's vehicle. (Courtesy of Bryan Holden, Utah DPS.)

Reference Samples for Fiber Evidence

A known sample should be submitted with each unknown item. If the reference sample is clothing (e.g., a sweater), then the entire item should be submitted. If it is a larger item such as carpeting from a room or an automobile seat, then a representative cutting may be substituted (Figure 16.5).

Paint

Paint evidence has been used in a variety of ways to prove association. Typically, it is encountered with hit-and-run and burglary cases as microscopic fragments or smears left behind after some type of contact. Like other forms of trace evidence, it can easily be overlooked and requires that the cold case investigator apply substantive thought to make the most of its potential value.

In the laboratory, an analyst will begin his/her analysis by examining vehicles, clothing, or tools for evidence of contact. He/she will collect any fragment or smears of paint and begin comparing them to submitted reference samples. There are two types of comparisons.

- *Paint layer comparison*
  Paint may be composed of multiple coatings, each with a potentially different composition. The more layers in the evidence, the greater the uniqueness and the stronger the association. Most analyses of this type resulting in a positive comparative report may describe many class features (e.g., color, chemical composition, etc.) but still not be sufficient to convey uniqueness.
- *Fracture match*
  Paint evidence associations can sometimes be unique. Similar to fitting a missing piece into a jigsaw puzzle, a paint fragment can be physically matched to a common origin. The caveat is that the evidence must be sufficiently large with enough detail for the laboratory analyst to perform the comparison.

Paint Data Query Database

The Paint Data Query (PDQ) database is a unique effort within the trace discipline to maintain a reference set of automobile paint samples. Managed by the Royal Canadian Mounted Police (RCMP), the PDQ database is an international, collaborative effort by forensic laboratories to use a database to provide automobile make/model information from paint evidence fragments to law enforcement. Not all laboratories participate in this effort; thus, cold case investigators are encouraged to work with their provider to identify a laboratory willing to assist them. Most forensic providers work in a spirit of mutual cooperation and are more than willing to assist other agencies.

Reference Samples for Paint Evidence

For cases involving automobiles, known samples should be collected nearest the point of suspected contact or where damage is evident but not within the area of damage itself. With respect to cold cases, the damage may have been repaired with new paint applied. In these situations, the investigator should be aware that the collection and comparison of case samples can be challenging and may require extra collaborative effort. All standards should be rigorously recorded by the investigator with both notes and photographs. This is necessary due to the variation in paint application processes on vehicles (e.g., automotive paint on metal parts is chemically different from paint on plastic parts), and the potential to collect a sample that may not be appropriate. Additional reference samples may need to be collected.

With regard to paint transfer from tools, the entire item should be submitted, if practical (Figures 16.6 and 16.7).

Glass

Glass fragments may be transferred to clothing and footwear and have a practical potential for adherence and retention to those items. If the case facts suggest a glass fragmentation event (e.g., broken window, display case, etc.), then it may worthwhile to have the laboratory examine the clothing, automobile, or other items for the presence of fragments.

The analyst may begin their analyses by looking in the pockets and the surface of outerwear or soles of shoes for embedded fragments and collecting those items for testing. Somewhat similar to paint, there are two types of comparisons.

Hit-and-run homicide

The victim was hit from behind on a paved country road. A white truck was seen in the area. At the scene, pieces of zip tie were collected near the impact area. The victim's clothing was sent to the lab along with the zip tie pieces. From the truck, paint samples were collected on the hood and on the side of the truck bed. Microscopic examination of the victim's paints revealed white paint smears and white multilayered automotive-type paint chips. These unknowns were compared to the comparison samples from the truck using microscopic and instrumental chemical analysis. Based on the testing, it was concluded that the paint chips on the victim's pants could have come from the same source as the paint on the hood of the truck. A physical match was made between the pieces of zip tie found at the scene and pieces of zip tie found under the truck hood, thereby conclusively tying the truck to the victim. The truck was also swabbed for the victim's DNA, but no profile was developed.

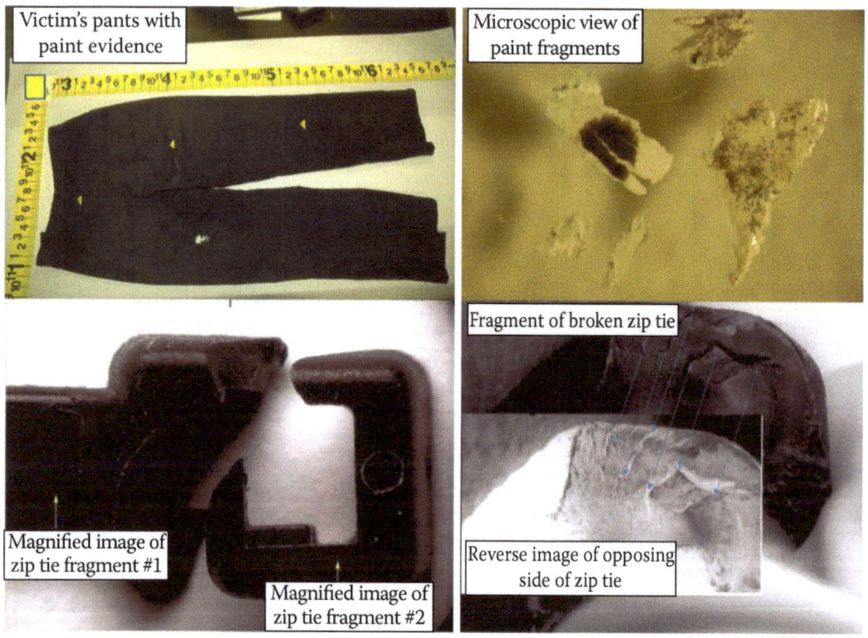

Figure 16.6 Paint fragments and physical match of zip tie in hit-and-run homicide. (Courtesy of Jennifer McNair, Utah DPS.)

- *Glass fragment comparison*
  Glass fragments are distinguished by their optical properties and chemical compositions. An analyst will measure each fragment's refractive index and evaluate its chemical makeup to determine consistency with submitted standards. Similar to other trace disciplines, most analyses of this type resulting in a positive comparative report may describe consistency in refractive index and elemental composition but still not be sufficient to convey uniqueness.
- *Fracture match*
  Similar to paint, a glass comparison can sometimes be unique. A glass fragment of sufficient size and detail may have the potential to be physically matched to show that the two compared items originally were one.

Trace cold case feature: Guarded Secrets

In 1991, Bryan Ruff, a security guard at Kennecott Copper Mine near Salt Lake City, went missing from his guard shack one evening. A search of the shack revealed no foul play. Dale Bradley was another security guard who often worked with Bryan. Dale Bradley became a suspect when investigators learned Bryan was having an affair with Dale's wife. Dale's 1974 orange-red Camaro was searched for GSR and blood and came up negative. When Dale later passed a lie detector test, he was no longer a suspect. One year later, hikers discovered the remains of Bryan Ruff 50 miles from the mine. An autopsy determined Bryan had been shot five times in the back with a .22-caliber handgun and buried in a shallow grave. Approximately 200 yards from the body, search, dogs found a cowboy boot that was identified as Bryan's. Fourteen years later, a Salt Lake County cold case detective received a call from a neighboring country's sheriff's office stating that Dale Bradley was a suspect in yet another murder. Dale was once again a suspect in the murder of Bryan Ruff. Dale's wife mentioned in an interview that Dale cleaned out his Camaro one day after the murder of Bryan Ruff, an uncommon event. The Salt Lake County detective examined the boot and observed a reddish smear on the bottom and remembered that Dale's car was of a similar color. Schneck was hired to determine if Camaros were painted in the trunk with the same color as the exterior of the vehicle and if the smear on the boot could have originated from the truck of the Camaro where it was believed Bryan may have been placed. Unfortunately the Camaro was sold as scrap in 1993. During the original search of the Camaro, an officer also collected red paint samples from the car. The red smear on the boot was compared to the control paint samples for the 1991 Camaro and a known reference paint sample from a 1991 Camaro acquired from NIST. Schneck identified orange–red lead chromate paint of similar color and chemical composition in all three samples using polarized light microscopy, scanning electron microscopy, energy dispersive spectroscopy, and infrared spectroscopy. Bryan Ruff likely was in the trunk of Dale Bradley's Camaro, and as he tried to kick the trunk open, some of the red paint transferred to his boot. This case was featured in Forensic Files, Episode 324, Guarded Secrets.

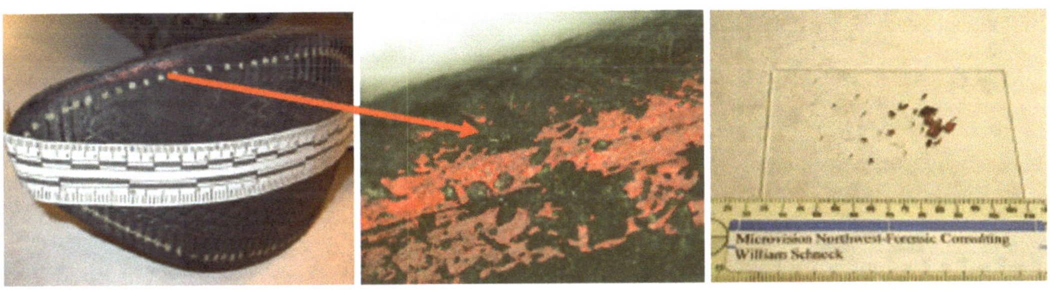

Boot | Close-up of boot | Paint from Bradley's Camaro

Figure 16.7 Paint cold case. (Courtesy of Bill Schneck, Microvision Northwest.)

Reference Samples for Glass Evidence

Glass reference samples should have been taken of the area nearest the breakage event.

Other Forms of Trace Evidence

The aforementioned trace evidence disciplines represent the most common laboratory requests. However, as mentioned at the beginning of this chapter, there is no strict definition of what type of evidence is considered trace. Thus, cold case investigators are encouraged to not limit themselves to just the typical discipline requests but to carefully consider the facts of each case, consult with their local forensic provider, and think

Candle-wax homicide

A request was submitted to the crime laboratory to determine if the wax on a suspect's clothing had come from a source found at a crime scene. The suspect denied being at the scene. The results of the examination revealed that the wax in the candle and the wax on the jeans were like one another with respect to their color, texture, and chemical characteristics. The candle wax in the jar could not be ruled out as a possible source for the wax on the jeans. This information was invaluable in placing the suspect at the scene. The case resulted in a conviction.

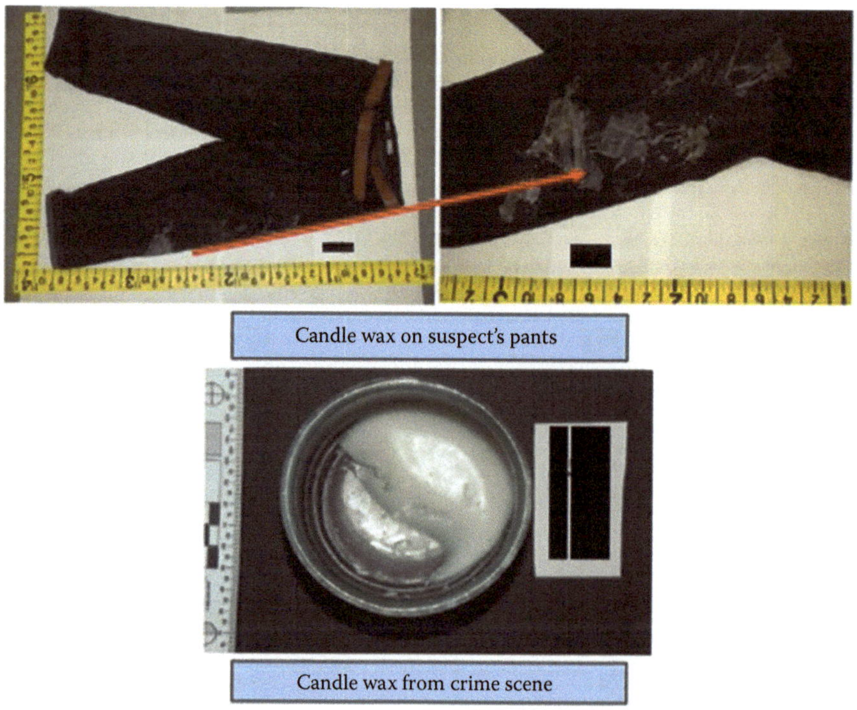

Figure 16.8 Candle-wax homicide. (Courtesy of Justin Bechaver, Utah DPS.)

deeply about the evidence in their case. Some additional considerations are cosmetics, soil, pollen, seeds, wood, and building materials, among others. The variation of physical evidence can be substantial and may not fit a traditional comparison category (Figure 16.8).

Where Is It Now?

As with law enforcement agencies, the evidence retention practices and policies of forensic providers vary greatly, and there is no national, standardized procedure. Hence, finding cold case trace evidence can be a challenge. The following represents some additional thoughts beyond what has already been discussed in previous chapters.

- *DNA swabs/cuttings:*

  Some laboratories adopted a practice of retaining biological evidence on all positive cases. Inquiries should be made regarding the location of those samples. Many cases have been solved with samples that have been stored in long-term evidence freezers or rooms. A not-uncommon practice has been for medical examiners to make two sets of swabs; one would be furnished to the law enforcement agency and the other maintained by the medical examiner. Although the agency's evidence may not be available, investigators should check with the medical examiner to ascertain their retention of any evidence

- *Hair/fiber lifts*

  Many providers have used water-soluble lift tape to process clothing and other items for hair and fiber evidence. Prior to accreditation of forensic laboratories, these lifts were sometimes stored on plastic sheets within the original case file itself. After a certain retention period, those case files may have been transferred to a long-term archives building.
- *Hair/fiber microscope slides*

  In the laboratory, forensic scientists would conduct their comparison analyses using microscope slides. For convenience, the slide, along with the potential evidence, was kept within the crime laboratory in a slide holder or in the case file itself. There may be a chance that those slides are still in the laboratory or in a long-term archives building.
- *Bullets*

  Often overlooked, projectiles (e.g., jacketed hollow points) are excellent collectors of evidence such as fibers, DNA, building materials, etc. A continuing practice of law enforcement is to rush to request the comparison of the bullets to the firearm in question but neglect considering the applicability of any trace evidence.
- *Autopsy and/or rape kits*

  Autopsy and rape kits are a great source of a variety of evidence. A review of each kit between the investigator and laboratory personnel is a great starting point. Most commercial kits contain packets labeled for trace evidence.

Acknowledgments

I wish to extend my deepest appreciation to Jay Henry, laboratory director for the Utah Department of Public Safety, for his contribution of this chapter. The case studies provide much insight into the experiences of team members in cold case investigations and lessons to be learned from the close cooperation of laboratory, investigative, and legal personnel. He was assisted in this endeavor by laboratory team members of the Utah Department of Public Safety—Bureau of Forensic Services, including Pilar Shortsleeve, Bryan Holden, Jennifer McNair, and Justin Bechaver, and to each, I also extend my deepest appreciation.

The National Missing and Unidentified Persons System (NamUs) 17

R. H. WALTON
SILVIA PETTEM

Contents

The number of cases of missing and unidentified persons reposing nationwide in the files of law enforcement and coroner/medical examiner offices has been called "the nation's silent mass disaster" (Ritter, 2007). These instances share a number of factors in common with cold case homicides. Included in these is that the true number of each is only an approximation, as many missing persons were never reported as such; many cold cases involved unidentified victims, and not all homicides are known to police.

In May 2016, it was reported that "4,400 unidentified remains are found every year and over 1,000 of these remain unidentified after one year" (NamUs Fact Sheet). Further, it was estimated that more than 40,000 unidentified human remains (UHR) cases continue to go unidentified. These are often kept in the offices of medical examiners/coroners, or cremated or buried.

Many of the missing are homicides but were never investigated as homicides. Compounding their resolution are the significant issues that occur when jurisdictional boundaries and state lines are crossed, involving different agencies and databases. For their families, the unknowing is a daily occurrence, perhaps in many cases the hardest aspect.

From decades of frustration among the families of the missing and the law enforcement and medicoforensic community evolved the National Missing and Unidentified Persons System (NamUs). This national database, which went online in 2009, is unlike others in that private citizens as well as law enforcement and the medical–forensic community can participate. Its initial development encompassed three phases between 2003 and 2009.

In 2003, the President's DNA Initiative resulted from a series of directives and meetings sponsored by the United States Attorney General and the National Institute of Justice (NIJ, the research and funding arm of the U.S. Department of Justice [DOJ]) seeking to reduce the backlog of DNA criminal cases and to streamline the nation's capacity to routinely and effectively utilize DNA as an investigative tool. Among topic discussions was the development of tools to facilitate investigation and resolution of missing persons and to identify unidentified remains. Almost concurrently, the International Homicide Investigators Association received some federal funding to explore and improve procedures for managing and identifying missing persons. The conception of NamUs drew on the pioneering efforts of Randy Hanzlick, MD, chief medical examiner of Fulton County, Georgia, and his office website listing unidentified cases. (He also represented the National Association of Medical Examiners.) Joining with others, they developed the Unidentified Decedent Reporting System (UDRS), with the inauguration of a pilot program in 2005. This remained the online system until 2007, when DOJ/NIJ began to provide funding to expand the system, and in 2007–2008, UDRS merged into an online national unidentified-persons database known as NamUs-UP.

Meanwhile, in 2005, the Identifying the Missing Summit took place in Philadelphia. Attendees included representatives of law enforcement, medical examiners/coroners, victims' families, scientists, and policy makers. A task force was created at the direction of the U.S. DOJ to identify available tools and create others to solve these cases. A problem evident to all was that while persons 17 years of age and younger had to be reported to the National Crime Information Center (NCIC; see Chapter 7), reporting of persons over 18 was voluntary, and there was and is no crime in voluntary "disappearance." This issue needed to be addressed so as to encompass all missing and unidentified. Policy among many agencies in the 1960s–1990s, in these authors' experiences, often minimized attention to cases involving late teens and adults, and efforts were minimal.

In 2009, the unidentified-persons database (NamUs-UP) was integrated with the missing-persons database (NamUs-MP), and NamUs went online. This provided a new and powerful investigative means that allowed simultaneous searching of missing-persons records with cases in the unidentified-persons index, by law enforcement, the medical examiner/coroner community, and the public.

Like all other databases, this system continues to expand and grow as more persons are added.

In addition to the online support, NamUs provides free forensic services, including odontology, anthropology, and fingerprint and DNA analysis for law enforcement and medical examiners'/coroners' offices. At the outset, the NIJ partnered with the National Forensic Science Technology Center in Largo, Florida, but transitioned to the University of North Texas Center for Human Identification (UNTCHI) in 2011. This fully accredited forensic laboratory is funded by the NIJ for its many services and managed in a partnership between both.

At its inception, the database contained only these two databases but added the unclaimed-persons database in 2012. Thus, as of mid-2016, the three databases include the (1) Missing Persons Database, (2) Unidentified Persons Database, and (3) Unclaimed Persons Database.

NamUs Missing Persons Database (MP)

The Missing Persons Database links to state and federal clearinghouses, law enforcement agencies, and missing-persons clearinghouses. In addition to basic descriptive data of a missing person, information may include characteristics that include demographics; anthropological features; and dental and other distinct features such as scars, marks, tattoos, surgery implants, and last-known clothing worn.

- Both medical/law enforcement and the public can enter data on missing persons into NamUs-MP, although cases submitted by the public have to be verified and given an NCIC number (or local report number) by law enforcement before they go live in the database.

- Basic case information includes first and last name, physical description, and known circumstances of disappearance. If any of this information is unknown, then "unknown" can be entered into the listing.
- Once the information is entered and saved, an MP case number is assigned. It is reviewed for case management purposes and assigned to a local officer in the appropriate jurisdiction. All attempts are made to involve the appropriate agency before it is published to the website.

The NamUs-MP database, however, is set up to hold much more detailed information, including photographs, physical characteristics and fingerprints, dental records, availability of DNA, and images of items such as clothing, jewelry, scars, and tattoos. New cases are added daily from around the nation, and agencies can easily share these online case files. As with the Combined DNA Index System (CODIS), Next Generation Identification (NGI), and other databases, cases must be entered in order to search against others in file, or for others to search against.

Searching the MP database may be done by keyword, quick search, and advanced search options. The search results page displays cases based on the entered criteria. The system offers other distinctive features, which, common to web-based databases, constantly undergo refinement and modifications.

NamUs Unidentified Persons Database (UP)

This database was designed to aid and assist in the identification of deceased persons. While it is searchable by anyone, only medical examiners, coroners, and/or their authorized official designees can enter cases into this database or close cases. The public cannot do so, and law enforcement can enter data only if they are the authorized designee. Searches are made using a variety of identifiers, including physical features and dental records, but also DNA, scars, marks and tattoos, clothing, jewelry, and prosthetics. These records are automatically searched against missing-persons records, and potential matches are provided investigators.

- Basic information to be entered includes a case number, the date the body or part was found, the county and state where the body or part was found, and the condition of the remains. "Unsure" or "cannot estimate" can be entered into the fields for age group, sex, weight, and height.
- Additional information, such as a morgue photograph, facial reconstruction, or artist's rendering, may also be added. Any sensitive data (such as a photograph of a decomposed body) can be blocked from public view.
- As with the NamUs-MP entries, the database provides the capability to enter much additional and detailed information.

When a new missing person or unidentified decedent case is entered into NamUs, the system automatically performs cross-matching comparisons between the databases, searching for matches or similarities between cases.

NamUs Unclaimed Persons Database (UCP)

Inaugurated in 2012, this database contains information about deceased persons who have been identified by name, but for whom no next of kin or family member has been identified or located to claim the body for burial or other disposition.

- Only NamUs staff and medical examiners and coroners may enter cases in the UCP database.
- This database is searchable by the public using a missing person's name and year of birth, and other methods, without registration, password, or user name.
- When a new missing person or unidentified remains are entered into NamUs, they are automatically checked through the other databases, searching for matches or similarities.

Using NamUs

- Cold case investigators should be aware that the U.S. is divided into eight regions, and each region has its own regional system administrator who can provide information, training, and support to individual investigators as well as agency training. Training can be accomplished by individual assistance from trained administrators, online, and in workshops at professional conferences. NamUs also provides free training to agencies upon request.
- Law enforcement and medical examiner/coroner inquiries enjoy automatic matches, while those of the public do not. Like other databases, the System can provide possible matches, which can be narrowed through refinement of parameters.
- Law enforcement users can enter information that can be withheld from public view but remains viewable by other law enforcement officers.

Entering and Searching in NamUs

NamUs is only as good as the information that is provided. As in cold case homicide investigations, it is recommended that all forensic work and expert opinions be reexamined before entering data. For best results,

- Investigators need to search from both sides of the System by manipulating the parameters of both NamUs-MP, on missing persons, and NamUs-UP, on unidentified remains.
- Every law enforcement agency needs to enter its cold missing-persons cases.
- All medical examiners/coroners should input information on their unidentified remains.
- Data on missing-persons cases can be entered by any registered user, but *the data will not go live until they are vetted by the appropriate law enforcement agency.*
- In addition to investigators, the public is encouraged to search the site and also to enter additional information such as jewelry regularly worn by the missing person.
- Some investigators also archive cases of missing persons who have been found, in the event that they go missing again. Others archive partial-remains cases, so as to readily identify additional partial remains that might be found in the future.
- The system offers case matching as an investigative tool for law enforcement and the forensic community and can flag possible leads based upon geography, chronology, and physical characteristics. Through forensic comparison, these can be excluded by a process of elimination.

Investigators are encouraged to monitor the NamUs website for enhancements, including consolidated registration and one-point entry.

University of North Texas Center for Human Identification

The UNTCHI is an accredited forensic laboratory located in Fort Worth, Texas. The forensics unit works with medical examiners' and coroners' offices, the National Center for Missing and Exploited Children (NCMEC), and law enforcement agencies throughout the United States in the submission, collection, and analyses of missing-persons samples.

- Missing-persons reports are filed with the law enforcement agency having jurisdiction where the individual was last seen or last resided. The agency may ask the person's family for a direct reference sample (DRS) obtained from articles belonging to the missing person. In addition, the agency may need to collect family reference samples (FRSs). FRSs can only be collected and submitted by the law enforcement agency. Family reference collection kits (with buccal swabs) and the required paperwork are provided *free of charge* by the UNTCHI. After analyses, the profiles are entered into the Federal Bureau of Investigation's (FBI's) DNA databases.
- Correspondence is mediated through the respective law enforcement agency. If a match occurs, the agency may notify the family as appropriate, and the law enforcement agency and medical examiner/coroner may need to submit samples of UHRs.

Other Resources

Many of the nation's law enforcement agencies do not know about their own state clearinghouses, or the four federal databases that may be of assistance in these investigations. These are the (1) NCIC, (2) CODIS (MP), (3) Integrated Automated Fingerprint Identification System (IAFIS), and (4) the FBI's Violent Criminal Apprehension Program (ViCAP).

FBI: NCIC, CODIS, and NDIR

NCIC

The Missing Person and Unidentified Person Files within the NCIC contain information referencing these topics. The Missing Person File contains personal identification information about missing persons, while the Unidentified Person File contains information on deceased persons or those whose identity cannot be determined. Shortly after an entry or modification of a record, NCIC generates two lists of possible matching records. One record consists of matching personal identifiers and the other of matching dental features. NCIC then messages the appropriate agencies if one of their records is a possible match to that of the agency file.

The Missing Person File contains six categories of persons. These are

- Endangered
- Disabled
- Involuntary
- Catastrophic victim
- Juvenile
- Other

The Unidentified Person File consists of three categories. These are

- Deceased person
- Living person unable to ascertain his/her identity
- Catastrophe victim

As does NamUs, the FBI offers assistance to appropriate law enforcement agencies in correctly entering data into these files. Further information may be obtained from the NCIC Investigative and Operational Assistance Unit. See Chapter 7.

In addition, the FBI offers additional services for identification of unknown deceased. These include forensic anthropology and forensic imaging. See Chapters 20 and 28.

CODIS and Missing and Unidentified Persons

In 2000, the FBI began development of the National Missing Person DNA Database program to be utilized in the investigation of missing and unidentified persons. CODIS, which went online as a pilot program in 1990 and became operational in 1998, contains three indices, which can be searched against each other. These are as follows:

- Missing Persons—contains DNA reference profiles of missing persons
- Unidentified Human Remains—contains DNA profiles from UHRs
- Biological Relatives of Missing Persons—contains DNA profiles voluntarily furnished by relatives of missing persons

For further information on CODIS, see Chapter 18.

National Dental Image Repository (NDIR)

This repository of images is maintained for law enforcement agencies who desire to post supplemental dental images that are related to missing, unidentified, and wanted persons in NCIC. Agencies convert their supplemental dental information to a specified format, and this is e-mailed to the Criminal Justice Information System (CJIS) Division at Clarksburg, West Virginia.

National Center for Missing and Exploited Children

See Chapter 31 on cold case resources.

Step-By-Step Checklist (Courtesy of FBI)

UNIDENTIFIED REMAINS

- ☐ Enter case into NCIC
- ☐ Autopsy/anthropologic examination
- ☐ Odontology examination
- ☐ Obtain nuclear DNA profile for CODIS entry
- ☐ Obtain mitochondrial profile for entry
- ☐ Produce facial reconstruction/3-D imaging/photographic

- ☐ Enter case into NDIR
- ☐ Enter case into ViCAP

MISSING PERSONS

- ☐ Enter case into NCIC
- ☐ Collect relevant identification information
- ☐ Collect DNA profiles of relatives for CODIS entry
- ☐ Enter case into NDIR
- ☐ Enter of case into ViCAP

In summary, the NamUs System has evolved to fill a void in national databases that have been developed since the last decades of the twentieth century. It is a central repository and resource center for matters related to missing persons, unidentified persons, and unclaimed deceased. Unlike the other federal and state databases, it is accessible to the public (with restrictions), thus increasing the ability of the relatives of missing persons to actively participate in the resolution of their case. Information can be submitted by law enforcement, missing-persons clearinghouses, and the general public (after vetting by law enforcement.) NamUs automatically cross-searches the missing-persons database against the unidentified-person database, and NCIC automatically does the same within its indexes.

Acknowledgments

We would like to express our deepest appreciation to Todd Matthews, director, case management and communications, of the University of North Texas (UNT) Center for Human Identification's Forensic Services Unit. He joined the NamUs management team in 2011 as the program transitioned, has served as a NamUs regional administrator (RA) and member of the advisory board for the development of the NamUs database and program, manages the NamUs RA staff, oversees quality assurance and quality control of NamUs data, performs outreach and training, and serves as media director.

Suggested Readings and Bibliography

NamUs Fact Sheet. (2016). namus.gov. Retrieved May 19, 2016.

Pearsall, B. and Weiss, D. (2007). Solving Missing Persons Cases. Report No. 265. National Institute of Justice.

Pettem, S. (2013). *Cold Case Research: Resources for Unidentified, Missing and Cold Homicide Cases*. CRC Press. Boca Raton, FL.

Ritter, N. (2007) Missing Persons and Unidentified Remains: The Nation's Silent Mass Disaster. Journal Issue 256. National Institute of Justice.

Unidentified Remains and Missing Persons. Laboratory Division, Federal Bureau of Investigation. Quantico, VA.

Walton, R.H. (2006). *Cold Case Homicides: Practical Investigative Techniques*. CRC Press. Boca Raton, FL.

Walton, R.H. (2013). *Practical Cold Case Homicide Investigations Procedural Manual*. CRC Press. Boca Raton, FL.

Combined DNA Index System (CODIS) 18

CONNIE MILTON

Contents

History

Recognition of the value of DNA as a means of individual identification in the late 1980s led to the Federal Bureau of Investigation's (FBI's) establishment of the Combined DNA Index System (CODIS) in 1990. The system initially began as a pilot project and served 14 states and local laboratories. In 1994, Congress passed Public Law 103-322, the DNA Identification Act (42 U.S.C. §14132). This act formalized the FBI's authority to establish a national DNA index for law enforcement and to establish DNA indexes for persons convicted of crimes, samples recovered from crime scenes, and samples recovered from unidentified human remains. On October 13, 1998, the FBI announced the operation of the National DNA Index System (NDIS).

How CODIS Is Used

CODIS is a collaborative effort among local, state, and federal law enforcement agencies. It is similar to the Integrated Automated Fingerprint Identification System (IAFIS), also operated by the FBI. Just as fingerprints from crime scenes are run through a computer system in search of a known individual with matching prints on file, CODIS allows a DNA profile found at a crime scene to be entered into a computer database in search of an individual with that DNA profile. These individuals may now include convicted offenders, known suspects, and arrestees, depending on the state in which the sample was collected. Law enforcement is thus able to identify or link possible suspects when no prior knowledge of the suspect existed.

Many in law enforcement contend that DNA is the most significant advance in criminal identification since fingerprints. The significance of this investigative tool in cold case homicide investigation cannot be overstated. In the past, jurisdictions tended to act independently in homicide investigations, failing to realize or admit that another jurisdiction may hold the key to solving their case. DNA and CODIS force the issue, bringing together the scene and offender.

System Design and Structure

CODIS utilizes a three-tier structure to input and access DNA profile data. The three levels are local level (LDIS), state level (SDIS), and national level (NDIS). The local level contains profiles of forensic samples developed through casework. Local databases may also contain the DNA profiles of suspects who gave samples for comparison in their respective cases. From the local level, DNA profiles from casework evidence (called forensic unknowns) are uploaded to the state level (SDIS). Local suspect DNA profiles are generally not uploaded to SDIS. Even when a match is achieved locally between a forensic unknown and the submitted known DNA sample from a suspect on the case, the forensic unknown can be uploaded to SDIS. In this way, it is possible to match to other forensic unknowns in other cities or states, thereby solving additional crimes that occurred in other jurisdictions (Figure 18.1).

If no match is achieved when a forensic unknown profile is uploaded to SDIS, eligible profiles will then be uploaded to NDIS for comparison to a national index of crime scene samples (forensic unknowns) and known offenders. NDIS is, in essence, a network of all the state DNA databases. If no match is achieved the first time a forensic unknown is searched against the LDIS, SDIS, or NDIS databases, the sample will be searched again periodically against those databases automatically, without any further effort on the part of the local laboratory or investigator. In this way, if an offender sample is entered well after the

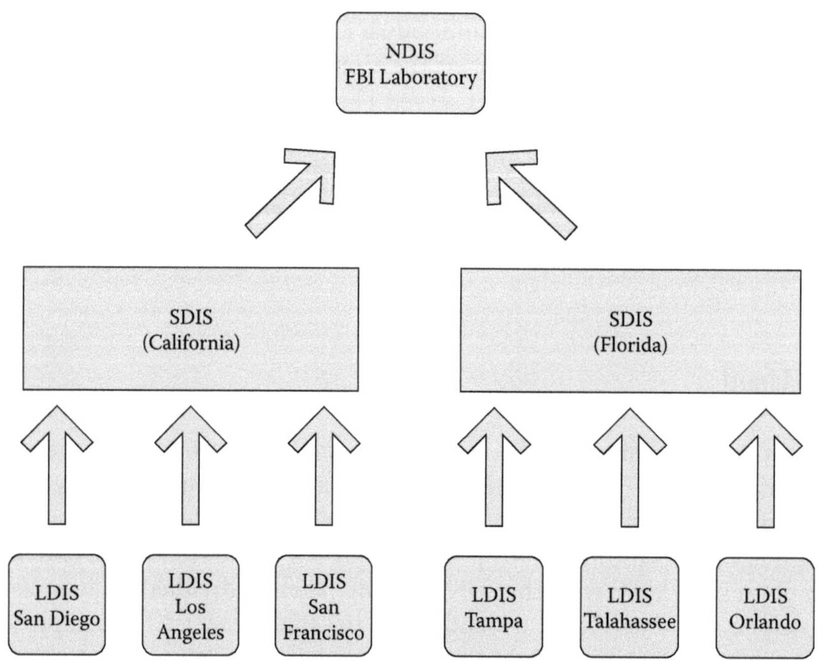

Figure 18.1 CODIS tier system. CODIS utilizes a three-tiered system. DNA profile information originates at the Local DNA Index System (LDIS) and can be uploaded to the State DNA Index System (SDIS). Ultimately these DNA profiles can be uploaded to the National DNA Index System (NDIS) operated by the FBI Laboratory. (Author's drawing.)

entry of the forensic unknown, a "hit" will be achieved. The separate databases are further described as follows:

- *LDIS—Local DNA Index System.* Casework samples such as semen stains are examined; DNA is extracted and profiled, and then entered into the local database. Suspect DNA profiles may also be loaded into the local database. Cases may be solved locally if a forensic unknown matches a suspect profile. Approved DNA profiles will be submitted to the state level of CODIS on a regular basis.
- *SDIS—State DNA Index System.* Offender samples are analyzed, and the DNA profiles are entered into SDIS by the state CODIS laboratory. These known-offender profiles are compared against the forensic unknowns from casework samples that are uploaded by the local crime laboratories in that state. The forensic unknowns are also compared against other forensic unknowns in the database. When forensic unknowns from multiple cases exhibit the same DNA profile (a case-to-case match), a crime series has been established. Eligible profiles will be routinely uploaded to the national level of CODIS.
- *NDIS—National DNA Index System.* This is the final level of CODIS and serves as a repository for DNA profiles submitted by all 50 states and the FBI. After submission and comparison at the local and state levels, eligible DNA profiles are entered into this national database and compared with a national index of forensic unknowns as well as offenders. As a result, NDIS allows states to exchange DNA profiles and to perform interstate comparisons of DNA profiles.

CODIS Loci

Forensic DNA typing kits are available from a number of different sources and manufacturers, each testing a number of different short tandem repeat (STR) markers. When CODIS was first implemented, 13 CODIS core loci were agreed upon, meaning that whatever kit or combination of kits was used by a laboratory to obtain a profile for entry into CODIS, they must have tested all 13 of the CODIS core loci. As the size of the database has grown to include several million known-offender samples, the chance for adventitious matches has also increased. In 2010, the FBI Laboratory empaneled a working group to evaluate the expansion of CODIS to include additional core loci.

After several years of research and validation studies by a number of different laboratories, they announced the expansion of the 13 original CODIS core loci to include an additional 7 loci. This means that all NDIS-participating laboratories need to have validated and available for casework an NDIS-approved forensic DNA testing kit that includes all of the new 20 CODIS core loci, as of January 1, 2017. In addition to the increased discrimination potential that these so-called megaplex kits provide, the expansion of the CODIS core loci will also allow for more sharing of DNA profiles with other countries, whose DNA testing kits may have many different STR loci than the 13 original CODIS core loci.

The Indexes

Forensic Index

This index contains DNA profiles from crime scene evidence, from both unsolved and solved cases. Matches made between profiles in the Forensic Index can link crime scenes to one another. Based upon a match that extends across political boundaries, police in those jurisdictions will learn of their common interest in a serial offender, and can then coordinate their respective investigations and share information and leads they developed independently. Samples entered into the Forensic Index will be classified as forensic unknowns, forensic partial, or forensic mixture samples. A mixed profile means that DNA was detected from more than one individual and that a specific DNA profile attributable to only one person cannot be determined. Many mixed DNA samples will not be suitable for entry into CODIS, period. Forensic partial means that full DNA typing results were not obtained at all genetic locations tested.

Offender Indexes

This index contains DNA profiles of known offenders and may consist of convicted offenders, arrestees, and known suspects. There are variations, state to state, in the classifications of the offenders who populate the databases. As of September 2011, all 50 states have passed legislation to allow profiles for all adult convicted feltons, and 30 states have passed legislation allowing for DNA sample collection for certain felony arrestees. Some states also maintain samples from suspects lawfully obtained during investigations. Prior to a change in federal law in 2006, arrestee samples were not eligible to be submitted to NDIS, but now they are; the arrestee index is the fastest-growing part of the database. Suspect known samples remain ineligible for upload to NDIS and will only be searched in LDIS and SDIS. Suspect known samples classified as "legal" may be uploaded to NDIS.

National Missing Persons DNA Database

Similar and parallel to the CODIS forensic unknown and offender indexes, there exists a DNA database for missing persons. The National Missing Persons DNA Database was initially outlined in 1996 but not funded by Congress until 1999. The goal is to match found unidentified human remains to DNA profiles of missing persons. DNA profiles representing these missing persons may have come from the individual's dentures, hair from a hairbrush, or some other secondary standard that individual left behind. In the absence of a reliable secondary DNA standard representing that individual, the DNA profiles of close relatives (parents, children, and siblings) of the missing person can be entered into the database. STR DNA information will be used if possible, but mitochondrial DNA will also be used in the missing-persons database. If the only sample recovered (from found remains) is weathered bone, it is likely that the only result that will be obtained will be a mitochondrial DNA type. Samples obtained from relatives of missing persons are not compared against crime scene samples entered into the forensic unknown and mixture indexes.

Unidentified Human Remains Index

Typically, when human remains are found, the local investigator will attempt to determine if there is a matching local case that explains the remains. When no clear matching case is obvious, a portion of the remains (usually a section of long bone, such as a femur) is sent to the state database laboratory that is handling found remains and missing persons. The state laboratory will attempt STR DNA profiling as well

Table 18.1 CODIS NDIS Search Table

INDEX	Forensic	Convicted Offender	Missing Person	Unidentified Human Remains	Relatives of Missing Persons
Forensic	•	•	•	•	
Convicted Offender	•		•	•	
Missing Person	•	•		•	
Unidentified Human Remains	•	•	•	•	•
Relatives of Missing Persons				•	

Note: This table demonstrates the search sequences that automatically occur when a DNA profile is entered into NDIS. As is shown, unidentified human remains are checked against all indexes.

as mitochondrial DNA typing. Just as convicted offenders and forensic unknowns are uploaded to search against a national database, there is a national database containing DNA information relating to missing persons and found human remains (Table 18.1).

Software

CODIS is a software system developed by the FBI. It blends computer technology and forensic science into a valuable means for solving violent crimes. CODIS is an automated DNA information-processing and telecommunications system that supports LDIS, SDIS, and NDIS. This system allows *public* forensic laboratories throughout the United States to exchange and compare DNA profiles electronically.

Criminal justice laboratories in the United States are linked by the Criminal Justice Information Services Wide Area Network (CJIS WAN) operated by the FBI. This system offers a secure Internet style of connectivity and is accessible only by authorized terminals within participating laboratories. LDIS and SDIS participants provide their own computer systems, and the FBI provides and installs CODIS software in these laboratories. In addition, the FBI provides free training and user support to any state and local law enforcement laboratories performing DNA analysis. CODIS is currently installed in more than 100 laboratories. Private laboratories do not have access to the CODIS database. Private consulting laboratories that develop DNA profiles would send those profiles back to the client laboratory for review and entry into CODIS by a local or state CODIS laboratory.

Sources of DNA Profiles

In contrast with IAFIS, CODIS has strict requirements as to the source of crime scene samples that may be entered. You must be reasonably certain that a DNA profile can be directly attributed to the perpetrator of a crime in order for it to be entered into CODIS. This may be more difficult to establish in a cold case where the original evidence documentation is limited. Also, as mentioned previously, many mixed DNA profiles are not suitable for entry into CODIS. DNA database legislation is constantly evolving as to the types of offenders who are being included in CODIS. Due to the changing nature of individual state requirements and mandates, cold case investigators should consult their local crime laboratory, state criminal justice laboratory, or attorney general for current status and requirements.

The Process Involved in a Hit

After first checking against the local DNA database, the local laboratory uses their CODIS computer to upload a *forensic unknown* (or *forensic mixture*) to the state DNA database. The forensic unknown is a DNA profile obtained from an item of evidence in a criminal case. The uploaded DNA profile from the forensic unknown is compared against the existing offender indexes and the forensic indexes at the state level.

If a hit is made between the forensic unknown and an offender in the database, the CODIS software system contacts the local laboratory to inform them of the potential match. If this is an unsolved case and the local lab confirms the match, usually, the state lab will reprofile the offender's known sample, to ensure that no sample switching occurred. At that point, a "hit report" is sent from the State laboratory to the local laboratory. This hit report provides additional information, including case information and the name and criminal ID number of the offender. Detectives at the local level would then be in a position to evaluate the evidence against the offender in this cold hit case. The hit report is considered probable cause to obtain a search warrant to obtain a new reference sample from the identified individual. Law enforcement investigators subsequently collect a fresh DNA sample from the identified offender, and this sample is forwarded to the local laboratory to confirm the DNA match.

Familial Searching

Familial searching is a deliberate search of the offender database conducted when a routine search has failed to yield an exact match. It is based on the concept that first-order relatives (such as parent/child or siblings) will share more DNA than unrelated individuals. Database searches done under different parameters allowing for nonidentical matches, but with a number of shared alleles, may indicate a close biological relationship. The United Kingdom has had much success with familial searching, conducting over 200 searches providing investigative information that has helped to solve over 40 serious crimes since 2003. Initially, the United States decided that familial searching would not be allowed in CODIS. NDIS later decided to leave it up to each state to decide on how to address familial searching at the SDIS level.

For jurisdictions that chose to perform familial searches, a strict protocol for searching is generally developed, and specially designed software (not CODIS) must be developed and validated to conduct these searches. Personnel with expertise in kinship analysis are needed to examine familial search results, and Y chromosome short tandem repeat (Y-STR) analysis may be required to confirm a potential familial match. For this reason, most forensic unknowns that will be good candidates for familial searching will be from serious unsolved cases with a single-source male DNA profile in CODIS that has failed to return an offender match.

Many state laws are silent on the issue of familial searching, and few states have actively begun performing such searches. California began conducting familial searches in 2008 with the approval of their attorney general. Other states have introduced legislation to formally permit familial searches, and some jurisdictions have laws that explicitly prohibit it. As of January 2017, California, Colorado, Florida, Michigan, Ohio, Texas, Utah, Virginia, Wisconsin, and Wyoming are the only states currently performing familial searching; however, other states are considering adopting this practice. Cold case investigators should consult their local or state crime laboratory to see if familial searching might be available to help solve their case. Currently, familial searching is not allowed in NDIS.

Acknowledgments

I would like to express my deepest appreciation to Connie Milton, supervising criminalist for the San Diego County Sheriff's Department, California, Regional Crime Laboratory. Before joining the sheriff's crime lab in 1996, she was a research scientist with the Salk Institute for Biological Sciences. She specializes in DNA analysis and supervises the DNA Rapid Response Team, a team of criminalists who deploy DNA technology to solve street crimes, including robberies, burglaries, and auto thefts. She has been instrumental in helping to solve some of San Diego's most infamous cases and is a longstanding member of the department's crime scene investigations team. She is an experienced law enforcement and forensics instructor and has presented throughout the United States, and in Mexico and the United Kingdom.

National Integrated Ballistic Information Network (NIBIN)

19

KATHARINE DYER
R. H. WALTON

Contents

The National Integrated Ballistic Information Network (NIBIN) is a database of digital images of fired bullets and cartridge cases from crime scenes and known firearms. NIBIN can generate investigational leads in shooting cases by informing the investigator if the firearm used in one crime was also used in another crime. NIBIN can help develop a suspect where there was none before on a case by linking it to another case that does have a suspect.

Every firearm has individual characteristics that are as unique to it as fingerprints are to human beings. When a firearm is fired, it transfers these characteristics in the form of microscopic scratches and indentations to the bullets and cartridge cases fired in it. The barrel of the firearm marks the bullet traveling through it, and the breech face, firing pin, and ejector mark the expended cartridge case. Efforts to match firearms to fired bullets and cartridge cases are found in criminal cases going back to the beginning of the twentieth century, and the forensic application of technology to this field began in earnest in the 1920s.

Direct comparisons can be made when both firearm(s) *and* bullets or cartridge cases are recovered during a criminal investigation. Firearms examiners use the microscopic marks for comparison to determine whether or not bullets and/or cartridge cases were fired from a suspect's firearm. Test-firing the weapon creates exemplar bullets and cartridge cases for future comparison as well. Bullets and cartridge cases found at one crime scene can also be compared with those found at another in order to link the crimes (Figure 19.1).

But what happens if an investigator has only a cartridge case at his/her crime scene, or just a firearm, and no idea of what other crime scene's evidence to compare it to? In the past, this has been a tedious and time-consuming process. Each cartridge case (or bullet, either test-fired or from the scene) was compared by hand under a microscope, piece by piece, to a large number of other cartridge cases (or bullets) previously collected at other scenes or test-fired by only that particular agency. No means of automatic comparison existed, let alone cross-jurisdictional. This manual process was hindered by limited available resources and time constraints, making matches less likely. This began to change in the 1990s.

Figure 19.1 Cartridges and cartridge cases. Cartridges expended in semiautomatic firearms account for the majority of expended cartridge cases recovered at crime scenes. (Author's photo.)

The Birth of Ballistic Imaging: CEASEFIRE, DRUGFIRE, BulletProof, and NIBIN

In 1992, the Bureau of Alcohol, Tobacco, Firearms, and Explosives (*BATFE*, commonly known as *ATF*), a federal law enforcement agency, developed and began to implement *CEASEFIRE*. This was an enforcement program aimed at addressing firearms-related violence in the wake of the spike in homicide rates of the 1980s and early 1990s. CEASEFIRE was a spin-off from the ATF program *Achilles*, a nationwide program enforcing provisions of the Armed Career Criminal and Comprehensive Crime Control Acts of 1984 targeting neighborhoods with high rates of violent crimes and creating mandatory minimum sentences. CEASEFIRE provided comprehensive and focused investigative assistance through the integration of ATF investigative expertise with new state-of-the-art technology. In the beginning, the plan sought to enter all data obtained from firearms seized as a result of investigation by ATF personnel into a national computer system. In addition, local and state law enforcement could utilize this system to enter and retrieve information for investigative purposes related to their own firearms-related criminal investigations. As a result, this system would serve as a central database for all data on firearms used in crimes.

In January 1993, the ATF viewed a presentation from Forensic Technology, Incorporated (FTI) of a new ballistic imaging system that allowed firearms examiners to rapidly examine large numbers of fired bullets (Figure 19.2). This system, known as *BulletProof*, also allowed data sharing among terminals, thus permitting tracking of mobile criminals. As a result, the ATF leased equipment from the firm and began exploring other uses for this technology. In 1995, the ATF formulated a set of principles for expansion of ballistic imaging technology sites and utilization of these resources by local law enforcement.

During this previous period, however, the Federal Bureau of Investigation (FBI) had implemented a computerized ballistic imaging system of its own called *DRUGFIRE*. Some agencies opted for the ATF system, and some had opted for DRUGFIRE. There was a glitch, however. The two systems were *incompatible* and did not communicate with each other. Data entered into one system could not be utilized by the other system. As a result, two different systems that could not be linked together were beginning to appear and spread in the nation's law enforcement forensic community. An independent evaluation of the BulletProof and DRUGFIRE systems ensued.

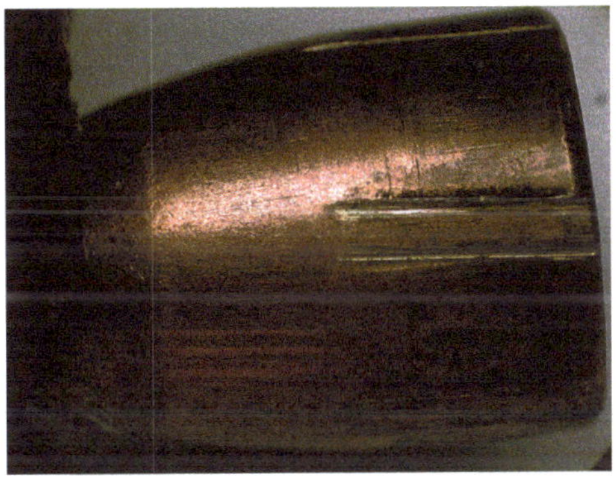

Figure 19.2 Fired bullet. Images of the land impressions offer the most accurate and dependable potential for a match. The land impression is the narrower image in the center, and the groove impression the wider impression on each side of the land impression. (Courtesy of Mike Grubb, San Diego Sheriff's Department Regional Crime Laboratory.)

Both ballistic imaging systems used computer-searching capabilities to match recovered crime scene evidence against information stored in a computer database and minimized the amount of nonmatching evidence that firearms examiners had to inspect in order to discover a match. The review found that processing both bullets and cartridge cases on one common versatile platform would offer the best solution to a need for ballistic imaging requirements. As a result of this review, FTI developed *BrassCatcher*, which would image cartridge cases using the same computer as BulletProof.

This development provided a platform that could evaluate both bullets and cartridge cases. FTI referred to this new system as the "Integrated Ballistics Identification System" (IBIS). IBIS comprised both BulletProof and BrassCatcher. IBIS provided for the first time a platform for evaluating both bullets and cartridge cases on the same system.

In January 1996, both the ATF and the FBI acknowledged a need for interoperability. In June of that year, the National Institute of Standards and Technology (NIST) issued a report to define minimal specifications for this interoperability. The report provided the manufacturers of IBIS and DRUGFIRE with specifications to make hardware and software modifications to their systems in order to achieve interoperability. In May 1997, the ATF and FBI entered into an agreement, the NIBIN Concept Paper, where each pledged to make no modifications to existing systems that would exacerbate the differences in the technology. From this agreement arose the term *National Integrated Ballistic Information Network (NIBIN)*. As a part of this agreement, the ATF agreed to stop referring to its ballistic imaging program as "CEASEFIRE," and the FBI agreed to stop using the term "DRUGFIRE" for its program.

The *NIBIN Board* was created in order to unify federal efforts to deploy ballistics technology. The three-member board comprised one member each from the ATF and FBI and a member from the state/local law enforcement community. Each agency continued to operate its own system, however. By the summer of 1999, after extensive testing and research by NIST into the potential for interoperability, the NIBIN Board made the decision to pursue the single-network goal in a different way, through interagency cooperation and joint deployment of only one system. Later that year, the ATF and FBI signed a memorandum of understanding (MOU) delineating each agency's role in the creation of NIBIN. The ATF was responsible for field operations, including purchase of equipment and training of users, while the FBI was responsible for providing a communications network.

In February 2000, the ATF completed its strategic plan to support the *rollout*—the change from DRUGFIRE to NIBIN. The plan included the creation and staffing of the NIBIN Branch as part of the Firearms Programs Division of the ATF to support NIBIN operations. It also became clear that it would be necessary to enable information sharing among more sites in the same region. This necessitated the creation of regional servers capable of correlating and storing more data and of communicating with more sites than under the previous hub configuration. FTI began developing a regional server to meet this need. Criteria were established to evaluate local law enforcement agencies for participation, including population served, firearms-related crimes, and number of firearms recovered. In late 2003, it was decided NIBIN would be more efficient if only one federal agency was involved, so the ATF took over all facets of running it, and it was placed in their Science and Technology Division. In 2013, realizing NIBIN could be more effectively used on the front lines of shooting cases, the ATF moved it from the Science and Technology Division to the Field Operations Division, where it could be utilized more proactively in criminal investigations.

Setup and Design

NIBIN setup has occurred on a regional basis. The initial design system divided the nation into 16 multistate regions with every major population center having access to integrated ballistic imaging technology (Figure 19.3).

In most cases, the ATF purchases IBIS equipment for deployment to local law enforcement agencies and contracts with FTI, now Ultra Electronics Forensic Technology, for training users from the approved sites. Some law enforcement agencies purchase the equipment on their own. But all agencies connecting to NIBIN must participate in an MOU and meet established criteria. The ATF ensures that the equipment is properly installed and that the sites' personnel are trained and qualified. Thereafter, the ATF provides for regular updates and service, as well as administering the network by which it communicates. It also

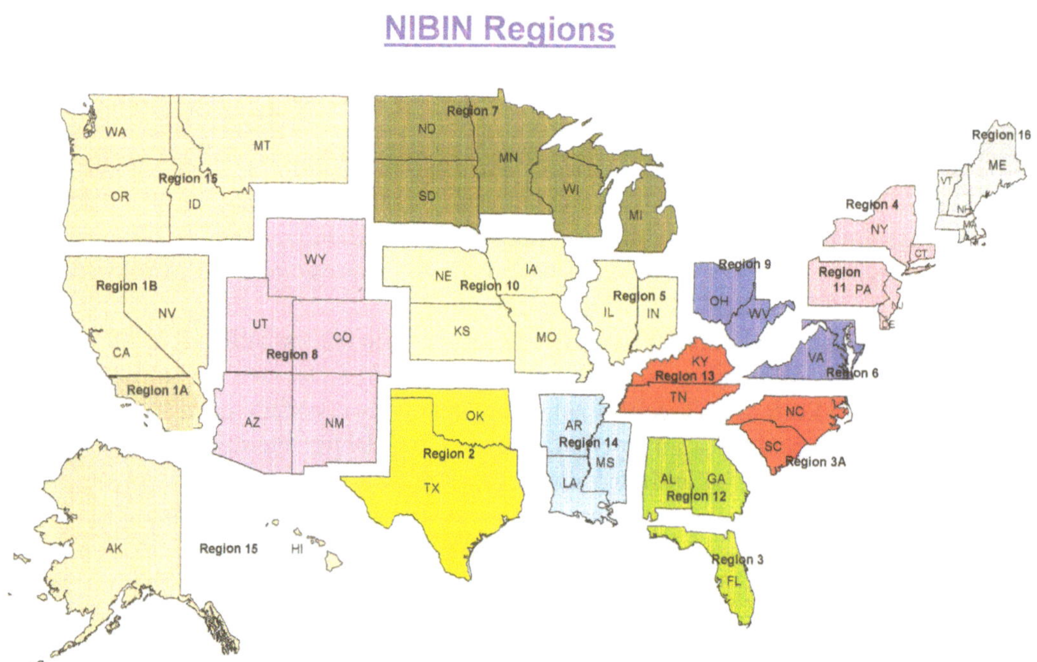

Figure 19.3. NIBIN regional map. (Courtesy of ATF.)

monitors use statistics to ensure that the equipment is being used to its maximal effectiveness. In turn, the law enforcement agency agrees to support the program by

- Providing adequate staff and resources
- Possessing a bullet/cartridge case recovery system for test firing
- Entering as much crime gun evidence as possible into their IBIS systems in a timely manner
- Sharing evidence and intelligence information with other law enforcement agencies in a timely manner
- Abiding by ATF regulations for system use

Equipment and Networking

NIBIN allows firearms technicians to acquire, digitize, and compare markings made by a firearm on bullets and cartridge cases quickly.

Four different types of IBIS equipment currently comprise NIBIN:

1. *IBIS TRAX-HD3D*—the latest in IBIS technology. The *BRASSTRAX* and *BULLETTRAX* are the main units of the IBIS high-definition three-dimensional system, each comprised of an automated digital imager (acquisition station) and a computer that will allow the viewing and validation of acquisitions. BRASSTRAX is for the high-definition topographical 3-D imaging of cartridge cases (rollout began in the United States in 2015), and BULLETTRAX is for the high-definition topographical 3-D imaging of bullets. These systems are locally installed but connected to NIBIN (Figure 19.4).
2. *IBIS TRAX-HD3D MATCHPOINT.* A desktop computer connected to a data concentrator that is used to compare and analyze correlations of the 2-D and 3-D images. This is locally installed but connected to NIBIN (Figure 19.5).
3. *IBIS Data Concentrator.* Compresses the high-resolution images taken by the acquisition stations and generates image signatures, which are then sent to the server for correlation. The concentrator can be installed locally or remotely.
4. *IBIS Regional Correlation Server.* Compares image signatures and generates the correlations. The servers are located within three ATF laboratories across the country.

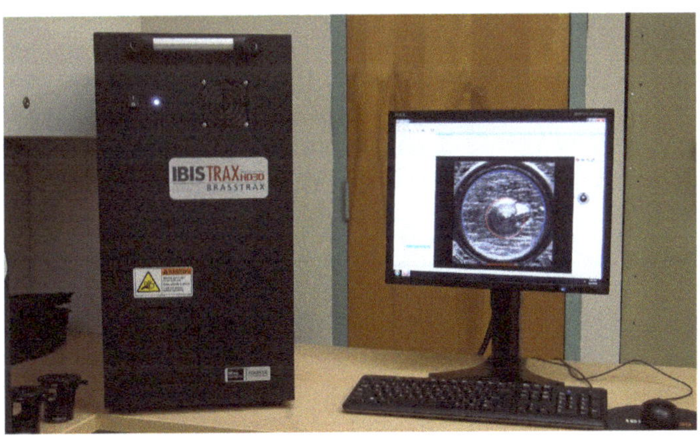

Figure 19.4 IBIS TRAX-HD3D BRASSTRAX. The main unit of the IBIS three-dimensional system that images cartridge cases comprises an automated digital imager (acquisition station) and a computer that will allow the viewing and validation of acquisitions. (Courtesy of K. Dyer, San Diego Sheriff's Regional Crime Laboratory.)

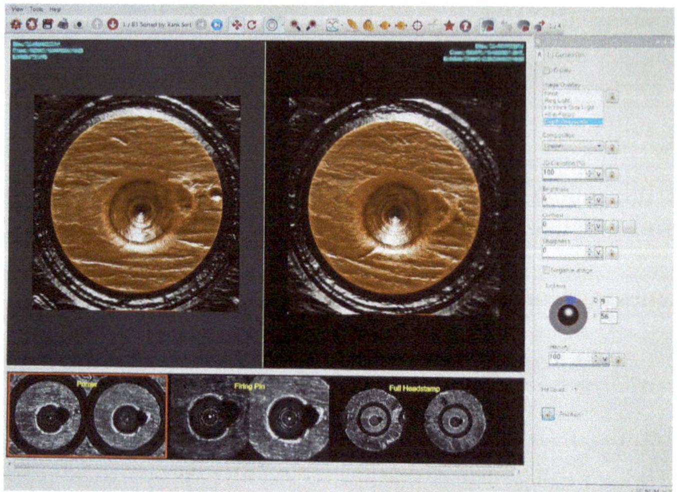

Figure 19.5 IBIS TRAX-HD3D MATCHPOINT. IBIS TRAX-HD3D MATCHPOINT monitor screen showing the latest 3-D technology. Ballistic imaging systems use computer search capabilities to match recovered crime scene evidence against information stored in a computer database. (Courtesy of K. Dyer, San Diego Sheriff's Regional Crime Laboratory.)

How It Works

For entry into NIBIN, a firearms examiner or technician, without needing extensive previous computer experience, is trained to take high-resolution digital images of the unique markings left on the crime scene or test-fired bullets and cartridge cases using the IBIS equipment. These images are then uploaded to the NIBIN database, in addition to recording the demographic information of the case such as crime type, date, and other information.

- For a cartridge case, the images acquired and correlated include (if present) the following:
  - *Breech face mark impression.* These impressions are made by marks on the breech face of the firearm left behind as a result of final finishing in the manufacturing process. The breech face is the largest surface for marks.
  - *Firing pin impression.* Images can also be made of the firing pin impression of rimfire cartridge cases. Differences in firing pin shapes and sizes assist in finding a match.
  - *Ejector mark.* The ejector mark is caused when the fired cartridge case contacts a projection of metal in the breech of the firearm when it is ejected.
- For a bullet, images of the *land impressions* are acquired and correlated. Markings on this engraved portion of the bullet after it leaves the barrel offer the most accurate and dependable potential for a match. However, it has been shown that "hits" (matches) with cartridge cases occur with much greater frequency than with bullets.

These images are then sent to the regional server for correlation against other images in the regional database. The system produces a list of potential candidates for a possible match, those that exhibit a high correlation of similar characteristics. Correlation results, a selection of images with very high correlation scores, are then sent back to the acquiring IBIS site. Search results alert the examiner to possible matches. The IBIS correlation analysis does not positively match bullets or cartridge cases fired from the same weapon. This must be done by a firearms examiner, who will examine the original evidence side by side on a comparison microscope to confirm the hit.

During the correlation, the images are compared against earlier entries into NIBIN. Because it has been observed by system users and detectives that firearms used for criminal purposes tend to travel in certain corridors, such as along the eastern seaboard or along the west coast, these searches are usually made against evidence from the same jurisdiction and neighboring jurisdictions. They can be made against jurisdictions across the country, but the investigator must let the technician know a specific city and state to search because only regional corridors are automatically checked. National searches are not routinely done.

It is important for investigators to work with the lab, and to give them information so they know which region to search.

"Hit" Defined

A hit is defined as a linkage of two different crime investigations by the user of the NIBIN technology, where previously there had been *no known connection* between the investigations. Other NIBIN linkages derived by investigative leads, hunches, or previously identified laboratory examinations are not hits according to this definition.

A hit must be confirmed by a firearms examiner examining the actual specimens under a microscope.

Key to the success of this program is input of data in the form of fired bullets and cartridge cases in a timely manner. As with any database, the more entries, the better it works. Similar to that of the AFIS and CODIS databases, it is important for law enforcement personnel to understand the importance of submitting shooting evidence for inclusion and search against the database. It is also important to get this evidence into the system in a timely manner to discover investigational leads that are still actionable. Since the beginning of the program, the ATF has encouraged use of the following priority order for entering evidence into NIBIN:

1. Bullets and cartridge cases from crimes where no firearm has been recovered
2. Test fires from firearms seized during criminal activities or search warrants

The ATF has determined that the higher the ratio of scene evidence (i.e., bullets and cartridge cases) to test fires, the more successful a laboratory can be in linking unsolved shooting cases.

Certain calibers make up the vast majority of those firearms used in crimes. These are

- .22LR
- .25 auto
- .380 auto
- 9mm
- .40 S&W
- .45 auto

By and large, these cartridge cases are recovered from a crime scene when they are expended from *semiautomatic* weapons (the 9mm and .45 may be found in and fired from fully automatic weapons). All nominal calibers of cartridge cases and bullets ranging from .22 up to .50 using pistols, revolvers, and rifles may be entered into the system, as well as shotgun shells from .410 up to 10 gauge. However, black powder firearms, firearms using blanks or pellets, and shotgun pellets or wadding cannot be entered into NIBIN.

By law, the NIBIN program is expressly *restricted* to the ballistic imaging of data associated with *crime guns*. Ballistics systems deployed to federal, State, or local authorities *cannot* be used to capture or store images acquired at the point of manufacture, importation, or sale, or any other data associated with such images. This includes information about the purchaser, firearm type, model, caliber, gauge, serial number, or date of manufacture.

However, there are no restrictions on NIBIN as to what *type* of crime the firearm was confiscated from. Anything from fired bullets and cartridge cases from crime scenes that are complete unknowns (e.g., drive-by shootings) should be entered into NIBIN, as should test-fired bullets and cartridge cases from crime guns, guns confiscated from suspects that were not used in that crime, or even "found guns" (who throws a gun into the bushes?) Even if a link is not established at the time of the initial NIBIN search, the case stays in the database, is searched against future cases, and may result in a match at a later time. Even if it seems there can be nothing done with a case, entering the evidence into NIBIN might just clear another investigator's case.

When multiple cartridge cases are found at the scene, all should be identified to each other to make sure each was fired from the same weapon, and if they are, then only one need be entered into NIBIN.

Organization and History of ATF

The forerunner of the ATF was historically the tax-collecting, enforcement, and regulatory branch of the U.S. Treasury Department. This agency derives its authority from Congress and cannot enact laws nor amend laws. The passage of the National Firearms Act in 1934 and the Federal Firearms Act four years later involved taxation of regulated weapons (e.g., machine guns). This taxation was assimilated with tobacco tax collection under the auspices of the Bureau of Internal Revenue until the early 1950s. In a 1952 reorganization, this bureau became the Internal Revenue Service (IRS), and firearms and tobacco taxation was delegated to the Alcohol and Tobacco Tax Division. This lasted until passage of the 1968 Gun Control Act, which added explosives regulation to the body. In addition, this act now required serial numbers be affixed to all firearms. The 1970 Organized Crime Control Act solidified ATF explosives authority, and the unit became known as BATFE Division. The 1982 Anti-Arson Act gave the ATF responsibility for nationwide investigation of commercial arson.

On July 1, 1972, the agency became a more autonomous unit within the Treasury Department and separated from the more revenue-collecting mission of the IRS. Since 9/11, the organization is now under the auspices of the U.S. Department of Justice.

Further ATF Cold Case Resources

Cold case investigators have conducted investigations in which they have sought to locate the firearms records of dealers who are no longer in business. If the name of the dealer is known, or becomes known, it is suggested that investigators attempt to contact the dealer for a statement, copies of records, and any other pertinent information that may be generated. In cases where the name of the dealer is unknown, but the make and serial number are recorded in the file (as in the case of a recovered weapon at some point during the investigation), the ATF may possess records pertinent to the investigation. Licensed firearms dealers, importers, or manufacturers who discontinue business are required to forward their business records to the ATF.

National Firearms Tracing Center

The National Firearms Tracing Center

- Traces the origins and ownership of recovered firearms used in crimes. This database information, which derives from recovered and traced firearms, is available to federal, state, and local law enforcement or foreign law enforcement authorities.
- Is the main repository of all the records of federal firearms dealers who are no longer in business (Figure 19.6).

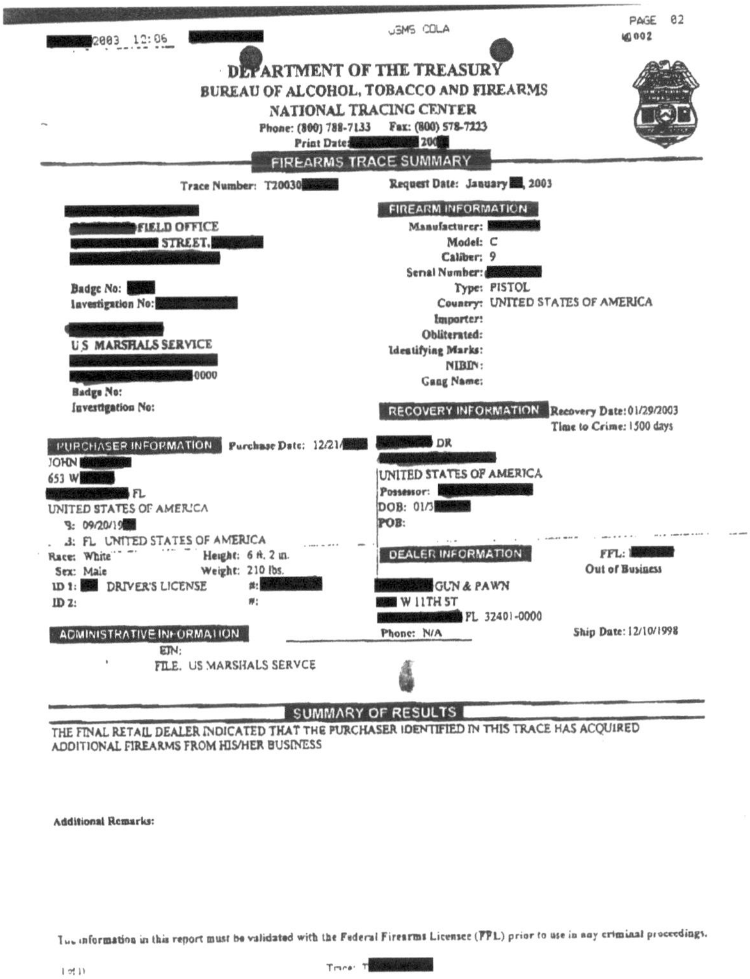

[redacted]2003 12:06 [redacted] USMS COLA PAGE 02

002

DEPARTMENT OF THE TREASURY
BUREAU OF ALCOHOL, TOBACCO AND FIREARMS
NATIONAL TRACING CENTER
Phone: (800) 788-7133 Fax: (800) 578-7223
Print Date: [redacted] 200[redacted]

FIREARMS TRACE SUMMARY

Trace Number: T20030[redacted] Request Date: January [redacted], 2003

[redacted]
[redacted] FIELD OFFICE
[redacted] STREET, [redacted]

Badge No: [redacted]
Investigation No: [redacted]

[redacted]
U.S. MARSHALS SERVICE
[redacted]0000
Badge No:
Investigation No:

FIREARM INFORMATION
Manufacturer: [redacted]
Model: C
Caliber: 9
Serial Number: [redacted]
Type: PISTOL
Country: UNITED STATES OF AMERICA
Importer:
Obliterated:
Identifying Marks:
NIBIN:
Gang Name:

RECOVERY INFORMATION Recovery Date: 01/29/2003
Time to Crime: 1500 days
[redacted] DR
[redacted]
UNITED STATES OF AMERICA
Possessor: [redacted]
DOB: 01/3[redacted]
POB:

PURCHASER INFORMATION Purchase Date: 12/21/[redacted]
JOHN [redacted]
653 W[redacted]
[redacted] FL
UNITED STATES OF AMERICA
DOB: 09/20/19[redacted]
POB: FL UNITED STATES OF AMERICA
Race: White Height: 6 ft. 2 in.
Sex: Male Weight: 210 lbs.
ID 1: [redacted] DRIVER'S LICENSE #: [redacted]
ID 2: #:

DEALER INFORMATION FFL: [redacted]
Out of Business
[redacted] GUN & PAWN
[redacted] W 11TH ST
[redacted] FL 32401-0000
Phone: N/A Ship Date: 12/10/1998

ADMINISTRATIVE INFORMATION
EIN:
FILE. US MARSHALS SERVCE

SUMMARY OF RESULTS
THE FINAL RETAIL DEALER INDICATED THAT THE PURCHASER IDENTIFIED IN THIS TRACE HAS ACQUIRED ADDITIONAL FIREARMS FROM HIS/HER BUSINESS

Additional Remarks:

The information in this report must be validated with the Federal Firearms Licensee (FFL) prior to use in any criminal proceedings.

1 of 1 Trace: T[redacted]

Figure 19.6 Firearms trace summary. A separate report is generated for each individual firearm subjected to a trace investigation. (Courtesy of ATF.)

The ATF has set up a convenient online avenue for law enforcement agencies to submit tracing requests called eTrace.

National Tracing Center
ATF/Records Center
244 Needy Road
Martinsburg, WV 25405
1-800-788-7133
http://www.atfonline.gov/etrace/

Federal Firearms Licensing Center

The Federal Firearms Licensing Center is responsible for licensing all manufacturers, importers, dealers, and collectors of firearms in the United States. The center's firearms records system provides the means to trace firearms and explosives.

Federal Firearms Licensing Center
244 Needy Road
Martinsburg, WV 25405
1-866-662-2750
FFLC@atf.gov

Acknowledgments

I wish to acknowledge and express my deepest gratitude to NIBIN Specialist Katharine Dyer of the San Diego County Sheriff's Department Regional Crime Laboratory for her gracious willingness and contribution to update this chapter. In the ensuing decade since the original contributions by ATF supervising special agent Lisa Kincaid, supervising criminalist Richard Grzybowski at the ATF laboratory in Walnut Creek, California, and supervising criminalist James Stam and criminalist Eugene LaChimia of the firearms unit at the San Diego Police Department forensic science section, our technology has expanded significantly.

A graduate of the University of California, San Diego, Katharine Dyer is the NIBIN firearms specialist for the San Diego County Sheriff's Department Regional Crime Laboratory. For more than a decade, she has helped the NIBIN grow and expand from its infancy to what it is today, applying NIBIN technology to the work of local, state, and federal law enforcement agencies.

Forensic Anthropology in Cold Cases

20

MADELEINE HINKES

Contents

Introduction

Such is the nature of cold cases that a body may not be immediately available for autopsy and analysis. Someone disappears; weeks, months, even years later, remains are found. They may be decomposed, incomplete, skeletonized, burned, ravaged by animals, or otherwise unrecognizable. Who is this person? What happened to him or her? How and when did he/she die? These are questions that need answers, for legal and humanitarian reasons. Now is the time to call in a forensic anthropologist, an individual uniquely qualified to assist in the recovery and identification of human remains.

Anthropology is the study of the human species. Cultural anthropologists examine human behavior in all its infinite variety around the world. Biological (or physical) anthropologists study humans as biological creatures and have built a long tradition of research in human growth and development, physiological adaptations, genetics, anthropometry (measurement of body segments), and human biological variation.

Forensic anthropologists are a subset of biological anthropologists who bring their training and experience to medicolegal problems, such as human identification. These experts are well-trained in human anatomy and osteology, as well as archaeological field techniques. They specialize in studying remains that may have lost the soft tissue components relied on for traditional autopsy, analysis, and identification. Those who make a profession of studying the human skeleton know that each person's skeleton has certain identifying features that can be interpreted by someone who knows how to read the clues.

Forensic anthropologists are usually found in anthropology departments at colleges and universities, often within the law enforcement jurisdiction. It is important to distinguish between a physical and a forensic anthropologist. Both may know bones, but only a forensic anthropologist is also skilled in evidence collection, report preparation, and court testimony. A forensic anthropologist knows how to function as a member of a medicolegal team, working with homicide investigators, medical examiners, attorneys, and crime lab personnel. The best place to find one is in the listing of the American Board of Forensic Anthropology (http://www.theabfa.org). The Board comprises PhD-level forensic anthropologists who have attained the requisite level of education, training, and experience to pass an intensive eight-hour examination. ABFA-certified diplomates are required to adhere to strict ethical standards and to maintain their continuing education in order to meet recertification requirements.

Search and Recovery

Remains pertinent to a cold case investigation are sometimes found accidentally: hikers come across a body, the family dog brings home a human bone. It may be that the accidental discovery of remains creates a case. At other times, a search for remains is actively undertaken, following evidence in response to a tip or other source of information. In any of these situations, the forensic anthropologist can provide valuable assistance to the search and recovery team by helping to develop a recovery strategy and adapting archaeological techniques to the special needs of a criminal investigation: recover the remains and preserve the evidence. This expert can also distinguish between human and nonhuman bone onsite, determine which body parts are accounted for and which are still missing, and estimate postmortem interval based on contextual information (such as bugs, plant life, and soil characteristics).

What is presented here is a brief overview of field techniques. Burns (2013) has written a guide that can be very useful to investigators. A surface find can be localized or scattered with the effects of decomposition and scavenger activity (Figure 20.1). In order to get an overview of the distribution, it is recommended that investigators walk the area in an organized manner and mark each item with a flag or Global Positioning System (GPS) reading as it is found. This may reveal patterns in interpretation of the scene. The search area should be expanded until no more remains are found, using trained dogs if necessary. It is crucial to thoroughly document the scene with photographs and verify the location and distances with good maps and GPS. As remains are bagged, the bags should be labeled to correlate with the position of the remains on the map.

Locating clandestine graves can be difficult, and a variety of techniques are used depending on finances and the availability of personnel and specialized equipment.

Figure 20.1 Scattered remains, one year postmortem.

The simplest method is a foot search of the suspicious area. Investigators walk an area in a systematic fashion, looking for surface irregularities, for inconsistencies in vegetation patterns or soil compaction, or for animal signs (e.g., a bone in or near a packrat nest). Trained dogs, a soil probe, or a metal detector can be used.

Remote sensing techniques such as aerial photography or infrared scanner (thermal) imagery might be useful, giving a "bird's eye view" of vegetation differences that might signal a gravesite. A variety of geophysical methods are available to detect a gravesite when no surface traces can be noted, using soil resistivity, electromagnetic survey, and ground-penetrating radar. The common feature of the techniques is that man-made signals are sent into the earth to detect subsurface structural or chemical anomalies. Disturbed, aerated soil is less dense and shows a different pattern of conductivity. Each anomaly can be investigated to determine if it is, in fact, a grave. All of these techniques require special equipment and trained personnel, and there are geophysical companies available to assist (for example, http://www.subsurfacesurveys.com). A good discussion of all these methods can be found in Killam (2004).

Some jurisdictions have their own specialized response/recovery teams. One such team is the Los Angeles County Special Operations Response Team (SORT). Team members, including archaeologists and criminalists, assist in search and recovery and also present skeletal recovery workshops (http://www.mec.lacounty.gov).

Necrosearch International is a nonprofit organization founded in 1991 to assist law enforcement agencies by providing training and assistance with on-site investigations. Their organization provides personnel and equipment in the areas of, to name a few, botany, cadaver dogs, entomology, geophysics, and remote sensing (http://www.necrosearch.org). Jackson (2002) tells the interesting story of how the organization came into being, with much information useful to investigators.

Once a grave site has been located, it is documented and excavated. As a crime scene, it is a potential source of evidence and must be handled with care by trained personnel. Recovery takes time and should not be rushed or performed under adverse conditions, such as darkness or heavy rain. The discussion here presents general guidelines only; more detailed methodologies can be found in Dupras et al. (2006), Blau and Ubelaker (2009), and Dirkmaat (2012), but no book can substitute for field training.

Excavation tools include shovels, trowels, brushes, bamboo or wooden picks for close work near remains, and buckets to haul soil to a screen for sifting (1/8 inch mesh is recommended). Photo and/or video documentation is essential. Initially, surface vegetation and leaf litter are removed, watching for any bits of evidence. The grave area is staked out and mapped, after establishing a reference datum point, preferably with GPS. Once the grave outline is defined, soil is removed in shallow layers and sifted. It is important to work horizontally, shovel scraping rather than digging vertically, to minimize damage to the remains. When the body is reached, it is photographed, and its positioning evaluated. If the grave is shallow, recovery personnel can dig down carefully to expose the remains in their entirety. As the remains are exposed, they are photographed and described in place. A deeper grave necessitates that the excavation area be expanded in order to have room enough for the excavators to work without stepping on the remains.

Figure 20.2 shows an untidy grave excavation. The limits are not well defined, topsoil is in danger of falling into the grave, and there is little room to work around the remains. In fact, some of the ribs were cracked as a result of excavators standing on the remains.

If the remains are fairly intact or wrapped or otherwise contained, recovery is less complicated; the remains can be lifted out as a whole. With skeletonized remains, bones are removed one by one and placed in labeled bags. Paper bags are preferred to prevent condensation.

Disinterment involves the body parts themselves, and possibly loose finger or toenails, hair, teeth, remnants of clothing, and personal effects. The anthropologist briefly inventories the remains to see what is present. Excavation of the grave continues down to sterile soil, sifting the soil beneath the body. Any insects

Figure 20.2 Untidy grave excavation.

can be saved for examination by an entomologist. The remains are then wrapped and labeled and prepared for transport back to the medical examiner's office. The final step is to clean up the site.

In some cases, cemetery exhumation might be required in order to reexamine the remains. Burial might have been in an above-ground crypt or subsurface grave. Cemetery personnel will have the skill and equipment to exhume these remains, under the watchful eye of the investigator. The closed container should then be transported to the medical examiner's office for opening and examination under controlled conditions. See also Chapter 22 in this volume.

Analysis

However the remains are recovered, whatever condition the remains are in, the forensic anthropologist follows the same basic analytical steps back at the lab or medical examiner's office. The completeness and preservation of the remains may affect the quality and quantity of determinations that can be made, but even incomplete or fragmentary remains can yield useful information to a person trained in their analysis. A good forensic anthropologist is equally comfortable with fleshed, decomposed, and skeletonized remains. Our main request of the investigator is to let us help with the recovery, if possible, and show us all the remains, rather than just bringing us a bone or two.

The timing of the initial exam may depend on the medical examiner. The ME may want the anthropologist there for the autopsy, or the anthropological exam can take place after the autopsy. If the remains are skeletal, the anthropological exam may serve as the autopsy. In any case, the first step is to lay out the remains in anatomic position, and document the inventory on paper and photographically. Most forensic anthropologists prefer to do their own photo documentation. Since it may be years before a case comes to trial, these photos will serve to refresh the anthropologist's memory, and they can also be useful teaching tools.

Any clothing present can be examined for sizing information as well as to ensure that no body parts are still in the clothing. Radiographs are usually taken as part of the autopsy protocol, but the anthropologist might request additional views. Any nonhuman bones or nonbone objects can be segregated. Evidence for commingling, in the form of duplicate bones, incompatible size or maturation stage, is noted

(Adams & Byrd 2014). At this time, the anthropologist might perform a preliminary assessment of sex, age, and ancestry, which will be reassessed after more detailed analysis.

Adherent soft tissue may need to be removed to facilitate osteological analysis, a process known as maceration. This is usually accomplished by soaking bones in hot water and mild powdered laundry detergent in a crockpot or similar setup. Low, consistent heat loosens the soft tissue without destroying the bone properties. Periodically, the murky water is poured off, and the soft tissue is gently scraped or pulled from the bone. This process may take hours or days to complete. A final soak in hot water and sudsy ammonia serves to degrease and deodorize the bones (Fenton et al. 2003). The use of bleach is not recommended, as it can damage some delicate bone structures. If there is an anatomical specimen preparation facility nearby, as at a medical school, they may have a beetle colony for rapid defleshing.

Bones are reconstructed as deemed necessary for analysis. This is especially useful for severe cranial trauma. Clean bone fragments are glued together, and the reconstructed fragments are placed in a sandbox to dry. This is a time-consuming process, but the results can pay off remarkably by defining entrance or exit gunshot wounds or a central focus of blunt force trauma.

At this point, a general biological profile can be constructed, including sex, age, biological ancestry, and stature. Features unique to an individual, such as skeletal anomalies, pathologies, or traumata can be assessed. The discussion that follows is not a how-to manual, but rather an illustration of what assistance a forensic anthropologist can offer. Each of these topics could itself fill a chapter. For detailed methodology and case examples, refer to Buikstra and Ubelaker (1994), Iscan and Kennedy (1989), Krogman and Iscan (1986), Rathbun and Buikstra (1984), Reichs (1986, 1998), Stewart (1979), Christensen et al. (2014), Katzenberg and Saunders (2008), Tersigni-Tarrant and Shirley (2013), and Byers (2010). Your forensic anthropologist will gladly explain and demonstrate the methods he or she uses.

Biological Profile

Sex

If the remains are fleshed, determination of sex is fairly straightforward. Skeletonized remains require the skills of a forensic anthropologist. The pelvis is the most dimorphic area of the skeleton, with the female showing morphology accommodated for childbearing. This results in a longer and narrower pubis, broader sciatic notch, and wider subpubic angle than in a male (Phenice 1969). Details and side-by-side comparisons can be found in an osteology text such as White et al. (2012). An experienced forensic anthropologist can correctly estimate sex from the pelvis over 90% of the time.

Lacking a pelvis, the cranium also contains many dimorphic features, though not as definitive as the pelvis. Areas to look at include the supraorbital ridges, external occipital protuberance, mastoids, and shape of the chin, all of which are more strongly developed in males. Many forensic anthropologists follow the scoring system in Buikstra and Ubelaker (1994). This takes an experienced eye, because some of these features are more population-specific, and there is a range of variability.

There are metric and statistical approaches to the determination of sex (Giles 1970; Jantz & Ousley 2005). There are more than 30 measurements that can be taken between defined landmarks of the skull, which requires considerable practice. The set of measurements on the unknown skull are then compared to reference populations in a database, using discriminant function analysis. This process has been facilitated by FORDISC, a computer software program developed at the University of Tennessee (Jantz & Ousley 2005). It is then up to the forensic anthropologist to interpret the results of the statistical analysis.

Males in general have larger bodies and heavier bones than females, and this is reflected in joint size (for example, the diameter of the femoral or humeral head) and areas of muscle attachment (France 1986).

Again, an understanding of inherent population variability is necessary. Simply looking at pictures in a book or taking measurements without understanding the morphology behind them does not suffice.

Children's (subadult) skeletons are much less dimorphic until puberty, and any assessment of sex should be offered with caution. When subadult skeletal remains are discovered, it is recommended that investigators consider missing children of either sex, in order to prevent stalling the investigation by focusing on what could be the wrong sex. DNA analysis should serve to confirm the sex.

Age

Age estimates are based on the development, maturation, and subsequent degeneration of the human frame. Growth and development of teeth and bones proceed at a fairly predictable pace, so it is usually not too difficult to estimate the biological age of a growing child within a narrow range, using tables developed on modern children around the world (Ubelaker 1989).

Fetal and infant age is assessed using the measured lengths of the long bones and an inventory of centers of ossification, the beginnings of the bones themselves (Fazekas & Kosa 1978). To the untrained eye, these centers might not even appear to be bone. For children, the anthropologist relies on dental calcification and eruption, long bone growth, and epiphyseal development and closure at the growth plates (Scheuer & Black 2000; Latham & Finnegan 2010). These developmental thresholds are closely correlated with chronological age.

For adults, after bone and tooth development have been completed, there are a few areas of the skeleton that are particularly useful. These include the pubic symphysis (Suchey & Katz 1986; Brooks & Suchey 1990), auricular surface of the ilium (Lovejoy et al. 1985), and costochondral junctions (Iscan et al. 1984). If only the cranium is present, the stage of suture closure can yield a general age estimate (Meindl & Lovejoy 1985; Nawrocki 1998).

Degenerative changes are also taken into account, such as changes in weight-bearing joints of the legs and lower back. However, these changes are not age-specific and may be hastened by obesity and heavy or repetitive physical activity during life.

Changes in long bone histomorphology can also be used to estimate age, but the microscopic techniques are complicated and best left to anthropologists who specialize in them (Kerley 1970; Kerley & Ubelaker 1978; Stout 1988; Robling & Stout 2008; Crowder & Stout 2011).

Accuracy of age estimation depends on the abundance of remains and the experience of the anthropologist. The estimated age range reflects individual variation. Precision diminishes with increasing age of the deceased.

Ancestry

Biological ancestry can be extremely difficult to evaluate in skeletal remains because living populations have few clear distinguishing features, and most of those are soft tissue features. Nevertheless, certain morphological features of the cranium, face, and teeth are found with greater frequency in certain populations and thus may serve to distinguish among European, African, and Asian or Native American ancestry (Gill & Rhine 1990; Berg & Ta'ala 2015). These features include length of the cranium, breadth of the face, projection of the jaws, morphology of the nasal root and aperture, and shoveled incisors, among others. No trait is 100% diagnostic. The assessment is complicated by admixture, generations of mixing among the basic ancestral groups. An appreciation of human variability, the hallmark of biological anthropology, is necessary, along with a measure of caution. The investigator also needs to realize that biological ancestry may not exactly reflect an individual's self-identification into a particular group. On a practical level, however, the investigator is not interested in a discourse on the anthropological theories of race and ancestry, so the anthropologist's responsibility is to give a best assessment of the skeletal evidence (Ousley et al. 2009).

As with sex determination, discriminant functions are available to assess ancestry, using similar measurements of the skull. These statistical techniques may be useful in supporting morphoscopic determinations (Giles & Elliot 1962). The Forensic Anthropology Data Bank at the University of Tennessee provides a valuable research tool in its ongoing collection of biological data on documented forensic cases. Reference groups include American White, American Black, Hispanic, Japanese, Chinese, Vietnamese, Guatemalan, and Native American. Measurements taken at specific landmarks on unknown crania (or other bones) can be compared statistically with the database using the FORDISC program (Jantz & Moore-Jansen 1988; Moore-Jansen et al. 1994; Ousley & Jantz 2012); version 3.1 has just been released (fac.utk.edu). Once again, the expertise of the forensic anthropologist is required, because FORDISC will classify the unknown skull into one of the reference populations, whether or not it actually comes from one of those populations, but it will also give the probability of the skull belonging to each group. Anthropologists are constantly testing these methods on populations worldwide and adding to the reference database.

In the absence of a skull, assessment of ancestry is more difficult. There are some metric and nonmetric methods that have been proven useful especially with the femur (Stewart 1979; Shirley et al. 2015), but assessments should be expressed with the appropriate degree of uncertainty.

Stature

Stature (height) is calculated using the measured length of a long bone (one of six bones in the arm or leg) in the sex-and-race-appropriate equation. These are a series of regression formulas developed in the 1950s to predict stature based on the measured length of a long bone (Trotter 1970). These equations are being refined in the Forensic Anthropology Data Bank to account for secular trends in modern populations and interpopulational variation; people today are taller than in previous generations (Jantz & Ousley 2005; Ousley 2012).

The length of an incomplete bone can be approximated by comparing it to intact bones in a study collection, and there are also formulas for estimating stature from portions of long bones (Steele 1970).

Weight is very difficult to estimate from skeletal remains, but associated clothing may give some clues. A heavy individual may show increased degeneration at the weight-bearing joints. Body build (or skeletal robusticity) is easier to assess, evaluating the development of areas of muscle attachment and shoulder and hip breadth.

Handedness can often be inferred based on asymmetric development of shoulder joints and arm bones, with the dominant side being larger or longer (Stewart 1979).

Skeletal Anomalies

Every person's skeleton is unique, due to aspects of genetics, growth and development, health, nutrition, and lifestyle. This fact is brought home to the forensic anthropologist at each analysis, and some of these anomalies may prove useful for identification, if antemortem information is available. Examples of some anomalies include different number of vertebrae in each segment of the spine, 11 or 13 pairs of ribs instead of the usual 12, accessory bones or articular facets, and a variety of discrete (nonmetric) traits such as a metopic suture (Berry & Berry 1967; Finnegan 1978; Hauser et al. 1989; Saunders & Rainey 2008). A sternal aperture (Figure 20.3), with its location near the heart, might be mistaken for a gunshot wound. In reality, it is a developmental defect resulting from incomplete fusion of the distal segments of the growing sternum (Barnes 1994). It can be distinguished from a gunshot wound by its smooth, even edges and lack of any other tissue damage.

Repeated mechanical stress on a particular part of the skeleton as a result of work or sports-related activities can affect the bony morphology, resulting in what anthropologists call occupational markers. A particular set of muscle attachments may be asymmetrically more developed. By knowing what muscles

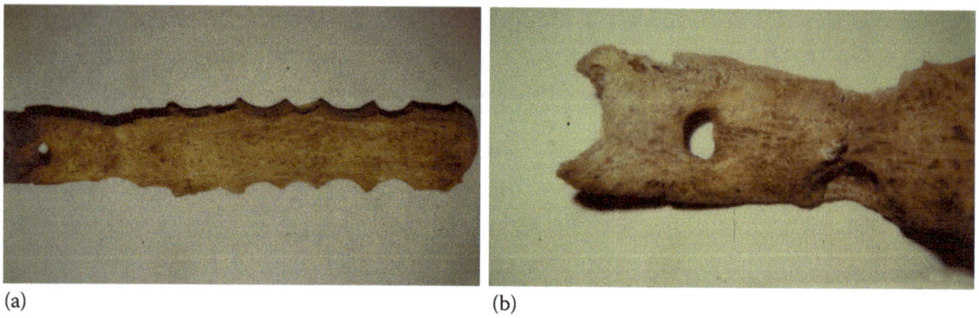

Figure 20.3 Sternal aperture, a skeletal variant. (a) View of the sternum. (b) Close-up of sternal aperture.

attach to particular areas of bones, and what actions those muscles facilitate, the anthropologist might be able to propose a particular activity that developed the markers (Kennedy 1989; Capasso et al. 1998). The author examined a femur in a 2011 case that had extremely well-developed attachments for the quadriceps muscle, a powerful knee extensor. It was later learned that the deceased had been a soccer player.

Stable Isotope Analysis

A new tool in establishing the biological profile of human remains is stable isotope analysis. Stable isotope analysis of bones and teeth has been used by anthropologists since the 1970s to identify paleodiets among archaeological populations (Schoeninger 1995). Diets high in corn or marine resources, for example, leave different carbon, nitrogen, and oxygen isotopic signatures in bones and teeth as these elements are incorporated into developing teeth and renewing bone. In addition, and more pertinent to forensic anthropology case investigations, stable isotope analysis can be used to track an individual's residence history based on signatures that reflect a particular drinking water source or geological region where food is grown (Katzenberg & Saunders 2008; Meier-Augenstein 2010; Bartelink et al. 2013). The signatures in teeth reflect childhood residence, while migrations can be tracked in bone as it replaces itself over time. In the average adult, cortical bone remodels every 10–15 years. Comparative worldwide studies of groundwater allow the comparisons to be made.

Juarez (2008) has used strontium isotope analysis in teeth as a means of identifying the home areas of deceased Mexican border crossers. Her original comparative sample included donated permanent teeth of Mexican-born individuals of known origin from four (Mexican) states. Strontium levels are tied to local geology, with the underlying bedrock affecting soils and water, so she was able to map the isotopic variation in modern Mexican tooth enamel. This map will allow for comparison with deceased border-crossers of unknown origin. This kind of analysis requires a thermal ionization mass spectrometer and other specialized equipment, along with the knowledge of how to interpret the findings, so it might not be easily available in a particular jurisdiction.

Antemortem Trauma and Disease

Many people break bones during their lifetime, due to falls, sports activities, vehicular accidents, or physical altercations (Rogers 2002). Generally, the younger you are, the more quickly and completely the fracture will mend. Years later, the only evidence of the fracture may be a slight surface irregularity on the bone. Other times, the deformity is more marked, or orthopedic pins may still be in place. Joint prostheses or other surgical interventions may be in place. Skeletal evidence for child abuse may be apparent in multiple fractures in various stages of healing (Kerley 1978; Harris et al. 1996; Walker et al. 1997).

A variety of diseases can affect bones, including vitamin deficiencies, tuberculosis, malignancies and metastases, infections, and metabolic disorders (Ortner 2003; Mann & Hunt 2005). Nutritional or age-related osteoporosis may be noted. While the specific pathogen might not be identifiable, the anthropologist can provide an accurate description of bony changes, which may facilitate a differential diagnosis.

Equally important might be what is not present. On January 12, 1965, a two-year-old girl died. Her death was attributed to post-traumatic cerebral hemorrhage, and circumstances were somewhat suspicious. This was reexamined as a cold case nearly 40 years later. The stepmother had alleged that the little girl fell a lot because she had weak ankles, which gave her trouble walking. After her remains were exhumed, the forensic anthropologist (the author) removed her feet above the ankles and macerated them to examine the bones. Bone development was found to be age-appropriate, with no anomalies, asymmetry, or pathology. The second autopsy determined that the cranial trauma was due to blows to the head, not a fall (Soto 2004).

A feature known as parturition scars or birth scars can sometimes be seen on the female pelvis as shallow depressions on the dorsal surfaces of the pubic bones near the symphyseal border (Stewart 1970; Suchey et al. 1979). Presence of these dorsal pits is strongly suggestive of a full-term pregnancy and vaginal delivery, but the number or size of the pits is only weakly correlated with the number of pregnancies.

Perimortem Trauma

While it is the legal responsibility of the medical examiner or coroner to determine cause and manner of death, the forensic anthropologist can often provide useful information based on an examination of skeletal remains, although not all causes of death leave a mark on the skeleton. "Perimortem" trauma is that occurring at or around the time of death, thus showing no evidence of healing and likely directly related to the death event. In skeletal terms, perimortem injuries are those that occur when the bone is still fresh. Fresh bone and dry bone have different mechanical properties and thus respond differently to trauma. Because the pace at which bone dries out varies with circumstances, it is not possible to put a definite upper time limit on the perimortem interval. The anthropologist's task is to document and describe the injuries and to comment on type and timing. Only a brief discussion is presented here. Increasingly, forensic anthropologists are moving beyond the biological profile to interpret bone trauma. Along with the experience they have gained working on cases alongside medical examiners, they are engaged in research and experimentation on nonhuman animal models.

Interpretation of trauma is complex and depends on an understanding of the mechanical properties of bone as a living tissue and how it responds to the application of force in compression, tension, or shear. Bone contains organic (protein) and inorganic (mineral) elements, which affect its strength and elasticity. Dry bone, having lost its organic component, is less elastic and fractures differently.

Bone fragments may need to be reconstructed. Radiography may be helpful. Magnification of the wound may provide details of tool marks. An expert in tool marks can give a better idea of the class of tool and perform comparisons. A casual stroll through the tool aisle of a hardware store reveals a stunning array of objects with distinctive edges that can be used to inflict damage on a human body.

Blunt force trauma results from the application of a low-speed force over a relatively large surface area, as from a blow or a fall. The anthropologist will describe the type, location, and nature of the fractures (transverse, spiral, depressed, concentric, et al.). It may be possible to determine the impact site(s), the number and sequence of impacts, directionality, amount of force, and possible weapon (Jones 1997; Galloway 1999; Rich et al. 2005; Wedel & Galloway 2013; Passalacqua & Rainwater 2015). The trauma in Figure 20.4 was inflicted with a hatchet. The concentric fracture line is the result of the bone collapsing inward around the impact site. Massive blunt force trauma can result from vehicular or aircraft accidents or falls from a great height.

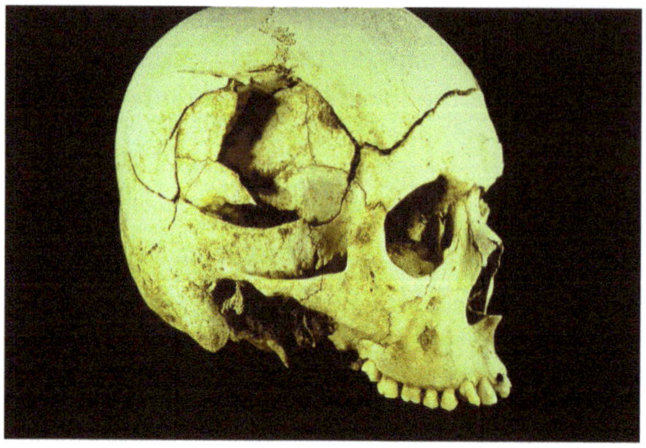

Figure 20.4 Blunt force trauma to the cranium.

A fractured hyoid bone is often cited as proof of manual strangulation, but its presence or absence is not definitive evidence. Ubelaker (1992) reports that just 34% of manual strangulation victims showed a fractured hyoid, and there are ways to fracture the hyoid that have nothing to do with homicide, such as motor vehicle accidents or severe coughing with neck muscle spasms (Dalati 2005). The adult hyoid bone results from the fusion of three component parts, so it must be ascertained if the bone is actually broken or simply unfused. The flexibility or brittleness of the bone and adjacent neck cartilages is affected by age.

Sharp force trauma results from an implement with a narrow or beveled edge or point. The characteristic punctures and incised wounds can be the result of stabbing, cutting, chopping, or sawing. All bones present should be carefully examined for cuts or nicks. In fresh or intact bodies with apparent neck trauma, the medical examiner might excise the neck area and give it to the anthropologist to macerate, so that the trauma can be better documented. Wound characteristics vary according to the angle at which the edge strikes bone, whether the edge is straight or serrated, and the type of bone (Symes et al. 2012). The anthropologist describes and documents the number, type, and location of wounds, even if he or she cannot interpret them with certainty. This may help narrow the search for the weapon. Cut marks and saw marks can be molded, using dental products, for more detailed analysis of the blade characteristics. Knowledge of the soft tissue anatomy in the vicinity of the bony trauma may help in the interpretation of the severity of the trauma.

Figure 20.5 shows a cervical vertebra with incised marks caused by the assailants' attempt to cut off the head of their victim after raping her. As they cut through the soft tissue, they would have severed the jugular vein and carotid artery.

Cut marks in areas of the skeleton that are normally protected within a joint, such as the head of the femur or the trochlea of the humerus, may represent dismemberment marks. The example presented here is the trochlea (elbow) of the humerus (Figure 20.6).

High-velocity projectile trauma most commonly results from bullets or shrapnel. This is high-speed force over a small surface area. A gunshot wound to the cranium will almost always produce fractures. Interpretation of this type of trauma again depends on the familiarity of the anthropologist with the biomechanical properties of bone. Thin bones of the face respond differently than the cranial vault or thick cortex of a long bone. The round versus keyhole shape, beveling along the edges, and pattern of radiating fractures may give indications of the direction of the shot, sequence of multiple shots, and type of firearm (Berryman et al. 2013).

Figure 20.5 Incised marks on cervical vertebra.

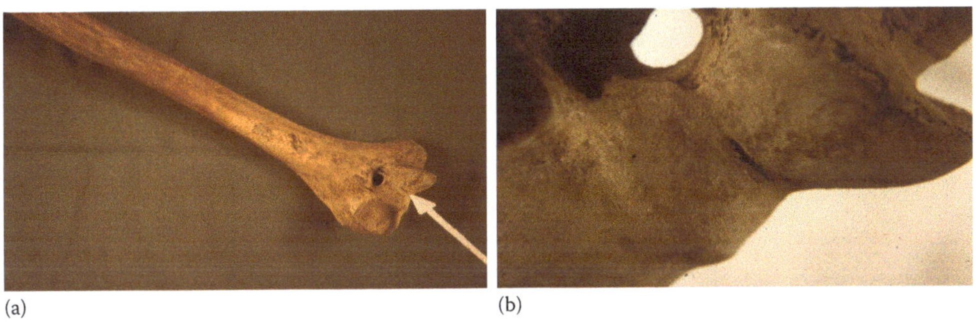

Figure 20.6 Dismemberment marks. (a) View of the humerus. (b) Close-up of cut mark on trochlea.

Burned Remains

Analysis of burned bone can be challenging, partly because the bone is very fragile and critical landmarks may have been destroyed. All burned remains require very careful handling to prevent further damage. But "burned beyond recognition" does not mean burned beyond identification.

Analyzing the pattern of burning may help in the interpretation of the temperature and duration of the fire, the position of the body, and the presence or absence of soft tissue or wrappings. Parts of the body protected by a heavy muscle layer may burn less than bones close to the skin surface. As part of the normal burn pattern, the dominant flexor muscles contract with the heat, producing the characteristic pugilistic posture, and this process may snap bones. The resultant chemical and histological alterations of bone produce color changes from charred black to calcined gray-white, fractures, warping, and delamination of the cranial vault (Schmidt & Symes 2008).

A determination must be made as to whether the burning occurred in the perimortem or postmortem interval. Bones burned when dry show a particular pattern of cracking and longitudinal splitting. This situation might occur as a result of a ground fire sweeping over an area where skeletal remains are already exposed on the surface. In contrast, bones that are burned "green" (i.e., fleshed, having a high moisture content) show curvilinear or transverse cracking and warping, due to the moisture being pulled out by the heat. This pattern indicates an individual who died in or shortly before the fire, which might be a significant factor in covering up a homicide.

Perimortem bone fractures due to trauma will need to be distinguished from heat-induced fractures. Characteristically, thermal fractures have sharp (rather than smooth) edges and are often parallel to the long axis of the bone. Thermal fractures do not travel into unburned bone.

Extremely hot fires (>800°C) or fires of long duration can cremate a body. The resulting cremains are usually small, brittle gray to white fragments. Only the teeth and smallest bones (carpals, phalanges) may still be intact, making it extremely difficult to assess biological parameters. Some anthropologists are called in on civil cases to analyze cremains from funeral homes in an attempt to determine whether these cremains are, in fact, the remains of the deceased or even human at all (Ubelaker 1989; Maples & Browning 1994; Correia 1997).

Postmortem Changes

Numerous factors can affect human remains, many of which are part of the natural taphonomic processes (Haglund & Sorg 1997, 2002; Pokines & Symes 2014). Taphonomy is the study of the processes that affect human remains from death until recovery. Bones exposed on the ground surface can show weathering, sun-bleaching, breakage, disarticulation, scavenging, and scattering. Small bones can be incorporated into packrat nests. The marks left by animal teeth (punch marks or crushing from carnivore teeth, parallel grooves from rodent gnawing) can, at first glance, simulate trauma or toolmarks. Magnification and a trained eye are useful in distinguishing real trauma from "pseudotrauma."

Postmortem fractures occur in dry bone, which has lost its elasticity so that it fails at lower loading forces. The breaks are less clean and more jagged, and concentric or radiating fractures are not seen (Maples 1986).

Buried remains are not entirely protected. Although sheltered from most animal activity, buried remains can be damaged or deteriorated by ground water, acidic soil, ground pressure, animal activity, and vegetation growth.

The recovery process itself might damage bones if not handled properly. Careless use of excavating tools or rough handling and inadequate packaging might break bones. These recent marks can be distinguished by differences in bone color at the new cut or break.

Estimation of Postmortem Interval

The ease of estimating postmortem interval diminishes with increasing time since death. Usually by the time an anthropologist is called in on the case, the remains are well along the path of decomposition, and postmortem interval is measured in weeks, months, or years, rather than hours or days. The pace of decomposition is affected by ecological factors, such as temperature, humidity, elevation, and shade. Remains can become skeletonized in as little as two weeks in the desert summer, or may retain soft tissue for years, if buried or wrapped in some way. Cold temperatures, burial, or immersion in water slows decomposition, while warmth and humidity accelerate the process.

The Anthropological Research Facility at the University of Tennessee, Knoxville (commonly known as "The Body Farm"), has devoted over 35 years to the study of decomposition of human remains under a variety of circumstances (Rodriguez & Bass 1983, 1985; Bass & Jefferson 2003). Their timeline works well in similar environments but does not have universal applicability. In the Southwest, for example, human bodies often pass through a dry mummification stage that is rarely seen in the Southeast (Galloway et al. 1989). Other outdoor research facilities are being developed at Western Carolina University and Texas State

University-San Marcos (http://www.txstate.edu/anthropology/facts/labs/farf.html). It makes sense for the investigator to consult the local experts.

Insects are a reliable line of evidence in the estimation of postmortem interval. There is a regular sequence of insects that visit a body, including flies, beetles, and ants. The timing of specific species activity provides the basis for estimating a postmortem interval. The forensic entomological literature is extensive (for example, Byrd & Castner 2010). The local natural history museum may have an expert.

Plant growth around or possibly invading the remains may help to set the upper or lower limits of postmortem interval, along with leaf fall. Another line of evidence comes from clothing or other materials in the grave or around the remains, which deteriorate at different rates (Morse et al. 1983; Rowe 1997).

A specialized area of research involves chemical analysis of the soil under the body, specifically the volatile fatty acids contained in the fluids of decomposition (Vass et al. 1992). This technique and other aspects of soil chemistry are promising for the future of time-since-death estimations.

Two cases, within four months of each other, allowed the author to appreciate the variability in postmortem changes. In September 2008, remains were excavated from under a concrete floor of a dwelling. The bones were in excellent condition and stained brown from the soil (Figure 20.7). A disposable underpad ("chux") was wrapped around the pelvic area. The only remnants of clothing were two thin lacy straps in the shoulder area, the rest of the clothing having deteriorated over time. The remains were identified as a woman who died in 1995 at age 47, from as yet unknown causes. Her husband (who continued to collect federal benefits for her) buried her in the backyard of their house and later poured a concrete slab over the grave. Subsequent owners of the house incorporated this slab into an addition they built onto the house. Investigators were lead to this scene by a tip.

In January 2009, remains were excavated from a backyard, based on information from the current resident. The remains were wrapped in bedding held closed by silver duct tape. When the layers of bedding were unwrapped, human skeletal remains were observed clothed in a sweater, white camisole, and white socks. The bones were extremely soft and mealy, and most had collapsed (Figure 20.8). A dark organic residue lay beneath the bones. These remains were identified as the 82-year-old mother of the current resident. Before she died 15 years prior, she had asked her son to bury her in the backyard, and he complied with her request but neglected to file a death certificate and continued to collect her federal benefits.

Figure 20.7 Excavation of remains, 13 years postmortem.

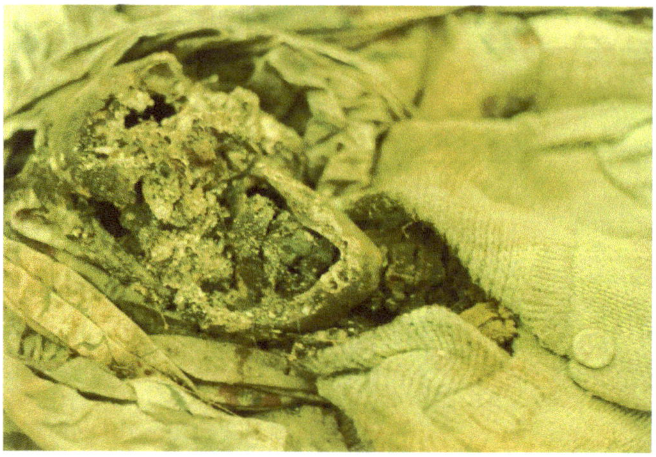

Figure 20.8 Recovered buried remains, 15 years postmortem.

The postmortem intervals were comparable, 13 and 15 years, but because the second woman had been wrapped in so many layers, the decomposition fluids had time to destroy the bones. Clothing made of natural fibers had deteriorated, while that containing synthetic fibers had preserved. Chux, apparently, are indestructible.

Identification

Identification of decomposed, fragmentary, incomplete, or skeletonized remains is not a simple process, but it is crucial to the investigation. Success depends on the nature of the remains and the quality of antemortem records (Thompson & Black 2007). After a long postmortem interval, fingerprints and visual recognition will not be possible. Personal effects may be available, but these should provide a starting point for an identification, not an endpoint.

A positive identification results from a combination of anatomic/biological detail sufficiently unique to provide convincing proof. It results from matching postmortem and antemortem biology, using fingerprints, radiographs of teeth or the body, or serology including DNA. A probable identification (also known as presumptive) is supported by all available evidence, but that evidence is insufficient for a positive identification, due to inadequate records or remains. Usually there is good circumstantial information to support this level of identification. At a much lower level of certainty is a tentative identification, based on clothing or personal effects or location of the body (for example, in a residence). The investigator can then focus on finding more definitive information. An exclusionary identification might be possible when everyone else from an incident has been identified and no antemortem data for the last individual are inconsistent with the remains (Christensen & Anderson 2014). Or, the remains may be a clear mismatch for the antemortem information.

The postmortem examination (autopsy) may yield the medical and surgical history of the deceased, along with tissues for serology and toxicology. Surgical implants may have the manufacturer's information and a serial number, which can be traced. If teeth or dental structures are present, a dental exam is performed by a qualified forensic odontologist. Even if no restorations are noted, an antemortem–postmortem match could be made on the anatomy of the dental root, pulp chamber, or alveolar bone. DNA can be extracted from tooth roots. See Chapter 21 in this book for a more detailed explanation.

If the case is cold because the remains were not found until long after death, bones and teeth may be the only sources of data for identification. Biological information can be determined from the remains, as described earlier, but these data are rarely specific enough for a positive identification. If antemortem radiographs are available (from a putative decedent), along with postmortem radiographs of the corresponding remains taken at a similar orientation and magnification, a comparison can be attempted. Besides dental x-rays, individuals might have had a sinus series, chest x-rays, or bone density studies. The antemortem and postmortem films can be compared side-by-side or superimposed. That anthropological knowledge of skeletal anatomy and variation again comes into play. The anthropologist looks for trauma or disease, but also normal variants in trabecular patterns, cranial sutures, bone contours, and foramina (Brogdon 1998). He or she needs to address a specific issue: are these antemortem and postmortem structures radiographically identical because they are the same in most people or because these are, in fact, films of the same individual? There can be no unexplainable differences.

Some research in a documented skeletal collection may be necessary to prove the point. Ubelaker (Scammell 1991) demonstrated this when he looked at frontal sinus patterns, which are now accepted as unique to an individual (Figure 20.9). These days, more films are from CT scans or MRIs rather than traditional radiographs, so anthropologists are learning to read these films too (Rogers 2002). Digital storing of the images alleviates the problem of storing large quantities of exposed films and may facilitate their availability for use. Poor antemortem film quality can often be enhanced through digitization or enlargement (Fitzpatrick et al. 1996).

If no antemortem radiographs are available for the putative decedent, medical or dental records, notes, and charts can be used, or even family recollections of injuries or diseases. Every little bit of information helps to strengthen the individuation.

DNA can often be recovered from skeletal or dental remains. Many jurisdictions require that samples routinely be taken and submitted for analysis. Nuclear DNA encodes genetic information about inherited characters unique to an individual, while mitochondrial DNA traces the maternal lineage (Boyer 2012). See Chapters 15 and 18 for more detail. DNA testing does not eliminate the role of the forensic anthropologist, however. The DNA may be too degraded to be of use. Since there is no universal DNA database, it may be the developed biological profile that narrows the list of potential comparisons. In some jurisdictions, it may be the anthropologist who actually collects the samples of teeth and bones to be sent for DNA analysis. DNA can serve to link widely scattered remains of a single individual once the anthropologist has suggested that these might be the same person. And, every so often, a database gives up a blind hit.

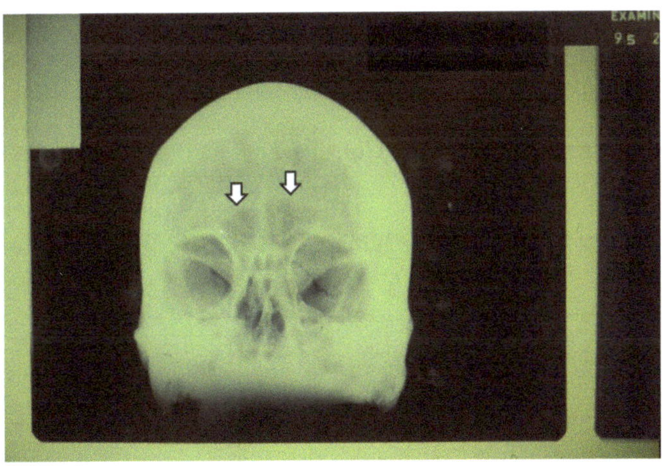

Figure 20.9 Radiograph showing frontal sinus, at arrows.

Facial reconstructions or approximations, either two dimensional or three dimensional, can be accomplished as a means to develop leads. These techniques put a face on a skull, so that the reconstruction can be published in the hope that someone will recognize it. This recognition does not make a positive identification. The technique requires artistic skill beyond the capabilities of many anthropologists, but their demographic data are useful to the artist (Iscan & Helmer 1993; Taylor 2001; Wilkinson 2007). Whether the anthropologist/artist uses the tissue depth method or the anatomical method, neither fully accounts for facial features that do not have an underlying bony structure, such as the ears, lips, or fleshy part of the nose.

Skull/photo superimposition is a technique using video or still cameras to compare the morphology of the skull with an antemortem photograph by overlaying the two. This necessitates a good idea of whose remains these might be. The skull should be reasonably intact and is placed in the same perspective as the photograph. It is a fairly straightforward process to overlay and compare points of concordance between bony landmarks and overlying soft tissue, such as the bridge of the nose, the distance between the eyes, and the most forward point of the chin (Helmer et al. 1989; Austin-Smith & Maples 1994; Clement & Ranson 1998; Sauer et al. 2012). If two photographs are used (for example, a frontal and side view), the possibility of error is greatly reduced. It is up to the anthropologist to decide whether the points match sufficiently to establish a probable identification or whether the match is excluded (Sauer et al. 2012). The latest procedure uses digitized images and computer-assisted image manipulation methods (Ubelaker et al. 1992). This technique was used successfully in the identification process of the Romanov family (Maples & Browning 1994) and of Joseph Mengele (Helmer 1987). Lacking the proper validation studies, however, this cannot be considered a means of positive identification.

Whichever techniques are used, it is important to recognize their limits and use multiple methods to secure a personal identification.

Suggested Readings and Bibliography

Adams, B.J. & J.E. Byrd. *Commingled Human Remains.* Academic Press, San Diego, CA, 2014.

Austin-Smith, D. & W.R. Maples. The Reliability of Skull/Photograph Superimposition in Individual Identification. *Journal of Forensic Sciences* 39(2):446–455, 1994.

Barnes, E. *Developmental Defects of the Axial Skeleton in Paleopathology.* University Press of Colorado, Niwot, CO, 1994.

Bartelink, E.J., R. Berry, & L.A. Chesson. Stable Isotopes and Human Provenancing, and case review. In Mallet, X. & T. Blythe (eds.), *Advances in Forensic Human Identification,* Taylor & Francis, Boca Raton, FL, pp. 157–184, 2013.

Bass, W.M. & J. Jefferson. *Death's Acre.* G.P. Putnam's Sons, New York, 2003.

Berg, G.E. & S.C. Ta'ala. *Biological Affinity in Forensic Identification of Human Skeletal Remains.* CRC Press, Boca Raton, FL, 2015.

Berryman, H.E., N.R. Shirley, & A.K. Lanfear. Basic Gunshot Trauma Interpretation in Forensic Anthropology. In Tersigni-Tarrant, M.A. & N.R. Shirley (eds.), *Forensic Anthropology, An Introduction.* CRC Press, Boca Raton, FL, pp. 291–306, 2013.

Berry, A.C. & R.J. Berry. Epigenetic Variation in the Human Cranium. *Journal of Anatomy* 101:361–379, 1967.

Blau, S. & D.H. Ubelaker. *Handbook of Forensic Anthropology and Archaeology.* Left Coast Press, Walnut Creek, CA, 2009.

Boyer, D. DNA Identification and Forensic Anthropology; Developments in DNA Collection, Analysis, and Technology. In Dirkmaat, D.C. (ed.), *A Companion to Forensic Anthropology,* Wiley-Blackwell, Malden, MA, pp. 462–470, 2012.

Brogdon, B.G. *Forensic Radiology,* CRC Press, Boca Raton, FL, 1998.

Brooks, S.T. & J.M. Suchey. Skeletal Age Determination Based on the Os Pubis: A Comparison of the Acsadi–Nemeskeri and Suchey–Brooks Methods. *Human Evolution* 5(3):227–238, 1990.

Buikstra, J.B. & D.H. Ubelaker. *Standards for Data Collection from Human Skeletal Remains.* Arkansas Archaeological Survey Research Series No. 44, 1994.

Burns, K.R. *Forensic Anthropology Training Manual*, 3rd edition. Prentice Hall, Upper Saddle River, NJ, 2013.

Byers, S.N. *Introduction to Forensic Anthropology*, 4th edition. Allyn & Bacon, Boston, MA, 2010.

Byrd, J.H. & J.L. Castner. *Forensic Entomology*, CRC Press, Boca Raton, FL, 2001.

Capasso, L., K.A.R. Kennedy, & C.A. Wilczak. *Atlas of Occupational markers on Human Remains.* Edigrafital SpA-S. Atto, Teramo, Italy, 1998.

Christensen, A.M. & B.E. Anderson. Methods of Personal Identification. In Christensen, A.M., N.V. Passalacqua, & E.J. Bartelink (eds.), *Forensic Anthropology: Current Methods and Practice*, Academic Press, San Diego, CA, pp. 397–420, 2014.

Christensen, A.M., N.V. Passalacqua, & E.J. Bartelink. *Forensic Anthropology: Current Methods and Practice*, Academic Press, San Diego, CA, 2014.

Clement, J.G. & D.L. Ranson. *Craniofacial Identification in Forensic Medicine.* Oxford University Press, New York, 1998.

Correia, P.M.M. Fire Modification of bone: A Review of the Literature. In Haglund, W.D. & M.H. Sorg (eds.), *Forensic Taphonomy.* CRC Press, Boca Raton, FL, 1997.

Crowder, C. & S.D. Stout. *Bone Histology: An Anthropological Perspective.* CRC Press, Boca Raton, FL, 2011.

Dalati, T. Isolated Hyoid Bone Fracture: Review of an Unusual Case, *International Journal of Oral & Maxillofacial Surgery* 34(4):449–452, 2005.

Dirkmaat, D.C. (ed.). *A Companion to Forensic Anthropology.* Wiley-Blackwell, Malden, MA, 2012.

Dupras, T.L., J.J. Schultz, S.M. Wheeler, & L.T. Williams. *Forensic Recovery of Human Remains: Archaeological Approaches*, 2nd ed. CRC Press, Boca Raton, FL, 2006.

Fazekas, I.G. & F. Kosa. *Forensic Fetal Osteology*, Akademiai Kiado, Budapest, 1978.

Fenton, T.W., W.H. Birkby, & J. Cornelison. A Fast and Safe Non-Bleaching Method for Forensic Skeletal Preparation. *Journal of Forensic Sciences* 48(1):274–276, 2003.

Finnegan, M. Non-Metric Variation of the Infracranial Skeleton. *Journal of Anatomy* 125:23–37, 1978.

Fitzpatrick, J.J., D.R. Shook, B.L. Kaufman, S.J. Wu, R.J. Kirschner, H. MacMahon et al. Optical and Digital Techniques for Enhancing Radiographic Anatomy for Identification of Human Remains. *Journal of Forensic Sciences* 41(6):947–959, 1996.

France, D. Osteometry at muscle origin and insertion in sex determination. *American Journal of Physical Anthropology* 76:515–526, 1986.

Galloway, A. (ed.) *Broken Bones: Anthropological Analysis of Blunt Force Trauma.* Charles C Thomas, Springfield, IL, 1999.

Galloway, A, W.H. Birkby, A.M. Jones, T.E. Henry, & B.O. Parks. Decay Rates of Human Remains in an Arid Environment. *Journal of Forensic Sciences* 34:607–616, 1989.

Giles, E. Discriminant Function Sexing of the Human Skeleton. In *Personal Identification in Mass Disasters*, T.D. Stewart (ed.), Smithsonian Institution, Washington, DC, pp. 99–110, 1970.

Giles, E. & O. Elliot. Race Identification from Cranial Measurements. *Journal of Forensic Sciences* 7:147–157, 1962.

Gill, G.W. & S. Rhine (eds.). *Skeletal Attribution of Race.* Maxwell Museum of Anthropology Anthropological Papers No. 4, Albuquerque, NM, 1990.

Haglund, W.D. & M.H. Sorg (eds.). *Forensic Taphonomy.* CRC Press, Boca Raton, FL, 1997.

Haglund, W.D. & M.H. Sorg (eds.). *Advances in Forensic Taphonomy.* CRC Press, Boca Raton, FL, 2002.

Harris, V.J., M.A. Lorand, J.J. Fitzpatrick, & D.K. Sofer. *Radiographic Atlas of Child Abuse.* Igaku-Shoin Medical Publishers, New York, 1996.

Hauser, G. & G.F. DeStefano. *Epigenetic Variants of the Human Skull.* E. Schweizerbart'sche Verlagsbuchhandlung, Stuttgart, Germany, 1989.

Helmer, R. Identification of the Cadaver Remains of Josef Mengele. *Journal of Forensic Sciences* 32(6):1622–1644, 1987.

Helmer, R.P., J.B. Schimmler, & J. Rieger. On the Conclusiveness of Skull Identification via the Video Superimposition Technique. *Canadian Society of Forensic Sciences Journal* 22:177–194, 1989.

Iscan, M.Y. & R.P. Helmer (eds.). *Forensic Analysis of the Skull.* Wiley-Liss, New York, 1993.

Iscan, M.Y. & K.A.R. Kennedy (eds.). *Reconstruction of Life from the Skeleton.* Alan R. Liss, Inc., New York, 1989.

Iscan, M.Y., S.R. Loth, & R.K. Wright. Age Estimation from the Rib by Phase Analysis: White Males. *Journal of Forensic Sciences* 29:1094–1104, 1984.

Jackson, S. *No Stone Unturned: The True Story of Necrosearch International.* Kensington Books, New York, 2002.

Jantz, R.L. & P.H. Moore-Jansen. *A Data Base for Forensic Anthropology: Structure, Content and Analysis: Report of Investigation 47.* Department of Anthropology, University of Tennessee, Knoxville, 1988.

Jantz, R.L. & S.D. Ousley. *FORDISC 3.0: Personal Computer Forensic Discriminant Functions.* The University of Tennessee, Knoxville, 2005.

Jones, N. *Craniofacial Trauma.* Oxford University Press, Oxford, 1997.

Juarez, C.A. Strontium and Geolocation, the pathway to Identification for Deceased Undocumented Mexican Border-Crossers: A preliminary Report, *Journal of Forensic Sciences* 53(1):46–49, 2008.

Katzenberg, M.A. & S.R. Saunders. *Biological Anthropology of the Human Skeleton*, 2nd edition, John Wiley & Sons, Inc, Hoboken, NJ, 2008.

Kennedy, K.A.R. Skeletal Markers of Occupational Stress. In Iscan, M.Y. & K.A.R. Kennedy (eds.), *Reconstruction of Life from the Skeleton*, Alan R. Liss, Inc., New York, pp. 129–160, 1989.

Kerley, E.R. Estimation of Skeletal Age: After About Age 30. In *Personal Identification in Mass Disasters*, T.D. Stewart (ed.), Smithsonian Institution, Washington, DC, pp. 57–70, 1970.

Kerley, E.R. The Identification of Battered-Infant Skeletons. *Journal of Forensic Sciences* 23(1):163–168, 1978.

Kerley, E.R. & D.H. Ubelaker. Revisions in the Microscopic Method of Estimating Age at Death in Human Cortical Bone. *American Journal of Physical Anthropology* 49:545–546, 1978.

Killam, E.W. *The Detection of Human Remains*, 2nd edition. Charles C Thomas, Springfield, IL, 2004.

Krogman, W.M. & M.Y. Iscan. *The Human Skeleton in Forensic Medicine.* Charles C Thomas, Springfield, IL, 1986.

Latham, K.E. & M. Finnegan. *Age Estimation of the Human Skeleton.* Charles C Thomas, Springfield, IL, 2010.

Lovejoy, C.O., R.S. Meindl, T.R. Pryzbeck, & R. Mensforth. Chronological Metamorphosis of the Auricular Surface of the Ilium. *American Journal of Physical Anthropology* 68:15–28, 1985.

Mann, R.W. & D.R. Hunt. *Photographic Regional Atlas of Bone Disease*, Charles C Thomas, Springfield, IL, 2005.

Maples, W.R. Trauma Analysis by the Forensic Anthropologist. In Reichs, K.J. (ed.), *Forensic Osteology.* Charles C Thomas, Springfield, IL, pp. 218–228, 1986.

Maples, W.R. & M. Browning. *Dead Men Do Tell Tales.* Doubleday, New York, 1994.

Meindl, R.S. & C.O. Lovejoy. Ectocranial Suture Closure. *American Journal of Physical Anthropology* 68:57–66, 1985.

Meier-Augenstein, W. *Stable Isotope Forensics*, John Wiley & Sons, Hoboken, NJ, 2010.

Moore-Jansen, P.H., S.D. Ousley, & R.L. Jantz. *Data Collection Procedures for Forensic Skeletal Material.* Report of Investigations No. 48, University of Tennessee Department of Anthropology, Knoxville, 1994.

Morse, D., J. Duncan, & J. Stoutamire (eds.) *Handbook of Forensic Archaeology and Anthropology.* Florida State University Foundation, Inc., Tallahassee, FL, 1983.

Nawrocki, S.P. Regression formulae for the estimation of age from cranial suture closure. In Reichs, K.J. (ed.), *Forensic Osteology: Advances in the Identification of Human Remains*, 2nd edition. Charles C Thomas, Springfield, IL, 1998.

Ortner, D.J. *The Identification of Pathological Conditions in Human Skeletal Remains*, 2nd edition. Academic Press, San Diego, CA, 2003.

Ousley, S.D. Estimating Stature. In Dirkmaat, D.C. (ed.), *A Companion to Forensic Anthropology.* Wiley-Blackwell, Malden, MA, pp. 330–334, 2012.

Ousley, S.D. & R.L. Jantz. FORDISC 3 and Statistical Methods for Estimating Sex and Ancestry. In Dirkmaat, D.C. (ed.), *A Companion to Forensic Anthropology.* Wiley-Blackwell, Malden, MA, pp. 311–329, 2012.

Ousley, S.D., R.L. Jantz, & D.L. Fried. Understanding Race and Human Variation: Why Forensic Anthropologists Are Good at Identifying Race. *Journal of Forensic Anthropology* 139(1):68–76, 2009.

Passalacqua, N.V. & C.W. Rainwater. *Skeletal Trauma Analysis*, John Wiley & Sons, Hoboken, NJ, 2015.

Phenice, T. A Newly Developed Visual Method of Sexing the *os pubis. American Journal of Physical Anthropology* 30:297–302, 1969.

Pokines, J.T. & S.A. Symes. *Manual of Forensic Taphonomy*, CRC Press, Boca Raton, FL, 2014.

Rathbun, T.A. & J.E. Buikstra (eds.). *Human Identification.* Charles C Thomas, Springfield, IL, 1984.

Reichs, K.J. (ed.). *Forensic Osteology.* Charles C Thomas, Springfield, IL, 1986.

Reichs, K.J. (ed.). *Forensic Osteology: Advances in the Identification of Human Remains*, 2nd edition. Charles C Thomas, Springfield, IL, 1998.

Rich, J., D.E. Dean, & R. H. Powers. *Forensic Medicine of the Lower Extremity.* Humana Press, Totowa, NJ, 2005.

Robling, A.G. & S.D. Stout. Methods of Determining Age at Death Using Bone Microstructure. In Katzenberg, M.A. & S.R. Saunders (eds.), *Biological Anthropology of the Human Skeleton*, 2nd edition, John Wiley & Sons, Inc, Hoboken, NJ, pp. 149–171, 2008.

Rodriguez, W.C. & W.M. Bass. Insect Activity and Its Relationship to Decay Rates of Human Cadavers in East Tennessee. *Journal of Forensic Sciences* 28:423–432, 1983.

Rodriguez, W.C. & W.M. Bass. Decomposition of Buried Bodies and Methods that May Aid in Their Location. *Journal of Forensic Sciences* 30:836–852, 1985.

Rogers, L.F. *Radiology of Skeletal Trauma*, 3rd edition. Churchill Livingstone, New York, 2002.

Rowe, W.F. Biodegradation of Hairs and Fibers. In Haglund, W.D. & M.H. Sorg (eds.), *Forensic Taphonomy.* CRC Press, Boca Raton, FL, pp. 337–351, 1997.

Saunders, S.R. & D.L. Rainey. Nonmetric Trait Variation in the Skeleton: Abnormalities, Anomalies, and Atavisms. In Katzenberg, M.A. & S.R. Saunders (eds.), *Biological Anthropology of the Human Skeleton*, 2nd edition, John Wiley & Sons, Inc, Hoboken, NJ, pp. 533–560, 2008.

Sauer, N.J., A.R. Michael, & T.W. Fenton. Human Identification Using Skull-Photo Superimposition and Forensic Image Comparison. In Dirkmaat, D.C. (ed.), *A Companion to Forensic Anthropology.* Wiley-Blackwell, Malden, MA, pp. 432–446, 2012.

Scammell, H. *Mortal Remains.* Harper Collins, New York, 1991.

Scheuer, L. & S. Black. *Developmental Juvenile Osteology.* Academic Press, San Diego, CA, 2000.

Schmidt, C.W. & S.A. Symes, (eds.). *The Analysis of Burned Human Remains*, 2nd edition, Elsevier Press, New York, 2015.

Schoeninger, M.J. Stable Isotope Studies in Human Evolution. *Evolutionary Anthropology* 4:83–98, 1995.

Shirley, N.R., E.E.A Fatah, & M. Mahfouz. Beyond the Cranium: Ancestry Estimation from the Lower Limb. In Berg, G.E. & S.C. Ta'ala. *Biological Affinity in Forensic Identification of Human Skeletal Remains.* CRC Press, Boca Raton, FL, pp. 133–153, 2015.

Soto, O.R. After Nearly 40 Years, A Murder Case Is Closed. *San Diego Union-Tribune* July 18, 2004, pp. A1, A20.

Steele, D.G. Estimation of Stature from fragments of long limb bones. In Stewart, T.D. (ed.), *Personal Identification in Mass Disasters*, Smithsonian Institution, Washington, DC, pp. 85–97, 1970.

Stewart, T.D. Identification of the Scars of Parturition in the Skeletal Remains of Females. In Stewart, T.D. (ed.), *Personal Identification in Mass Disasters*, Smithsonian Institution, Washington, DC, pp. 127–135, 1970.

Stewart, T.D. *Essentials of Forensic Anthropology.* Charles C Thomas, Springfield, IL, 1979.

Stout, S.D. The Use of Histomorphology to Estimate Age. *Journal of Forensic Sciences* 33:121–125, 1988.

Suchey, J.M. & D. Katz. Skeletal Age Standards Derived from an Extensive Multiracial Sample of Modern Americans. *American Journal of Physical Anthropology* 69:269, 1986.

Suchey, J.M., D.V. Wiseley, R.F. Green, & T.T. Noguchi. Analysis of Dorsal Pitting in the Os Pubis in an Extensive Sample of Modern American Females. *American Journal of Physical Anthropology* 51:517–540, 1979.

Symes, S.A., E.N. L'Abbe, E.N. Chapman, I. Wolff, & D.C. Dirkmaat. Interpreting Traumatic Injury to Bone in Medicolegal Investigation. In Dirkmaat, D.C. (ed.), *A Companion to Forensic Anthropology.* Wiley-Blackwell, Malden, MA, pp. 340–389, 2012.

Taylor, K.T. *Forensic Art and Illustration.* CRC Press, Boca Raton, FL, 2001.

Tersigni-Tarrant, M.A. & N.R. Shirley. *Forensic Anthropology, An Introduction.* CRC Press, Boca Raton, FL, 2013.

Thompson, T. & S. Black, (eds.). *Forensic Human Identification.* CRC Press, Boca Raton, FL, 2007.

Trotter, M. Estimation of Stature from Intact Limb Bones. In Stewart, T.D. (ed.), *Personal Identification in Mass Disasters.* Smithsonian Institution, Washington, DC, pp. 127–135, 1970.

Ubelaker, D.H. *Human Skeletal Remains: Excavation, Analysis, Interpretation*, 2nd edition. Taraxacum Manuals on Archeology, Washington, DC, 1989.

Ubelaker, D.H. Hyoid Fracture and Strangulation. *Journal of Forensic Science* 37(5):1216–1222, 1992.

Ubelaker, D.H., E. Bubniak, & G.E. O'Donnell. Computer-Assisted Photographic Superimposition. *Journal of Forensic Sciences* 37:750–762, 1992.

Vass, A.A., W.M. Bass, J.D. Wolt, J.E. Foss, & J.T. Ammons. Time since Death Determinations of Human Cadavers Using Soil Solution. *Journal of Forensic Sciences* 37:1236–1253, 1992.

Walker, P.L., D.C. Cook, & P.M. Lambert. Skeletal Evidence for Child Abuse: A Physical Anthropological Perspective. *Journal of Forensic Sciences* 42(2):196–207, 1997.

Wedel, V.L. & A. Galloway. *Broken Bones*, 2nd edition. Charles C Thomas, Springfield, IL, 2013.

White, T.D., M.T. Black, & P.A. Folkens. *Human Osteology*, 3rd edition. Academic Press, Inc., New York, 2012.

Wilkinson, C. Facial Anthropology and Reconstruction. In Thompson, T. & S. Black (eds.), *Forensic Human Identification*. CRC Press, Boca Raton, FL, pp. 231–255, 2007.

Forensic Dentistry in Cold Cases[1]

21

NORMAN D. SPERBER
ANTHONY R. CARDOZA

Contents

Introduction

Cold cases are solved using a variety of means and methods. Modern technological developments are a leading factor, especially in the area of genetics (DNA). The discipline of forensic odontology (forensic dentistry) can assist cold case homicide investigators in a variety of situations. This chapter presents the practical use of forensic odontology in cold case homicide investigation through its use in the identification process and the role of bite mark analysis.

Dental Identification

Since approximately 1980, several advances have occurred in this field. The states of California, Texas, and Washington developed data processing that linked missing persons' *dental* information with that of unidentified deceased individuals, including unidentified living persons. Comparisons with *reported missing individuals* eliminated the necessity for impractical, expensive, and complex procedures, which would have required the entry of dental information from *all* living persons. Following California's success in the positive identification of dozens of individuals employing a central clearinghouse supervised by the Department of Justice, Sacramento, Missing and Unidentified Unit, the United States government developed a computerized

[1] Updated by Anthony R. Cardoza, DDS.

dental identification system through the National Crime Information Center (NCIC) for the identification of human remains. Dr. Irvin Sopher has excellently addressed the rationale for dental identification as follows:

> "The individuality or specificity of the dentition is based upon the multiple points of comparison inherent in a variable combination of events, which alter the status of a given set of thirty-two teeth, each comprising five anatomic surfaces. Such events include (1) hereditary, congenital, or developmental alterations; (2) acquired, natural, or traumatic alterations; (3) the presence or absence in multiple combinations of one, many, or most of the thirty-two units; and (4) the combinations and permutations in the variable construction, constitution, and morphology of a various array of restorable procedures, materials, and prosthetic devices employed by the dental profession. In addition, the innumerable features of the dental and jaw structure, as revealed by the roentgenogram, further enhance the criterion of individuality. The instance where chronologic age exercises a role in the identification, the added dimension of time and its effect on the teeth is introduced as a measurable criterion.
>
> More concisely put, the presence of 160 available dental surfaces (32 teeth times 5 surfaces) subject to alteration by decay and restoration, the latter process including numerous materials of varying shape and size, as well as the innumerable combinations of one or more missing teeth at variable locations, impart uniqueness or specificity to the dental medium.
>
> Indeed, a basic premise of dental identification is that no two mouths are identical. Theoretically, this may represent a true statement; however, in actuality the reliability of this statement depends upon the number of points of specificity available for the comparison between the ante-mortem and the post-mortem data in any particular case. The greater the number of quantitative and qualitative points of comparison, the more reliable is the comparison and the more nearly one approaches the axiom. Computer models have shown that there are more than 2.5 million possibilities in charting the human mouth. Much effort is currently being expended in evaluating the efficacy of computerized dental charts as a means of classifying mass identification data." (Sopher 1976, p. 58)

Cold Case Identification of Unknown Persons through Dental X-Rays

Positive identification of an individual who cannot be recognized by the usual means such as viewing the body, fingerprints, scars, marks, tattoos, personal possessions, or identification papers, is often successfully accomplished through dental means. The dentition (teeth, soft tissue, and the supporting bone) is unique for every individual. This identification can be accomplished years, even decades, after death (Figure 21.1).

Dental records usually denote x-rays and written records. These records are now typically created and stored electronically, so the term *written* will be used versus *electronic*. Since written records are sometimes inaccurate, most experts in the field will agree that x-rays are by far the most important and reliable method because they readily demonstrate the morphology (shape) of existing restorations (fillings) or crowns, fixed bridges, root canal procedures, implants, and missing teeth (Figure 21.2). In addition, forensic dentists can observe the shape of the roots, the shape of the crowns (portion of the tooth visible above the gingiva [gum]), the relationship of the roots to anatomical landmarks such as the maxillary sinus to adjacent teeth, as well as the shape of the nutrient canals (trabecular bone patterns) within the jawbones. These relationships become exceptionally important when an individual has no dental restorations in place. In some states, labeling of removable full dentures and partial dentures is required. However, an unmarked denture found near a body can be linked to the body if the forensic dentist is convinced that the denture "fits" in all respects. This facet can be determined if little or no decomposition has occurred (Figure 21.3).

If the identification of the decedent is unknown in a cold case investigation, several steps can be considered by the investigator(s):

1. Have dental records been created (full-mouth x-rays of all remaining teeth)?
2. What agency (federal, state, or local) has custody of said x-rays?

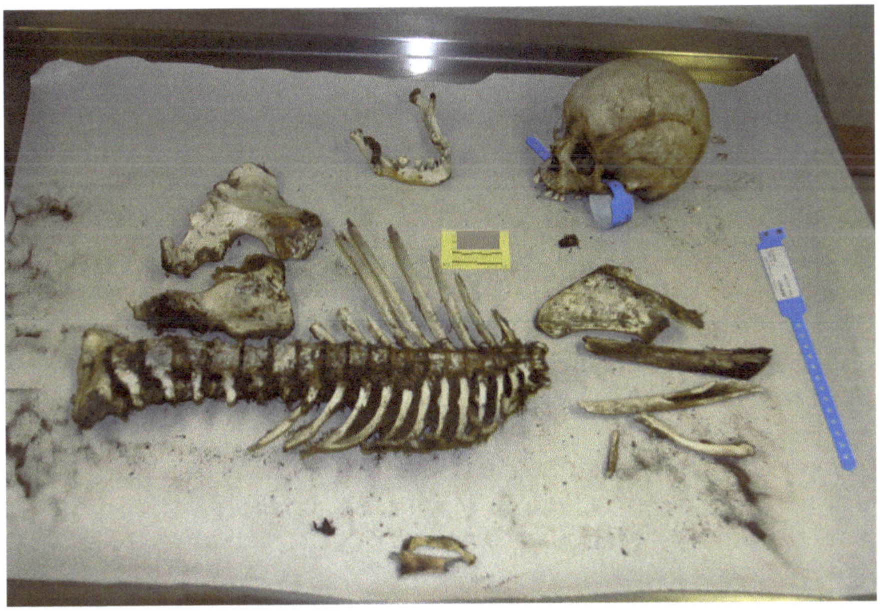

Figure 21.1 Skeletonized remains of a John Doe. (Courtesy of Dr. Anthony R. Cardoza.)

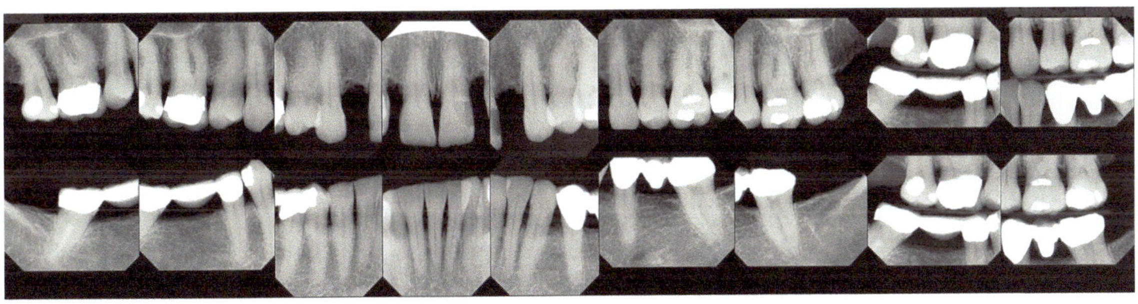

Figure 21.2 Postmortem full-mouth dental radiographs. (Courtesy of Dr. Anthony R. Cardoza.)

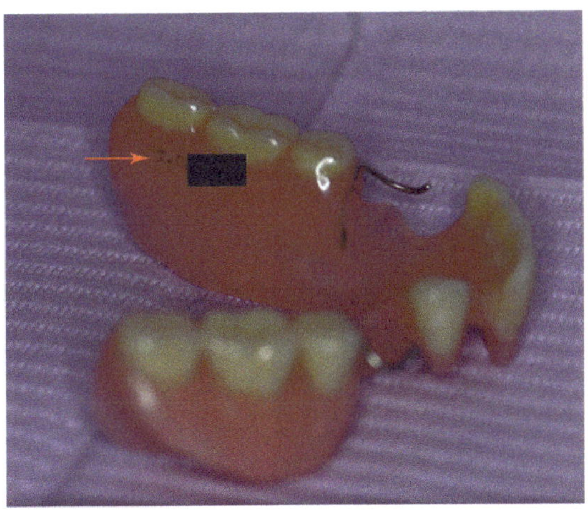

Figure 21.3 Mandibular partial denture recovered on an unidentified decedent. The denture led to the identification of the individual. (Courtesy of Dr. Anthony R. Cardoza.)

3. If this evidence has not been collected, is exhumation of the body possible, or has the body been cremated?
4. If the dental x-rays exist, has the information therein *been distributed to local, state, or federal systems*?
5. Have there been recent submissions or inquiries to the agencies listed previously?
6. Are there existing antemortem x-rays in the possession of investigators?
7. If antemortem and postmortem are records are available, has a certified forensic dentist compared them? A list of such individuals is available online by visiting the website of the American Board of Forensic Odontology.

Thus, when case circumstances are such that investigators have an unknown decedent with dentition (teeth present), check with the following:

1. Your state coroner's office or state medical examiner's office if there is such an agency.
2. In California, the Department of Justice's Missing and Unidentified Persons System (MUPS), which includes the Unidentified Persons System (UPS) and the Missing Persons System (MPS). Their telephone number is 916-227-3290.
3. FBI/NCIC (unidentified dental files established in 1983, updated in 2004).
4. National Dental Image/Information Repository (NDIR), established in 2006.
5. National Missing and Unidentified Persons System (NamUs), established in 2007.

Possible Sources for Antemortem X-Rays

1. Private dental sources (private dental offices, dental schools)
2. Union sources if the employment of the individual is known
3. Insurance companies
4. Federal sources (military records, NCIC, NamUs, NDIR)
5. Custodial (prisons or jails)

NCIC Missing Person and Unidentified Person Files

Cold case investigations may be stalled, often for years, due to the inability to recover the body and learn what it can tell us. Cases that begin as a missing-persons report not uncommonly become a homicide case, but until the body is located, the case may languish in a state of limbo. Sadly, this is all too common for reported missing children. Not infrequently, bodies or their parts may repose in the medical examiner's office in one jurisdiction and other parts from the same body in the coroner's office in another jurisdiction.

In an effort to unite information between those agencies that recover unidentified bodies or body parts and those agencies that hold missing-persons reports, the NCIC has set up a system for data entry by these agencies in efforts to obtain a match between the two databases. This may offer a significant resource to cold case investigators. However, investigators are reminded that the information in the computer is only as reliable and accurate as what was entered into the data system. The system is not perfect. If information is miscoded on the entry forms, or if erroneous information due to error on the part of the person filling out the forms occurs, a match between these two databases may not occur.

NCIC Missing Person File

This file inputs data through a Missing Person Packet. Entry of a missing person into this index is accomplished by the completion of a form and its submission to NCIC by the responsible agency. This packet seeks information that includes

- Initial report completed by the reporting officer and entered into NCIC immediately.
- Personal descriptors. Information completed by parent, legal guardian, or next of kin, and returned to the police agency that completed the initial report.
- Jewelry description.
- Medical/optical information.
- Medical release forms.

See Figures 21.4 and 21.5.

In addition, a list of personal descriptors is offered to investigators to further define a missing person. These descriptors include

- Artificial body parts and legs
- Eye disorders
- Deafness
- Deformities
- Fractured bones
- Medical devices
- Missing body parts/organs
- Moles
- Needle or "track" marks
- Other physical characteristics
- Scars, marks, tattoos
- Skin discolorations
- Medical conditions and diseases
- Drugs of abuse
- Therapeutic drugs

Dental History Information

Dental characteristics are a significant feature in the Missing Person File. A packet of forms detailing requested information is provided by NCIC for data entry. The information supplied in this packet is designed to be completed by a *dentist* familiar with the missing person as his/her patient or as a previous patient. The dental report is extremely comprehensive and was designed for entry into the NCIC for comparison with dental data of unidentified individuals. This format has changed over the years, however. While information sought through these descriptors is best supplied by a trained dentist, in some instances, these forms have been filled out by the patrol officer taking a missing-persons report or by investigators. The result has been less than satisfactory in many instances. Certainly, a law enforcement officer, unless he/she is a dentist, should not fill out dental forms. In addition to patient information, information sought includes

- Date of last patient treatment
- Charting dentist contact information
- Whether x-rays are available
- Date last x-rays were taken
- Whether dental models are available
- Whether photographs of teeth are available
- Whether all 32 teeth are present without decay, restoration, or any unusual characteristics
- Tooth restorations including caries and types of fillings and crowns and combinations

NCIC Missing Person File
Data Collection Entry Guide

Agency Case #________________

NCIC Initial Entry Report

Message Key **(MKE)** (*See Categories, page 2*)
☐ Disability (EMD) ☐ Catastrophe Victim (EMV) ☐ Other (EMO)
☐ Juvenile (EMJ) ☐ Involuntary (EMI)
☐ Endangered (EME) ☐ Caution

Date

Reporting Agency **(ORI)**

Name of Missing Person **(NAM)**

Sex **(SEX)** ☐ Male (M) ☐ Female (F)

Aliases

Race **(RAC)** ☐ Asian or Pacific Islander (A) ☐ American Indian/Alaskan Native (I) ☐ Black (B) ☐ White (W) ☐ Unknown (U)

Place of Birth **(POB)**

Date of Birth **(DOB)**

Date of Emancipation **(DOE)**

Height **(HGT)**

Weight **(WGT)**

Eye Color **(EYE)** ☐ Black (BLK) ☐ Blue (BLU) ☐ Brown (BRO) ☐ Gray (GRY) ☐ Green (GRN) ☐ Hazel (HAZ) ☐ Maroon (MAR) ☐ Pink (PNK) ☐ Unknown (XXX) ☐ Multicolored (MUL)

Hair Color **(HAI)** ☐ Brown (BRO) ☐ Black (BLK) ☐ White (WHT) ☐ Sandy (SDY) ☐ Gray or Partially Gray (GRY) ☐ Red/Auburn (RED) ☐ Blond/Strawberry (BLN) ☐ Blue (BLU) ☐ Green (GRE) ☐ Orange (ONG) ☐ Pink (PNK) ☐ Purple (PLE) ☐ Unknown or Completely Bald (XXX)

FBI Number **(FBI)**

Skin Tone **(SKN)** ☐ Albino (ALB) ☐ Black (BLK) ☐ Dark (DRK) ☐ Yellow (YEL) ☐ Dk. Brown (DBR) ☐ Fair (FAR) ☐ Light (LGT) ☐ Lt. Brown (LBR) ☐ Medium (MED) ☐ Medium Brown (MBR) ☐ Olive (OLV) ☐ Ruddy (RUD) ☐ Sallow (SAL)

Scars, Marks, Tattoos, and Other Characteristics **(SMT)** (*See Checklist, page 8*)

Has the missing person ever been fingerprinted?
☐ No
☐ Yes, by whom?________________

Other Identifying Numbers **(MNU)**

Fingerprint Classification **(FPC)***

Social Security Number **(SOC)**

Operator's License Number **(OLN)**

Operator's License State **(OLS)**

License Expiration **(OLY)**

Missing Person **(MNP)**
☐ Missing Person (MP) ☐ Catastrophe Victim (DV)
☐ Child Abduction (CA) ☐ AMBER Alert (AA)

Date of Last Contact **(DLC)**

Originating Agency Case Number **(OCA)**

Miscellaneous **(MIS)** Information such as build, handedness, any illness or diseases, clothing description, hair description, should be included. If more space is needed, attach additional sheet.**

Missing Person Circumstances **(MPC)**
☐ Abducted By Stranger (S)
☐ Runaway (R)
☐ Abducted By Non-custodial Parent (N)

License Plate Number **(LIC)**

State **(LIS)**

Year Expires **(LIY)**

License Plate Type **(LIT)**

Vehicle Identification Number **(VIN)**

Year **(VYR)**

Make **(VMA)**

Model **(VMO)**

Style **(VST)**

Color **(VCO)**

Rev 2/06 * Fingerprints, if available, may be submitted electronically via the CJIS Wide Area Network or in hard copy to the FBI, CJIS Division, Post Office Box 4142, Clarksburg, West Virginia 26302-9929.
** All dental information should be recorded on the NCIC Missing Person Dental Report and entered into NCIC as supplemental information.

4

Figure 21.4 NCIC initial entry form, missing persons, page 1. (Courtesy of Dr. Anthony R. Cardoza.)

NCIC Missing Person File
Data Collection Entry Guide

Agency Case #________________

Caution and Medical Conditions **(CMC)**

Code	**Description**	**Code**	**Description**	**Code**	**Description**
00 ☐	Armed and dangerous	25 ☐	Escape risk	65 ☐	Epilepsy
05 ☐	Violent tendencies	30 ☐	Sexually violent predator - contact ORI for detailed information	70 ☐	Suicidal
10 ☐	Martial arts expert			80 ☐	Medication required
15 ☐	Explosives expertise	50 ☐	Heart condition	85 ☐	Hemophiliac
20 ☐	Known to abuse drugs	55 ☐	Alcoholic	90 ☐	Diabetic
		60 ☐	Allergies	01 ☐	Other

Has the missing person ever donated blood? **(MIS)**
☐ Yes
☐ No

Blood Type **(BLT)**

☐ A Positive (APOS)	☐ B Positive (BPOS)	☐ AB Positive (ABPOS)	☐ O Positive (OPOS)	☐ Unknown (UNKWN)
☐ A Negative (ANEG)	☐ B Negative (BNEG)	☐ AB Negative (ABNEG)	☐ O Negative (ONEG)	
☐ A Unknown (AUNK)	☐ B Unknown (BUNK)	☐ AB Unknown (ABUNK)	☐ O Unknown (OUNK)	

Circumcision? **(CRC)**
☐ Was (C) ☐ Was Not (N) ☐ Unknown (U)

Footprints available? **(FPA)**
☐ Yes (Y) ☐ No (N)

Body X-Rays? **(BXR)**
☐ Full (F) ☐ Partial (P) ☐ None (N)

Does the missing person have corrected vision? **(SMT)**
☐ Yes ☐ Glasses
☐ No ☐ Con Lenses

Corrective Vision Prescription **(VRX)**

Jewelry Type **(JWT)** *(See Checklist, page 20)*

Jewelry Description **(JWL)** *(See Checklist, page 20)*

DNA Profile Indicator **(DNA)**
☐ Yes (Y) ☐ No (N)

DNA Location **(DLO)**

Complainant's Name

Complainant's Address

Complainant's Telephone Number

Relationship of Complainant to Missing Person

Missing Person's Occupation **(MIS)**

Missing Person's Address

Close friends/relatives

Places Missing Person Frequented **(MIS)**

Possible destination **(MIS)**

Reporting Officer

Reporting Agency Telephone Number

Investigating Officer and Telephone Number **(MIS)**

Complainant's Signature

Date

NCIC Number **(NIC)**

Rev 2/06 5

Figure 21.5 NCIC initial entry form, missing persons, page 2. (Courtesy of Dr. Anthony R. Cardoza.)

NCIC Missing Person File
Data Collection Entry Guide

Agency Case # ____________

NCIC Missing Person Dental Report

SECTION 1

Patient's Name: ____________ Age at Disappearance: ______ NCIC #: ____________

Completed by: ____________ Date Completed: ____________

Address: ____________

Telephone #: ____________ Email Address: ____________

X-Rays Available? ☐ Yes ☐ No Dental Models Available? ☐ Yes ☐ No Dental Photographs Available? ☐ Yes ☐ No

Section 2 ***DENTAL CHARACTERISTICS***

Upper Right

01 (18) ____________
02 (17) ____________
03 (16) ____________
04 (15) ____________ (A)
05 (14) ____________ (B)
06 (13) ____________ (C)
07 (12) ____________ (D)
08 (11) ____________ (E)

Upper Left

09 (21) ____________ (F)
10 (22) ____________ (G)
11 (23) ____________ (H)
12 (24) ____________ (I)
13 (25) ____________ (J)
14 (26) ____________
15 (27) ____________
16 (28) ____________

(Numbers in parentheses represent FDI system.)

(Letters in parentheses represent deciduous dentition.)

Lower Right

32 (48) ____________
31 (47) ____________
30 (46) ____________
29 (45) ____________ (T)
28 (44) ____________ (S)
27 (43) ____________ (R)
26 (42) ____________ (Q)
25 (41) ____________ (P)

Lower Left

24 (31) ____________ (O)
23 (32) ____________ (N)
22 (33) ____________ (M)
21 (34) ____________ (L)
20 (35) ____________ (K)
19 (36) ____________
18 (37) ____________
17 (38) ____________

SECTION 3 ***DENTAL CODES***

X = Tooth has been removed or did not develop
V = Tooth is unrestored or no information (Default Code)
M = Mesial Surface Restored
O = Occlusal/Incisal Surface Restored
D = Distal Surface Restored
F = Facial or Buccal Surface Restored
L = Lingual Surface Restored
C = Lab Processed or Prefabricated Restoration
R = Endodontic Treatment
/ = Tooth present but clinical crown missing (i.e., fractured)*

(*The codes V and / are used differently in the Missing Person Dental Report than in the Unidentified Person Dental Report.)

SECTION 4 ***DENTAL REMARKS***

☐ **ALL** (All 32 teeth are present and unrestored) ☐ **UNK** (No dental information available)

(Rev 11/08) 30

Figure 21.6 NCIC missing-persons dental report form. (Courtesy of Dr. Anthony R. Cardoza.)

- Dentures/partial dentures and replacement teeth
- Other forensic odontological descriptors

See Figure 21.6.

NCIC Unidentified Person File

The Unidentified Person Packet is used for initial and immediate data entry into the NCIC system. Criteria for entry into the NCIC Unidentified Person File are as follows:

- Unidentified deceased. Any unidentified deceased person and/or body parts when a body has been dismembered.
- Unidentified living person. A living person of any age who is unable to ascertain his/her identity. This can include those with amnesia, victims, infants, etc. There may be consent issues involved in this category.
- Unidentified catastrophe victim. Any unidentified victim or body parts dismembered as a result of a disaster.

See Figures 21.7 and 21.8.

Antemortem personal descriptors in this file include those designed to correspond to the MPS, including

- Artificial body parts and aids
- Eye disorders
- Deafness
- Deformities
- Fractured bones
- Medical devices
- Missing body parts/organs
- Moles
- Needle track marks
- Other physical characteristics
- Scars
- Tattoos
- Skin discoloration
- Medical conditions and diseases
- Drugs of abuse
- Therapeutic drugs
- Jewelry type
- Optic information

Dental Information Includes

- Coroner/medical examiner case number
- Charting dentist's name and address
- Whether x-rays are available
- Date last x-rays were taken
- Whether dental models are available
- Whether photographs of teeth are available

NCIC Unidentified Person File
Data Collection Entry Guide

Agency Case #________________

NCIC Initial Entry Report

Message Key **(MKE)** *(See Categories, page 2)*

☐ Unidentified Deceased (EUD) ☐ Unidentified Living (EUL)
☐ Unidentified Catastrophe Victim (EUV)

Date

Reporting Agency **(ORI)**

Body Parts Status **(BPS)**

☐ All 15 parts recovered - fresh **(ALF)**
☐ All 15 parts recovered - decomposed **(ALD)**
☐ All 15 parts recovered - skeletal **(SKL)**

Body Parts Status **(BPS)** if incomplete body or skeleton, see body diagram page 7 for coding corresponding parts
N - Not Recovered D - Recovered Decomposed F - Recovered Fresh S - Skeletal

1	2	3	4	5	6	7	8	9	10	11	12	13	14	15
☐	☐	☐	☐	☐	☐	☐	☐	☐	☐	☐	☐	☐	☐	☐

Sex **(SEX)**

☐ Male (M) ☐ Female (F)
☐ Unknown (U)

Race **(RAC)**

☐ Asian or Pacific Islander (A) ☐ American Indian/Alaskan Native (I) ☐ Unknown (U)
☐ Black (B) ☐ White (W)

Estimated Year of Birth Range **(EYB)**

☐☐☐☐-☐☐☐☐

Estimated Date of Death **(EDD)**

☐☐-☐☐-☐☐☐☐

Date Body Found **(DBF)**

☐☐-☐☐-☐☐☐☐

Approximate Height Range **(HGT)**

☐☐☐-☐☐☐

Approximate Weight Range **(WGT)**

☐☐☐-☐☐☐

Eye Color **(EYE)**

☐ Black (BLK) ☐ Green (GRN) ☐ Unknown (XXX)
☐ Blue (BLU) ☐ Hazel (HAZ) ☐ Multicolored (MUL)
☐ Brown (BRO) ☐ Maroon (MAR)
☐ Gray (GRY) ☐ Pink (PNK)

Hair Color **(HAI)**

☐ Brown (BRO) ☐ Sandy (SDY) ☐ Blue (BLU) ☐ Purple (PLE)
☐ Black (BLK) ☐ Gray or Partially Gray (GRY) ☐ Green (GRE) ☐ Unknown or Completely Bald (XXX)
☐ White (WHT) ☐ Red/Auburn (RED) ☐ Orange (ONG)
☐ Blond/Strawberry (BLN) ☐ Pink (PNK)

Scars, Marks, Tattoos, and other Characteristics **(SMT)** *(See Checklist, page 8)*

Fingerprint Classification **(FPC)***

☐☐☐☐☐
☐☐☐☐☐

Originating Agency Case Number **(OCA)**

Miscellaneous **(MIS)** Information such as build, handedness, clothing description, hair description, weather conditions at the time of death, place where the individual was found, should be included. If more space is needed, attach additional sheet.**

* Fingerprints, if available, may be submitted electronically via the CJIS Wide Area Network or in hard copy to the FBI, CJIS Division, Post Office Box 4142, Clarksburg, West Virginia 26302-9929.

** All dental information should be recorded on the NCIC Unidentified Person Dental Report and entered into NCIC as supplemental information.

Rev 2/06 4

Figure 21.7 NCIC initial entry form, unidentified persons, page 1. (Courtesy of Dr. Anthony R. Cardoza.)

NCIC Unidentified Person File
Data Collection Entry Guide

Agency Case #________________

Blood Type **(BLT)**

☐ A Positive (APOS)	☐ B Positive (BPOS)	☐ AB Positive (ABPOS)	☐ O Positive (OPOS)	☐ Unknown (UNKWN)
☐ A Negative (ANEG)	☐ B Negative (BNEG)	☐ AB Negative (ABNEG)	☐ O Negative (ONEG)	
☐ A Unknown (AUNK)	☐ B Unknown (BUNK)	☐ AB Unknown (ABUNK)	☐ O Unknown (OUNK)	

Circumcision? **(CRC)**	Footprints available? **(FPA)**	Body X-Rays available? **(BXR)**	Does the Unidentified Person have corrected vision? **(SMT)**	Corrective Vision Prescription **(VRX)**
☐ Was	☐ Yes	☐ Full (F)	☐ Yes ☐ Glasses	
☐ Was Not	☐ No	☐ Partial (P)	☐ No ☐ Con Lenses	
☐ Unknown		☐ None (N)		

Manner and cause of Death **(CDA)**	Describe
☐ Natural Causes (N) ☐ Suicide (S)	
☐ Accidental (A) ☐ Unknown (U)	
☐ Homicide (H)	

Jewelry Type **(JWT)** *(See Checklist, page 20)*	Jewelry Description **(JWL)** *(See Checklist, page 20)*

DNA Profile Indicator **(DNA)**	DNA Location **(DLO)**
☐ Yes	
☐ No	

Medical Examiner/Coroner Agency Name and Case Number **(MAN)**	Medical Examiner/Coroner Locality **(MAL)**
Medical Examiner/Coroner Telephone Number **(MAT)**	Investigating Officer and Telephone Number **(MIS)**
NCIC Number **(NIC)**	

Rev 2/06 5

Figure 21.8 NCIC initial entry form, unidentified persons, page 2. (Courtesy of Dr. Anthony R. Cardoza.)

- Whether all 32 teeth are present without decay, restoration, or any unusual characteristics
- Tooth restoration including caries and types of fillings and crowns and restorations
- Dentures/partial dentures and replacement teeth
- Other forensic odontological descriptors

See Figure 21.9.

NCIC Unidentified Person File
Data Collection Entry Guide

Agency Case #__________

NCIC Unidentified Person Dental Report

SECTION 1

ME/Coroner Case #: __________ NCIC #: __________

Completed by: __________ Date Completed: __________

Address: __________

Telephone #: __________ Email Address: __________

X-Rays Available? ☐ Yes ☐ No Dental Models Available? ☐ Yes ☐ No Dental Photographs Available? ☐ Yes ☐ No

SECTION 2 ***DENTAL CHARACTERISTICS***

Upper Right		Lower Right
01 (18)		32 (48)
02 (17)		31 (47)
03 (16)		30 (46)
04 (15) (A)	(Numbers in parentheses represent FDI System.)	29 (45) (T)
05 (14) (B)		28 (44) (S)
06 (13) (C)		27 (43) (R)
07 (12) (D)		26 (42) (Q)
08 (11) (E)		25 (41) (P)
Upper Left		**Lower Left**
09 (21) (F)	(Letters in parentheses represent deciduous dentition.)	24 (31) (O)
10 (22) (G)		23 (32) (N)
11 (23) (H)		22 (33) (M)
12 (24) (I)		21 (34) (L)
13 (25) (J)		20 (35) (K)
14 (26)		19 (36)
15 (27)		18 (37)
16 (28)		17 (38)

SECTION 3 ***DENTAL CODES***

X = Tooth has been removed or did not develop
V = Tooth is present and unrestored
M = Mesial Surface Restored
O = Occlusal/Incisal Surface Restored
D = Distal Surface Restored
F = Facial or Buccal Surface Restored
L = Lingual Surface Restored
C = Lab Processed or Prefabricated Restoration
R = Endodontic Treatment
/ = Postmortem Missing or Not Recovered (Default Code)

(*The codes V and / are used differently in the Unidentified Person Report than in the Missing Person Dental Report.)

SECTION 4 ***DENTAL REMARKS***

☐ ALL (All 32 teeth are present and unrestored) ☐ UNK (No dental information available)

Rev 2/06 30

Figure 21.9 NCIC unidentified-person dental report form. (Courtesy of Dr. Anthony R. Cardoza.)

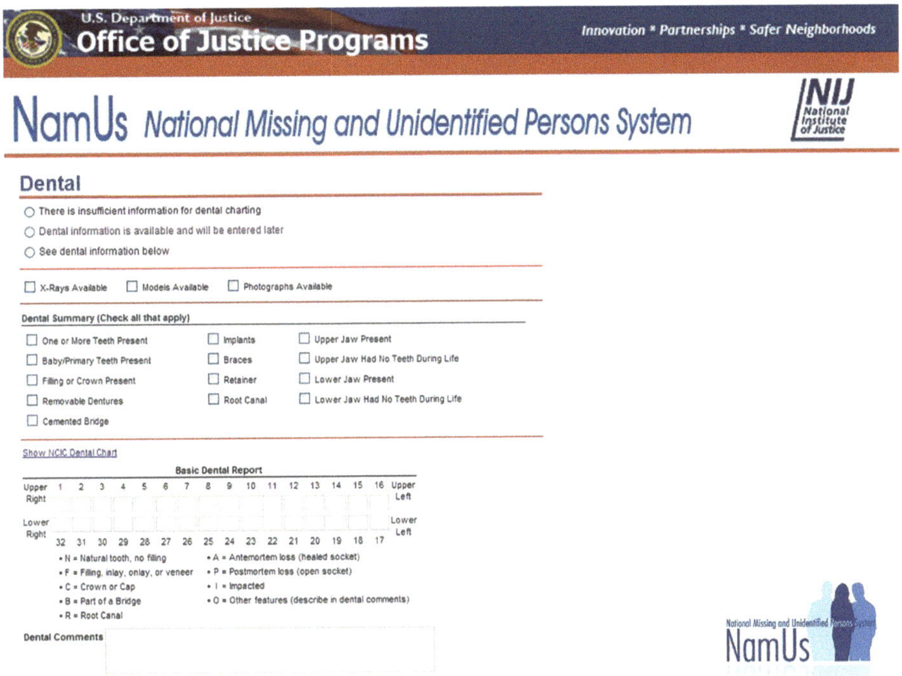

Figure 21.10 NamUs unidentified-persons dental report form. (Courtesy of Dr. Anthony R. Cardoza.)

National Dental Image Repository

NDIR is a supplement to NCIC to be used by forensic dentists. It is found on the Law Enforcement Online (LEO) CJIS website, and it contains the missing/unidentified (MUP) wanted-person form, the digitized copy of the NCIC record, the digitized copy of the dental condition worksheet, and the digitized dental radiographs.

National Missing and Unidentified Persons System

NamUs was created in 2007 as the first online repository for missing persons and unidentified remains when the National Missing Persons Task Force, through the National Institute of Justice, identified the need to improve access to database information by people who can help solve cases of missing and unidentified deceased persons. It brings together two innovative programs and their online, searchable databases: http://identifyus.org (for information on unidentified human remains) and http://www.findthemissing.org (for information on missing persons). NamUs allows the general public to actively participate in providing access to resources, information, and nationwide tools for missing adults (Figure 21.10).

Bite Marks on Victims or Perpetrators

Bite mark evidence in felony crimes such as homicide, child abuse, and sex crimes has been recognized by the courts in numerous jurisdictions for several decades. When properly preserved and protected, these marks may provide an important link between a victim and his/her assailant. While bite marks on victims are seemingly the most commonly encountered during law enforcement investigations, equally incriminating may be those inflicted by the victim on the assailant (Figure 21.11).

Analysis of bite marks on perpetrators and victims is one of the responsibilities of modern forensic dentistry (Figure 21.12). Bite mark analysis is more *interpretive* and less objective than, for example, toxicology or DNA procedures. In fact, several cases of positive comparisons logged by a number of odontologists have been reversed by DNA analysis. (As of 2016, there have been 27 cases nationally that have been reversed where bite mark testimony was used as a contributor to the original conviction.) There have been far too many criticisms of existing procedures in legal literature. Bite mark analysis has been termed a

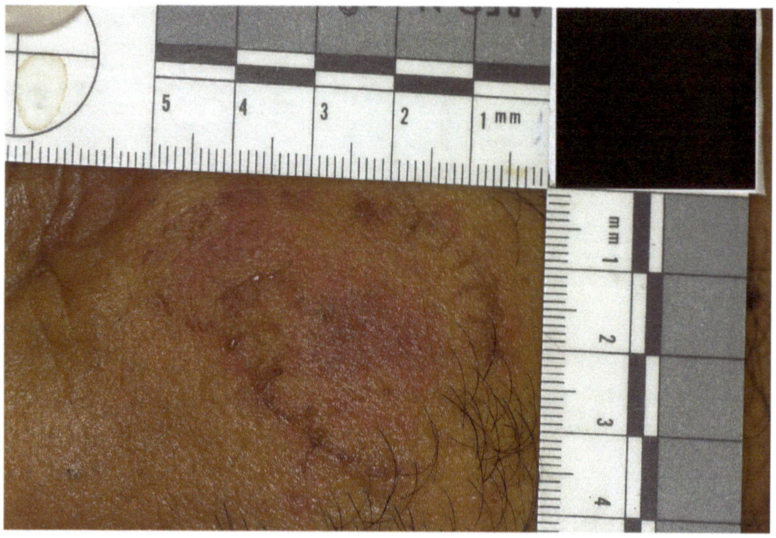

Figure 21.11 Close-up view of a human bite mark found on the face of a decedent. Note that a scale is in place. (Courtesy of Dr. Anthony R. Cardoza.)

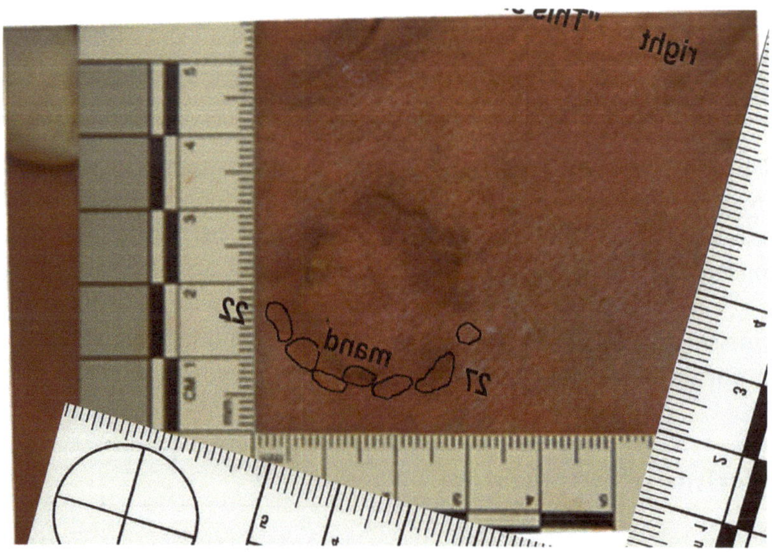

Figure 21.12 Human bite mark pattern with suspect bite overlay in place for comparison. Note that scales on both images correspond to a 1:1 size orientation. (Courtesy of Dr. Anthony R. Cardoza.)

"junk science." Some experts in the field believe that it is not a science at all, especially when lesions occurring during resuscitative attempts by medical personnel or insect marks found on the body have been falsely identified as bite marks. The field of odontology has always urged the collection of saliva for DNA analysis and now considers the collection of trace salivary evidence on a suspected bite mark to be the *critical step* in bite mark analysis.

Not uncommonly, case or file review will reveal the presence of bite marks on either the victim or a suspect. Investigators should consider the following:

- Were swabbings of the alleged bite mark accomplished (critical step)?
  - What swabbing procedure was used (dual-swab technique)?
  - Have these swabbings been located?
  - Is there an original DNA report?
  - Have the swabbings been reexamined?
  - What were the results?
- Is clothing that was over the bite mark available for DNA testing?
- If DNA results were obtained, were they entered into the Combined DNA Index System (CODIS)?
- Were salivary specimens secured from the victim or suspect?
- If photographs are available, were they examined by a certified forensic dentist?

In these instances, cold case investigators should consult with a qualified forensic odontologist.

Bite Mark Photography

A number of issues may confront cold case investigators when reviewing past photographs of purported bite marks. These photographs may be valuable evidence, but a number of factors may affect their usefulness and reliability. Camera angle and scale placement (if any) may be important considerations in evaluating the reliability of these photographs. In reviewing the photographs and this record, investigators should consider the following:

- How long after the crime were the photographs taken?
- What was the distance from the camera to the bite mark?
- Is this record sufficiently documented?
  - Date
  - Time
  - Photographer
- Are there both black-and-white and color photos available? Black-and-white photographs cannot differentiate between, for example, freckles and an actual bite mark.
- At what camera angles were the photographs taken? Right-angle photography eliminates distortion.
- Were the photographs taken before or after the autopsy?
- *Was a ruler or scale placed next to the alleged bite mark during photography (critical photographic step)?* (Other objects such as a coin may be used if a scale is not available.)
- Who took the photographs?
  - Is this photographer still available?
  - Does he/she have any notes, records, or other photographs?

If the photography is distorted, a forensic dentist may be able to use Adobe Photoshop software to correct this problem.

Bite Mark Impressions

Similar considerations as in conditions of swabbings or photography should be considered when reviewing bite mark impressions. In addition, cold case investigators need to know the following:

- Were they taken by a forensic odontologist, dentist, or experienced lab technician?
- What materials were used?
- What procedures were used or followed during this process?

It is also important to point out that in some cases, tooth marks have been found in objects such as chewing gum, apples, cheese, duct tape, Styrofoam, weather stripping, etc.

Standard procedures in evaluating bite mark cases are as follows:

1. Orientation photographs
2. Swab for DNA evidence (dual-swab technique)
3. Close-up photography
4. Impressions of bite mark if perforations are noted

Exhumations of Embalmed Bodies with Bite Marks

Usually at autopsies, photographs of suspected bite marks are taken by pathologists. On occasion, these bite mark lesions may not be recognized at the time of autopsy. If this is the case, an exhumation may result in the completion of better photographic images with corresponding rulers in place. It should be understood that the embalming process is not always effective and the lesion may not be as obvious or objective as the original preautopsy photographs might have been had they been collected at that time. Also, collecting bite mark evidence postautopsy can result in a distorted bite mark due to the surgical manipulation of the body during autopsy.

Qualified forensic dentists may be located through the following:

American Board of Forensic Odontology
http://www.abfo.org
American Academy of Forensic Sciences
PO Box 669
Colorado Springs, Colorado 80901
1-719-636-1100
(http://www.aafs.org)

For further information:

Anthony R. Cardoza, DDS
Diplomate, American Board of Forensic Odontology
9530 Cuyamaca Street, Suite 101
Santee, California 92071

Acknowledgments

I wish to extend my deepest appreciation and gratitude to Dr. Norman D. "Skip" Sperber for his authorship of this chapter. Dr. Sperber has been repeatedly acknowledged as perhaps the world's leading forensic odontologist, and his leadership efforts in this field have contributed greatly to the betterment of the forensic and law enforcement spectrum for over 50 years. Prior to his graduation from the New York University College of Dentistry in 1954, Dr. Sperber worked for the New York Chief Medical Examiner's Office in New York City. After passing his board exams in New York and California, he practiced in his field and served 10 years as a dental officer in the U.S. Navy. In 1963, Dr. Sperber was appointed the forensic dentist for the San Diego County Coroner's Office, California (later medical examiner), and has served continually since.

Dr. Sperber has instructed law enforcement officers in aspects of forensic dentistry for over 30 years. In 1983, he attended and completed, on his own time, the San Diego Police and Sheriff's Reserve Academy and became a reserve police officer.

Dr. Sperber helped devise the first civilian dental identification computer system in the United States in 1978, one used extensively to identify over 100 of 144 victims from a midair collision over San Diego the following year. As a result of a U.S. congressional appointment, he devised the dental section of the NCIC computer relating unidentified-persons data to missing-persons data, and he continues today as a consultant in that capacity. This was the first national dental identification system in the history of the United States. He has testified in over 215 trials, including the first U.S. court-martial bite mark case, and as a primary forensic bite mark expert in the cases against Ted Bundy and Jeffrey Dahmer.

Dr. Sperber has served as director of the American Board of Forensic Odontology, in addition to chair positions and other duties and accomplishments. He has served as vice president of the American Academy of Forensic Sciences (AAFS) and as chair of the Odontology Section of this highly respected organization. In 2000, he and a codentist were named the first distinguished fellows from the dental section of the AAFS. He was one of three dentists to design the first state system (California) for body identification and continues to the present as chief forensic dentist for the California Department of Justice's statewide identification system.

I further wish to recognize and extend my deepest gratitude to Anthony R. Cardoza, DDS, D-ABFO, for his contributions to this chapter. Dr. Cardoza is a 1985 graduate of the Northwestern University Dental School and maintains a general dental practice in Santee (San Diego County, California). He began his affiliation with the San Diego County Medical Examiner in 1992 under the mentorship of Dr. Norman Sperber. Dr. Cardoza is a diplomate of the American Board of Forensic Odontology (ABFO), a fellow of the AAFS, and a member of the American Society of Forensic Odontology (ASFO) and the California Society of Forensic Dentistry (CSFD). Dr. Cardoza serves as a forensic dental consultant for the Office of the Medical Examiner, County of San Diego; Office of the Coroner, County of Imperial; Office of the Coroner, County of Riverside; Department of Justice, Sacramento; the San Diego Police Department; and the San Diego County Sheriff's Department, California. He is also a member of the California Dental Identification Team (CalDIT) and the California Office of Emergency Services (CalOES).

Dr. Cardoza maintains a busy forensic caseload due to the proximity of the San Diego and Imperial Counties to the Mexican border. He has performed numerous postmortem dental examinations, comparisons, and identifications and most recently was involved with the identifications of victims of the Southern California wildfire disasters.

Suggested Readings and Bibliography

Bowers, C. M. 2010. *Forensic Dental Evidence*. Second Edition. Burlington, MA: Elsevier.

Senn, D. R. and R. A. Weems. 2013. *Manual of Forensic Odontology*. Fifth Edition. Boca Raton, FL: American Society of Forensic Odontology.

Sopher, I. M. 1976. *Forensic Dentistry*. Springfield, IL: Charles C Thomas.

III Investigative Tools

Forensic Exhumation

22

R. H. WALTON

Contents

Introduction

For the purposes of this book, a forensic exhumation is the legally sanctioned act or process of disinterring or digging up a previously lawfully buried human body for law enforcement–associated forensic purposes. This form of exhumation may be undertaken at the direction of a court order or, in some cases, may result from consent by those persons with standing to give such sanction. Normally, these would include close family members. A forensic exhumation is normally conducted at the grave site within a cemetery or in a mausoleum under the auspices of law enforcement, forensic personnel, medical examiner or coroner personnel, and cemetery representatives. During a forensic exhumation, the search for evidence is usually more specifically focused, and this focus underlies the legal procedure preceding and governing the exhumation process.

Considerations in the Exhumation Process

This act is differentiated from the recovery of the remains of an otherwise buried person, as would be exemplified by a forensic excavation or body recovery of a crime victim from its burial location.

During such an excavation, the excavation site is treated as a crime scene, and appropriate recording and obtaining of photographic record is conducted. During the course of an excavation, the investigation is usually in a more general stage and the search for evidence is a primary factor among investigative considerations.

Why Conduct a Forensic Exhumation?

With the increased use of DNA as an investigative tool, a forensic exhumation has become a more commonplace procedure in the criminal investigation process. Modern technology and advanced criminal investigation methods have enhanced the application of this technique to make it a viable procedure under some circumstances during the investigation process (Figure 22.1).

A forensic exhumation may be utilized by cold case homicide investigators for the following purposes:

- Obtaining biological material for mitochondrial or nuclear DNA testing to aid in identification of the remains
- Obtaining biological material for use in mitochondrial DNA (mtDNA) testing to determine DNA profiles of those related to the deceased
- Facilitating 3-D facial reconstruction
- Exclusion of persons of interest
- Investigation purposes to determine whether injuries were compatible with witness statements or other case investigation information
- Anthropological or medical examination to support or disaffirm a proposed defense version of events as to how injuries were received
- Secondary autopsy
- Forensic odontological purposes, including identification

Figure 22.1 Forensic exhumation. Tree roots and no remains. The condition of the remains will be unknown until the casket is opened. In this example, few remains have been found due to severe decomposition. Note the tree roots throughout the casket. (Courtesy of Connie Milton, San Diego County Sheriff's Department.)

Role of the Death Certificate in Forensic Exhumation

The death certificate is a legal document that contains important information for use in consideration of a forensic exhumation (Figure 22.2). Information to be found on this document may include the following:

- Disposition of remains. This would indicate whether the remains were buried or cremated, or other information. As in any other investigation, however, investigate and confirm any reported disposition.
- Date of disposition of the remains.
- Name and address of the cemetery or crematory.
- Name and address of attending physician.
- Name and license number of embalmer, if applicable.
- Name of funeral director or person acting on his/her behalf.

When reviewing the death certificate, it is suggested that a check be made with the registrar to ascertain if any supplements or amendments to the death certificate were subsequently added. Further discussion of the death certificate can be found in Chapter 10.

Disposition of Human Remains

What happens to the body after death and the autopsy may become a significant issue in cold case homicide investigations. There are a number of possible dispositions of the physical remains. These are as follows:

- Cremation. The remains are burned in a crematorium and (if properly conducted) reduced to ashes. These remains become known as *cremains*. Cremated remains may be scattered at sea, or they may be scattered on private property with any appropriate health or other permits. In addition, some churches have separate interment areas known as a *niche* for cremated remains. Remains or cremated remains may also be buried in some veterans' cemeteries. Examinations including DNA, toxicology, and similar testing cannot normally be conducted upon remains in this condition.
- Burial in ground without embalming.
- Burial in ground after embalming.
- Entombment in mausoleum/crypt (embalming is normally required by cemetery).
- Burial at sea.

Investigative Considerations

Cold case investigators may be faced with a number of issues when considering a forensic exhumation. Among these may be the following:

- What is the purpose of the exhumation? A primary consideration in the decision to conduct a forensic exhumation is to establish the specific information that such an exhumation will provide cold case investigators. For example, are samples sought for DNA testing or for anthropological examination?
- Are the remains to be removed or examined on site? This will assist in the determination of whether the remains are to be removed from the grave, and the necessity for proper transportation equipment, or whether the necessary requirements may be accomplished on site and without the necessity to remove the remains.

CERTIFICATE OF DEATH
STATE OF CALIFORNIA
USE BLACK INK ONLY / NO ERASURES, WHITEOUTS OR ALTERATIONS
VS-11 (REV 1/03)

STATE FILE NUMBER — LOCAL REGISTRATION NUMBER

DECEDENT'S PERSONAL DATA
1. NAME OF DECEDENT --- FIRST (Given) | 2. MIDDLE | 3. LAST (Family)
AKA. ALSO KNOWN AS --- Include full AKA (FIRST, MIDDLE, LAST) | 4. DATE OF BIRTH mm/dd/ccyy | 5. AGE Yrs. | IF UNDER ONE YEAR Months Days | IF UNDER 24 HOURS Hours Minutes | 6. SEX
9. BIRTH STATE/FOREIGN COUNTRY | 10. SOCIAL SECURITY NUMBER | 11. EVER IN U.S. ARMED FORCES? ☐ YES ☐ NO ☐ UNK | 12. MARITAL STATUS (at Time of Death) | 7. DATE OF DEATH mm/dd/ccyy | 8. HOUR (24 Hours)
13. EDUCATION --- Highest Level/Degree (see worksheet on back) | 14/15. WAS DECEDENT SPANISH/HISPANIC/LATINO? (If yes, see worksheet on back.) ☐ YES ☐ NO | 16. DECEDENT'S RACE --- Up to 3 races may be listed (see worksheet on back)
17. USUAL OCCUPATION --- Type of work for most of life. DO NOT USE RETIRED | 18. KIND OF BUSINESS OR INDUSTRY (e.g., grocery store, road construction, employment agency, etc.) | 19. YEARS IN OCCUPATION

USUAL RESIDENCE
20. DECEDENT'S RESIDENCE (Street and number or location)
21. CITY | 22. COUNTY/PROVINCE | 23. ZIP CODE | 24. YEARS IN COUNTY | 25. STATE/FOREIGN COUNTRY

INFORMANT
26. INFORMANT'S NAME, RELATIONSHIP | 27. INFORMANT'S MAILING ADDRESS (Street and number or rural route number, city or town, state, ZIP)

SPOUSE AND PARENT INFORMATION
28. NAME OF SURVIVING SPOUSE --- FIRST | 29. MIDDLE | 30. LAST (Maiden Name)
31. NAME OF FATHER --- FIRST | 32. MIDDLE | 33. LAST | 34. BIRTH STATE
35. NAME OF MOTHER --- FIRST | 36. MIDDLE | 37. LAST (Maiden) | 38. BIRTH STATE

FUNERAL DIRECTOR/ LOCAL REGISTRAR
39. DISPOSITION DATE mm/dd/ccyy | 40. PLACE OF FINAL DISPOSITION
41. TYPE OF DISPOSITION(S) | 42. SIGNATURE OF EMBALMER | 43. LICENSE NUMBER
44. NAME OF FUNERAL ESTABLISHMENT | 45. LICENSE NUMBER | 46. SIGNATURE OF LOCAL REGISTRAR | 47. DATE mm/dd/ccyy

PLACE OF DEATH
101. PLACE OF DEATH | 102. IF HOSPITAL, SPECIFY ONE ☐ IP ☐ ER/OP ☐ DOA | 103. IF OTHER THAN HOSPITAL, SPECIFY ONE ☐ Hospice ☐ Nursing Home/LTC ☐ Decedent's Home ☐ Other
104. COUNTY | 105. FACILITY ADDRESS OR LOCATION WHERE FOUND (Street and number or location) | 106. CITY

CAUSE OF DEATH
107. CAUSE OF DEATH — Enter the chain of events --- diseases, injuries, or complications --- that directly caused death. DO NOT enter terminal events such as cardiac arrest, respiratory arrest, or ventricular fibrillation without showing the etiology. DO NOT ABBREVIATE. | Time Interval Between Onset and Death | 108. DEATH REPORTED TO CORONER? ☐ YES ☐ NO REFERRAL NUMBER
IMMEDIATE CAUSE (Final disease or condition resulting in death) → (A) | (AT)
Sequentially, list conditions, if any, leading to cause on Line A. Enter UNDERLYING CAUSE (disease or injury that initiated the events resulting in death) LAST
(B) | (BT) | 109. BIOPSY PERFORMED? ☐ YES ☐ NO
(C) | (CT) | 110. AUTOPSY PERFORMED? ☐ YES ☐ NO
(D) | (DT) | 111. USED IN DETERMINING CAUSE? ☐ YES ☐ NO
112. OTHER SIGNIFICANT CONDITIONS CONTRIBUTING TO DEATH BUT NOT RESULTING IN THE UNDERLYING CAUSE GIVEN IN 107
113. WAS OPERATION PERFORMED FOR ANY CONDITION IN ITEM 107 OR 112? (If yes, list type of operation and date.) | 113A. IF FEMALE, PREGNANT IN LAST YEAR? ☐ YES ☐ NO ☐ UNK

PHYSICIAN'S CERTIFICATION
114. I CERTIFY THAT TO THE BEST OF MY KNOWLEDGE DEATH OCCURRED AT THE HOUR, DATE, AND PLACE STATED FROM THE CAUSES STATED. Decedent Attended Since (A) mm/dd/ccyy | Decedent Last Seen Alive (B) mm/dd/ccyy | 115. SIGNATURE AND TITLE OF CERTIFIER | 116. LICENSE NUMBER | 117. DATE mm/dd/ccyy
118. TYPE ATTENDING PHYSICIAN'S NAME, MAILING ADDRESS, ZIP CODE

CORONER'S USE ONLY
119. I CERTIFY THAT IN MY OPINION DEATH OCCURRED AT THE HOUR, DATE, AND PLACE STATED FROM THE CAUSES STATED. MANNER OF DEATH ☐ Natural ☐ Accident ☐ Homicide ☐ Suicide ☐ Pending Investigation ☐ Could not be determined | 120. INJURED AT WORK? ☐ YES ☐ NO ☐ UNK | 121. INJURY DATE mm/dd/ccyy | 122. HOUR (24 Hours)
123. PLACE OF INJURY (e.g., home, construction site, wooded area, etc.)
124. DESCRIBE HOW INJURY OCCURRED (Events which resulted in injury)
125. LOCATION OF INJURY (Street and number, or location, and city, and ZIP)
126. SIGNATURE OF CORONER / DEPUTY CORONER | 127. DATE mm/dd/ccyy | 128. TYPE NAME, TITLE OF CORONER / DEPUTY CORONER

STATE REGISTRAR | A | B | C | D | E | FAX AUTH. # | CENSUS TRACT

Figure 22.2 Death certificate. (Author's file.)

When investigators determine that the exhumation of remains is necessary for investigation purposes, there are a number of preliminary issues to be considered. Among these are the following:

- Confirm the physical location of the human remains. This would include the name and address of the cemetery or mausoleum, and the plot or grave number, if applicable. Confirmation of the location of the remains should be made, as postinterment actions may have resulted in the removal and other disposition of the remains that are not reflected in the initial investigation or records available to investigators. In some cases, family members may have disinterred the remains for reburial at another location at a later date. This information may be available from the cemetery or from the city/county health department.
- Determine what treatments were applied to the remains.
  - Embalmed?
  - Cremated?
  - Buried without embalming?

Visit the Cemetery and Grave Location

Prior to exhumation, cold case investigators may seek to visit the cemetery and grave location, and to meet with representatives of the cemetery. Investigators may seek to review cemetery records if these records are available, although a court order may be necessary. Most burial requirements are regulated at the state level, and these vary from state to state. Similarly, record-keeping systems and retention policies may also vary.

Depending on age, remaining paper records may be in the format of the whole file, or may be a book summary or card file only. During this review, investigators may seek to identify the following:

- Names in these records that are not found in the case investigation file.
- Who paid for the funeral and/or burial expenses.
- *Visitor's log.* This document is normally returned to the family at the conclusion of services, and cold case investigators may ask family members for this log for investigative review. This document may be reviewed with selected family members to identify friends, associates, or other relations to the victim.
- *Burial record or record of funeral.* Depending upon the funeral home, this may provide everything from make and model of casket to services provided, such as makeup and embalming.
- "*Arrangement sheets.*" These list relatives to grandchildren and include information from family members for the death certificate, planning of services, etc.
- *Type of burial container.* Was it a metal coffin or a wood coffin? A vault is a concrete enclosure into which is placed the coffin. This in turn is covered by a concrete lid. This may factor into preservation of the remains after passage of time and soil and moisture conditions. In addition, coffins may have gaskets or seals. Less expensive coffins, whether metal or wood, may lack these seals, and this may affect preservation of remains.
- Any permits for burial or other disposition, including transfer of remains.
- Copies of any checks written for cemetery services.
- Copies of any worksheets.
- Logs of family conversations, i.e., any problems or other concerns.
- *Removal sheet.* This is the form cemetery personnel fill out when they pick up the body for transport to the cemetery. This will contain vital information, including social security number, when deceased was last seen by a physician, name of primary physician, time of death, and next of kin, and personal effects on the body are noted if brought in.

- *Hospital sheet.* Vital information from hospital containing much of the same information on the removal sheet. This serves as a check for the removal sheet.
- *Clothing sheet.* Clothing brought in by family for dressing the deceased.
- *Name of the "case arranger."* This is the cemetery person who oversees the interment process. It may be beneficial to inquire if any photographs were taken, or whether there was new media coverage at the time of the service.
- *Name of the funeral director.* This person handles the funeral as set up per the case arranger.
- *Other persons who are involved in arrangements and interment.* Some institutions have a "super director," who handles both mortuary and cemetery aspects, but this varies from place to place.
- *Embalming report.* This report describes the physical condition and review of the body and its preparation for interment.

390249

APPLICATION AND PERMIT FOR DISPOSITION OF HUMAN REMAINS

USE BLACK INK ONLY — MAKE NO ERASURES, WHITEOUTS OR OTHER ALTERATIONS

1A. NAME OF DECEDENT—FIRST (GIVEN) | 1B. MIDDLE | 1C. LAST (FAMILY) | 2. DATE OF BIRTH MONTH, DAY, YEAR | 3. DATE OF DEATH MONTH, DAY, YEAR | 4. SEX

5A. CITY OF DEATH | 5B. COUNTY OF DEATH — OUTSIDE CALIF., ENTER STATE | 6. NAME, RELATIONSHIP, FULL MAILING ADDRESS AND ZIP CODE OF INFORMANT

7A. TYPED NAME AND ADDRESS OF CALIFORNIA - FUNERAL DIRECTOR OR PERSON ACTING AS SUCH | 7B. CALIF. LICENSE NUMBER — IF APPLICABLE

8A. SIGNATURE OF APPLICANT—Person taking permit | 8B. DATE SIGNED

ACKNOWLEDGEMENT OF APPLICANT — I hereby acknowledge as applicant that the proposed disposition stated herein is one of the dispositions authorized by Section 103055 of the Health and Safety Code, and was authorized pursuant to Section 7100 of the Health and Safety Code.

PERMIT

AUTHORIZATION OF LOCAL REGISTRAR

ANY CHANGE IN DISPOSITION REQUIRES A NEW PERMIT TO SHOW FINAL DISPOSITION

THIS PERMIT IS ISSUED IN ACCORDANCE WITH PROVISIONS OF THE CALIFORNIA HEALTH AND SAFETY CODE AND IS THE AUTHORITY FOR THE DISPOSITION SPECIFIED IN THIS PERMIT.
NOTE: THIS PERMIT GIVES NO RIGHT OF DISPOSAL OUTSIDE OF CALIFORNIA

9A. AMOUNT OF FEE PAID | 9B. DATE PERMIT ISSUED | 9C. SIGNATURE OF LOCAL REGISTRAR ISSUING PERMIT

9D. ADDRESS OF REGISTRAR OF DISTRICT OF DEATH — IF DEATH OCCURRED IN CALIFORNIA | 9E. ADDRESS OF REGISTRAR OF DISTRICT OF DISPOSITION — IF DISPOSITION IS TO OCCUR IN ANOTHER DISTRICT IN CALIFORNIA

10. AUTHORIZED DISPOSITION(S) CHECK APPLICABLE ITEMS

- ☐ A. BURIAL (INCLUDES ENTOMBMENT)
- ☐ B. CREMATION
- ☐ C. DISPOSITION OF CREMATED REMAINS OTHER THAN IN A CEMETERY
- ☐ D. SCIENTIFIC USE
- ☐ E. TEMPORARY ENVAULTMENT
- ☐ F. DISINTERMENT
- ☐ G. SHIP IN TO CALIFORNIA
- ☐ D. TRANSIT TO OUTSIDE OF CALIFORNIA

FOR CORONOR'S USE ONLY

- ☐ I. DISPOSITION PENDING — REMAINS LOCATED AT (Name and Address)

COMPLETE ALL APPLICABLE ITEMS

BURIAL	11A. NAME AND ADDRESS OF CALIFORNIA CEMETERY	11B. DATE BURIED	11C. SIGNATURE OF PERSON IN CHARGE OF BURIAL
CREMATION	12A. NAME AND ADDRESS OF CALIFORNIA CREMATORY	12B. DATE CREMATED	12C. SIGNATURE OF PERSON IN CHARGE OF CREMATION
SCIENTIFIC USE	13A. NAME AND ADDRESS OF CALIFORNIA FACILITY RECEIVING REMAINS	13B. DATE RECEIVED	13C. SIGNATURE OF PERSON IN CHARGE OF FACILITY
TRANSIT	14A. NAME AND ADDRESS IN RECEIVING STATE OR COUNTRY WHERE REMAINS OR CREMATED REMAINS ARE TO BE SHIPPED	14B. DATE SHIPPED	14C. ADDRESS AND SIGNATURE OF PERSON IN CHARGE OF PLACING WITH THE CARRIER
SCATTERING/BURIAL AT SEA OR DISPOSITION OTHER THAN IN A CEMETERY	15A. ADDRESS, NEAREST POINT ON SHORELINE, OR OTHER DESCRIPTION SUFFICIENT TO IDENTIFY FINAL PLACE AND CA DISTRICT OF DISPOSITION. IF BURIAL AT SEA, ONLY ENTER LATITUDE AND LONGITUDE	15B. DATE OF DISPOSITION	15C. SIGNATURE OF PERSON IN CHARGE OF DISPOSITION — 15D. LICENSE NUMBER OF CREMATED REMAINS DISPOSER — IF APPLICABLE

COPY 1 OF THE PERMIT ACCOMPANIES THE REMAINS TO THE STATED PLACE OF DISPOSITION. THE PERSON IN CHARGE OF DISPOSITION IS RESPONSIBLE FOR COMPLETING AND FORWARDING THE PERMIT WITHIN 10 DAYS OF DISPOSITION TO THE REGISTRAR OF THE DISTRICT IN WHICH DISPOSITION OCCURRED OR THE DISTRICT NEAREST THE POINT WHERE THE CREMATED REMAINS WERE SCATTERED AT SEA. THE LOCAL REGISTRAR MAY DESTROY ANY ORIGINAL OR DUPLICATE PERMIT AFTER ONE YEAR FROM ISSUE DATE.

COPY 1 — STATE OF CALIFORNIA, DEPARTMENT OF HEALTH SERVICES, OFFICE OF STATE REGISTRAR — VS9 (REV. 3/03)

Figure 22.3 Application and permit for disposition of human remains. Forensic exhumation and disinterment may require permits as well as a separate permit to reinter the remains. (Author's file.)

By meeting with cemetery personnel, investigators may establish a single liaison person, someone with authority to get things done. Keep in mind that cemetery personnel may be sensitive to the image or negative publicity aspects of disinterment procedures. In addition, they may have concerns regarding publicity, security, etc. Any disinterment is usually done in view of visiting public, or ongoing interment services, and investigators should be cognizant of these concerns.

When meeting with these representatives, cold case investigators should seek to identify specific permits, procedures, or other costs associated with disinterment and reinterment (Figure 22.3). Among the permits that may be required are the following:

- City exhumation permit.
- County health department exhumation permit.
- Separate reinterment permit.
- Other permits or fees.
- An exhumation may require the use of cemetery personnel and the use of specialized equipment, including backhoes (Figure 22.4). Investigators should inquire whether the cemetery will absorb the cost of the disinterment and reinterment, or whether the law enforcement agency will be responsible for these costs (and these costs are approved *before* you start digging). In some cases, the cemetery may absorb the costs of the procedures when ordered to do so by court order but will charge when requested to do so by consent of a family member. It cannot be overemphasized that it is best to have cemetery personnel actually do the digging, or at least someone who is experienced. Most cemeteries will want to do this to preserve the grounds, and whether they charge for their service or not, it is well worth it. If the selected dig site is the wrong one or, worse, it's the wrong grave, the situation is greatly minimized if it is their people doing it.

Figure 22.4 Backhoe. Depending upon burial circumstances, specialized equipment may be necessary for ease of exhumation. Check with the cemetery prior to exhumation to determine the necessity for any specialized equipment. (Courtesy of Connie Milton, San Diego County Sheriff's Department.)

Observations at the Grave

- Soil moisture and drainage. Is the grave in a swampy location where water accumulates, or is it in a location that has facilitated drainage?
- Water table level. Swampy?
- Vegetation. Are there trees or tree roots crowding the grave location?
- Soil conditions. Is the grave site collapsed, or does it appear flat and level?
- Any other obstacles that may inhibit or complicate the exhumation process?

Unidentified Remains

Depending upon state law, protocols and procedures for unidentified remains may be expedited when the purpose is for identification of a Jane Doe or John Doe. Check with the health department or other regulatory or legal resources (Figure 22.5).

AFFIDAVIT
FOR
DISINTERMENT–REMOVAL–REINTERMENT PERMIT

Request is hereby made and permission given to:

____
(Name of Mortuary or person Acting as such) (Address)

____
(City) (County) (State) (Zip)

for the DISINTERMENT/REINTERMENT of: ____________________
(Name of Decedent)

who is buried at ______________ Cemetery, ______________
(Address)

____
(City) (County) (State) (Zip)

Reinterment will be in the ____________________ Cemetery,

____
(Address) (City) (County) (State) (Zip)

on approximately ____________.
(Date)

I do hereby certify that I am the next of kin and have the legal authority to request and authorize said disinterment/reinterment.

____
(*Signature) (Relationship)

____
(Address)

____
(City) (State) (Zip)

Dated this ____ day of ________, 20___.

Subscribed and sworn to before me on ________________.

My commission expires ____________.

____
(Signature of Notary Public)

Mail the original notarized affidavit with a copy of *your driver's license to:

Colorado Department of Public Health and Environment
Vital Records Section HSVR-VR-A1
4300 Cherry Creek Drive South
Denver, CO 80246-1530

Attention: Notification to the County Clerk will need to be done if remains are being disinterred /reinterred from/on private property to another location i.e., cemetery, etc. The Clerks Office will update their records accordingly.

I:\OSRVS\FORMS\DATAMANAGEMENT\2007FORMS M-Revised 9/2010

Figure 22.5 All-in-one permit. (Courtesy of Detective Steve Ainsworth, Boulder County Sheriff's Office, Boulder, Colorado.)

Drafting the Request for a Forensic Exhumation

This is a process with significant legal considerations and should be accomplished with the support and assistance of a deputy district attorney or similar counterpart. A representative of this office may wish to be present at the exhumation. The specific format may vary, depending upon local rules and procedures, but a good rule of thumb when considering drafting a request for an exhumation and an application for a court order is to think of it as an affidavit in support of a search warrant. As such, the purpose is to lay out for the magistrate what you want to do, where you want to do it, and why you want to do it. This would include the following:

- Name of affiant.
- Position or title of affiant.
- Location where property (remains) is sought.
- Reason for affiant's belief that the property (remains) sought is at the subject location.
- Persons authorized or permitted to take part in the exhumation procedure, sampling, or forensic examination and testing procedures.
- Description of property sought. This may indicate the actions to be taken at the exhumation, including whether the remains are to be examined on scene or removed to another location. If the remains are to be removed to another location, this should be spelled out in the affidavit, including who is to take custody of the remains, where they are specifically to be removed to, and the purpose to which the remains will be subjected, i.e., forensic anthropological examination, removal of biological matter for DNA testing purposes, etc.
- Reinterment considerations.
- Date of affidavit.
- Signature of affiant.
- Statement of probable cause. This is the narrative that explains to the judge the history of the case and why this exhumation is necessary. This would include the following:
  - A summary of the initial investigation, including names, dates, and events.
  - A summary of any follow-up investigations after the initial investigation.
  - A summary of the reactivation of the case, including names, dates, and events leading to the request for an order for exhumation.
  - Why the exhumation is necessary. This would include description of what examinations, if any, were previously conducted upon the remains and why the proposed examinations are to be conducted at this time (i.e., advances in DNA technology, etc.). If necessary, investigators may also wish to include a discussion of the technology to educate the magistrate in this area.
  - Other information as dictated by specific case factors or legal considerations.

The Court Order

A court order should be issued by the court with jurisdiction to do so, preferably a superior court. The order would be issued in the name of the People of the State, similar to that of a search warrant. Included within a court order for exhumation would be (Figure 22.6) the following:

- Name of the body to be exhumed
- Name of cemetery, memorial park, or other location where the body is to be exhumed from
- Specific location, including street address and plot or grave site identifying number, where body is to be exhumed from

SUPERIOR COURT OF THE STATE OF CALIFORNIA

FOR THE COUNTY OF SAN DIEGO

THE PEOPLE OF THE STATE OF CALIFORNIA,	**ORDER**
CONTINUIING HOMICIDE INVESTIGATION EL CAJON POLICE DEPARTMENT CASE #XXX	No.

ORDER

I HEREBY ORDER that the body of X be exhumed from Greenwood Memorial Park and Mortuary, Rest Haven area, Lot x, site x, 4300 Imperial Avenue, San Diego, California. I FURTHER ORDER that a representative of the Medical Examiner's Office either take a part of his remains graveside, or, if necessary, I ORDER the transportation of his remains, or a part thereof, to the Medical Examiner's Office. I FURTHER ORDER that a portion of his remains then be transported to the San Diego Sheriff's Department, Crime Laboratory, at 5255 Mt. Etna Dr., San Diego, California for the needed examination and DNA testing. Upon completion of testing, I ORDER the remains of x to be re-interned at Greenwood Cemetery at its original location.

Dated this day of, 2004.

Hon. X
Judge of the Superior Court
State of California, County of San Diego
East County Division

Figure 22.6 Court order for exhumation. This court order mandates that the body be removed from a described location under the auspices of a representative of the medical examiner's office, or that a portion of the remains be removed and transported to the sheriff's department crime laboratory. The order further states that upon completion of the examination, the remains be reinterred at their original location. (Courtesy of Deputy District Attorney Dan Lamborn, San Diego County District Attorney's Office.)

- Specific definition of who (i.e., representative of medical examiner's office) will take a part of the remains graveside, or, if necessary, orders that the remains, or parts thereof, be transported to a specific location (i.e., medical examiner's office, crime laboratory, or other location described by address) for the needed examination (and DNA testing, if applicable)
- Orders that, upon completion of examination and testing, the remains of (name of body) are to be reinterred at the identified cemetery at its original location

The Exhumation

- Normally, the removal of the earth above the coffin is accomplished by heavy equipment or by laborers using hand tools.
- Specialized equipment may be required to remove a cement cap overlying the top of the vault or coffin, if present.
- Arrangements for opening the coffin should be negotiated and understood between law enforcement personnel and cemetery personnel. Knowledge of burial container type is of importance, as in some cases, a *coffin key* may be required to unlock the casket. This is a universal tool used to secure casket lids (Figure 22.7).
- Assure that all properly equipped and authorized personnel are present at the appointed time and place.
  - Medical examiner/coroner representative to physically handle the remains?
  - Are the remains to be removed fully, or are samples to be taken at the gravesite?

Recording the Exhumation

- Record names of all persons present.
- Make a photographic record.
- Prepare written reports in accordance with standard reporting procedures, including date, time, and other information detailing the exhumation process.
- Note any unusual conditions or observations encountered during the exhumation (Figure 22.8).

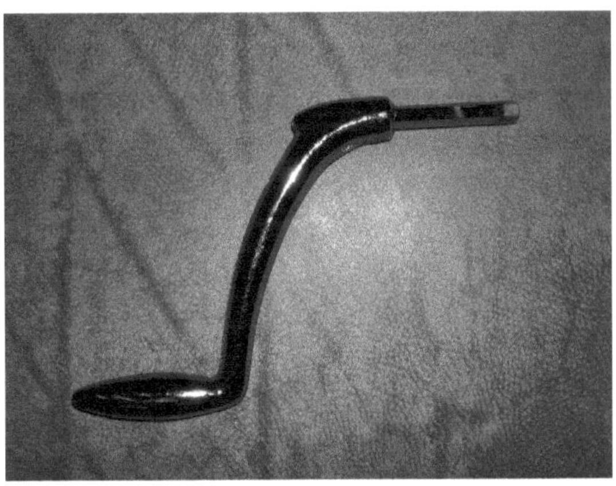

Figure 22.7 Coffin key. A coffin key may be necessary to open a locked coffin. This universal tool may be available from the cemetery. (Author's file.)

Figure 22.8 When a forensic exhumation is necessary and the remains are to be transported for forensic purposes, this is a solemn procedure necessitating respect by all parties. In the "Boulder Jane Doe" case, a local mortuary donated the services of a hearse to respectfully transport her remains for processing. (Courtesy of Detective Steve Ainsworth, Boulder County Sheriff's Office, Boulder, Colorado.)

The Embalming Process

For many homicide investigators, knowledge or involvement in the disposition of the remains postautopsy are minimal. The embalming process is essentially a preservation and disinfection procedure applied to the body after the autopsy and prior to interment. This procedure results in additional trauma and alteration of the body, and these procedures may be of significant importance to later cold case investigators. It is usually accomplished in three steps.

Step 1. The body is positioned, and the features are set. This stage includes eye and mouth closure. The mouth is wired or sewn shut, eye caps are set under the eyes, and hands are set properly. Factors included in this process include the amount of trauma and cause and manner of death, and different scenarios require different fluid mixtures.

Step 2. An incision is made above the clavicle, the carotid artery is raised, and a small incision is made in the vein. A canula from the embalming machine is placed into the incision, and embalming fluid is injected into the body through the carotid while at same time, blood is drained out thru the vein. About 3 gallons of fluid, a formaldehyde-and-water mix, is usually put into body. The body is bathed, cleansed, and massaged for even distribution of the fluid.

Step 3. The third stage in this process occurs when a *trocar* is inserted into the abdomen approximately two fingers above the navel. This is a long instrument hooked up to an aspirator (Figures 22.9 and 22.10). The main internal organs, including heart, lungs, liver, and intestines, are aspirated, and full-strength cavity fluid is injected into the cavity for preservation and disinfection. Once this is done, incisions are sewn and sealed, and the body is cleansed. Head hair is washed, the body is bathed and dried, the hair is dried, and the body is made ready for dressing and application of appropriate cosmetics.

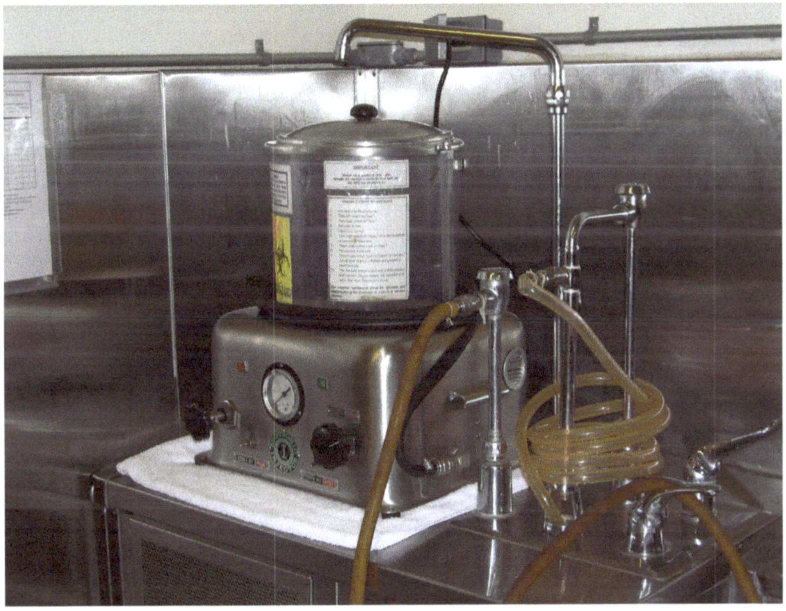

Figure 22.9 Embalming machine. (Author's file.)

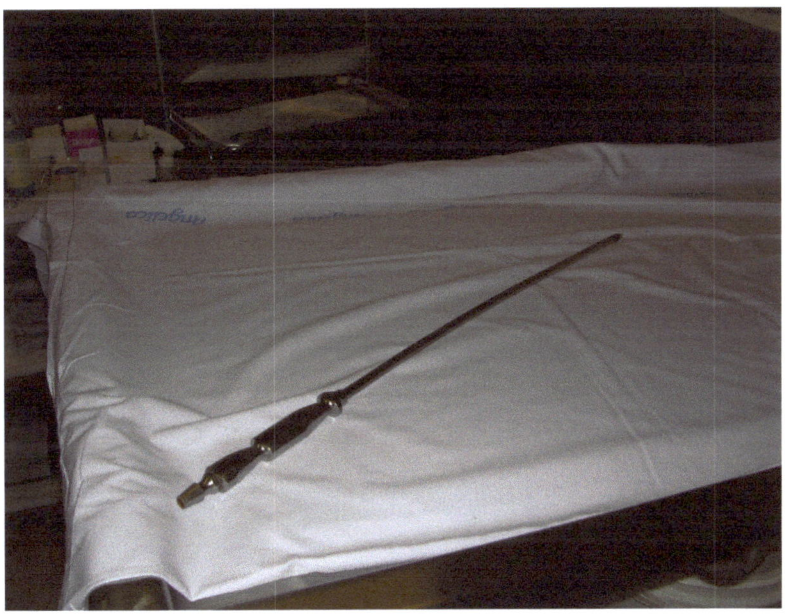

Figure 22.10 Trocar. (Author's file.)

During the embalming process, not all blood is drained out, and some remains with the fluid. Embalming and burial practices vary, and embalming is not required by law in some states.

In addition, embalming may bring out bruises not necessarily noticed during previous examinations. After embalming, bite marks may remain visible, although there may be a lesser chance for their survival in an unembalmed body.

The Embalming Report

This is a report that records information about the body at the time of receipt by the embalmer and the procedures and processes subsequently utilized (Figures 22.11 and 22.12). It will record the date and case number. It will further report the following:

Identification of the deceased:

- Name
- Gender
- Age
- Eye and hair color
- Estimated height and weight
- Date of death
- Place of death
- Date removed
- Removed from
- Removed by
- Personal effects
- Elapsed time between death and embalming
- Receiving location

Condition of deceased prior to embalming:

- Normal
- Edema
- Emaciated
- Skin slip
- Lividity
- Pacemaker
- Purge
- Tissue gas
- Jaundice
- Rigor mortis
- IV leakage
- Organ donor
- Autopsy
- Mutilations present
- Discolorations
- Identifying marks
- Whether deceased was refrigerated

Disinfection treatments, posing features (such as mouth and eyes), and embalming techniques will be further reported and described in detail in the report. This may include:

- Plastic garments used (yes/no) and type
- Dry chemicals used (yes/no) and type

Embalming Report

IDENTIFICATION:

Date: ____________ Case Number: ____________

Deceased Name: ____________ I.D. Tag Present: No ☐ Yes ☐

Gender: ______ Age: ______ Estimated Weight: ______ Estimated Height: ______

Color of Eyes: ______ Color of Hair: ______ Beard/Mustache? No ☐ Yes ☐

Place of Death: ______ Date of Death: ______ Time: 0:00 AM

Removed From: ______ Date Removed: ______ Time: ______

Removed By: ____________ Personal Effects? No ☐ Yes ☐ See HMIS

Elapsed Time between Death and Embalming ______

Receiving Location: Greenwood Memorial Park & Mortuary

CONDITION OF DECEASED PRIOR TO EMBALMING DECEASED:

☐ Normal ☐ Emaciated ☐ Lividity ☐ Purge ☐ Jaundice

☐ Edema ☐ Skin Slip ☐ Pacemaker ☐ Tissue Gas ☐ Rigor Mortis ☐ IV Leakage

☐ Organ Donor (skin) (eyes) (bone) (internal organs)

☐ Autopsy (full) (thoracic) (abdominal) (cranial)

Mutilations Present: ____________

Discolorations: ____________

Identifying Marks: ____________

* *Use Anatomic Outline Chart To Indicate Body Areas affected and general comments*

Deceased Refrigerated? No ☐ Yes ☐ How Long? ______

DISINFECTION:

☐ Eyes ☐ Other body orifices ☐ Body orifices packed

☐ Nose ☐ Deceased bathed with antiseptic soap

☐ Mouth ☐ Hair Washed

POSING FEATURES:

Mouth Closure: ☐ Suture ☐ Needle Injector ☐ Other

Mouth Shaping: ☐ Natural ☐ Dentures ☐ Mouth Former ☐ Other

Eye Closure: ☐ Cotton ☐ Eye Caps ☐ Stay Cream ☐ Donor

EMBALMING TECHNIQUE:

Arteries Injected:

Carotid ☐ Right ☐ Left Iliac ☐ Right ☐ Left

Subclavian ☐ Right ☐ Left Femoral ☐ Right ☐ Left

Axillary ☐ Right ☐ Left Radial ☐ Right ☐ Left

Brachial ☐ Right ☐ Left Ulnar ☐ Right ☐ Left

Veins Drained:

Jugular ☐ Right ☐ Left

Axillary ☐ Right ☐ Left

Iliac ☐ Right ☐ Left

Femoral ☐ Right ☐ Left

Injection Pressure: ______ lbs. Rate of Flow: ☐ slight ☐ ¼ ☐ ½ ☐ Full

Injection Method: ☐ Intermittent ☐ Continuous

Drainage Method: ☐ Intermittent ☐ Continuous ☐ Restricted ☐ Heart Tap

Condition of Arteries: ______ Drainage Received: ______

FLUID DILUTIONS:

Pre/Co injection: ______ Oz. ______ Gal.; Index ____

1st Injection: ______ Oz. ______ Gal.; Index ____

2nd Injection: ______ Oz. ______ Gal.; Index ____

3rd Injection: ______ Oz. ______ Gal.; Index ____

BRAND OF FLUID & TOTAL CONCENTRATE USED:

Pre/Co Injection: ______ Oz. ____

Arterial: ______ Oz. ____

Humectant: ______ Oz. ____

Dye: ______ Oz. ____

Other: ______ Oz. ____

CAVITY TREATMENT:

☐ Hydro Aspirator ☐ Trocar Button

☐ Electric Aspirator ☐ Suture

Condition of Abdominal Area: ____________

Total Cavity Chemical Used: Oz.: ______ Index: ______ Fluid Name: ______

Were Cavities Treated Immediately Following Arterial Injection? ☐ Yes ☐ If No, How Long? ______

Total Cavity Chemical Used (Autopsy): Oz.: ____ Index: ______ Fluid Name: ______

Total Cavity Chemical Used (Viscera): Oz.: ____ Index: ______ Fluid Name: ______

Chemical Powder: ☐ Yes ☐ No

Figure 22.11 Embalming report. This report provides information about postautopsy processing of the remains. (Courtesy of Dan Williams, Greenwood Mortuary, San Diego, California.)

- Embalmer's signature and license number and date
- Provisional embalmer's/apprentice's signature and date
- Dressed by, signature and date
- Casketed by, signature and date
- Cosmeticized by, signature and date

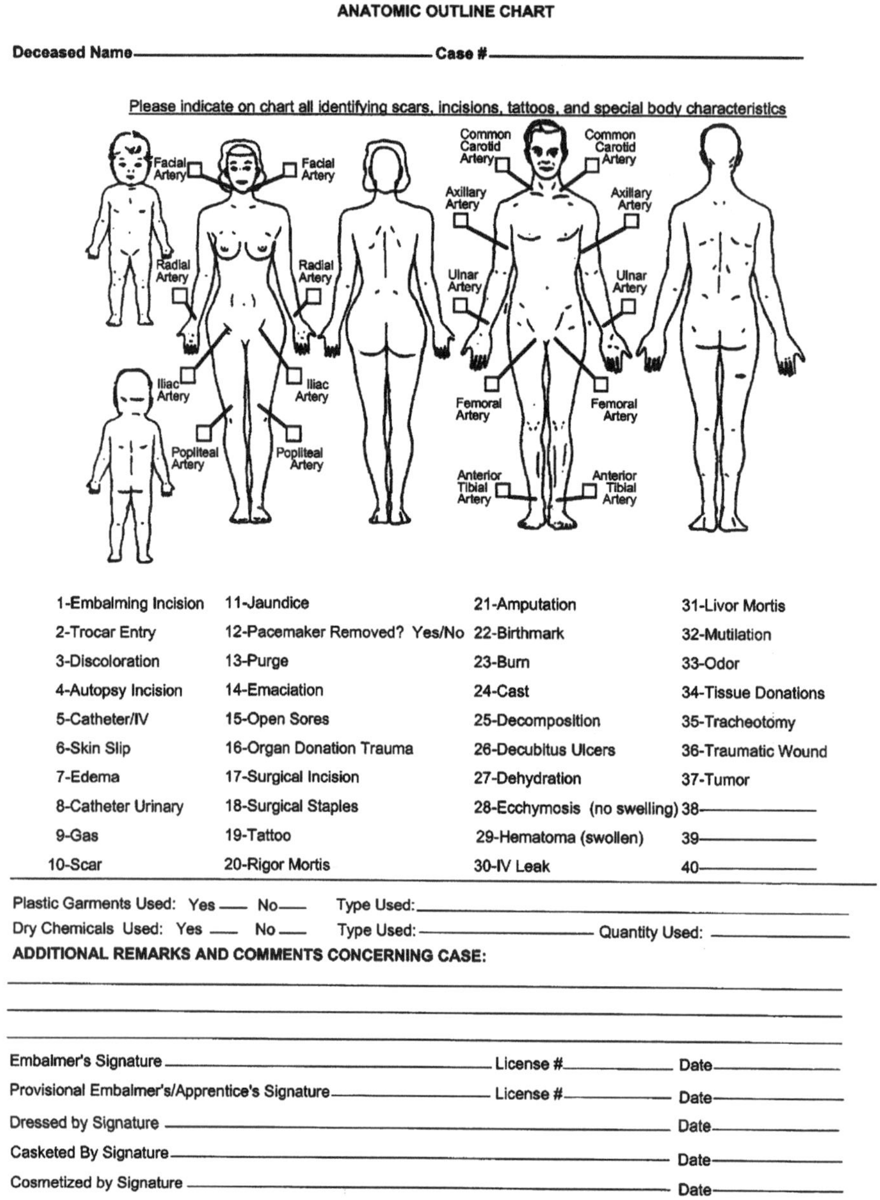

ANATOMIC OUTLINE CHART

Deceased Name__________ **Case #**__________

Please indicate on chart all identifying scars, incisions, tattoos, and special body characteristics

1-Embalming Incision	11-Jaundice	21-Amputation	31-Livor Mortis
2-Trocar Entry	12-Pacemaker Removed? Yes/No	22-Birthmark	32-Mutilation
3-Discoloration	13-Purge	23-Burn	33-Odor
4-Autopsy Incision	14-Emaciation	24-Cast	34-Tissue Donations
5-Catheter/IV	15-Open Sores	25-Decomposition	35-Tracheotomy
6-Skin Slip	16-Organ Donation Trauma	26-Decubitus Ulcers	36-Traumatic Wound
7-Edema	17-Surgical Incision	27-Dehydration	37-Tumor
8-Catheter Urinary	18-Surgical Staples	28-Ecchymosis (no swelling)	38-____
9-Gas	19-Tattoo	29-Hematoma (swollen)	39-____
10-Scar	20-Rigor Mortis	30-IV Leak	40-____

Plastic Garments Used: Yes __ No __ Type Used: __________

Dry Chemicals Used: Yes __ No __ Type Used: ______ Quantity Used: ______

ADDITIONAL REMARKS AND COMMENTS CONCERNING CASE:

Embalmer's Signature __________ License # ______ Date ______

Provisional Embalmer's/Apprentice's Signature __________ License # ______ Date ______

Dressed by Signature __________ Date ______

Casketed By Signature __________ Date ______

Cosmetized by Signature __________ Date ______

Figure 22.12 Anatomic outline of embalmment. This portion of the embalming report provides further information about procedures affecting the remains. (Courtesy of Dan Williams, Greenwood Mortuary, San Diego, California.)

Finding Usable DNA

The ability to extract usable DNA after burial or interment is dependent upon numerous factors. These factors may include the following:

- Degradation due to severe deterioration of all biological matter. Such deterioration may be brought about through the following:
  - Extreme or long-term moisture
  - Extreme or long-term heat

- Soil conditions
- Severe physical decomposition prior to burial
- Degree of severity of decomposition after burial (Figure 22.13)

Desirable locations for successful retrieval of DNA after burial include bone, teeth, fingernails, and toenails (Figure 22.14). Experienced investigators have found that the further back a tooth is, the better the possibility of finding usable DNA. In order of preference, one might start with a wisdom tooth, then a molar, and then a premolar. It is recommended to collect more than one when feasible.

Figure 22.13 Femur with roots. This portion of the femur removed during a forensic exhumation from unembalmed remains illustrates a potential source of remaining DNA, although there would be concern of degradation as very little bone material remains. Note the roots. (Courtesy of Connie Milton, San Diego County Sheriff's Department.)

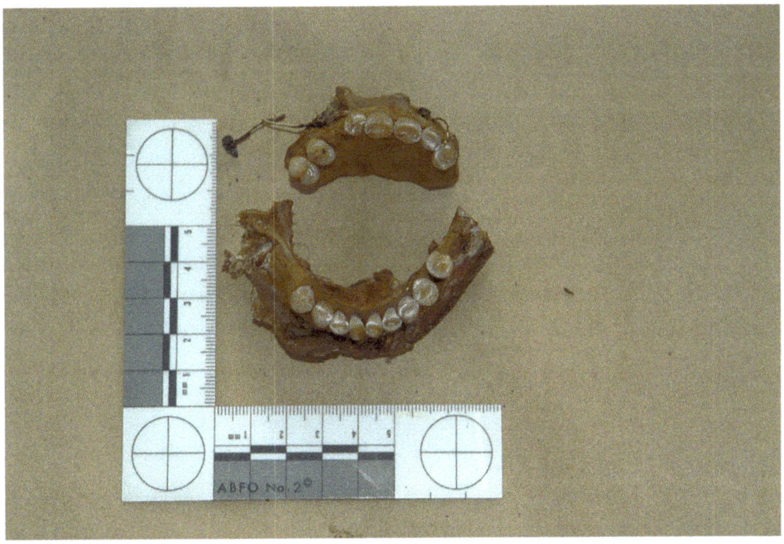

Figure 22.14 Teeth with scale. The pulp within teeth may offer a remaining source of DNA. Teeth and bone, however, require significant additional processing by the laboratory in order to attempt to extract DNA. (Courtesy of Connie Milton, San Diego County Sheriff's Department.)

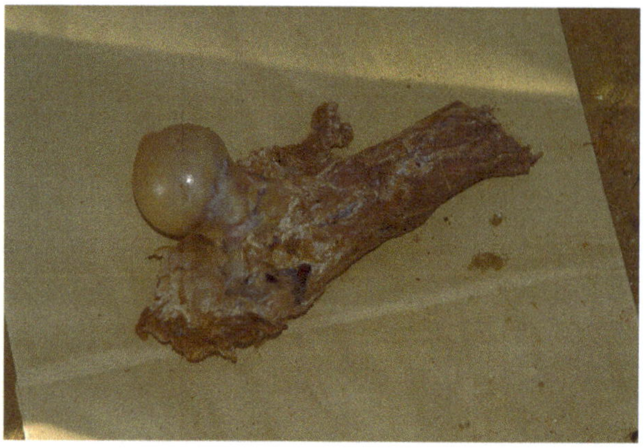

Figure 22.15 Good femur with muscle. This femur from the embalmed body was removed during a forensic exhumation and was a good source of DNA. (Courtesy of Connie Milton, San Diego County Sheriff's Department.)

Bone and teeth require significant additional processing prior to DNA analysis. Fingernails or toenails may assist in expediting DNA analysis. Hair is often a source of last resort for successful DNA retrieval. The embalming process should not interfere with the ability to extract viable DNA, especially when the primary samples used for DNA analysis from exhumed remains are bone, teeth, fingernails, or toenails. The embalming fluid is not going to enter these samples to any significant degree. In addition, deep muscle tissues, if present, may also provide successful DNA results (Figure 22.15).

Figures 22.16a and b illustrate conditions that investigators may encounter due to differences in burial containers and embalming.

PKU Cards—An Overlooked Forensic Resource

PKU (phenylketonuria) cards, sometimes called Guthrie cards, contain DNA and have been on file since 1966. Their existence is often unknown to even experienced investigators, and this method of identification may be used to identify unknown remains, as well as link them to missing persons, or confirm identify.

- These direct DNA samples, taken from the heels of infants immediately after birth, are retained by health departments in all 50 states, but each health department varies, widely, in the amount of time the dried blood is kept on file. (Google individual state health departments for specific information.)
- DNA extracted from a drop of blood on a PKU card may be used to find a missing person and make a positive identification of unidentified remains. The cards may prove especially helpful for missing children who were adopted and for whom no biological parents are known, or available, for family reference samples.

Case History: "Boulder Jane Doe"

In April 1954, two college students discovered the nude body of a young female while hiking near Boulder, Colorado. A pathologist later concluded that the victim had been alive when thrown down an almost 30-foot embankment into Boulder Creek. She suffered a skull fracture and numerous broken bones and injuries. When found, she had been ravaged by animals (Figure 22.17). No identifying features except for

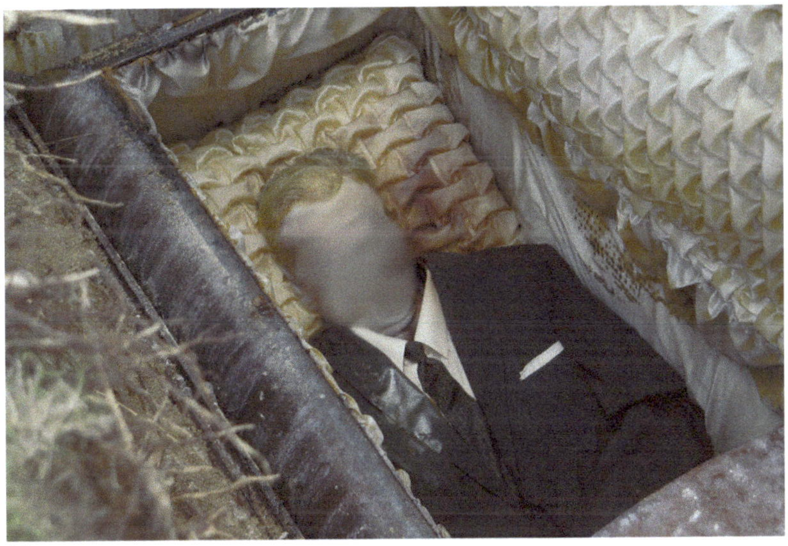

(a)

(b)

Figure 22.16 (a) Embalmed remains buried in a metal casket and exhumed after 30 years. (b) Non-embalmed remains buried in a wooden casket 16 years later. Both were buried in same soil conditions. (Courtesy of Connie Milton, San Diego County Sheriff's Department.)

an appendectomy scar were discovered, and she had no fillings in her teeth that might offer assistance for dental records at the time. Her identity could not be established.

News of the discovery and lack of identity of this person became a major story for the Boulder and Denver newspapers. In doing so, these records preserved in-depth details about the victim, the circumstances, and the names of those involved in the discovery and investigation. A local pathologist performed an autopsy, and the coroner held a *coroner's inquest* that ultimately concluded that the victim died "...from shock caused by severe beating by person or persons unknown, with felonious intent" (Boulder County Coroner's Office, Inquest).

Ultimately, no clothing or murder weapon was found, and she was listed simply as "unidentified woman." Local townspeople, in the spirit of the Mountain West, took up a collection to buy her a plot in

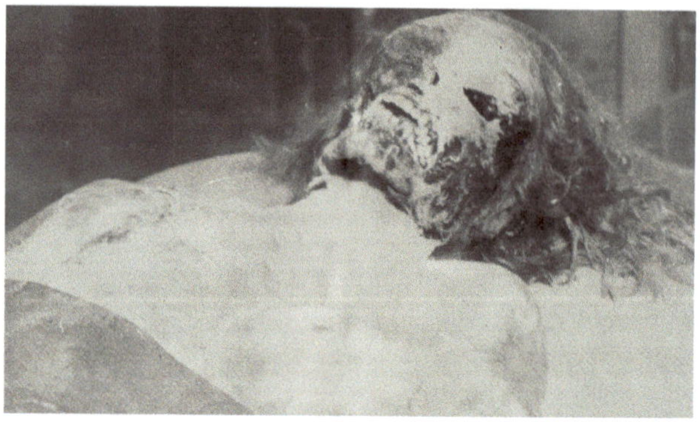

Figure 22.17 Original morgue photo. Due to resultant publicity, a citizen came forward with a photograph of the victim taken in the county morgue in 1954. Not uncommonly, photos in cold cases surface as a result of media publicity and word of mouth during these investigations. (Name withheld at owner's request.)

the Columbia Cemetery and marked her final resting place with a granite marker. The casket was donated by a local mortuary, and a Catholic Priest donated his time for the funeral service. Unfortunately, she was one of an unknown number of John and Jane Does whose cases have long gone unsolved (Figure 22.18).

For nearly a decade, Silvia Pettem, a Boulder-area historian and newspaper columnist and now renown cold case author and authority, had been interested in the case and had compiled newspaper accounts of it.

Figure 22.18 Boulder Jane Doe headstone. (Courtesy of Detective Steve Ainsworth, Boulder County Sheriff's Office, Boulder, Colorado. Used with permission of *Rocky Mountain News*.)

Figure 22.19 The body dump scene today as re-located by Silvia Pettem. The historian–journalist based her search upon detailed newspaper accounts that reported the location as 300 yards from a known location along a described roadway. In her quest, Pettem consulted highway maintenance records and learned that the last major improvement on this gravel road occurred when it was regraded in 1953, one year before the crime. She located the river site and then used original newspaper photographs to compare rock formations then and now. (Courtesy of Silvia Pettem.)

In the course of her research, she utilized original newspaper narrative descriptions and photographs of the crime scene to re-locate the homicide location from almost 50 years before (Figure 22.19).

In September 2003, due to the advances in forensic technology, she approached the Boulder County Sheriff's Office and inquired if it were possible for the body to be exhumed and possibly identified. A search of the sheriff's files found no remaining records or evidence (not unusual after such a length of time in many jurisdictions, although it was suspected that this and other cases were removed several decades before by a disgruntled official), and investigators began reconstructing the cold case homicide almost from scratch, including original newspaper reports.

Pettem discovered that the pathologist who conducted the original autopsy was still alive and, at age 85, still retained *his copy* of his autopsy report. He was one of only a few surviving original persons in this case. In addition, they discovered the coroner's inquest *report*. These documents, coupled with appropriate interviews and detailed newspaper accounts, became the basis for the reactivation of this cold case homicide.

The news media picked up the case, and donations to defray the costs of exhumation and forensic analysis were donated by the community. Pettem learned of the services of the Vidocq Society from the Department of Justice and made inquiry of this organization for possible assistance in the investigation. Forensic specialists associated with the Vidocq Society responded to assist the local authorities, and the body was exhumed. The following is the affidavit that became the basis for a court order for the exhumation.

Affidavit for Search Warrant

The following affidavit was utilized in this forensic exhumation:

The affiant is Detective Steven G. Ainsworth, a duly commissioned officer of the Boulder County Sheriff's Office. The affiant has been a law enforcement continuously since 1977 and has investigated in excess of 350 death of all manners, including homicides. The affiant also is a certified death investigator certified through the Colorado Coroner's Association, and has attended numerous courses on death investigation, including homicides. The affiant, being duly sworn, deposes and states:

> On October 2, 2003, I met with Detective Lieutenant Phil West, and duly commissioned officer of the Boulder County Sheriff' Office, and Silvia Pettem, a local author. Pettem had newspaper articles detailing an apparent homicide of a female, whose body was found 300 feet east of Boulder Falls in the creek bed of Boulder Creek, in Boulder Canyon, County of Boulder, State of Colorado. The female's nude body was found by two CU students on April 8, 1954, according to the newspaper accounts. Also, according to newspaper accounts, the pathologist who performed the autopsy, Dr. Freburn L. James, said the victim had been dead from three to seven days. The accounts were photocopies printed in the *Denver Post*, the *Rocky Mountain News*, and the *Boulder Daily Camera*. The case was never solved and the victim remains unidentified. Pettem's reasoning for giving us this information was to determine if there was a possibility that the victim could be identified and a possible suspect identified through technological advances which have been made since 1954. Pettem told us, and newspaper accounts bear out the fact that the victim was buried on April 22, 1954 at the Columbia Cemetery bounded by Pleasant and College Streets on the north and south respectively, and Ninth and Eighth Streets on the east and west sides, in the City of Boulder, County of Boulder, State of Colorado. Additionally, I found a *Record Of Funeral*, serial number 7896 generated by Howe Mortuary of Boulder which details the expenses and arrangements for the funeral of "Unidentified Murdered Girl" buried on April 22, 1954. The cemetery indicated on the form is "Columbia."
>
> Pettem also produced a photocopy of a handwritten verdict of a coroner's inquest which is attached to and incorporated herein by reference. The inquest verdict, across the top of which is handwritten "Verdict of Jury," was that the death of the unidentified woman was due to shock "caused by a severe beating by person or persons unknown, with felonious intent." I obtained a copy of the unidentified victim's death certificate from the Boulder County Coroner's Office, issued by the State of Colorado. It states the victim's death was a homicide, "caused by shock and exposure to fracture of skull, fracture of left arm, fracture of 4 ribs left, multiple abrasions." It also states the injuries occurred "near Boulder, Boulder County, Colo." and was signed on April 21, 1954 by George W Howe, Coroner.
>
> Lt. West, Pettem, and I went to the Colorado State Archives to attempt to locate Boulder County Sheriff reports and/or Boulder County Coroner reports which document the homicide, but were unable to locate any. We later went to Columbia Cemetery and Pettem showed us the unidentified victim's grave, which is marked with a black granite headstone with the inscription:
>
> JANE DOE
APRIL 1954
AGE ABOUT
20 YEARS.
>
> I noted that the graves on either side, both of which were interred several years later, were sunken, indicating their caskets had broken and collapsed. The Jane Doe grave was relatively even with the surrounding soil, indicating that it had probably not collapsed.
>
> On October 7, 2003, I spoke with Dr. Mike Dobersen, the Arapahoe County Coroner. I know Dr. Dobersen personally and know that he is a board certified forensic pathologist. I asked Dr. Dobersen if he has had any experience with exhuming a body. For the purposes of conducting forensic testing and he told me he has done seven or eight exhumations for that purpose. I asked him if he had an opinion to a reasonable degree of medical certainty if DNA samples would be available and a facial reconstruction would be possible in a body which has been buried for 49 years, as has "Jane Doe." He said one of his exhumations was on a body which had been buried for twenty years and there certainly was enough material in that case. He said that, even if the casket had collapsed over the past forty nine years, the compaction should have been at a slow enough rate as to not crush the skull, enabling a successful reconstruction.

Dr. Dobersen also said that mitochondrial DNA would be obtainable from the pulp of a tooth and possibly from the hair and a DNA profile would be obtainable for comparison to a known sample for positive identification purposes.

On October 22, 2003, I went to Howe Mortuary–Boulder and spoke with the owner, Danielle Vandiver, about this case. I asked if she could determine from the *Record of Funeral* in what type of casket Jane Doe was buried. She looked at the record and said she did not know but it was probably a cloth covered fiberboard one, as one of the newspaper accounts described it as gray cloth covered. I then showed her a photograph of the graveside service which showed the casket and she said it was a metal one. I also checked Howe's records from that time period and finally found the 1954 records combined in the 1955 file. I found an envelope containing flower cards which were sent to the funeral by several people in the community. There were no other records in the file.

On October 29, 2003, I checked the City of Boulder website and found an interactive site of the Columbia Cemetery. I had previously learned that Columbia is not an active cemetery and is administered by the City of Boulder Parks Department. I found that, on that website there is an index where one enters the name of the deceased and is able to access location information as well as a photo of the grave. I selected the Js, then "Jane Doe," which took me to a file with a photo of the small granite headstone I had seen personally. It gave the official location as Section B, Lot 015, Grave 3NE. It also brings up a map of the entire cemetery which shows where the queried grave is located. I noted the spot indicated on the map was where I had personally been and had seen the Jane Doe grave.

In researching leads sheets generated in the original case, I found that several reports of missing women had not been properly followed up by today's standards, in that more can be done to determine if the missing person reported is, in fact Jane Doe. I also found at least two entries on the *Doe Network* website of missing women whose physical descriptions and the time of disappearance match Jane Doe. The *Doe Network* is a website dedicated to finding leads in missing persons cases and in cases where a body is unidentified. These leads can be narrowed further by characteristics unique to the Jane Doe case, then DNA compared from the old cases to Jane Doe's DNA.

The affiant believes sufficient probable cause has been shown to believe the offense of Murder in the First Degree, contrary to CRS 40-2-1 and 40-2-3, was committed between April 1, 1954 and April 5, 1954 at or about the Boulder Falls area of Boulder Canyon Drive, County of Boulder, State of Colorado by a person or persons unknown.

The affiant further believes that there is specific physical evidence which is located in the plot know as the Jane Doe gravesite, Section B, Lot 015, Grave 3NE at Columbia Cemetery located at Ninth and College Streets, City of Boulder, County of Boulder, State of Colorado, which could be of great assistance in identifying the victim and furthering the criminal investigation of her murder, to wit:

1. The physical remains of Jane Doe
2. Trace evidence

The affiant therefore requests the court issue a warrant authorizing the search of the above named location and seizing the above named evidence from that location at this time.

____

AFFIANT

Subscribed in my presence and sworn to before me this ______ day of ________________, 2003, County of Boulder, State of Colorado

____

JUDGE

On February 4, 2004, a World Wide Web page was launched by Silvia Pettem to solicit information and provide investigative assistance relating to this case.

On June 8, 2004, the exhumation process began. The event was filmed by a television camera crew from *America's Most Wanted*; sheriff's personnel and Boulder County forensic anthropologist Beth Conour were assisted and supervised by Dr. Richard Froede, a forensic pathologist, Dr. Walter Birkby, a forensic anthropologist, and Dr. Robert Goldberg, a medical doctor. A backhoe was used for initial earth movement, but the process soon became a forensic anthropological dig (Figures 22.20 through 22.23).

Fifty years of water and earth movement had caused substantial deterioration of the coffin and disturbance of the remains, and it took two days to complete the forensic exhumation. The recovered bones were released to Dr. Birkby and transported to his Human Identification Laboratory in Tucson, Arizona (Figures 22.24 and 22.25).

Luck can be a solvability factor in cold case homicide investigation. Due to the publicity, a subject came forward a few months later with a magazine photo taken of the victim while she lay in the morgue. It had reportedly been taken by a university student who worked in the morgue at the time and published in an "off campus sex magazine." At the time, this photo provided investigators with the only known photo remaining from the original period. Subsequently, other photos surfaced anonymously but were taken by a local newspaper editor at the request of the mortuary (Figure 22.17).

Reautopsy, as could be conducted, confirmed the original injuries and identified an additional injury not noted in the coroner's report. The right patella had been fractured, an injury consistent with being struck by a moving automobile. Investigation by Detective Ainsworth and Pettem discovered facts and circumstances strongly indicating that Jane Doe was a heretofore unidentified victim of serial killer Harvey Glatman, who murdered a series of young women in Southern California in 1957–1958 and who travelled between there and his mother's home in Denver, where he had previously assaulted other women. They identified the vehicle he was known to drive at the time, and per request, this author conducted follow-up

Figure 22.20 Forensic exhumation shovel work. A forensic exhumation may involve a variety of tools to access the site for further exhumation. (Courtesy of Detective Steve Ainsworth, Boulder County Sheriff's Office, Boulder, Colorado.)

Figure 22.21 Forensic anthropologist at work. Forensic anthropologist Beth Conour of the Boulder County Coroner's Office, Colorado, spent many hours tediously removing dirt to gain access to Jane Doe. Forensic anthropology work is not always glamorous and conducted inside a laboratory setting. (Courtesy of Detective Steve Ainsworth, Boulder County Sheriff's Office, Boulder, Colorado.)

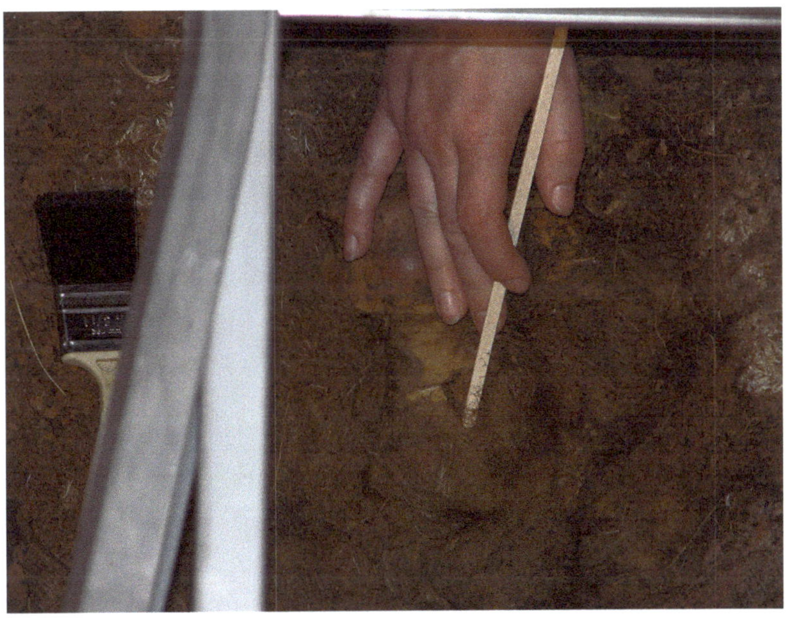

Figure 22.22 Tools of the trade. Once the dirt and other material is removed, recovery is a slow process using simple hand tools. Here, the hair and remains are recovered. (Courtesy of Detective Steve Ainsworth, Boulder County Sheriff's Office, Boulder, Colorado.)

Figure 22.23 Remains uncovered. Working slowly and carefully, the forensic recovery team uncovered the sought-after remains in their attempt to begin the identification process. (Courtesy of Detective Steve Ainsworth, Boulder County Sheriff's Office, Boulder, Colorado.)

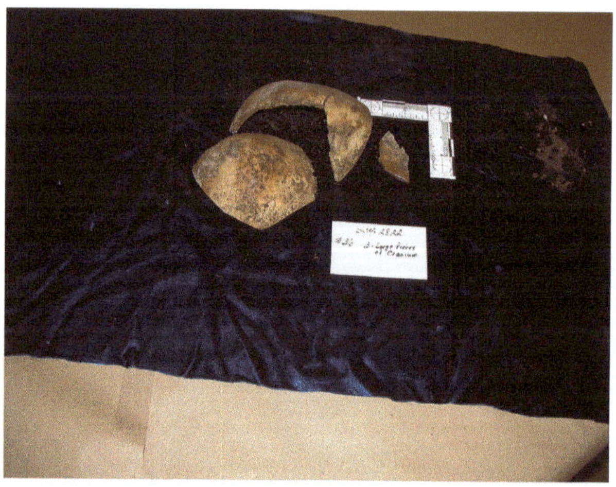

Figure 22.24 Pieces of skullcap. The skull reconstruction took three months to complete as it was in 171 pieces and the skullcap was sprung, all due to soil compaction. (Courtesy of Detective Steve Ainsworth, Boulder County Sheriff's Office, Boulder, Colorado.)

investigation to determine the disposition of Glatman's vehicle. Detective Ainsworth found a fully restored identical vehicle, and specific measurements, suggested by reautopsy findings, corresponded "exactly" with where Jane Doe's injuries were located. It was subsequently theorized that Jane Doe had been struck by a vehicle and thrown into the creek. A simulated reconstruction, utilizing a dummy of approximately the victim's height and weight, resulted in abrasion patterns and a landing position consistent with this theory and manner of disposal. Pettem discovered original interview transcripts by legendary Los Angeles Police

Figure 22.25 Facial bones. Due to water conditions and earth movement, the coffin had collapsed. The skull bones were recovered in large and small pieces. Many hours of analysis and reconstruction were to follow. (Courtesy of Detective Steve Ainsworth, Boulder County Sheriff's Office, Boulder, Colorado.)

Department detective Pierce Books after Glatman was arrested for these homicides. Brooks asked him if there were other victims in Denver, and Glatman responded, "…not unless they were run over" (Los Angeles Police Department, Criminal Report 255 504). Glatman was executed in 1959.

The skull was reconstructed by Dr. Birkby, and ultimately, it was sent to the anthropology laboratory at Michigan State University, where it was photographed (Figure 22.26). This laboratory specializes in identification of human remains and possesses extensive forensic capability. Using photo superimposition techniques, two women identified by Pettem as missing during the approximate time period were excluded from further consideration. One rolled fingerprint from Jane Doe had been recovered, as the others were destroyed by animal action. It was retained until 1993, when it was reportedly destroyed by the FBI.

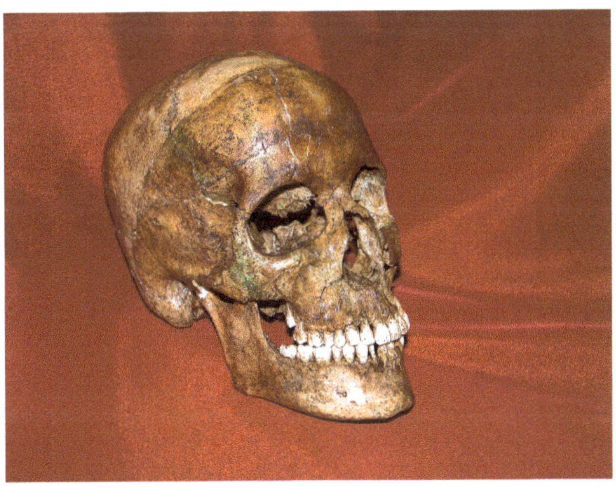

Figure 22.26 Reconstructed skull. Reconstruction of the many small skull fragments by forensic experts began to put a "face" back on Boulder Jane Doe. (Courtesy of Detective Steve Ainsworth, Boulder County Sheriff's Office, Boulder, Colorado.)

Of several possible candidates, a Katharine Farrand Dyer, also reported missing in the Denver area shortly before Jane Doe's body was found, could not be excluded. This name, and thus identity, however, could never be confirmed at the time despite extensive research.

The skull was sent to Frank Bender, forensic sculptor and cofounder of the Vidocq Society, for reconstruction of the victim's facial features. Bender had been highly successful in reconstructing features of unidentified deceased persons or age-enhancing fugitives. His works appeared on the *America's Most Wanted* television show, and on June 13, 2005, Bender as the Boulder County Sheriff's Office unveiled a reconstructed likeness of Jane Doe. Local and national news media gave the case widespread publicity (Figures 22.27 and 22.28).

Figure 22.27 The reconstructed skull was forwarded to Vidocq Society founder and the late forensic sculptor Frank Bender. Bender's uncanny ability to reconstruct lifelike features from a skull or to age-enhance fugitives has resulted in numerous identifications and fugitive apprehensions. The Boulder County Sheriff's Office subsequently unveiled the bust with a press conference that sought media exposure of the case in the hopes that someone might recognize the bust and come forward with information that will help identify Boulder Jane Doe. (Courtesy of the late Frank Bender, VSM.)

Figure 22.28 Detective Ainsworth at *America's Most Wanted*. (Courtesy of Silvia Pettem.)

Experienced homicide investigators understand that, in life, "stuff happens." So it was in this case. The remains lingered for four years in storage at the sheriff's office and then were reinterred in the same cemetery (Figure 22.29). Pettem was recognized for her work by the Vidocq Society with its Medal of Honor. Subsequently, an elderly woman in Australia—known there as Barbara Thompson—was being moved into a nursing home by a caregiver when an old address in her possession showed the name "Katharine Farrand Dyer." An Internet research yielded Pettem's name and the case. Katharine was alive and well. Extensive international and national media brought forth an inquiry by a college student searching for her long-lost great aunt, Dorothy Gay Howard. Investigation showed she had gone missing from the Phoenix, Arizona, area shortly before her 18th birthday, and the physical description fit Jane Doe "exactly." A surviving sister was located, and buccal swabs were obtained and forwarded to Mitotyping Technologies, LLC, a private laboratory in Pennsylvania that had already profiled DNA from Jane's tooth. Comparison, at no charge, showed a match.

Follow-up investigation provided in-depth victimology information, including a prior runaway incident. Dorothy resided in Phoenix and, without telling anybody where she was going, most likely had travelled to Denver to visit her aunt, who lived in the same neighborhood where Glatman had assaulted some of his other victims. Dorothy never arrived. As she was unexpected, no report there was ever made.

Figure 22.29 Dorothy Howard's headstones today in Boulder, Colorado. (Courtesy of Detective Steve Ainsworth, Boulder County Sheriff's Office, Boulder, Colorado.)

Significant Cold Case Issues

This case represents a significant number of cold case investigation techniques and situational circumstances discussed throughout this textbook, including long-term missing-persons investigations. Among these are the following:

- Extensive (50-year) cold case period
- Newspapers used as source of case information ultimately contributing as an official record of events when agency records no longer exist
- Newspaper photos and descriptions used to rediscover original crime scene
- Identification of living original case participants (pathologist) and recovery of vital documents
- Discovery and recovery of coroner's inquest report
- Use of death certificate as official record of homicide and source of investigative information
- Disappearance of original law enforcement agency case file
- Lack of remaining physical evidence
- Use of state archives for records search
- Inquiry and inspection of mortuary/funeral home records
  - Identification and utilization of mortuary records
  - Identification of casket material to evaluate potential for continued existence of remains
  - Comingling of records
- Visit to grave scene and recording of observations
- Investigative use of the Doe Network in the course of identification of remains
- Referral to the Vidocq Society for forensic and other assistance
- Forensic exhumation of victim's remains
  - Affidavit for search warrant to recover specific physical evidence from an unsolved homicide utilizing newspaper records in combination with independent investigation and recovery of few remaining official records
  - Application of forensic anthropology methods
- Utilization of advanced technology for identification purposes, including
  - Mitochondrial DNA testing
  - Nuclear DNA testing
  - Potential for advanced fingerprint-lifting capability using superglue
  - Forensic reconstruction and use of photographic superimposition techniques
- Locating period automobiles through museum resources for potential reconstruction purposes
- Reconstruction and simulation of theorized events yielding substantiating suggestion of event sequence
- Forensic artistry constructing an image of the victim based upon anthropological features for media usage
- Media role and publicity
  - Internet web page dedicated to this specific Jane Doe case
  - Use of Doe Network for possible identification purposes
  - Citizen coming forward with only known original photograph of victim
  - Local and national news coverage
  - Additional photos surfacing, apparently taken by newspaper photographer
- Determination that suspect in Canadian disappearance was excluded by polygraph examination and other investigation circa 1953
- International scope of local case

Acknowledgments

Many persons contributed to this chapter. I wish to extend my deepest appreciation to supervising criminalist Connie Milton of the San Diego County Sheriff's Department, California, Crime Lab. Her experiences and expertise in the exhumation process and DNA processing have greatly contributed to this textbook. In addition, I wish to express my deepest appreciation to Agent Jon Wooddell of the El Cajon Police Department, California, and to Officer Robert Anderson of the Murrietta Police Department, California, for sharing their experiences and expertise in the exhumation process. I also wish to acknowledge the great contribution of Daniel Williams, mortuary manager of the Greenwood Cemetery and Memorial Park, San Diego, California, for his professional expertise and contribution to this segment.

In addition, I wish to acknowledge and extend my deepest gratitude to Detective Steve Ainsworth and Division Chief Phil West of the Boulder County Sheriff's Office, Colorado, for their assistance in the preparation of this case history. As do Agents Anderson and Woodell, Detective Ainsworth represents the tenacity and personal and professional determination that so exemplify cold case investigators. In addition, I wish to recognize and acknowledge the efforts of Silvia Pettem for her dedication on behalf of this and all other "Does" whose murders or disappearances have remained unsolved, and to note her "bulldog tenacity." Further, this case exemplifies the spirit of the Vidocq Society and its members, who contribute in a voluntary manner so much to solving unsolved cases.

Suggested Readings and Bibliography

Goldberg, R. and West, P. (2004) Boulder Colorado's Jane Doe: Part II. *Vidocq Society Journal.* (Fall). 15/4. pp. 1–4.

Pettem, S. (2004). Vidocq Expertise and the reopening the case of Boulder's Jane Doe Homicide. *Vidocq Society Journal.* (Summer). 15/3. pp. 8–11.

Pettem, S. (2009). *Someone's Daughter: In Search of Justice for Jane Doe*, Taylor Trade. Lanham, MD. Electronic edition.

Pettem, S. (2013). *Cold Case Research: Resources for Unidentified, Missing and Cold Homicide Cases.* CRC Press. Boca Raton, FL. http://doenetwork.us.

Criminal Investigative Analysis in Cold Case Investigations

23

SHARON PAGALING HAGAN

Contents

> In solving a problem of this sort, the grand thing is to be able to reason backward. That is a very useful accomplishment, and a very easy one, but people do not practice it much. In the everyday affairs of life it is more useful to reason forward, and so the other comes to be neglected...Let me see if I can make it clearer. Most people, if you describe a train of events to them, will tell you what the result would be. They can put those events together in their minds, and argue from them that something will come to pass. There are few people, however, who, if you told them a result, would be able to evolve from their own inner consciousness what the steps were which led up to that result. This power is what I mean when I talk of reasoning backward, or analytically.
> **—Sherlock Holmes**
> *From* A Study *in Scarlet, by Sir Arthur Conan Doyle*

Homicide cases often remain unsolved because pertinent information or evidence was either overlooked or misinterpreted. Upon close inspection and analysis of an unsolved case, investigators sometimes discover that theories originally pursued regarding the motive, the manner in which the crime was committed, and the primary suspect(s) are inconsistent with the crime scene, the physical and/or trace evidence, and wound pathology. These common pitfalls are magnified with the passage of time.

The purpose of this chapter is to provide investigators with an introduction to the analysis of a cold homicide from a behavioral perspective. The degree to which an investigator understands human behavior, and is able to apply such understanding to a crime scene, is directly related to their ability to be successful in homicide investigation. Unfortunately, over time, homicide investigation has become increasingly focused upon forensic analysis of trace and biological evidence to solve cases, while the behavioral component has been neglected.

Criminal investigative analysis is a behavioral analytic process that integrates information regarding the victim, the initial crime scene investigation, physical and trace evidence, wound patterns, toxicological examination results, geographical information (including demographics and crime patterns), witness accounts, and an indirect personality assessment of any potential suspects.

Investigators tasked with a cold homicide investigation can benefit from the process of criminal investigative analysis in

- Organizing old case files
- Prioritizing cases based upon solvability factors
- Identifying elements of the original investigation that require follow-up
- Providing new focus to the investigation by integrating a prediction of human behavior with the most recent advancements in forensic science

Historical Perspective

Criminal investigative analysis is an investigative tool developed by the Federal Bureau of Investigation's Behavioral Science Unit. During the 1970s, special agents assigned to the unit believed that a detailed understanding of the behaviors exhibited by an offender during the commission of a violent crime could assist investigators in the identification, investigation, and successful prosecution of the subject. The agents began conducting research on violent offenders to identify commonalities and behavioral patterns that could assist police investigators in the detection of such offenders.

Robert Ressler, Ann Burgess, and John Douglas provided an early example of such research in *Sexual Homicide* (Ressler et al. 1988), which compiled information obtained from interviews and background investigations of 36 sexual killers. Ressler and Douglas identified commonalities shared by the offenders, including the habitual use of violent pornography from an early age, dysfunctional relationships with their parents, and social isolation from peers. Although their study gathered data from a relatively small number of subjects, the information offered clinicians and criminal justice professionals insight into the behavioral traits, personality characteristics, and patterns of social interaction, which might assist the criminal justice system in the identification and management of such individuals.

Although criminal investigative analysis, commonly termed "psychological or criminal profiling," has received much attention from the media and has been popularized in television, movies, and books, the potential benefits of this investigative tool continues to be misunderstood. The most common misconception is that criminal profiling is identical to criminal investigative analysis; in fact, profiling is only one element of criminal investigative analysis. A behavioral profile, or description of an unidentified offender's personality and lifestyle, may assist investigators in the identification of an offender by narrowing the focus of an investigation to a more restricted pool of potential suspects. A profile may be particularly useful in cases in which a potential suspect is not identified during the initial investigation, because the profile can then be used to reevaluate those people who have already been contacted that bear similarity to the profile. However, while such a description may be useful to investigators during their search for the offender, profiles have rarely if ever led to the actual identification of an offender. Further, "profiling" information is not admissible in court to prove the guilt or innocence of a defendant.[1]

Criminal investigative analysis refers to a range of functions related to the behavioral analysis of violent crimes, and the perpetrators who commit such crimes. The types of analytical services available to investigators and prosecutors include

- Crime scene analysis and reconstruction
- Indirect personality assessment
- Threat assessment
- Interview and interrogation strategies
- Crime linkage analysis
- Equivocal death investigation
- Trial and cross-examination strategy
- Expert testimony[2]

Criminal investigative analysis is currently conducted by a small group of highly skilled crime analysts who are trained in numerous disciplines including the psychology of persons who commit violent crimes, forensic science disciplines such as DNA analysis, comparative analysis, trace evidence, toxicology, bloodstain interpretation, wound pathology, threat assessment, interview and interrogation, crime scene analysis, and crime scene reconstruction. These analysts, who are sworn or retired law enforcement professionals, have completed a structured training and certification program under the supervision of the International Criminal Investigative Analysis Fellowship (ICIAF). Investigative assistance and expertise is available from members of the ICIAF to requesting investigators and/or prosecutors within the United States, Canada, Australia, and several European countries, often at no expense to the requesting agency.

Investigative Role

Criminal investigative analysis can assist investigators to organize existing case materials, identify "good" cold cases, prioritize cases based upon solvability factors, and identify issues that require additional investigative follow-up. Although advances in forensic science have enabled law enforcement agencies to solve crimes through biological evidence that identifies the perpetrator, investigators still need help to accurately interpret crime scenes that reveal such evidence.

Investigators who are confronted with the task of reactivating an unsolved homicide investigation typically face a variety of challenges resulting from the passage of time. Such challenges include the retirement and/or death of the original investigators; missing or deteriorated physical evidence; misplaced or lost case notes; incomplete or partial case files; poor documentation of previous investigative efforts; photographs that are of poor quality and/or insufficient quantity; and the death or unknown location of key witnesses.

[1] Testimony regarding behavioral profiles of offenders who commit various types of crimes has been ruled to be potentially prejudicial and/or of limited probative value in the determination of the facts relevant to a specific crime or defendant.
[2] Expert testimony has been allowed regarding crime scene analysis, crime scene reconstruction, and staging.

A thorough and fresh evaluation of the case by newly assigned detectives who have no prior commitment or loyalty to the theories that were originally developed regarding the motive or responsible person(s) has proven instrumental in solving many cold homicides. However, recontacting and establishing a positive relationship with the original investigators can be helpful. It is essential that the newly assigned investigators not criticize the original investigation or point out any investigative errors that may have been identified by reactivation of the investigation. The original investigators may have saved their investigative notes, know the whereabouts of missing case materials, and/or recall information pertinent to the crime that was not documented in reports.

The passage of time has also proven beneficial to the successful resolution of many unsolved homicide cases by offering investigators the opportunity to reinterview potential witnesses, persons associated with the victim, and any potential suspects for pertinent information that developed after the initial investigation was concluded. Likewise, deteriorated relationships may allow investigators to access information withheld by witnesses who were originally motivated by loyalty or fear.

Investigative Materials

Ideally, before a comprehensive analysis of the crime is initiated, investigators should compile as much of the following materials as possible:

- Complete historical information regarding the victim(s)
- Natural/candid photographs of victim(s) in life
- Initial and follow-up investigative reports
- Media accounts, including newspaper clippings, videotapes of television news, etc.
- Geographical information, including map(s), crime rates, and similar crimes committed during that period of time
- Narrative description(s) of crime scene(s)
- Photographs of crime scene(s)
- Photographs of decedent(s) at scene
- Crime scene diagram(s)
- Laboratory reports and analyses
- Autopsy report(s), diagrams, and photographs

Victimology

Criminal investigative analysis begins with an in-depth study of the victim's personality and lifestyle. To this end, a thorough background investigation of the victim is essential to shed light on such questions that may help focus the investigation. For example: Why was it "necessary" for this particular person to die? Did someone perceive them as an obstacle? What was their risk level of becoming the victim of a violent crime? Was the victim "specifically selected" by the offender, or was his or her interaction with the offender the result of opportunity and circumstance? Did the geographic location where the crime was committed effect the victim's risk level? Was the victim "security conscious," or did he or she feel comfortable leaving windows and doors unlocked? Did lifestyle place the victim in contact with persons who potentially posed a physical threat? Had the victim previously been the victim of a violent crime or expressed concern regarding their safety? Had the victim ever discussed how they planned to defend themselves if they were threatened or assaulted? What was the victim's medical and psychological history? Was the victim involved in any high-risk behaviors such as drug or alcohol abuse, domestic violence, extramarital sexual encounters, sexual deviation(s), or criminal enterprise?

Experience has shown that most homicides are the result of interpersonal conflict, and the offender can be found in the victim's family, social network, or work environment. Homicides that are motivated by interpersonal conflict are an attempt by the perpetrator to "solve a problem" he or she is experiencing with the victim. As such, consideration of any potential problems and conflicts that may have either been present in the victim's personal life, or perceived as a problem or conflict by a potential offender, is often effective in narrowing the search for the perpetrator. Experience has shown that with the passage of time, persons who had close personal relationships with the victim become more willing to divulge sensitive or unflattering information regarding the victim's lifestyle and activities.

Investigators should make every effort to obtain an understanding of the victim's background, personality, lifestyle, and interpersonal relationships, with particular attention to compilation of a detailed timeline of the victim's activities and contacts with other persons during the last 72 hours of life. Investigators should produce a detailed timeline of everyone the victim had contact with during this 72 hour window that precedes the murder, including telephone conversations and written messages. In most cases, the decision to commit a murder is made within a relatively short period of time prior to initiation of the assault. As a result, the perpetrator can typically be found within the group of persons who had contact with the victim within the last few days, hours, and sometimes minutes that preceded the murder.

Geographic Information

Information regarding the geographic location, accessibility and the area surrounding the crime scene(s) is important to the analysis. How and where did the offender encounter the victim? What types of crimes were common to the area during that period of time, and were there any crimes that bore resemblance to the behaviors the offender displayed during the murder of the victim? Information should be accumulated regarding traffic patterns, accessibility to and from major thoroughfares, lighting conditions, and environmental factors including weather. Was the victim vulnerable to an assault by a stranger, or could the victim have only been contacted in that particular location, at that particular time, by someone familiar?

Geographic analysis can assist in narrowing the search for an offender responsible for a crime or a series of crimes that involve multiple locations. If possible, investigators should consult with a geographic profiler to identify the most probable area the offender may be found (see Chapter 30). Because offenders can often be found a short distance from the crime scene, a less formal technique involves marking the areas on a map that approximates a one-half mile radius around each location, and then concentrating the search for the offender in any areas that overlap and are therefore geographically common to the scenes.

Crime Scene Analysis

Crime scenes depict the final outcome of the behavioral interaction between the offender(s) and the victim(s). Unfortunately, this simple truth is complicated by the fact that the locations are typically not sterile environments prior to initiation of the murder and therefore contain various evidence items not related to the crime. Consequently, in order to most effectively filter out such misleading items and identify only those pertinent to the homicide investigation, investigators must make a concerted effort to determine the preexisting condition of the crime scene. As specific information is often unavailable regarding the condition of the crime location on a particular day and time, investigators may be limited to whatever information they can obtain regarding the "normal" appearance of the scene. This process is essential since many homicide investigators rely heavily upon forensic examination of biological and physical evidence recovered from the scene to identify the perpetrator. Scientific testing of items that are not associated with the murder, and which erroneously identify innocent persons, will confuse the investigation and may even exonerate the responsible party.

Physical evidence from a crime scene is the product of behaviors that were exhibited by an offender(s) and a victim(s). A crime scene (cs) may be represented by the equation: cs = o (offender) + v (victim). Analysis of a crime scene from this perspective encourages investigators to more fully consider the contribution the victim's behavior likely had on the crime scene, which is essential in order to avoid the all-too-frequent error of attributing the scene solely to behaviors exhibited by the offender. Further, analysis from this perspective allows investigators to acquire an accurate assessment of the manner in which the offender behaved by acquainting themselves with the victim's personality and behavioral patterns, and "subtracting," so to speak, the victim's behavior from the crime scene. This concept can be represented as follows: o = cs – v. Theoretically, once the victim's behavior is subtracted from the scene, the behavioral evidence that remains can more appropriately be attributed to the offender. The following case description illustrates the importance of understanding the "preexisting" condition of the crime scene, as well as the behavioral patterns of the victim.

Case Study

Investigators responded to a single-family residence located in a new housing development at approximately noon on a weekday regarding the homicide of a 38-year-old pregnant female. The victim's husband told detectives he had discovered his wife's body several minutes earlier when he came home to drive her to a counseling appointment. The residence was in significant disarray. Furniture was overturned, drawers were emptied, and the contents scattered. A waterbed had been punctured and was leaking onto the carpet, and a large entertainment center situated in the living room had been overturned. Many household items were scattered in the backyard, including several televisions, the dining room chairs, and the contents of the kitchen cabinets and refrigerator. All of the upholstered living room furniture had been cut and were heavily stained with the victim's blood. A blood trail led from the living room into the master bathroom. The victim was located in the bathtub in the master bathroom, covered by a plastic jug, which was partially filled with coins, and a laundry hamper. The body was in a semi-seated position, and the victim was wearing a dress, bra, panties, and a wristwatch. Although there was no water in the bathtub, a bloody bathtub ring was visible in the tub, and blood spatter was visible on the adjacent wall. Chemical burns were present over portions of the right side of the victim's body and both shoulders; her hair appeared to have been bleached, and a small portion of her hair had been shaved above her right forehead. Barber shears, scissors, tweezers, and a bloodstained towel were found beneath her body. A racial slur was written on the bathroom mirror in toothpaste. The victim's cause of death was manual strangulation; however, she also suffered five stab wounds to her right back and buttocks and blunt force trauma to her head, left breast, face, and left leg. She suffered fractures to her nose and two ribs and had many bruises and abrasions to her arms and legs, and there was no evidence of defense-style injuries. During the course of the investigation, detectives learned the victim had a volatile temper and on a previous occasion had slashed the furniture after becoming angry. The couple had a limited history of domestic violence and had argued repeatedly during the preceding days. According to a female friend of the victim who had visited the residence on the morning of the murder, the victim had admitted causing nearly all of the damage to the home after her husband left for work. Interviews of the couple's neighbors revealed the victim's husband had arrived at the residence approximately 15 minutes prior to the time he had given to the investigators. He was subsequently arrested and convicted of the murders of his wife and unborn child.

As illustrated by this case, essential information regarding the behavioral sequence that occurred during the crime, the probable motive for the crime, the type of relationship the victim likely had with the perpetrator, and the type of person most likely to have committed the crime can be garnered through analysis of the crime scene and victimology. This information can also be useful during the interview or interrogation of suspects, and by prosecutors to distinguish between planned and impulsive homicides.

Information regarding the sequence of behaviors that occurred at the scene may be obtained through careful consideration and integration of the crime scene characteristics with the physical evidence. These characteristics may include, but are not limited to,

- The amount of risk the offender accepted to commit the crime
- The manner in which the offender approached the victim
- The size of the crime scene
- Bloodstain patterns
- Items taken or left behind
- Positioning and disposition of the body
- Wound patterns
- Indications of postmortem activity at the crime scene
- Indications of sexual activity

Some murders involve multiple crime scenes, which may include a point of abduction, initial assault, murder, body storage, and body and evidence disposal sites. When multiple crime scenes are involved, it is typically more difficult for investigators to locate pertinent physical evidence and information regarding the behavioral interaction of the offender and the victim.

Offender Risk

The offender determines the time, place, and circumstances under which the murder occurs. Since the offender is in control of these factors, investigators can learn a great deal by examining the environmental factors (location, time, lighting conditions, and traffic patterns in the area where the crime occurred), and assessing the amount of risk the offender was willing to accept in order to commit the crime.

Regardless of the time or location the offender selects for the murder, the offender cannot be absolutely certain he or she will not be seen by witnesses. An offender may reduce that risk by altering their appearance or committing the murder during late night or early morning hours. In general, however, the anxiety an offender has regarding the possibility of being seen by witnesses depends on several factors: the type of relationship the offender has with the victim; the extent to which the offender "belongs" at the location where the crime will occur; and the number of potential witnesses the offender believes will likely be present in the vicinity when the crime is committed.

An offender who has a close personal relationship with his or her victim often has less concern about being seen by other persons while either with the victim or at the location. An offender who "belongs" at a location, because he or she resides in, works in, or frequently visits the area, is often unconcerned that his or her presence at the scene will be noticed and considered unusual by potential witnesses. Persons who have a legitimate reason for being in the area (for example, service workers) are often not reported to investigators during the neighborhood canvasses that are typically conducted in the hours immediately following discovery of the victim's body and during the subsequent investigation. Potential witnesses are not usually asked questions regarding *all persons* seen in the area, but rather are primarily focused on persons who were perceived as being somehow *unusual*.

Offenders who are strangers to the victim and do not frequent the area where the crime occurs also tend to be less concerned that other persons will be able to accurately identify them to law enforcement as potential suspects. These offenders are often careful not to return to the area of the crime in order to avoid being recognized.

Another type of risk an offender likely considers both before and after commission of the murder is the likelihood that he or she will eventually be identified as the person responsible for the victim's death. Criminally sophisticated offenders may take precautions to either reduce or eliminate physical and trace evidence from the scene by wearing gloves, using condoms, cleaning the crime scene after the murder, and removing items from the scene they believe might reveal their identity. However, given the dramatic strides in forensic science, even the most knowledgeable and criminally sophisticated offenders can no longer be confident that they did not leave potentially incriminating evidence at the scene.

Prior to the commission of a planned homicide, and frequently during the commission of a more spontaneous killing, offenders consider the likelihood they will be interrupted during the commission of the crime by unexpected persons or events. Unexpected visitors, the premature arrival of other residents to the location, mail delivery, or even incoming unanswered telephone calls may sharply curtail the amount of time the offender is willing to spend at the scene. Offenders may take precautions to reduce the number of potential interruptions, including familiarizing themselves with the victim's schedule and routine behaviors, unplugging or disabling telephones, and extinguishing all interior and exterior lights.

If the murder involved prior planning, the offender may have taken precautions to facilitate his or her escape from the scene in order to avoid being apprehended. In these instances, offenders may plan their escape route, prop windows and doors open, and position a vehicle, bicycle, or other means of transportation in a location that is out of view but easily accessible.

Method of Approach

Analysis of the manner in which an offender likely gained access to the victim often supplies investigators with valuable insight regarding the offender's perception of his/her own talents and weaknesses, as well as identification of behaviors he or she is willing to exhibit. Although homicide scenes frequently lack conclusive evidence regarding the exact manner in which the offender was able to access the victim, criminal justice professionals are frequently able to accurately theorize the method that was employed through an analysis of the crime scene, the victim's personality, lifestyle and circumstances, and the "process of elimination."

Hazelwood and Warren (2001) suggest sexually motivated offenders employ three methods to approach victims: the con, the blitz, and the surprise. Offenders who are confident in the strength and persuasiveness of their interpersonal skills prefer the con approach. These offenders attempt to literally talk their victims into positions of vulnerability and/or persuade them to accompany them to locations that afford the offender a sufficient degree of privacy in order to perpetrate the crime. The blitz-style approach is the immediate application of debilitating force against the victim in order to incapacitate and render them incapable of physically resisting. Offenders who select the surprise approach use their physical strength to quickly gain control of the victim. Offenders who are more confident of their physical prowess than their social skills prefer the surprise approach. The correct identification of the method of approach an offender uses during the commission of a violent crime can help identify and facilitate the interview and prosecution of the perpetrator.

Few crime scenes exhibit evidence of forced entry. Because most homicides are the result of interpersonal conflict, it is common for victims to have admitted the offender to the location or willingly spent time with the offender immediately before the murder. Knowledge of the victim's habits is often helpful in determining whether other persons would have had access to the crime scene location, whether the victim routinely left doors and/or windows open or unlocked, or would have answered the door to an unexpected visitor or stranger.

Size of the Crime Scene

A crime scene that is littered with overturned furniture is behaviorally quite different from a small, contained scene that is limited to the location of the body. Expanded crime scenes may result from several scenarios, including recognition by the victim that the offender posed a significant threat prior to initiation of the assault; a substantial attempt by the victim to defend him/herself; an inability by the offender to effectively control the victim during the assault; and/or the possibility there was an escalation of violence, from a verbal argument to a physical assault. Expanded crime scenes are also more likely to be found in homicides that were not carefully planned by the offender, and in cases where the victim and the offender were of comparable size and strength. Conversely, smaller, more contained scenes are more likely to be found in premeditated murders, or cases where the offender is either significantly larger and/or stronger than the victim, or was able to exert and maintain effective control of the victim throughout the assault.

Bloodstain Patterns and Deposits

Accurate analysis of the bloodstain patterns and deposits found at the crime scene may provide police investigators with extremely valuable information regarding the physical movements of the offender and the victim during the murder. Conversely, misinterpretation of bloodstain patterns may cause a homicide to remain unsolved. Analysis of bloodstain patterns from an unsolved homicide depends upon the quality and quantity of photographs taken of the crime scene.

It is important when inferring behavior from bloodstain patterns to differentiate between blood from the victim and blood from the offender. In some cases, careful analysis has enabled investigators to discover that blood previously assumed to have come from the victim was actually deposited by the perpetrator. Investigators are encouraged to seek an informed opinion regarding any blood deposits associated with an unsolved murder in order to obtain an enhanced understanding of the behaviors that likely occurred at the scene.

Items Taken or Left Behind

Did the offender use items he or she found at the scene to facilitate the murder, or did the offender bring all of the items to the scene for the specific purpose of perpetrating the crime? What, if anything, is missing from the scene? Were there any items left at the scene that do not belong?

There are several possible explanations as to why an offender may have utilized items available at the crime scene, such as knives and heavy objects as weapons, or clothing items as bindings. These include (1) a murder that involved little or no prior planning; (2) a murder in which the offender was familiar with the location where the crime was committed and was confident the items could be found there; or (3) the offender was not willing to risk being found in possession of weapons, tools, or binding materials as he or she approached or left the crime scene.

Offenders who choose to bring specific objects to the scene may do so because they are routinely in possession of the item (e.g., a pocket knife, handgun), the crime involves a significant degree of prior planning, or the items utilized by the offender are of special significance to him/her.

Offenders who are criminally sophisticated—or who are forensically knowledgeable—are hesitant to leave transportable items behind that could lead to their identification. Homicides committed by such an offender may show evidence that the offender attempted to "clean up" prior to departing the scene, and any incriminating evidence was taken and discarded a safe distance away. In contrast, offenders who utilize weapons, bindings, or other items that have special meaning or significance (e.g., linked to their sexual fantasy) are often unwilling to discard them, and choose to retain possession of them so they can use them again. In these instances, investigators are often able to recover the items from the offender's possessions months or even years after the crime was committed.

Positioning and Disposition of the Body

The manner in which the victim's body was left often provides investigators with valuable information regarding the relationship, if any, the offender had with the victim, the emotional state of the offender immediately following the murder, and any logistical problems that the offender perceived following the murder.

Offenders can choose among numerous options once they are satisfied the victim is dead. They may choose to leave the victim's body at the crime scene without any further manipulation, transport the body to another location, or conceal or cover the body, or in rare instances, the perpetrator may position and "display" the body in a manner that will likely be particularly provocative or shocking to the person who finds the body.

In most instances, offenders are anxious to distance themselves from the crime scene and the victim's body shortly after the commission of the murder. They are aware that continued association with the victim's body increases their risk of being discovered. Consequently, only offenders who have serious/severe mental impairments, are driven by a specific need (usually sexual), or believe they must alter the death scene somehow in order to avoid detection will remain in contact with the body.

Offenders who are confident that other persons are not aware of their association with the victim are more likely to leave the body at the crime scene. However, offenders who had a close personal relationship with the victim, or who believed their association with the victim near the time of death was witnessed or known by others, may attempt to transport or conceal the body in hopes of either delaying or preventing discovery of the murder.

The amount of time and contact an offender has with the victim's body following the murder is a function, at least in part, of the offender's personality and ability to function under pressure. Offenders who had a close personal relationship with the victim or who cannot tolerate touching a deceased person may have more difficulty controlling their emotions sufficiently in order to move or manipulate the deceased. Crime scenes sometimes reflect evidence that the offender "changed their mind" and aborted an attempt to move or transport the victim's body.

The offender's ability to transport the victim's body is influenced by such factors as physical strength, access to a vehicle, and a sufficient opportunity. Disposition of the body is influenced by the physical strength of the offender, a significant disparity in size between the victim and the offender, the physical layout of the murder scene, the degree of privacy the murder scene affords the offender, and the offender's ability to easily and covertly access an appropriate means of transportation. For instance, did the residence where the crime was committed have an attached garage, or could the vehicle only be parked in an open area in view of potential witnesses? How many persons were present and active in the area during the time immediately following the murder? Was there any indication the offender remained at the murder scene for an extended period after the death, waiting for nightfall? Were window coverings manipulated; did the offender engage in extensive cleanup; and/or did the offender eat, sleep, launder clothing, or bathe at the crime scene?

Cause of Death and Wound Patterns

Significant information regarding the sequence of events at the crime scene is available by examination and assessment of the victim's wounds. Factors that are often relevant to the behavioral analysis of a murder include the presence of blunt force trauma, the presence or absence of defense-style injuries, identification of patterned injuries, analysis of the lethality of multiple wounds, estimation of the time period during which the wounds were inflicted, the cause of death, and postmortem activity. It is essential that the wounds be considered within the context of the scene, and background information regarding the victim's personality, history of drug and alcohol use, medical history, and lifestyle. In some instances, a thorough analysis may reveal the death was not the result of homicide. This was illustrated by the following case, which was initially suspected to be a homicide.

Case Study

The 20-year-old male college student resided in a private room on the second floor of a fraternity house, which was located in a low crime-rate area. He was academically successful, had an active social life, had a steady girlfriend, and had a positive relationship with his family. He had a minor criminal history, resulting from several incidents during which he had been drinking alcoholic beverages. He had no reported enemies, and no history of physical or psychological problems. Shortly before his death, his parents said he had been anxious regarding his course of study, and had suffered bouts of insomnia. Two fraternity house roommates told investigators they last saw him at approximately 1 a.m. when he retired to his room, following a quiet evening of television. During the next two days, his roommates said they knocked on the deceased's door and called his name; however, when they got no answer, they assumed he was visiting friends.

His roommates obtained a key to his room from the company that managed the house and discovered the deceased in bed, partially covered by a comforter. The room was dark, music was playing, and the deceased was wearing earplugs. Bloodstains were apparent on three walls, the rug, desk, and bedding. His shirt, shorts, and sock bottoms were bloodstained. His shirt had numerous defects, which corresponded to numerous of his 25 stab wounds and 4 incised wounds to his face, scalp, neck, chest, and wrists. He had also suffered fatal stab wounds to his chest, which penetrated both lungs and his heart, a fatal four-inch-deep incised wound across his neck, and moderately deep horizontal incised wounds to both wrists. There was no evidence of blunt force trauma, broken bones, torture, bindings, or sexual assault. Several minor abrasions and cuts were found on the fingers of his right hand; however, there was no indication of defense-style injuries. A toxicological examination revealed no traces of alcohol or drugs. A bloodstained knife was found on the bed, and all of the fingerprints on the knife were matched to the decedent. There was no indication of forced entry or a struggle involving a second person. None of the deceased's roommates reported hearing any sounds emanating from the deceased's bedroom or finding any evidence that an intruder had been present in the house.

Analysis of the deceased's wounds revealed that all of the stab wounds were uniform and had no jagged edges (which would be consistent with a struggle); many were superficial and all of the wounds were located within his reach. Although stabbing is the least common method of suicide, experience has shown that suicide cannot be eliminated from consideration based upon the severity of the wounds. Since the deceased had no history of suicidal ideation, his family and friends, as well as numerous investigators, were reluctant to accept a finding of suicide. However, an integrative analysis of his personality, wounds, and the physical evidence brought perspective to the case and convinced all parties he had committed suicide.

Detectives involved in a cold homicide investigation should carefully review the postmortem medical examination report and photographs, and consult with a forensic pathologist to obtain a thorough understanding of the victim's wounds, the manner and mode of death, and an estimate of the time the victim could have remained ambulatory before succumbing to such wounds. Investigators are often reluctant to thoroughly review the autopsy report and photographs because they have little or no training in wound pathology, and find the medical terminology used in the autopsy report difficult to understand. Consequently, after determining the victim's cause of death, they do not adequately consider the implications of any other injuries.

Minor injuries such as bruising to the victim's face are important to the analysis of a homicide because they may indicate that an escalation of violence occurred. Murders motivated by interpersonal conflict often begin as verbal arguments that escalate to physical assaults. The possibility that the victim exchanged blows with the offender should be considered. The presence of defense-style injuries or bruising to the victim's body is also consistent with the possibility that an argument and physical struggle preceded the murder. Recognition of these types of wounds may be an indication that the offender did not originally approach the victim with the intent to kill. In such cases, the offender may have had a personal but problematic relationship with the victim, and he/she may have rationalized the murder as justifiable.

Offenders intent on ensuring the victim's death often inflict multiple potentially fatal injuries. Infliction of serious injury that does not cause immediate death may motivate the offender to resort to another mode of attack (e.g., manual strangulation followed by a gunshot wound; a gunshot wound followed by throat slashing; stomping of the abdominal region followed by stabbing injuries). A pathologist is usually able to estimate the amount of time necessary for the victim to succumb to each of the potentially fatal injuries. The following case summary is an example of a homicide that involved multiple fatal injuries.

Case Study

The 22-year-old female was last seen entering her apartment with her 2-year-old child at approximately 1 a.m. after playing cards at her next-door female neighbor's apartment. Residents in the complex told investigators they had been awakened several hours later by loud noises, including voices arguing, a baby crying, and several loud "thumps." The victim was found dead in her locked apartment approximately 36 hours later, when the apartment manager went to the victim's apartment to investigate the source of water leaking into the unit immediately below.

Evidence at the scene indicated a struggle had occurred in the living room; the victim's body had been dragged into the bedroom and then partially covered with newspaper. She was dressed in her normal sleeping attire; however, her bra had been pushed up, exposing her right breast. The child was unharmed. The victim's cause of death was listed as internal hemorrhage due to blunt force trauma to her abdomen. A patterned bruise was faintly visible on the victim's abdomen. She suffered blunt force injury to her head and neck, and all of the injuries were consistent with stomping and kicking injuries. She had numerous bruises on her face, left knee, and left elbow. She had facial suffusion, conjunctival hemorrhages, and scalp edema, caused by mechanical compression of her neck. The victim had a stab wound to her neck, which occurred prior to death, and five additional stab wounds to her abdomen, which were inflicted between the perimortem and postmortem states. There were no injuries to the victim's hands, no evidence of binding, or sexual assault. The victim had a trace amount of alcohol in her system; however, no drugs were found. A knife stained with the victim's blood was found stored with other knives in a butcher block on the kitchen counter. After a prolonged investigation, the boyfriend of the victim's next-door neighbor was eventually identified as the perpetrator. He told investigators he had gone to the victim's apartment for sexual purposes. She had refused him and he became enraged. He admitted taking the victim's door key, returning to her apartment the day following the murder, and turning the water on in order to ensure the safety of the child.

Analysis of this case provided investigators with valuable information regarding the sequence of events that led up to the victim's death. The analysis was used to narrow the focus of the investigation to persons who were known to the victim, and later provided investigators with information that was useful during the interview and subsequent prosecution of the offender.

Sexual Activity

A thorough understanding of the crime scene is necessary before investigators can efficiently search for and identify trace evidence left by an offender. While some crime scenes contain obvious indications the offender had sexual contact with the victim close to the time of the murder, evidence of sexual activity is often difficult to identify. Various types of sexual activity may occur during a homicide, including masturbation by the offender onto the victim's body, oral copulation, penile vaginal penetration, and/or penetration with a foreign object. Sexual activity may occur prior to, during, or following the victim's death.

Sexual activity by the offender can offer investigators an opportunity to identify the perpetrator of an unsolved homicide. Although it is relatively common for sexually motivated offenders to experience sexual dysfunction, recent advances in forensic science have enabled scientists to identify and retest extremely small deposits of trace evidence. In cold case investigations, detectives should request forensic scientists review all physical evidence to determine the utility of conducting further laboratory tests for identifiable material. Items that have been previously analyzed using older, less sensitive and/or discriminating forensic techniques, or evidence not previously analyzed, should be carefully evaluated.

Experience has shown that serology DNA test results are often misinterpreted. Even experienced investigators are prone to misinterpreting the conclusions drawn from test results. For instance, are the test results consistent with sexual contact? Are any of the samples tested inconsistent with the victim? How many donors contributed to the sample(s) that were tested? Was the victim's consensual sexual partner(s) excluded? Have all potentially relevant samples been tested? Investigators should consult with forensic scientists to thoroughly review all of the biological and trace evidence associated with the crime to gain a thorough understanding of the meaning of the test results and determine whether further testing is feasible. See Chapters 15 and 16.

The following case was submitted for analysis to determine whether the victim's death was the result of sexual misadventure, as the defendant claimed, or homicide.

Case Study

The 55-year-old male victim was a successful businessman, lived alone, and was openly homosexual. He drank excessively and frequented several local bars where he flashed significant amounts of money and enjoyed giving others the impression he was wealthy. The victim was described as security conscious and routinely locked and secured his doors and windows. His neighbor said the residence had appeared secure at 5:30 p.m.; however, at 7:45 p.m., the garage door was standing open and the victim's car was gone. When she was unable to contact the victim by telephone, the neighbor called the police.

The police entered the residence through an unlocked garage door that led into the kitchen and observed an empty liquor bottle on the table. The telephone had been unplugged. The victim's nude body was lying on his bed in the unlit master bedroom. An electrical cord had been wrapped around the victim's neck five times, and the lamp to which it was attached was hanging down toward the floor. Minor lacerations were visible on the victim's face, chin, and chest. Semen that did not match the victim's DNA profile was recovered from the victim's chest and a towel that was lying near the corner of the bed. The victim's DNA and the unidentified DNA profile were recovered from an empty glass on the bedside table. A dresser drawer had been overturned near the foot of the bed, and several items were missing from the residence, including the victim's vehicle, a briefcase, a gold ring, a jewelry box, and the victim's wallet, which contained his identification and credit cards. The vehicle was recovered the following day in a residential area where it had been abandoned, and bloodhounds trailed to a nearby bus stop. A latent fingerprint was located on the base of the lamp. The fingerprint was matched to a young married man approximately one year later, following his arrest for theft.

The analysis integrated information regarding the victim's lifestyle and sexual habits with the victim's wound patterns and physical evidence found at the scene. Investigation of the victim's behavioral patterns showed that he had no history of using ligatures or other devices to restrict his breathing during sexual activity, and no information was found to indicate the victim had any suicidal intent. The wound patterns found on the victim's face, chin, and chest were consistent with the base of the lamp that was found attached to his neck, suggesting the item had likely not been applied with the victim's consent. The prosecutors used the analysis to effectively refute the defendant's claim of consensual sexual misadventure, and the defendant was convicted of murder.

Staged Crime Scenes

The Crime Classification Manual defines staging as the alteration of the death scene in order to either direct the investigation away from the perpetrator or to protect the deceased or their family from potential embarrassment (Douglas et al. 1992). In homicides, staging involves a variety of behaviors that may be exhibited at the scene following a death, including alteration of the scene so that it appears to have been financially or sexually motivated, or reporting the victim to law enforcement authorities as a missing person. When a death scene is staged, it is nearly always accomplished by a person who had a close personal relationship to the deceased.

One of the most common instances in which staging is encountered is in a domestic homicide in which a spouse is murdered at their shared residence. In these cases, the perpetrator is aware that if the spouse's body is discovered at the unaltered scene, he or she will immediately become the primary suspect. The perpetrator will therefore attempt to rearrange the scene to suggest an alternative motive for the crime, provide misleading statements to investigators, and/or clean the scene, hide the body, and report the victim as a missing person.

Staged scenes are often recognizable because the circumstances surrounding the victim's death or disappearance are inconsistent with the physical evidence and victimology. Domestic homicides are typically committed by offenders who are criminally inexperienced and who are therefore unaware of the appearance of a genuine crime scene. Their inexperience, combined with the likelihood they attempted to alter the crime scene while agitated and/or in a highly emotional state, inhibits their ability to think clearly. As a result, individuals who stage scenes often make unintended errors, termed "red flags," that reveal that the scene is inconsistent with an actual burglary, sexual assault, kidnapping, or missing person case (Douglas et al. 1992).

Criminal investigative analysts can assist investigators and prosecutors in the identification of the sometimes-minute inconsistencies reflected in the scene or in problematic statements made to the investigators. The case example that follows illustrates numerous crime scene indicators often found in a staged domestic homicide.

Case Study

The victim was an attractive, physically fit middle-aged woman who resided with her husband of 30 years. Their home was located in an upscale neighborhood that had a low rate of violent crime. The victim had many friends, was socially active, and was a part-time teacher. On the day of her death, the victim taught a morning class, and then purchased coffee and a pastry before returning to her residence to prepare for an afternoon lesson. At approximately 1:40 p.m., the victim's husband returned to the residence in the company of two of the couple's friends and found the front door standing open. He found the victim's body lying head first near the bottom of the basement stairs fully dressed, with the exception of one of her shoes, which was located on a step above her body. After summoning his friends and asking them to telephone for help, the victim's husband pulled her body onto the cement basement floor and attempted resuscitation. Emergency personnel who responded to the scene were unable to revive the victim and she was pronounced dead at the scene.

The victim's husband tearfully told investigators he had warned the victim the shoes she had been wearing that day were not appropriate for the basement stairs and that she had slipped before. There was no sign of forced entry; however, the couple was not security conscious and had often left doors and windows unlocked. None of the neighbors reported seeing any strangers in the area, heard any dogs barking, or heard loud voices or screams in the time period during which the victim died. There was no evidence of ransacking or theft, although many items of value were openly displayed. Examination of the residence with luminol revealed the presence of blood on a kitchen chair, on the kitchen floor through the main hallway to the area at the top of the basement stairs, and bloody drag marks on the last seven steps in the basement. Blood had been cleaned from the kitchen floor, the hallway, and the area at the top of the basement stairs, and the blood was matched to the victim.

The postmortem examination revealed the victim's cause of death was massive head injury and manual strangulation. She suffered multiple lacerations to the back of her head, her skull was fractured, and she had numerous bruises and lacerations to her forehead, left cheek, eyes, lips, and jawline. She had defense-style injuries to her left arm and wrist. During the investigation, detectives discovered the victim's husband had uncharacteristically removed vegetation from a back gate, making it operational, several days before her death. A financial investigation revealed the couple had depleted most of their financial assets during the preceding several years. A search of the vehicle operated by the victim's husband produced a shirt and shoes stained with the victim's blood, which had been hidden beneath the driver's seat. Analyses of his cellular telephone records were inconsistent with the locations he claimed to have visited during the time his wife was killed.

In order to obtain a better understanding of this murder, the assigned investigators requested the assistance of a criminal investigative analyst shortly after this crime was committed. Following a careful review of the victimology, physical evidence, witness statements, and wound pathology, the analyst prepared a detailed written report that delineated the "red flags" that were present in the crime scene. During the trial of the victim's husband, the prosecutor consulted with the analyst during cross-examination of the defendant and used the report to effectively describe the elements of staging during his closing statement to the jury. The defendant was convicted.

Evaluation of Eyewitness Evidence

Detectives involved in cold homicide investigations often rely heavily upon the accuracy of eyewitness accounts, particularly in cases with no physical or biological evidence.

Since the 1970s, researchers have been studying the causes of eyewitness errors (Loftus 1979). The unreliability of eyewitness accounts and identifications has been dramatically illustrated by recent court cases in which DNA evidence exonerated individuals wrongfully convicted of violent crimes. Many wrongful convictions have been based almost exclusively on testimony from eyewitnesses who remained convinced that their identifications were accurate. Despite the fallibility of such evidence, testimony from eyewitnesses is often perceived as the most compelling trial evidence.

Misconceptions regarding the manner in which human memory functions and the factors that influence an eyewitness's ability to accurately make an identification are common not only in the general population but also throughout the criminal justice system. Historically, criminal investigators have routinely relied upon statements from witnesses to develop investigative leads, identify perpetrators, and exonerate the innocent. Additionally, criminal prosecutions have frequently been based exclusively upon identifications by individuals who claim to have seen either the victim or suspect engaged in normal noncriminal behaviors prior to the commission of the crime. DNA evidence, on the other hand, is often difficult for jurors to understand (Ainsworth 1998).

Despite belief to the contrary, the identification process does not operate like a videotape recording system. Scientific research has shown that several cognitive processes are involved in "identification memory," which enables a person to accurately select a person from a photographic or live presentation. These processes, which consist of encoding, storage, and retrieval, operate separately; however, each is essential to the identification process. Identification memory is a complicated process that is vulnerable to alteration by numerous factors, including the nature of the instructions given to the eyewitness regarding identification, the amount of time between the witnessed event and identification, the presentation format, the emotional state of the eyewitness, environmental factors such as lighting and duration of the event, and the degree of familiarity the eyewitness had with the potential suspect. As a result, memories are vulnerable to change by internal and external conditions, interactions with other persons, and exposure to additional information.

One of the most prevalent techniques used within the criminal justice system to evaluate the accuracy of eyewitness statements is an assessment of the level of confidence the witness reports. Although it has been popularly assumed that confidence is predictive of accuracy, researchers have found a relatively weak correlation, which would likely be functionally worthless in real-life settings (Wells & Loftus 1984; Sporer et al. 1995). Research has confirmed that a witness's confidence level is affected by factors unrelated to accuracy, such as receiving affirmative feedback, which confirms the accuracy of their identification (Wells & Bradfield 1998, 1999). This finding has important implications for homicide investigations. It is common for investigators to solicit a self-confidence rating from the witness regarding the accuracy of their identification, and to use their confidence level as a basis for prioritization of leads. Investigators and prosecutors also use the witness's confidence level to make a determination of whether there is sufficient probable cause to make an arrest and/or file charges.

Another misperception is that an eyewitness who was highly emotional at the time of the event is a more reliable and accurate witness. It is assumed that a witness or victim will not forget a person they saw during a violent or threatening encounter and that human memory regarding this type of event is essentially unaffected by the passage of time. Researchers have determined that high levels of stress actually interfere with a person's ability to encode information, and that people who are only moderately aroused are more likely to make accurate identifications (Deffenbacher 1983; Christianson 1992).

The role that familiarity plays in accurate identification is another issue that is frequently misunderstood. Higher rates of misidentification have been found with persons who had previously been seen than for total strangers; however, higher confidence ratings were reported in identifications of persons rated as familiar (Read 1994). Researchers believe witnesses are often unable to distinguish between two or more memories, possibly because they perceive them to be similar in quality, content, or characteristics. Accurate identification requires that the person recall the exact context in which he or she saw the person, and not base identification on exposure to media accounts, viewing mug shots, or conversations with other persons

(Reed 2004). This finding has significant implications during assessment of statements from neighbors or persons who regularly saw the person they identified, and for identifications that followed publicity of the crime. Research by Shapiro and Penrod (1986) found that the only characteristic predictive of identification accuracy was distinctiveness of appearance.

Detectives should carefully review the procedures utilized and the circumstances under which eyewitnesses made identifications. Close scrutiny should be given to any witness who became more confident over time regarding the accuracy of their report; reported details or events they could not have witnessed due to distance, impaired eyesight, insufficient lighting, or position; or reported new details or modification of their account following exposure to other witnesses or media coverage.

Witnesses who were young children at the time of the event require special consideration. Criminal justice professionals should review *Children Who Witness Homicide and Other Violent Crimes* (Boychuk-Spears 2002) for recommendations regarding appropriate interviewing procedures and analyses of statements given by children.

Unfortunately, procedures utilized by police investigators regarding eyewitness identifications have not comprehensively integrated the findings of psychological researchers. Although a collaboration of researchers and criminal justice professionals in 1999 produced the U.S. Department of Justice's publication, *Eyewitness Evidence: A Guide for Law Enforcement* (Technical Working Group for Eyewitness Evidence 1999), their recommendations regarding double-blind testing and sequential presentation format have not been commonly adopted (Wells et al. 2000).

Conclusion

Criminal Investigative Analysis is a valuable tool that can bring fresh focus to the investigation of a cold case by providing a comprehensive understanding of the manner in which the crime was committed. The technique integrates information regarding the victim, the initial crime scene investigation, physical and trace evidence, wound patterns, toxicological examination results, geography, witness accounts, and an indirect personality assessment of potential suspects. This comprehensive analysis process can serve as a means of organizing numerous sources of investigative information from a cold case file that might otherwise remain dormant for many years. The passage of time is both an enemy and ally with regard to a cold homicide case. New insights spawned by a comprehensive analysis of the case are possible through integration of all available information, including behavioral analysis of the interaction of the victim and offender, forensic evidence, and a determination of the feasibility of conducting scientific tests on evidentiary items that may have been overlooked or misinterpreted. Criminal investigative analysis is available to investigators and prosecutors upon their request from members of the International Criminal Investigative Analysis Fellowship (ICIAF).

Acknowledgments

I wish to express my deepest gratitude and appreciation to Sharon Pagaling Hagan for her authorship and contribution of this chapter. Hagan is a clinical psychologist and retired Special Agent Supervisor of the California Department of Justice's Violent Crime Profiling Unit. She studied criminal investigative profiling and crime scene analysis in conjunction with the International Criminal Investigative Analysis Fellowship and the FBI's National Center for the Analysis of Violent Crime, and has provided investigative assistance to law enforcement agencies and prosecutors throughout California and nationally regarding homicide, sexual assault, threat assessment, and child abduction cases.

Suggested Readings and Bibliography

Ainsworth, P. B. (1998). *Psychology, Law and Eyewitness Testimony.* West Sussex, England: John Wiley & Sons, Inc.

Boychuk-Spears, T. (2002). *Children Who Witness Homicide and Other Violent Crimes* (pp. 91–115). San Diego, CA: Specialized Training Services.

Christianson, S. A. (1992). Emotional stress and eyewitness memory: A critical review. *Psychological Bulletin, 112,* 284–309.

Deffenbacher, K. (1983). The influence of arousal on reliability of testimony. In S. M. A. Lloyd-Bostock & B. R. Clifford (Eds.), *Evaluating Witness Evidence: Recent Psychological Research and New Perspectives* (pp. 235–251). Chichester, England: Wiley.

Douglas, J. E., Burgess, A. W., Burgess, A. G. & Ressler, R. K. (1992). *Crime Classification Manual* (pp. 249–258). New York: Lexington Books.

Hazelwood, R. R. & Burgess, A. W. (2001). The behavioral-oriented interview of rape victims: The key to profiling. In Hazelwood, R. R. & Burgess, A. W. (Eds.), *Practical Aspects of Rape Investigation: A Multidisciplinary Approach,* Second Edition (pp. 118–119). Boca Raton, FL: CRC Press.

Loftus, E. F. (1979). *Eyewitness Testimony.* Cambridge, MA: Harvard University Press.

Read, J. D. (1994). Understanding bystander misidentifications: The role of familiarity and contextual knowledge. In D. F. Ross, J. D. Read & M. P. Toglia (Eds.), *Adult Eyewitness Testimony: Current Trends and Developments* (pp. 56–79). New York: Cambridge University Press.

Reed, S. K. (2004). *Cognition: Theory and Applications* (pp. 111–115). Belmont, CA: Wadsworth/Thomson Learning.

Ressler, R. K., Burgess, A. W. & Douglas, J. E. (1988). *Sexual homicide: Patterns and motives.* New York: Lexington Books.

Shapiro, P. N. & Penrod, S. D. (1986). Meta-analysis of facial identification studies. *Psychological Bulletin, 100,* 139–156.

Sporer, S., Penrod, S., Read, D. & Cutler, B. L. (1995). Choosing, confidence and accuracy: A meta-analysis of the confidence-accuracy relation in eyewitness identification studies. *Psychological Bulletin, 118,* 315–327.

Technical Working Group for Eyewitness Evidence (1999). *Eyewitness Evidence: A Guide for Law Enforcement* (Booklet). Washington, DC: United States Department of Justice, Office of Justice Programs.

Wells, G. L. & Bradfield, A. L. (1998). "Good, you identified the suspect": Feedback to eyewitnesses distorts their reports of the witnessing experience. *Journal of Applied Psychology, 83,* 360–376.

Wells, G. L. & Bradfield, A. L. (1999). Distortions in eyewitnesses' recollections: Can the post identification feedback effect be moderated? *Psychological Science, 10,* 138–144.

Wells, G. L. & Loftus, E. F. (1984). *Eyewitness Testimony: Psychological Perspectives.* Cambridge, MA: Cambridge University Press.

Wells, G. L., Malpass, R. S., Lindsay, R. C. L., Fisher, R. P., Turtle, J. W. & Fulero, S. M. (2000). From the lab to the police station. *American Psychologist, 55 (6),* 581–598.

Warming Up with Wiretaps

24

ROBERT P. HICKEY

Contents

The wiretap is an underutilized and overfeared tool in the investigation of cold homicides. The purpose of this chapter is to demystify the use of wiretaps and to suggest how and when to use them to solve cold case homicides. While wiretaps or, more accurately put, *electronic intercepts* require substantial resources, they should not be overlooked because of the fear of the unknown. Instead, they should be thought of as a glorified search warrant that requires additional executive approval and often a fairly significant commitment of resources. Most jurisdictions require approval from the Presiding Judge, Chief of Police, Sheriff, or Agency Head *and* the District Attorney, or Attorney General. Significant resources are required to monitor the "lines" and compliment the intercept with surveillance and proactive investigative methods commonly referred to as "tickling the wire." That said, the payoff can be immense. When all, or nearly all, else fails, a wiretap can be the best chance to capture the suspect's conversations about the murder or cover-up of the murder.

Wiretaps may be used in cold homicide investigations to establish a *target's* motive to commit the murder, to record a target crafting a bogus alibi, to catch targets planning additional murders, and to prosecute people close to the killers in order to leverage them into cooperating in a murder investigation. Wiretaps have been used extensively to put the final pieces of the puzzle together in successful murder investigations and prosecutions.

What Is a Wiretap?

A wiretap is an order from a judge authorizing a law enforcement agency to intercept wire, electronic digital pager, or electronic cellular telephone communications. This includes common telephone conversations over a hard line, cellular phone, or cellular phone with a "walkie-talkie" feature, and text messages to or from a pager or telephone.

Wiretaps and the Resources to Run Them Are Available in Most Jurisdictions

Wiretaps are available under federal jurisdiction and in most states. Figure 24.1 illustrates jurisdictions with statutes authorizing interceptions (U.S. courts). Note the frequency, or infrequency, of wiretap orders granted in a particular jurisdiction in 2014 to gauge whether or not it will take a pioneer-like effort to get a wiretap application through the process.

Wiretaps are usually only available in investigations of certain serious crimes listed in the authorizing statute. I am unaware of a state wiretap statute that does not include murder as a qualifying crime, but check for this or other limits specific to the jurisdiction before investing any time or effort into obtaining a wiretap order.

The next question is the availability of a "wire room" or facility where the telecommunications company can send the data and where law enforcement can receive, monitor, and collect the conversations or text messages. Few city or county agencies have these facilities, but most local Federal Bureau of Investigation (FBI) and Drug Enforcement Administration (DEA) offices have modern wire rooms and are usually willing to make their assets available to local law enforcement. Contacting the FBI's Violent Crimes Task Force responsible for the jurisdiction is the best first move to find a wire room and to get technical advice. Federal agencies are particularly helpful if the murder, suspect, or investigation has a tie to narcotics activity.

Finally, make sure your agency has, or another agency can provide, qualified agents/officers to monitor the intercept. Wiretap statutes typically require that the intercepts be monitored by people with specific qualifications. Check the statute and with the prosecutor's office.

Application to Cold Homicides

Wiretaps can be useful in warming up a cold homicide; however, the status of the investigation and circumstances of the crime must be appropriate. For instance, you would not expect to gain anything from a wiretap for a murder committed by a lone perpetrator, without an accomplice after the fact, and without a person to whom the perpetrator has confessed or to whom the perpetrator would be expected to confess. What pertinent conversations could you hope to intercept? Much more promising are murders involving multiple perpetrators, subjects who helped the killer plan the offense, subjects who provided weapons or information to the killer, subjects who helped the killer conceal the crime or murder weapon, or subjects in whom the killer has confided about the killing.

Multiple Perpetrators

The possibilities of obtaining incriminatory conversations among subjects who committed a murder together are a great foundation for obtaining a wiretap and either jump-starting or putting a cold case over the top. Even after many years, you could expect fellow killers to talk about their crime or evasion of arrest, particularly if one is a weak link or less culpable. In fact, the passage of time could help by wearing on one of the perpetrators' conscience. The trick is finding probable cause to believe that the subjects would be discussing the crime after several or many years. Tips from a family member or friend to whom one of the perpetrators confessed or evidence that the killers are still in constant contact are helpful facts, but you still may need to engage in proactive measures both to obtain probable cause to get the intercept and to gain incriminatory conversations during the wiretap. Such techniques are up to the investigator's imagination, and some suggestions will be discussed in this chapter.

Accomplices Before or After the Fact

Even if your target committed the murder alone, look to see if you have a subject who in any way helped the target. Did someone supply the murder weapon with or without knowledge of its intended use? Did someone tell the killer where to find the victim with or without knowledge of the killer's intent? Did someone

Table 1
Jurisdictions with Statutes Authorizing the Interception of Wire, Oral, or Electronic Communications Effective During the Period January 1 Through December 31, 2014 [1]

Jurisdiction	Statutory Citation [2]	Reported Use of Wiretap in 2014	Number of Orders Authorized in 2014
Federal	18 U.S.C. §§ 2510-2522	Yes	1,279
Alaska	Alaska Stat. §§ 12.37.010 et seq.	No	-
Arizona	Ariz. Rev. Stat. Ann. §§ 13-3001 et seq.	Yes	24
California	Cal. Penal Code §§ 629.50 et seq.	Yes	971
Colorado	Colo. Rev. Stat. § 16-15-102	Yes	162
Connecticut	Conn. Gen. Stat. §§ 54-41a et seq.	No	-
Delaware	Del. Code Ann. tit. 11, §§ 2401 et seq.	Yes	1
District of Columbia	D.C. Code §§ 23-541 et seq.	No	-
Florida	Fla. Stat. §§ 934-01 et seq.	Yes	162
Georgia	Ga. Code Ann. §§ 16-11-60 et seq.	Yes	27
Hawaii	Haw. Rev. Stat. §§ 803-41 et seq.	No	-
Idaho	Idaho Code Ann. §§ 18-6701 et seq.	No	-
Illinois	ch. 720 Ill. Comp. Stat. act 5, §§ 14-1 et seq.	Yes	52
Indiana	Ind. Code §§ 35-33.5-3-1 et seq.	Yes	17
Iowa	Iowa Code §§ 808B.1 et seq.	No	-
Kansas	Kan. Stat. Ann. §§ 22-2514 et seq.	Yes	3
Louisiana	La. Rev. Stat. Ann. §§ 15:1302 et seq.	Yes	10
Maine	Me. Rev. Stat. tit. 15, §§ 709 et seq.	No	-
Maryland	Md. Code Ann., Cts. & Jud. Proc. §§ 10-401 et seq.	Yes	76
Massachusetts	Mass. Gen. Laws ch. 272, §§ 99 et seq.	Yes	1
Minnesota	Minn. Stat. §§ 626A.01 et seq.	No	-
Mississippi	Miss. Code Ann. §§ 41-29-501 et seq.	Yes	7
Missouri	Mo. Ann. Stat. tit. 37, §§ 542.400 et seq.	No	-
Nebraska	Neb. Rev. Stat. §§ 86-290 et seq.	No	-
Nevada	Nev. Rev. Stat. §§ 179.410 et seq., 199.540, 200.610 et seq.	Yes	175
New Hampshire	N.H. Rev. Stat. Ann. §§ 570-A:1 et seq.	No	-
New Jersey	N.J. Stat. Ann. §§ 2A:156A-1 et seq.	Yes	106
New Mexico	N.M. Stat. Ann. §§ 30-12-1 et seq.	Yes	7
New York	N.Y. Crim. Proc. Law §§ 700.05 et seq.	Yes	273
North Carolina	N.C. Gen. Stat. §§ 15A-286 et seq.	Yes	30
North Dakota	N.D. Cent. Code §§ 29-29.2-01 et seq.	No	-
Ohio	Ohio Rev. Code Ann. §§ 2933.51 et seq.	Yes	14
Oklahoma	Okla. Stat. tit. 13, §§ 176.1 et seq.	Yes	7
Oregon	Or. Rev. Stat. §§ 133.721 et seq.	No	-
Pennsylvania	18 Pa. Cons. Stat. §§ 5701 et seq.	Yes	78
Puerto Rico	P.R. Laws Ann. tit. 25, §§ 971 et seq.	No	-
Rhode Island	R.I. Gen. Laws §§ 12-5.1-1 et seq.	No	-
South Carolina	S.C. Code Ann. §§ 17-30-10 et seq.	No	-
South Dakota	S.D. Codified Laws §§ 23A-35A-1 et seq.	No	-
Tennessee	Tenn. Code Ann. §§ 40-6-301 et seq.	Yes	63
Texas	Tex. Code Crim. Proc. Ann. art. 18.20	Yes	4
Utah	Utah Code Ann. §§ 77-23a-1 et seq.	No	-
Virgin Islands	V.I. Code Ann. tit. 5, §§ 4101 et seq.	No	-
Virginia	Va. Code Ann. §§ 19.2-61 et seq.	No	-
Washington	Wash. Rev. Code §§ 9.73.010 et seq.	No	-
West Virginia	W. Va. Code §§ 62-1D-1 et seq.	No	-
Wisconsin	Wis. Stat. §§ 968.27 et seq.	Yes	1
Wyoming	Wyo. Stat. Ann. §§ 7-3-701 et seq.	Yes	4

[1] Pursuant to provisions of the Omnibus Crime Control and Safe Streets Act of 1968, 18 U.S.C. § 2519.
[2] Includes only those jurisdictions that enacted legislation during or before calendar year 2014.

Page 1 of 1

Figure 24.1 Wiretap—jurisdictions with statutes authorizing the interception of wire, oral, or electronic communications effective—during the 12-month period ending December 31, 2014. (From http://www.uscourts.gov/statistics/table/wire-1/wiretap/2014/12/31, retrieved June 18, 2016.)

help the killer dispose of the body? Did someone help the killer get rid of the weapon with or without knowledge of the murder? Your target could be expected to speak with anyone fitting these descriptions under the proper circumstances.

Persons in Whom the Killer Has Confided or May Confide

Oftentimes, cold homicides are revived when a *source* close to the killer comes forward with information based upon his/her observations of the killer and/or statements made by the killer. Obviously, you would first consider employing the new source, if cooperative, to place recorded consensual/*pretext* calls to the killer—no wiretap needed. But consider if the source is not cooperative (e.g., an anonymous tipster who you have identified), or if you learn about the source's information from a third party (e.g., "My sister told me her ex-husband killed someone in a robbery, but she won't work with you because he's the father of her children"). It is not difficult to think of ways to manipulate even an uncooperative or unknowing source into eliciting incriminatory statements from the killer.

Would it not be possible to use someone like a sibling or spouse to unwittingly gain an incriminatory statement from your killer? With the right pressure, you could expect the source to call the killer and question him/her about the murder. The police may not need to manipulate the players in the gang or criminal enterprise scenario.

Remember, criminals are known to brag.

Building a Wiretap Affidavit

States derive the power to authorize wiretaps through the federal wiretap statute, so they follow similar requirements. Most statutes require that the affidavit (1) demonstrate that all other investigative techniques have been exhausted to the point that a wiretap is necessary in order to build a prosecutable case; (2) identify a *target subject*; (3) identify a *target telephone*; and (4) establish probable cause to believe that the target phone will be used by a subject to discuss a qualifying target offense. Check the applicable statute, but expect to meet these requirements.

Exhaustion of Other Law Enforcement Techniques and Necessity

All jurisdictions require, in some form and to some degree, that the affidavit contain an explanation regarding why a wiretap is needed. In other words, you must lay out what evidence you have, what investigative techniques you have tried, and why other techniques not yet attempted would not likely succeed. Explain why a wiretap is necessary to make the case or to lead the investigation toward a prosecutable case. Look no further than the other traditional techniques discussed in this text to get an idea of other techniques you must discount as sufficient to make a prosecutable case.

Although not complete, start with the following: undercover police officers, confidential informants, surveillance, search warrants, pen registers and phone tolls, grand jury subpoenas and immunity, trash searches, mail cover requests, closed-circuit television monitoring, consensual recordings/pretext calls, financial investigations, and if you have used prior wiretaps, why they did not meet the objectives of the investigation.

The Target Telephone

The affidavit must identify a *target telephone*. The phone number can come from any lawful source such as informants, a tip, subpoenaed records, or pretext calls. Use a search warrant or administrative subpoena to obtain subscriber information such as the provider telecommunications company, the person who owns the number, how long the line has been in service, and the billing address. If the person who owns or primarily uses the phone is not the suspect, explain how the subscriber is connected to the suspect. Depending on the jurisdiction, the target telephone need not be the killer's but could be that of someone who witnessed the crime, an accomplice, or someone with whom the killer is expected to speak.

Some jurisdiction may require, and I recommend, that you obtain call/toll records or *pen registers* for the phone beforehand. (Identifying the parties the target speaks with regularly will help you monitor and manipulate the parties during the intercept.) Most of this process is only getting easier with the spread of cellular phones and digital cable phone lines.

The Target Subject

The *target subject* or person you expect to use the phone to discuss the murder with should be named if known or otherwise described as best as possible. If you can identify the *target*, provide information such as residence, occupation, and criminal history. If not, describe the *target* by his/her relationship to the target phone and other parties to the murder. Describe how and why there is probable cause to believe that this person is linked to the murder. This will be the meat of the probable cause supporting the intercept.

Relationship between the Target, the Phone, and the Crime

The affidavit must include language explaining why you believe that the *target's* conversations will be captured on the *target telephone* and why you believe that at least one conversation will be related to the murder or cover-up. Consider the following questions. Has a source reported that he/she spoke to the killer about the murder over the telephone? Has a source reported that a third party spoke to the killer about the murder over the telephone? Can you demonstrate through records or witnesses that this is a telephone the *target* uses or calls frequently? Many of these questions will be answered through the investigation, but others will require the investigator's opinions about criminal behavior. Be sure to articulate the foundation for those opinions in the affidavit. In a cold homicide, you will need to explain why, after years, you expect the *target* to speak about the murder at all. If necessary, lay out your plans to *tickle the wire* and get the *target* talking, without revealing tactical details that could compromise future investigations.

Some jurisdictions or agencies, including the United States Department of Justice, require what is commonly referred to as a "dirty call"—meaning evidence of a specific call by the *target subject* on the target telephone about criminal activity. Check the statute and seek the advice of the prosecuting agency to determine if and to what extent you must meet this requirement.

Additional Approval and Procedural Requirements

As previously noted, wiretaps require approval from the top level of every agency involved. That could mean the Presiding Judge, Chief of Police, Sheriff, or Agency Head *and* the District Attorney, or Attorney General. Involve the prosecuting attorney's office as soon as you begin to consider seeking a wiretap. The prosecutor's office may have policies in place as to when and how they will seek a wiretap. Providing a draft of the affidavit to the appropriate judge ahead of time is recommended so that he/she will be knowledgeable about the wiretap before you seek his/her approval.

You must also make advanced contact with the telecommunications company to assure that the intercept is in place as soon as possible after the judge signs the orders.

Once the wiretap is in place, follow the recording and reporting requirements specific to your jurisdiction. These will include the *minimization* process (only monitoring and recording pertinent calls), the manner in which the intercepted calls are recorded (digital or tape) and how they are sealed, and the requirements for how to report the status of the intercept to the authorizing judge.

Tickling the Wire—Tips to Warm Up a Cold Case during a Wiretap

Because this is a cold case, you will most likely need to engage in proactive methods of investigation to provoke the *target* into making incriminatory statements over the telephone. The tactics are only limited by the law and your imagination. Sensitivity in your approach is the key. A blunt frontal attack on the *target* is more likely to lead to no statement rather than a confession. Find a "dupe." Approach people you know the *target* speaks to over the phone. Think of cokillers, accomplices, family members, and the sources who helped you create probable cause for the intercept. If it makes sense to discuss the murder with the *dupe*, do not necessarily mention the *target*—maybe describe the *target* to the extent that the *dupe* will know whom you are talking about. If you need to discuss the *target* with the *dupe*, do not necessarily mention the murder—maybe ask general questions about the *target* around the time of the murder. Get the *dupe* and the *target* talking about the investigation over the phone and continue to tickle.

Suggested Wiretap Procurement Procedure

Here is a basic chronology of how to approach a wiretap once your department thinks it has the need to seek one:

- Find the relevant statute in your jurisdiction to learn particular probable cause requirements and monitoring and reporting requirements.
- Determine which county or state has jurisdiction (typically where the hard line is located or, if a cellular phone, where the calls originate or where the phone is located).
- Contact the prosecuting authority.
- Find a wire room (you may need to work with the local office of the FBI or DEA).
- Find authorized officers/agents to monitor the wire.
- Determine the strategy and resources needed to monitor and *tickle the wire.*
- Subpoena phone record and toll information (if necessary or wanted).
- Determine which judge can sign and authorize the intercept.
- Draft the affidavit and submit to the prosecuting authority.
- Contact the telecommunications company.
- Provide a draft of the affidavit and sample orders to the judge.
- Draft instructions and schedules for wire monitors.
- Finalize the affidavit and orders and submit them to the judge.
- Once signed, deliver or fax the orders to the telecommunications company.

Acknowledgments

I wish to extend my deepest gratitude and appreciation to Robert Hickey for his authorship and contribution of this chapter. Hickey has been a Deputy District Attorney in San Diego County, California, for almost 20 years and spent 4 years as the assistant chief of the gang prosecution unit. Hickey graduated from the University of San Diego School of Law in 1994 and also practiced law at a large international law firm for a year and a half. Hickey was the first San Diego prosecutor to use state wiretaps in cold case homicides and gang violence investigations and has overseen hundreds of wiretaps. Hickey has also worked with investigators to bring four cold case homicides to prosecution and conviction, is a recipient of the prestigious FBI Director's Award, and was the 2001 Prosecutor of the Year.

Bloodstain Pattern Analysis in Homicide Cold Case Investigations

25

TOM BEVEL

Contents

Introduction

The chronology of a homicide that goes unsolved for several years may be classified as still active, but often goes from a proactive investigation to a reactive investigation. This means that work is completed on the case only when new leads come in. The unsolved case is shoved back in priorities to allow more investigative time for recent cases with greater solvability factors. At some point, the unsolved case is sent to a cold case unit if the agency has one.

Investigating homicide cold cases usually requires looking at three different areas. The first is relationship oriented. People involved in the case may now be willing to talk to the investigators due to divorce, deaths, or other changed relationships. The second area is new technology oriented, where we need only identify what new forensic techniques or tools are available today that were not available at the time of the crime; DNA is the most common new forensic discipline used in cold case investigations. The third area is to ensure that all available forensic disciplines were originally used. For some crimes, we simply need to use all of the forensic tools that were in place at the time, but, for whatever reason, were never applied in the case in question. One forensic tool that has often been overlooked in past cases is bloodstain pattern analysis (BPA). Crimes of violence frequently produce bloodstains which, when properly studied, will aid in reconstructing the occurrences that took place to produce the patterns found at the scene, on victims or suspects, and on their clothing. This discipline adds another investigative tool for determining what happened, how it occurred, who was or was not involved, number of blows struck, which hand was used to deliver the blows in a beating and the position of the victim and suspect during the attack and subsequent movement (Bevel, 1992). One of the best properties of blood spatters is that they will always appear in a manner that is consistent with the events that produced them. Even in staged crime scenes where blood is used to set up the scene, the bloodstains will look consistent with the staging event that produced them.

While BPA has a long history of use in violent crime investigations, the value of this discipline is still today often overlooked in many investigations. Thus, it is not too surprising that BPA may not have been applied to many older case investigations.

A Brief History of Bloodstain Pattern Analysis

Studies and research in BPA, as a forensic discipline, are documented in several European countries in the late 1800s. As far back as 1220–1235, Germanic law in the *Sachsenspiegel* dealt with the raising of the "hue and cry" and the necessity of proving one's innocence when a criminal was caught in the act or caught with blood on his or her hands (Bevel and Gardner, 2002). Today, we would all recognize the importance of identifying that the substance on the person's hands is blood, whether it is animal or human and whether it is the victim's blood. From its early day application of little in-depth analysis, the BPA discipline has grown dramatically to where today it can reveal a vast amount of information about what happened during and after the crime.

An early application of BPA in police investigations was documented in 1875 in Denver, Colorado. Sheriff David J. Cook used bloodstain interpretation to reconstruct the violent killing of four Italian musicians on October 21, 1875. When the suspects were caught several days later, they were found to still have dried blood stains on their undershirts. The suspects confessed to the crime and confirmed Sheriff Cook's theory of the murders. Due to the confessions, the reconstruction, based partly on BPA, did not get used at trial (Adair, 1999).

One of the early judicial uses of BPA in America was in the case of *State of California v. Jack Ryan* in 1925. Dr. Ernst A. Victors and Edward Oscar Heinrich (sometimes called the Wizard of Berkeley or the American Sherlock Holmes) combined forces and used BPA to identify blood spatter locations and direction of travel on the coat of Jack Ryan, who was accused of killing Henry Sweet and Carmen Wagner. This case is discussed in the Introduction.

Another early and renowned court case in which BPA was admitted in American courts was the *State of Ohio v. Samuel Sheppard* in 1955. This was in the form of an affidavit by Dr. Paul Kirk explaining his analysis of the crime scene, which included BPA. Due to Dr. Kirk's analysis having been recorded in an affidavit, his reasoning and logic are explained in detail and is quite fascinating reading for anyone interested in BPA or crime scene reconstruction. Dr. Kirk's affidavit can be obtained from many different sources, including the internet.

Methodology of BPA in Homicide Cold Cases

Unique to cold case investigations is that the investigator no longer has the ability to personally view the crime scene, as it has long ago been processed and released. The cold case investigator has to depend on what others have done long before the analyst became involved in the case. The quality of the crime scene documentation, collection, and preservation of physical evidence dictates the quality and extent to which the BPA expert can go in their analysis and opinions. Some of the items needed for an analysis include the following:

- Investigative reports by responding officers
- Investigative reports by detectives
- CSI reports on scene processing and evidence collection
- Witness or accused statements, interviews, or depositions

- Autopsy protocol
- Photographs of the crime scene, autopsy, and physical evidence
- Lab reports from serology, DNA, firearms, fingerprints, toxicology, etc.
- Crime scene diagrams
- Reports by EMTs
- All physical evidence that is still available

When the case is assigned to a cold case unit or investigator, the assigned investigator has to read the complete case file to understand what has been done, needs to be done, or redone. In this process, the investigator will evaluate the reports, photographs, and evidence to understand all the minute details of the events that encompass the crime and original investigation. In this process, the investigator continually attempts to understand what events or actions by the attacker and to the victim took place during and immediately after the time of the crime. The investigator will compare the physical evidence analysis against statements given by witnesses or the accused. This is often referred to as a *statement analysis.* This involves comparing the statements against the physical evidence, looking for areas that can be supported by the physical evidence or refuted by it.

The same process followed by the case investigator applies equally to the BPA expert. Bloodstain pattern analysis should always be viewed in a holistic approach and never in a vacuum all by itself. This means that the opinions coming from the bloodstain analysis should be compared against all the other information and evidence. If the BPA opinions are supported and corroborated by other case information and evidence outside of BPA, then it makes the foundation for the BPA opinions even stronger. If the other information or physical evidence is in disagreement with the BPA analysis, then this is a "red flag" that should cause analysts to reanalyze their opinions and attempt to reconcile why there is disagreement. This practice is similar to the "audit" used in crime scene analysis and reconstruction (Adair, 1999).

The *investigative reports* by responding officers and detectives will give an overview of the entire case and investigation. These reports will furnish needed information about the victim, who called the crime into dispatch, when and where the victim was found, and any additional witness information. This will help acquaint the analyst with the crime, crime scene, its layout and the victim's position as found before examination and transport.

The *CSI reports* on scene processing and evidence collection give an understanding of the scene layout, the size and measurements between items of evidence, and the location in the scene where each item was found. From this information, the analyst is able to identify evidence relationships and the interpretive value between items of related evidence.

The *witness or suspect statements*, interviews, or depositions are used after the bloodstain patterns are identified and analyzed. The statements are tested against the bloodstain patterns and other physical evidence to identify consistencies or inconsistencies in the statements.

The *autopsy protocol* will assist in identifying the type and location of wounds. This will assist in supporting or refuting opinions related to the type of blood staining. For example, if some blood patterns appear to be from an arterial spurt, there should be a wound to the victim's body that will produce such a gush of blood volume. Absent a breached artery on the victim, you may need to look at other possibilities. If blood spatter is believed to be from expectorate, then blood should be found in the mouth or nose of the victim. Identifying types of wounding mechanism such as knives, firearms, or blunt force instrument should be compared against the expected type of blood spatter or castoff stains from each type of weapon and subsequent wound. The autopsy protocol will also address the clothing worn by the victim and what effect they may have on blood patterns or the possible blocking of blood patterns.

Next to bloodstained evidence such as a weapon or suspect clothing that is still in custody, photographs of the crime scene, autopsy, and physical evidence are the most important documentation for the bloodstain pattern analyst. Once all the photographs are in hand, they should be divided into groups. The divisions might include: (1) outside and approach to the scene, (2) the victim at the scene, (3) the victim at autopsy, (4) the room or area where the victim was found, (5) evidence, (6) suspects, and (7) any other division that is logical. Once the photographs are in logical groups, each one should be sequentially numbered. During the analysis, as important points are shown in the photographs, your notes should also include the number of the photograph so that it can easily be retrieved when needed at a later time.

Another important aspect, the first provided by *in situ* photographs, is the ability to see how the bloodstains on the victim and his or her clothes appeared before the victim was disturbed by the various investigators and transportation to the hospital or morgue. Because we can never collect evidence without losing a portion of its meaning, photographs help to separate "investigative transfer," which is accidentally altered evidence during the collection or processing of the scene and body movement versus actual evidence from the crime itself. Predictably, with movement the still wet blood will create additional bloodstained areas and may disturb or alter existing stains as well as add additional stains. It is important for the analyst to distinguish between stains associated with the crime and those that are created by processing, movement and transportation by the investigators. Equally important is the ability to recognize when this distinction can not be made. In this instance little to no value can be placed on such stains in forming your opinions.

The autopsy photographs will assist in identifying the type, number and location of bleeding wounds. This information will be correlated to bloodstain patterns found at the scene and items of evidence from the scene.

Photographs of victim, his or her clothing and the surrounding area where the victim was found are very important in identifying what type of blood spatter is found or is expected to be present. This will later be contrasted against any blood spatter found on other evidence such as the weapon, suspect, or suspect's clothing. If there is impact spatter from a blunt trauma beating on the suspect's clothing then there should be consistent blood spatter on and around the victim.

The *lab reports* from serology, DNA, firearms, fingerprints, toxicology, etc., will identify that the suspected blood is or is not in fact blood and to whom it belongs. Firearms will identify which bullets were fired from which weapons and fingerprints will identify who created the latent prints found at the scene or on the evidence collected and if any of the prints were made in blood. Also important is whether there are any identifiable prints or DNA that have not been identified as belonging to anyone.

The *crime scene diagrams* will be an invaluable aid in locating where within the scene items of evidence were located as well as an understanding of the physical confines of the scene. Scene photographs tend to always make the area photographed look larger than it really is. Comparing the photographs to the crime scene diagrams will help to understand the spatial relationships as well as place what area within the scene certain photographs are taken of and from what angle and direction.

The *reports by the EMTs* will assist in identifying how the EMTs entered the scene, what they touched, how they first observed the victim, and how they moved the victim. Of critical importance is the question of blood in the mouth or nose of the victim upon the EMTs first arrival. Photographs of the victim's mouth or nose may show blood that came after movement of the body during lifesaving attempts or during the medical examiner's or investigator's examination of the body. It is important to also question the first responders, police, firefighters or EMTs as to what they noted about blood in the mouth or nose of the victim before the body was moved.

Examine all physical evidence that is still available. While you want to consider what others in the original investigation found, documented, and reported on the physical evidence, you also need to personally examine the physical evidence. This is to verify that what others reported is still there and to ensure that evidence important to BPA was not omitted due to a lack of BPA knowledge or was simply missed. The more items you can personally examine versus taking someone else's description of what is there, the better. In a cold case, visiting the crime scene may not be an option that is still available. If the scene can still be visited, even if it has long ago been released by law enforcement, make every effort to view the physical site of the crime. At the very least, this will give the investigator an understanding and feel for the spatial relationships within the scene. On multiple occasions, I have visited an old crime scene and was able to find bloodstain patterns reported by the first investigators *still in place*. On several cases, I was able to find blood patterns not reported or that were missed by the first investigators. Some of these blood patterns were crucial in forming a foundation as to what could be opined about the events during the crime.

Identifying Expectorate Blood Spatter

As blood is shed, stains will be found in areas consistent with what has actually occurred to produce the stains. The geometry and direction of travel of these stains will also be consistent with the event that produced them. This allows BPA to assist in understanding the blood-producing events and ultimately in identifying what is consistent or inconsistent in the statements that are considered to have caused the spatter. If the statement by the accused person is that he or she received blood on his or her clothing from moving and performing CPR on the victim, then the investigator will go through a check list to support or refute this statement or identify that insufficient information does not allow an opinion to be formed. If the victim is breathing, he or she may be expelling blood out of the mouth or nose, which will break up the blood and project it on surrounding areas. This usually occurs when the victim is trying to clear blood from the air passages to allow easier breathing. First, check any physical evidence that would indicate that the victim had evidence of blood in the air passage:

1. Check with the first responders to the scene; did they observe blood in the mouth or nose of the victim before the victim was moved?
2. Next check the autopsy report. Is there evidence that blood was aspirated? (Aspirated refers to breathing in as opposed to expectorate, which is breathing out.) Evidence that there was blood aspiration is consistent with breathing by the victim after wounding.
3. Study the photographs of the victim to determine if you are able to see blood in or surrounding the mouth or nose.
4. Check on the clothing of the accused and the victim to see if they were collected in the original investigation.
5. If this clothing is still available, analyze it for spatter the correct size and location consistent with expectorate blood coughed out while trying to clear the victim's airway or forced out from CPR. Look for lighter-in-color spatter due to the blood's being mixed with saliva or mucus. Look for bubble rings where air was mixed with blood projected from the mouth or nose producing bubbles that then burst, leaving bubble rings in the blood spatter. Look for an elevated level of amylase, a digestive enzyme that occurs at a much reduced level in blood than in saliva.

If the first responders report no blood in the mouth or nose, and the autopsy indicates there was no blood aspiration and these are consistent with the photographs of the victim at the scene, then expectorate blood can be eliminated as a mechanism that produced any spatter that may be on the clothing in question. Having eliminated expectorate blood as the mechanism directs the analyst to some other event producing the spatter found on the clothing of the accused. The elimination of expectorate may refute the statement of the accused as to how the blood spatter got on his or her clothing. Obviously, if the physical evidence supports and is consistent with expectorate blood produced from CPR or the victim coughing up blood onto the clothing of the accused, this supports the witness statement and is equally helpful information that may in fact assist in eliminating this person as a possible suspect. There will also be cases in which the analyst is not able to eliminate either possibility of expectorate spatter or spatter from the impacts consistent with the attack. This is exactly how it should be reported, that both are equally possible.

Chemical Enhancements

The application of any chemical enhancements should always be one of the last steps to be taken on the analysis of physical evidence. The addition of any fluid dilutes any substances such as blood that may be present on the area being processed. Before any chemical application, ensure that all other processing has been completed and that documentation of the evidence, such as close-up photographs with proper scales of reference, has been completed.

If the case indicates that no blood was found at the scene and the possibility exists that a cleanup took place before the original investigators arrived, then the use of blood chemical enhancements may be needed. Chemicals such as Luminol, Fluorescein, Blue Star™; TMB (tetramethyl-benzidine); LMG (Leucomalachite Green); LCV (Liquid Crystal Violet); or Amido black work very well with old and diluted blood even many years later. These or other chemical enhancements can be applied to suspected scenes, clothing, or other items of evidence in search for the presence of blood that will not be visible to the unaided eye. Any of the chemical enhancements are only presumptive for blood, and additional confirmatory tests will be needed. With the ever increasing sensitivity of confirmatory tests, even minute amounts of blood may be identified as blood, human or animal, and, if human, whose blood it is. Establishing that the scene or other evidence was cleaned and that it was the victim's blood that was found, are great clues in directing the new investigation, as someone not living at the location of the murder would have little to gain in cleaning the scene.

The application of any chemical enhancement, when looking for small traces of blood, should be done by a trained analyst who is aware of the many false positives and the safety precautions that should be taken when using such chemicals. A trained analyst will also be able to take the timed photographic exposures required to properly document their findings and to take the most promising samples for confirmatory tests. Further discussion of this topic can be found in Chapter 26.

A Methodology for Examining Clothing and Other Physical Evidence

The first step in looking for blood spatter on clothing or other evidence is viewing the article with a good light source and some type of magnification. Then, using the knowledge of the events that took place and the type of bleeding wounds that were present, predict what type of spatter would result. This often requires the analyst to mentally reenact events and actions to identify where blood spatter would go onto the clothing. In some cases, this may also require a physical reenactment to properly visualize relationships between body movement, clothing, and other issues. Look in the expected locations for the type of blood staining that would result from movement and actions involved in the crime. In one case where this methodology was employed, my mental reenactment directed me to look inside the cuff of a white dress shirt. Directional spatter was found high up inside the cuff. While others had examined the shirt and found spatter and directional stains on the outside of the shirt cuff, they were too few in number, and thus the opinion was inconclusive about what occurred to produce them. However, there was enough spatter when both the inside and outside of the cuff were viewed together. Thus, an opinion could be given as to the events that would be consistent in producing them. In any mental or physical reenactment, be sure to consider what witnesses said they did, such as rendering CPR. Also consider other known actions that occurred during the crime such as the attack on the victim. Both possibilities should be given equal consideration in searching for the predicted type and location of possible blood staining. If no bloodstains are found, remember the axiom written by Dr. Carl Sagan that states, "Absence of evidence is not evidence of absence" (Sagan, 1977). The original quote was not directed toward forensic science, but its meaning works well for science and the discipline of BPA. In forensic science as it relates to BPA, if there are no bloodstains, all you can say is that there is an absence of bloodstains, and be very careful about taking your opinion further. You can always say much more about the possibilities when there are bloodstains present than when none are found.

Dark-colored clothing poses quite a challenge to find and document small to mist-sized spatter. After the visual exam with good lighting and magnification, examine the clothing with a microscope from 10× to 60× magnification. Two additional techniques to consider are the night vision setting on a video camera and infrared photography. Many of the newer video cameras can view objects and film them in near-zero light levels. When blood spatters are present on dark clothing the video camera's night vision tends to create a visible contrast between the dark clothing and the dark spatter. This will direct you to the suspected spatter locations and allows testing with a presumptive and further lab testing if the presumptive is positive. Another photographic method is to use infrared (IR) film. This method also gives a contrast between the dark clothing and the blood spatter and documents what is found. Presumptive and further lab testing, if the presumptive is positive, is still required.

Any chemical enhancement on clothing should always be the last resort. The application of any chemical further dilutes any blood that may be present and more dilution makes confirmation tests more difficult or impossible.

Applying the Scientific Method to Your Analysis

Many bloodstain patterns have more than one mechanism or event that is capable of creating the patterns. An example is expectorated spatter versus backspatter from a gunshot. Both are capable of producing mist-sized spatter. As a result, the analyst often has to consider different, viable mechanisms that might have created the pattern in question. The best methodology to use, in identifying which event is the best explanation to account for the pattern, is the scientific method. An example of the steps taken in this process is shown in Figure 25.1.

If after applying the scientific method to multiple viable possibilities and finding that none of the possibilities can be eliminated, the answer is that each mechanism is possible. However, the goal is to identify which of the possible mechanisms is the best explanation. This can only be done by proving each of the hypotheses wrong. When you are unable to prove one hypothesis wrong then this hypothesis becomes the best explanation. The best explanation has to be supported with and by the facts in the case.

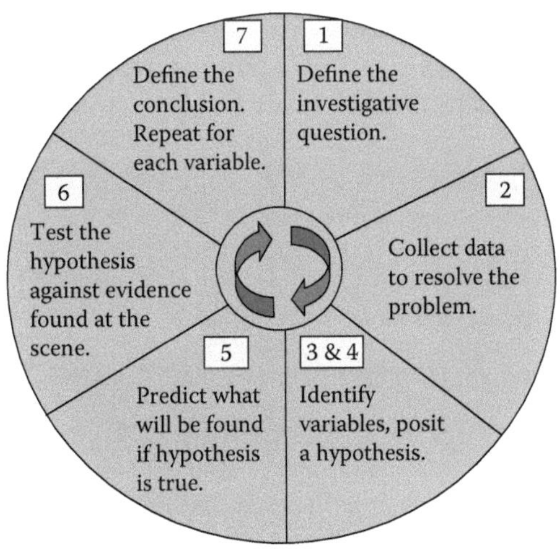

Figure 25.1 The scientific method is shown in a clockwise-moving circle process. This method encourages the analyst to adequately consider all viable actions that could explain the question being analyzed. This method is referred to as a self-correcting circle process that leads to the best explanation, and often leads to additional questions.

Case Analysis Examples

Case 1

A case example of applying the scientific process has multiple mist-sized bloodstains and blood, human tissue, bone, or hair on the lower center of a suspect's T-shirt. The subject wearing the shirt is the husband of the adult female victim and father to the two juvenile victims. When the husband drove up to his garage and opened the garage overhead door he observed his wife supine on the garage floor beside the open passenger door of their two-door older Ford Bronco. After checking his wife and determining that she was dead from a gunshot to her head, the subject looked into the rear of the vehicle. His daughter was sitting in the right rear passenger's seat; seatbelted in and slumped over to her left. The daughter also appeared to be dead from a gunshot wound to the head. The subject next looked to his son, who was slumped part way over the left rear passenger's seat and shot one time in the upper left side. Believing his son might be alive; the subject lifted him out of the vehicle, laid him on the ground next to the boy's mother and performed CPR on him. The subject then called police.

One of the investigative questions in this case is: How did the spatter and bone fragment get on the front of the subject's T-shirt (Figures 25.2 and 25.3)? Viable ways the spatter and bone fragment could have gotten on the shirt include:

1. Back spatter from gunshot to victim
2. Expectorate from doing CPR to victim
3. A hand slap into blood
4. Rehydrating spatter by contact with the wet T-shirt and then transferring to shirt

Possibilities number one and two were offered by the prosecution, and possibilities three and four were offered by the defense. Each of the identified possibilities are formed into a hypothesis and tested, trying to prove each false as shown below.

Hypothesis (H)-1 *The spatter is from backspatter that occurred when the juvenile female was shot.*
I would predict that:

- There will be spatter consistent in size and location surrounding the victim of the gunshot.
- The spatter and bone on the shirt will be identified to this victim.

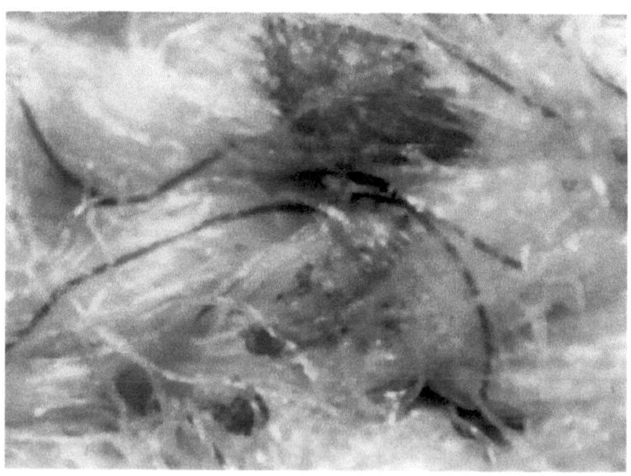

Figure 25.2 This close-up photograph shows one of the blood spatters on the front of the husband's T-shirt.

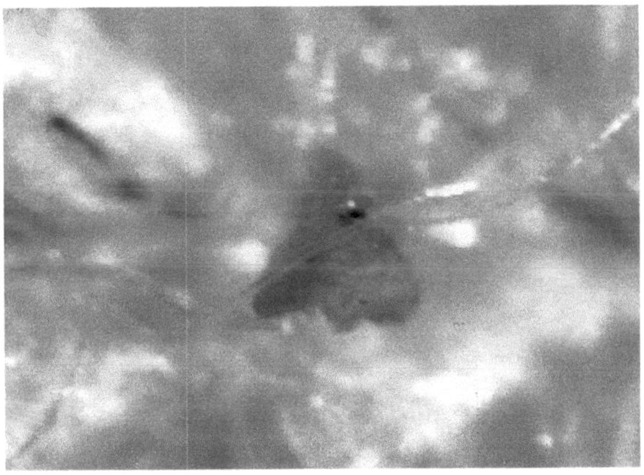

Figure 25.3 Shows the human tissue on the front of the husband's T-shirt.

- This area of the T-shirt would be exposed and in proximity at the time of the shooting.
- The spatter will be driven into the weave of the T-shirt.
- The spatter will not be diluted from rehydrating.

All of the above predictions are compared against the physical evidence and lab reports and are consistent with the spatter in question. The juvenile female in the right rear of the vehicle has mist-sized spatter consistent with back spatter from a gunshot above her on the roll bar and headliner and to her right on the window glass and hard plastic side molding. The entire mist-sized spatter pattern area is consistent with her head gunshot while she is sitting in the right rear seat. The mist-sized spatter on the T-shirt of the accused is identified through DNA to belong to the juvenile female. The spatter on the T-shirt is driven into the weave consistent with projected back spatter. *H-1 is not proved false.*

H-2 *The spatter is from performing CPR on the juvenile male victim.* I would predict that:

- The spatter will be identified to the juvenile male victim as the accused stated he did CPR on him.
- There is evidence on and around the juvenile victim consistent with the size of the misting stains on the T-shirt.
- This victim will have a wound to bone capable of creating the bone fragment found on the T-shirt.

In testing the predictions, the blood spatter and bone were identified through DNA as coming from the female and not the male victim. *H-2 is proved false.*

H-3 *The spatter is from a hand slap into blood.* I would predict that:

- There will be evidence that the accused got the juvenile female's blood on his hand.
- The blood-covered hand was held in an orientation and location capable of producing a vertical, linear, spatter pattern onto the front lower center of the T-shirt.

In testing the predictions against the physical evidence at the scene and the statements, the accused stated that he did not touch the female victim. He further stated that he did not enter into the rear seat area where this victim was located.

A hand orientated to produce a similar linear pattern from a hand slap in front of the tee shirt while wearing the shirt is very difficult to position. Such a position would require an effort to accomplish and thus would be a purposeful act and highly improbable in this case. The subject did not give a statement about blood on his hand or any statement about a hand slap. *H-3 was proved false.*

H-4 *The spatter is from the wet T-shirt contacting and rehydrating spatter and transferring the rehydrated spatter onto the tee shirt.* I would predict that:

- There will be evidence that spatter at the scene from a gunshot was rehydrated and transferred.
- There is a location in the vehicle and around the juvenile female victim that would allow the T-shirt to come into contact with the spatter in a straight in and straight out movement with little to no lateral movement.
- Recreating like spatter and transfer will be possible by experimentation under like conditions.
- The accused will state that he was in the area around the juvenile female victim.
- The blood transfer onto the wet T-shirt will produce diluted stains and there will be lateral movement observed.

Experiments under like conditions were not able to create similar spatter by re-hydrating spatter and then transferring them to a wet tee shirt. The accused stated that he did not enter into the area where the juvenile victim was located. In experiments, the spatter that was rehydrated and then transferred to the wet T-shirt was visibly diluted and showed lateral movement. *H-4 was proved false.*

Hypothesis H-1 is the best explanation for the mist-sized spatter to the front lower center T-shirt of the accused. The spatter is consistent with backspatter from a gunshot into the juvenile female's head and consistent with spatter found around her in the vehicle. The bone fragment is also consistent with the gunshot to the victim's head when the T-shirt was present at the time of the shooting.

Case 2

A husband returning from work found his wife dead on the master bathroom floor. Upon rolling her from her right side to her back, her head hit into a pool of blood on the floor, creating spatter. The husband then jumped over the victim to the floor on her right side. From her right side the husband performed CPR on

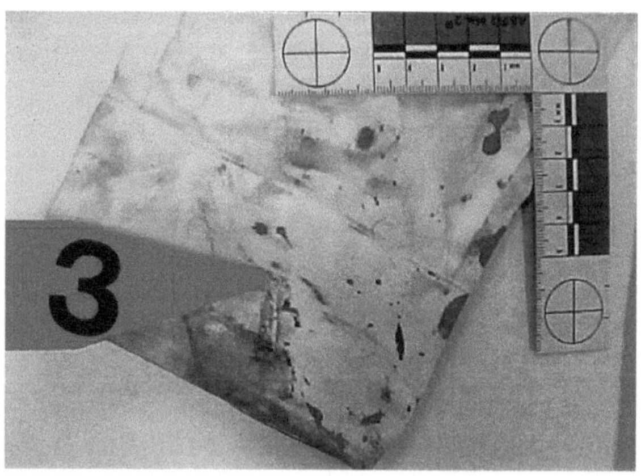

Figure 25.4 Bloodstains on the outside cuff of the suspect's dress shirt.

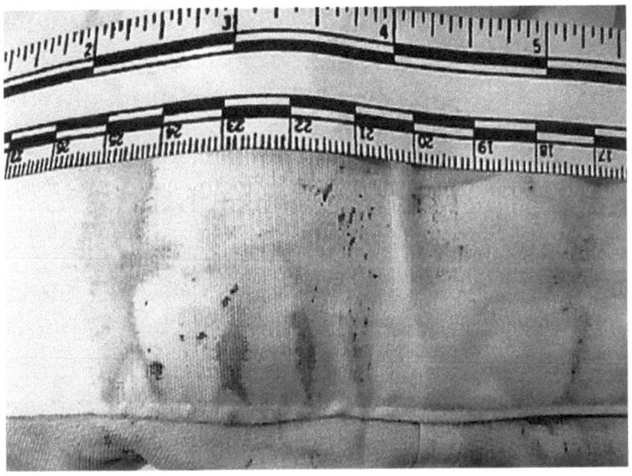

Figure 25.5 The inside of the dress shirt cuff. Considering both the inside and outside of the cuff in concert, there are enough spatters to form an opinion as to what actions occurred to produce these stains.

his wife. He held his wife's head and it slipped out of his hand and hit into a pool of blood on the floor, producing a second spatter event. The husband's right shirt sleeve cuff had soaked blood, directional spatter, and transfers on the outside of the cuff (Figures 25.4 and 25.5). There were not enough stains to allow an opinion as to what produced them.

In applying the scientific method, mental and physical reenactments, I predicted what type of bloodstains would be produced in doing CPR and predicted where they would be found. Upon examining the shirt, no such spatters were found. In also mentally and physically reenacting how the victim's wounds were created, I predicted what type of spatter would be created and where it would be found. The multiple blunt trauma blows to the victim's head would produce spatter and directional spatter to the outside of the long sleeve cuff and possibly to the inside of the cuff. The outside did contain such spatter, but not enough to form an opinion. In examining the inside of the same cuff, additional directional spatter was found some distance up into the cuff. With the spatter on both the outside and the inside of the cuff, taken in concert, there was enough to offer an opinion. Possible ways the spatter could have been created on both the outside and the inside of the right cuff included: (1) CPR, (2) head hitting into pool of blood on floor, and (3) impact blows to the victim's head. In applying the scientific method to consider the possible ways this spatter could be created, three hypotheses were formed:

H-1 *Performing CPR created spatter onto both outside and inside of the right cuff.* I would predict that:

- The victim's mouth and nose will have blood in them. There will be consistent spatter around the victim's mouth and upper torso consistent with spatter on the shirt cuff.
- The shirt cuff and forearm will be held in an alignment allowing spatter to get onto the inside and outside of the shirt cuff.
- I would look for bubble rings and spatter that is lighter in color as it is mixed with saliva.

H-1 is tested against the above predictions and is proved false as there is not consistent spatter around the victim's mouth or upper torso. There is neither blood in her mouth and no bubble rings nor lighter in color spatter. A consistent alignment with the cuff and forearm is not impossible, but it is improbable. *H-1 is proved false.*

H-2 *The victim's head impacting into the blood pool on the floor created spatter onto both the outside and inside of the right shirt cuff.* I would predict that spatter created from the victim's head hitting into a blood pool on the floor will require the cuff and forearm to align parallel with the floor and in front of the impact. H-2 is tested against the above predictions and is proved false as the alignment from rolling her onto her back or from dropping her head into a pool of blood will not allow the correct alignment of the cuff and forearm. *H-2 is proved false.*

H-3 *Impacts to the victim's skull created spatter onto the inside and outside of the shirt's right cuff.* I would predict that the cuff and forearm would be in a correct alignment to get directional spatter onto both the inside and outside of the right cuff. H-3 is tested against the above predictions and is not proved false. As the other possibilities, H-1 and H-2, were eliminated or highly improbable, then the best explanation that remains is H-3, spatter created at the time the victim was struck with a blunt instrument to her head.

H-3 is tested against the above predictions and is *not* proved false.

As the other possibilities, H-1 and H-2, were eliminated or highly improbable, then the best explanation that remains is H-3, spatter created at the time the victim was struck with a blunt instrument to her head.

Case 3

In another case, for seven years the husband was ruled a hero for shooting an intruder who was attacking his wife with a hammer. According to the husband, after hearing a strange noise he retrieved a .45 caliber handgun from his bedroom and ran down a hallway toward the dining area. He saw his wife in a fetal position on the floor with the intruder behind her, beating her head with a hammer. The husband stated that the intruder was facing toward the husband as the husband was running down the hallway. The husband shot the intruder in the head and the man fell backwards onto the carpet, landing supine on the floor. The husband continued running up to the man, straddled him, and shot him in the head at close range as the man lay on the carpeted floor. A study of the photographs indicated two areas with blood evidence that caused concern. The first contained both spatter and cast-off bloodstains on the wall beside the female victim's right shoulder and directional cast-off on the ceiling traveling toward the wall with the spatter on it (see Figures 25.6 and 25.7).

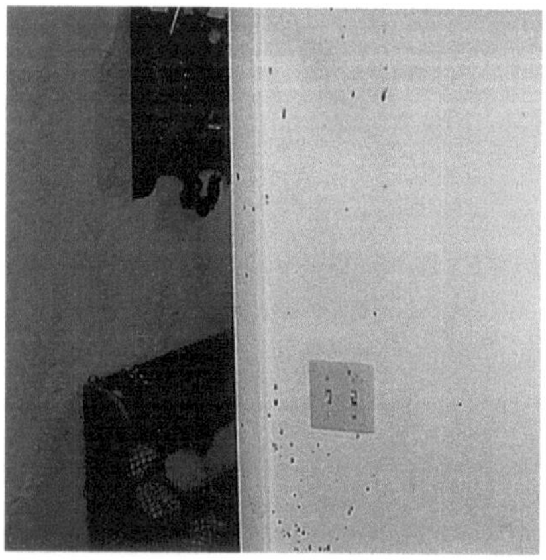

Figure 25.6 The wall above, below, and around the light switch has both spatter and cast-off bloodstains. The likely position to create consistent stains is facing the wall at a 90-degree angle; however, this position would not allow the correct bullet trajectory into the intruder's head. The position described by the husband would rotate the intruder 45 degrees, placing the intruder's right shoulder toward the wall with the spatter. This position would allow a correct bullet trajectory, but would not allow the correct position to create the spatter and cast-off stains.

Figure 25.7 There are two separate blood pools in the carpet. According to the husband's statement, there should only be one. Having two separate blood pools indicates that the intruder's body was in one area long enough to form a pool, then in a separate area also long enough to form a blood pool. The distance between the two pools is consistent with rolling the person over from front to back.

In considering where the female's body was found and where her blood pool on the carpet was located, in conjunction with the husband's statement of the intruder facing toward the husband as the husband ran down the hallway, you are able to predict how the bloodstains should appear. The cast-off blood and impact spatter should be found extending along the wall and not extended from the floor to the ceiling. The spatter and cast-off blood were not consistent with the position described by the husband. It was consistent with the intruder facing toward the wall and not facing down the hallway. But, if the intruder is facing the wall, the bullet trajectory into the intruder's head becomes inconsistent. The second area of concern was two different blood pools from the intruder as his body lay on the carpeted floor as shown in Figure 25.7.

The husband stated that, after the first shot, the man fell over backward onto the carpet and onto his back. The husband continued running up to the intruder and shot him again in the head at close range. The husband stated he did not move the intruder. The first responders stated that they only moved the intruder from the carpet up to a gurney for transport out of the scene. They were sure they did not move or roll the intruder over to create a second pool of blood. A study of the photographs of the intruder at the scene indicated that the passive blood flows and blood transfer on his forehead were consistent with his being rolled from face-down onto his back. This would explain how two different blood pools were created. Again, this was not consistent with the actions stated by the husband.

In the above case, the clothing of all three of the involved people was still available for analysis. DNA examinations that had not been conducted in the original investigation were completed for the second investigation. This revealed that the type, location, and direction of the blood spatter on each of the participants' clothing was consistent with the husband killing his wife with the hammer and in shooting the reported intruder. The intruder had been lured to the scene by the husband in a premeditated plan to get rid of his wife and to put the blame on the reported intruder. A lot of additional information was used in the successful prosecution of the husband at trial. The BPA evidence was used in concert with the additional information to assist in explaining what events took place during the commission of the two murders.

Summary

Bloodstain pattern analysis is one of the forensic disciplines that should be considered in the reinvestigation of any homicide cold case. As the above case examples demonstrate, BPA can greatly assist in identifying what events took place during the commission of a crime as well as provide the best explanation as to how questioned bloodspatter was produced onto items of evidence such as the suspect's clothing. Of equal importance is the verification of the statements being consistent with the physical evidence and bloodstain pattern analysis. It is just as beneficial for the investigation to verify statements as true as it is to identify false statements, as both will assist in directing the investigation.

Acknowledgments

I wish to recognize and thank Captain Tom Bevel for his valuable contribution to this book with this chapter.

Captain Bevel (Ret.), served 27 years with the Oklahoma City, Oklahoma Police Department. He is the coauthor of the text book *Bloodstain Pattern Analysis with an Introduction to Crime Scene Reconstruction*, now in its second edition. Captain Bevel has been a consultant in questioned death cases in 46 U.S. States and nine foreign countries. He is a Distinguished Member of both the International Association of Bloodstain Pattern Analyst and The Association for Crime Scene Reconstruction. He has been a case consultant for the U.S. Inspector General, U.S. Justice Department, Federal Bureau of Investigation and several U.S. Attorney General Offices. Captain Bevel is a graduate of the Scenes of Crime Officers Course, Metropolitan Police Academy, Hendon, England and the Medical Legal course at London Medical College. Cases he has consulted on have been presented on New Detectives, Medical Detectives, 20/20, Biography, 60 Minutes, 48 Hours, and Court TV.

Suggested Readings and Bibliography

Bevel, T., A Basic Overview of Bloodstain Pattern Analysis, Southern Police Institute, University of Louisville, Homicide Investigation Handout, 1992.

Bevel, T. and Gardner, R.M., *Bloodstain Pattern Analysis—With an Introduction to Crime Scene Reconstruction*, 2nd ed., CRC Press, Boca Raton, FL, 2002, p. 6, 7.

Adair, T., Recognition of Bloodstain Evidence in Historical Denver, Colorado, *International Association of Bloodstain Pattern Analysts NEWS*. December 1999, Volume 15, Number 3.

Sagan, C., *Dragons of Eden*, Ballantine Press, New York, 1977, p. 7.

Blood Enhancement

26

ROD ENGLERT

Contents

Introduction

Luminol is a presumptive test for the presence of blood. Luminol does not identify the source of the blood; rather, it suggests that a suspect pattern or stain may have originated with blood-based compounds. While luminol is a law enforcement tool often utilized during the investigation of fresh homicides, it is a very useful instrument in cold case homicide investigations. Interestingly enough, while some law enforcement agencies have used this tool extensively, others have not heard of it. This chapter presents the practical use and value of luminol in cold case investigations. Also illustrated is amido black, a general protein stain that reacts with proteins found in blood yet is not specific just for blood.

Composition and Background

The chemical name of luminol is 3-aminophthalhydrazide. It is a very sensitive chemical compound. Luminol can detect, and thus illuminate, one part blood in one million. This is analogized to 1 drop of blood in 999,999 drops of water. A luminol test is predicated on the fact that certain hemoglobin derivatives significantly enhance the chemical luminescence exhibited by luminol when it oxidizes in an alkaline solution. As a compound, the effective use of luminol is dependent upon the proper mixture of the compounds and appropriate application. Luminol is not a confirmatory test for blood. When applied to a surface of containing possible blood, it gives off a blue–green luminescence. The presence of this luminescence only presumes that the suspect material providing luminescence may be blood. Once a suspected pattern is revealed, further confirmatory testing is required. The spraying of luminol does not impede further confirmatory testing or DNA typing.

Luminol was reportedly first synthesized in Germany in 1902 and underwent further refinement and investigation in the succeeding decades. It was not until the late 1920s, however, that the compound was named luminol, producer of light. During the late 1930s, applications of luminol indicated the presence of blood in water, clean and soapy, and sewage. The presence of blood was also detected from application of a spray mixture on paper, fabrics, and iron pipes that had been exposed to the elements for three years. The test for the detection of blood works better on old bloodstains, as opposed to fresh blood. The blood needs to degrade for some time prior to giving a stronger luminescence.

The forensic use of luminol was first proposed in 1937. A luminol reagent was sprayed on a test pattern of blood that had been allowed to dry for two weeks and exposed to the elements. When the luminol reagent was sprayed onto the blood, all bloodstained areas exhibited a blue light for 10–15 minutes. These early experiments also reported that while the luminescence disappeared, it would reappear with a fresh application. This is analogous to the drying and cracking of old paint that has been exposed to the elements.

The reaction of luminol on aged bloodstains is more pronounced due to the oxidation process that has occurred during the intervening time period. That older, dried blood exhibits a stronger luminescence than fresh blood holds true today. In 1942, the luminol test was further recommended for use in forensic blood detection. Further investigation and experimentation continued into the 1970s, when its forensic application became somewhat more utilized.

Usage of Luminol

Some Misconceptions

As a presumptive test, luminol *presumes* the luminescence may be blood. Through its application, luminol *illuminates* the patterns resulting from the suspected substance.

Confirmation of the suspected stains, however, must be accomplished by other lab tests such as DNA, which can provide the donor. The legal and scientific use of luminol has been accepted in some states and sparingly in other states. A few states disallow the use of the tool because of misinformed reasons, which include the following:

- ❑ "It is carcinogenic."
  - ! It is not reported to be carcinogenic.
- ❑ "It cannot be properly photographed."
  - ! It can be photographed.
- ❑ "Spraying of luminol will create patterns not previously present."
  - ! It does not produce false patterns but, if oversprayed, will create a false background.
- ❑ "Luminol will destroy potential for subsequent DNA examination."
  - ! DNA testing and other confirmatory tests are *not* affected by the use of luminol.

Common Uses of Luminol

The most common uses of luminol in cold case homicide investigations may include the following:

- ❑ *Examination of evidence*—Use of luminol in this instance may include articles or evidence containing suspected blood not yet visible to the unaided eye. These may include clothing, weapons, and other articles. The use of luminol may be especially useful if evidence has been stored without exposure to the elements or other degrading circumstances.

- ❑ *Examination of a suspected homicide scene*—Use of luminol in this instance may be exemplified by instances in which investigators seek to determine whether a homicide may have occurred at a particular location. This may be in response to informant information, admissions, confessions, or other investigative activity. Luminol may be used to cover large crime scenes in fresh or cold case homicides, thus producing the original pattern. While luminol may be used on outdoor crime scenes within a short period after the offense, it may also be used on indoor crime scenes even after a lengthy period of time has passed. Its use in cold case homicide investigations is most effective when applied to areas that have been protected from the elements, including
    - Vehicle interiors, including dashboards, floor mats, and other coverings such as seats, trunk carpets, and so forth
    - Floor surfaces of homes, offices, storage facilities, and similar structures including concrete slabs, wood floors, and rugs or carpets
    - Cracks and crevices in floors and walls, in areas in which suspected cleaning has occurred
    - Wall surfaces
    - Furniture

In addition, luminol may also illuminate

- Blood tracks
- Drag marks
- Hand impressions
- Swipes
- Blood spatter impacts

The question is asked: "Which is better, luminol or BLUESTAR?" Both are luminol-based with very little difference in application. Both are mixed at the scene: luminol by combining three powders in distilled water and BLUESTAR by dropping tablets in a solution. Luminescence varies slightly as well as the liquid's stability on items sprayed. Although both are good, experience with BLUESTAR had a slight edge:

- The sprayed object is brighter.
- There is less running of the pattern. BLUESTAR holds to the pattern, and luminol solution runs slightly more.
- BLUESTAR's luminescence lasts a little longer than luminol, allowing for a longer photography period.

Both products, if mixed and sprayed properly, yield very good results. The most important factor is proper photography of the luminescence, which can be tricky without a lot of practice and experience.

Application and Use

Luminol is prepared at the scene or in the laboratory by a qualified, experienced analyst. When mixed with distilled water, premeasured quantities of sodium perborate and sodium carbonate must be shaken well before application. Application occurs, creating an aerosol mist from a spray container. Prior to application, however, a controlled sample of known blood must be sprayed to test the mixture. Luminol has minimal shelf life and should be applied immediately after it is mixed. The longer the time span between its mixture and application, the lesser the reaction of luminescence. Practically speaking, this could begin to occur within 24 hours. A fresh amount should be prepared for each day's use.

The application of luminol involves a number of procedures. These include

- Identification of suspect exhibit areas to be treated and examined
- Mixture and application of luminol
- Observation of the pattern resulting from the application of luminol
- Photographing the resulting pattern
- Documentation of the examination

Application is most often accomplished under darkened conditions to facilitate and reveal the luminescence. The analyst does not concentrate on the luminescence but, rather, upon the pattern that cannot be seen with the naked eye. While many objects will glow, a pattern will not be present on items such as metal rivets on a pair of jeans, cleansers used to clean toilet bowls and bathroom sinks, certain plant material with iron in the pulp, as well as some other substrates.

Many cases involve gunshots where the perpetrator is so close to the victim when shots are fired that blood spatters back toward the shooter in specks so small that the naked eye cannot detect them (Figure 26.1). A pattern is created, however (Figure 26.2), and when the analyst discovers the pattern with luminol, a representative sample must be taken for DNA analysis.

In cold case homicide investigations, an advantage of luminol is that it gives off a *more intense* luminescence when applied to *aged* bloodstains. This does not mean, however, that one can determine the age of the bloodstains from the intense chemical luminescence that occurs from older blood.

Luminol does not contaminate follow-up testing for DNA and other confirmatory tests. Chemicals used in the cleaning of any suspected items of evidence may give a false-positive reaction with what appears to be a blood pattern of significance. Additional DNA testing is necessary to confirm the presence of blood before giving an opinion about the pattern.

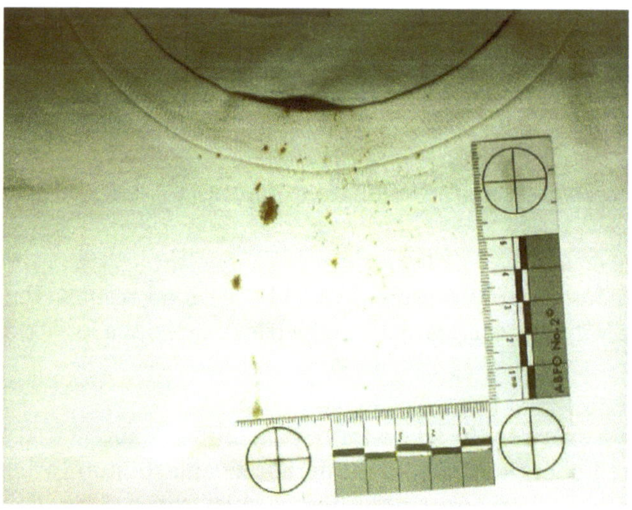

Figure 26.1 High-velocity stains on a T-shirt. In a case where a husband shot his wife, this photo illustrates the distribution of blood from high-velocity impact spatter from the wife onto the husband's shirt. (Courtesy of Rod Englert.)

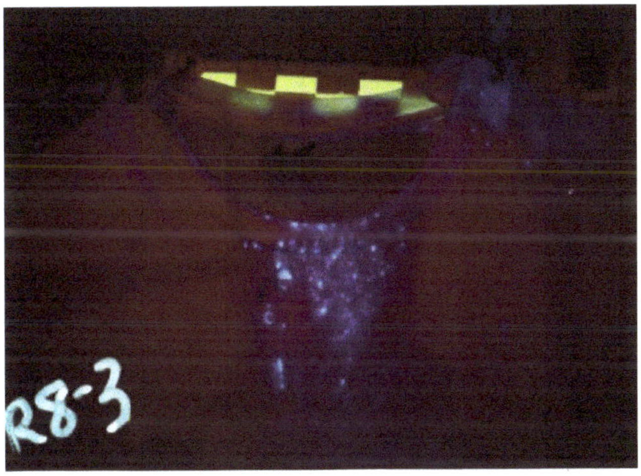

Figure 26.2 V-shaped blood pattern. Application of luminol on the T-shirt shown in Figure 26.1 revealed the V-shaped pattern created by an outer garment. (Courtesy of Rod Englert.)

Photography

The utilization of luminol necessitates the proper photography and documentation of its application. It is recommended that this should be undertaken by those experienced in this technique. Experiments in the early 1970s identified means and methods to obtain good photographic records of bloodstains as revealed by application of luminol, and this was recommended for adoption as a standard practice.

Luminol is very difficult to photograph, as this process must occur under conditions of little or no light. Photography of a luminol application without expensive commercial photographic equipment requires patience and skill, utilizing a cable release to operate an open shutter. The trick is knowing when to *close* the shutter, for if it is closed too soon, the picture's gone. You only get *one* good chance to obtain a good photograph as a documentation record, because the spraying of luminol may distort or change the original pattern, dependent upon the surface of what the blood is on. As an example, if luminol is sprayed on the metal of a car door, the suspected pattern will run and create another type of pattern not representative of the original crime scene (Figure 26.3). This also illustrates the necessity of using more than one camera during the application and photographic process, as chances are good that one of the cameras will capture the image.

During the photography of the luminescence, it is important to provide enough lighting to ensure that one captures the luminescence as well as the subject being photographed. Whether it be a light switch, piece of furniture, or article of clothing, the jurors not only can see what you describe as a blood transfer on a switch when it is presented in court; they can also observe the glowing pattern around the light switch.

Excluded Surfaces and False Positives

A disadvantage to luminol addresses its application on certain surfaces. These include those metals with copper salts. Bronze and brass, and similar alloys containing copper, may give a false reaction. These materials may be found on locks, door handles, and other similar materials. Other materials that may produce a false-positive reading include

- Grease and oils with trace amounts of copper
- Some cleaning materials

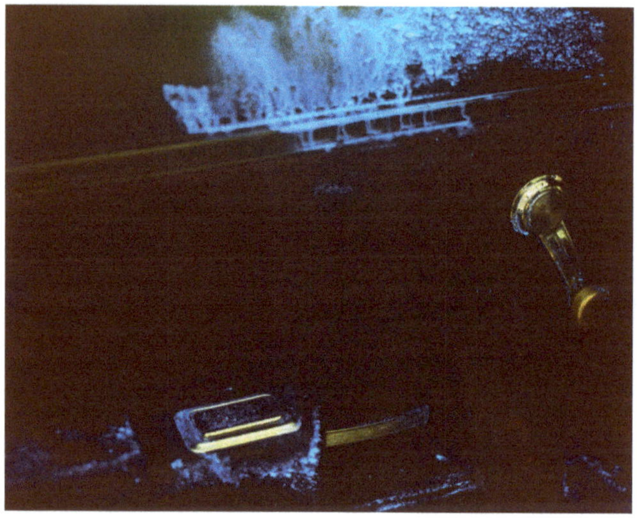

Figure 26.3 Overspray of luminol on car door. (Courtesy of Rod Englert.)

- Certain plant matter and vegetables, including horseradish, turnips, potatoes, onions, apples, apricots, and blackberries
- Some paints
- Some ceramic tiles and grouts
- Certain body materials including bone marrow, brain tissue, spinal fluid, intestinal and lung tissue, as well as leukocytes and mucus

Postincident Cleaning

During the intervening time period since commission of the offense and investigative response and detection, suspects may clean their clothing. Luminol may still be effective despite the passage of time. Patterns may be revealed despite washings of clothes, depending on the number of times the clothes were washed, soap used, and how well the clothing was washed. Dry cleaning, however, pretty much eliminates the patterns that may be illuminated by the use of luminol.

Case History

In 1992, a family of four in Southern California was found murdered. The young mother and her three children each had been shot in the head as they lay asleep in their separate beds. The father was missing at the time but, one week later, was found dead in his vehicle. The cause of his death was determined to be cyanide poisoning. The case was investigated by detectives, and the answer to what occurred lay in a piece of evidence taken during a search of the residence. That piece of evidence was a maroon-colored housecoat (Figure 26.4).

The jurisdiction investigating the five deaths came under attack by the media for being unable to resolve the case. The case attracted international attention, which involved Interpol, the Central Intelligence Agency (CIA), and the victim's family in another country. In 1995, the bathrobe removed from the home of

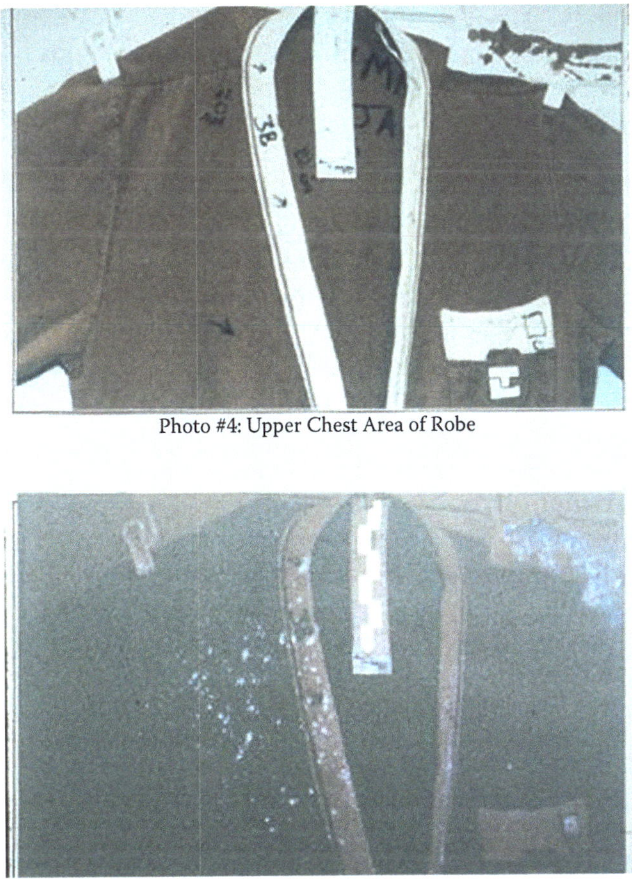

Figure 26.4 Housecoat. The housecoat in natural light (upper photo). The same housecoat (lower photo) after application of luminol revealing blood spatter on the upper chest area. (Courtesy of Rod Englert.)

the victims was treated with luminol. The results were positive and revealed that family members donated to the blood patterns on the robe. DNA tests were subsequently conducted on the areas that luminesced, revealing patterns resembling back spatter of blood from gunshots in the form of high-velocity mist. When the family members' blood was projected onto the sleeve and chest area of the dark red (blood-colored) housecoat, the DNA results told the story. The father had been observed wearing the bathrobe at the time of the murders by the housekeeper, who went to the residence on her day off. The evidence left no doubt that the father killed each member of the family prior to committing suicide because of heavy debt and possibly other reasons that will never be known.

Retrieving Bloody Fingerprints from Cloth

A very successful technique *using amido black* is the blood enhancement method to retrieve fingerprints from smooth cloth, i.e., bedsheets, T-shirts, nylon jackets, jeans... material not consisting of a heavy, distorted, or uneven weave. Very few fingerprint laboratories employ the technique, and little is mentioned in the literature regarding bloodied fingerprints on cloth.

If during a homicide investigation, bloodied grab patterns are observed on articles of clothing, the material should be submitted to an identification lab with experience in this type of blood enhancement. The King County Sheriff's Office in Seattle, Washington, has been doing fingerprints on clothing for many years and is quite skilled in the process.

Case Example

Briefly stated, a suspected article of clothing (T-shirt) and bedsheets were submitted from an Akron, Ohio, homicide. The ID lab in King County was successful in getting a fingerprint from the victim's blood on the suspect's T-shirt when he handled the shirt after the bloodshed. The victim had been sexually assaulted, stabbed, and cut over 100 times while tied to her bed.

During the trial, a representative from King County, Washington, explained to the jurors the process for locating the bloody fingerprint. It was explained that the T-shirt with a bloody grabbing pattern on the front left sleeve was submersed into the chemical amido black and hung up. The amido black reacts and fixes the entire blood pattern. The shirt is then bathed by spraying water on it while hanging allowed to dry. Digital photos are then taken and scanned into a computer. A computer program is able to separate the blood pattern via subtracting the cloth weave. The fingerprint becomes visible, allowing a fingerprint expert to determine the number of points. The defendant was convicted and later executed. The bloody fingerprint and other substantial evidence helped find justice in this brutal murder (Figures 26.5 through 26.7). Also see Chapter 13.

Figure 26.5 Jeans dipped into amido black.

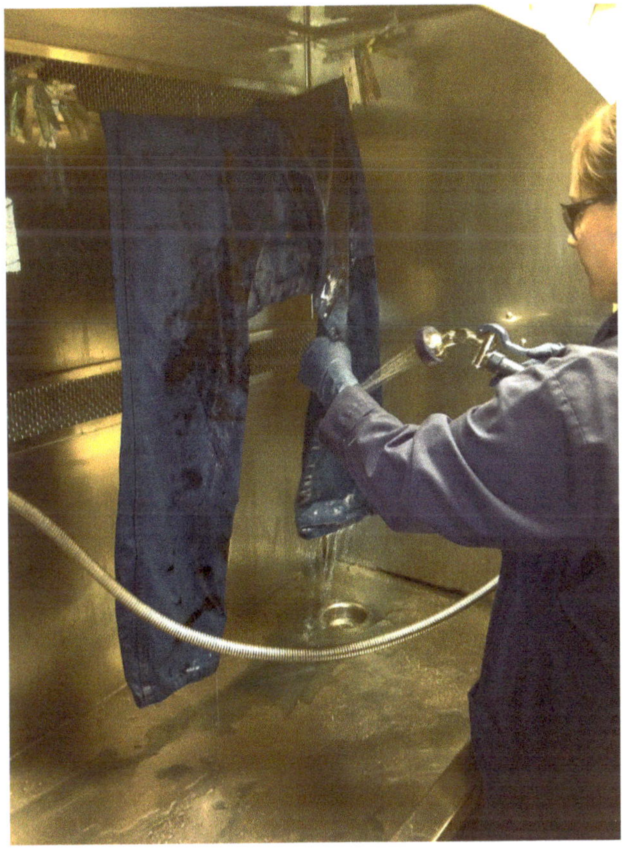

Figure 26.6 Water removing amido black solution, leaving dark stain.

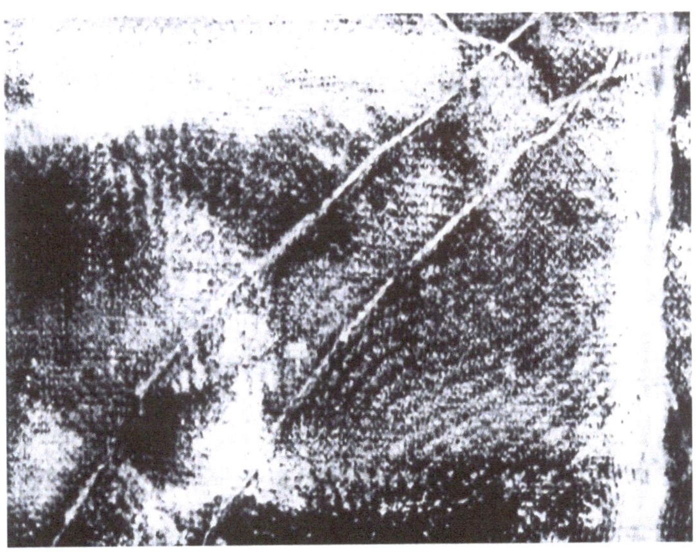

Figure 26.7 Fingerprint raised using amido black on cloth.

Conclusion

Luminol is a viable tool for law enforcement to determine the possible presence of human blood on evidence or at a scene, or to illuminate blood-based impressions left as a result of the criminal act. When applied by a competent professional and properly photographed, luminol preserves a record for the court and the jury to see. Luminol may illuminate that which was not known previously during an investigation and, as a result, help provide answers and contribute to the solution of cold case homicides.

For further information:

Rod Englert
Englert Forensic Consultants
PO Box 605
West Linn, Oregon 97068
1-503-656-0953
rod@englertforensics.com

Acknowledgments

I wish to express my deepest gratitude and appreciation to Rod Englert for his authorship and contribution of this chapter. Chief Deputy (Retired) Rod Englert, a 54-year veteran of law enforcement, retired as Commander of the Operations Division, Multnomah County Sheriff's Office, Portland, Oregon, in 1995. He started his career with the Downey, California Police Department after graduating from the Los Angeles Police Academy. In 1969, Chief Deputy Englert moved to Portland, Oregon and joined the Multnomah County Sheriff's Office. A large portion of Chief Deputy Englert's career has been associated with working on major crimes, narcotics, and homicide. His expertise is in the area of homicide crime scene reconstruction and blood spatter interpretation. After retirement, he became a member of the Multnomah County Sheriff's Office Cold Case Homicide Team.

Rod Englert received a bachelor's degree in police administration from California State University at Los Angeles, California. He is a graduate of the FBI National Academy, where he was president of the 159th session.

Chief Deputy Englert has conducted over 600 lectures and training seminars on managing criminal investigations, solving unresolved homicides, blood spatter interpretation, and crime scene reconstruction to law enforcement personnel, district attorneys, and private attorneys in 35 states as well as in Canada, Russia, England, France, Portugal, and South America. He has consulted in over 460 homicides in the United States and Canada. He has testified and is a qualified court expert in crime scene reconstruction and blood pattern analysis in 26 states.

Englert is a member of the International Homicide Investigator's Association and several states' Homicide Investigator's Associations; a fellow, distinguished member, president (2001–2002), and chairman of the board (2002–2003) of the Association of Crime Scene Reconstructionists; a fellow in the American Academy of Forensic Sciences; and a former president of the International Association of Blood Pattern Analysts. He has received the Lecturer of Merit and Distinguished Faculty Awards from the National College of District Attorneys.

Rod Englert is the author of *Blood Secrets: Chronicles of a Crime Scene Reconstructionist* (Thomas Dunne Books/St. Martin's Press, 2010). Part autobiography and part casebook, *Blood Secrets* has earned praise from respected sources such as *Publishers Weekly,* which dubbed it "a fascinating journey into the study of crimson drops….deftly balanc[ing] real-life examples and scientific analysis."

Suggested Readings and Bibliography

Grispino, R.J. (1990). "The Effect of Luminol on the Serological Analysis of Dried Human Blood Stains." *Crime Laboratory Digest*. Vol. 17, No. 1, pp. 13–23.

Gross, A.N., Harris, K.A., and Kaldun, G.I. (1999). "The Effect of Luminol in Presumptive Tests and DNA Analysis Using Polymerase Chain Reaction." *Journal of Forensic Sciences*. Vol. 44, No. 4, pp. 837–840.

Hesskew, D. (1997). *Law and Order Magazine*. November 1991.

Laux, D.L. (1991). "The Effects of Luminol on the Subsequent Analysis of Blood Stains." *Journal of Forensic Sciences*. Vol. 36, No. 5, pp. 1512–1520.

Montpetit, D.A. (2000). "A Novel Approach to Obtaining Reliable PCR Results from Luminol Treated Blood Stains." *Forensic Science*. Vol. 45, No. 4, pp. 886–890.

Forensic Document Examination

27

MARIE DURINA

Contents

The Forensic Document Examiner

A *questioned document* is any form of written or machine-printed material whose origin, source, or authenticity is in question. A *forensic document examiner* is an expert who makes a close and critical study of any material or portion of a questioned document. This may include examinations to resolve issues concerning

- Handwriting examination and comparison
- Altered documents
- Erasures
- Obliterations
- Indented writing
- Tracings
- Inks and writing instruments
- Watermarks and trademarks
- Dating a document (paper, inks, sequence of strokes)

- Methods of creating a document (printing processes used, cut-and-paste techniques, stapling of pages, etc.)
- Check-writer machines
- Burned or charred document reconstruction
- Shredded document reconstruction
- Rubber stamps
- Photocopies, photographs, faxes, and other machine-printed documents

Various methods used to perform these types of examinations may include

- Visual.
- Microscopic.
- Examinations of documents under various wavelengths of radiation such as ultraviolet and/or infrared.
- Examinations with instrumentation to detect indented impressions.
- In some cases, chemical processing may be required; however, it should be noted that these examinations are destructive. They should only be performed *after* forensic document examination has taken place and should be employed only as a last resort.

Individuals who enter the profession of forensic document examination as trainees may work in a government crime laboratory under the direction of a forensic document examiner, or they may be privately employed to undergo apprenticeship training by another qualified forensic document examiner. The minimum training period for a qualified forensic document examiner is at least two years. To be eligible for training as a forensic document examiner, one must possess a bachelor's degree and undergo an extensive training program in all facets of forensic document examination. Upon completion of training and performance of actual casework, forensic document examiners testifying in court are subject to *voir dire*, a line of questioning in which they must describe the details of their education and training before the court determines if they are qualified to render expert testimony.

Graphologists

Graphology or graphoanalysis attempts to predict character traits from handwriting examination, and those who engage in this practice are known as *graphologists*. Graphologists are *not* forensic document examiners. Legitimate forensic document examination involves the analysis and comparison of questioned documents with known material in order to determine their origin, source, or authenticity. Some graphologists call themselves handwriting analysts or document examiners and are therefore often confused with legitimate forensic document examiners. In *U.S. v. Bourgeois*, 950 F. 2nd 980 (5th Cir. 1992), the court rejected the testimony of a proffered handwriting examiner, in part, because his training was completed through a correspondence school with a strong emphasis on graphoanalysis. Those seeking to retain qualified forensic document examiners should be aware that persons who advertise themselves as handwriting analysts may be self-trained, or trained as graphologists. Unfortunately, groups outside the mainstream forensic science organizations abound, so great caution is necessary when vetting the qualifications of any person professing to be a forensic document examiner. See the section "Retaining a Qualified Expert Forensic Document Examiner" in this chapter.

Scientific Basis for Handwriting Examination and Comparison

About the time the average writer graduates from high school, he/she has experimented with various types of handwriting and/or signatures; has eliminated the juvenile characteristics or traits from his her handwriting; and thereby has attained graphic maturity. From this point on in people's lives, their handwriting becomes fixed and may only change when affected by factors such as illness, age, or other physical impairment. By early adulthood, a writer attains a certain level of skill, which will also become fixed. It is extremely difficult, if not impossible, for a writer to exceed his/her fixed level of skill.

Although many research studies have been done to attempt to prove otherwise, no two individuals have ever been found to write exactly alike. These studies included those done on the handwriting of identical twins, members of the same families, and those who attended the same schools as children and were taught to write by the same teachers.

Every individual's writing can be identified *if all of the following are true*:

- It was written with natural speed and comfortable posture.
- The *questioned* writing provided is of sufficient quantity and quality.
- An adequate quantity of *known* sample writing specimens is provided to the forensic document examiner for comparison purposes.

Obtaining Handwriting Exemplars

Handwriting exemplars are samples of handwriting whose source is known. Exemplars are obtained by investigators and provided to forensic document examiners to enable them to do a side-by-side comparison of the known handwriting (on the exemplars) with the document in dispute (the questioned documents.) Obtaining a handwriting exemplar is not a violation of the Fourth, Fifth, or Sixth Amendments to the Constitution.

If the court orders that a handwriting exemplar be produced for the court, it can hold the subject/defendant in contempt if he/she only provides disguised handwriting (where the most conspicuous features are deliberately changed by the writer to avoid detection).

The following guidelines may be of assistance when preparing, collecting, and preserving handwriting evidence.

First, investigators should review the files or documents that are the subject of the investigation. If there are questions, the investigator should speak directly to the attorney assigned to the case. If criminal or civil litigation is pending, ensure that the attorneys on both sides have communicated and that there are no objections to exemplars being obtained.

If a court order is required to obtain handwriting from a living subject, be certain the following wording is included: "normal handwriting in the amount, type and wording as directed by the investigator."

This wording allows the investigator to control the quantity and quality of the handwriting specimens that are obtained.

For example, investigators can instruct the writer to

- Write faster or slower
- Write smaller or larger
- Write with a backhand or forehand slant
- Write with the opposite hand
- Write in cursive handwriting or hand printing

Investigators should try to make the writer comfortable when obtaining handwriting exemplars and should also try to duplicate the conditions under which the questioned document was written. This should include use of the same type of paper, writing instrument, and even writing position (i.e., sitting or standing) if this is known.

Known writing specimens are documents whose source(s) or origin(s) is known. They are used for comparison to the questioned material. There are two kinds of known writing specimens:

- *Dictated* (or requested) exemplars, also known as "requested writing"
- *Collected* (or undictated) specimens, also known as "normal course-of-business writing"

Dictated Handwriting Exemplars

These are writings dictated by the investigator to the writer. Dictated writings are beneficial because they mimic the content and format of the document in question, and therefore allow for a comparison of comparable words, letters, and letter combinations.

Investigators obtaining handwriting exemplars should abide by the following *rules for obtaining dictated exemplars*:

- *Never* allow the subject to see the questioned document(s).
- *Always* dictate the contents of the writing to the subject one specimen at a time, removing each specimen from view after it is completed. This prevents the subject from copying what he/she had previously written.
- *Watch* the subject as he/she is writing. Look for attempts at disguise, such as slowing down, changing slant, or making grotesque letter forms.
- *Consider* obtaining specimens written with the writer's opposite hand, while the writer is standing, or at different time periods.
- *Note* the following:
  - Age of writer
  - Medical conditions or handicaps of the writer
  - Whether the writer is under the influence of drugs or alcohol
  - Time, place, and date specimens were obtained

Collected Writing Specimens

These are writings completed by the subject prior to the investigation. They are writings prepared in the course of daily living and are not likely to be disguised or distorted. Collected specimens are beneficial as they permit the forensic document examiner to assess the subject's normal, natural writing.

Some good sources of course-of-business writings are as follows:

- Cancelled checks
- Signed receipts
- Job applications
- Letters
- Telephone books
- Diaries/journal entries
- Department of Motor Vehicles (DMV) records
- Court records
- Booking/arrest record information

- Military records
- Voter's registrations
- Insurance applications
- Notebooks
- Customer/membership ID cards or completed forms
- Exam papers or written school assignments
- Calendar entries
- Real estate documents
- Completed forms
- Expense accounts
- Tax records
- Medical records
- Accident reports

Points to Consider When Obtaining Writing Specimens

- With collected or undictated standards, the principal points to consider are as follows:
  - The amount and quality of writing available must be sufficient.
  - The writing should be comparable. There should be a sufficient quantity of comparable words, numbers, letters, and letter combinations to that seen in the questioned document.
  - There should not be a big disparity in relative dates of questioned and known writing. Both classes of documents should have been completed around the same time period. Conditions under which the specimens were prepared should be noted (plenty of time, done in haste, etc.).
  - The type of writing instrument used should be similar to that seen on the questioned document.
  - The type of writing substrate used (paper, cardboard, plastic surface, etc.) should be similar to that of the questioned document (Figure 27.1).
- With dictated (requested) standards, the principal points to consider are as follows:
  - The material must be dictated with no help with spelling, punctuation, or grammar.
  - Dictated text must have similar words, numbers, letters, and letter combinations, and should be repeated several times.
  - There must be an adequate amount of writing. The amount required depends on the nature of the case. As a general rule, obtain all of the following:
    - 20–30 repetitions of signatures
    - 15–20 repetitions of check exemplars
    - 3–4 repetitions of entire written letters

  Obtain even *more* if possible. Remember, there is no such thing as too many specimens. More is *always* better!
  - The type of writing instrument should be similar.
  - The type of substrate used should be similar.
  - The dictation session should allow a sufficient amount of time for multiple repetitions to be obtained.

Terminology Regarding Signatures

- *Spurious signature*—A fraudulent, freehand signature with no apparent attempt at simulation of the genuine signature. This usually occurs when the writer has no idea of what the genuine signature looks like.

101 SOURCES OF HANDWRITING SPECIMENS

1. Account books
2. Affidavits
3. Assignments
4. Autographs
5. Automobile insurance applications
6. Automobile license applications
7. Automobile title certificates
8. Bank deposit slips
9. Bank safe deposit entry slips
10. Bank savings withdrawal slips
11. Bank signature cards
12. Bank statements, receipts for
13. Bible entries
14. Bills of sale
15. Bonds
16. Books, signatures of owner in
17. Building "after hours" registers
18. Business license applications
19. Charity pledges
20. Check book stubs
21. Checks, including endorsements
22. Church pledges
23. Convention registration books
24. Contracts
25. Cooking recipes
26. Corporation papers
27. Criminal records
28. Credit applications
29. Credit cards
30. Deeds
31. Deeds of trust
32. Depositions
33. Diaries
34. Dog license applications
35. Drafts
36. Drive-it-yourself applications
37. Drivers licenses and applications
38. Druggists' poison registers
39. Employment applications
40. Envelopes
41. Fishing licenses
42. Funeral attendance registers
43. Gas service applications
44. Gasoline mileage records
45. Gate records at defense plants
46. Greeting cards, Christmas, etc.
47. Hospital entry applications, etc.
48. Hotel and motel guest register
49. Hunting license
50. Identification cards
51. Inventories
52. Leases, real property
53. Letters
54. Library card applications
55. Light company applications
56. Life insurance applications
57. Loan applications
58. Mail orders
59. Manuscripts
60. Marriage records
61. Membership cards
62. Memoranda of all kinds
63. Military papers
64. Mortgages
65. Newspaper advertisement copy
66. Occupational writings
67. Package receipts
68. Parents signatures on report cards
69. Partnership papers
70. Pawn tickets
71. Passports
72. Payroll receipts
73. Pension applications
74. Permit applications
75. Petitions, referendum, etc.
76. Photograph albums
77. Pleadings
78. Postal cards
79. Probate court papers
80. Promissory notes
81. Property damage reports
82. Receipts for rent, etc.
83. Registered mail return receipts
84. Releases of mortgages
85. Rental contracts for equipment
86. Reports
87. Retail store sales slips
88. School and college papers
89. Social security cards and papers
90. Sport and game score cards
91. Stock certificates, endorsements on
92. Surety bond applications
93. Tax estimates and returns
94. Telegram copy
95. Telephone service applications
96. Time sheets
97. Traffic tickets
98. Voting registration records
99. Water company service applications
100. Wills
101. Workmen's compensation papers

This list has been around for a long time and may appear dated, but is only added here as a starting point.

Figure 27.1 101 Sources of Handwriting Specimens. This is a list of possible sources of *collected specimens* (writing executed in the normal course of business).

- *Simulated signature*—A fraudulent signature that was executed purely by imitating the appearance of the genuine signature (such as a freehand simulation or tracing of the genuine signature). This signature usually appears to have been drawn, rather than quickly and fluently written.
- *Cut-and-paste signature*—A reproduction of a genuine signature that is placed on a fraudulent document. This may be accomplished by a *physical* cut-and-paste method, such as photocopying a genuine signature, cutting the image out with scissors, pasting it onto a fraudulent document, and recopying that document; or it may be done by electronic means with the use of software such as Adobe Photoshop. In an *electronic* cut and paste, the original signature is scanned as a digital

image. The image is then electronically copied and pasted onto the fraudulent document. *Note: When either method is used, the resulting signature is not an inked signature but is made up of either ink-jet printing or toner used to create the fraudulent document.*

- *Traced simulation*—A fraudulent signature executed by following the outline of a genuine signature using one of the following:
  - *Transmitted light*—The original is viewed with a light source behind the document, allowing the simulator to trace it onto a spurious document.
  - *Indented or pencil outline*—The original is traced over with a stylus or pencil, which causes an indented outline or pencil guideline on the copy beneath. This indented outline or pencil guideline is then overwritten with an ink stroke.
  - *Carbon paper or carbonless paper*—Such a spurious document can be produced with the aid of carbon or carbonless paper, where the original signature is traced using carbon or carbonless paper between the legitimate and spurious document. This spurious signature image is then overwritten with an ink stroke. (Often, a felt-tip pen is used as this covers up more of the carbon outline.)

Forensic Document Terminology

- *Baseline*—A real or imaginary line upon which writing rests. It can be straight, curved, or diagonal.
- *Cursive writing*—Writing in which individual letters of words are generally joined.
- *Hand printing*—Any disconnected style of writing in which each letter is individually executed.
- *Disguised writing*—Deliberately altered writing with the intention of changing established characteristics. Usually, features changed most frequently are as follows:
  - Size
  - Slant
  - Capital letters
  - Hesitation, patching, slowly drawn strokes
  - Writing with the opposite hand

Most writers have a difficult time maintaining a disguise for any length of time. When disguise is suspected, it is important to get many repetitions of the writing in question. Studies have shown that the majority of writers who disguise their writing will resort repeatedly to the same method of disguise each time.

- *Forgery*—Because the crime of forgery is a specific-intent crime, this term is not used by forensic document examiners. Forgery implies that a nongenuine document was issued with the intent to defraud, and forensic document examiners do not address the issue of intent. They can only opine as to whether or not a document derived from a particular writer or source.
- *Individualizing characteristic*—A characteristic or feature in writing that is highly personal or peculiar and is unlikely to have been generated by another writer.
- *Initial/beginning stroke*—A stroke leading into the first letter of a word.
- *Terminal/ending stroke*—The final stroke associated with the ending letter of a word.
- *Line quality*—Refers to how smoothly handwriting is executed. Factors as speed, rhythm, and smoothness of movement can affect line quality.
- *Model signature*—A genuine signature that is used as a sample to prepare a simulated or traced forgery.
- *Pen lift*—Interruption of a written line (usually in cursive writing) by temporarily removing the writing instrument from the document.

- *Pen pressure*—The force with which the pen contacts the paper (if heavy, may cause indentations on the page beneath).
- *Ratio or Proportion*—The ratio between the sizes of the tall letters such as *l* and *t* and all capitals, and the short letters such as *a*, *e*, *i*, *o*, and *u*. This is also known as *height relationship*.
- *Retouching*—Retracing or altering a defective portion of a written stroke (in an attempt to make it look more like the model signature). This may also include *patching*, where portions of letters are overwritten or completed using multiple strokes.
- *Slant*—Angle or inclination of the vertical axis of letters or numerals.
- *Spacing*—Distances between individual letters in a word, between words, and/or between lines.
- *Traced simulation*—A fraudulent signature executed by following the outline of genuine writing (or a model signature) with a writing instrument.
- *Tremor*—The condition of a written line usually portrayed by irregular, shaky strokes that lack smooth and continuous direction. Tremor may or may not indicate nongenuineness. It is common for the elderly or physically impaired to have tremor within their normal writing.
- *Variation*—Every person's writing contains what is known as a range of natural variation. Some writers have alternate writing styles and therefore would possess a *wide range of variation*. Others write or print their letters in a similar way each time and would be considered to have a *narrow range of natural variation*. There is some degree of variation, however, within every writer's handwriting:
  - No individual ever writes exactly the same way twice. For example, it will not be possible to superimpose any signatures written by the same person, as each one will vary slightly.
  - No two people write exactly the same way.
  - Variation is introduced in every writing sample each time a person writes.
  - Variation is inherent. Human beings are not machines, and it is impossible for them to make exact reproductions of their own writing each time.
  - If an *exact* duplication of a writing *is* seen, it is a signal that something is wrong. The writing may have been traced, photocopied, or reproduced fraudulently by electronic means.

Handwriting Characteristics

Handwriting is identifiable due to the fact that individualizing characteristics are present within all writings. Writers are often not even aware of the individualizing characteristics within their own writing. These individualizing characteristics are what make writing identifiable.

When evaluating and comparing individualizing characteristics of handwriting, forensic document examiners take into account many features present within the writing and must assess each writer's full range of natural variation. To enable a complete assessment of a writer's skill level, ability to write with alternate writing styles, and range of natural variation, it is important to submit as much known writing as possible to the forensic document examiner.

Other Types of Forensic Document Examinations

Indented Impressions

Documents such as notes, letters, calendars, diaries, and journal entries may contain indented impressions not visible to the naked eye. These can often be visualized through the use of an Electrostatic Detection

Apparatus (ESDA®), found in the laboratory of any qualified forensic document examiner. Indented impressions have been recovered up to seven layers below the original writings and have been known to last more than 50 years provided the papers are not mishandled.

Alterations, Obliterations, and Substitutions

Alterations, obliterations, erasures, and page substitutions not visible to the naked eye can often be detected through used of an instrument known as a Video Spectral Comparator (VSC®). This device uses radiation filtered at various wavelengths to visualize reactions in different inks and papers used to prepare a document. Often, material that has been added, altered, or eradicated can be restored or deciphered for investigators through this method.

Burned, Charred, or Shredded Documents

Various lighting and reconstruction techniques are available to forensic document examiners that may aid in the possible decipherment of material on burned or charred documents, and in the reconstruction of shredded documents.

Typewritten and Machine-Printed Documents

Typewritten documents and documents printed with ink-jet or laser printers, fax machines, and photocopiers can often be sourced to particular makes or models of machines, or even to a specific machine. Printing processes used to prepare questioned documents can also be identified. These can include possible counterfeit documents such as passports, driver's licenses, vehicle titles, or other identification documents. When possible, always obtain known standards, ribbons, etc. from any machine in question. Submit the machine itself as evidence when possible.

Other Miscellaneous Types of Document Examinations

Questioned documents bearing rubber stamp impressions, embossed seals, watermarks, trademarks, or other mechanically printed marks may also be submitted for examination. Examinations of folds, sequencing of ink strokes, and other subtle features present on a document may aid in determining possible dates of preparation of the questioned document(s). When possible, it is important that investigators obtain any suspected devices associated with the questioned document that may have been involved in its preparation. This includes, but is not limited to, writing instrument(s), papers or other substrates, rubber stamp(s), sealing devices (such as notarial seals), and printing devices or mechanisms (Figures 27.2 through 27.4).

Obtaining Fingerprints from Documents

The most common method used to obtain fingerprints from paper documents is a chemical called *ninhydrin. Caution:* This is a destructive chemical technique that will render the document useless for subsequent examination of indented impressions, ink analysis, sequence of strokes, and paper examination. Before submitting any important questioned document for fingerprints, it is important that the document be submitted to a forensic document examiner for examination *prior* to any processing of the document for latent print development (Figure 27.5).

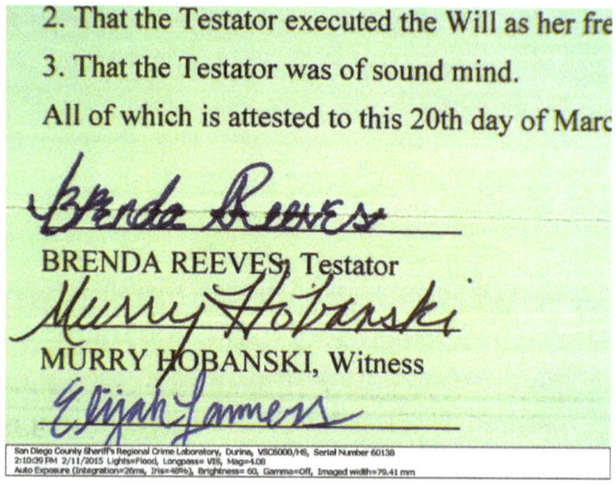

Figure 27.2 Folds in a document. Was the writing done before or after the fold? Folding disturbs the paper fibers, which results in the absorption and spreading of the ink. If writing is done before the paper is folded, ink spreading does not occur. Ballpoint ink often just skips across the fold, leaving a deposit of excess ink. This signature was placed on the document after the document was folded.

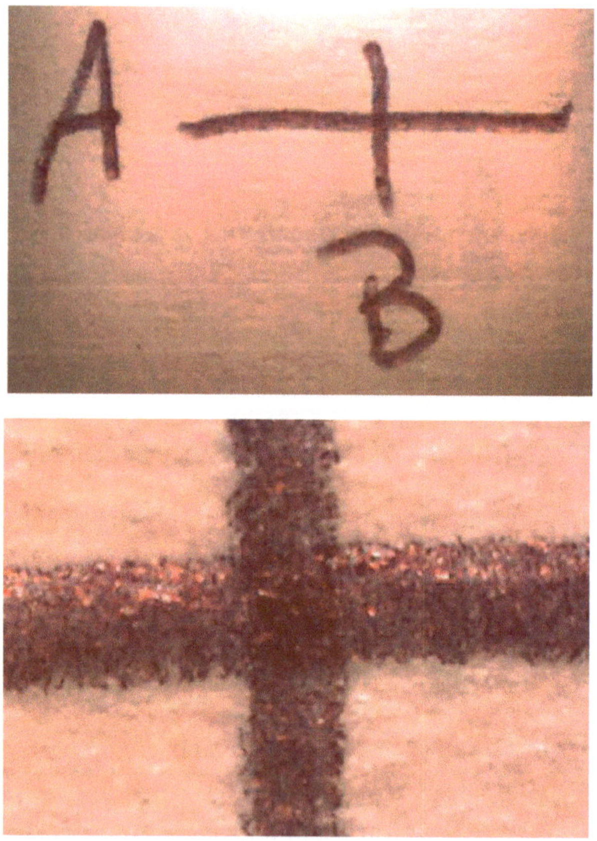

Figure 27.3 Line crossings. A visual exam may be deceptive, as a dark line intersecting with a lighter line will always appear to be on top. Line crossings are affected by the type of writing instrument, type of ink, writing material, and age of the writing. Which line was written first—A or B? The top photo was taken at 10×, the bottom photo at 60×.

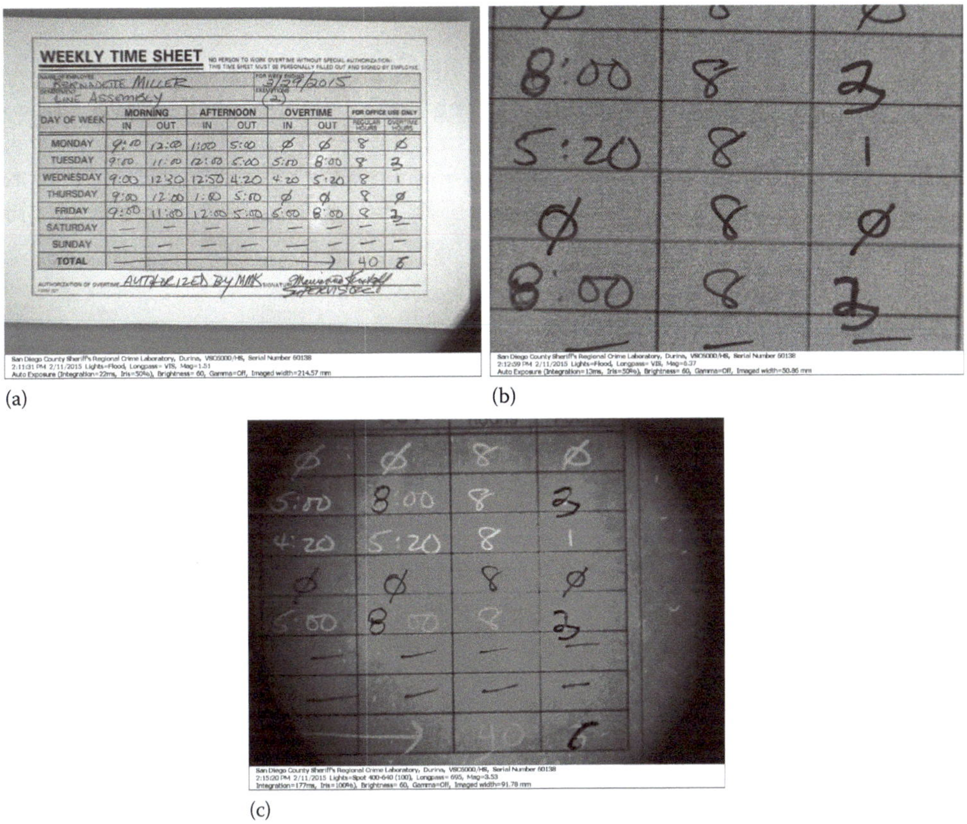

Figure 27.4 These figures depict a time sheet that has been erased and/or altered to change the number of hours worked. (a) Time sheet as viewed under visible light. (b) Close-up of altered numbers on time sheet. (c) Close-up of altered numbers on time sheet as viewed with infrared radiation (which enables us to visualize the different inks used).

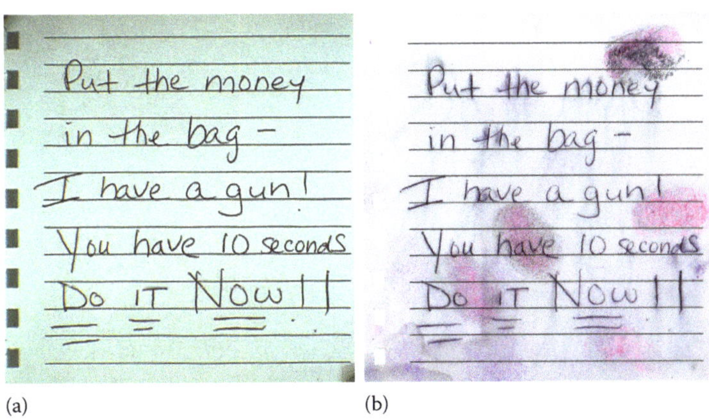

Figure 27.5 Ninhydrin. Use *caution* before proceeding with any chemical processing. Ninhydrin is a destructive chemical process and should *never* be used on a document to attempt to obtain fingerprints, until the document is first examined by a forensic document examiner. (a) Document before fingerprint processing. (b) Document after fingerprint processing.

Fax Copies

The quality of facsimile-transmitted documents is often a limiting factor in examination because of this digitized appearance of the writing or printing on the document that results in a notched or stepped effect. However, examinations of facsimile-transmitted documents are often performed to determine the identification of a particular make or model of the machines that sent or received the facsimile transmissions, or to determine if segments of the faxed document were altered or substituted (Figure 27.6).

"Washed" Documents

A "washed" document is one that is dipped in one of a number of solvents to remove the handwritten entries without removing the printing that was printed by the manufacturer. This may be a check, business form, deed, diploma, or vehicle title. Forensic document examiners can use a wide array of lighting techniques to visualize the alterations and attempt to recover the eradicated content (Figures 27.7 and 27.8).

Figure 27.6 Fax copy. The quality of facsimile-transmitted documents often place quality limitations on the examinations due to their notched or stepped effect. The original, or at least first-generation photocopies, are preferred for any examination.

Figure 27.7 Washed check. A washed check is dipped in a chemical solution (such as acetone, bleach, or a number of other chemicals), and the handwritten ink is removed. The check is then dried, and new, fraudulent entries are made. This check was originally made payable to Southern California Gas Company in the amount of $27.73 on January 2, 1993.

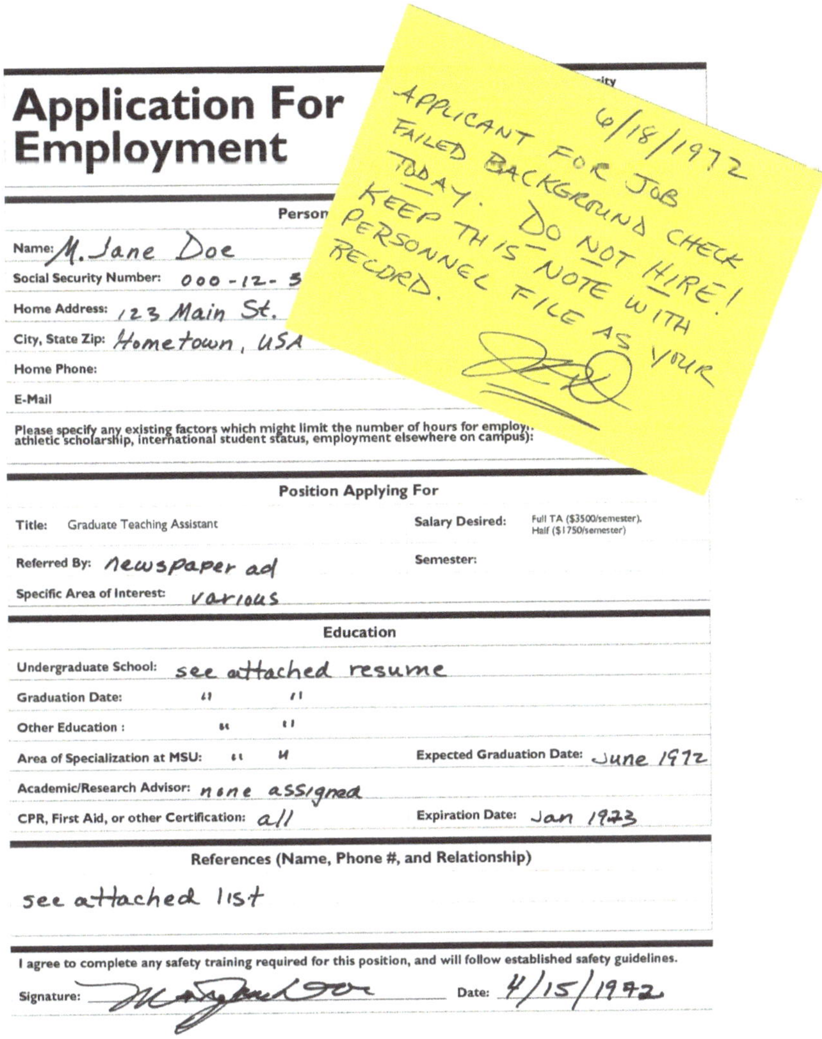

Application For Employment

Personal

Name: M. Jane Doe

Social Security Number: 000-12-5

Home Address: 123 Main St.

City, State Zip: Hometown, USA

Home Phone:

E-Mail

Please specify any existing factors which might limit the number of hours for employ... athletic scholarship, international student status, employment elsewhere on campus):

APPLICANT FOR JOB 6/18/1972 FAILED BACKGROUND CHECK TODAY. DO NOT HIRE! KEEP THIS NOTE WITH PERSONNEL FILE AS YOUR RECORD.

Position Applying For

Title: Graduate Teaching Assistant | Salary Desired: Full TA ($3500/semester), Half ($1750/semester)

Referred By: newspaper ad | Semester:

Specific Area of Interest: various

Education

Undergraduate School: see attached resume

Graduation Date: " "

Other Education: " "

Area of Specialization at MSU: " " | Expected Graduation Date: June 1972

Academic/Research Advisor: none assigned

CPR, First Aid, or other Certification: all | Expiration Date: Jan 1973

References (Name, Phone #, and Relationship)

see attached list

I agree to complete any safety training required for this position, and will follow established safety guidelines.

Signature: | Date: 4/15/1972

Figure 27.8 Post-it notes. Post-it adhesive was created by accident in the early 1970s by 3M. The Post-it note was invented by Art Fry in 1974. In 1977, it was test-marketed but failed. Post-it brand notepads were introduced nationally in 1980 and internationally in 1981. If a document contains a Post-it note and predates the above, it can be identified as a spurious document.

Preserving Questioned Documents

Careful handling of documents prior to their submission to a forensic document examiner is of extreme importance.

- Never handle a document excessively. Wear gloves when handling an original document. Never mark a document. Mark only the packaging or container *prior* to placing the documents inside. This will avoid the placement of nonevidentiary indented impressions on the document.
- Keep these documents in protective envelopes (archival quality is best), and do not fold, remove, staple, or unstaple any pages. Keep all document evidence in its original condition. Have the

documents examined by a forensic document examiner *prior* to any other processing such as latent print development, DNA analysis, etc.
- Protect the document from environmental conditions such as strong light or moisture.
- Always submit the *best evidence*. Obtain originals when possible. Limiting factors include documents that are photocopied, faxed, or digitally scanned, and documents whose quality and quantity are inadequate to allow for comparison.

Retaining a Qualified Expert Forensic Document Examiner

Qualifications of a forensic document examiner are as follows:

- Bachelor's degree (four years)
- Apprenticeship training with a qualified forensic document examiner of at least two years
- Full-time employment as a forensic document examiner
- Memberships in organizations such as the American Society of Questioned Document Examiners (ASQDE) and/or professional certification by the American Board of Forensic Document Examiners, Inc. (ABFDE)
- Technical research, presentations, and publication

Beware of "pseudo experts" such as the following:

- Investigators (such as private or law enforcement fraud investigators with investigative experience but without forensic science backgrounds)
- Criminalists or forensic scientists/examiners with no background, experience, or specific training in document examination
- Self-taught, self-proclaimed "document examiners" (including those taught by correspondence or online courses only)
- Graphologists and/or profilers, who claim to discern personality traits through handwriting analysis
- Part-time document/handwriting examiners, hobbyists, and charlatans

For more information, contact the following listed organizations, or visit their websites:

- American Academy of Forensic Sciences (AAFS) Questioned Document Section, (719) 636-1100, http://www.aafs.org/.
- American Society of Questioned Document Examiners (ASQDE), (312) 558-1684, http://www.asqde.org/.
- American Board of Forensic Document Examiners (ABFDE), (713) 784-9537, http://www.abfde.org/.
- Midwestern Association of Forensic Sciences (MAFS) Questioned Document Section, (517) 336-6628, http://www.mafs.net/.
- Mid-Atlantic Association of Forensic Scientists (MAAFS), http://www.maafs.org/.
- Northeastern Association of Forensic Scientists (NEAFS), http://neafs.org/.
- Scientific Working Group for Forensic Document Examination (SWGDOC), http://www.swgdoc.org/.

- Southwestern Association of Forensic Document Examiners (SWAFDE), http://www.swafde.org/.
- Southeastern Association of Forensic Document Examiners (SAFDE), http://www.safde.org/.
- Canadian Society of Forensic Science, http://www.csfs.ca/.
- Australasian Society of Forensic Document Examiners Inc. (ASFDE Inc.), http://www.asfdeinc.org/.
- Australian and New Zealand Forensic Science Society (ANZFSS), http://anzfss.org.au/.

Acknowledgments

I wish to acknowledge and express my deepest gratitude to Senior Forensic Document Examiner Marie Durina of the San Diego County Sheriff's Department Regional Crime Laboratory for her contribution and efforts in updating and expanding this chapter, which was originally prepared by the late Paul Edholm. Durina joined the Sheriff's Crime Lab in 1998 as an evidence technician in the Crime Scene Investigations (CSI) Unit and began her training as a forensic document examiner in 2003 under the tutelage of Dr. Linton Mohammed. She was promoted to Forensic Document Examiner in 2005 and to Senior Forensic Document Examiner in 2011. She holds a bachelor's degree in business administration from Baruch College, City University of New York (CUNY); a certificate of achievement in criminal investigations from Miramar College in San Diego; and a graduate certificate of academic studies in the forensic examination of questioned documents from Oklahoma State University.

Durina has published five papers related to forensic document examination in forensic science journals and has given numerous presentations and workshops to various forensic organizations and law enforcement agencies. She is certified by the American Board of Forensic Document Examiners (ABFDE) and has served on this certifying body's board of directors. Durina is also a member of the American Society of Questioned Document Examiners (ASQDE) and a member of the American Academy of Forensic Sciences Questioned Documents Section (AAFS). Since 2010, Durina has also been as a member of the Scientific Working Group for Document Examination (SWGDOC) and works with this group's committees to prepare standards and protocols for the profession of forensic document examination.

Forensic Art in Cold Cases

28

KAREN T. TAYLOR

Contents

Introduction to Forensic Art

By their nature, cold cases may require that the investigator delve into his or her most creative processes. Perhaps that *might* include a little forensic art. The combination of *art and science* or even *art and investigation* could sound incongruous. Yet elements of forensic art have proven to be a valuable tool for resolving many long-term unsolved cases. During my years as a forensic artist at the Texas Department of Public Safety and now as a freelancer, requests for my investigative-related art have often been linked to cold cases. Inherently, many forensic art processes are done as a "last resort," usually after more traditional investigative methods have been unsuccessful. This chapter synopsizes some of the methods to aid investigators that are described more expansively in my textbook ***Forensic Art and Illustration*** (Taylor 2001). Suggestions are offered here for ways in which creative use of forensic art might enhance various types of cold case investigations.

This chapter will enable you to

- **Understand the basic techniques of forensic art**
- **Consider whether a forensic art technique might be useful in your investigation**
- **Identify what the forensic artist needs from the investigator**
- **Select a qualified forensic artist**

Scope of Forensic Art

Forensic art is "any art that is of a forensic nature; that is, art used in conjunction with legal procedures." A working definition of **forensic art is any art that aids in the identification, apprehension, or conviction of criminal offenders, or that aids in the location of victims, or identification of unknown deceased persons.**

Many law enforcement officers have come to know the power of forensic art. They have seen a composite drawing lead to the perpetrator they seek, or a facial reconstruction help reveal the identity of a homicide victim. Age progressions help officers recover abducted children and locate fugitives who have been at large for many years. Many have witnessed the profound impact and clarity that forensic art can bring to court proceedings.

While not every forensic art attempt is successful and not every cold case lends itself to the use of forensic art, this work does contribute significantly in many criminal investigations. The increasing options for image enhancement and modification that computers allow mean this role is likely to escalate in the future. **It is incumbent upon all who bear the responsibilities of criminal investigations and prosecutions to understand more about forensic art.**

Four Categories of Forensic Art Methods

1. **Composite imagery.** Graphic images made up from the combination of individually described component parts (may include full body drawings or object/evidence drawings).

   Composite images are likely the most familiar type of forensic art. A suspect composite image enables officers and the public to better focus on a suspect's appearance based on the witness's description rather than on a potentially erroneous image in their own minds derived solely from a verbal or written description. The term *composite* is sometimes erroneously used to describe child age progressions, fugitive updates, postmortem images, or facial reconstructions. But **composite images refer specifically to images produced with the assistance of witness input**, not those based on photographs or skulls. **Composites may be hand-drawn, hand-assembled, or computer-aided.**

2. **Image modification and image identification.** Methods of manipulation, enhancement, comparison, and categorization of photographic images.

   Most criminal investigations include use of photographic images of various types. These may be crime scene photos, morgue photos, victim injury photos, suspect mugshots, surveillance images, and others. Review of facial or other images by a forensic artist may result in a needed boost to a cold case. This could involve assessment, comparison, and sometimes enhancement or modification. It is logical that forensic artists, who are usually also "facial identification specialists," become involved in these procedures. **Child age progressions or fugitive updates are examples of image modification that require knowledge of craniofacial growth and aging, respectively**. Such appearance updates encourage the viewer to visualize a present-day likeness of a given face rather than an outdated image. **Photo-to-photo comparisons or video-to-photo comparisons are examples of image identification that also require a solid foundation in anatomical knowledge of the face.**
3. **Demonstrative evidence.** Visual information for case presentation in court as trial displays.

   Art for court presentation aids both judge and jury in the visualization and understanding of complex crime scenes and events. Certain forensic artists specialize exclusively in demonstrative evidence preparation. These displays may be two- or three-dimensional or computer-generated. Skillfully prepared trial displays may be particularly important in the presentation of resolved cold cases. In addition to clarifying the past events of the crime itself, the investigator and prosecutor may also need to explain the long-term course of the investigation. (It is not within the scope of this chapter to cover preparation of trial displays, since an entire book could be written on that topic alone.)
4. **Facial reconstruction and postmortem identification aids.** Methods to aid in the identification of human physical remains in various conditions.

   Artwork in this category is intended to provide a link between an unidentified person and the records needed to positively identify him or her. This is especially significant since an unidentified body likely means a murder unsolved and a murderer walking free. *In cold cases, identification of the victim is sometimes the critical first step for all the investigative pieces to fall into place.* **Postmortem imagery is a method of forensic art done when bodies are in good enough condition for the artist to develop a reasonable facial likeness based on morgue or crime scene photographs or by viewing the actual body**. For aid in the identification of semi-skeletal or skeletal remains, **facial reconstruction from the skull may be done two-dimensionally by drawing or three-dimensionally by sculpting**. Ideally, the artist and anthropologist collaborate to construct the facial features of the unknown individual on the basis of the underlying cranial structure. In some skeletal cases, a team approach method of **superimposition comparison** may be used for assessing the likelihood of a match between a skull and a missing person's facial photograph. While not generally considered a means of positive identification, a reasonable congruence between skull and photo would point to the next logical step, such as DNA comparison. The method may be indicated when few antemortem records for a missing person exist.

Composite Imagery in Cold Cases

Circumstances for Doing Composite Images

Normally, the request for a composite image is made soon after a major crime has occurred and police have a witness they believe capable of providing a good description of the perpetrator. **In cold case investigations,**

you may consider the potential usefulness of producing *new* composite images. These might be totally new or re-dos of old composites. Development of full body images or object or evidence drawings may also be undertaken.

Procedural Considerations for the Composite Interview

Overall Significance of the Composite Interview

To prepare a high-quality composite image, the interview is everything. The skill and care taken to interview individuals for the purpose of developing composite images, whether by hand-drawn, mechanically assembled, or computer-generated methods, cannot be overemphasized. **For new or revised composites in cold cases, it is advisable that only the most skilled and experienced composite artists and/or interviewers be used**.

Any artist or software technician who produces composites must have a solid grasp of the **processes by which our minds encode memories** and the **effects of trauma on memory**. Essential, too, is a working **knowledge of facial anatomy**, particularly as it relates to our abilities to recognize faces. The psychological and medicolegal literature provides a wealth of studies and articles about cognition and perception, memory and trauma, victimology, facial recognition, eyewitness identification, and interviewing methods.

Many researchers in the psychological literature describe a **three-stage memory process: the acquisition stage, the retention stage, and the retrieval stage**.

In ***Forensic Art and Illustration***, the method of cognitive interviewing is presented as a recommended approach to optimum memory retrieval for successful composite interviews. A **composite-specific method of interviewing** is described in which cognitive interviewing is incorporated with **use of reference cues** in the form of facial photographs to trigger recognition ability and augment recall.

Other Interview and Memory Factors…FACE FACTS

There are numerous other factors that may have significance in the interview and composite generation process as well as the recognition and identification processes. Composites should be prepared with these concepts in mind. Understanding them may help determine the wisdom or appropriateness of new or revised composites. I like to call them ***Face facts***.

- **We encode faces in memory *as a whole***. The single most important factor for attaining likeness and individuality in composites, thus hopefully triggering recognition, is **proportion or layout**. I call this capturing the ***gestalt* of a face**. By this I mean that the image of the face as a whole is more important, and probably more recognizable, than any of its individual parts. We encode faces into memory holistically rather than as individual component parts.
- **We place more importance on some features than others for recognition**. Hair is usually remembered and described most frequently from memory, followed by eyes and eyebrows, nose, and general facial structure. By contrast, the cheeks, mouth, and forehead seem less important for recognition. While encoding of a face in memory is usually done as an overall "grasp," when looking at certain faces, we may quickly focus our attention on odd features such as huge ears, crooked noses, or crossed eyes. Good examples would be the face (and nose) of comedian Bob Hope and the face (and birthmark) of former Soviet premier Mikhail Gorbachev.
- **We tend to place more importance on the upper half of the face in memory**. Psychological studies indicate this as does my case experience drawing thousands of composites.
- **Memories of faces come back in flickering, elusive glimpses not like photographs you can hold at will in your mind**. Sketch artists must understand this and work to assist the witness in bringing back the needed information again and again throughout the drawing process.

- **We can *recognize* more than we can *recall*.** This fact makes a strong case for the use by composite artists of an interview methodology that integrates both cognitive interviewing for free recall and use of photo references as triggers to recognition. This usually promotes optimum use of memory for faces. Recall is a *verbally conveyed* skill, so the mental processing of a *visual* image can be difficult in words alone. Using visual photographic cues may make the task easier.
- **All faces are *not* created equal.** Studies have shown that some faces are simply easier to describe and recognize than others. Faces that are either particularly attractive or particularly unattractive seem to better capture our attention. This appears to suggest that **distinctiveness rather than typicality is what makes faces more recognizable.**
- **All witnesses are *not* created equal.** In a perfect world of forensic art, every witness would observe the suspect under excellent conditions, for the needed period of time, and be able to describe the face in exquisite detail. Of course, this does not happen. To further complicate matters, studies have determined that **a witness who appears to be giving a good description may, in fact, not be as good at recognizing.** The witness may simply be *fluent* or *confident* in describing a face, yet the description may turn out to be less than accurate. This may mean that other witnesses, disregarded in the early stages of an investigation because of a perceived lack of confidence, might be worth reinterviewing.

Reinterviewing Witnesses

Certainly the reinterviewing of witnesses is a well-known means of generating new or additional information in a case. Surprisingly, it is sometimes possible to reinterview witnesses and develop useful composites, even after the passage of a lot of time. However, potential candidates for reinterviewing should be carefully assessed.

For an event to be encoded into memory, it must first be perceived and experienced. **In general, witnesses who have experienced trauma in association with the event may have a stronger memory, though this is by no means a hard and fast rule.**

Simple physical and environmental obstacles inherent in the event, or so-called **situational factors**, should be considered when assessing a witness, such common sense things as

- **Duration of view.** The longer a person has to look at something, the better his or her memory will be.
- **Point of view.** The primary point of view by the witness should dictate the view of the facial drawing done by the composite artist.
- **Obstructions to view.** Any object that interferes with the witness's sight of the subject can pose serious difficulty.
- **Lighting conditions.** The artist must determine the lighting conditions under which the target suspect's face was seen.
- **Distance from subject.** Subjects viewed at closer distances are better perceived than those viewed at long distances.
- **Movement or motion.** Motion can diminish the time that the witness is allowed to view the face and blurring of features may occur.
- **Time since event.**

A number of researchers have assessed the effects of time elapsed in relation to the retrieval aspect of memory. They have attempted to define variables based on both accuracy of verbal descriptions and facial identification success. Results have varied according to the type of material studied, such as visual vs. verbal, and according to the form of the memory test.

As a *very* general guideline, it is better to do composite interviews with less traumatized victim/witnesses promptly after an event. "Promptly" may mean an hour, a day, or a week.

Severely traumatized victims may require more time to regain their bearings and be emotionally ready to do a composite interview. Most people benefit from, at minimum, a night's sleep and a sort of "regrouping" period after a traumatic event. The time required for trauma victims to be prepared to do a composite interview may vary considerably from days to many weeks or even longer, depending on their physical and emotional injuries. Remember the many months that passed before young Mary Catherine Smart was emotionally prepared to acknowledge and describe her sister Elizabeth's abductor.

It is important to acknowledge that memories held regarding a situation of severe trauma may be lifelong and quite vivid. This may be described as **extended retention**. Most people, when asked to recall their circumstances upon hearing of certain tragedies, find that their memories were quite clear. Where were you when you found out that President John Kennedy had been assassinated? Or that Princess Diana had died? Or on September 11, 2001?

This **extended retention** may benefit the cold case investigator. Witnesses who were unavailable for composite interviews in the early stages of an investigation, because they were too traumatized or perhaps too young, might actually be able to do a sketch later in time. It should be remembered, however, that such a sketch would be potentially viewed with greater scrutiny in court if it led to a perpetrator. The best use of a sketch like this might be quietly rather than in a public release, a judgment call that must be made case to case.

When assessing individuals for potential reinterviews, the investigator should also consider other **victim/witness factors**. Clearly, the degree of involvement by the victim/witness may have a marked effect on his or her abilities during the acquisition stage of memory and on ability to convey information after the crime has occurred. **Witnesses tend to fall into three categories with regard to involvement in an event: active, passive, and inactive.**

- **Active witnesses** may be actual victims of crime, or close observers who have felt personally threatened.
- **Passive witnesses** are usually impartial observers who view an incident from a safe distance and feel no personal threat.
- **Inactive witnesses** generally have no knowledge that a crime has taken place or that something they have seen may be significant.

Witnesses who are actively or passively involved usually have better recollection of an event than those who are merely bystanders. All of these issues are highly complex, and it is recommended that input from a qualified mental health professional be sought in circumstances where there is any doubt about potential psychological harm to a crime victim.

Other victim/witness factors may relate to perceptions of the individual witness due to their age, race, sex, or personal experience or prejudices. For example, for each of us, our own age affects how we describe the age of others, as does our physical build, our skin color, and so on. The witness's use of drugs or alcohol or any other handicaps due to deficiencies in eyesight, hearing, or mental faculties may also come into play.

Redoing preexisting composites should only be done after careful consideration of the potential ramifications. These days, we see more and more that new images are released at the direction of media entities or even bereaved victim family members. I know that certain forensic artists actually *encourage* victim family members to go outside of law enforcement to commission composites if they are unsatisfied. I consider this an unethical practice that can actually jeopardize investigations. Certainly, the existence of multiple composite images creates a prime opportunity for defense attorneys to question the drawings in trail, possibly developing reasonable doubt. In addition, who will check out tips from composites not authorized by police?

The potential upside of new composite images is that they can be used as tools to generate new interest in an old investigation. If there is a new witness who has not done a composite in the past, it is not the same sort of complicated matter as redoing existing images. On rare occasions, there are situations where there was a problem with the preparation of a drawing and a witness is simply not satisfied with the original composite. Investigators might ask another artist to attempt to produce an image that will be more acceptable and accurate to the witness. In this case, the preparation of a new composite would be reasonable.

We tend to think composites and other graphic images are produced only for the purpose of release to the media and exposure to the general public. However, **in some instances, it may be useful to reserve the composite information for limited distribution to a targeted area or group of people**. It may also be produced strictly for the quiet use of the investigator to generate new leads.

Composite Drawing Examples

Figure 28.1 shows a composite sketch based on the description of a victim of sexual assault. While the sketch was prepared fairly close to the time of the event, it was not given much distribution. Later, the subject was arrested on an unrelated auto theft charge. Vehicle theft investigators happened to notice a resemblance to the sketch that had been circulated around the police agency. This led to the subject being charged and convicted of the sexual assault.

Figure 28.2 shows a composite sketch drawn from the description of a young victim of aggravated sexual assault. This witness had seen her husband brutally murdered in her presence as he prayed for her safety. The likeness is notable even though the drawing was not prepared until many months after the event occurred. It was a key feature in the prosecution of the offender.

Types of Composite Systems

Composite images may be produced by hand in the form of sketches, by hand-assembly kits, or by use of computer-based composite systems. **The quality of the interview process and the knowledge of both memory function and anatomy are far more important than the choice of method.**

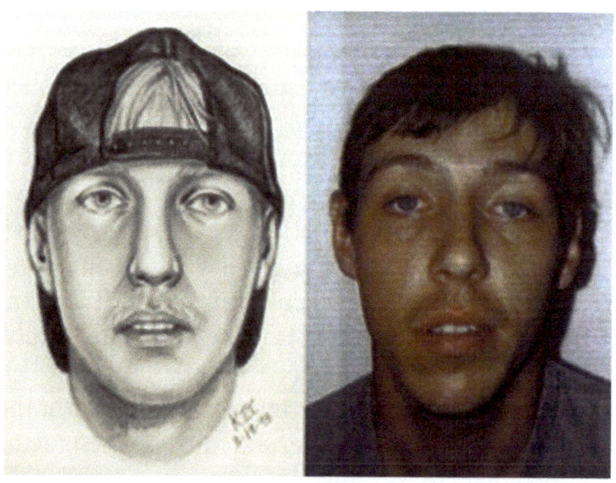

Figure 28.1 Composite drawing by KTT of suspect as described by a sexual assault victim (left) and photo of the subject identified (right). (Courtesy of Karen T. Taylor.)

Figure 28.2 Composite drawing by KTT of suspect as described by a victim in a sexual assault/homicide case (left) and photo of the subject identified (right) with bandana added. (Courtesy of Karen T. Taylor.)

A particularly notable phenomenon is the benefit of "sketch quality" versus "photographic quality" in the production of composite images. My friend Tom Macris, a highly successful police artist formerly with the San Jose, California Police Department, addresses this point in his paper "Composite Art: General Principles for Man and Machine":

> **Sketch quality in a composite has always offered one key advantage over photo detail.** This advantage is that when viewing a completed composite sketch, one is forced to apply a very fruitful margin for interpretation. The accomplished police artist knows how the addition of superfluous detail is an overkill, which defeats the purpose of the composite.
>
> **In a photographic composite, when such precise details are included and visually totaled, they may result in a product that precisely suggests an absolute identity.** This tempts the viewer to interpret what the composite is trying to say very narrowly, thereby leaving many potential stones unturned in the investigation. It is as if twentieth century man, raised on the precise nature of photographic images, maintains a knee-jerk response to expect all photographic images to be precise representations of the subject. This misleading quality is compounded by the fact that much of the detail or subtlety was not even initially requested by the witness. It simply (and unnecessarily) came with the image (Macris 1987).

It is my opinion that choice of a composite system, if other than hand-drawn sketches are to be used, should involve careful consideration of this "sketch quality" versus "photo quality" phenomenon. Also important in product selection is the effectiveness of the tools for easy modification that a given system contains. There should be high-quality, flexible graphic tools capable of producing various adjustments as needed.

A good system should allow the production of

- Both male and female faces
- Faces of any age group
- Faces of any racial/ancestral or ethnic group
- Facial hair as needed
- Assorted headgear and eyewear
- Basic facial expressions

Drawings Other than the Face

It is possible that a thorough case review might trigger ideas for other drawings that might be useful to the cold case investigation. Witness statements might include descriptions of items in words alone. Basically, mostly anything that a witness can describe, a good forensic artist can draw.

Such drawings could depict

- Full body
- Unique body parts
- Vehicles, including aircraft and marinecraft; vehicle interiors; logos of vehicle manufacturers; bumper stickers or decals; exterior painted designs
- Details of interiors of locations
- Weapons
- Articles of clothing or footwear; printing on T-shirts; printing or logos on ball caps, footwear, or clothing brands, or other clothing details; monograms, jewelry, or watches; and eyeglasses
- Unusual or personalized drug paraphernalia
- Gang- or organized-group-related insignias
- Tattoos, moles, scars, or deformities

On several occasions, I have sketched physical body parts or unique characteristics of perpetrators, usually sex offenders, which victims were able to describe in great detail. When such traits appear on a suspect, the evidence can be very damaging, particularly when the specific trait would not be observable while the person was clothed.

Considerations for the Investigator

- Are there any witnesses who could be interviewed or reinterviewed to provide descriptions of faces?
- What were the physical situational factors and circumstances of the viewing?
- Was the witness actively, passively, or inactively involved in the event?
- What is their current psychological state?
- Would it be useful to have drawings of other items as part of the investigation?
- Should these images be distributed widely or used only for investigative purposes?

What the Artist Needs

- Enough insight into the investigation to properly interview the witness
- Some background information about the witness
- Ideally, experience in complex interviews

Image Modification: Child Age Progressions in Cold Cases

Circumstances for Doing Child Age Progressions

As parents know, children change and grow so quickly that photographs taken of them become out-of-date after a very short period of time. In the cases of missing and abducted children, the need for an "up-to-date" look of the child is critical. **Child age progression, either hand-drawn or computer-generated, helps provide a more current and effective facial image for distribution of case information regarding a missing child.**

There are no hard rules about the timeframes in which child age progressions may be done. However, some forensic artists decline cases of children who fall in an age group so young that no growth data exist to aid in prediction of the face. Others rely more heavily on genetic trends and facial patterns influenced by heredity and will attempt any case for which there are family photographs.

It is likely that the best child age progressions are based on a balance of genetic prediction of likeness combined with quantifiable growth data. And hopefully, new growth data sets are being developed all the time to aid with this work.

The odds are also better for cases in which there are excellent photos from which to work.

Procedural Considerations for Child Age Progressions

Choice of Method for Child Age Progressions

Effective child age progressions have been done by hand-drawn methods, on computer, or using a combination of both. Because of the volume of work done at the National Center for Missing and Exploited Children, the computer-generated method is best known. Forensic artists may specialize in one method or another or may offer various approaches, depending on the particular case needs.

Importance of Artist's Knowledge

As previously stated with regard to composite images, it matters less whether an image is hand-drawn or computer-generated than that the artist is a skilled interviewer with knowledge of facial anatomy. With child age progressions, the same logic applies with regard to foundational knowledge of how faces grow and mature.

Neither the most technically skilled computer technician nor the finest portrait artist can produce high-quality child age progressions without an understanding of craniofacial growth. The importance of this knowledge cannot be overemphasized.

Artists must understand that there are certain growth trends that effect growth on all our faces and then incorporate these with specific elements observed within an individual family. The very obvious proportional change in the *amount* of lower face is one of the most fundamental aspects of facial growth. Over time, young children's faces grow downward and forward. There is usually a strong retention of a "look" in the eye area as we grow. Childhood expressions may last a lifetime.

The forensic artist who attempts child age progressions must also have a general understanding of the **eruption patterns of the teeth**. Lack of attention to the teeth can produce a very incorrect or even distorted look in a finished updated image.

Also beneficial is reliable background information on the child regarding health or possible lifestyle. These topics aid the artist in determining whether to make the child appear more or less robust or healthy-looking in the age progression. Any insights about habitual expressions or behaviors might also be subtly incorporated.

Forensic Art and Illustration offers a series of photographs showing growth in the same face from age 18 months to age 25, accompanied by an explanation of the anatomical dynamics involved.

Photographs for Child Age Progressions

The quality of available photographs may also play a significant part in the determination of which method to use. If the photographs are of high quality and the required angles of view are available, then the logical choice would be a computer application. If the photographs are inferior and cannot be scanned effectively, a hand-drawn facial image might be the better choice using the photographs just for reference input. Video images may be of such low resolution that they cannot be effectively used as stills; in such cases, they should be used only for the insights they afford into the child's appearance.

As preparation for a child age progression, you should attempt to get the best quality photographs available. It is beneficial to have multiple photos of the child in various views, particularly those taken near the time of disappearance.

Artists who use a computer approach must collect, sort by age, and store photographs of various unrelated children to incorporate into their child age progressions as needed. For example, a hairstyle or shirt collar may be pulled from the photo of any child of appropriate age, sex, and ancestry. School photographs of children are ideal for this purpose.

Good quality photographs of family members from both sides may be beneficial for assessing and gathering facial details. A child's face should be carefully studied and compared to any available family photographs. There may actually be a resemblance of specific features to grandparents or other relatives that is stronger than resemblance to parents.

Ideally, facial photographs of parents and/or siblings are in the same angle of view as the target photo of the missing child that will be scanned and updated. **Photos of parents and siblings at the age to which the child's face will be progressed are most beneficial.** Of course, in cases of parental abduction, family photographs from the abducting parent's side may be unavailable.

Child Age Progression Case Example

Figure 28.3 shows a hand-drawn age progression based on photographs of a male child at 2½ years of age, projecting the appearance to 18 years. After his location, photographs of the boy at age 18 were compared to the age progression, adding facial hair to resemble his own.

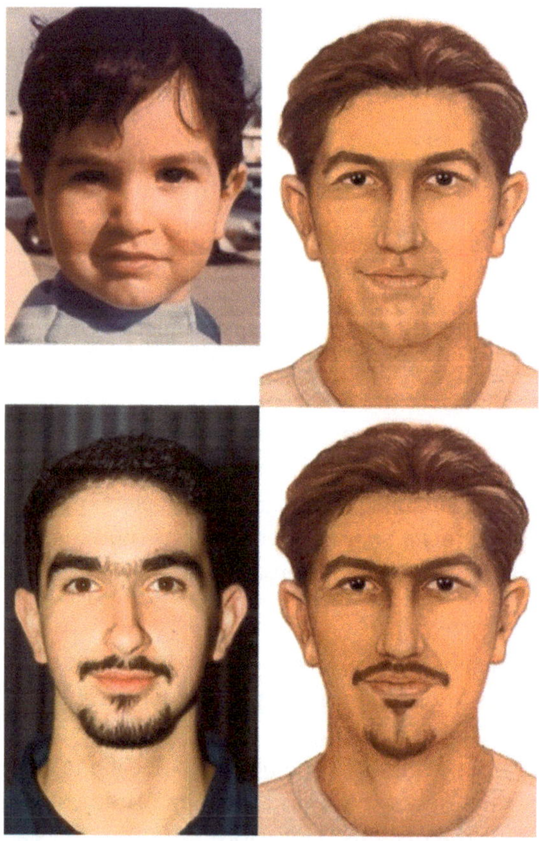

Figure 28.3 Hand-drawn age progression by KTT based on photograph of a male child at 2½ years of age (upper left), projecting the appearance to 18 years of age (upper right), photo of young man when located at age 18 (lower left), and age progression with facial hair added (lower right). (Courtesy of Karen T. Taylor.)

Considerations for the Investigator

- Would a child age progression benefit this investigation?
- Do good quality photographs of the child exist? How many? What facial views?
- Are there available photographs of the parents? Siblings? Grandparents or other close relatives?
- Are there any known habits that might aid in the age progression process?
- How about health or lifestyle factors?

What the Artist Needs

- Enough insight into the investigation to properly prepare the child age progression
- Some background information about the child and his/her family
- Knowledge of craniofacial growth
- The best available photographs of the child in multiple views
- Photographs of family members, particularly at the age to which the target child will be advanced

Image Modification: Adult Age Progression in Cold Cases

Circumstances for Doing Adult Age Progression

Adult age progression may be done in circumstances where an "updated" image might lead to new case information or even case resolution. Either innocent missing persons or sought-after fugitives may be age-progressed, though the fugitive updates are far more commonly done. **Both the terms "adult age progression" and "fugitive updates" are used, depending on the status of the target individual.**

Adult age progression, either hand-drawn or computer-generated, helps provide a more current and effective facial image for distribution of case information regarding a missing adult or fugitive.

An age-old problem in the corrections aspect of law enforcement is the reality that incarcerated prisoners sometimes escape. The concept of "updating" the appearance of long-term missing fugitives has gained popularity in the last two decades or so. In the United States and several other countries, the medium of television has encouraged the production of age progressed images of adult individuals to augment stories of sought-after criminals, usually fugitives. Adult age progression is sometimes done in cases of long-term absent adults who are classified as missing persons as part of the investigative effort to locate them.

Most cases in which adult age progressions or fugitive updates are done involve high-profile criminals or missing persons sought by members of law enforcement for many years. The most logical circumstances for use of the method include cases in which there are at least fairly good photographs available of the subject, even though they are out-of-date.

There is no specified time frame after which updates should be done, though common sense dictates that enough time should have passed for significant aging to have occurred. In addition, it may be especially beneficial to produce updates when investigators have gained intelligence information regarding the person's current appearance to include such things as weight changes, and hair or facial hair changes.

In some cases, the production of an age progression is precipitated by an event such as an upcoming anniversary of a major crime or a planned media story about the crime. **The age progression can encourage renewed interest in the investigation and hopefully generate new leads.**

Procedural Considerations for Adult Age Progression

Choice of Method for Adult Age Progressions

Effective adult age progressions have been done by hand-drawn methods, on computer, or using a combination of both. They have also been done sculpturally as was the well-documented case of fugitive John List by forensic artist Frank Bender.

The most significant factor is the artist's foundation in anatomical knowledge about the face, not the type of method used.

Importance of Artist's Knowledge

As with all other aspects of forensic art, the artist should carefully study and assess each case individually rather than assume that every person will have precisely the same indications of age on the face. A sound understanding of the physical mechanics of the facial aging process helps to promote reasonable judgments and predictions.

Neither the most technically skilled computer technician nor the finest portrait artist can produce high-quality adult age progressions without an understanding of craniofacial aging. The importance of this knowledge cannot be overemphasized.

Throughout our lives, the changes that occur in our faces are influenced by genetics, environment, and lifestyle. Forensic artists who attempt to project the advanced appearance of faces must first study the facial morphology of the target face, assess genetic predisposition to the extent possible, and learn what they can about the possible environment and lifestyle of the person.

The cold case investigator should search out and provide any reliable background information on the target person regarding health and lifestyle factors. This helps the artist determine the relative harshness or mildness with which the face should be aged. For example, the face of a health-conscious person should be aged differently from the face of a known drug abuser or alcoholic. Smoking and inclination toward sun exposure should also be considerations.

Forensic Art and Illustration gives detailed decade-by-decade information as a resource for artists who employ this method, along with a reference gallery of photographs for additional guidance.

Knowledge about the creation of facial expressions and their role in the development of wrinkles is important for the artist. Expressions may contribute to a certain "look" throughout life. While this **"lifelong look"** does not absolutely hold true for all people, it is true for a large number of them. Therefore, the maintenance of the "look" should be a goal of adult age progressions. This nebulous quality is what allows us to recognize childhood and adolescent friends as adults when we see them at class reunions.

Photographs for Adult Age Progression

When investigators have spent many years searching for a particular fugitive, they generally develop a thick file of information on their subject. This usually includes multiple photographs. It is beneficial and wise to review any available photographs of a subject to be aged. Certainly, each of us has different looks in different photographs taken under different circumstances, and photographs can be very deceiving. Most people hate to think that they really look like their driver's license photographs!

The more photographs made available to the forensic artist for assessment, the better. Even if a frontal view is to be developed, oblique or lateral views should be studied if provided in the case file.

As with the projection of craniofacial growth in child age progressions, the process of projecting age may be made **more accurate if the artist has access to photographs of family members**. It is sometimes possible to discern a trend or tendency within a family that can be incorporated into the age progression. Predictably, fugitives' families may not be cooperative in providing photographs of family members. Law enforcement officers may, however, have access to photos such as those in driver's license or arrest records. High school or college yearbooks may also be a source.

Depending upon the age of the target subject, parents' photos or siblings' photos may be assessed. I have found older siblings' photos to be particularly useful.

Fugitive Update Case Example

Figure 28.4 shows the case of **Virgilio Paz Romero**. A Cuban national, Paz was part of a conspiracy in the political assassination of former Chilean ambassador Orlondo Letelier and a young aide. The murders, resulting from a car bomb in a busy area of Washington, DC, in 1976, led to strained relations between the United States and Chile for over a decade. The fugitive update was prepared from very poor quality photocopies of a photo of Paz from years earlier. He was captured after 15 years at large, three days after the update drawing aired on "America's Most Wanted" in 1991. At the time of his capture, he was considered one of the most wanted men in the world. There was a lot of teasing because I chose to draw him with a red shirt and he was apprehended wearing an identical red shirt!

Considerations for the Investigator

- Would it be useful to have an updated facial image of a primary person in the case?
- Are there good quality photos of that person? How many?
- What about photos of members of his or her family? Are they obtainable?
- Are there any known health or lifestyle factors that might be helpful in the age progression process?
- Are there any characteristic facial expressions attributable to the person? Do photos of the expressions exist or are there associates who could describe them?

What the Artist Needs

- Enough insight into the investigation to properly prepare the adult age progression
- Some background information about the subject and his/her family
- Knowledge of craniofacial aging and expressions
- The best available photographs of the subject in multiple views
- Photographs of family members, particularly at the age to which the target subject will be advanced

Figure 28.4 Virgilio Paz Romero in poor-quality photocopy (left), fugitive update by KTT (center), and after capture (right). (Courtesy of Karen T. Taylor.)

Image Identification in Cold Cases

Circumstances for Doing Image Identification

In today's investigative world, there are many occasions in which it would be beneficial to know the identity of a particular facial image or whether two faces are one and the same. We are photographed and videotaped in many aspects of our lives, and these images often enter into criminal investigations. This will likely escalate in the years ahead.

Because of the nature of their work, **forensic artists are often considered "facial identification specialists"**. Over time, I began to be asked more and more to give opinions regarding facial images even when no drawing was needed.

In recent years, I have been asked to assess photographs of people believed to be fugitives, missing children, long-lost relatives, missing-in-action war veterans, celebrities caught topless, literary figures, historical personages from presidents to outlaws of the Wild West, and many others.

I do not relish this role, since it is often one of very little certainty, a lot of speculation, and a great risk of being totally wrong. For these reasons, I rarely give a specific or firm opinion regarding arbitrary face-to-face comparisons. A phrase I use is, "I find nothing to indicate it is not the person," rather than "it is the person." I believe the former is a far more appropriate response for a possible match, considering the nature and limitations of such comparisons.

Yet with all this said, there are times when the "eye" of a forensic artist may offer the cold case investigator some valuable insights. I try to offer any insights that are reasonable, always with many caveats about the limited nature of face-to-face comparisons.

Methods of assessing, comparing, or identifying facial photographs vary considerably. In this chapter, I address only those done artistically rather than those done by computer means. **By whatever method an image is assessed, the most important factor once again is a solid foundation in anatomical knowledge of the face.**

As a state police forensic artist in Texas, my job duties would routinely include the visual assessment and comparison of facial images. Crime analysts and officers request assistance in determining whether or not two images could actually be the same person. Fraud cases in which individuals have multiple forms of identification in different names are always prevalent. Fugitive case investigators sometimes ask that known mug photos are compared with surveillance photographs of individuals whom they believe might be the subjects they seek. Sadly, on occasion, I am asked to review child pornography, comparing faces shown with the facial photos of missing children.

In all of these cases, my evaluations are made almost solely by just looking at the photos. **The anatomical morphological traits of faces are compared to one another, strictly on a visual basis. This approach may prove accurate if the evaluator is skilled and experienced, but it is far from scientific or definitive.**

As part of certain investigations, I have been asked to simply review photographs to see if there might be something that I see that others have missed. A few years ago, I was presented with crime scene photographs from a two-year-old unsolved homicide case. In this murder of a senior citizen, police believed that they were seeking a lone assailant. Upon study of the photos, I could readily see and define three distinctly different sets of footprints, which changed the course of the investigation. I can't claim to fully understand why some of us have better **pattern recognition** cognitive abilities than others, but it does seem to be the case. So, at times, there are real advantages of a "fresh look" at an unsolved cold case, especially with an "artist's eye."

Procedural Considerations for Image Identification

Face-to-face comparisons may be approached in different ways. Sometimes an anatomical morphological evaluation is made. In other instances, a more electronic, technology-based assessment is made. There may be benefit to a team approach that makes use of the expertise of multiple individuals. For example, a comparison of two facial images might involve

- Bony cranial structure assessment by an anthropologist
- Facial feature comparison by a forensic artist, an anatomist, or even a plastic surgeon
- Dental assessment and comparison by a dental specialist or forensic odontologist
- Evaluation of the effects of lighting and exposure in the photograph by a photographer or digital imaging specialist

Forensic Art and Illustration includes suggested guidelines for simple evaluation and comparison of facial photographs and a discussion of the factors to consider. This is meant for use in investigative-related assessment of the facial characteristics to determine the *possibility* that certain photos may or may not depict the same individual. **This approach is not appropriate or legally valid for determination of a positive identification**.

A methodical step-by-step approach is recommended for evaluation. Multiple factors must be considered when reviewing facial images. Some fundamental concerns are the angle of view and the age of the subject in the image. Some elements of the facial "look" are simply natural, such as weight change or expression, while others may be intentional alterations of appearance. It can be helpful to assess the primary factors first and then consider other aspects and features one at a time.

In certain rare instances, an experienced facial identification specialist, anatomist, or anthropologist may give an opinion as to a match. However, such visual assessment comparisons **may be useful tools to eliminate an individual as a possible match** or simply **may indicate that further investigation is warranted**.

Image Identification Case Example

Image identification may involve face-to-face comparison of photos or other images, or it may be related to developing some type of forensic art to aid with identifying a subject captured on a surveillance system. Figure 28.5 shows a person sought in a homicide case that involved the brutal murder of an elderly man on Christmas day. Texas Rangers located a surveillance image of the suspect's face and wanted to improve its quality for distribution. Video, photographic, and electronic methods of enhancement proved unsuccessful, so I was asked to do a drawing of the person in the still frame. With some speculation, the frontal drawing was produced, but there was no identification for several years. Subsequently, the case was presented on "America's Most Wanted," and a tip was called in from across the United States, leading to the positive identification of the murderer through comparison of his fingerprints to latent prints from the crime scene. An important lesson learned from this case is that no matter how accurate a forensic art image might be, *it must be seen by the right person for it to prove successful*. Sometimes it's just a matter of luck or serendipity.

Considerations for the Investigator

- Who might be the best person for the job of comparison? A forensic artist? An anthropologist? An anatomist? A dental specialist? A photographer? A digital imaging or video specialist? Or *all* of them?
- What are the potential sources for comparison photos? High school year books? 50 state DL checks for name or alias names?

Figure 28.5 Surveillance image of suspect in a homicide case (top) from which a facial drawing was prepared by KTT (lower left) and the subject identified (lower right). (Courtesy of Karen T. Taylor.)

What the Artist Needs

- Enough insight into the investigation to properly do the face-to-face assessment
- Some background information about the subject and his/her lifestyle
- Knowledge of craniofacial anatomy
- The best available photographs of the subject in multiple views

Postmortem Imagery in Cold Cases

Circumstances for Doing Postmortem Drawing or Imagery

Postmortem drawing or imagery is a method of forensic art done when bodies are in good enough condition for the artist to develop a reasonable likeness based on morgue or crime scene photographs or by viewing the actual body. If the art is developed by hand sketching, it is generally called *postmortem drawing*. If it is done by means of computer-assisted graphics, it is referred to as *postmortem imagery*.

The primary purpose of postmortem drawing is to attach a name to the body as a result of someone viewing the facial image, so that medical records of a missing person can be compared to the body and lead to a legally valid positive identification. I often refer to my role as forensic artist as being the "middle man." The artwork is intended to provide a link between an unidentified person and the records needed to positively identify him or her.

It is the reanimation of the face from a deceased photograph that is one of the most difficult but necessary aspects of postmortem drawing. Adding that look of "life" is a difficult-to-describe, intangible action that the forensic artist must learn to accomplish.

Forensic artists are usually requested to do postmortem drawings in cases that fall into two broad categories. The first group includes unidentified deceased persons whose photographs are inappropriate for media distribution or viewing by possible family members because of trauma or postmortem effects on the face. The second group includes unidentified deceased individuals who have been buried for a period of time before personal identification has taken place and only photographs remain.

Postmortem drawings may be done in cases of various types of death and to depict faces in different postmortem stages. **For the cold case investigator, the unidentified person likely would be a victim of homicide or unnatural death, but could also be a long-term unidentified individual who died of apparent natural causes.**

Cases in Which Postmortem Drawing Is Used

- Suicides, natural deaths, or homicides
- Traffic fatalities
- Blunt or sharp trauma fatalities
- Gunshot would fatalities
- Drowning or boating accidents
- Some other transportation disasters
- Non-extensive conflagrations or fires
- Other miscellaneous types of homicidal violence

Cases in Which Postmortem Drawing Is Generally Not Used

- Extensive conflagrations
- Explosions
- Air disasters

Procedural Considerations for Doing Postmortem Drawing or Imagery

Choice of Method for Postmortem Drawing or Imagery

If good-quality facial photographs of the deceased are available, it may be preferable to do computer-based facial images, using tools in software to "clean up" the areas of damage to the face. If the photos are of poorer quality, taken at less than ideal angles with poor lighting, a hand-drawn approach is probably indicated.

Importance of Artist's Knowledge

Forensic art is a field that merges artistic skills with academic knowledge about a number of subjects. If an artist is to attempt unidentified deceased cases, there must be yet another entire new body of anatomical knowledge skills acquired. **The benefit of collaboration between the artist and the scientist cannot be underestimated in forensic art, particularly in unidentified deceased cases.**

Photography for Postmortem Drawing or Imagery

A primary difficulty in postmortem drawing cases is the lack of access to the body for viewing or photography. If a body is available for viewing by the artist, this is recommended. Although not a pleasant experience, the act of personally viewing the body may provide insights into the facial appearance not possible from photos alone.

Ideally, deceased photographs are taken in **frontal and lateral views**, including a scale or ruler with attention paid to avoiding distortion. The **scale** should be placed perpendicular to the camera lens so that it can be accurately read. If it is hanging, the **jaw should be raised** into as normal a position as possible.

In some jurisdictions, it may be possible to request that additional photographs be made for the artist's purposes. **More than likely, in cold cases, the photographs already taken will be the only ones available.** The odds are that the body has been long buried before the artist ever receives the request to do a postmortem drawing.

Depending upon the available material in the case file, the artist may benefit from access to **full-body photographs** in addition to facial ones. This gives a sense of body weight and body style, useful information for determining facial fullness. Full-length figure drawings depicting the clothing and appropriate body style may also be done (see Figure 28.7). Photos of **specific body details** such as the hands, any scars, marks or tattoos, or other unique traits may also form the basis for drawings. When photographs are inappropriate for public viewing, drawings can be prepared of most any other needed features. Examples might be tattoo drawings based on photos of decomposing skin or clothing details based on tattered soiled garments found with the body. I have also drawn hands with jewelry in the correct placement as found on the body, including nail shapes and nail polish color.

Photographs of the **dentition**, particularly if there are unique traits, may be used to draw the mouth in a slightly open fashion to reveal the teeth. With good photographs, the teeth can be drawn very specifically. In fact, the teeth may be the most reliable trait in cases of decomposed faces, since they are not subject to easy change as are the soft tissues.

When I receive cases with poor-quality photographs, I must decide if the face represented in the photographs is in good enough condition for me to develop a reasonable facsimile in drawing form. I also factor into my decisions the thought that my drawing may be the only opportunity that this person ever has to be identified and laid to rest. **If the photographs do not provide adequate information or the condition of the body is too bad, the postmortem drawing should not be attempted.**

Scientific Input for Postmortem Drawing or Imagery

In an ideal situation, the artist would have full access to discussions with the forensic pathologist or other scientific specialists who examine the body. This is not often the case. It is very important for the artist to receive copies of the autopsy or other scientific reports such as odontological or anthropological information. Typically, the artist might need clarification of such things as correspondence of body weight to facial fullness, or distinction between postmortem changes and antemortem traits. In photographs, insect bites may be difficult to distinguish from small moles.

In ***Forensic Art and Illustration***, there is information about postmortem changes that affect the face to aid the artist with reanimation of the face in the forensic artwork. Methods for use of dental information and photos are described so that the artist might better correct for the common slack-jawed position after death. There are specific palpebral changes that often occur in the eye area that must also be understood.

For me, postmortem drawing is probably the most difficult type of forensic art, or at least the type about which I feel most tentative. I am far more comfortable with a totally skeletonized case in which I have the skull to study.

Postmortem Drawing Case Examples

Figure 28.6 shows a case in which an oblique angle morgue photo was used to develop a postmortem drawing, approximately two years after the deceased body was found. She had been sexually assaulted, stabbed, beaten in the head with a claw hammer, and dumped from a bridge. The murder victim was identified and her assailant was subsequently tied to a series of murders.

Figure 28.6 Oblique morgue photograph of unidentified homicide victim (left), postmortem drawing by KTT drawn by rotating the face (center), and life photo (right). (Courtesy of Karen T. Taylor.)

Considerations for the Investigator

- Would a postmortem drawing or image be useful in the case?
- What sort of photographs are available of the deceased? From the crime scene? From the morgue? Full body photos? Detail photos? Photos of the teeth?
- How about photos of associated items like clothing, hats, jewelry, dentures?
- Is the body too decomposed for postmortem imagery from photos alone?
- Do sufficient antemortem records exist to confirm identity if a name surfaces from the forensic art? Dental records?
- Should the tissue be removed to provide the artist with a cleaned skull for reconstruction? Cost? Potential ramifications?

What the Artist Needs

- Enough information about the investigation to properly prepare the postmortem drawing
- Both crime scene photographs and autopsy photographs if available
- Specimens or good photos of available items like hair, dentures, eyeglasses, clothing, hats
- Access to autopsy or other scientific reports
- Knowledge of taphonomic changes that affect the face such as rigor mortis, livor mortis, autolysis, putrefaction, insect, and animal activity

Two-Dimensional Facial Reconstruction in Cold Cases

Circumstances for Doing Two-Dimensional Facial Reconstruction

The technique of two-dimensional facial reconstruction from the skull is a method of forensic art used to aid in identifying skeletal remains. The artist and the anthropologist collaborate to construct the facial features of the unknown individual on the basis of the underlying cranial structure.

We automatically think of all of the various scientific methods of identifying bodies today that we have seen used so often on television: fingerprint comparisons, radiograph and dental comparisons, and DNA. Yet the simple fact is that these are all **comparative methods**, which means that **there must first be records in order for them to be compared to a body**.

Again, I characterize my forensic artist role as that of the "middle man." Ideally, my **artwork provides the needed connection between an unidentified deceased person and the records needed to identify that person**. Placing an item of forensic art in the public media or in police publications may generate a lead or tip that results in a possible name attached to the body. Then science can do its job of comparing the body to a missing person's records and positively identifying the body by any of various available means.

For the cold case detective, the identification of the murder victim may be the most critical step needed to get the investigation started. This is particularly true since statistics indicate that so many victims of homicide died at the hands of a close associate. **Establishing the identity of the victim may lead to all of the pieces of the investigative puzzle coming together**.

Law enforcement agencies and medical examiners are regularly presented with difficult cases of unidentified victims of homicide or unexplained death. It is their **statutory and moral obligation to make every attempt to identify** these individuals. There are numerous reasons to identify bodies. Doing a representation of an individual's visage may be the only hope of ever identifying that person. For every life, there is someone somewhere who cares. Missing persons who are never located or identified may leave behind complicated legal issues such as inheritances and other business matters. Especially significant is the knowledge that **an unidentified body likely means a murder unsolved and a murderer walking free**.

Due to situational and climactic factors, human remains may be found in a great variety of physical conditions. When bodies are severely damaged or in advanced stages of decompositional change, postmortem drawings may not be possible. In instances of semi-skeletal or totally skeletonized remains, a method of reconstructing the face from the skull may be necessary.

Procedural Considerations for Doing Two-Dimensional Facial Reconstruction

Choice of Method for Facial Reconstruction

Both two- and three-dimensional facial reconstruction methods have proven successful, but some cases may be better done by either one or the other method. The artist may prefer one method or have greater skill in a particular method.

Extremely fragile skulls, either forensic or historical cases, may not be strong enough to bear the weight of clay for a sculptural reconstruction. In such cases, particularly if the damage is in the facial area, a two-dimensional approach may be taken.

Three-dimensional reconstruction offers the advantage of viewing and photographing the sculpture in multiple views. In addition, actual items recovered at the scene with the skeletal body, such as eyeglasses, jewelry, or clothing, may sometimes be placed directly on the finished sculpture of photography. These days, technology even allows that the forensic sculpture may be scanned and placed on websites, showing it in a rotating or 360° fashion.

A plus with the drawing approach is that it is somewhat less expensive, and the skull is left uncovered so that it is available for other types of analyses to be conducted. With the drawing approach, it is also easy to alter the hair, facial hair, or eye color using matte acetate overlays, without purchasing wigs or prosthetic eyes. It is also simple to scan a drawn facial reconstruction into graphics software and manipulate the hair or facial hair, add glasses, and so forth.

On several occasions, I have been asked to prepare reconstructed faces on available radiographs/x-rays in cases where the body has been buried, but I decline to do this for several reasons. My two-dimensional technique is based on certain formulas applied to life-size, undistorted photographs of a skull, using discernible bony landmarks. In a radiograph, it cannot be assumed that the image is life size, since most equipment produces a variable enlargement factor of an indeterminate percentage. The use of calculations would therefore be incorrect. Further, **from a radiograph alone, it is not possible to accurately locate many of the bony landmarks needed for reconstruction**.

In some cases, it is possible to do methods of facial reconstruction based on **damaged or incomplete skulls.** However, such restoration can prove very challenging and is no job for the inexperienced.

Importance of Artist's Knowledge

As emphasized in all other sections of this chapter, the artist must have the appropriate anatomical and technique knowledge base to enter into each type of forensic art. Just because an artist draws effective composites does not mean that he or she can do unidentified deceased cases without training specifically for that area. An entirely new set of skills and knowledge are needed for facial reconstruction.

The artist must gain enough understanding of technical and anatomical language in order to communicate with scientific professional and interpret their reports.

Forensic Art and Illustration includes a chapter on **Skull Protection and Preparation for Reconstruction,** coauthored by Betty Pat. Gatliff and myself. We outline specific procedures that should be followed to prepare a skull for reconstruction whether the forensic art project will be done two-dimensionally or three-dimensionally. It is critical that care be taken to protect the integrity of the skull as an item of evidence, and to ensure appropriate transferal from person to person or "chain of custody". Equally important is physical protection of the skull since certain parts are extremely fragile.

Occasionally, it is necessary to restore missing or incomplete areas of the skull before reconstruction is attempted. Guidance for this is also included in the above-mentioned chapter.

The textbook also includes in-depth chapters on **Two-Dimensional Facial Reconstruction from the Skull** and **Three-Dimensional Facial Reconstruction on the Skull.** Included are step-by-step procedures for each method along with hundreds of illustrations and photographs.

The artist should receive a **cleaned, uncontaminated skull,** transferred using the **evidence transferal procedures** for the particular jurisdiction. It is important that the teeth are carefully attended to and inventoried.

Scientific Input for Facial Reconstruction

Again, the benefit of collaboration between the artist and the scientist cannot be overemphasized in forensic art, particularly in unidentified deceased cases.

Before the artist attempts any skull restoration or facial reconstruction, as much information as possible should be gathered concerning a particular case. Various scientific specialists may need to be consulted, particularly a skilled **physical or forensic anthropologist**. Only through anthropological evaluation to determine age, sex, and ancestry can the artist select the appropriate tissue depth date as preparation for rebuilding a face on the skull.

It may be **important that specimens of the teeth or areas of bone be removed before the artist is given the skull.** The investigator should determine whether any needed specimens should be taken, to insure that there is no contamination from cements or other artistic materials potentially used by the forensic artist, or even by handling of the skull by the artist.

The dentition of the skull should always be considered to be an extremely important aspect for identification. If reconstruction will be done, the investigator should attempt to **retrieve all available teeth** for the artist to use. The evaluation and input of a **trained dental professional** is particularly helpful to the artist who does facial reconstruction.

Photography for Two-Dimensional Facial Reconstruction

Photography is an integral part of the two-dimensional facial reconstruction process and **must be done very precisely.** The procedure that I developed in the mid-1980s requires that tissue depth markers first be cut and glued to the skull. Then, frontal and lateral photographs are made with the skull in an orientation called the Frankfort horizontal. The needed photography method is outline specifically in ***Forensic Art and Illustration.***

(a)

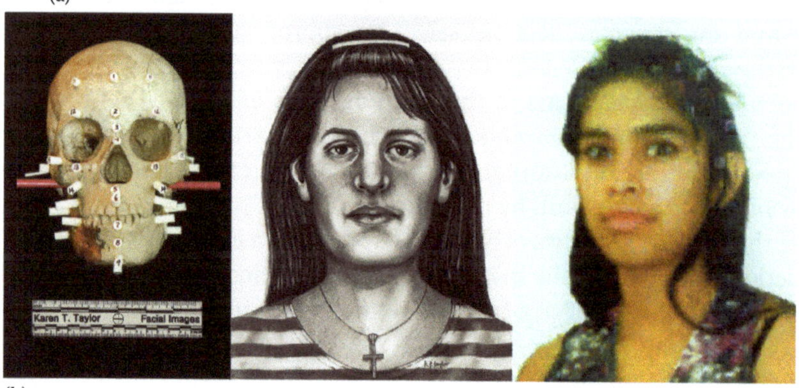

(b)

Figure 28.7 (a) Drawing of full body by KTT on a poster used to show clothing, jewelry, and body style of a now-identified homicide victim. In the first edition of this text, the victim was unidentified but as a result of this image and investigation, her identity became known. (b) Fragmentary skull with more than half the face and the dentition rebuilt in clay by KTT (left), two-dimensional facial reconstruction by KTT (center), and life photo (right). (Courtesy of Karen T. Taylor.)

Some officers have requested that I do two-dimensional facial reconstruction from photographs that they have taken of a skull. I decline to do this because of the need for precision photography with the tissue depth markers in place.

Two-Dimensional Facial Reconstruction Examples

Figure 28.7a shows a poster from an unidentified deceased case in which the full figure has been drawn. I used photographs of clothing and jewelry items found with the remains to prepare the drawing. An effort was also made, based on the scientific reports, to depict the petite stature and short-legged body style. See Figure 28.7b for the resulting victim identification.

Figure 28.8 shows a case in which two-dimensional facial reconstruction led to the identity of a young female homicide victim. Most of the teeth were recovered with the remains along with a hair specimen. These were provided to me by the investigator for inclusion in the drawing.

Figure 28.9 is a homicide case in which only the cranium and upper teeth were recovered. With anthropological input, I was able to approximate the mandible and develop two-dimensional reconstruction drawings that aided in the victim's identification.

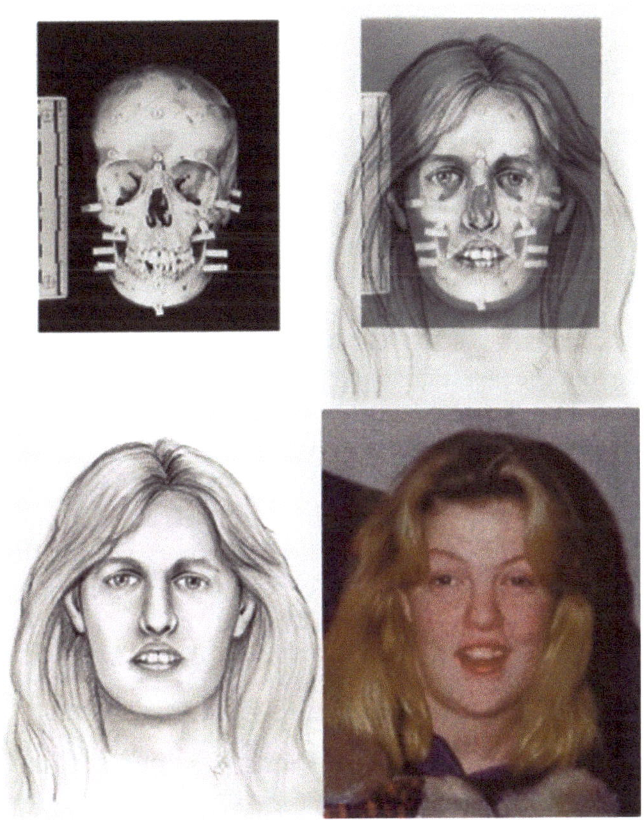

Figure 28.8 Skull (upper left), two-dimensional facial reconstruction by KTT with skull visible beneath (upper right), two-dimensional facial reconstruction (lower left), and victim identified (lower right). (Courtesy of Karen T. Taylor.)

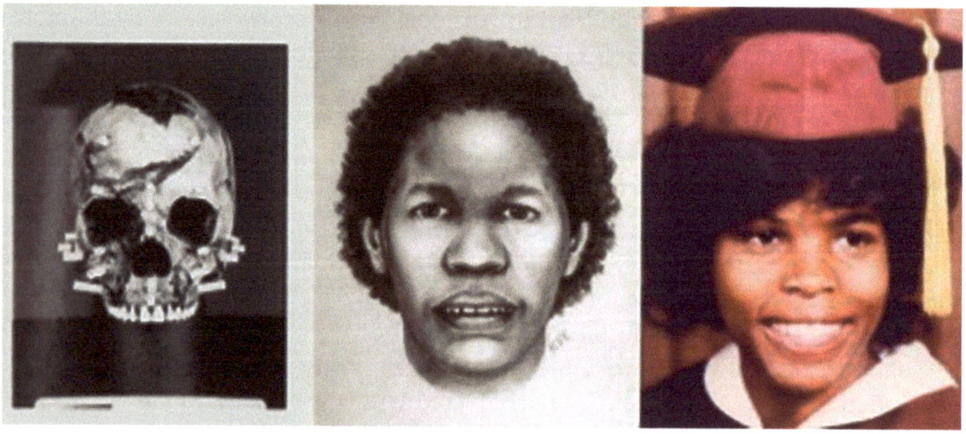

Figure 28.9 Skull with missing mandible (left), two-dimensional facial reconstruction by KTT (center), and victim identified (right). (Courtesy of Karen T. Taylor.)

Considerations for the Investigator

- Will the unidentified body have to be exhumed to perform this procedure? Is the burial location known?
- Will it be possible to get the skull cleaned for transferal to the artist?
- Have all available teeth been recovered and provided with the skull?
- Are there any hair specimens, glasses, dentures, items of clothing, hats, or other artifacts that the artist should see?
- Have all the necessary specimens of teeth or bone for potential DNA use been obtained before the skull goes to the artist?

What the Artist Needs

- Enough information about the investigation to properly prepare the facial reconstruction
- Cleaned, uncontaminated skull
- Input from a qualified anthropologist and dental specialist if possible
- Access to autopsy or other scientific reports
- Any available photos from the scene that show the body or its accoutrements
- Specimens or good photos of available items like hair, dentures, glasses, clothing, hats
- Knowledge of taphonomic changes that affect the face

Three-Dimensional Facial Reconstruction in Cold Cases

Circumstances for Doing Three-Dimensional Facial Reconstruction

Facial sculpture, synonymous with facial or skull reconstruction, restoration, approximation, and reproduction, is a method of forensic art used to help identify skeletal remains. The artist and the anthropologist collaborate to construct the facial features of the unknown individual on the basis of the underlying cranial structure.

Procedural Considerations for Doing Three-Dimensional Facial Reconstruction

Choice of Method for Facial Reconstruction

See the discussion in the section on two-dimensional facial reconstruction to help determine whether a drawn or sculptural approach is best for your case.

In the area of forensic sculpture or three-dimensional facial reconstruction, there are **two primary approaches:** the **anatomical method** and the **tissue depth method**.

Generally, in the anatomical method of facial reconstruction, muscles are defined individually to flesh out the face, and tissue depth data are not utilized. The anatomical method is associated originally with the Russians and is most commonly used in England. It is also preferred by museum preparators who develop exhibits based on ancient skulls. Due to the nature of the method, it tends to be more time consuming.

The tissue depth method involves use of data gained in anthropological studies as a guide for building up to the facial surfaces. It is considered the "American Method" and is the approach most commonly used in law enforcement cases. Generally, it is faster to do than the anatomical method.

It is my belief that the most advantageous method for law enforcement use is probably a combination of both the anatomical approach and the tissue depth approach that I call the **combination method**.

Importance of Artist's Knowledge

See the discussion in the section on two-dimensional facial reconstruction.

Scientific Input for Three-Dimensional Facial Reconstruction

See the discussion in the section on two-dimensional facial reconstruction.

Photography for Three-Dimensional Facial Reconstruction

The photography of the finished forensic sculpture may be simple or elaborate, but it **should be distortion free**. The usual five views that are shot are frontal, oblique left, lateral left, oblique right, and lateral right.

Take care to light the sculpture in such a way that the morphological details are shown, not diminished. While dramatic lighting may be desirable in portrait photography, the goal here is to convey information rather than to flatter. A backdrop that is solid in color and neutral will also help emphasize the face. Soft, diffuse lighting is preferable.

With forensic reconstructions, it is usually relatively simple to generate media attention, if desired. Members of the media find the sculpted face of a homicide victim an interesting subject. While beneficial and necessary for distribution of the facial replica, such interviews should be carefully controlled. Caution should be taken by the investigator to **control the facial views given to the media to ensure that they don't simply use distorted photos shot for their dramatic appeal, rather than for maximum definition of the face**.

When using digital cameras, particular attention should be paid to preventing distortions. Use of a tripod helps prevent upward or downward angles, since they distort the features. The sculpted face should be photographed very straight on or in direct profile.

Three-Dimensional Facial Reconstruction Example

Figure 28.10 shows the skull with tissue depth approximation markers attached, along with the sculpted facial reconstruction by Karen T. Taylor. At right is a life photo of the young woman who was identified once the forensic sculpture was aired on ***America's Most Wanted***.

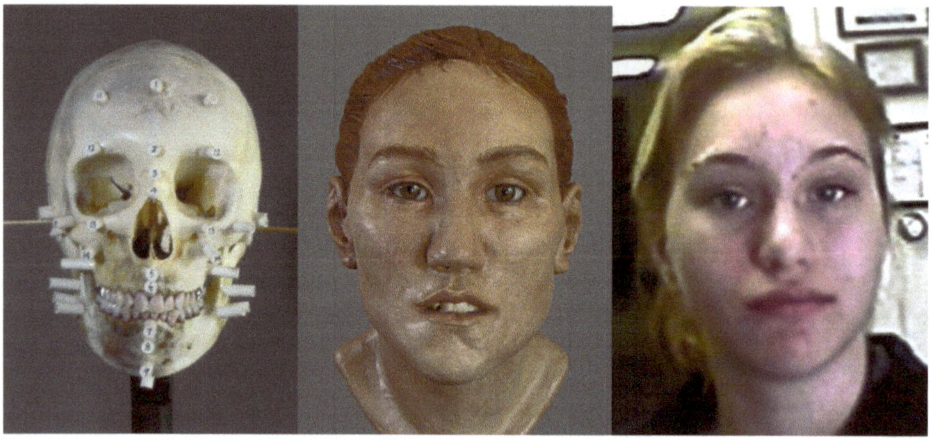

Figure 28.10 Skull (left), three-dimensional facial reconstruction by KTT (center), and victim identified (right). (Courtesy of Karen T. Taylor.)

Considerations for the Investigator

- Will the unidentified body have to be exhumed to perform this procedure? Is the burial location known?
- Will it be possible to get the skull cleaned for transferal to the artist?
- Have all available teeth been recovered and provided with the skull?
- Are there any hair specimens, glasses, dentures, items of clothing, hats, or other artifacts that the artist should see?
- Have all the necessary specimens of teeth or bone for potential DNA use been obtained before the skull goes to the artist?

What the Artist Needs

- Enough information about the investigation to properly prepare the facial reconstruction
- Cleaned, uncontaminated skull, sturdy enough to bear the weight of the clay sculpture
- Input from a qualified anthropologist and dental specialist if possible
- Access to autopsy or other scientific reports
- Any available photos from the scene that show the body or its accoutrements
- Specimens or good photos of available items like hair, dentures, glasses, clothing, hats
- Knowledge of taphonomic changes that affect the face
- Sculpture skills

Superimposition Comparison in Cold Cases

Circumstances for Doing Superimposition Comparison

There is one other method that I will include in brief, in which the **artist may act as part of a team of facial identification specialists.**

When semi-skeletal or skeletal bodies are found and investigators have no idea at all as to the identity of the deceased, a method of facial reconstruction is indicated. However, **there are some cases in which crime analysts or investigators have suspicions that the body might be a certain missing person**. If there are no dental or other antemortem records for comparison, a method of superimposition comparison might be helpful, especially if good photographs of the missing person exist.

A practical factor is that **superimposition comparisons may save investigative dollars in the long run**. The procedure may quickly eliminate a possible missing person as a match for the unidentified deceased. Or, it may be a strong indicator that the next step, perhaps time-consuming or pricey tests, would be well-warranted.

While **not generally considered a means of positive identification**, a reasonable congruence between the skull and the photo would point to the next logical step such as DNA comparison.

Procedural Considerations for Doing Superimposition Comparison

Superimpositions have actually been done for over 100 years and have recently developed into a more technologically useful tool for assessing identification of unknown skeletal remains. **These techniques fall into three general categories: photographic, video, and computer-aided**. It is likely that each technique has unique advantages and disadvantages.

Undoubtedly, further technological advances in computer digitization and photographic enhancement will yield a degree of accuracy not yet obtainable by today's methodology (Glassman 2001).

Forensic Art and Illustration includes a chapter by forensic anthropologist Dr. David Glassman on **Methods of Superimposition**. The chapter discusses the critical variables necessary to develop an accurate comparison and describes the video superimposition procedure and subsequent analysis technique. Also specified is the type of video equipment needed.

Essentially, superimposition comparisons focus on **orientation and scale**. The skull must be placed so that it is in the same orientation and at the same scale as the face in the photograph used for comparison. This is far easier said than done. Dr. Glassman and I have worked on many cases, primarily using the video approach.

The artist is often the member of the team tasked with achieving the correct orientation, using experience and skill gained through other forensic art tasks. Usually the science part of this art/science task is a **forensic anthropologist**. At times, other team members might be a pathologist, an anatomist, an odontologist, dentist, orthodontist, or others. There should also be photographic and video specialists.

Once the correct scale and orientation are achieved through trial and error, then the critical variables may be assessed. These include, but are not limited to, positioning, size, distortion, features to be used for comparison, and the defining limits for concluding a possible match or exclusion.

In general, the comparison is more effective and has **greater odds for accuracy if several views of the missing person's face are available**. Photographs from various angles should be overlaid if possible, reorienting the skull with each new photo. Straight frontal views and profile views are the simplest to position. Oblique views are more complicated and may result in inaccurate interpretation.

When recovered with a skull, the anterior or **frontal teeth can be very useful as part of the superimposition process**. If the investigator can find smiling photographs of the missing person and they reveal the teeth clearly, this is an added plus.

Skeletal remains do not need to be complete to be useful in superimposition comparisons. Missing mandible cases or those with areas of damage may be used.

It is important to note that the artist may be a valuable member of the team, but **the scientist should make any judgment calls regarding the identity of the deceased**. The artist is not qualified to do this.

Video Superimposition Comparison Example

Figure 28.11 shows a case of superimposition comparison done jointly by Dr. David Glassman and myself. The skull was quite fragmentary and had to be reassembled. Then, we were able to overlay it with photos of

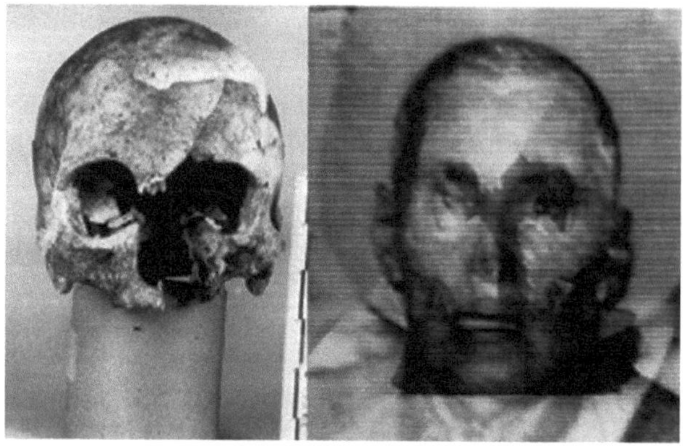

Figure 28.11 Superimposition comparison by KTT and forensic anthropologist David Glassman, PhD, of a fractured cranium (left) and a photographic image (right). (Courtesy of Karen T. Taylor.)

a missing person known to have disappeared from the general area where the remains were found. Time-since-death estimations and physical parameters from Dr. Glassman's report were also consistent, though there were no antemortem dental records available. Using video equipment, we established a congruence that indicated further investigation in this direction was appropriate, ultimately leading to his positive identification.

Considerations for the Investigator

What the Artist Needs

- Enough information about the investigation to properly assist with the superimposition procedure
- Knowledge of craniofacial anatomy
- Working environment within a team of qualified science professionals
- Assistance of photographic or video experts with knowledge of the superimposition process
- Video equipment that includes two cameras, a monitor, and an image mixing capability
- Skull, with mandible in place and front teeth accurately affixed in the sockets, if available
- Photographs of the missing person for comparison, preferably multiple facial angles

Qualifications of the Forensic Artist

Training and Education

To aid in your selection and hiring of an artist practitioner, you should have some understanding of the training and qualifications of forensic artists. This might also help to guide the training for individuals within your agency who have demonstrated an aptitude for this work.

The forensic art field does not have a specific set of educational requirements or defined career paths. Many forensic artists today are capable of performing a wide spectrum of art functions to assist in criminal investigations and case presentations. However, some artists specialize almost exclusively in one aspect of forensic art such as composite imagery, facial reconstruction from skulls, or child age progression.

Most police agencies in the United States utilize a forensic artist on as "as needed" basis, either using someone on staff in another capacity or hiring a freelancer. Certain agencies employ a full-time artist, but such instances are rare and usually occur in federal or state agencies or in very large cities.

Practitioners in this business tend to enter the field from various directions. Many are police officers who began doing forensic art out of necessity on cases within their own agencies. Others are civilian employees working within police agencies who demonstrated artistic talent and were recruited by detectives to help with their investigations. Some are trained artists who contract with law enforcement agencies on a freelance basis.

Depending upon which forensic art specialty practitioners choose, their education should be geared accordingly, with the intention being to "fill the gaps" of their own previous training and experience. For example, experienced police officers who have spent many years conducting interviews and testifying in court may require additional art training. Civilian artists, whether employed in law enforcement or freelancers, must learn about functioning within the proper restraints of the laws of the jurisdiction within which they work.

Training for artists should also facilitate the specific area of forensic art to be done. Anyone who prepares composite images should have training in interview techniques and sensitivity to crime victims. Serious composite artists should consider this an area for career-long improvement. Such artists can never have too much knowledge about memory-enhancing interview techniques, and they should feel compelled to constantly read literature involving research in this area.

Those artists who work with image modification, particularly by computer methods, should seek training and expertise in software packages that allow the manipulations and enhancements they require. Image modifications such as age progressions that project growth in a child's face require study of the complex patterns of craniofacial growth. Age progressions of the faces of long-term missing fugitives require knowledge of facial aging. Both types of age progressions can be enhanced by an understanding of human dentition and the associated patterns of dental eruption in children as well as modifications that occur in the forms around the mouth with aging and dental attrition.

Artists who prepare demonstrative evidence or trial displays must have a wide array of skills. This field has become so multifaceted that many have chosen to specialize in a particular category. Displays can be hand-drawn, graphic art, photographic, computer-assisted, three-dimensional, or animated. They may be as simple as an enlargement of two side-by-side fingerprints for comparison or as complex as elaborately animated reenactments of an event.

Those who do postmortem imagery or facial reconstruction from the skull must delve into an entirely different base of learning. Postmortem drawings require a working knowledge of taphonomic changes that occur with death and their effects on the face. Facial reconstructionists work very closely with physical or forensic anthropologists and often gain knowledge in that field that directly benefits their work. Trained medical illustrators are "naturals" for going into facial reconstruction because of their strong foundation in facial anatomy.

Methods of superimposition comparison of skulls to photographs of missing persons are generally best approached as a team effort. The forensic artist, as one member of the team, provides knowledge of the morphological structures of the face that aids in the orientation of the skull into the correct position for overlay comparisons. The scientifically trained experts make the assessments that can lead to identification.

Again, **the benefit of collaboration between the artist and the scientist cannot be** underestimated in forensic art, particularly in unidentified deceased cases.

Experience

It is worth emphasizing that **forensic art is extremely experience-based**. Investigators are encouraged to utilize the skills of artists who are experienced in identification-specific work rather than just portrait or other artists. **Because artwork in cold cases may be complex, the skills of experienced artists are ideal**.

On the other hand, if no funds for an experienced artist are available, maybe a talented volunteer beginner might be worth a shot.

As with any other profession, it is always advisable to check an artist's credentials, experience, and references. Ask to see a portfolio of drawings and sculptures to assess basic art skills. Ask to view photographs of previous forensic art cases, especially if you are hiring a freelancer. Ask about solved cases and be prepared to verify any claims of previous "hits." **Consider the training needed for the specific task you need. Are you choosing the best artist for the job? Have they had the training needed to do the work?**

Certification

There is a certification program for forensic artists within the International Association for Identification. This is the **only existing certification process under the auspices of a professional organization and involves a testing procedure and peer review.**

Some artists attend a workshop and receive a "certificate" upon completion of the course. Such a certificate is a "certificate of attendance" and means only that the person attended the workshop for the required time. The certificate may be important documentation of the hours of training received, useful in court testimony or when applying for certification. However, a **"certificate of attendance" is not a "certification."**

Fee Structure

Salaries and fees in the forensic art field vary tremendously throughout the United States and Canada. There is also variation in the ways in which jobs are assigned and valued. **As with any field, experience and demonstrated success bring higher fees**. Only a handful of artists are full-time employees with law enforcement agencies. Freelance or contract employees may charge by the job or by the hour.

Dealings between the Artist and the Investigator

Important aspects of artist/investigator interaction include

- Good communication
- Proper evidence transferals when needed
- Possible use of NDAs or nondisclosure agreements, if necessary, with a freelancer

It is my hope that the contents of this chapter will aid cold case investigators to have greater understanding and insight into my field, and encourage them to consider use of forensic art methods. It has been said that **the pen is mightier than the sword**...if used correctly, **so is the pencil...**

Acknowledgments

I wish to extend my deepest gratitude and appreciation to Karen T. Taylor for her gracious contribution and authorship of this chapter. Of international renown, Karen Taylor is considered by many to be one of America's leading forensic artists. Taylor attended the School of Fine Arts at the University of Texas and the Chelsea School of Fine Arts in London, where she was also a freelance portrait sculptor for Madame Tussaud's Wax Museum. She worked as a forensic artist for 18 years for the Texas Department of Public Safety in Austin, Texas. Her crime-fighting work for law enforcement agencies and FOX television's "America's Most Wanted" has involved a variety of art services to aid in the apprehension and conviction of criminals or further efforts to identify unknown, deceased persons.

In addition, her work has been featured on FOX, ABC, CBS, CNN, Court TV, the Discovery Channel, the History Channel, Telemundo, and the BBC. The popular CBS drama "CSI" created a forensic artist character based on Taylor, and her hands and artwork have appeared on the show.

The successes of her forensic art have led to Taylor being named one of the "Texas Women of the Century." She has served as a forensic art instructor at the FBI National Academy and other law enforcement academies, universities, and medical schools in the United States and Canada, and now devotes her in-depth knowledge of the human face to the training of fine artists. She is the author of *Forensic Art and Illustration* and the upcoming work *Understanding the Human Face.* (http://www.Karenttaylor.com.)

Suggested Readings and Bibliography

Glassman, D.M., Methods of superimposition, in *Forensic Art and Illustration*, Taylor, K.T., Eds. Boca Raton, FL: CRC Press, 2001.

Macris, T.F., "Composite art, general principles for man and machine," *Identification News*, August, 1987.

Taylor, K.T., *Forensic Art and Illustration*. Boca Raton, FL: CRC Press, 2001.

Cold Case Polygraph

29

PAUL REDDEN

Contents

Introduction

The polygraph, more commonly referred to as the lie detector, is another excellent tool available to the cold case investigator that cannot be overlooked or forgotten. In cold case homicide investigations, the polygraph can play a valuable role in assisting and assessing a person's knowledge of or involvement in a case under investigation. In addition, review of cold case files may reveal that subjects involved in the unsolved case had been polygraphed in decades past (see Figure 29.1). Have an examiner review the polygraph charts. Techniques and equipment have changed. Do not assume that the examiner will agree on the earlier conclusions. If the subject is available, and he is a possible suspect or have valuable information for your investigation, he should probably be retested. The revived investigation could have produced some new information and questions that now need to be addressed. Sometimes individuals will take a private polygraph examination. Again, do not assume the results are accurate. The information provided to the examiner about the case came from the individual who was tested and could have been inaccurate, which would have played a significant role in the results of the test. The private polygraph examiner will be happy to produce his polygraph file for your review as long as it does not violate any attorney–client privilege.

Role of the Polygraph

There are several things to take into consideration when deciding to use the polygraph in a cold case investigation. Remember, the polygraph is an *aid* to the investigator and should never be considered a substitute or a shortcut to a thorough investigation. The polygraph can be used not only to determine a suspect's involvement in a crime but can also assist in verifying witness information or knowledge in a particular crime. Although polygraph results are generally inadmissible in court, the information obtained or statements made to the examiner are. This can also play an important role in pointing the investigation in the right direction.

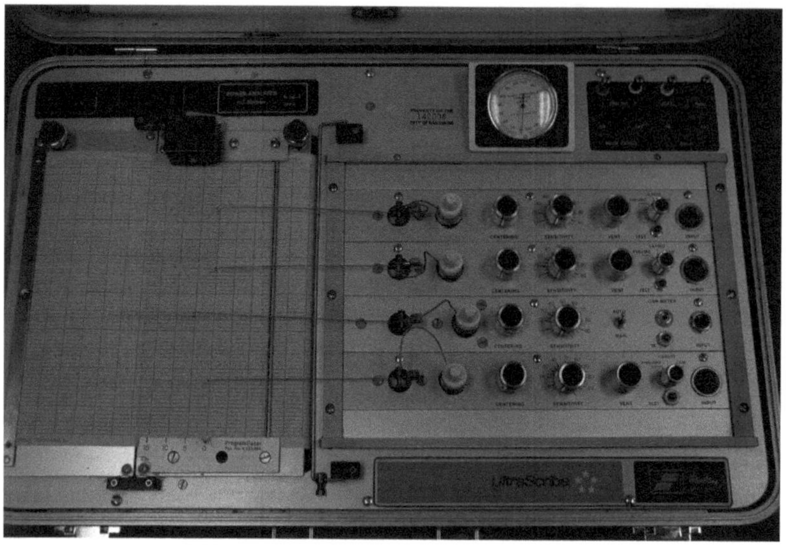

Figure 29.1 Old-style analog polygraph. (Author's collection.)

Selection and Qualifications of Polygraph Examiner

If an agency does not have its own polygraph examiner, several things need to be considered in selecting a polygraph examiner. First and foremost, did the examiner receive training at an approved polygraph school? The American Polygraph Association (APA) or the American Association of Police Polygraphists (AAPP) can provide information concerning approved or recognized polygraph schools. Successful completion of an approved polygraph school is a requirement to become a member APA, AAPP or a State Polygraph Association.

Limitations on Examination

Prior to scheduling the polygraph examination, the investigator should be aware of conditions that might prohibit the examination. Persons with physical disabilities, severe heart conditions, pregnancy, or severe psychological disorders are examples of people who may not be suitable for a polygraph examination. Additionally, people who are intoxicated or under the influence of drugs should not be tested. Ideally, the subject should be well rested and nourished. If subjects are taking prescribed medication, they should continue to take their medication as prescribed. The polygraph examiner has the final decision as to whether subjects are suitable for an examination.

Prior to the Examination

The investigator should not interrogate the subject prior to the polygraph examination and should stop all questioning once the subject has agreed to submit to the exam. Continued questioning could have a serious impact on the results of the exam. In addition:

- Do not attempt to explain the polygraph to the subject.
- Do not go into detail about what questions the examiner will ask.
- Never suggest to the subject that the examiner will ask only questions about the investigation.
- Tell subjects that the examiner will explain the entire process and they will be given the opportunity to ask the examiner any questions about the polygraph procedure.

In deciding to use the polygraph in an investigation, think about what there is to gain from the examination. There is a lot of information that is important for the investigation, but in a polygraph examination,

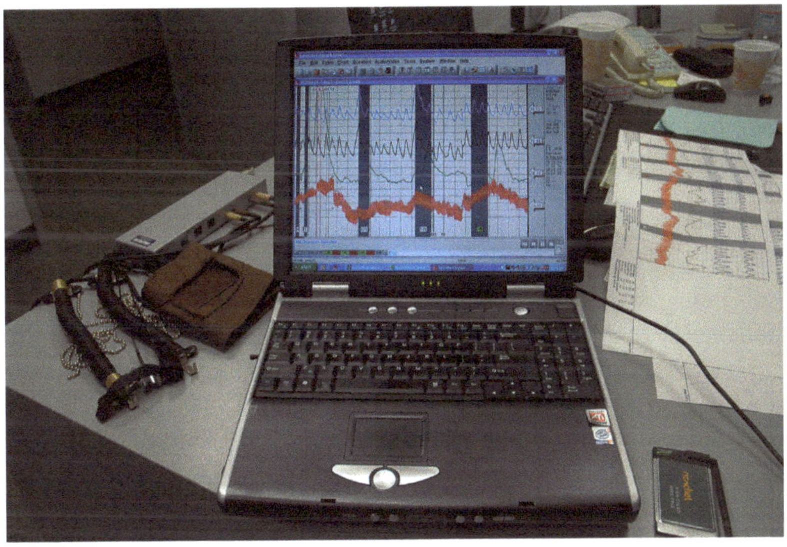

Figure 29.2 Computerized polygraph. (Courtesy of Paul Redden.)

target the questions to the most important piece of information that the subject may possess or have knowledge about. There are only three or four relevant questions that can be asked in a polygraph examination, so consider what is the most important question to be answered.

A conference with the investigator and polygraph examiner is extremely necessary prior to the polygraph examination. The investigator needs to discuss all of the case facts with the examiner and should not withhold any information that could assist the examiner during the exam. Remember, the subject could be the perpetrator, and it is imperative that the examiner be aware of all the case facts and information. If subjects think that the examiner is misinformed or uniformed, they will try to use that to their advantage, which could play a role in gaining or losing a confession or valuable information that could assist you in the investigation.

If investigators can observe the polygraph, I encourage them to watch the entire examination. Information often surfaces that they may not be aware of and that can be of assistance in the investigation. If they are there to hear it, they can start using that information immediately. Also, the examiner may need help from the investigator to clarify issues or to ask questions about some of the information that has surfaced during the interview of the subject.

It is my opinion that all polygraph examinations should at least be tape recorded. This protects all involved and may later be extremely valuable in replaying what was said in the polygraph room during the examination. Video taping is even better, as it provides a visual reference to all of the subject's behavior during the examination. Computerized polygraph equipment is capable of digitally recording both audio and video of the examination. The computerized equipment is portable and allows for webcam audio/video recording in virtually any situation (see Figure 29.2).

The Examination Process

The polygraph is conducted on a voluntary basis. No one can be forced to take a polygraph exam, and it cannot be rushed. A properly conduced examination will last a minimum of 90 minutes and could take several hours to cover a complex case. The examination consists of several different phases, more commonly referred to as pre-test, testing, and post-test phases.

Pre-Test Phase

During this phase, or pre-test interview, the examiner gathers personal information about the subject's background. The examiner will explain how the polygraph works. What components will be physically attached to the subject and what each component is recording, as well as a description of the psycho-physiological aspect of lying, will be explained to subject, who will be given the opportunity to explain what he or she knows about the crime under investigation and will give his or her version of what he or she knows or the role he or she played in the crime under investigation.

The examiner is looking for any changes in the original statement made to the investigator or any additional information that may not have been previously disclosed. This is an interview phase and the examiner will not challenge the subject but will ask questions to clarify any questions that might arise. The examiner will then formulate the questions that will be asked of the subject in the polygraph examination. All of the questions are first reviewed with the subject.

During this review, the individual will be asked to explain the meaning and his or her understanding of the relevant questions that are going to be asked. The examiner does this to make sure he or she understands what is going to be asked in the examination and to ensure the questions have the same meaning to both the examiner and the subject.

Test Phase

This is the actual polygraph examination. The examiner will attach the components to the subject. The components consist of two pneumo tubes, an expandable tube that measures respiration. One goes around the chest and one goes around the stomach. The galvanic skin response (GSR) plates are attached to the fingers and measure the skin response, and the cardio cuff goes around the arm and measures the pulse rate, increases or decreases in blood pressure, and the strength of the heart beat. All of the components are measured simultaneously on the polygraph chart. Subjects will be instructed to remain completely still during the exam and to answer the questions only with a yes or no answer, as previously reviewed. The examiner will adjust the instrument to the subject's physiological level and administer the examination. There is an approximate 25-second time period from one question to the next. This allows time for the subject to react to and recover from any question that poses a threat to their well-being.

There are several types of exams that the examiner can use. Each type of examination has a specific purpose:

- The **S-K-Y** exam, containing three relevant questions, is used to help determine suspicion, knowledge, personal involvement, or lesser involvement in the crime under investigation.
- A **YOU** phase exam contains two or three relevant questions. It is used to determine a specific role in the crime, i.e., "Did you fire the shot that resulted in the death of John Doe?"
- An **Exploratory** exam contains three or four relevant questions and is used to determine the different roles a subject might have committed, i.e., "Did you drive the getaway car? Were you the lookout man?" etc.
- The **Peak of Tension** exam can be used to determine specific knowledge that only the perpetrator should know, i.e., "If you shot John Doe, did you use a .22, .38, .45 …?" etc. This must be an item of information that is known only to the individual and the investigators and has not been publicly disclosed.

Upon conclusion of the polygraph examination the examiner will probably advise the subject of the results of the examination. The examiner may first ask for a quality control of the charts from another examiner, if readily available, before advising the subject of the findings (see Figure 29.3).

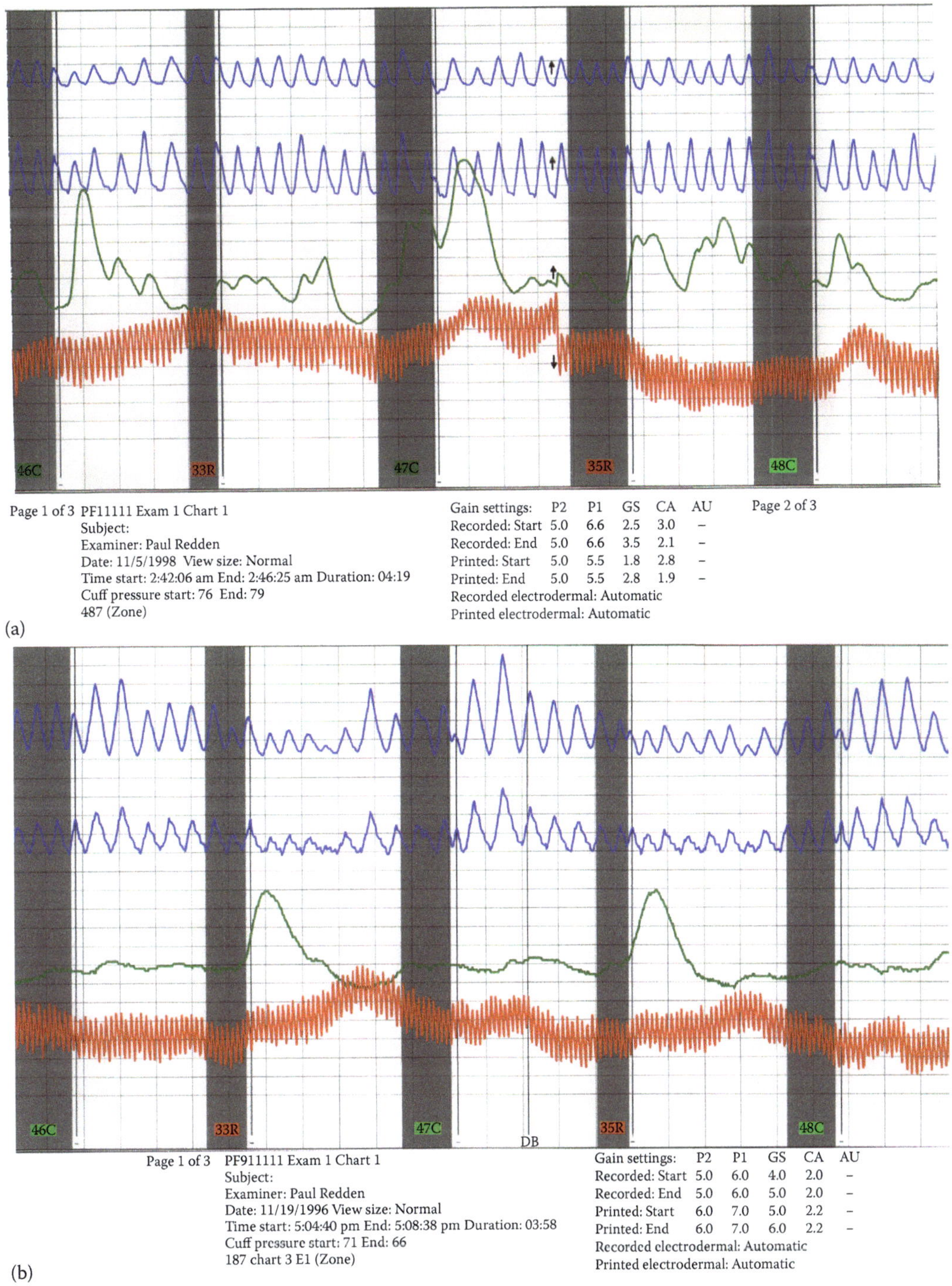

Figure 29.3 (a) An example of a truthful chart. Numbers 46C, 47C, and 48C are comparison questions. 33R and 35R are the Relevant Questions. They ask, "Did you do the crime?" The subject's blood pressure (red) and the GSR (green) shows subject is reacting to comparison questions and is therefore considered innocent of the crime under investigation; (b) is a deceptive homicide chart. Blood pressure increases, and there is a significant rise in the GSR as well as suppressed cycles in the breathing on the Relevant Questions (33R and 35R). This is an example of a person who is being deceptive as to relevant issues in a crime under investigation. (Author's collection.)

Post-Test Phase

The post-test phase follows the completion of the examination after the examiner has reached a conclusion. If the subject does not appear to be attempting deception to the relevant questions, he or she will probably be advised that he or she does not appear to be involved in the crime under investigation. If the individual appears to be attempting deception to the relevant questions, however, the examiner will begin the interrogation process.

The subject being tested will be told that he or she has failed the polygraph examination with regard to the relevant questions, and be given the opportunity to explain his or her reactions. The examiner will confront the individual with his or her reactions and attempt to resolve the issue under investigation. Any statements or confessions the subject makes are admissible. A trained and qualified polygraph examiner will usually not give up very easily at this point. The examiner knows that the subject has failed the test and is probably involved in the crime under investigation.

The examiner wants to verify the reactions that have been collected on the polygraph charts and the subject will be given the opportunity to explain his or her involvement in the crime and the reason the incident occurred. If the subject confesses, the examiner should bring in the investigator and have the subject repeat his or her role to the investigator. Often, additional details of the crime remain to be resolved and the investigator needs to know what the subject has revealed.

Effect of Time on Cold Case Polygraph

I do not think that time produces a significant problem in the use of the polygraph. Short of a medical problem or physical injury people remember significant things that have occurred in their lives. The individual still does not want to get caught and that fear of detection of deception will continue to produce reactions in a polygraph examination.

Conclusion

The polygraph is an excellent investigative tool available to the investigator. I encourage its use in cold case homicide investigations. Discuss its capabilities with the examiner. Information obtained in a polygraph examination frequently plays an important role in assisting the investigator and steering the investigation in the right direction.

Acknowledgments

I wish to thank Paul Redden for his authorship of this chapter. Redden, a polygraph examiner (retired) for the San Diego, California, Police Department, began his law enforcement career in 1969. In 1981, he graduated from the Backster School of Lie Detection and became a polygraph examiner for the San Diego Police Department in 1985. He has administered over 7000 polygraph examinations. He is a certified instructor for the Lafayette Computerized Polygraph and instructs at the school of lie detection from which he graduated. He has taught polygraph examiners throughout Mexico, and the National Police of Bulgaria. In 2003, he was selected Outstanding Polygraph Examiner of the year by the California Polygraph Examiners Association and the Region 1 Outstanding Polygraph Examiner of the year for the American Association of Police Polygraphists at their annual seminar in 2004 in Vancouver, British Columbia.

Geographic Profiling in Cold Case Investigations[1]

30

D. KIM ROSSMO

Contents

[1] For more information on geographic profiling, see Rossmo, D. K. (2000). *Geographic Profiling*. Boca Raton, FL: CRC Press.

Introduction

Cold case detectives are time travelers. They face problems of faded memories, missing witnesses, retired police officers, misplaced evidence, and altered crime scenes. Their criminal investigative expertise must be combined with historical research skills. By definition, cold cases are the hardest because they are the unsolved ones. But while these investigations are challenging, they do have certain advantages. A cold case detective brings a fresh perspective and a different way of thinking to the investigation, free of any original problematic mindsets and organizational pressures (Rossmo, 2009). Witnesses, accomplices, and family and friends of the offender are sometimes more willing to talk to police with the passage of time. And advances in forensic techniques and behavioral analysis allow the application of new investigative methodologies originally unavailable to investigators.

Many unsolved rapes and murders are stranger crimes. Most homicides are cleared for the simple reason that people are usually killed by someone they know. If there is no relationship between the offender and the victim, the crime is usually much more difficult to solve. Stranger crimes, however, may be part of a larger series. The investigation of serial crime, while a complex and information-intensive task, is actually easier in some respects than single stranger crimes. Special techniques for analyzing intercrime patterns become available to detectives in such cases. Every crime in the pattern can be considered a piece in a jigsaw puzzle. The more pieces, the more information; the more information, the more detailed the overall picture.

Cold case detectives investigating the 1995 shooting of a Baskin-Robbins restaurant owner in Laguna Beach, California, were stymied until they connected the murder to three other Orange County robberies. Identifying a series allowed the robberies to be analyzed as a pattern, rather than as isolated crimes. Each case file contained separate witness descriptions of the offender, in particular, information about a tattoo on his neck. One victim reported the tattoo was a word, a second remembered some of the letters, and a third recalled it was in script writing (L. Velarde, personal communication, May 21, 2005). Detectives Dan Lowrey and Bob Romaine used this integrated description to search a computer database of known gang members. They found Gilberto Corrales Garcia, a violent convicted felon and heavily tattooed former gang member (Welborn, 2003). Garcia was convicted of the murder in 2003 and is currently serving a life sentence with no possibility of parole.

The application of scientific studies of criminal behavior has led to the development of several serial crime investigative techniques, including linkage analysis systems, behavioral (psychological) profiling, geographic profiling, and crime-specific statistical databases. Geographic profiling is a criminal investigative methodology that analyzes crime locations to determine the most likely area of offender residence. Under the appropriate circumstances, it can be a useful tool in cold case investigations.

In this chapter, we first consider the nature of the criminal investigative process. Next, we discuss linkage analysis, an important step in the investigation of stranger serial crime. Then, we examine geographic profiling and its associated investigative strategies. Finally, we present a historic case example.

Criminal Investigative Process

A criminal investigation can be divided into two essential tasks: (1) finding the offender and (2) proving his or her guilt. Both tasks must be completed for a crime to be solved. These requirements are not chronologically ordered. Detectives may know who the offender is, but still lack sufficient evidence to prove their guilt.[2]

[2] The establishment of guilt is not a police prerogative and can only be done by a judge or jury. The police therefore never legally "know" who committed a crime before trial. In some cases, however, investigators become convinced a particular person committed the crime, and consequently focus their investigative efforts on collecting evidence against that individual—not on finding other suspects. Theoretically, the evidence collection process should confirm or refute the police theory.

Table 30.1 The Criminal Investigative Process

Find Offender				Prove Guilt
Collect Suspects		Prioritize	Evaluate	Direct/Indirect Evidence
Public	*Databases*	Physical description	Opportunity	Witness
Tips	Criminal records	Behavior	Motive	Confession
Witnesses	Police files	• General	Means	Physical evidence
Informants	DMV	• Specific	Modus operandi	
Friends	Other agencies	Geography	Composite sketch	
Family		• General	Video	
Neighbors		• Specific	Alibi	
			Suspect interview	
			Interviews of family, friends, and neighbors	

Conversely, they may be able to prove guilt, but not know the offender's identity. The first situation was the one facing investigators in the 2002 murder of Laci Peterson. Detectives felt strongly that her husband, Scot Peterson, had killed her and her unborn child. Their job was to prove the case in court. The second situation describes the case of the Baton Rouge serial murders that occurred from 2001 to 2003. Police had recovered DNA evidence from the crime scenes, so once the offender was identified his guilt could be established. Of course, sometimes investigators do not know who committed the crime, and could not prove their guilt even if they did. Such cases have a low chance of being solved.

Establishing guilt can be accomplished in one of only three ways: (1) a confession, (2) a witness, or (3) physical evidence (Klockars & Mastrofski, 1991). The task of finding an offender involves collecting, prioritizing, and evaluating suspects. Table 30.1 provides a schematic of the criminal investigative process. It is a simplification of the tasks facing "whodunit" criminal investigations. It does not include every possible investigative approach, and some of the categories overlap. Within these limitations, however, the table provides a framework for strategy development and progress assessment (Rossmo, 2004).

The investigative process is based upon information—its proper collection, analysis, and sharing. The Rand study of the criminal investigation process found the information that led to solved crimes typically came from the public, then from patrol officers, and third, from detectives (Chaiken, Greenwood, & Petersilia, 1991). This underlines the importance of effective channels of communication between the police and the community, and within the police organization. But not all information has the same value, and investigators must be wary of static or noise or useless or misleading information. And because investigative efforts can produce hundreds and even thousands of potential suspects, difficulties with information overload often develop. This is the classic needle in the haystack situation. Information management problems are sometimes the reason an investigation ends up as a cold case file.

Linkage Analysis

When FBI Special Agent Clarice Starling finds a black witch moth (*Erebus odora*) chrysalis lodged in the throat of serial killer Buffalo Bill's latest victim, a connection is soon made to another murder. But real crimes, unlike those in Thomas Harris' popular novel *Silence of the Lambs* (1988), are often much more difficult to link. "Prostitute strangled, dumped at the side of the road, no physical evidence," is a depressingly familiar crime scene description.

Establishing which offenses belong to a series is an important and essential task in the investigation of serial crime. This process is known as linkage analysis or comparative case analysis. Realizing the extent of the crime pattern helps determine the appropriate level of police response, facilitates information sharing between investigators and jurisdictions, outlines case similarities, and identifies common suspects. If and when the case is solved, additional crimes are cleared and the court delivers a more appropriate sentence (including dangerous offender or habitual felon designations). Knowing all the pieces of the puzzle allows a comprehensive picture of the offender to be formed and prevents linkage blindness from occurring.

There are three main methods used by police investigators to link crimes prior to an offender's apprehension: (1) physical evidence, (2) offender description, and (3) crime scene behavior. Each method has its strengths and weaknesses. It is not uncommon for a series of crimes to be connected together through a combination of these means.

Physical Evidence

Physical evidence provides the most certain means of linking crimes, though evidence of a type suitable for doing so may not be present in every case. One of the more powerful forensic methods, DNA profiling, has been heralded as the most revolutionary technology in the field of criminal investigation since the development of the Henry System for fingerprinting (Bigbee, Tanton, & Ferrara, 1989; Gaudette, 1990; Kelly, Rankin, & Wink, 1987). As blood, semen, hair, and skin contain DNA, the potential for ascertaining and verifying links in cases of violent and sexual crimes is significant. The establishment of centralized indices to facilitate computerized searches and comparisons is a necessary step in realizing this potential (Miller, 1991).

The FBI's National DNA Index System (NDIS) became operational in 1998 (Weedn & Hicks, 1998). Designed for the compatible storage and comparison of DNA records, the Combined DNA Index System (CODIS) consists of two investigative indices—the forensic index, for unsolved crimes, and the convicted offender index, for known felons. As of August 2016, there were 726,709 forensic profiles, 2,462,335 arrestee profiles, and 12,517,059 offender profiles in NDIS. CODIS has produced over 343,341 hits and assisted in more than 329,460 investigations.

One of the important functions of such a system is the establishment of crime series (Brown, 1994). For example, DNA pattern matching linked 18 unknown suspect serial cases together in Minnesota, eventually helping to solve them by matching specimens of two offenders to the crime scenes. Such results are common in Britain where a DNA database has been in existence for some time ("DNA profiling," 1995). It has been responsible for thousands of hits—defined as a match between crime scenes or between crime scene and offender. Canada has now also established a national DNA data bank.

Automated fingerprint identification systems (AFIS) allow comparisons and matches that sheer volume would have previously precluded (Sparrow, 1994). Programs such as the *Integrated Ballistics Identification System* (*IBIS*), networked into the joint ATF/FBI National Integrated Ballistic Information Network (NIBIN), link crimes committed with firearms through computerized comparisons of microscopic bullet striation patterns and shell casing marks (Dees, 1994; Strandberg, 1994; see also Di Maio, 1985). The British Shoeprint Image Capture and Retrieval System (SICAR) is a national database that connects crime scenes through the geometrical shapes associated with stored images of footprint evidence.

Offender Description

Descriptions of offenders have provided a common and long used method of linking crimes. Mug shot books, while still in existence, are being replaced by computerized photographic databases that allow for certain physical description parameters to be used to narrow the search. But this is all predicated upon the assumption that there was a witness to the crime. There may not be one in the case of murder or arson. Even in a sexual assault, the victim must see, remember, and accurately recall (acquisition, retention, and retrieval) the offender's description. The ability for investigators to obtain an accurate physical description depends upon such factors as lighting conditions, whether the offender was masked, if the attack was from the rear, and the level of victim trauma, stress, fright, alcohol use, forgetfulness, and cooperation (see Thomas, Aitken, Lucy, & Feist, 2004).

Individual physical appearance is also subject to modification. Weight changes slowly, hair more quickly, and clothing daily. Even more stable descriptors such as age, race, height, and build will be viewed subjectively by different victims. Ted Bundy, for example, was able to vary his description as can be seen from his photographs and police wanted posters (Michaud & Aynesworth, 1983; Winn & Merrill, 1979).

The prevalence of video cameras has enhanced the ability of police to use offender descriptions. Most banks and financial institutions, and many businesses, transportation centers, and building lobby areas have been outfitted with video cameras. Closed-circuit television (CCTV) coverage of city centers, parking lots, and other public places is now common in Britain. Police agencies make routine use of the photographs and videotape from these cameras to assist in their investigations.

Automated recognition systems for digital facial images now exist and are used for both comparison and identification purposes (Mardia, Coombes, Kirkbride, Linney, & Bowie, 1996). Distance and angle measurements are taken between certain facial points (e.g., from lower point of the ear to nose tip, the tangent to chin tip and nose tip, etc.) for both anterior (front) and profile (side) views. Horizontal and vertical landmarks are calculated to produce a mathematical profile of the face. These landmark-based data then provide the means of determining correlations between facial images.

These systems can be connected to video cameras placed within airport terminals and used to scan custom and immigration lines. A match with an image in the facial database alerts officials to the possible presence of a person of interest, such as a criminal, missing person, fugitive, abducted child, or terrorist. Police investigators have also used computerized facial recognition systems to assess the probability that two robbers captured on bank cameras are, in fact, the same person. These methods increase the value of offender image data, and echo the early work of Alphonse Bertillon in criminal identification through body measurement.

Crime Scene Behavior

The behavioral analysis of crime scenes provides a third, and rapidly developing, methodology for offense comparison. Linking crimes behaviorally requires comparing similarities versus differences for both related and unrelated crimes (see Robertson & Vignaux, 1995). Like crimes should show more similarities than differences, and unlike crimes, more differences than similarities. These comparisons are usually assessed in terms of proximity in time and space between offenses, comparable modus operandi (method of operation), and the presence of signature.

Crimes that take place close together in space and time are obviously more likely to be connected than those separated by significant distance and occurring years apart. This is not to say that some offenders do not travel great distances, change residence, or interrupt their criminal activity for personal, employment, or institutional reasons. It only means that geographic and temporal factors affect the probability of offense linkage, with those more proximate more likely to be connected (Bennell & Canter, 2002).

Modus operandi (M.O.) involves the mechanics of the crime and can be broken down into three chronologically ordered stages comprising the methods used by an offender: (1) to hunt (find and attack the victim); (2) to commit the crime; and (3) to escape from the scene. These three stages can be further subdivided into offensive (what is done to accomplish the crime) and defensive (what is done to avoid identification or apprehension) actions (Rossmo, 2000). The matrix in Table 30.2 illustrates M.O. behavior.

M.O. is not constant, but rather varies and changes for a variety of reasons. Like all human behavior, it is subject to individual deviation and random fluctuations. M.O. is responsive to environmental influences,

Table 30.2 M.O. Matrix

Action/Stage	Hunt	Crime	Escape
Offensive			
Defensive			

such as victim reaction, the physical conditions of a crime setting, and ongoing police activities and media attention. Displacement may result from police activities and can take the form of changes in the spatial, temporal, target, tactical, or functional characteristics of the crimes (Gabor, 1978; Reppetto, 1976). Over time, an offender's method of operation often evolves as the result of education, maturity, and experience; fantasy progression and development can also occur.

Unlike M.O., signature is constant, though certain aspects of its expression may evolve and improve over time (Keppel, 1995). Signature is defined as behavior that goes beyond the actions needed to commit the crime; it is a fantasy-based ritual or combination of rituals that represent a unique and personal expression of the offender (Douglas & Munn, 1992). When present, it provides a useful method for establishing links between crimes and can indicate certain underlying needs of the offender.

Staging is another consideration when examining crime scene behavior (Douglas & Munn, 1992). Staging occurs when the crime scene is purposely altered. This is usually done by the offender in an attempt to mislead the police and typically involves a criminal who knew the victim and hopes to create a convincing alternative scenario. Crime scenes have also been changed by family members to protect the victim from embarrassment (e.g., in cases of autoerotic fatalities).

The reality, however, is that the ability of the police to link serial crimes is limited. Establishing offense connections is often a difficult exercise, especially so in busy urban environments characterized by high levels of crime. The backdrop of other, similar offenses can interfere with the process, and such background noise can make it difficult to know who is responsible for what. Consistency and constancy are not characteristics of many criminal offenders, and when an analysis does indicate that certain crimes are connected, the links are usually referred to in terms of probabilities rather than certainties. This is made all the more difficult when multiple offenders are involved.

A further complication is that the links might be between different incident types. In the case of a serial rapist who breaks into apartments to attack women, for example, police must review not just other rapes and attempts but also sexual assaults, residential burglaries, and prowlings. Correctly establishing a serial criminal's pattern can involve analyzing hundreds or even thousands of crimes.

The major response to these problems has been the establishment of computer systems containing centralized investigative information networks. The idea of a national computer database to link murders originated with Pierce Brooks, a retired captain of detectives in the Los Angeles Police Department (LAPD) homicide unit (Brooks, 1984; Howlett, Hanfland, & Ressler, 1986). During his investigation of California serial killer Harvey Glatman in the late 1950s, Brooks found he had to resort to combing various newspaper files in order to locate murders that might fit the pattern from outside LAPD's jurisdiction (Newton, 1998).

Brooks' efforts led to the establishment of the Violent Criminal Apprehension Program (ViCAP), which became operational in 1985 under the auspices of the FBI's National Center for the Analysis of Violent Crime (NCAVC). ViCAP uses a standardized form containing a series of behaviorally oriented questions concerning the crime, victim, and offender that allows for computerized matching of similar cases from a national database. Several states have also developed their own computerized crime linkage systems, some of which feed into ViCAP (Collins, Johnson, Choy, Davidson, & MacKay, 1998; Cryan, 1988; Keppel & Weis, 1993a,b).

The Canadian Violent Crime Linkage Analysis System (ViCLAS), developed by the RCMP for murder and sexual assault cases, went national in 1995 (Johnson, 1994). Since then, ViCLAS has achieved international recognition and has now been adopted for use by several European countries, Australia, and certain American states (Collins et al., 1998). In the United Kingdom, the Serious Crime Analysis Section (SCAS), National Crime Faculty, is mandated to conduct comparative case analysis for murders, rapes, and abductions.

A major difficulty with computerized linkage systems is low reporting rates. This causes a serious data shortage problem because case matches are an exponential function of reporting level (Rossmo, 2000). For example, if only 50% of the crimes are entered, then only 25% of the potential linkages can be identified; with a 20% reporting rate, the linkage ability drops to 4%. It is paradoxical that some police officers, who typically possess little faith in offender rehabilitation, fail to see the value in a comprehensive criminal tracking system.

One of the common reasons quoted for failure to report cases is the time it takes an investigator to complete the input forms, which can involve over 150 questions. Therefore, the choice of behaviors used in the analysis is critical. Both discrimination and utility are important. Certain offender actions are so common (e.g., vaginal intercourse) as to be poor discriminators. Other behaviors are so rare (e.g., the offender writes on the victim's body) that they are unlikely to be encountered. Crime linkage is a holistic process and the questions must also provide a full understanding of events. System designers need to balance the requirement for parsimony with the necessity for a comprehensive assessment of crime scene behavior.

An underlying assumption of linkage systems is that the analyzed behaviors are more or less consistent across offenses. An examination of child abduction murders in the United States showed that victim gender and use of bindings were the most important and consistent linkage variables (Hanfland, Keppel, & Weis, 1997). Offender speech forms have been found to be consistent and useful in connecting rape cases (Dale & Davies, 1994), and the London Metropolitan Police Sexual Assault Index analyzes verbal themes as part of the process of linking crimes (Copson, 1993). But FBI research on 108 serial rapists determined that 58% of the 119 behavioral variables they examined reflected zero or minimal consistency across crimes (Warren, Reboussin, & Hazelwood, 1995). Alone, such questions make a poor basis for a case linkage system; together, they may point to common underlying fantasies or behavioral themes.

The true strength of these systems therefore lies in their ability to make concurrent comparisons between multiple variables. A study of British serial rapists found that 28% of the offenders took steps to prevent their face from being seen by the victim (Davies & Dale, 1995). In the FBI research, it was noted that 70% of rape contact sites occurred indoors, and 60% within the victim's home (Warren et al., 1995). These are not powerful discriminators separately, but assuming independence between questions, they can be combined in powerful ways. A burglary rapist who covers his face might only represent 17% of the offender population. Additional matching variables can help narrow the investigative focus.

The process of recognition—whether it be of faces, scenes, automobiles, voices, architecture—is based less on individual elements than on the relationships between them. Humans are much better than serial-processing computers at image and complex pattern recognition. As of today, most computerized case linkage systems are only designed to manage and search through large volumes of information, leaving the ultimate determination of case association to the analyst. As the volume of information collected by these databases increases, the need for expert system support becomes more crucial.

Grubin, Kelly, and Ayis (1996) caution that because of "the softer and more fluid substance of behavioral 'evidence' … [the process of linking crimes] must be based on scientific principles rather than on a combination of intuition, experience and theory" (pp. 12, 20). They summarize the practical problems in using offender behavior to link crimes as follows: (1) consistent but common behaviors; (2) consistent but uncommon behaviors; (3) preciseness of behavior description; (4) behavior influenced by victim response;

(5) weighting and relative importance of behaviors; (6) variation in behavior consistency; (7) evolution of behavior; and (8) interpretation of behaviors.

The idea that linked crimes should be interconnected provides one simple method for pattern determination. If crime A shows similarities to crime B, and crime B shows similarities to crime C, then crime C should also show similarities to crime A (Rossmo, 2000). If this is the case, then the probability of these crimes being connected increases. The results from the case variable matrix can then be plotted in a case linkage chart, which depicts the strength of association, in terms of the behavior variables of interest, between the different crimes. The proper selection and phrasing of crime scene behaviors (variables) are important parts of this analysis.

In summary, crime linkage methods can be outlined as follows:

1. Physical evidence
2. Offender description
3. Crime scene behavior
   a. Proximity in time and place
   b. M.O.
      i. Find and attack the victim
      ii. Commit the crime
      iii. Escape from the scene
   c. Signature

Geographic Profiling

Geographic profiling is an investigative methodology that uses the locations of a connected series of crime to determine the most probable area of offender residence (Rossmo, 2000). It is typically applied in cases of serial murder, rape, arson, robbery, and bombing, though it can be used in single crimes that involve multiple scenes or other significant geographic characteristics. Geographic profiling was developed from research conducted at Simon Fraser University's School of Criminology. Crime pattern theory, developed by Professors Paul Brantingham and Patricia Brantingham, provides the conceptual basis for geographic profiling (Brantingham & Brantingham, 1981, 1984, 1993). It states that crime locations are not distributed in space randomly, but rather are influenced by the features and road networks of the physical environment. An understanding of these patterns provides a means for determining the most probable area of offender residence.

A mathematical representation of this understanding was encoded in the criminal geographic targeting (CGT) computer algorithm. The CGT model is used to produce jeopardy surfaces—three-dimensional probability surfaces—that outline the most probable area of offender residence. These are displayed through color geoprofile maps that provide a focus for investigative efforts (see Figures 30.1 and 30.2).

While geographic profiling can be used as the basis for several investigative strategies, it is important to stress that it cannot solve crimes. Its purpose is to help manage the large volume of information typically generated in major crime investigations. Geographic profiling should be regarded as one of several tools available to detectives, and is best employed in conjunction with other police methods. Address information is an element of most record systems, and geographic profiling can be applied in a variety of contexts as a powerful decision support tool. Geographic crime patterns are clues that, when properly decoded, point in the direction of the offender.

For example, in the investigation of a series of over 20 rapes from 1988 to 1996 in St. Louis, Missouri, Detective Mark Kennedy employed both psychological and geographic profiling to prioritize a list of some 90 suspects for DNA testing. In addition to a residential focus, the geoprofile drew attention to the St. Louis

Figure 30.1 Jeopardy surface: armed robbery series, Vancouver, BC.

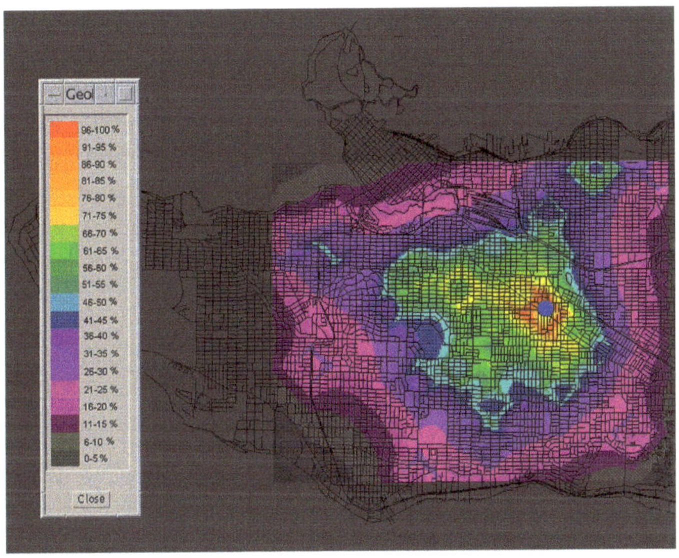

Figure 30.2 Geoprofile: armed robbery series, Vancouver, BC.

State Hospital, and to what appeared to be likely commuting routes used by the offender. When the Southside Rapist was identified through DNA testing subsequent to a burglary arrest, it was found that he moved several times during the crime series. The geoprofile identified his residential area during his most active rape period—one home was in the top 2% (0.4 mi^2), and the other, across the street from the St. Louis State Hospital, in the top 5.6% (1.2 mi^2) of the hunting area. The offender, 43-year-old Dennis Rabbitt, pled guilty in January 2000 to 49 counts of rape, sodomy, and burglary, and received five consecutive life terms.

The knowledge gained through research and experience of how and where criminal predators hunt for victims has both practical and theoretical implications. Geographic profiling is now an investigative support service offered to law enforcement agencies in cases of both violent and property crime. It has been used in criminal investigations in Canada, the United States, the United Kingdom, Europe, Africa, the Middle East, and Australia.

Geoprofiling Considerations

The ability to identify the existence of a serial offender is the starting point of the process. The extent and accuracy of the linkage analysis is important as the more crimes, the more accurate the geographic profile.

But providing there is no spatial bias, and not too many locations are missed, unlinked crimes are not a critical problem. The CGT algorithm is also quite robust and its results are not significantly affected by the mistaken inclusion of an unconnected crime; generally, at least 90% of the information should be accurate.

While primarily empirical, geographic profiling has both quantitative (objective) and qualitative (subjective) components. The objective component uses a series of geostatistical techniques and quantitative measures, such as the CGT program, to analyze and interpret the point pattern formed by target sites. Because the validity of these measures depends upon the number of locations, they are inappropriate for smaller crime series. The subjective component of geographic profiling is based upon the reconstruction and interpretation of the offender's mental map (Homant & Kennedy, 1998). A behavioral (psychological) profile is not a necessary precursor for a geographic profile, but the insights it provides to offender personality, behavior, and lifestyle are useful, particularly in cases involving only a few locations. A geographic profile, in turn, helps refine a psychological profile, focus its application, and increase its utility. The two types of profiles optimize each other, and act in tandem to assist investigators in developing a picture of the person responsible for the crimes in question.

In 1996, the RCMP investigated a series of 14 arsons of house carports in Burnaby, British Columbia, and requested psychological and geographic profiles. When a suspect who closely matched both profiles came to the attention of the investigator, he carefully focused on him, initiating surveillance and then interviewing strategies. The offender confessed. He closely matched the behavioral profile, and literally lived across the street from the highest part of the geoprofile, in 0.6% of the hunting area (0.02 mi^2).

Many different crime factors and environmental elements are considered in the construction and interpretation of a geographic profile. The most relevant ones include

1. Crime locations—offense locations and times are the most important data in a geographic profile. Also significant are the number and type of crime sites.
2. Offender type—the type and number of offender(s) affect crime geography. If multiple criminals living apart are involved, the geoprofile will focus on the dominant one's residence. Large, amorphous gangs may not be suitable for geographic profiling because of changing group composition. Psychological profiling assists in interpreting offender behavior by providing information on personality, background, and level of organization.
3. Hunting style—criminal hunting methods (used to search for, and then attack, victims or targets) influence crime site patterns. An offender's hunting style, therefore, is an important consideration in geographic profiling (see the following section for a more detailed discussion on criminal hunting methods).
4. Target backcloth—constrained or patchy target backcloths limit the degree of offender choice, and may influence the importance of certain crime site types for the profile.
5. Arterial roads and highways—people, including criminals, do not travel as the crow flies. Not only must they follow street layouts, but they are also most likely to travel along major arterial routes, freeways, or highways. Crimes often cluster around freeway exits and entrances.
6. Bus stops and rapid transit stations—offenders without vehicles may use public transit or travel along bicycle and jogging paths. The locations of these routes and stops are important considerations.
7. Physical and psychological boundaries—people are constrained by physical boundaries such as rivers, ocean, lakes, ravines, and highways. Psychological boundaries also influence movement. For example, a criminal of low socioeconomic status may avoid an upper class area, or a black offender might not wish to go into a white neighborhood.
8. Zoning and land use—zoning (e.g., residential, commercial, industrial) and land use (e.g., stores, bars, businesses, transportation centers, major facilities, government buildings, military institutions) provide keys as to why someone may be in a particular area. Police in Britain conduct site surveys and location inventories in the area surrounding a crime to help identify what may have

brought an offender to a particular location. Similarly, information about the peak area in a geoprofile provides insight to a criminal's anchor point, and zoning classification helps determine if this is a residence or workplace. For example, the geographic profile for a series of bank robberies occurring just afternoon fell on a commercially zoned area of the city. The time and location factors correctly suggested an offender who was committing the crimes during his lunch break. The anchor point for his crimes—and the focus of the geoprofile—was therefore his work site, not his home.

9. Neighborhood demographics—some sex offenders prefer victims of a certain racial or ethnic group. These groups may be more common in certain neighborhoods than in others, affecting spatial crime patterns.
10. Victim routine activities—the patterns of routine victim movements may provide insights as to how the offender is searching for targets.
11. Singularities—single offenses that do not appear to fit the overall pattern of the crime series are often a source of important clues, so are worthy of careful review.
12. Displacement—media coverage or uniformed police presence can cause spatial displacement, affecting the locations of subsequent crime sites. The geographic profile has to compensate for any displacement issues.

Criminal Hunting Methods

The hunting process can be broken down into two components: (1) the search for a suitable victim and (2) the method of attack. The first component influences selection of victim encounter sites, and the second, body dump or victim release sites. A criminal hunting typology can be produced by combining these search and attack elements.

The following four victim search methods have been identified for violent predatory crime:

1. Hunter—an offender who sets out specifically to search for a victim, basing the search from his or her residence
2. Poacher—an offender who sets out specifically to search for a victim, basing the search from an activity site other than his or her residence, or who commutes or travels to another city during the victim search process
3. Troller—an offender who, while involved in other, nonpredatory activities, opportunistically encounters a victim
4. Trapper—an offender who has an occupation or position where potential victims come to him or her (e.g., nursing), or by means of subterfuge, entices victims into a home or other location they control (e.g., by placing want ads)

The following three victim attack methods have been identified:

1. Raptor—an offender who attacks a victim upon encounter
2. Stalker—an offender who, upon encounter, follows a victim and then attacks at a different location and later time
3. Ambusher—an offender who attacks a victim after he or she has been enticed to a location, such as a residence or workplace, controlled by the offender

Hunters are those offenders who specifically set out from their residence to look for victims, searching through areas in their awareness space they believe contain suitable targets. This is the most commonly used method of criminal predators. Westley Allan Dodd, a serial killer executed for the murder of three children in the state of Washington, wrote in his diary, "Now ready for my second day of the hunt…. Will start at about 10 a.m. and take a lunch so I don't have to return home." He was worried, however, that if he murdered a child in the park through which he was searching, he'd lose his "hunting ground for up to two to three months" (Westfall, 1992, p. 59). The crimes of a hunter are generally confined to the offender's city of residence. Conversely, poachers travel outside of their home city, or operate from an activity site other than their residence, in search for targets. While the differentiation between a poacher and a hunter can be difficult, there are certain indicators that help in the assessment process (see the following section).

Trollers are opportunistic offenders who do not specifically search for victims, but rather encounter them during the course of other, usually routine activities. Their crimes are often spontaneous, but many sexual predators fantasize and plan their crimes in advance so they are ready and prepared when an opportunity presents itself (premeditated opportunism).

Trappers have an occupation or position that results in potential victims coming to them (e.g., nurse, hospital orderly, etc.). They also entice victims into their home or other location they control by means of subterfuge. This may be done through entertaining suitors, placing want-ads, or taking in boarders. Black widows, angels of death and custodial killers are all forms of trappers, and most female serial murderers fall into this category (Hickey, 1986; Segrave, 1992).

Raptors, upon encountering a victim, attack almost immediately. This is the most common method used by criminal predators. Stalkers follow and watch their targets, moving into the victim's activity space, waiting for an opportune moment to strike. The attack, murder, and/or body dump sites of stalkers are thus more strongly influenced by their victims' activity spaces. Jon Berry Simonis, the ski mask rapist, attacked women in Florida, Georgia, North Carolina, Ohio, Michigan, Wisconsin, Mississippi, Louisiana, Texas, Oklahoma, and California from 1978 to 1981, becoming progressively more violent before he was eventually arrested by the Louisiana State Police. Simon sometimes stalked his victims, and through his work at a hospital, had access to victims' medical records including their address, marital, and work details (Michaud & Hazelwood, 1998).

Ambushers attack victims they have brought or drawn into their web someplace where the killer has a great deal of control, most often their home or workplace. The bodies are usually hidden somewhere on the offender's property.[3] While victim encounter sites in such cases may provide sufficient spatial information for analysis, many ambushers select marginalized individuals whose disappearances are rarely linked, even when missing person reports are made to the police.

This hunting typology resembles that for burglars proposed by Bennett and Wright (1984), which includes planners, searchers, and opportunists. Surprisingly, it is also remarkably similar to Schaller's (1972) description of hunting methods used by lions in the Serengeti, where he observed ambushing, stalking, driving (direct attack), and unexpected (opportunistic) kills. Offenders may employ different hunting methods, but they usually adopt and stay with one, or at the most two approaches. For example, while trolling is not a primary criminal search technique, it is part of many offenders' repertoires.

Criminal target patterns are determined by offender activity space, hunting method, and victim backcloth. Hunting style is therefore helpful in determining which crime locations are the best predictors of an offender's anchor point under different circumstances. Another purpose of this typology is the identification of those situations where an analysis of the relationship between offender activity space and crime location geography is appropriate. This allows for the elimination of those cases where such an analysis is either impossible or redundant. Poachers, for example, who live in one city and commit their crimes in another, may not reside within their hunting area. Stalkers, whose crime locations are driven more by the activity spaces of their victims than by their own, produce more complex target patterns requiring different analytic methods.

[3] This is probably the result of the fact that ambushers are often also trappers, and the latter rarely exhibit significant mobility.

Poacher Indicators

The following factors are indicators of possible offender poaching (also known as commuting). They should be considered in relationship to each other and within the context of the specific details of the crime series.

Target Area

- The crimes occur in a very small area (a few square blocks).
- There is a specific but rare target/victim type or a patchy target backcloth.
- The crimes occur in the central business district or a nonresidential area.
- The crimes occur in wealthy neighborhoods (unlikely areas of offender residence) or neighborhoods with demographics (race/ethnicity/age) inconsistent with the offender's.
- The crimes occur along a major thoroughfare or highway.
- Alternative anchor point possibilities exist (e.g., drug market, freeway exit, metro stop, etc.).

Criminal/Crimes

- Spatial displacement has occurred (as a result of increased police presence or target hardening in the offender's neighborhood).
- There are only a few crimes in the series (less than five); by chance, an offender who is not actually a poacher/commuter may appear to be one if he or she has only committed a few crimes.
- The travel pattern of the crimes shows a definite directional trend.
- The offender is a professional criminal (e.g., a traveling bank robber, high-end burglar, gypsy, etc.).
- The offender is a stalker who follows his or her victims from a fishing hole or trap line, or else uses a nongeographic-based hunting method (e.g., finding targets from notices of estate sales in newspapers, or by reading luggage nametags at airports, etc.).
- Poaching/commuting is suggested by previous experience with local crime patterns.[4]

Crime Locations

Crime locations are the basis of a geographic profile, and a given murder can involve separate encounter, attack, murder, and body dump sites. But other locations that are not crime sites per se may also be connected to an offense. Examples of such locations include credit or bank card use, mailings, telephone calls, vehicle rentals or drops, witness sightings, and found property or evidence sites. In these cases, it may be possible to geographically profile a single crime, depending upon the number and types of locations.

In October 1995, two teenaged girls in the municipality of Abbotsford, British Columbia, were attacked on the street at night by a man with a baseball bat. One victim was murdered and dumped in the Vedder Canal, some 20 miles away; the other was left for dead but somehow managed to revive and make her way to a nearby hospital. A few days later, the Abbotsford killer began a series of bizarre actions starting with several taunting 9-1-1 telephone calls. He then stole and defaced his murder victim's gravestone, and dumped it in the parking lot of a local radio station. Finally, he threw a note wrapped around a wrench through a house window; in the note he admitted to other sexual assaults. These actions provided 13 different sites for the geographic profile. He was eventually caught through a local-based strategy initiated by the Abbotsford Police Department. His residence was in the top 7.7% of the geoprofile (0.6 mi^2).

[4] For an analysis of differences in crime scene behaviors between commuter and marauder patterns in U.S. serial rapists, see Chapter 6 (pp. 201–235) of Warren et al. (1995).

A geoprofile may result in two peak areas, an indication the offender has more than one anchor point. Manley Eng, responsible for a series of arsons in Saanich and Victoria, British Columbia, left a crime pattern that resulted in dual peaks—one that contained his residence, and the other, his probation office. Information regarding land use, zoning, and area characteristics helps interpret such outcomes. Examples of multiple anchor points include

- Residence and work sites
- Residence and social or family sites
- Present and previous residences
- Two or more offenders living apart

Between 1994 and 1998, the Mardi Gra bomber was responsible for a total of 36 explosive devices, most in the Greater London area (Cooper, 1999). These were mailed or delivered to locations near bank machines, supermarkets, payphones, businesses, and residences. Scotland Yard requested a geographic profile from the Vancouver Police Department. Even though the targets and delivery methods varied, the underlying spatial pattern of the crimes was consistent. The resulting geoprofile had two high-probability regions, a primary area around Chiswick in west London and a secondary peak in southeast London. When police detectives arrested two elderly brothers, it turned out they lived in Chiswick, and their family resided in southeast London. The geoprofile identified the convicted offender's home in the top 3.4% (9.1 mi^2) of the hunting area.

Questions

Investigators may benefit from a geographic perspective on their crimes, independent of a formal profile. It is not just what offenders do, but also what they do not do, that is of interest. Some specific questions worth considering include the following:

- Locations
  - ❑ What are the location types connected to this crime or crime series?
  - ❑ Where are these locations? Map them.
  - ❑ What are the distances and travel times between them?
- Time
  - ❑ When did the crimes occur (date, time, and weekday)?
  - ❑ What was the weather?
  - ❑ How much time was there between crimes?
- Site selection
  - ❑ How are the crime locations accessed?
  - ❑ What else is in the general area?
  - ❑ How might the offender have known of these locations?
  - ❑ What purpose did the crime locations serve?
- Target backcloth
  - ❑ Where is the target group (and where is it not)?
  - ❑ How much control did the offender have over the choice of crime locations?
  - ❑ Has displacement (in space or time) occurred?
- Hunting
  - ❑ What hunting method did the offender use?
  - ❑ Why these sites and not others?
  - ❑ What was the offender's likely transportation?

The *Rigel* Computer System

Rigel is a computerized geographic profiling workstation based on the patented CGT algorithm. It incorporates an analytic engine, geographic information system (GIS) capability, database management, and powerful visualization tools. Crime locations, which are broken down by type (e.g., victim encounter, murder, and body dump sites for a homicide), provide the input and are entered by the optional means of street address, latitude and longitude, or digitization. This reflects the realities of policing in which crimes can happen anywhere—houses, parking lots, back alleys, highways, parks, rivers, mountain ravines, and so on. Latitude and longitude coordinates can be determined from a handheld global positioning system (GPS) that reads the user's position from a satellite fix.

Scenarios, wherein crime locations are weighted based upon certain theoretical and methodological principles, are next created and examined. Output is a geoprofile, a color map showing the most likely area of offender residence. Suspect addresses can be evaluated according to their position on the geoprofile (expressed as a hit score percentage on a *z*-score histogram), allowing the prioritization of known criminals, registered sex offenders, task force tips, and other information.

Rigel was developed by Environmental Criminology Research Inc. (ECRI) of Vancouver, British Columbia (http://www.ecricanada.com). This provides the computing power for the 1,000,000 or so calculations of the CGT algorithm a typical analysis requires. Geoprofiles and jeopardy surfaces can be rotated and visually manipulated in a variety of ways, facilitating their interpretation. Orthodigital photographs may be overlaid on the peak geoprofile area, assisting the user in viewing land use within the region of interest. Large databases, including sex offender registries, major case management programs, and crime linkage systems (e.g., ViCLAS, ViCAP, etc.), can be searched and their entries prioritized by address. *Rigel* is designed to enable law enforcement agencies to geographically optimize their limited resources. It is the main tool used in geographic profiling.

Investigative Strategies and Tactics

Certain police strategies and tactics can be more effectively and efficiently conducted with a geographic profile. While specific applications are best determined by the investigators responsible for the case in question, suggested approaches are presented below. The development of these strategies has been an interactive process involving detectives, profilers, and academics. Case examples are used to illustrate these strategies, but it should be made clear that the crimes were not solved by geographic profiling; they were resolved by the assigned investigators. Profiling plays a support role, the importance of which can vary, and it is only one of many techniques in the investigator's repertoire.

While the most common anchor point is the offender's residence, some cases involve other bases of criminal activity. Clifford Olson used body dump locations near Agassiz Mountain Prison where he had once been incarcerated. John Collins hunted in the area around Eastern Michigan University where he was a student and summer employee. Aileen Wuornos based her "hitchhooking" from truck stops and freeway entrances in the town of Wildwood. Inmate records, enrollment and employee registries, and field checks were all potentially useful sources of investigative information in these cases. As important as residence is in structuring activity space, the value of business and institutional records should not be overlooked.

Suspect Prioritization

The geographic profile, in conjunction with a behavioral profile, can help focus follow-up investigative work. The problem in many serial violent crime investigations is one of too many suspects rather than too few. Profiling can help reassess and prioritize hundreds or even thousands of suspects, leads, and tips.

The South Side rapist in Lafayette, Louisiana, committed a series of 14 burglary rapes from 1984 to 1995. Detective McCullan Gallien refused to close the file and requested a geographic profile, which resulted in the identification of a neighborhood not previously considered by investigators. This was used as the basis for suspect and tip prioritization (there were approximately 1,000 suspects and 2,000 tips). One tip involved a sergeant with the Lafayette Parish Sheriff's Department who fit the FBI's psychological profile and lived in the peak area of the geoprofile at the time of the crimes. DNA obtained from a cigarette butt discarded by the suspect matched samples from the crime scenes. The offender confessed, pled guilty, and was sentenced to life in prison. The geoprofile located the rapist's address in the top 2.2% (0.5 mi^2) of the hunting area.

Police Information Systems

Additional investigative leads may be obtained from information contained in various computerized police dispatch and record systems (Rebscher & Rohrer, 1991). Offender profile details and case specifics can help further focus the search. Police agencies with computerized records containing description, address, and M.O. of local offenders can also use profiling information, including probable area of residence, as the basis for developing search criteria. Many departments maintain files for parolees and specific types of criminals (Pilant, 1994; Skogan & Antunes, 1979). Sex offenders often have nuisance crimes (e.g., loitering, trespassing, peeping, etc.) in their backgrounds, and the locations of their past offenses may overlap with the present ones.

Task Force Management

Task force operations formed to investigate a specific series of crimes often collect and collate their information in some form of computerized major case management system, such as the British HOLMES or FBI Rapid Start programs (Federal Bureau of Investigation, 1996; U.S. Department of Justice, 1991). Cases suffering from information overload will benefit from the prioritization of data and the application of correlation analysis (Keppel & Birnes, 1995). Geographic profiling can assist in these tasks through the ranking of street addresses, zip or postal codes, and telephone number (NNXs) areas.

This process may also be linked to information available in CD-ROM telephone directory databases listing residential and business names, telephone numbers, addresses, zip or postal codes, business headings, and standard industrial classification (SIC) codes. The details of the specific task force computer database software, including information fields, search time, number of records, and correlational abilities, determine the most appropriate form the geographic profile should take to maximize its usefulness to the police investigation.

Sex Offender Registries

Violent sex offender registries are a useful information source for geographic profiling in cases of serial sex crimes. By providing a list of addresses of known sex criminals, these registries can be used with a geographic profile to help prioritize suspects. The U.S. *Violent Crime Control and Law Enforcement Act of 1994* "requires states to enact statutes or regulations which require those determined to be sexually violent predators or who are convicted of sexually violent offenses to register with appropriate state law enforcement agencies for ten years after release from prison," or risk the reduction of Federal grant money (U.S. Department of Justice, 1994).

Sex offender registries are powerful tools for monitoring and controlling criminal predators who, unfortunately, are more prevalent than is commonly believed. Washington State established the first such registry, and according to the Seattle Police Department Special Assault Unit, in May of 1995, the city of Seattle had a total of 859 registered sex offenders, an average of 10 per square mile. This figure does not include the 20% of released sex offenders who fail to register.

Government and Business Databases

Data banks are often geographically based, and information from parole and probation offices, mental health outpatient clinics, social services offices, schools, and other agencies located in prioritized areas can also prove to be of value (it has been estimated that approximately 85% of all records contain an address). Several commercial companies offer law enforcement agencies the ability to search numerous personal information databases. Seisint, Accurint LE, ChoicePoint, and LexisNexis each have their own data mining algorithms, which sample and select mega-quantities of data bits electronically, and assign them to individual profiles.

A partial listing of the information sources tapped into by these systems includes

1. Public records, such as bankruptcies, tax liens and judgments, professional licenses, boat/aircraft ownership, vehicle registrations and driver's licenses in some states, workers' compensation appeals, state/local civil and criminal court filings, federal civil and criminal court filings, dog licenses, tax assessments, real property ownership, and others
2. Commercial records, such as magazine subscriptions, warranty card information, utility bills, credit headers (uses name/address/date birth/social security number, etc., from debtor identification data rather than actual credit worthiness data), telephone listings, unlisted phone numbers (most often obtained from people calling toll-free numbers, thus giving out their home telephone number by default), and others

In 2001, a serial rapist in Fort Collins, Colorado, assaulted seven women after breaking into their apartments. When investigators submitted a DNA sample from one of the crime scenes to a national databank, a match was found to a crime series 1,750 miles away in Philadelphia, Pennsylvania (Gibbons, McCoy, & Fish, 2001). The Center City rapist had preyed on women in the Rittenhouse Square area of Philadelphia from 1997 to 1999, raping five victims and strangling another. He then disappeared until reappearing in Fort Collins two years later. Detectives used commercial database services to develop lists of individuals who lived in Philadelphia from 1997 to 1999, and in Fort Collins in 2001. A geographic profile prepared for the Philadelphia Police Department helped narrow down the specific zip codes used in the search. The two lists were cross-referenced to identify individuals who appeared in both, resulting in approximately 700 names. From this, only a dozen or so individuals matched the suspect description parameters (e.g., gender, ethnicity, approximate age) and had moved in the proper direction—from Pennsylvania to Colorado. Follow-up investigation by detectives led to the arrest of Troy Graves. He pled guilty to both sets of crimes and was sentenced to life imprisonment in 2002 (Dale, 2002).

Motor Vehicle Registrations

A geographic profile can be integrated with suspect vehicle and offender descriptions to search registered motor vehicle and driver's license files, contained in state or provincial computer record systems. This is often done by first using the geoprofile to prioritize zip or postal codes most likely associated with the offender's residence. The description and geographic parameters act as a linear program to produce a small set of records containing the appropriate data. This strategy results in areas of manageable size for major police investigations.

For example, a new red station wagon driven by a tall white middle-aged male, with dark hair, may seem to be somewhat vague information. But the description actually contains several parameters: (1) vehicle style—station wagon; (2) vehicle color—red; and (3) vehicle year range—last five years. Further focus can be obtained from the various driver descriptors (e.g., sex, race, age range, height, hair color, etc.), though the assumption that the driver is the vehicle's registered owner may be incorrect. These parameters can narrow down hundreds of thousands of records to a few dozen vehicles or drivers when combined with a prioritized list of zip or postal codes. This is sufficient discrimination to allow detailed police follow-up.

A case involving a violent child sex offender illustrates this point. The geoprofile was first used to prioritize the postal codes for the neighborhood within where the crimes had occurred. Planning and zoning maps were then studied to eliminate industrial, commercial, and other nonresidential areas. Socioeconomic and demographic census data were also consulted to adjust the priority of those neighborhoods inconsistent with the socioeconomic status of the offender as suggested by the behavioral profile.

The final list of postal codes, ranked by priority of probability, could then be used to conduct a computer search of the provincial motor vehicle department records, which contain postal codes as part of the address associated with the vehicle registered owner and driver's license files. Suspect vehicle and offender descriptions had been developed by detectives, and this information was combined with the geographic data to effectively focus the search.

Bloodings

During a sexual murder or rape investigation, British police may conduct large-scale DNA testing of all men from the area of the crime ("How the DNA 'Database'," 1995). The first such case was the Narborough Murder Enquiry, when "all unalibied male residents in the villages between the ages of seventeen and thirty-four years would be asked to submit blood and saliva samples voluntarily in order to 'eliminate them' as suspects in the footpath murders" (Wambaugh, 1989, pp. 220–221). Close to 4,000 men from the villages of Narborough, Littlethorpe, and Enderby were tested during the investigation.

Considerable police resources and laboratory costs are involved in such "bloodings," and therefore British police follow intelligence-led DNA screens in which individuals are prioritized based on proximity to crime scene, criminal record, age, and other relevant criteria (National Crime Faculty, 1996; Rossmo, Davies, & Patrick, 2004). In cases of serial crime, geographic profiling can further refine the selection process through targeting by address, or zip or postal code, resulting in more efficient and systematic testing procedures. U.S. and Canadian police are also using this strategy. The Baton Rouge serial murders and the Wichita BTK strangler investigations both conducted large-scale DNA suspect testing. Geographic profiles had been prepared for investigators in both cases. When 11 sexual assaults occurred in just over one month in Mississauga, Ontario, Peel Regional Police detectives collected 312 suspects. Combining the geographic and behavioral profiles with description and interview information, detectives prioritized the suspects into groups and obtained DNA samples from the most probable individuals. The offender was identified in the first lot. He resided within the top 2.2% (0.03 mi^2) of the area under consideration.

Peak-of-Tension Polygraphy

In presumed homicides with known suspects but no bodies, polygraphists have had success in narrowing down the search area for the victim's remains through peak-of-tension (POT) tests (Hagmaier, 1990; see also Cunliffe & Piazza, 1980; Raskin, 1989). POT polygraphy (also known as guilty knowledge polygraphy) involves monitoring a subject's reaction to photographs, objects, or maps, as opposed to answering verbal questions. A deceptive response to queries concerning the type of location where the victim's body was hidden (e.g., cave, lake, marsh, field, forest, etc.) can help focus a search. Because POT tests often involve maps or area photographs, their usefulness is enhanced when results are combined with a geographic profile.

Missing Bodies

In certain missing person cases that are suspected homicides, geographic profiling can help determine probable body dump site areas. In November 1993, a teenage boy was found shot dead in his car outside St. Antoine, New Brunswick. His girlfriend was missing, and presumed kidnapped. The murderer was identified through rifle ballistics but disappeared before he could be arrested. After unsuccessfully pursuing various leads and tips, the RCMP began to theorize that the missing female victim had been killed and the offender had committed suicide. Two searches by police and military teams of the rural Bouctouche region failed to find evidence of either body. A geographic profile was then requested. Employing techniques of path analysis, journey-to-crime estimates, and time–distance–speed calculations, the geoprofile outlined two prioritized search areas. A third search effort later located effects of the offender in a river under a railway trestle and the body of the female victim in a field; the former was found in the highest prioritized area of the geoprofile, and the latter in the second highest.

Austin Ripper

Twenty years after the end of the Civil War, Austin, Texas, was plagued by a series of horrific axe murders (Corcoran, 2000; Hollandsworth, 2000; Humphrey, 1985; Plohetski, 2004; Saylor, 2000). From New Year's Eve 1884 to Christmas Eve 1885, eight people were killed in the capital city of 23,000. The victims were predominantly black females, cooks and maids, taken from their homes at night and "outraged" (to use the newspaper vernacular of the time). The serial killer operated with impunity, not so surprising considering that at any one time, there were only four police officers on duty. The media used monikers such as the Austin Ripper, the Austin Axe Murderer, or the Austin Servant Girl Annihilator.[5] Like Jack the Ripper, his later and more famous cousin, the Austin murderer was never caught and the case remains unsolved.

Bloody Work. A Fearful Midnight Murder on West Pecan—Mystery and Crime.[6]

The first attack occurred on Wednesday morning, early New Year's Eve, December 31, 1884, at 901 West Pecan (now Sixth) Street. Mollie Smith, a mulatto female, worked for W. K. Hall, and lived in a small apartment at the rear of his house, just back of the kitchen. Sometime between 3 a.m. and 4 a.m. she was dragged outside, assaulted, and murdered with an axe. She was found behind a small outhouse, 50 steps from the room where she slept. Her boyfriend, Walter Spencer, was also attacked and injured. There was a trail of bare footprints in the fresh snow that led from the murder scene to Shoal Creek, a block away.

The Foul Fiends.... Another Deed of Deviltry in the Crimson Catalogue of Crime.

The next victim was Eliza Shelly, a black female, who lived in a small one-room cabin on the property of Dr. L. B. Johnson, 302 East Cypress (now Third) Street, at San Jacinto Boulevard. The Central Railway line ran in front of the house on the Cypress Street side. Shelly's cabin was some 40 or 50 steps to the rear of Dr. Johnson's neat cottage, separated by a high fence with a connecting gate. An alley ran behind the cabin. Around 6 a.m., Thursday, May 7, 1885, Shelly was found murdered in her cabin, her head nearly cleaved in two. The weapon used was possibly a hatchet. Bare footprints were found at the crime scene.

More Butchery. Another Colored Woman Terribly Stabbed by an Unknown Fiend.... When Will It End?

Irene Cross, another black female, was attacked on Saturday, May 23, 1885, shortly after midnight. She lived in the yard of Whittman, 1737 San Jacinto Boulevard, at Linden (now Seventeenth) Street, across from Scholz's Beer Garden. The murder weapon was apparently a knife. Cross's arm was nearly chopped in two, and her head was cut as if she had been scalped. Her nephew claimed to have seen the assailant. "He said that the intruder was a 'big, chunky negro man, barefooted and with his pants rolled up.' He had on a brown hat and a ragged coat."

[5] This name was given to the killer by the writer O. Henry (William Sydney Porter), who was residing in Austin at the time of the murders.
[6] The quotations in this section are from the *Austin Statesman*.

An Atrocious Crime.... One of the Most Horrible Occurrences on Record.

The fourth victim was Mary Ramey, an 11-year-old black girl who lived with her mother, Rebecca Ramey, in the kitchen of the premises of V. O. Weed, 300 East Cedar (now Fourth) Street, at San Jacinto Boulevard. Sometime between 4 a.m. and 5 a.m. on Sunday, August 30, 1885, the killer dragged Mary from the kitchen where she was sleeping with her mother to a washhouse outside. Rebecca had been "sandbagged" (knocked unconscious). Mary was "ravished," and an iron pin driven through her ear and into her brain. The ground was damp and the killer's bare footprints could easily be seen. They went in and out of the backyard, through the alley gate, and into the alley. Bloodhounds followed the trail, which ended at some nearby stables.

Slain Servants. Monday Morning's Horrible Butchery.

On Monday morning, September 28, 1885, a double murder occurred. Gracie Vance and Orange Washington lived common-law in a small wooden shanty at 2408 West San Marcos (now Guadalupe) Street, catty-corner from the new University of Texas campus. Between 1 a.m. and 2 a.m., the killer entered the shanty and hit Washington on the skull with an axe, killing him; he was the only male victim in the series. Vance was dragged 75 yards from her room to just back of some stables where she was raped and murdered, "her head almost beaten into a jelly." Two other women, Lucinda Boddy and Patsie Gibson, asleep in the shanty at the time, were also attacked and injured. Vance, Washington, Boddy, and Gibson were all black. A man was seen running toward "Nigger Town." Tracks from the crime scene disappeared in a creek.

The Demons Have Transferred Their Thirst for Blood to White People!

Austin's citizens were shocked by the events of Christmas Eve 1885. The killer struck twice in one night, and for the first time his victims were white. Sometime before 11:30 p.m. on Thursday, December 24, 1885, Susan Hancock, "one of the most refined ladies in Austin," was dragged out of her house at 203 East Water (now First) Street, in the neighborhood of Germantown. She was found dead in the backyard by her husband, William H. Hancock, her head split open by an axe.

The Monsters in Human Shape Who Have Been Doing the Devil's Bidding.

An hour later, Friday morning, at 12:30 a.m., December 25, 1885, Eula Phillips became the second victim of the night. Her nude body was found outside her home, a "dozen squares away" (0.7 miles, a 15-minute walk). Phillips lived at 302 West Hickory (now Eighth) Street, at Lavaca Street, on the same property as the parents of her husband, James Phillips, Jr. Her forehead had been bashed in with the butt end of an axe. James was also attacked and injured, though the couple's baby boy was not harmed. A bloody trail showed Eula was dragged from her house onto the gallery, through the backyard, across another gallery, which connected her house with her husband's parent's house, then into another backyard to some outbuildings. She "had been outraged and most brutally maltreated." Tracks led from the crime scene to Shoal Creek.

Two attacks in the same night and both against white women—predictably, the community reacted with fear and outrage. A half-dozen black men were arrested on mere suspicion immediately following these murders. During 1885, a total of 400 people, mainly black men, were arrested and "severely examined" by police. One man was tried, but ultimately acquitted. Things became complicated, however, when it was discovered that Eula Phillips worked in May Tobin's house of assignation, at 103 Congress Avenue, as a "nymph du pave"—a prostitute. Was the killer one of her customers? The theories were as varied as they were speculative. Then, just as mysteriously as they began, the murders stopped. The crimes were never solved.

The Austin Ripper case is now more than 130 years old, and the murderer is long dead. It is a historical, not a cold case. What can a geographic profile tell us after so much time? Well, at the least it allows us to reassess what is already known, and perhaps provides a geographic perspective on the cast of characters and places.[7] The following locations of importance are in the peak area of the geoprofile for the Austin Ripper case:

- May Tobin's brothel, 103 Congress Avenue.
- Guy Town, a racially mixed district of prostitution, gambling, and saloons, located roughly between Colorado Avenue on the east and Guadalupe Street on the west, and Live Oak (now Second) on the south and Cedar (now Fourth) Street on the north.
- Pearl House, 221 Congress Avenue. Maurice, a Malay cook employed in 1885 at the Pearl House, disappeared in January 1886. He was presumed by some to be the Austin Ripper.
- Union Depot, 100 block West Cypress (now Third) Street. It is possible the killer worked at the train station, or travelled into the city by train.

While the crimes of the Austin Ripper are likely to remain forever a mystery, it is interesting to imagine what detectives might have accomplished given modern forensic and behavioral analysis techniques.

Conclusion

Geographic profiling can provide cold case investigators with a compass for prioritizing suspects and managing information. It is an appropriate technique in cases of serial crime, or those involving multiple locations. Geographic profiling cannot directly solve a crime, but it is a valuable addition to the detective's toolbox. The challenges of cold cases necessitate a comprehensive set of investigative strategies. The use of geography strikes a chord with practitioners, a resonance explained by the old police truism: "When all else fails, return to the scene" (Barrett, 1990, p. 90).

Acknowledgments

I wish to extend my deepest gratitude and appreciation to Dr. D. Kim Rossmo for authoring and contributing this chapter. D. Kim Rossmo is a research professor and the director of the Center for Geospatial Intelligence and Investigation (GII) in the School of Criminal Justice at Texas State University. Formerly, he was a management consultant with the Bureau of Alcohol, Tobacco, Firearms and Explosives (ATF), the director of Research for the Police Foundation, and the detective inspector in charge of the Vancouver Police Department's Geographic Profiling Section. Over the course of his 21-year policing career, he worked assignments in organized crime intelligence, emergency response, patrol, crime prevention, and community liaison. He holds a PhD (Simon Fraser University) in criminology and has researched and published in the areas of policing, offender profiling, and environmental criminology. He is a member of the International Association of Chiefs of Police (IACP) Advisory Committee for Police Investigative Operations and is a full fellow of the International Criminal Investigative Analysis Fellowship. He is also an adjunct professor at Simon Fraser University and sits on the editorial board for the international journal *Homicide Studies*.

[7] A similar analysis was done on the murder locations of Jack the Ripper in Whitechapel, England, with interesting results (see Rossmo, 2000).

Suggested Readings and Bibliography

Barrett, G. M. (1990). *Serial murder: A study in psychological analysis, prediction, and profiling.* Unpublished master's thesis, University of Louisville, Louisville, KY.

Bennell, C., & Canter, D. V. (2002). Linking commercial burglaries by *modus operandi*: Tests using regression and ROC analysis. *Science & Justice, 42*, 153–164.

Bennett, T., & Wright, R. T. (1984). *Burglars on burglary: Prevention and the offender.* Aldershot, Hants: Gower.

Bigbee, D., Tanton, R. L., & Ferrara, P. B. (1989). Implementation of DNA analysis in American crime laboratories. *The Police Chief*, pp. 86–89.

Brantingham, P. J., & Brantingham, P. L. (1984). *Patterns in crime.* New York: Macmillan.

Brantingham, P. L., & Brantingham, P. J. (1981). Notes on the geometry on crime. In P. J. Brantingham & P. L. Brantingham (Eds.), *Environmental criminology* (pp. 27–54). Beverly Hills: Sage.

Brantingham, P. L., & Brantingham, P. J. (1993). Environment, routine and situation: Toward a pattern theory of crime. In R. V. Clarke & M. Felson (Eds.), *Routine activity and rational choice* (pp. 259–294). New Brunswick, NJ: Transaction.

Brooks, P. R. (1984). *VICAP.* Lecture presented at Washington Criminal Justice Training Center seminar, Seattle, WA.

Brown, J. R. (1994). DNA analysis: A significant tool for law enforcement. *The Police Chief*, pp. 51–52.

Chaiken, J. M., Greenwood, P. W., & Petersilia, J. (1991). The Rand study of detectives. In C. B. Klockars & S. D. Mastrofski (Eds.), *Thinking about police: Contemporary readings* (2nd ed.) (pp. 170–187). New York: McGraw-Hill.

Collins, P. I., Johnson, G. F., Choy, A., Davidson, K. T., & MacKay, R. E. (1998). Advances in violent crime analysis and law enforcement: The Canadian Violent Crime Linkage Analysis System. *Journal of Government Information, 25*, 277–284.

Cooper, S. (1999). *Welcome to the Mardi Gra experience.* London: Blake Publishing.

Copson, G. (1993). *Offender profiling.* Presentation to the Association of Chief Police Officers Crime Sub-Committee on Offender Profiling, London, England.

Corcoran, M. (2000). Rediscovering Austin's Jack the Ripper. *Austin American-Statesman.*

Cryan, M. P. (1988). Halt program joins VICAP in hunting serial criminals. *Trooper Magazine*, (May/June), 8–9.

Cunliffe, F., & Piazza, P. B. (1980). *Criminalistics and scientific investigation.* Englewood Cliffs, NJ: Prentice-Hall.

Dale, A., & Davies, A. (1994). *Developments in the analysis of rapists speech.* Unpublished manuscript, Police Research Group, Home Office Police Department, London.

Dale, M. (2002). Airman pleads guilty to Philadelphia killing, rapes. *The Daily Camera.*

Davies, A., & Dale, A. (1995). *Locating the stranger rapist* (Special Interest Series: Paper 3). London: Police Research Group, Home Office Police Department.

Dees, T. M. (1994). Automation of forensic ballistics. *Law Enforcement Technology*, pp. 44, 47.

Di Maio, V. J. M. (1985). *Gunshot wounds: Practical aspects of firearms, ballistics, and forensic techniques.* Boca Raton, FL: CRC Press.

DNA profiling. (1995). *DNA Database*, p. 2.

Douglas, J. E., & Munn, C. (1992). Violent crime scene analysis: Modus operandi, signature, and staging. *FBI Law Enforcement Bulletin, 61*(2), 1–10.

Federal Bureau of Investigation. (1996). *Rapid Start Information Management System: Reference Guide.* Washington, DC: Author.

Gabor, T. (1978). Crime displacement: The literature and strategies for its investigation. *Crime and Justice, 6*, 100–106.

Gaudette, B. D. (1990). DNA typing: A new service to Canadian police. *RCMP Gazette*, 52(4), 1–7.

Gibbons, Jr., T. J., McCoy, C. R., & Fish, L. (2001). DNA links Center City rapist to Col. assaults. *Philadelphia Inquirer.*

Grubin, D., Kelly, P., & Ayis, A. (1996). *Linking serious sexual assaults.* Unpublished manuscript, Police Research Group, Home Office Police Department, London.

Hagmaier, B. (1990). *Ted Bundy, a case study.* Lecture presented at the FBI National Academy retraining session, Bellingham, WA.

Hanfland, K. A., Keppel, R. D., & Weis, J. G. (1997). *Case management for missing children homicide investigation.* Seattle: Washington State Office of the Attorney General.

Harris, T. (1988). *Silence of the lambs.* New York: St. Martin's Paperbacks.

Hickey, E. W. (1986). The female serial murderer 1800-1986. *Journal of Police and Criminal Psychology, 2*(2), 72–81.

Hollandsworth, S. (2000). Capital murder. *Texas Monthly*, pp. 106–111, 131–134.

Homant, R. J., & Kennedy, D. B. (1998). Psychological aspects of crime scene profiling: Validity research. *Criminal Justice and Behavior, 25*, 319–343.

How the DNA 'Database' & 'Caseworking' Units will function! (1995, February). *DNA Database*, p. 2.

Howlett, J. B., Hanfland, K. A., & Ressler, R. K. (1986). The Violent Criminal Apprehension Program—VICAP: A progress report. *FBI Law Enforcement Bulletin, 55*(12), 14–22.

Humphrey, D. C. (1985). *Austin: An illustrated history*. Northridge, CA: Windsor Publications.

Johnson, G. (1994). ViCLAS: Violent Crime Linkage Analysis System. *RCMP Gazette, 56*(10), 9–13.

Kelly, K. F., Rankin, J. J., & Wink, R. C. (1987). Method and applications of DNA fingerprinting: A guide for the non-scientist. *The Criminal Law Review*, 105–110.

Keppel, R. D. (1995). Signature murders: A report of several related cases. *Journal of Forensic Sciences, 40*, 670–674.

Keppel, R. D., & Birnes, W. J. (1995). *The Riverman: Ted Bundy and I hunt for the Green River Killer*. New York: Simon & Schuster.

Keppel, R. D., & Weis, J. G. (1993a). HITS: Catching criminals in the Northwest. *FBI Law Enforcement Bulletin, 62*(4), 14–19.

Keppel, R. D., & Weis, J. G. (1993b). *Improving the investigation of violent crime: The Homicide Investigation and Tracking System* (NIJ Publication No. NCJ 141761). Washington, DC: U.S. Government Printing Office.

Klockars, C. B., & Mastrofski, S. D. (Eds.). (1991). *Thinking about police: Contemporary readings* (2nd ed.). New York: McGraw-Hill.

Mardia, K. V., Coombes, A., Kirkbride, J., Linney, A., & Bowie, J. L. (1996). On statistical problems with face identification from photographs. *Journal of Applied Statistics, 23*, 655–675.

Michaud, S. G., & Aynesworth, H. (1983). *The only living witness*. New York: Penguin Books.

Michaud, S. G., & Hazelwood, R. R. (1998). *The evil that men do: FBI profiler Roy Hazelwood's journey into the minds of sexual predators*. New York: St. Martin's Press.

Miller, J. V. (1991). The FBI's forensic DNA analysis program. *FBI Law Enforcement Bulletin, 60*(7), 11–15.

National Crime Faculty. (1996). *Intelligence led DNA screening: A guide for investigating officers*. Bramshill: Author.

Newton, M. (1998). *Rope: The twisted life and crimes of Harvey Glatman*. New York: Simon & Schuster.

Pilant, L. (1994). Information management. *The Police Chief*, pp. 30–38, 42–47.

Plohetski, T. (2004). On a killer's trail. *Austin American-Statesman*, pp. A1–A12–A13.

Raskin, D. C. (Ed.). (1989). *Psychological methods in criminal investigation and evidence*. New York: Springer.

Rebscher, E., & Rohrer, F. (1991). Police information retrieval systems and the role of electronic data processing. In E. Kube & H. U. Störzer (Eds.), *Police research in the Federal Republic of Germany: 15 years research within the "Bundeskriminalamt"* (pp. 241–251). Berlin: Springer-Verlag.

Reppetto, T. A. (1976). Crime prevention and the displacement phenomenon. *Crime and Delinquency, 22*, 168–169.

Robertson, B., & Vignaux, G. A. (1995). *Interpreting evidence: Evaluating forensic evidence in the courtroom*. Chichester: John Wiley & Sons.

Rossmo, D. K. (2000). *Geographic profiling*. Boca Raton, FL: CRC Press.

Rossmo, D. K. (2004). Geographic profiling as problem solving for serial crime. In Q. C. Thurman & J. D. Jamieson (Eds.), *Police problem solving* (pp. 121–131). Cincinnati: Anderson Publishing.

Rossmo, D. K. (2009). *Criminal investigative failures*. Boca Raton, FL: Taylor & Francis.

Rossmo, D. K., Davies, A., & Patrick, M. (2004). *Exploring the geo-demographic and distance relationships between stranger rapists and their offences* (Special Interest Series: Paper 16). London: Research, Development and Statistics Directorate, Home Office.

Saylor, S. (2000). *A twist at the end*. New York: St. Martin's Press.

Schaller, G. B. (1972). *The Serengeti lion: A study of predator-prey relations*. Chicago: University of Chicago Press.

Segrave, K. (1992). *Women serial and mass murderers: A worldwide reference, 1580 through 1990*. Jefferson, NC: McFarland.

Skogan, W. G., & Antunes, G. E. (1979). Information, apprehension, and deterrence: Exploring the limits of police productivity. *Journal of Criminal Justice, 7*, 217–241.

Sparrow, M. K. (1994). Measuring AFIS matcher accuracy. *The Police Chief*, pp. 147–151.

Strandberg, K. W. (1994). FBI's "Drugfire." *Law Enforcement Technology*, pp. 50–51.

Thomas, N., Aitken, C., Lucy, D., & Feist, A. (2004). *Predicting the accuracy of stranger rape victims' statements* (Special Interest Series: Paper 15). London: Research, Development and Statistics Directorate, Home Office.

US Department of Justice. (1991). *Serial Murder Investigation System Conference* (Federal Bureau of Investigation). Washington, DC: US Government Printing Office.

US Department of Justice. (1994). *Violent Crime Control and Law Enforcement Act of 1994* (Fact Sheet No. NCJ-FS000067). Washington, DC: US Government Printing Office.

Wambaugh, J. (1989). *The blooding*. New York: Bantam Books.

Warren, J. I., Reboussin, R., & Hazelwood, R. R. (1995). *The geographic and temporal sequencing of serial rape* (Federal Bureau of Investigation). Washington, DC: US Government Printing Office.

Weedn, V. W., & Hicks, J. W. (1998). *The unrealized potential of DNA testing* (NIJ Publication No. NCJ-170596). Washington, DC: U.S. Government Printing Office.

Welborn, L. (2003). Trial nears end in '95 slaying. *The Orange County Register*, p. A1.

Westfall, B. (1992). Westley Allan Dodd. *Police*, *16*(7), 58–60, 84.

Winn, S., & Merrill, D. (1979). *Ted Bundy: The killer next door*. New York: Bantam Books.

Resources and Conclusion

IV

31 "Who You Know" Resources in Cold Case Homicide Investigation

R. H. WALTON

Contents

Case Review and Related Assistance

National Center for Missing and Exploited Children (NCMEC)

In 1982, Congress enacted the Missing Children's Act. This legislation authorized the entry of missing-child information into the National Crime Information Center (NCIC). Prior to this, guns and vehicles were entered into this national database, but not children.

By an Act of Congress in 1984, the Missing Children's Assistance Act established the National Center for Missing and Exploited Children (NCMEC). This quasi-government agency was an experiment in public–private partnership and was established to serve as a national clearinghouse and resource center on the issue of missing and exploited children. Today, this IRS 501(c)(3) corporation serves to help find missing children and help reduce and prevent child sexual exploitation and victimization. Expertise is contributed by others in the medico-legal, forensic, and law enforcement professions. The name of this organization is perhaps a misnomer, as the NCMEC provides expert assistance to law enforcement for missing, long-term missing children, and unidentified-remains cases of persons believed to be under the age of 21. These services are provided at *no cost* to law enforcement agencies. NCMEC further categorizes a missing child as one who is "critically missing." These are cases in which the missing child is at an elevated risk of danger if not located quickly due to the circumstances surrounding the disappearance. Factors considered in this category include age, physical condition, and family situation.

Background

In the early 1980s, a series of high-profile cases involving missing and abducted children highlighted a defect in the way American law enforcement reacted to reports of missing children. Included in these cases were those of Adam Walsh of Hollywood, Florida; Etan Patz of New York; and 26 missing and murdered children in Atlanta. These cases illuminated the then-common police practice of a mandatory waiting period before agencies would take a missing-children or missing-persons report. The prevailing wisdom was that children were runaways, and if they did not return home within this period, law enforcement would then take a report. When agencies did take a report, however, it was usually handled internally. This may be a significant factor in missing-children cases that are still unresolved and have become long-term missing-person's cases with a high potential to be cold case homicides.

As a result, investigation was delayed and, unfortunately, often nonexistent. There was no national response system between local, state, and federal law enforcement agencies. Communication and coordination among these agencies was lacking, or at most, minimal. For the families of the victims, there was no central resource. The extent of unsolved cases lacking remaining official records in local law enforcement agencies from this period is unknown.

Not unexpectedly, unresolved missing-children cases have usually experienced a series of investigators over the intervening years. Similar to cold case homicides, these cases may not have been assigned a high priority for investigation, due to the press of current cases and resource utilization. Each investigator brought a different perspective, but ultimately, interest in the case diminished, and the case went unresolved. These long-term missing-children or missing-person cases are not infrequently assigned for investigation to cold case homicide investigators. See Figure 31.1 and Chapter 5.

The following discussion is summarized and excerpted from the World Wide Web pages of NCMEC.

Programs and Services

NCMEC offers more than 20 programs and services to assist families of missing and exploited children as well as those tailored to assist law enforcement. These include programs to assist in cases both

Figure 31.1 Endangered missing. Karen Mitchell is one of an unknown number of runaway, missing, endangered missing, or murdered children and young adults. The National Center for Missing and Exploited Children offers a number of services to law enforcement to assist in these cold case investigations. (Courtesy of NCMEC.)

domestic and international in scope. Regional offices are maintained in Florida, California, Texas, and New York.

Law enforcement-oriented services may be categorized as forensic or investigative.

- **Forensic Services** include facial reconstruction and age regression or progression techniques, access to databases such as CODIS, NCIC, NGI/AFIS, and many other specific forensic disciplines that may aid in the solution of these cases. Investigators are urged to contact NCMEC for further details.
- **Investigative Services** include expert and on-site assistance offered at no cost to law enforcement through PROJECT ALERT and TEAM ADAM.
  - *PROJECT ALERT (America's Law Enforcement Retiree Team).* This is a team of approximately 170 retired local, state, and federal law enforcement personnel who volunteer their time and expertise as unpaid consultants to the national law enforcement community. Their purpose is to assist the agency to resolve long-term missing-child cases and those cases involving the remains of missing children. This program began in 1992 and is endorsed by numerous leading national law enforcement associations. In the course of their service with the NCMEC, personnel have received special instruction in cold case investigation. According to NCMEC, these investigators will provide assistance to the law enforcement agency at no cost to the agency, including
    - Long-term case review
    - Organization and analysis
    - Recommendations for investigative strategies
    - Follow-up of leads
    - Coordination of meetings with law enforcement personnel to discuss additional resources

- *TEAM ADAM.* This program is patterned after the National Transportation Safety Board's method of sending specialists to the scene of transportation incidents. This team is composed of retired law enforcement professionals with years of investigative experience. This team can respond to the site of serious child abductions and cases of child sexual exploitation. Services offered include
  - Search and rescue
  - Technical support
  - Investigative recommendations and analysis
  - Equipment and resources

Team Adam also provides assistance and support to family members, including (1) family advocacy services, (2) personal assistance, (3) stress management, and (4) media relations.

Other Services

- *CyberTipline.* This tipline allows the public and electronic service providers to report via online or toll-free instances of online efforts that target children for sexual exploitation, child pornography, child sex trafficking, and other means of child sexual exploitation.
- *Posters and Media.* NCMEC may offer assistance with major media to provide broadcast material to generate public awareness and exposure of cases. They assist in generating new posters as well as validating the information on older posters. Investigators are cautioned to check with originating agencies before taking action regarding a child or abductor depicted in any poster on their website or one not containing the official NCMEC logo. International posters may not have criminal warrants attached to the case, and it is suggested that investigators contact NCMEC during these investigations.
- *Case Analysis Unit.* This unit provides direct analytical support to law enforcement for cases involving missing or unidentified deceased child cases.
- *Missing children database* to search for missing children using known parameters.
- *Child Victim Identification Program.*
- *Sex Offender Tracking Team.*
- *Biometrics Team.* This team coordinates the collection of dental records, DNA, and other individual identifiers from family members or others to assist in the search for potential matches in databases.
- *Family Abduction Unit.* The unit encompasses case management teams providing technical support and assistance for law enforcement agencies and attorneys for domestic and international cases.

In addition, the NCMEC collects information about abductions, including short-term "abduct and release incidents and other suspicious incidents involving children." These, as well as trends identified in attempted abductions, are analyzed to identify patterns and thus potentially aid law enforcement's efforts in these cases.

Legal Services

NCMEC provides information for cases including

- Legal technical assistance to law enforcement, prosecutors, and other professionals
- Domestic family abductions

- International family abductions
- Information about the International Child Abduction Attorney Network
- Information about legal technical assistance regarding missing children who have run away
- Information about child sexual exploitation, including state and federal laws
- Additional legal resources

Other Written Resources

In addition, the NCMEC provides written resources for investigators. Among these are an *Investigator's Package*, and publications that may be downloaded onto a computer

- "Long-Term Missing Child Guide for Law Enforcement"
- "Missing and Abducted Children: A Law-Enforcement Guide to Case Investigation and Program Management"

Contact information:
National Center for Missing and Exploited Children
Charles B. Wang International Children's Building
699 Prince Street
Alexandria, Virginia 22314-3175
24 Hour Call Center: 1-800-843-5678 (national hotline)
http://www.missingkids.org

Vidocq Society

The Vidocq Society was founded in 1990 in Philadelphia, Pennsylvania, by William Fleisher, then second-in-command special agent for the U.S. Customs Service in that city; well-known forensic sculptor Frank Bender; and Richard Walter, a Michigan state prison psychologist. This trio wanted to establish a setting at which similarly minded persons would gather to discuss and consider crimes and mysteries. Other federal, state, and local law enforcement persons subsequently sought to join the group, and attention grew regarding the criminal investigative expertise of this enlarging body. In time, the society narrowed its mandate to focus on unsolved cold case homicides, and in some cases, disappearances.

Society membership is limited to 82 regular Vidocq Society Members (VSMs), one for each year of the life of the organization's namesake, Eugène Francois Vidocq. Vidocq was a brilliant eighteenth-century French crook-turned-cop who rose to become a famous detective and later became the first chief of the Sûreté in 1811. Vidocq Society membership is currently in excess of 150 regular and special members from a variety of disciplines, including law enforcement, forensics, psychology, business, and other diverse backgrounds. These persons donate their time and efforts for the public good.

Members of the Vidocq Society and invited guests normally meet over lunch on the third Thursday of each month at a site in downtown Philadelphia. At these meetings, they listen to guest presenters share the facts of a case and apply their collective forensic skills and experience to cold case homicides and unsolved deaths. At these meetings, the VSMs evaluate, refocus, breathe new life into, and attempt to solve the unsolved deaths officially brought to them by representatives of law enforcement organizations or victims' families. The Vidocq Society does not conduct independent investigations; it assists in the investigation of unsolved deaths and homicides only when law enforcement agencies accept their support, and the investigating agency directs *all* Vidocq Society efforts.

The Vidocq Society is a 501(c)(3) organization and has been recognized as a cold case resource by the U.S. Justice Department. An example of their work may be found in Chapter 22, "Boulder Jane Doe."

For law enforcement agencies, the Vidocq Society is a forensic resource at a great price, a team of experts whose consultative skills and talents are always free. Among the talents and skills VSMs may offer cold case homicide investigators include the following:

- Accident investigation and reconstruction and related civil disciplines
- Anthropology reconstruction and forensic anthropology
- Bloodstain pattern analysis
- Document examination
- Financial investigation, forensic accounting, and white-collar crime
- Firearms, arson, and bombing investigation
- Forensic odontology
- Forensic pathology
- Homicide investigation and events reconstruction
- Interview and interrogation
- Latent fingerprints
- Organized crime
- Polygraph
- Postconviction investigation
- Crime assessment and profiling

Case Selection and Intake Criteria

The society chooses its cases carefully and works closely with, and at the request of, local investigators and prosecutors. All work is done at no cost to victims' families or law enforcement and is pro bono as part of the society's commitment to public service. Detailed requirements and procedures for case submission and review are found at their World Wide Web site shown at the end of this section.

For the Vidocq Society to consider an unsolved death or homicide case, specific criteria include the following:

- The victim cannot have been engaged in dangerous or illicit activity of any kind.
- The agency with investigating jurisdiction must invite the Society to assist their effort.
- At minimum, the case should have a body, known crime scene, and physical evidence.

If the death falls within Vidocq Society guidelines, forward a letter by U.S. Postal service to

Vidocq Society Case Referrals
1704 Locust Street, Second Floor
Philadelphia, Pennsylvania 19103

The letter should include only photocopies of any police reports, forensic summaries, or other relevant documents or newspaper clippings. Prior to submitting required materials by U.S. Mail, questions may be submitted to the *Director of Case Management* at the Vidocq Society website.

Case Review Process

Upon receipt of the data sent with the request for investigation, along with any other facts gathered independently by the society personnel, a determination will be made to ascertain whether the case or matter meets Vidocq's basic acceptance criteria. If it is decided that the crime may qualify, the case is assigned to additional experts for further review and analysis. Some cases become Vidocq meeting presentations.

Case Presentation

The presenter of a cold case homicide at a Vidocq Society meeting could be a law enforcement professional who has investigated the murder over the years and continues to carry it on his/her caseload (or his/her successor), a VSM, or a presenter meeting Vidocq criteria.

Following the presentation, formal discussions by attending membership include a question-and-answer session. This is a collaborative effort that involves members and invited guests. Case presentations conclude with a call for VSMs interested in jointly pursuing the matter. In some cases, a working group is assembled to more intensively advance that specific investigation.

Confidentiality and Media Concerns

Information provided to the Vidocq Society is maintained in a confidential manner. The Vidocq Society's policy is to neither confirm nor deny any role in any investigation. The Vidocq Society is a private organization and is not obligated to provide access, information, or explanations to the media or to the public.

The Vidocq Society does not provide real-time media access to investigations. If the Vidocq Society is assisting in any investigation, any information would come from the law enforcement agency. The Vidocq Society recognizes the valuable role that the media can afford in the truth-gathering process and the role that publicity may play in advancing the cause of an investigation of an unsolved death. At the request of the investigating law enforcement agency, the Vidocq Society will alert local media that a particular death is being presented or investigated. Any case and crime details, however, would be provided by the investigating agency and not the Vidocq Society.

The Vidocq Society is a nonprofit charitable organization under section 501(c)(3) of the Internal Revenue Code. The society obtains its financial support from membership dues and voluntary contributors willing to help underwrite their pro bono services.

Contact information:
Vidocq Society
1704 Locust Street, Second Floor
Philadelphia, Pennsylvania 19103
1-215-545-1450
http://www.vidocq.org

Cold Case Review Teams

Many states and jurisdictional entities have established state, regional, or local cold case review teams. These teams usually consist of representatives from a variety of disciplines, including homicide investigation, medical examiner, forensic, and behavioral disciplines. A presentation is made by an agency submitting the case for review, and this procedure gives a fresh pair of eyes to the case. The following is a sampling of such teams and programs, and investigators are advised to contact the team or check for more local teams for case submission and review requirements.

Colorado Cold Case Review Teams

More localized cold case homicide review teams have been successful. Created and mandated by the Colorado legislature in 2007, this unfunded unit operates under the auspices of the Colorado Bureau of

Investigation. It addresses cold case homicides and long-time missing persons. At a meeting of assembled members, an agency presents its unsolved case, most often in PowerPoint© format, after which review team members ask questions and offer suggestions. The presenting agency subsequently is e-mailed an electronic account of the presentation as well as a list of the questions asked and suggestions given by the team. As with the Vidocq Society, all matters are confidential within law enforcement. Meeting two to four times a year, it includes representatives from

- Prosecutors' offices
- Forensic disciplines
- Homicide investigators
- Behavioral experts
- Victim advocates
- Forensic pathologists

This is a not uncommon model, bringing together multiple disciplines for case review.

Mid-Atlantic Cold Case Homicide Investigators Association (MACCHIA)

Along with similar organizations, MACCHIA provides training, networking, and related cold case homicide information-sharing services. For many years, they have partnered with the Naval Criminal Investigative Service to hold an annual training session and case review roundtable in Annapolis, Maryland (http://www.coldcasehomicide.org).

Sheriff's Association of Texas, Major Crimes Assessment Committee (MCAC) Cold Case Review Team

Since 1985, this team has brought together multiple disciplines, including medicolegal, forensic, and crime lab resources; the Department of Public Safety Special Services; the Texas Rangers; and seasoned investigators to provide assistance to law enforcement in solving cold cases. Meeting on a quarterly basis, they seek to integrate the expertise of participating membership (http://www.txsheriffs.org/comm_cold case.htm).

Military Cold Case Resources

Each branch of the U.S. Armed Forces includes a unit to investigate criminal violations as well as violations of the Uniform Code of Military Justice. Names vary but may include "Office of Special Investigations" or similar. A principal factor in investigation by military (cold case) units is that there is a military nexus, i.e., the victim or perpetrator was an active-duty (or in some cases, inactive) member. Unfortunately, due to budget and other considerations, these units have operated on a come-and-go basis. The result has been, in some instances, less than a focused and continuous effort, despite the best abilities of personnel assigned.

A little-known fact is that if an active service member commits a homicide or other crime, and ultimately separates from service, the Uniform Code of Military Justice provides for jurisdiction, even decades later.

Investigators seeking contact or assistance with cases that might involve military assistance are advised to contact the World Wide Web site for that agency, and the following is provided for further reference.

United States Navy
Naval Criminal Investigative Service

Russell Knox Building
27130 Telegraph Road
Quantico, Virginia 22134-2253

United States Army
U.S. Army Criminal Investigation Command
Russell Knox Building
27130 Telegraph Road
Quantico, Virginia 22134-2253
1-571-305-4009

United States Air Force
Office of Special Investigations
Russell Knox Building
27130 Telegraph Road
Quantico, Virginia 22134-2253

Unites States Coast Guard
Coast Guard Investigative Service
Department of Homeland Security
Office of the Inspector General
Office of Investigation
Building 410
245 Murray Drive
Washington, District of Columbia 20528

American Academy of Forensic Sciences

The American Academy of Forensic Sciences (AAFS) was founded in 1948. The distinguished and diverse membership includes many of the world's leading forensic scientists, and now numbers over 7000 members worldwide. The AAFS consists of 11 sections that represent a wide range of forensic disciplines, including anthropology, criminalistics, digital and multimedia sciences, engineering sciences, a general section, jurisprudence, odontology, pathology/biology, psychiatry and behavioral science, questioned documents, and toxicology. This professional association is committed to the application of science to law. In this regard, the AAFS promotes professional development and education in conjunction with the elevation of accuracy, precision, and specificity in the forensic sciences. It accomplishes these goals through annual meetings, educational programs and seminars, newsletters, and other venues.

The AAFS may assist cold case homicide investigators in a variety of areas through identification of qualified forensic scientists in a wide range of disciplines.

Contact information:
American Academy of Forensic Sciences
410 N. 21st Street
Colorado Springs, Colorado 80904-2798
1-719-636-1100
http://www.aafs.org

International Association for Identification

The International Association for Identification (IAI) is the world's oldest professional forensic association (1915), whose members represent an extensive body of experience and knowledge that seeks to educate others in various forensic disciplines, to critique and publish techniques and methodologies, and to conduct research in these areas. Their members work worldwide in various fields of forensic identification. The IAI prescribes professional standards for certification in a variety of forensic disciplines. These include (1) bloodstain patterns, (2) crime scenes, (3) footwear, (4) forensic art, (5) forensic photography, (6) forensic video, (7) latent prints, and (8) tenprint identifications.

Contact information:
International Association for Identification
2131 Hollywood Boulevard, Suite 403
Hollywood, Florida 33020
http://theiai.org

Victim–Witness Unit Cold Case Programs

Generally speaking, victim–witness units have been established in almost all jurisdictions nationwide, and often within the prosecutors' offices. A variation of this concept, as implemented by the Denver Police Department, Colorado (DPD), is a specialized program focusing on victim–witness issues solely in cold cases, both in homicides and sexual assaults. This has proven to be of great assistance to investigators and prosecutors. When a perpetrator is apprehended and charged, past events are suddenly at the emotional forefront for the families of the victim. The passage of time does little to dim the shock and loss, and questions about the case and the legal future of it will abound. Shock, disbelief, or denial—even anger—rises to the surface. The reaction may be extreme, and a victim program specialist accompanying or assisting the detectives can assist greatly in preparing families for the legal road ahead.

In 2004, the DPD obtained a grant from the National Institute of Justice, and the idea was conceived to form a cold case victim outreach coordinator as part of the cold case unit.

In 2008, a cold case grant allowed for additional detectives, an additional prosecutor, and a victim program specialist, who was incorporated into the DPD cold case investigation unit. The DPD cold case victim assistance program has become a model for others. Utilizing a team approach, the unit works closely with detectives assigned to cold cases, and when notified, the program specialists step in immediately to guide and assist the families. A cold case victim program specialist acts as an agent of the DPD and serves as an advocate. The specialist accompanies detectives to make initial notification to the family, and to answer questions and address issues that may be brought up, as well as give emotional support. In addition, they meet with victims' families to assist in identification of resources or other needs. They serve as a source of informational updates and as a point of contact until the case is filed by the district attorney.

After the case is filed, the district attorney's victim advocate and an investigator assigned to the case will work closely with the family. The victim advocate attends meetings with the assigned prosecutor and investigator, and will

- Make sure the family is notified of all critical stages of prosecution and guided through the judicial process

- Be present with family or witnesses if they are subpoenaed to court and will assist with the victim impact statement if so requested
- Otherwise ensure that the mandates of the Colorado Victim's Rights Amendment are complied with

Readers are referred to "Serving Survivors of Homicide Victims during Cold Case Investigations: A Guide for Developing a Law Enforcement Protocol" (National Sheriffs' Association 2011). This resource offers suggestions on identified issues including (1) definitions and terminology, (2) staffing issues and issues for rural agencies, (3) investigative strategies, (4) training and education, (5) communications with survivors, and (6) collaboration with other entities.

The Denver Police Department also provides victims with a guide, *Homicide Cold Case Investigations: A Guide for Victims and Their Families.* See Suggested Readings and Bibliography.

Volunteers

With no formal law enforcement in Old World England, when an emergency occurred, the *hue and cry* went out for citizens to respond. In frontier America, *posse comitatus* was the basis for local law enforcement putting together a posse of volunteers to assist officials in enforcement of law. Such concept has carried over in law in many states; thus, the concept of volunteers to assist is nothing new.

American law enforcement never has sufficient resources to fully optimize their mission. In the cold case and long-term missing-persons spectrum, volunteers—carefully selected and vetted—can contribute significantly to agency efficiency and mission fulfillment. Volunteers may be utilized in a variety of cold case–related functions including evidence and investigation report reviews. They serve as a means to give a preliminary review of unsolved homicide cases and to filter and detect follow-up leads for investigators. The following is excerpted from the website of the Charlotte-Mecklenburg Police Department (2016, with permission).

> The Charlotte-Mecklenburg Police Department formed a Cold Case Unit in April of 2003. The ***Homicide Cold Case Unit*** consists of homicide detectives, a civilian review team with law enforcement experience, and civilian volunteers from a wide array of life experiences. Initially, a case is assigned to a civilian review team member. That team member will read over the case file and identify any leads that need to be followed. They will also organize the paperwork and provide the detectives with a detailed summary of the available information relating to the case. This review and organization of the case information saves the detective valuable time. Subsequently, the detective can immediately begin working on the relevant leads. The review process generally takes approximately five months.

Experience has shown that many who volunteer in cold case programs are not uncommonly retired law enforcement, other criminal justice professionals, or interested civilians whose professional or occupational backgrounds provide a fit to assist the agency. Such is the experience of the Charlotte-Mecklenburg Police Department. This cold case unit intentionally recruited a member of the community with no law enforcement or investigative experience to bring an outside, fresh perspective to case reviews, and this has been working well. Remember—it is the initial review with a fresh pair of eyes that, not uncommonly, provides the segue for successful investigation and resolution. The selection process for volunteers varies, but a critical requisite is confidentiality and security. If the department already has in place policies and procedures for citizen volunteers, review of these in context of access to these files may be appropriate.

The following describes the Charlotte-Mecklenburg requirements for volunteers:

> Opportunities for volunteers are provided without regard to religion, creed, race, national origin, age, sex or disability. All volunteers must be at least 18 years of age. Each volunteer must complete an application, driver's history check and criminal history check, an interview and a drug screen. Volunteers may also be required to submit to a polygraph test prior to acceptance if the volunteer position involves sensitive security issues. These steps are taken to ensure that our volunteers adhere to the high standards set by our police department.

Academically Trained and Student Volunteers

Professor Elizabeth Gardner of the University of Alabama, Birmingham, offers an undergraduate- and graduate-level course, Cold Case Analysis, in their Justice Sciences program (Gardner 2012) (Figure 31.2). Using the first edition of this textbook as their course text, the objective of the course is *"to provide the student with comprehensive and in-depth understanding of the theory and practice involved in examining and re-analyzing criminal cold cases through the analysis of data from a solved case that will be investigated in teams. This course will utilize a blended format combining in-classroom and on-line media applications via UAB's course management system"* (University of Alabama 2014).

Contact information:
Elizabeth Gardner, PhD
Associate Professor of Forensic Science
Department of Justice Sciences
University of Alabama, Birmingham
1201 University Boulevard Office Building, Suite 316
1-205-934-2069
egard@uab.edu

The Doe Network

Founded in 2001, the Doe Network is an all-volunteer organization dedicated to assisting law enforcement in resolving unsolved missing- and unidentified-persons cases, both nationally and internationally. They attempt to do this by providing exposure of cases via website, by assisting responsible agencies by providing credible potential matches between missing- and unidentified-persons cases, and by utilization of media for case exposure. To accomplish this, they work with law enforcement agencies, medical examiners' and coroners' offices, and missing-persons organizations.

Case submission is accomplished through their World Wide Web site listed at the end of this section.

Unidentified persons are profiled on the website if the person is located, either living or deceased, at least two years prior to the current year and if the case is on file with a law enforcement agency, medical examiner's office, or medical facility. If the unidentified-person (living or deceased) case is less than two years prior to the current year, the investigating agency may opt to enter it as a "hot case." A case intake form is available online.

Missing-persons cases are similarly entered. At time of this writing, Doe policy features long-term missing persons, and criteria for entry require that the person must have gone missing at least nine years prior to the current year. Cases more recent can be added only at the request of law enforcement and will be profiled in the *Hot Cases* site.

UAB

Justice Sciences JS 465-2E Syllabus:
Cold Case Analysis

Spring Semester 2014
CRN: 36308

INSTRUCTOR:

Elizabeth A. Gardner, Ph.D.;
1201 University Boulevard Office Building, Suite 316
934-0668 (direct-dial); 934-2069(JS office tel) / 934-2067(fax)
egard@uab.edu (on-campus)
Office hours –Tues./Wed./Thurs. 11-12 or by appointment

CLASS HOURS: 2:00- p.m., Room UBOB 222

OBJECTIVE: To provide the student with comprehensive and in-depth understanding of the theory and practice involved in examining and re-analyzing criminal cold cases by the analysis of a solved cold case that will be investigated as a team.

This course will utilize a blended learning format combining in-classroom and on-line media applications via UAB's Blackboard.

TEXTBOOK: **Cold Case Homicides*: Practical Investigative Techniques*** (1st Ed 2006) and other assigned readings to be posted via UAB's WebCT Dashboard / Blackboard or direct email after each class and from week to week.

PRE-CLASS ASSIGNMENTS: A 5 question Blackboard quiz will be due at 12 noon on lecture days. The quiz will be worth 5 points and based on the assigned readings.

IN-CLASS ASSIGNMENTS: Assignments will also be given during class. They may cover several days and require out-of-class work.

ALL ASSIGNMENT HANDOUTS WILL ALSO BE POSTED ON BLACKBOARD.

GRADING:	Final Exam	25%
	Assignments	20%
	Cold Case Analysis/Individual	30%
	Cold Case Analysis/Group	25%

MISSED EXAMS and EVALUATED EVENTS: Make-ups for examinations and evaluated events, with the exception of documented emergencies, must be arranged before the due date and time with a legitimate excuse approved by the Instructors. Technical difficulties or computer operator error not attributable to Blackboard system failure is not a legitimate basis for requesting make-up.

Figure 31.2 Syllabus from graduate-level cold case course, University of Alabama, Birmingham. (Courtesy of Elizabeth Gardner.)

Each case is provided a unique identifier number intended only for Doe Network organizational purposes, and this should not be given to other agencies. If available, the Doe Network has provided the submitting agency's case number as well as NCIC number (United States and Canada only).

Resources

Doe provides an online resource list/link to many local/state/national websites, including international websites. The Doe Network does not normally contact a victim's family. They are open, however, to contact by the family of the victims and may be able to offer support or general help, depending upon the circumstances. In addition, they provide information regarding the NCIC Missing Person File and NCIC Unidentified Person File. Also see Chapter 8.

Contact information:
The Doe Network
http://www.doenetwork.org

Tips and Other Ideas and Resources

PKU (Phenylketonuria) Cards—A DNA Forensic Resource

PKU/Guthrie cards contain DNA and have been on file since 1966. Their existence is often unknown to even experienced investigators, and this method of identification may be used to identify unknown remains or confirm identity, as well as link them to missing persons.

- These direct DNA samples, taken from the heels of infants immediately after birth, are retained by health departments in all 50 states, but each health department varies, widely, in the amount of time the dried blood is kept on file. (Google individual state health departments for specific information.)
- DNA extracted from a drop of blood on a PKU card may be used to find a missing person and make a positive identification of unidentified remains. The cards may prove especially helpful for missing children who were adopted and for whom no biological parents are known, or available, for family reference samples. (By permission of Silvia Pettem.)

Cold Case Playing Cards

Special Agent Tommy Ray of the Florida Department of Law Enforcement conceived the idea of brief summaries of long term missing person (LTMP) and cold case homicide victims by putting their pictures and a brief case description on decks of playing cards. Modeled on the U.S. military's cards distributed to troops in Iraq to help identify wanted fugitives, they are printed and distributed in local jails and prisons, and are the only decks available for Florida inmates in all of the state's prisons (Figure 31.3).

The cards were funded by the Crime Stoppers Trust Fund, administered by the Florida attorney general. A toll-free number is listed on each card, and no identifying information is obtained from the callers—the callers are free to remain anonymous. Following the Florida model, cold case playing cards have been produced in several other states including Texas, South Carolina, California, Washington, Kansas, Oregon, New York, Kentucky, Minnesota, Oklahoma, Maryland, Virginia, Missouri, and Colorado, as well as Queensland, Australia.

Crime Stoppers International and Crime Stoppers USA

Since 1976, this organization has involved citizens in fighting crime in their communities by offering the opportunity to share information anonymously with, and at the behest of, law enforcement. Many cities and counties nationwide utilize this program, which includes posters, signs, and other forms of notice to those who have, or would, perpetrate crime. Through use of social media, funding for efforts to identify and prevent crime, and other programs, by 2016, this organization has factored in over 686,000 arrests and 9,000 homicides, and facilitated the payout of over $105,000,000. (http://www.crimestoppersusa.com.)

Figure 31.3 Cold case playing cards. (Courtesy of Tommy Ray.)

Acknowledgments

I wish to express my deepest appreciation and gratitude to Gerald N. Nance, case manager for the Special Case Unit at the National Center for Missing and Exploited Children, for his assistance in the original preparation of the section "National Center for Missing and Exploited Children (NCMEC)." A former special agent for the U.S. Naval Criminal Investigative Service, Nance wrote the cold case protocol used by that agency and supervised their cold case squad. Upon retirement, he joined the National Center for Missing and Exploited Children and was instrumental in establishing the Special Case Unit, which addresses long-term missing-children and unidentified-remains cases of persons believed to be under the age of 21. Version update May 2016, from http://www.missingkids.org.

I wish to extend my deepest gratitude and appreciation to Sara Chakin of the Denver Police Department for her gracious time and assistance in compiling the information in this chapter. Her energy and diligence have fostered and enhanced the ability of the Denver Police Department to reach out to and assist victims of cold case homicides as well as sexual assaults.

In addition, I wish to similarly express this same to Sgt. Darrell Price of the cold case/sexual assault unit of the Charlotte-Mecklenburg Police Department. A veteran of 34 years with the department, the past 27 years in criminal investigation, he supervises 7 detectives and 14 volunteers as of this writing. He graciously assisted this author in compilation of material for this and other chapters, and his philosophy of utilizing various viewpoints of civilians as well as law enforcement has proven highly successful in the mission of this department. As vice president of MACCHIA, he has extended his skill and expertise to assist others. Lastly, I wish to acknowledge and express my gratitude for the assistance of Silvia Pettem on discussion of state review teams, drawn from her book, suggested below.

Suggested Readings and Bibiliography

Charlotte-Mecklenburg Police Department. http://charmeck.org/city/charlotte/CMPD/organization/Investigative/ViolentCrimes/Homicide-ADW/ColdCase/Pages/home.aspx. Retrieved May 23, 2016.

Denver Police Department. *Homicide Cold Case Investigations: A Guide for Victims and Their Families*. https://www.denvergov.org/Portals/720/documents/VAU_Cold_Case_Program_Homicide_Booklet_2012.pdf. Retrieved June 15, 2016.

Gardner, E. (2012). Justice Sciences JS-465-565 7M Syllabus. Cold Case Analysis. Spring Semester, 2012. University of Alabama. Birmingham.

Lord, V.B. (2005). Implementing a Cold Case Homicide Unit: A Challenging Task, *FBI Law Enforcement Bulletin*, 74(2): 1–6.

Lowery, R.G. (2010). Team Adam. *Police Chief Magazine*, December 2010.

National Sheriffs' Association. (2011). Serving Survivors of Homicide Victims during Cold Case Investigations: A Guide for Developing a Law Enforcement Protocol. http://www.sheriffs.org/sites/default/files/uploads/guidefordevelopingalawenforcementprotocolaugust172011.pdf. Retrieved June 15, 2016.

Pettem, S. (2013). *Cold Case Research: Resources for Unidentified, Missing and Cold Homicide Cases*. CRC Press. Boca Raton, FL.

Price, D. Personal Interview. June 14, 2016.

Regensburger, D. (2001). Law Enforcement Volunteers: An Essential Tool in the Investigation of Cold Case Homicides. *Sheriff Magazine* 63(3):22–23.

The Doe Network. http://www.doenetwork.org. Retrieved May 23, 2016.

University of Alabama. (2014). Course Syllabus, Birminghan Course JS 465–2E. Spring.

Concluding Thoughts

In his textbook *Practical Homicide Investigation: Tactics, Procedures, and Forensic Techniques*, Vernon Geberth wrote that "as far as homicide detectives are concerned, there are two types of homicide: one in which the suspect is caught quickly, and the unsolved homicide."

He also noted that murder is the ultimate crime, and that each case deserves a thorough and complete investigation. In most instances, this has probably occurred. In some, it did not, and we would be naive to assume otherwise. Despite the best efforts of many, however, some homicides have gone unsolved.

He made no reference, however, to *when* we should stop looking, when we should stop investigating. I opine that he did not because we should *never* stop looking. We should *never* cease in our efforts to solve unsolved homicides. Why? Because we owe it to the victims, to their families, and indeed, to our civilization that we never cease in our efforts to bring accountability to those who have murdered another human being. In the past three decades, indeed, since the first edition of this text, many cold cases once thought unsolvable have been solved. They have been solved because dedicated investigators poured through old files and boxes of papers and evidence, or followed up on a tip. Or reprocessed old evidence and made startling new discoveries. Some, appreciatively, through the expanded knowledge gained by investigators who read through these pages.

I further believe, however, that we should never cease in our efforts to learn the truth, and to reinvestigate those cases in which, just perhaps, the wrong person was convicted and sentenced. After all, in those instances, someone did get away with murder, while someone else paid the penalty.

Unfortunately, many of America's cold case murders may never be solved. Despite this, we can hold out hope that perhaps one day, some of these will be solved. As we have seen in this text, the pendulum of time has become our biggest asset in this regard. Through changes in relationships, technology, and other factors, cold cases are being solved and will be solved in the future by the dedicated and professional men and women—such as those who so willingly gave of their time and expertise to contribute to this text—who comprise the cold case investigation team: the investigators, the prosecutors, and the laboratory.

Thank you, Anne Marie, Tad, Bennett, Edwardo, Peter, Mike, Jay, Silvia, Connie, Katharine, Madeline, Skip and Rick, Sharon, Robert, Tom, Rod, Marie, Karen, Paul and Kim: My life has been so enriched by our abiding friendships, and through these pages, we have given something back to society. To all cold case homicide investigators, past, present, and future, I say, "Thank you." I hope that these pages have facilitated, or will facilitate you in your struggles, and that you never cease in your efforts to bring whatever passes for justice in this world to the victims and their families.

In granting Jack Ryan a posthumous pardon on the grounds of innocence in 1996, the governor of California noted,

> We must remember that a just society may not always achieve justice, but it must constantly strive for justice. This means that we must not excuse the guilty nor fail to exonerate the guiltless. As the philosopher Sir Francis Bacon said some 380 years ago, 'If we do not maintain Justice, Justice will not maintain us.'

Index

Page numbers followed by f and t indicate figures and tables, respectively.

B

C

E

H

I

M

N

O

P

Q

R

T

W

Kolibri 360 GmbH
Ferdinand-Jühlke-Straße 7
99095 Erfurt, Deutschland
produktsicherheit@kolibri360.de